AMERICAN CORPORATE IDENTITY 2008

AMERICAN CORPORATE IDENTITY 2008

David E. Carter
Suzanna MW Stephens

COLLINS | DESIGN
An Imprint of HarperCollins*Publishers*

HarperCollins books may be purchased for educational, business, or sales promotional use. For information, please write: Special Markets Department, HarperCollins Publishers, 10 East 53rd Street, New York, NY 10022.

First Edition

First published in 2007 by:
Collins Design
An Imprint of HarperCollins*Publishers*
10. East 53rd Street
New York, NY 10022
Tel: (212) 207-7000
Fax: (212) 207-7654
collinsdesign@harpercollins.com
www.harpercollins.com

Distributed throughout the world by:
HarperCollins*Publishers*
10 East 53rd Street
New York, NY 10022
Fax: (212) 207-7654

Book and cover design by

Suzanna & Anthony Stephens

Additional photography by Anthony Stephens

Library of Congress Control Number: 2007930307

ISBN: 978-0-06-125573-1
ISBN-10: 0-06-125573-4

Produced by Crescent Hill Books, Louisville, KY.
Printed in China by Everbest Printing Company.

First Printing, 2007

TABLE of CONTENTS

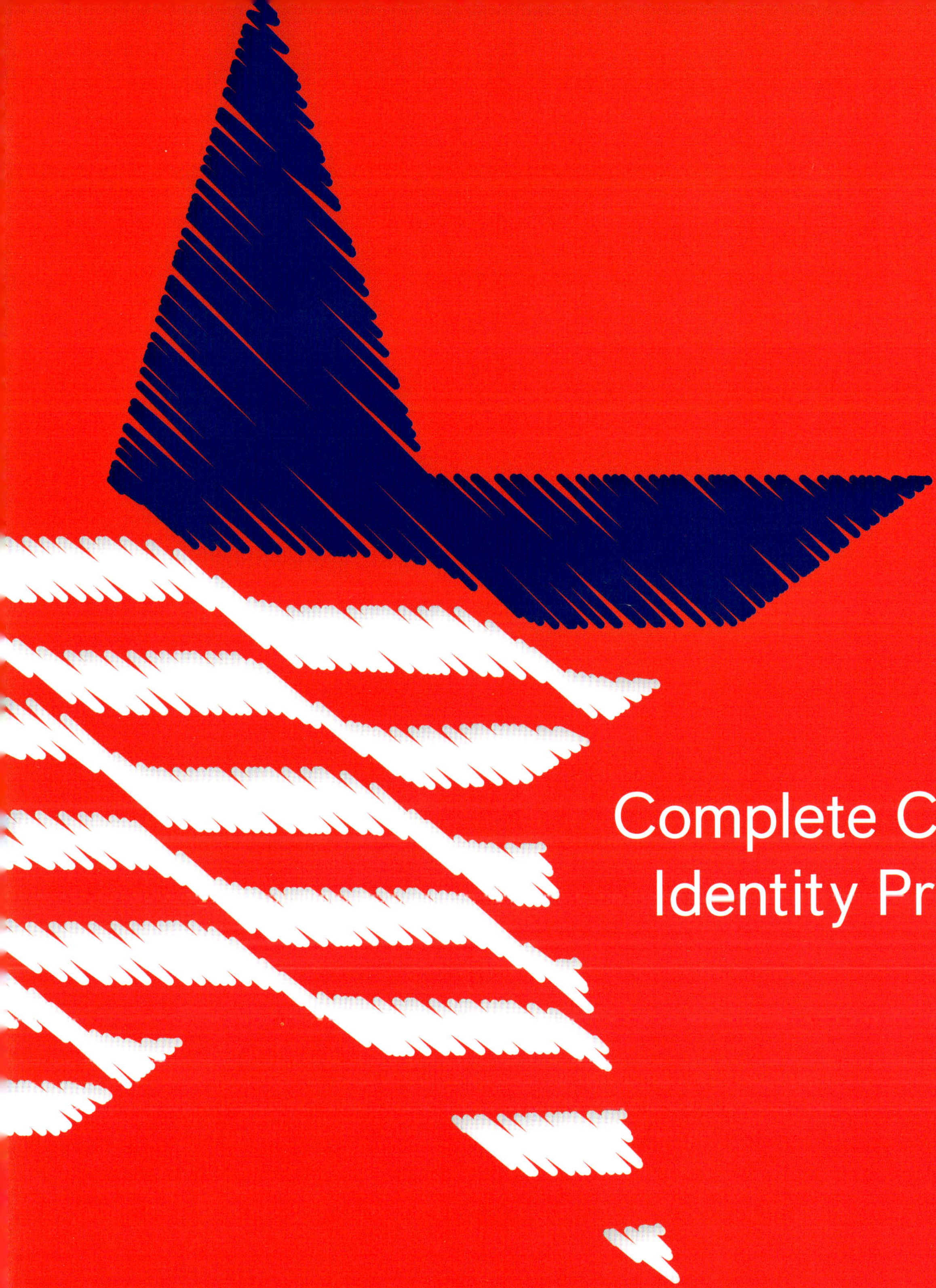

Complete Corporate Identity Programs

American
Paper

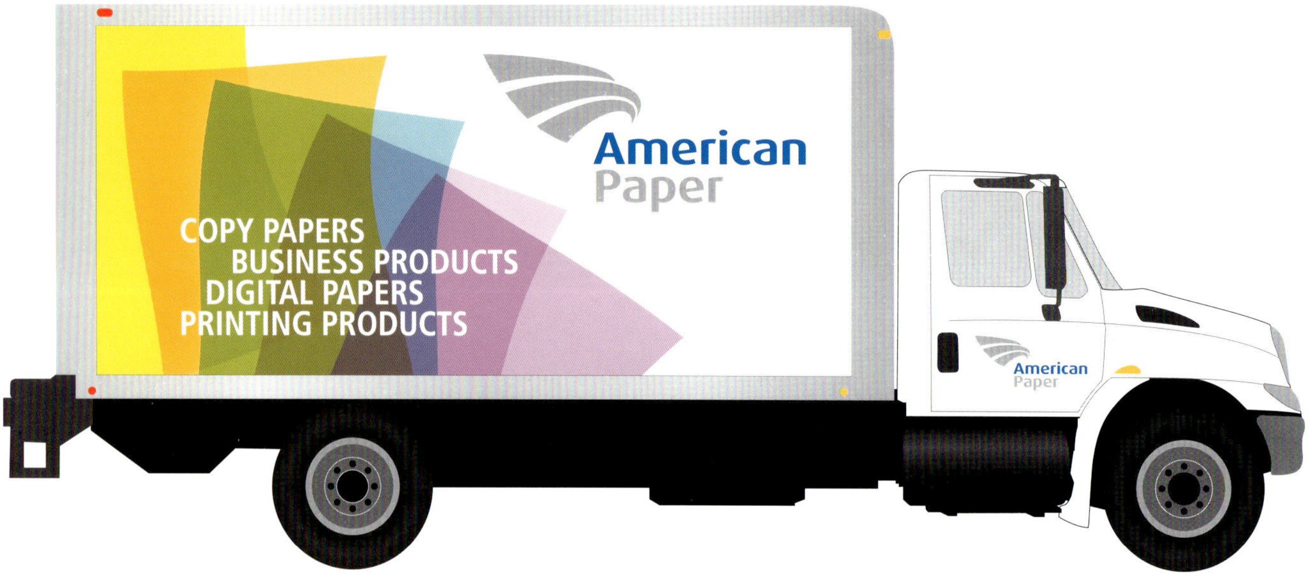

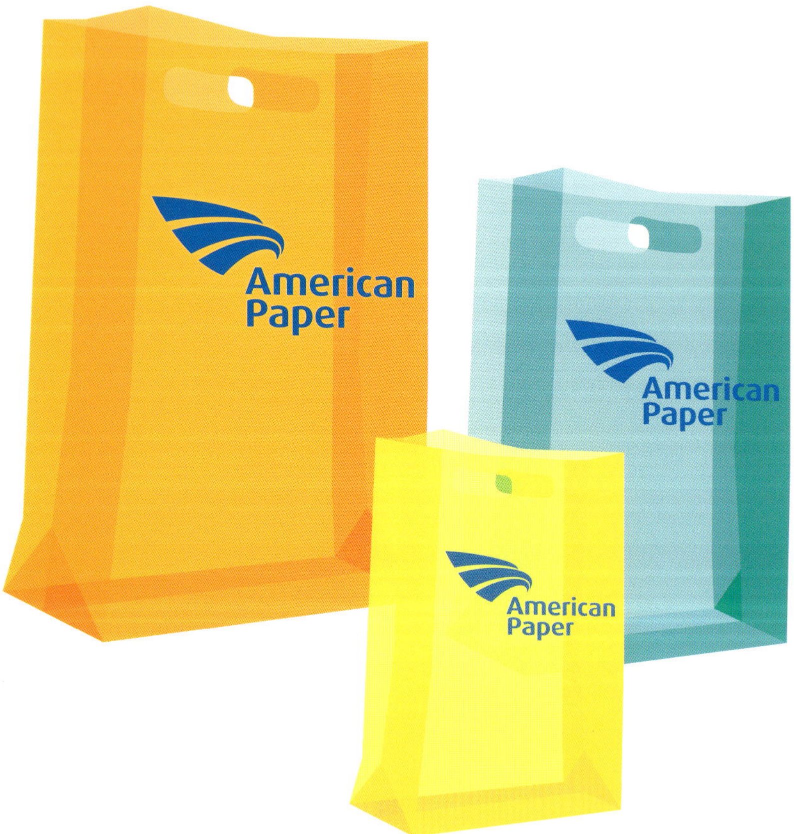

client
American Paper Corp.
design firm
ID Group
idgrouppr.com
designers
Jorge Colón,
Abner Gutiérrez,
Mayra Maldonado

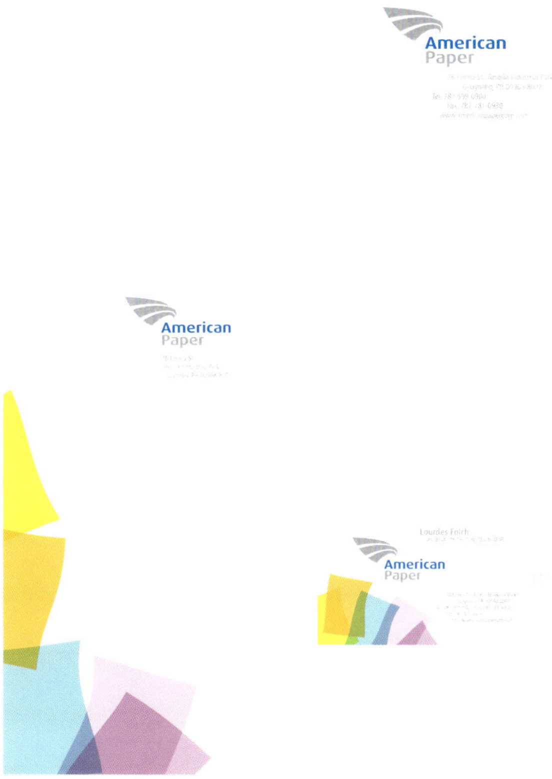

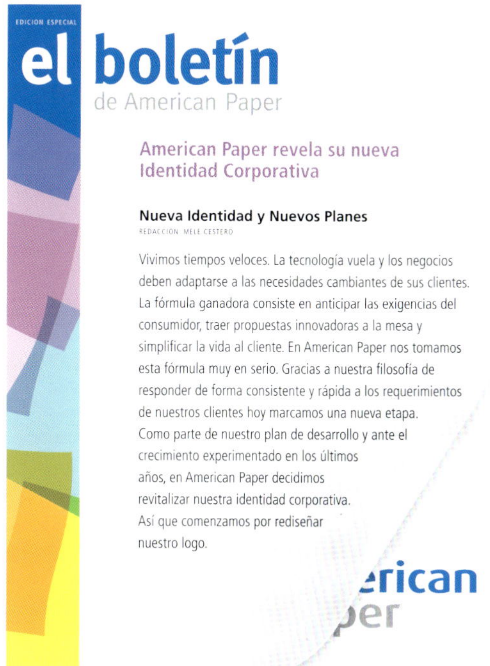
EDICION ESPECIAL

el boletín
de American Paper

American Paper revela su nueva Identidad Corporativa

Nueva Identidad y Nuevos Planes

REDACCION: MELE CESTERO

Vivimos tiempos veloces. La tecnología vuela y los negocios deben adaptarse a las necesidades cambiantes de sus clientes. La fórmula ganadora consiste en anticipar las exigencias del consumidor, traer propuestas innovadoras a la mesa y simplificar la vida al cliente. En American Paper nos tomamos esta fórmula muy en serio. Gracias a nuestra filosofía de responder de forma consistente y rápida a los requerimientos de nuestros clientes hoy marcamos una nueva etapa. Como parte de nuestro plan de desarrollo y ante el crecimiento experimentado en los últimos años, en American Paper decidimos revitalizar nuestra identidad corporativa. Así que comenzamos por rediseñar nuestro logo.

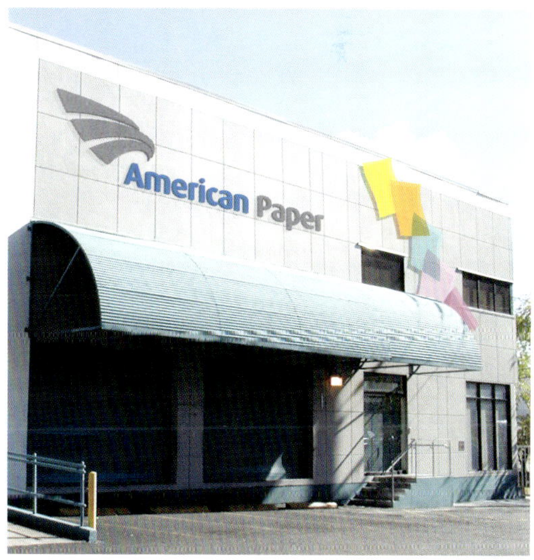

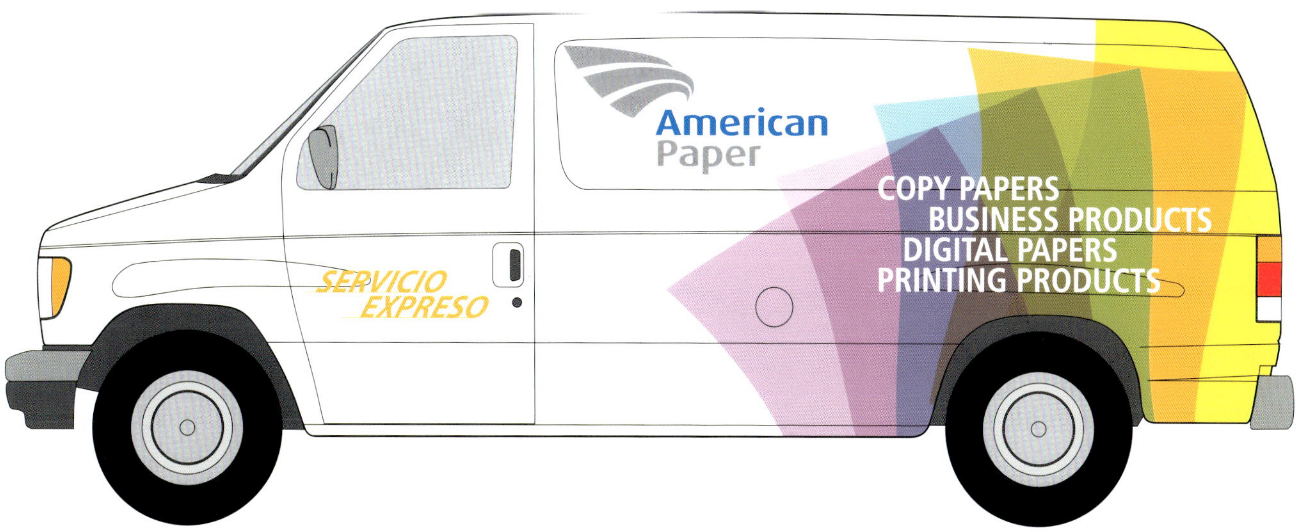

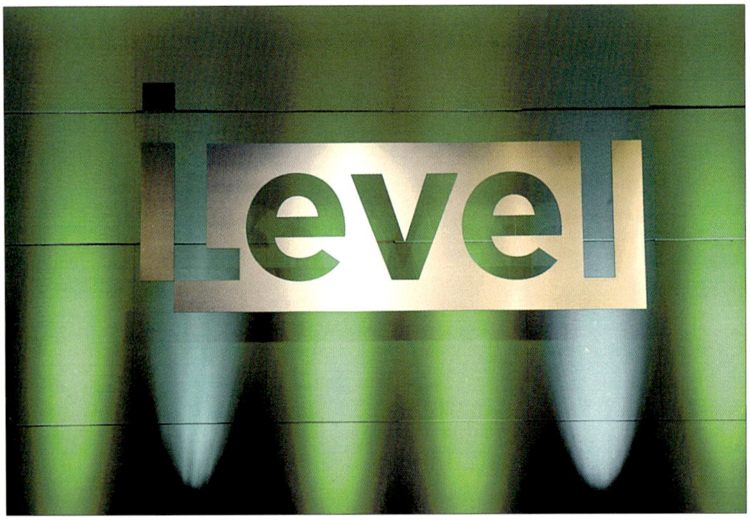
iLevel

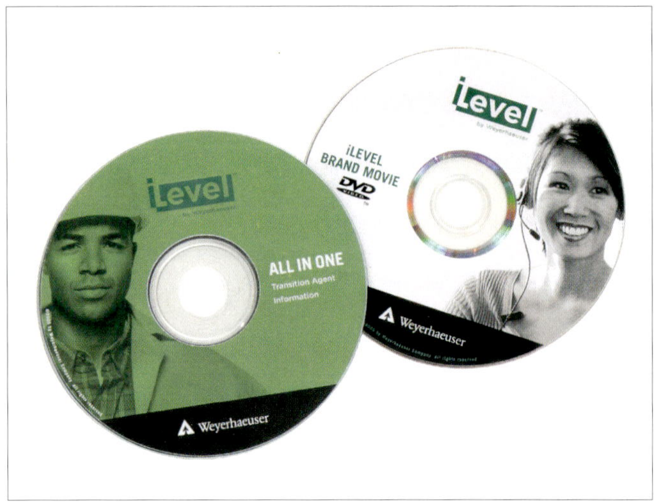
iLevel
iLEVEL
BRAND MOVIE
DVD
ALL IN ONE
Transition Agent
Information
Weyerhaeuser

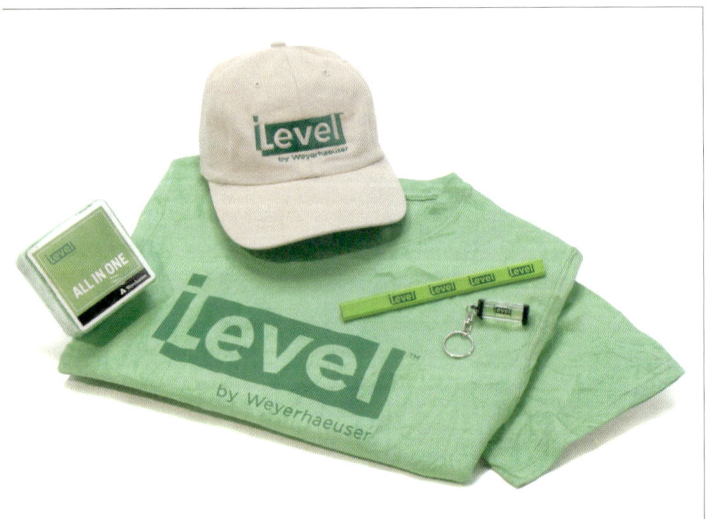
iLevel
by Weyerhaeuser
ALL IN ONE

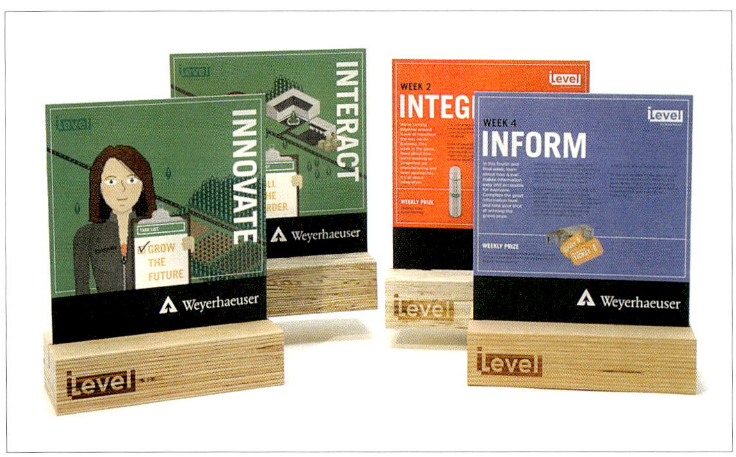
INNOVATE
GROW
THE
FUTURE
INTERACT
WEEK 2
INTEG
WEEK 4
INFORM
Weyerhaeuser
iLevel

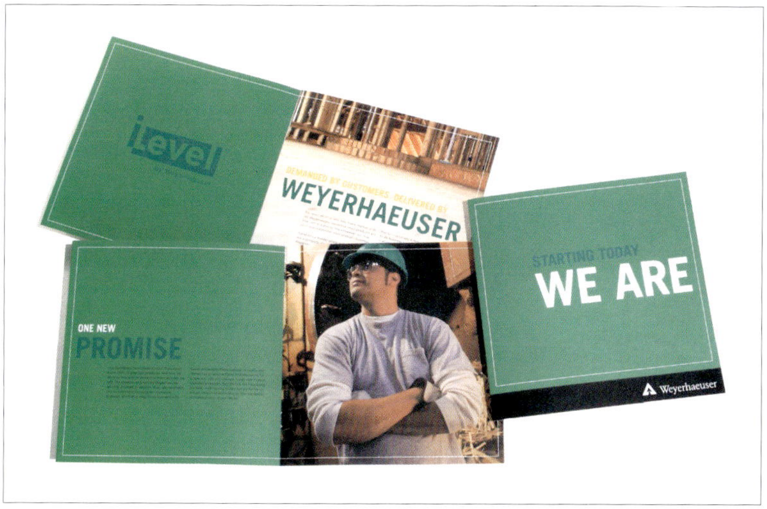

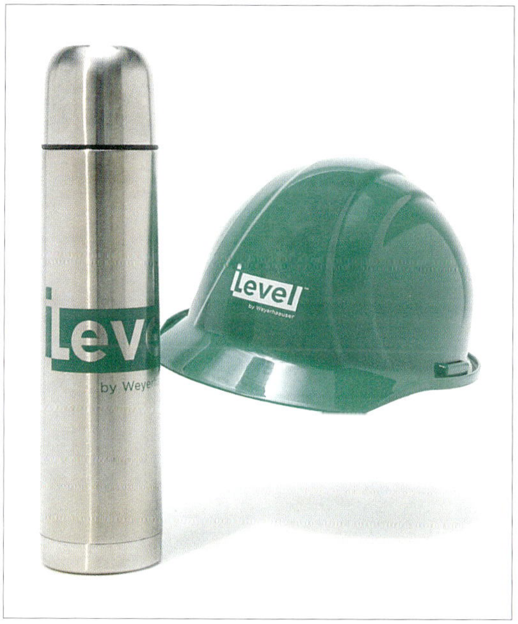

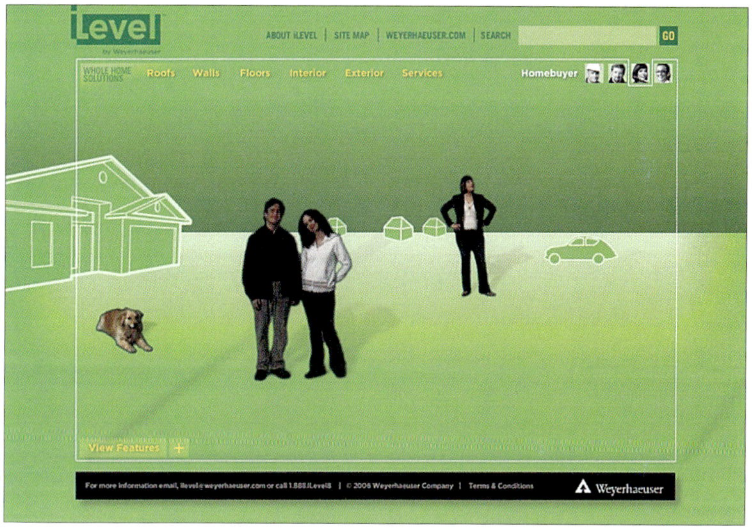

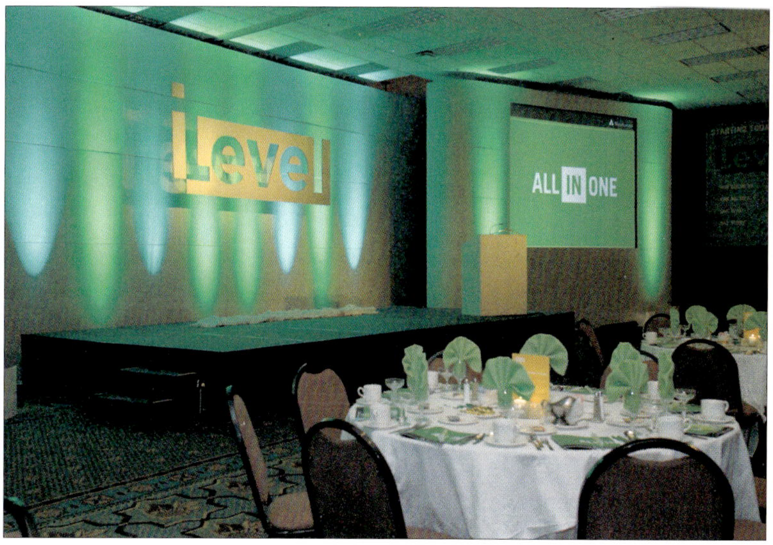

client
Weyerhaeuser Corporation
design firm
Hornall Anderson Design Works
www.hadw.com
designers
Jack Anderson, James Tee,
Andrew Wicklund, Elmer dela Cruz,
Holly Craven, Jay Hilburn, Hayden Schoen,
Belinda Bowling, Yuri Shvets, Michael Connors

CREASIA

client
Creasia LLC
design firm
Creasia LLC
creasiadesign.com
designer
Carmen Li

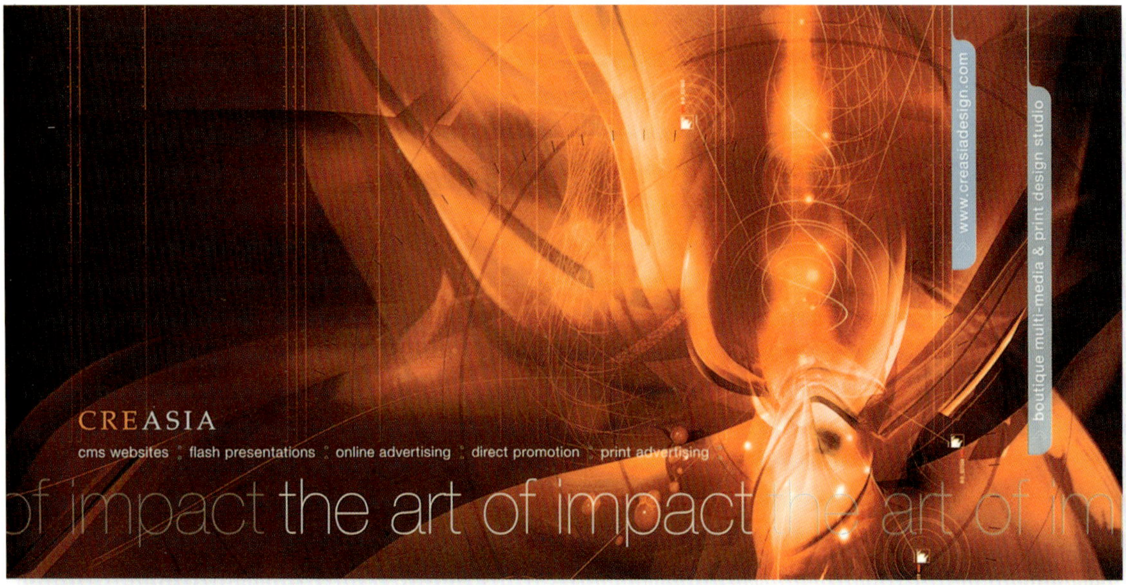

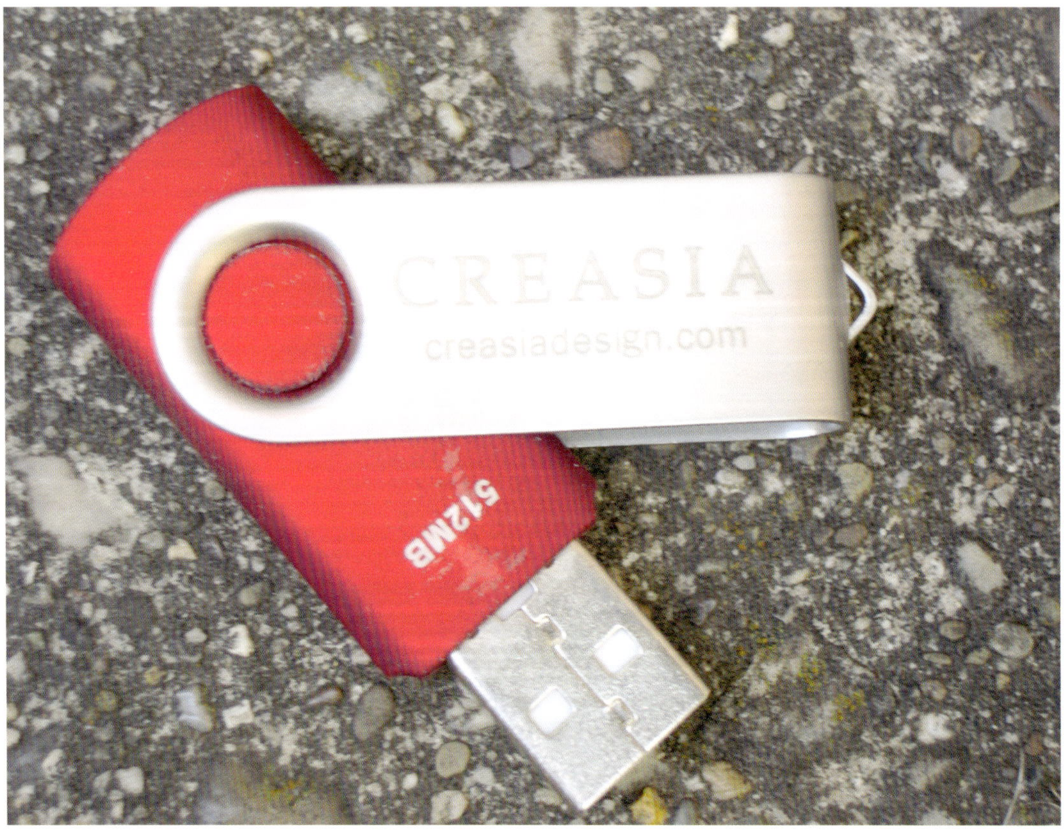

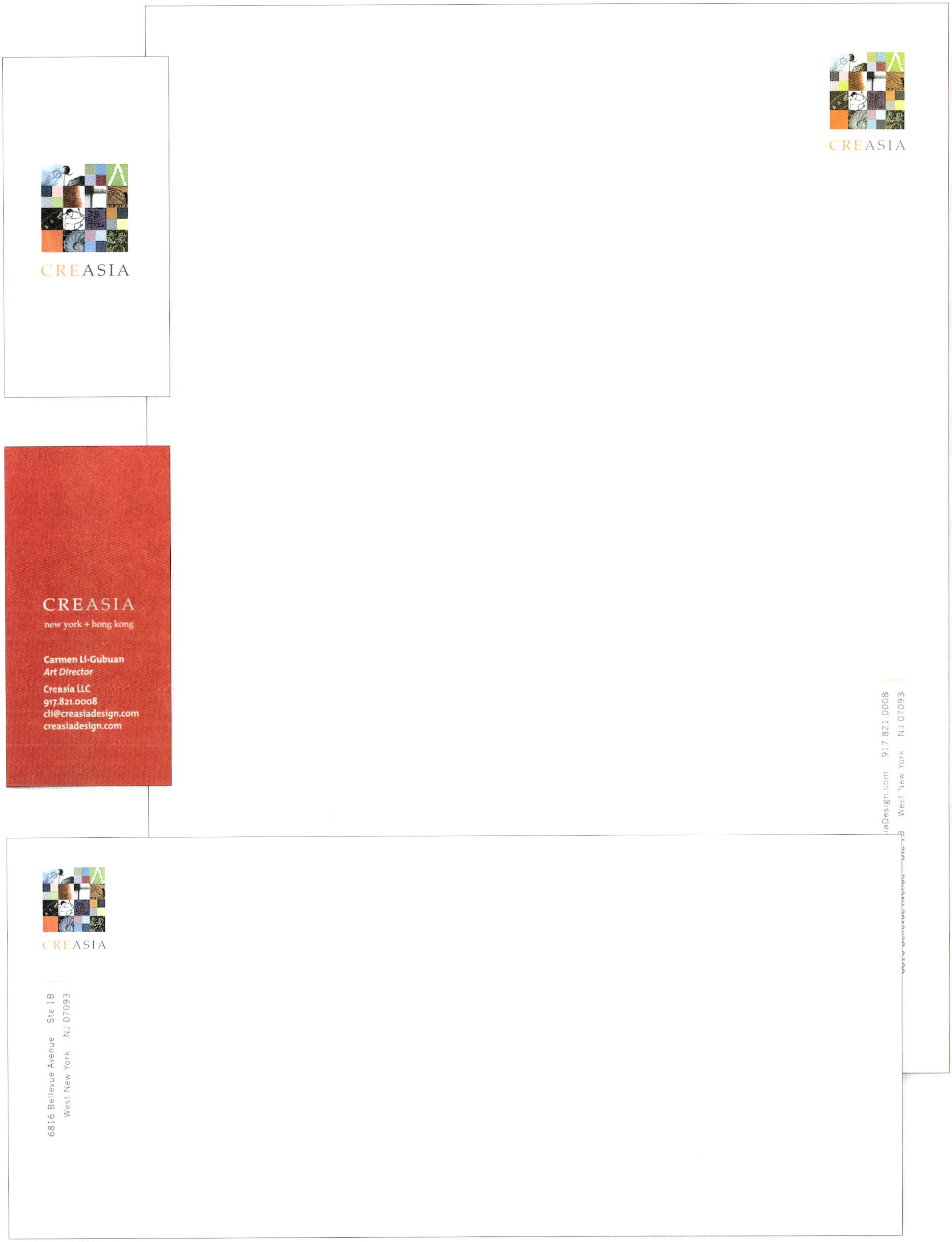
CREASIA
CREASIA
CREASIA
new york + hong kong
Carmen Li-Gubuan
Art Director
Creasia LLC
917.821.0008
cli@creasiadesign.com
creasiadesign.com
917.821.0008
West New York · NJ 07093
CREASIA
6816 Bellevue Avenue · Ste 1B
West New York · NJ 07093

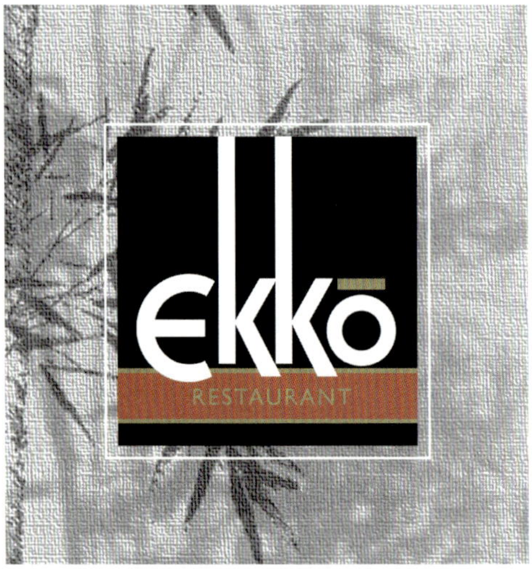
ekko
RESTAURANT

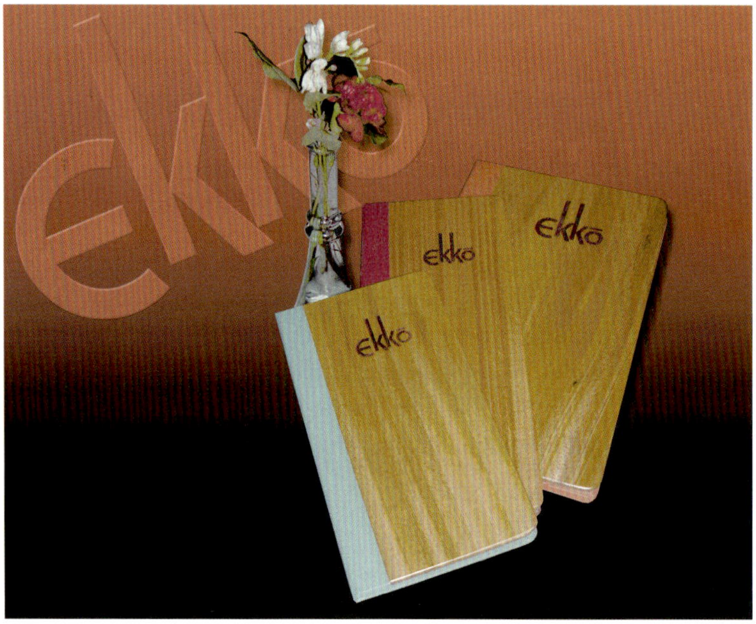
ekko
ekko
ekko
ekko

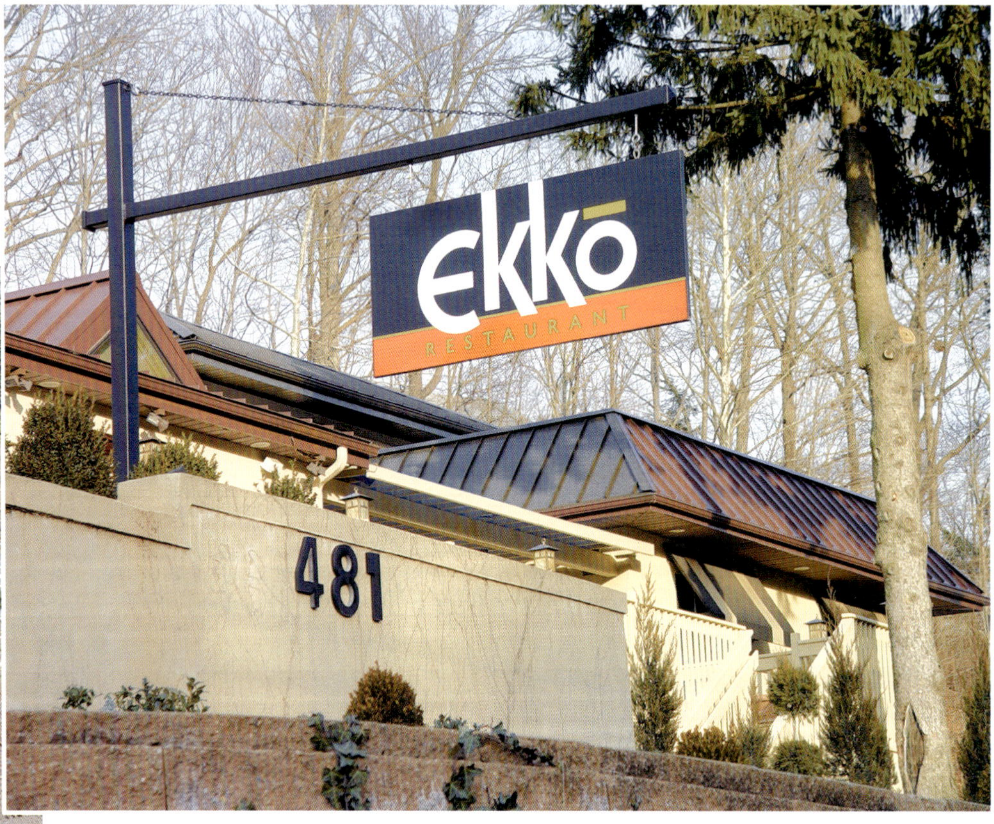
ekko
RESTAURANT
481

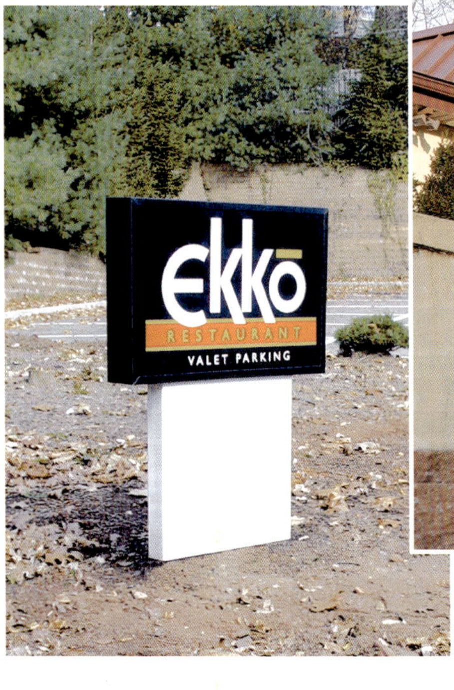
ekko
RESTAURANT
VALET PARKING

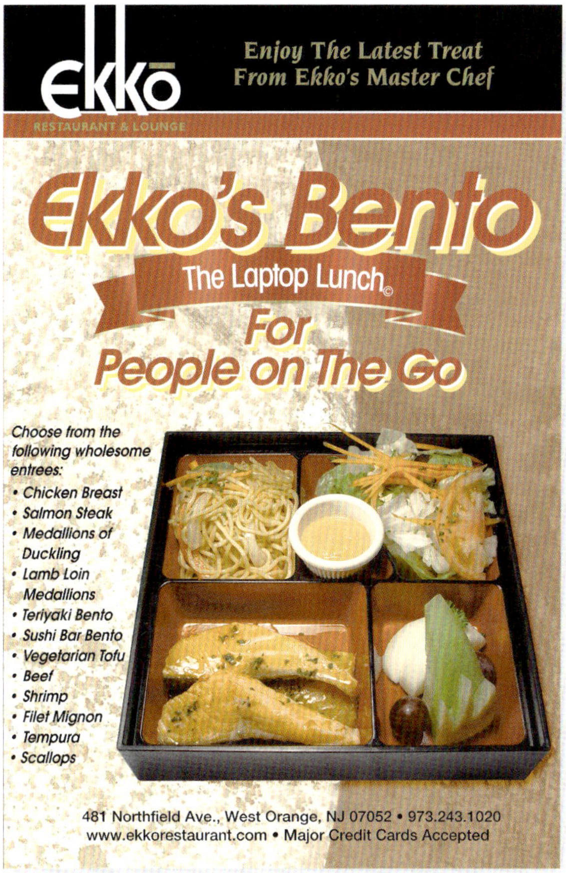

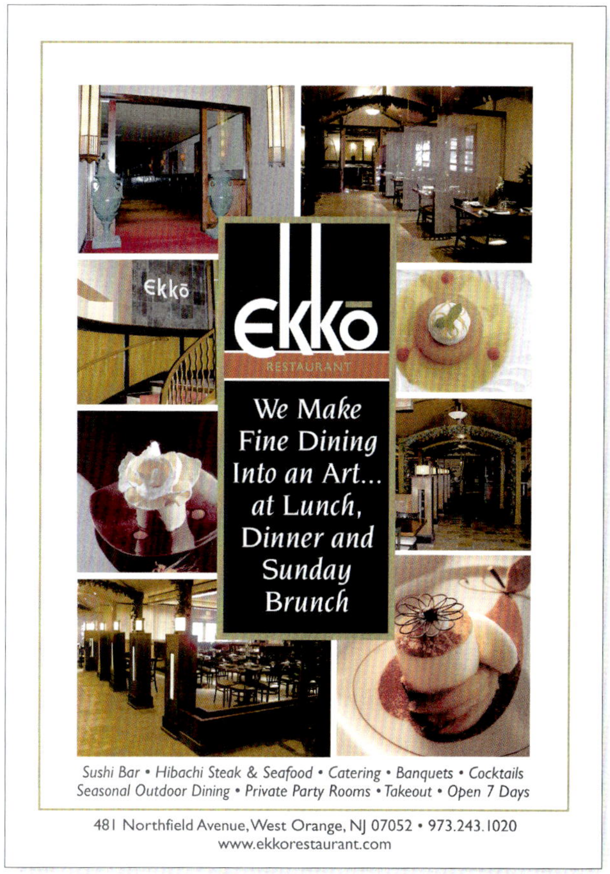

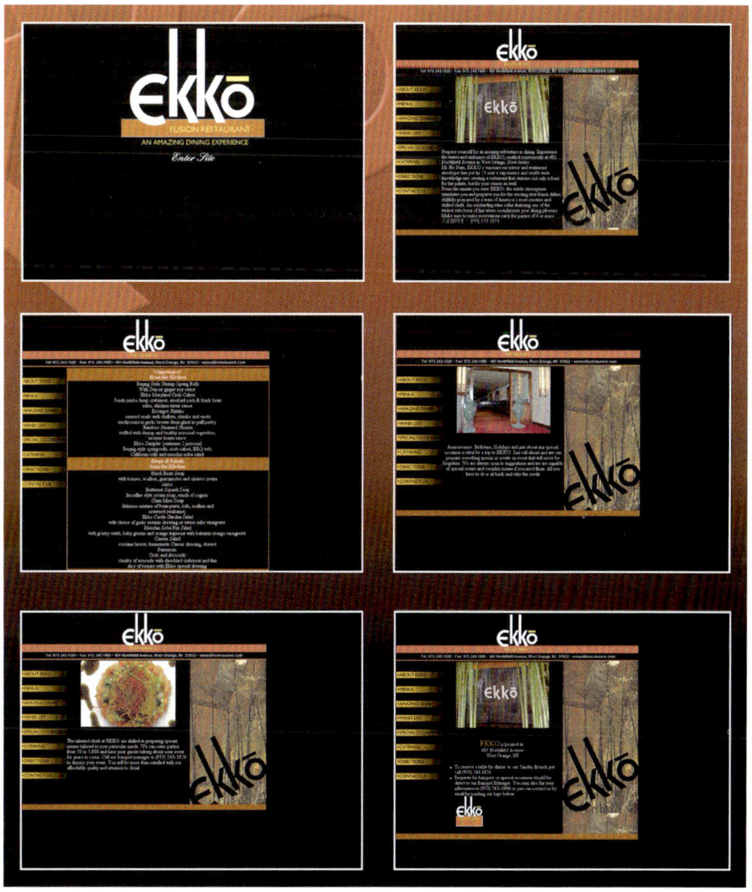

client
Ekko Restaurant
design firm
Stephen Longo Design Associates
designer
Stephen Longo

INVESTMENT PROPERTIES OF AMERICA

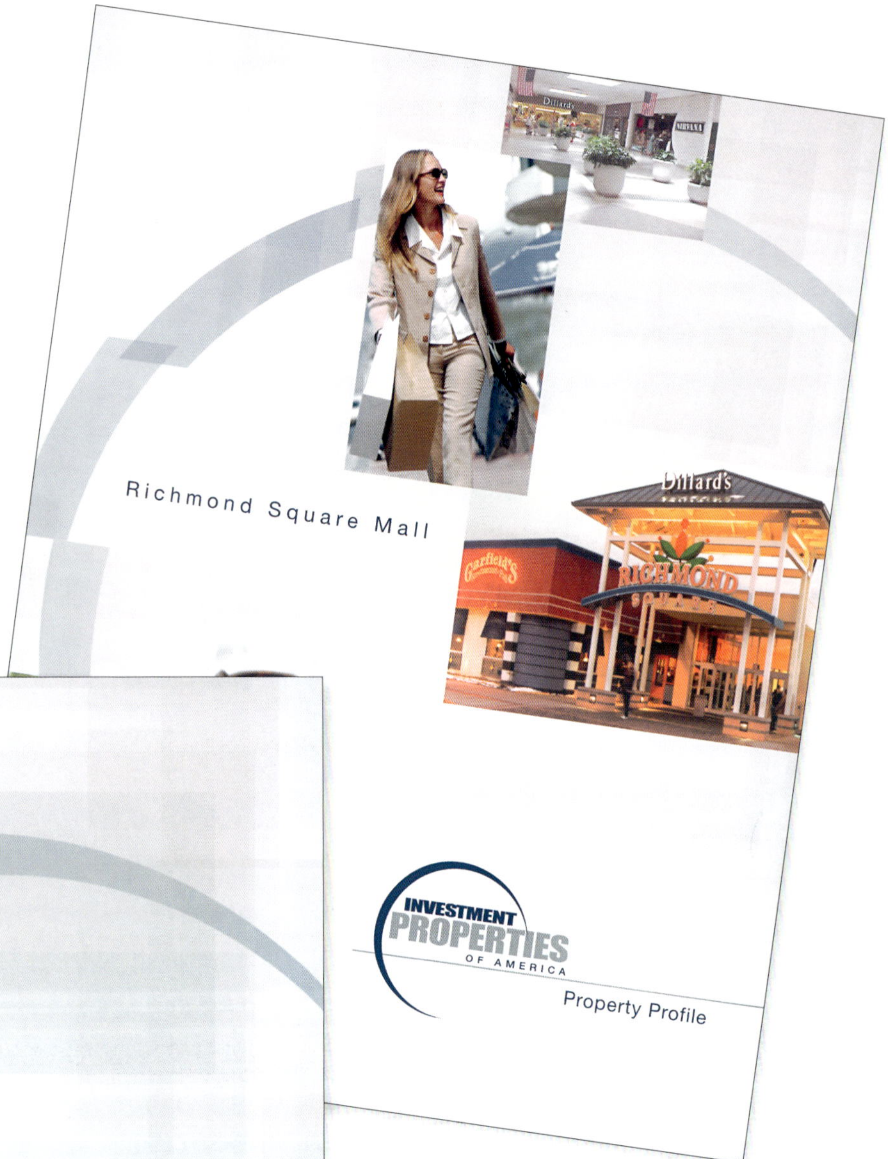

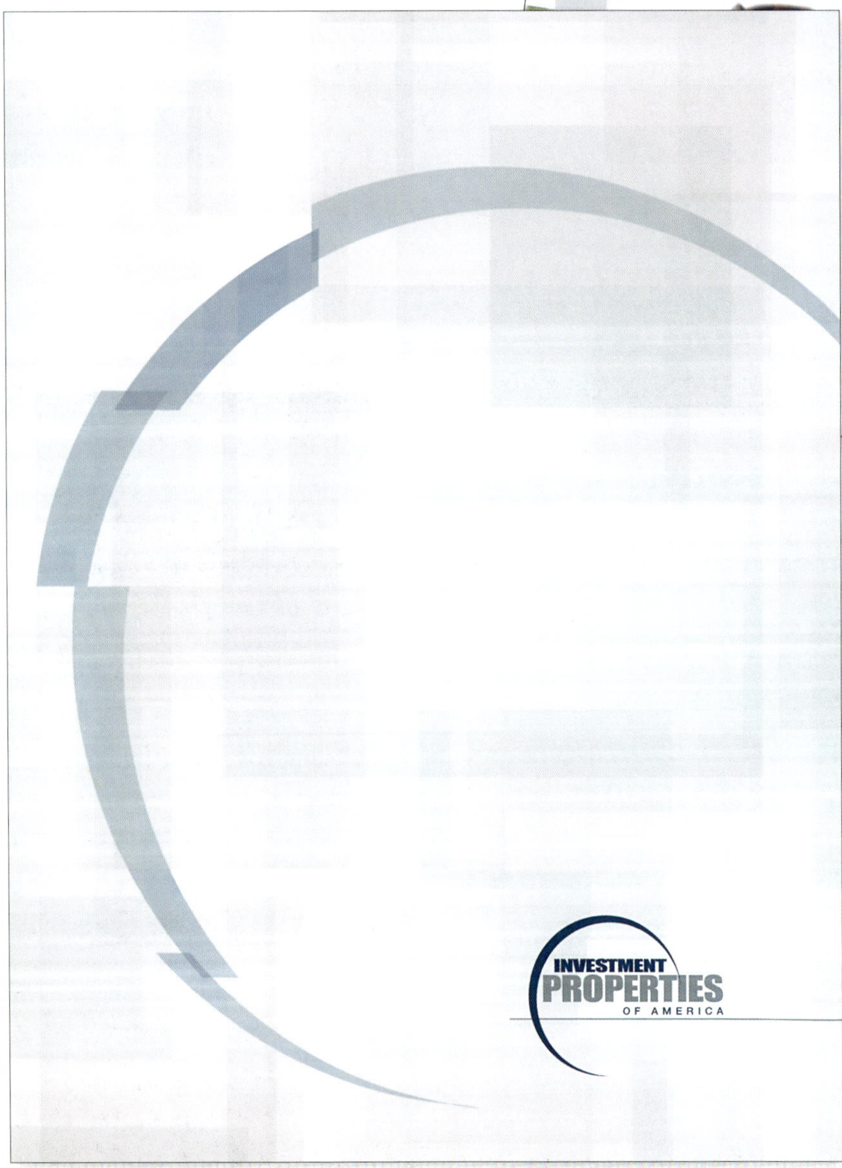

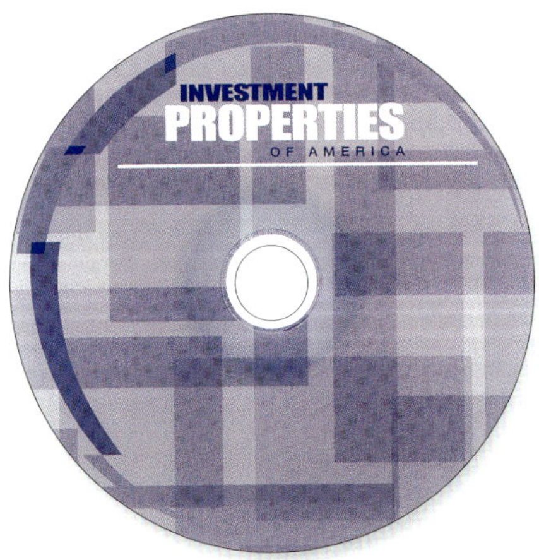

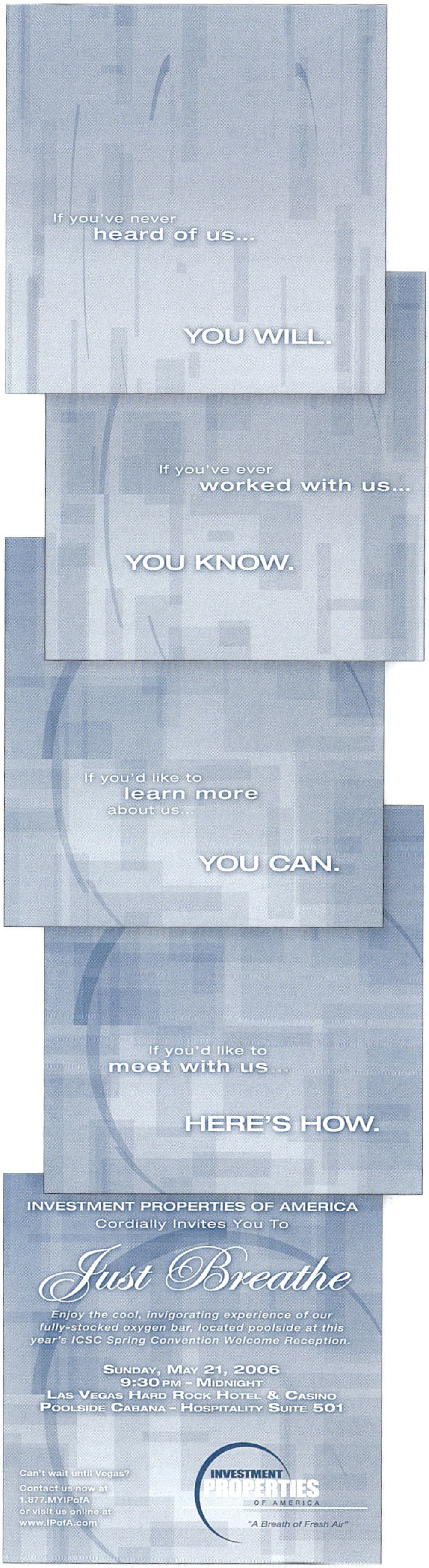

client
Investment Properties of America
design firm
Gibson Group
www.gibsongrp.com
designer
Diane McGuire

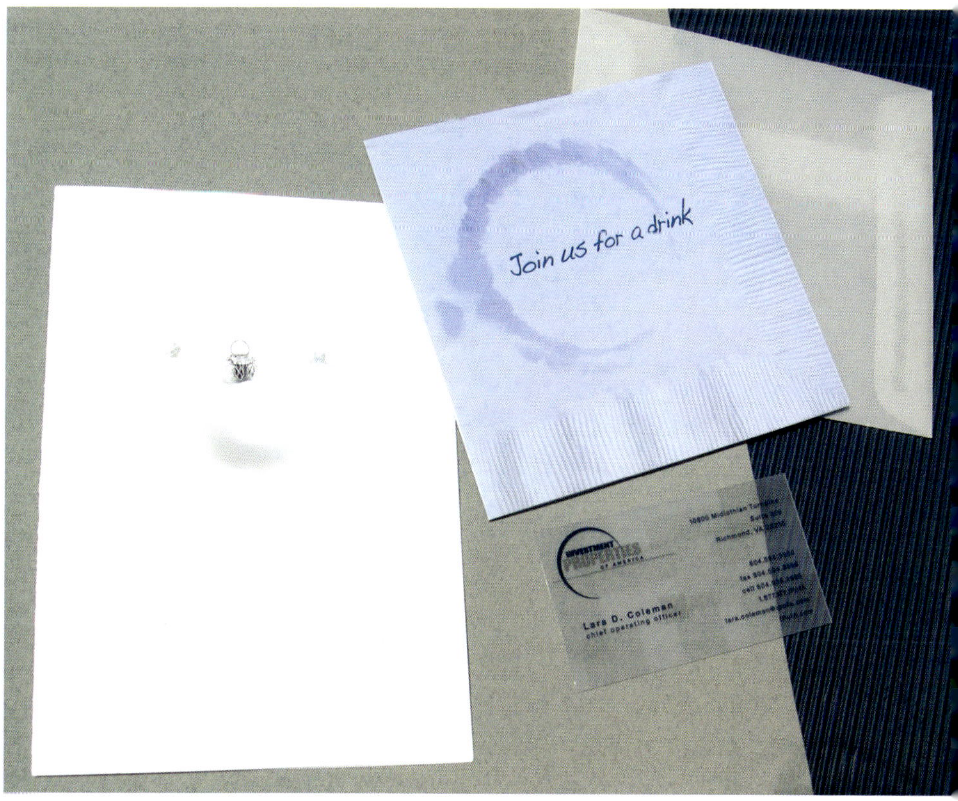

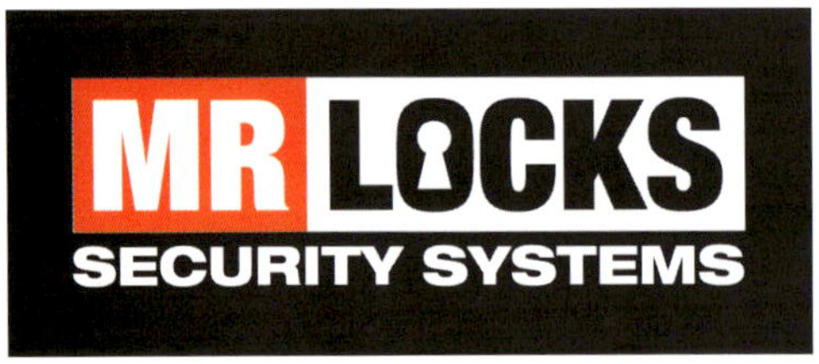

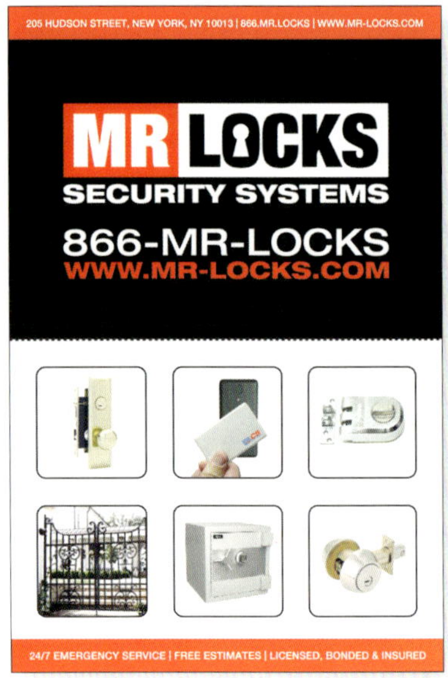

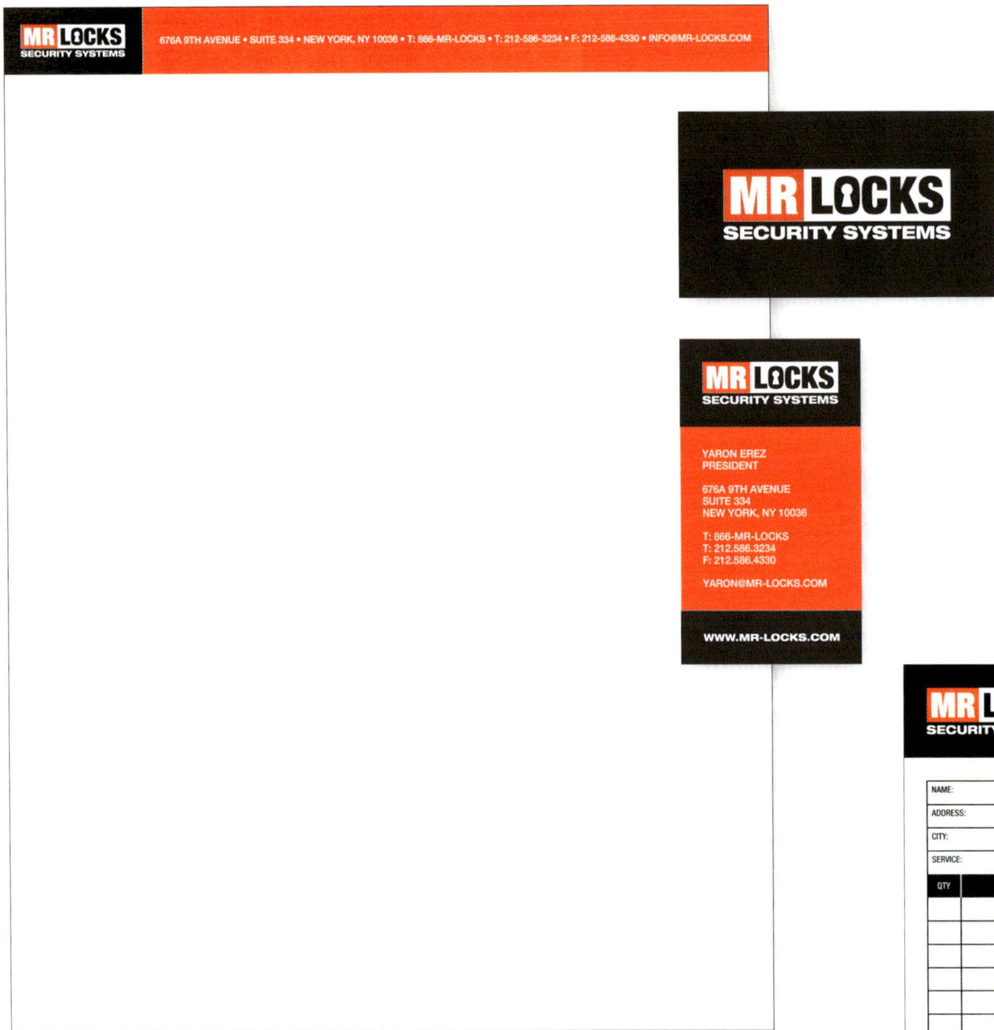

client
Mr Locks
design firm
Graphic Advance
www.graphicadvance.com
designer
Aviad Stark

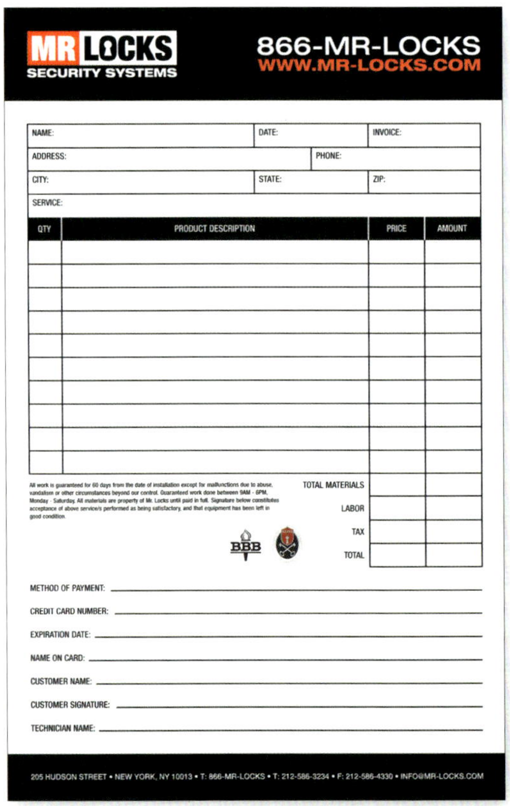

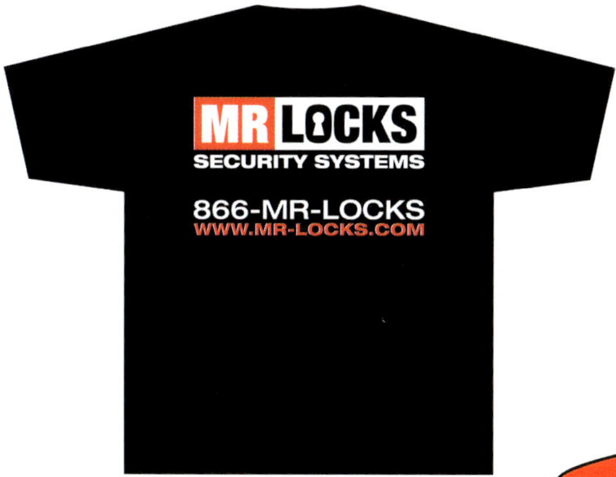
MR LOCKS
SECURITY SYSTEMS
866-MR-LOCKS
WWW.MR-LOCKS.COM

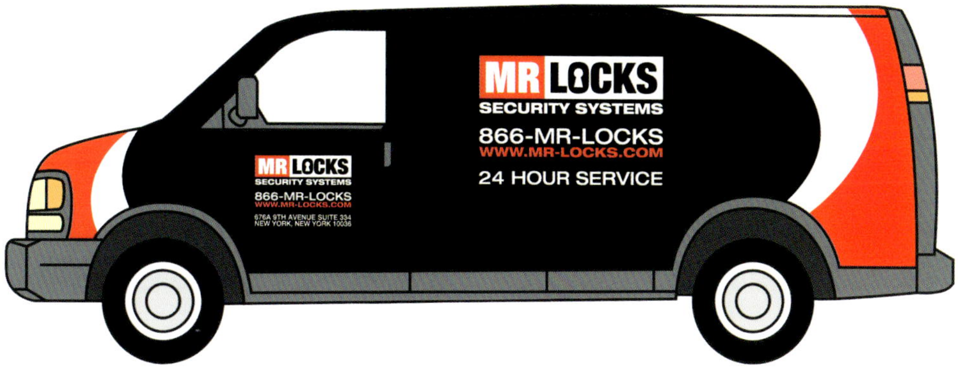
MR LOCKS
SECURITY SYSTEMS
866-MR-LOCKS
WWW.MR-LOCKS.COM
676A 9TH AVENUE SUITE 334
NEW YORK, NEW YORK 10036
MR LOCKS
SECURITY SYSTEMS
866-MR-LOCKS
WWW.MR-LOCKS.COM
24 HOUR SERVICE

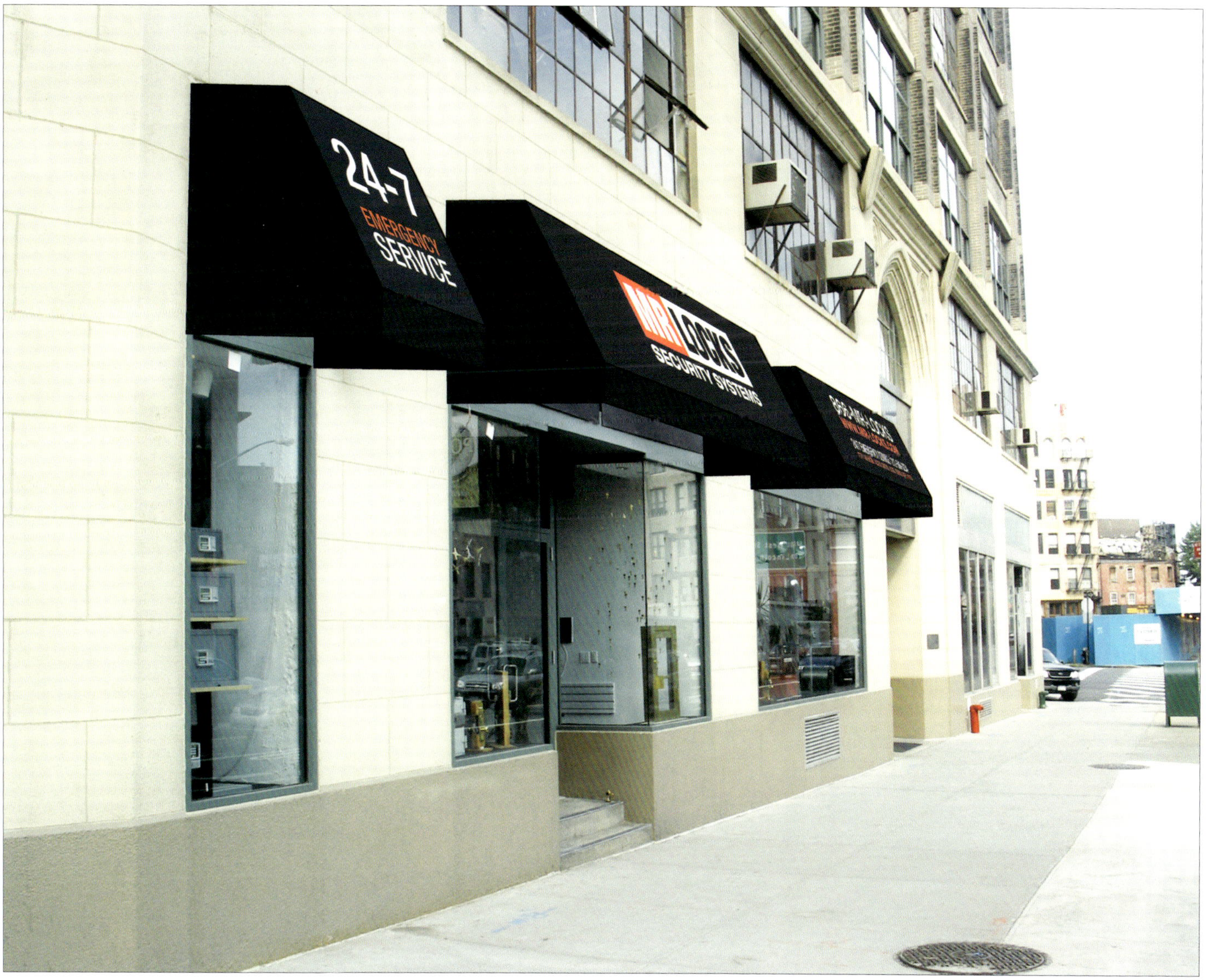
24-7
EMERGENCY
SERVICE
MR LOCKS
SECURITY SYSTEMS

Morgan Waterfront Estates

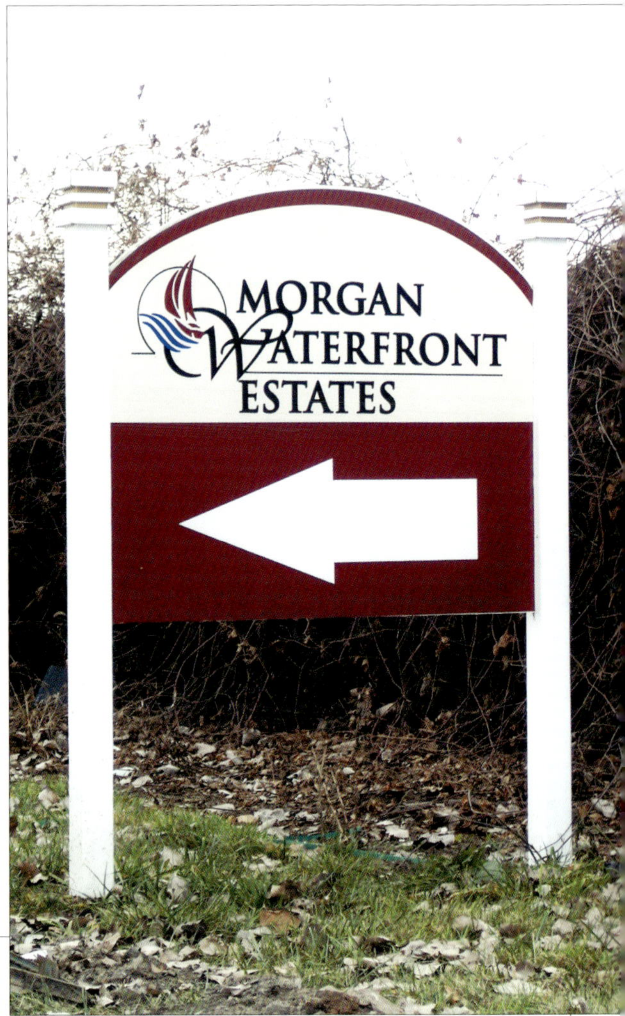

client
Morgan Development
design firm
Group Fifty-Five Marketing
www.group55.com
designers
Heather Sowinksi, Jeannette Gutierrez

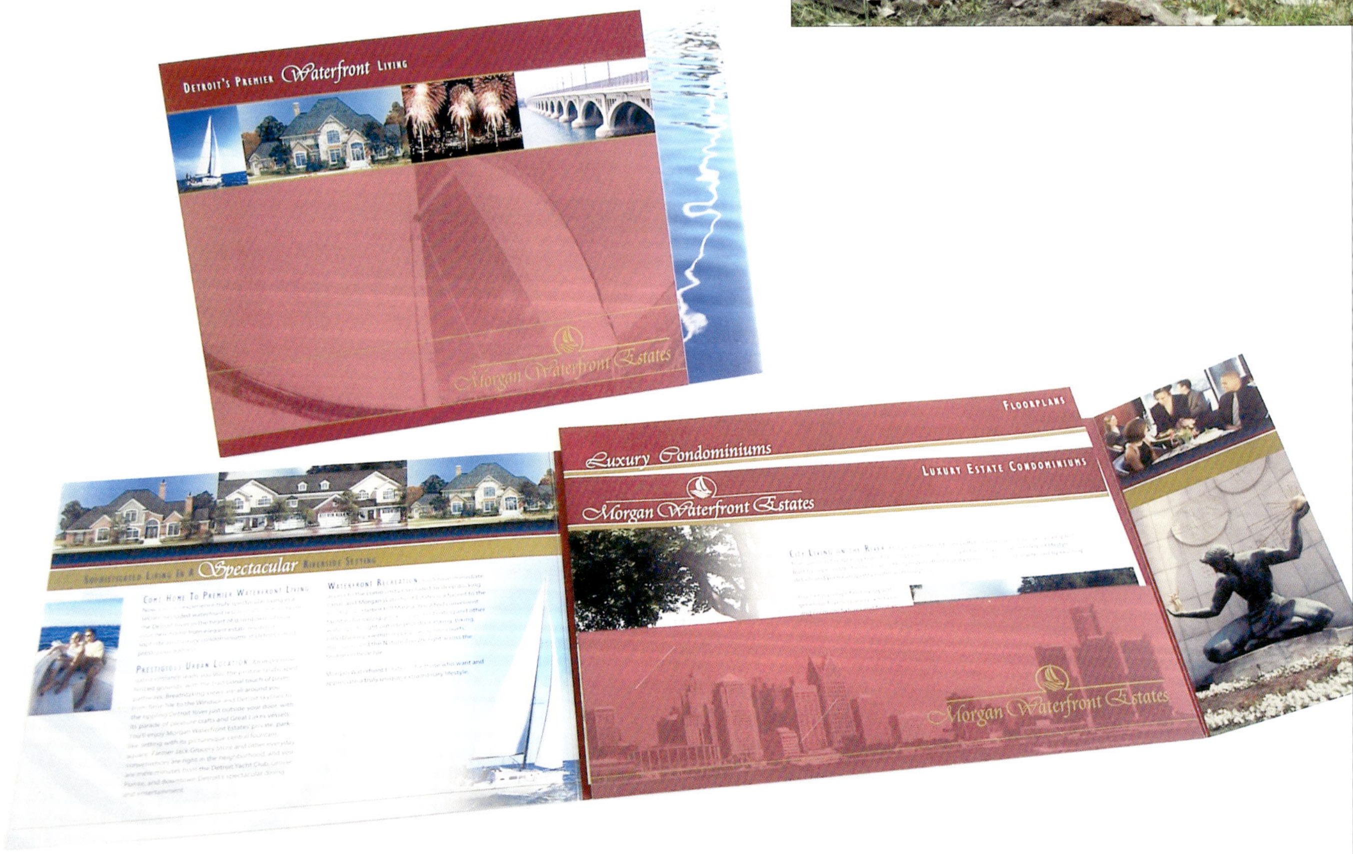

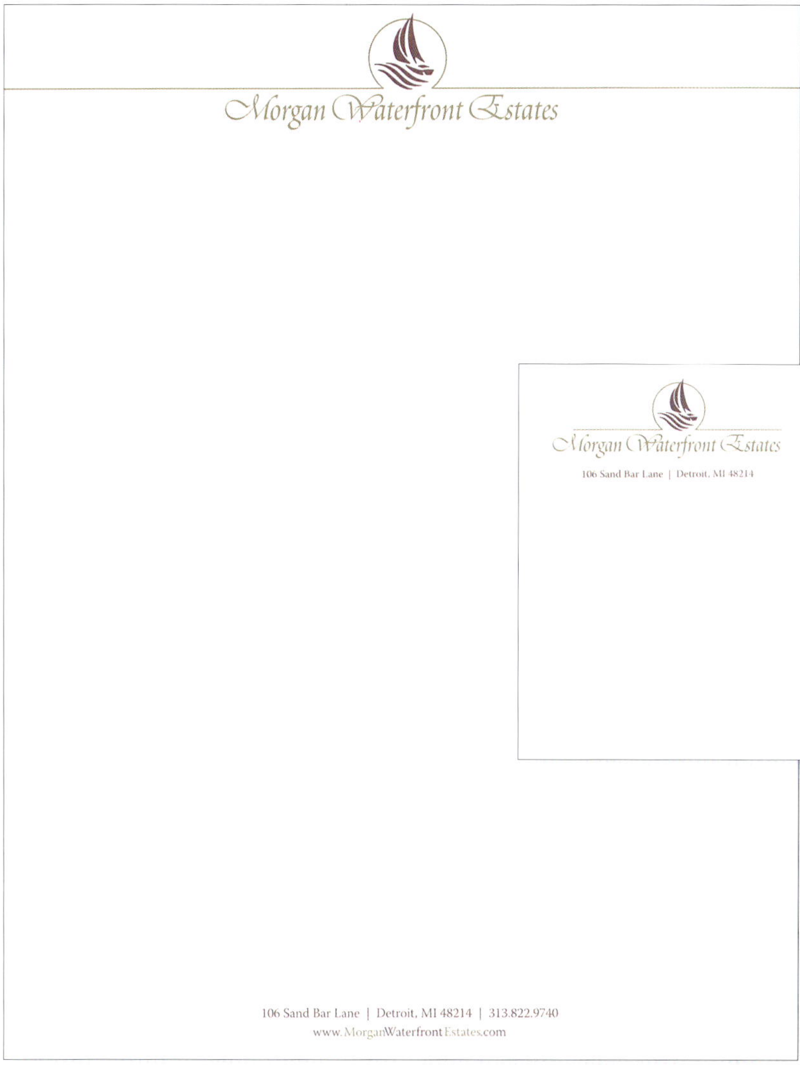
Morgan Waterfront Estates
106 Sand Bar Lane | Detroit, MI 48214 | 313.822.9740
www.MorganWaterfrontEstates.com

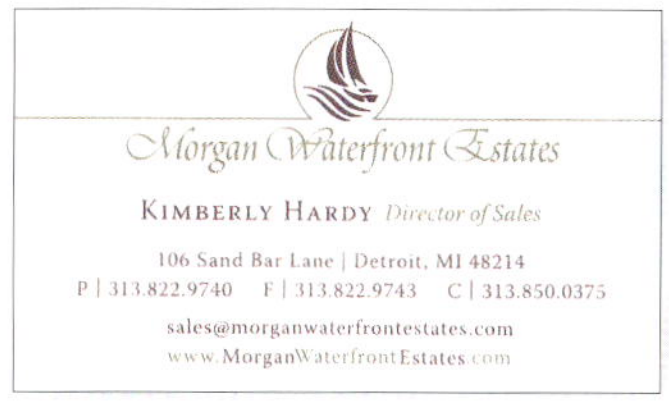
Morgan Waterfront Estates
Kimberly Hardy Director of Sales
106 Sand Bar Lane | Detroit, MI 48214
P | 313.822.9740 F | 313.822.9743 C | 313.850.0375
sales@morganwaterfrontestates.com
www.MorganWaterfrontEstates.com

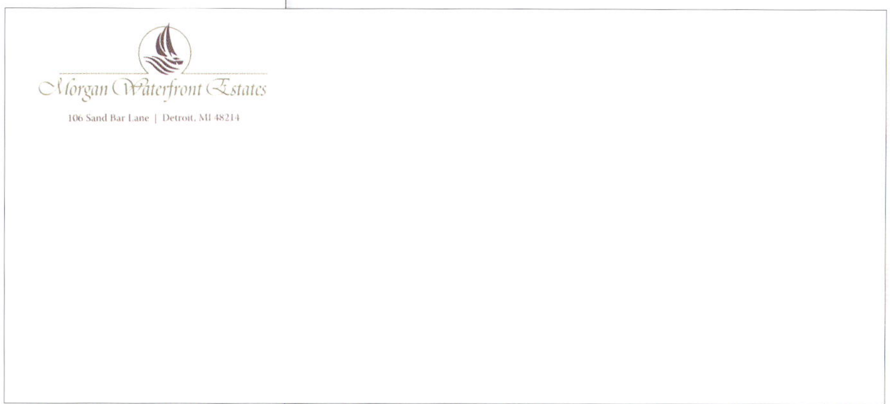
Morgan Waterfront Estates
106 Sand Bar Lane | Detroit, MI 48214

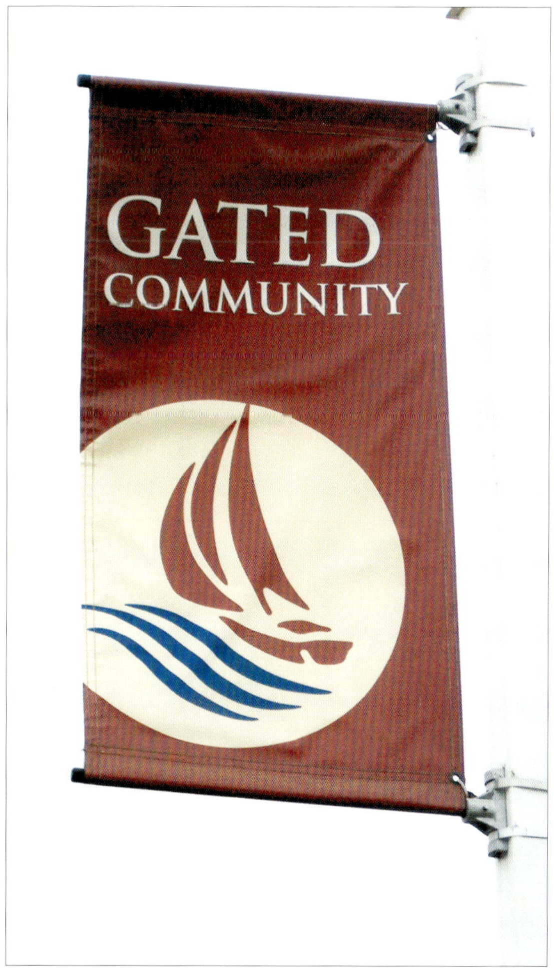
GATED
COMMUNITY

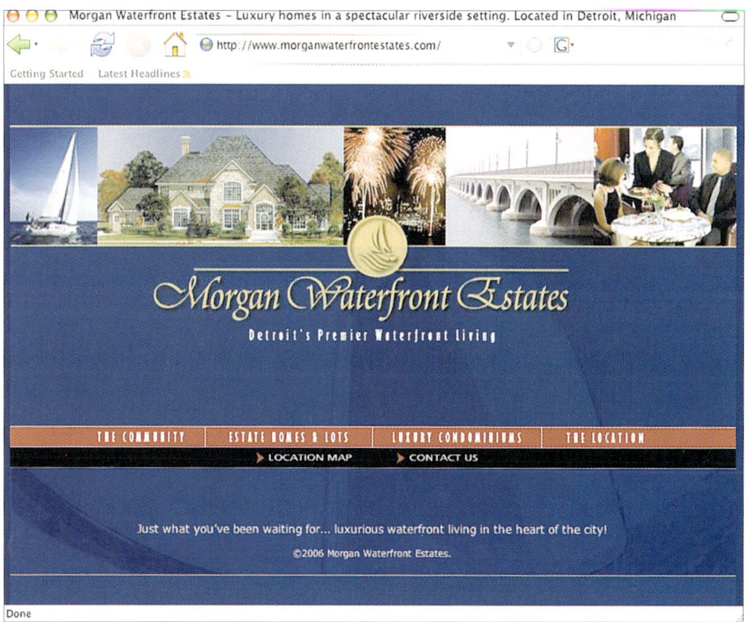
Morgan Waterfront Estates - Luxury homes in a spectacular riverside setting. Located in Detroit, Michigan
http://www.morganwaterfrontestates.com/
Getting Started
Latest Headlines
Morgan Waterfront Estates
Detroit's Premier Waterfront Living
THE COMMUNITY
ESTATE HOMES & LOTS
LUXURY CONDOMINIUMS
THE LOCATION
LOCATION MAP
CONTACT US
Just what you've been waiting for... luxurious waterfront living in the heart of the city!
©2006 Morgan Waterfront Estates.
Done

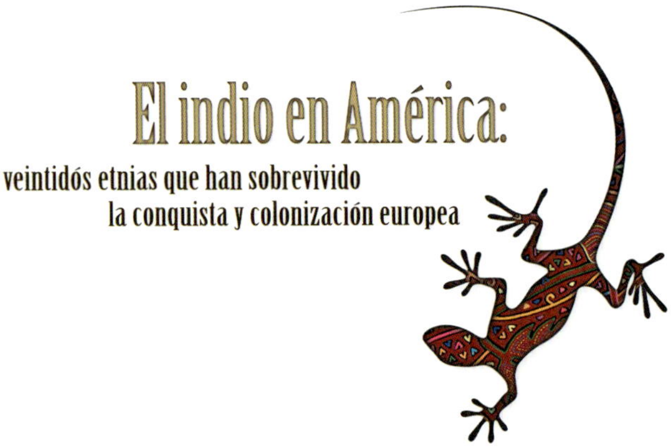
El indio en América:
veintidós etnias que han sobrevivido
la conquista y colonización europea

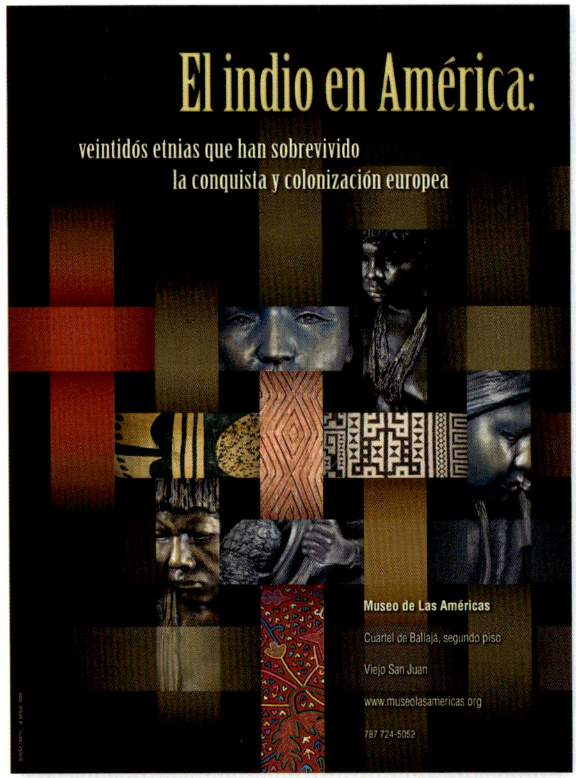
El indio en América:
veintidós etnias que han sobrevivido
la conquista y colonización europea
Museo de Las Américas
Cuartel de Ballajá, segundo piso
Viejo San Juan
www.museolasamericas.org
787 724-5052

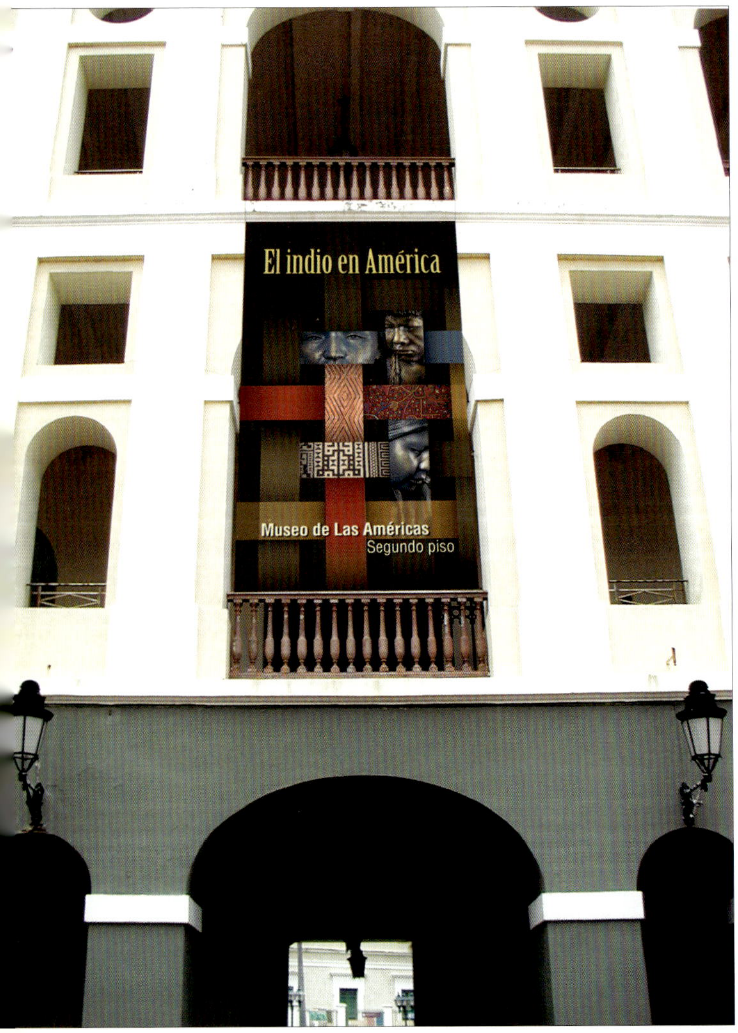
El indio en América
Museo de Las Américas
Segundo piso

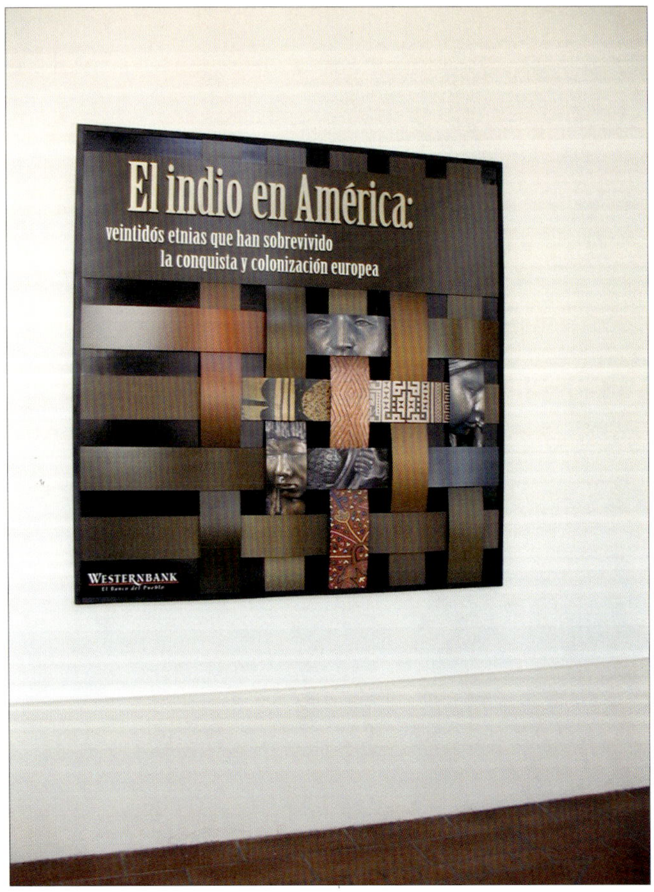
El indio en América:
veintidós etnias que han sobrevivido
la conquista y colonización europea
WESTERNBANK

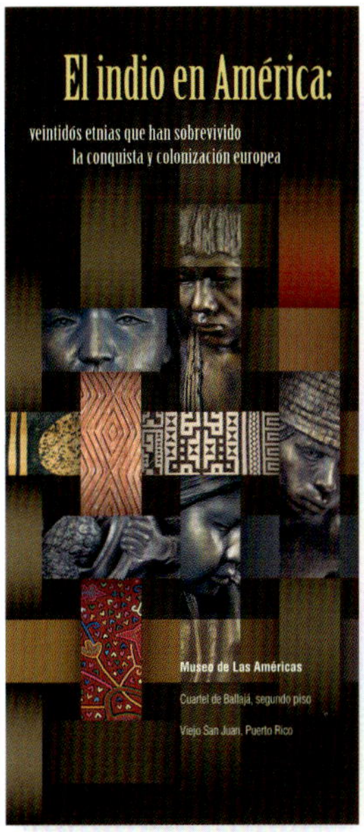

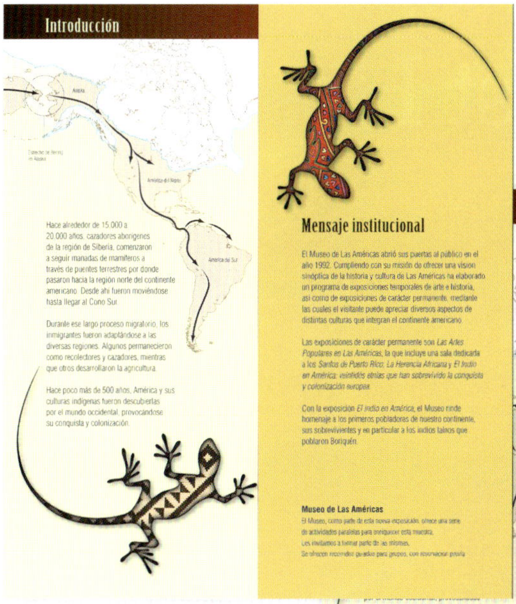

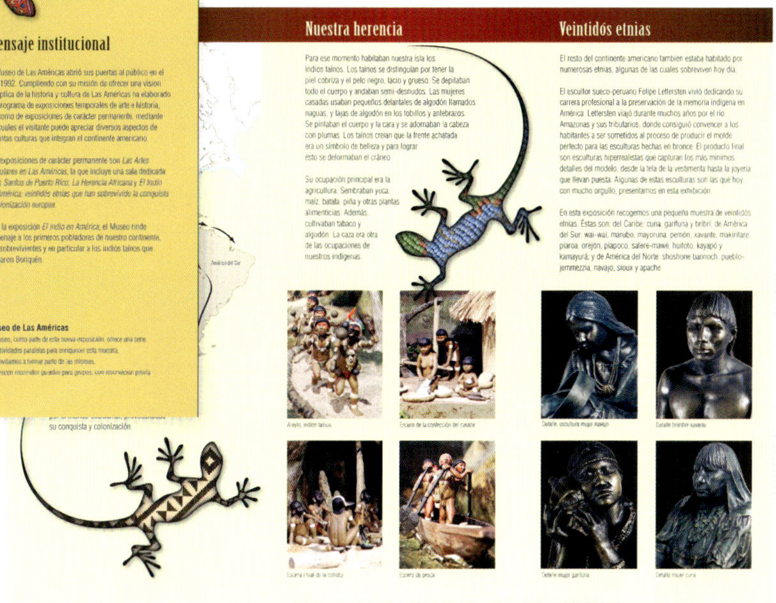

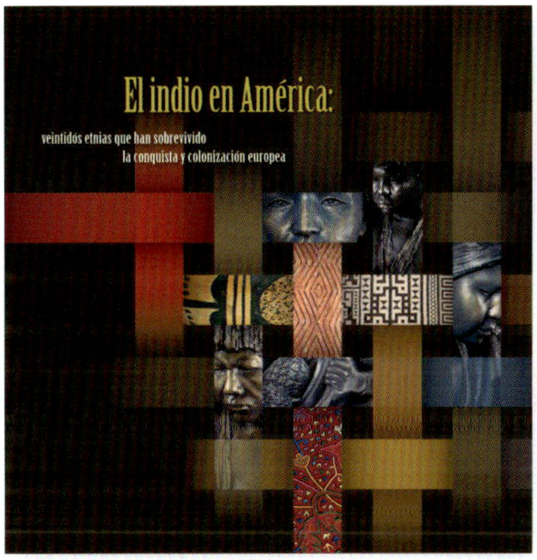

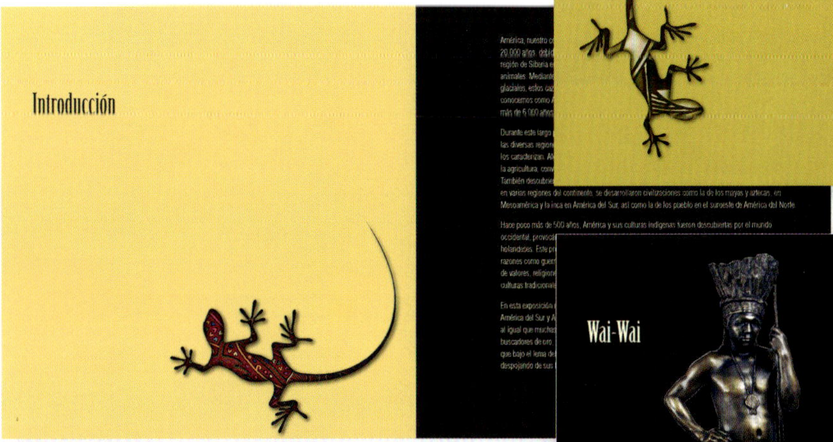

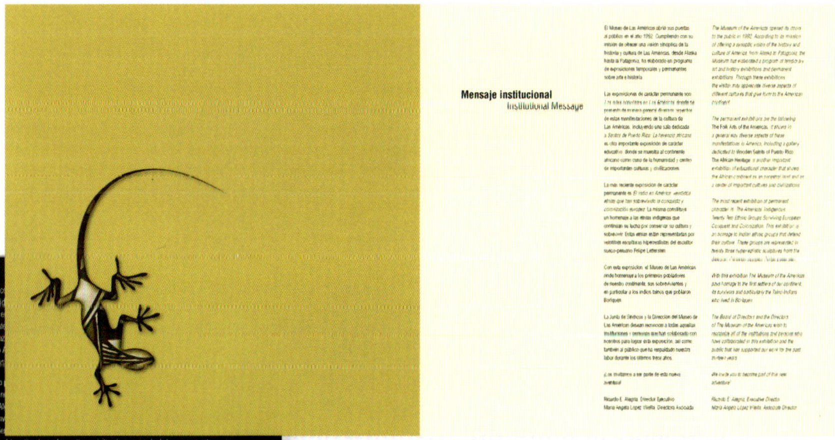

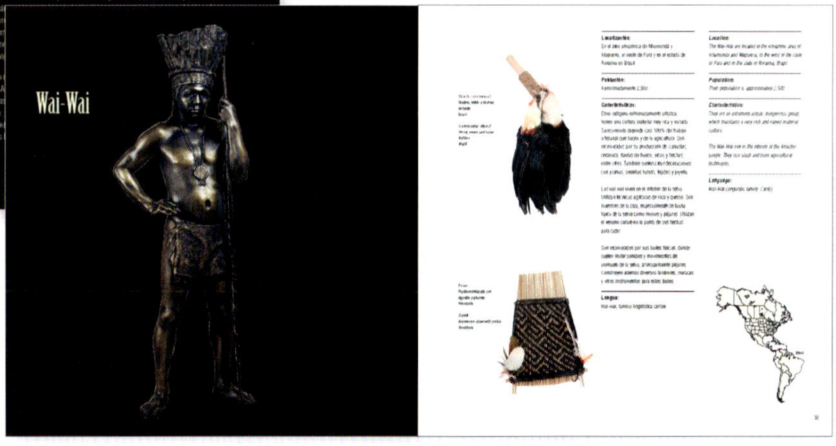

client
Museo de las Américas
design firm
ID Group
idgrouppr.com
designers
Mayra Maldonado,
Abner Gutiérrez,
Jorge Colón

Porter Adventist Hospital

Centura Health

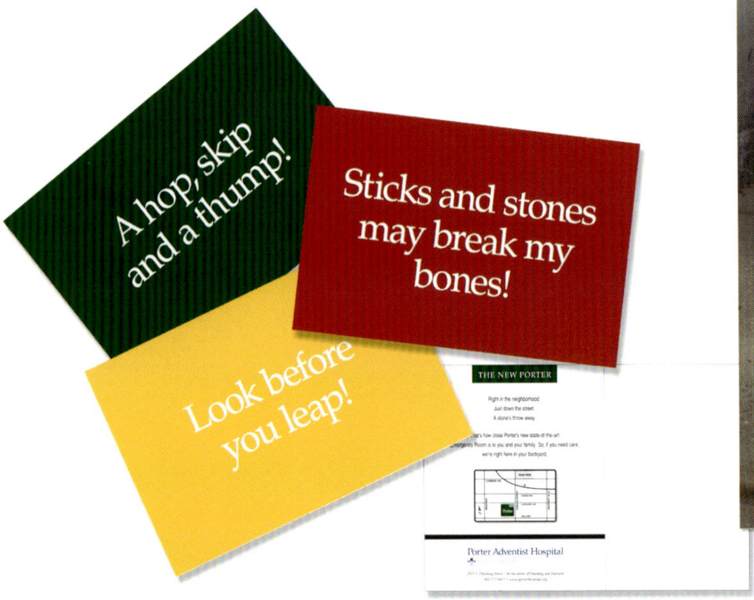

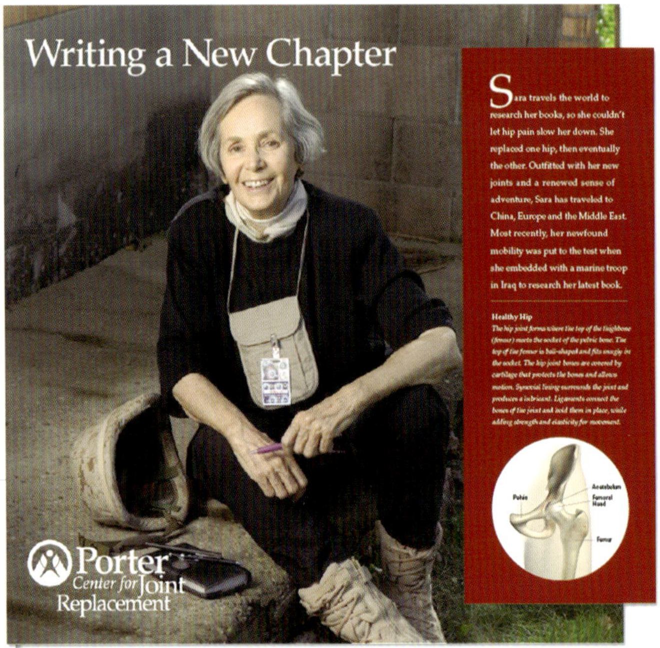

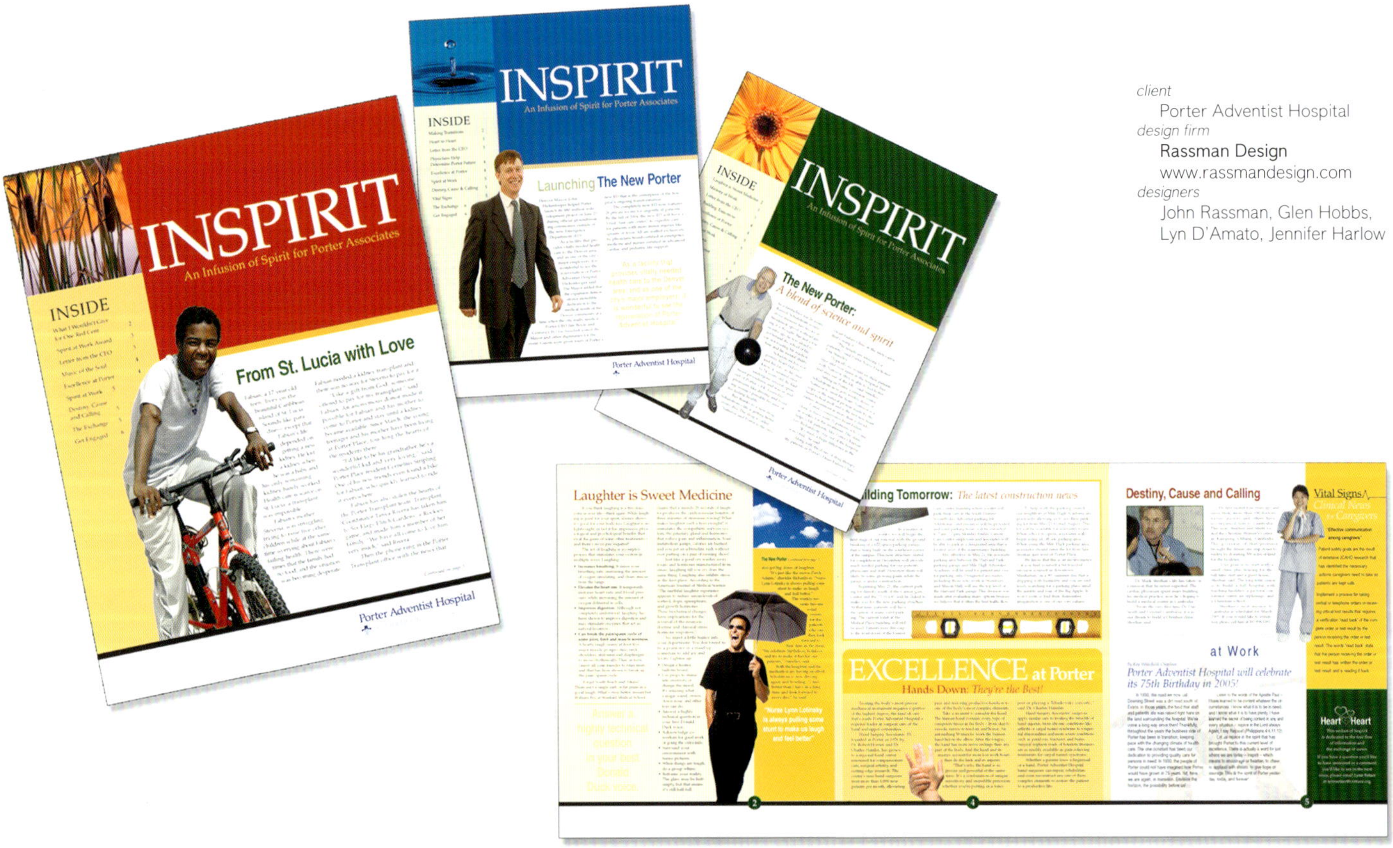

client
Porter Adventist Hospital
design firm
Rassman Design
www.rassmandesign.com
designers
John Rassman, Glen Hobbs, Lyn D'Amato, Jennifer Harlow

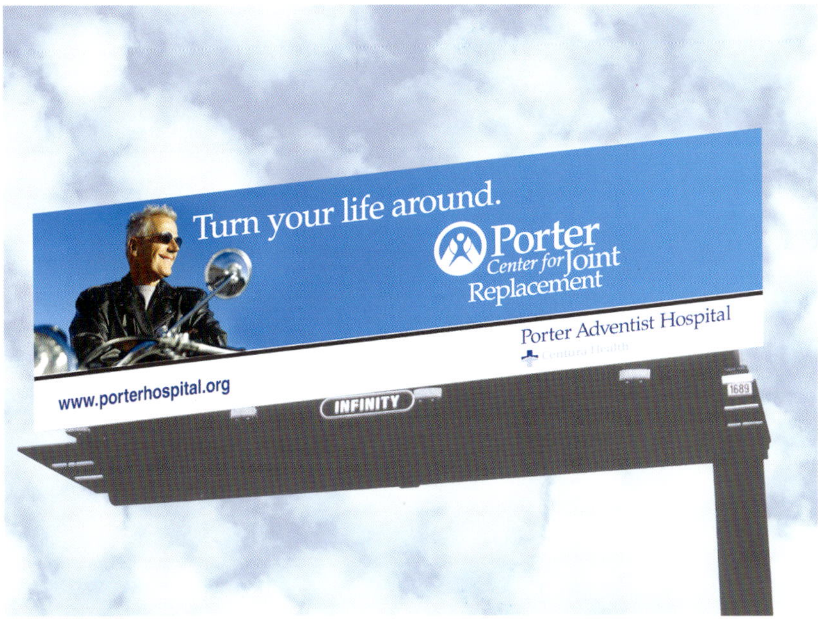
Turn your life around.
Porter
Center for Joint
Replacement
Porter Adventist Hospital
www.porterhospital.org
INFINITY

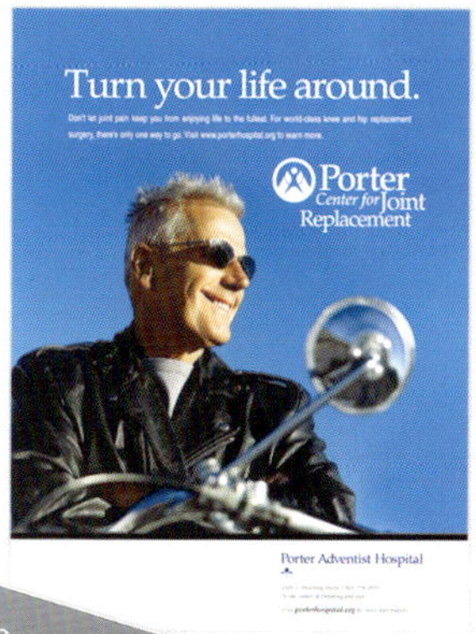
Turn your life around.
Porter
Center for Joint
Replacement
Porter Adventist Hospital

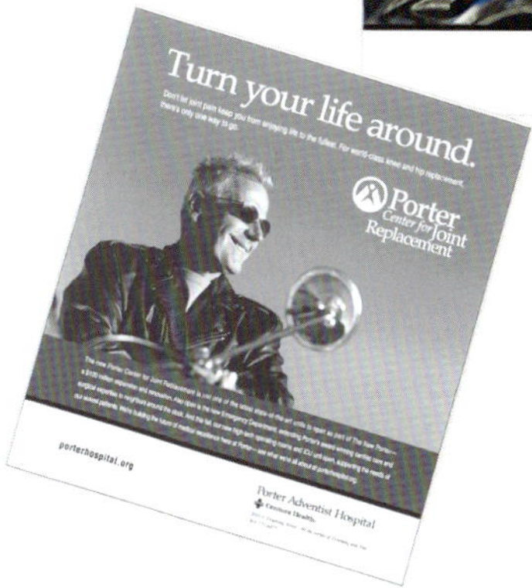
Turn your life around.
Porter
Center for Joint
Replacement
Porter Adventist Hospital

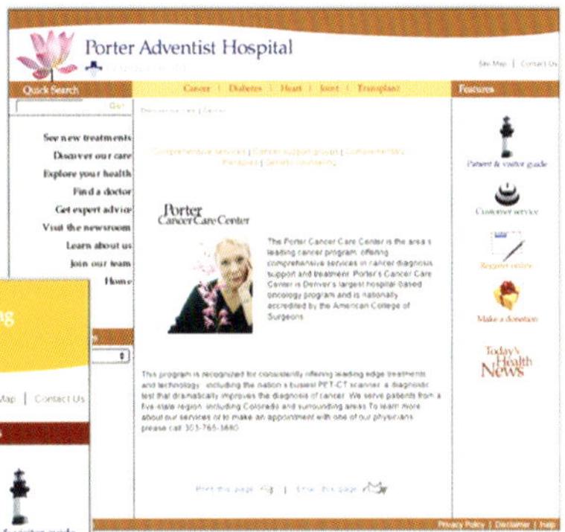
Porter Adventist Hospital
Quick Search
Features
Porter
Cancer Care Center
Today's Health News

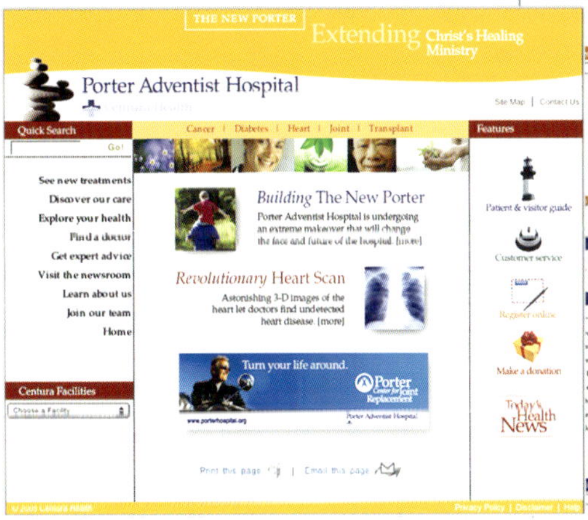
THE NEW PORTER
Extending Christ's Healing Ministry
Porter Adventist Hospital
Quick Search
Cancer | Diabetes | Heart | Joint | Transplant
Features
See new treatments
Discover our care
Explore your health
Find a doctor
Get expert advice
Visit the newsroom
Learn about us
Join our team
Home
Building The New Porter
Revolutionary Heart Scan
Turn your life around.
Centura Facilities
Today's Health News

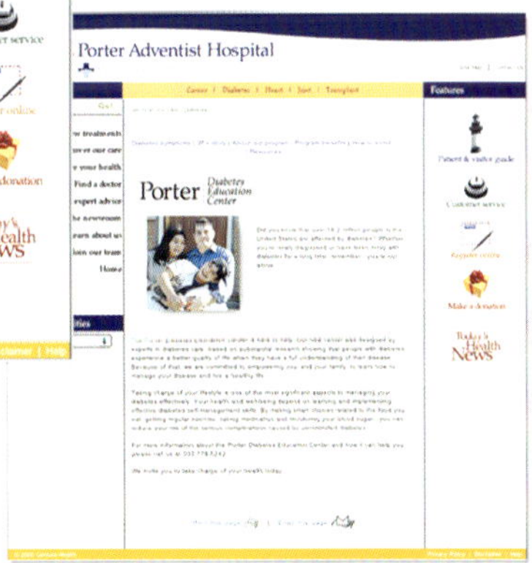
Porter Adventist Hospital
Features
Porter
Diabetes
Education
Center
Today's Health News

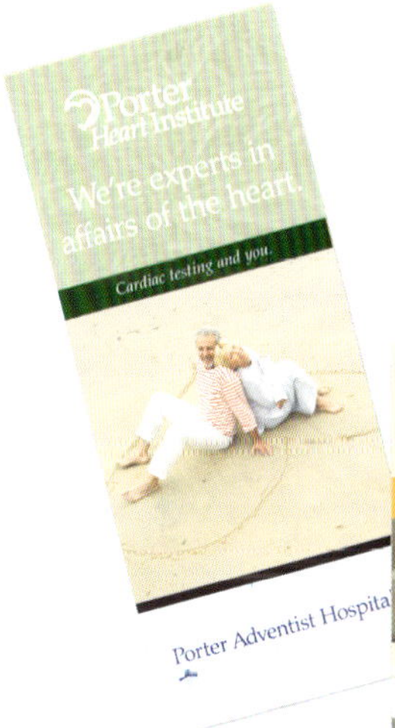
Porter
Heart Institute
We're experts in
affairs of the heart.
Cardiac testing and you.
Porter Adventist Hospital

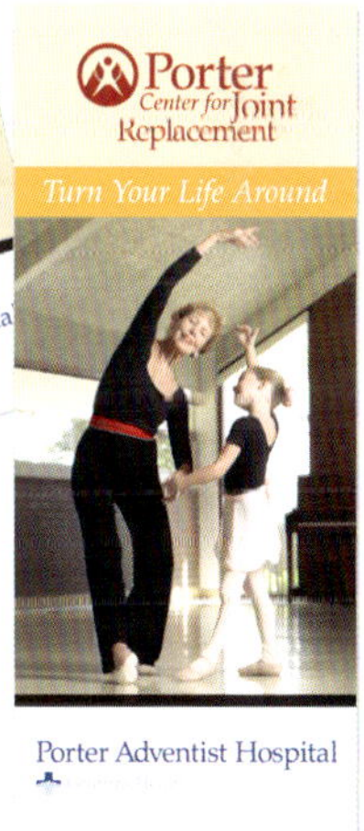
Porter
Center for Joint
Replacement
Turn Your Life Around
Porter Adventist Hospital

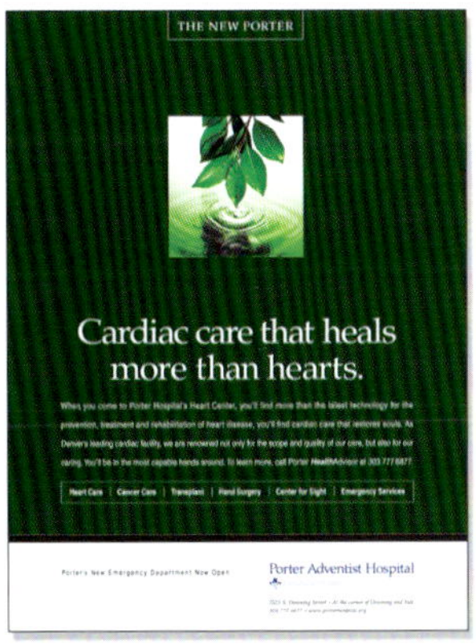
THE NEW PORTER
Cardiac care that heals
more than hearts.
Porter Adventist Hospital

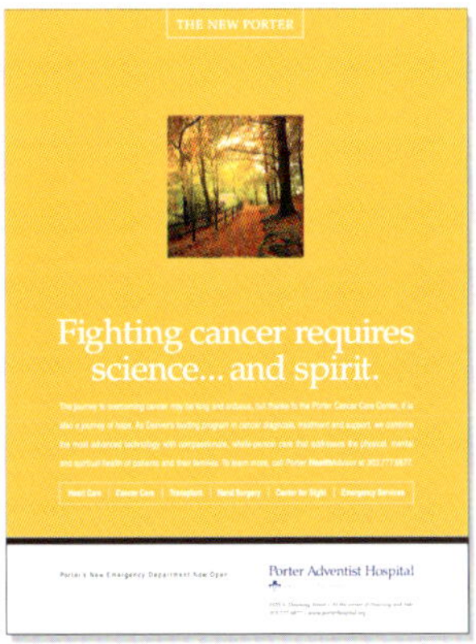
THE NEW PORTER
Fighting cancer requires
science... and spirit.
Porter Adventist Hospital

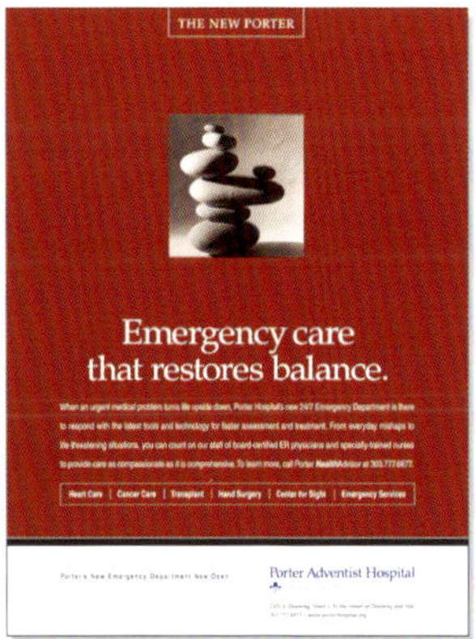
THE NEW PORTER
Emergency care
that restores balance.
Porter Adventist Hospital

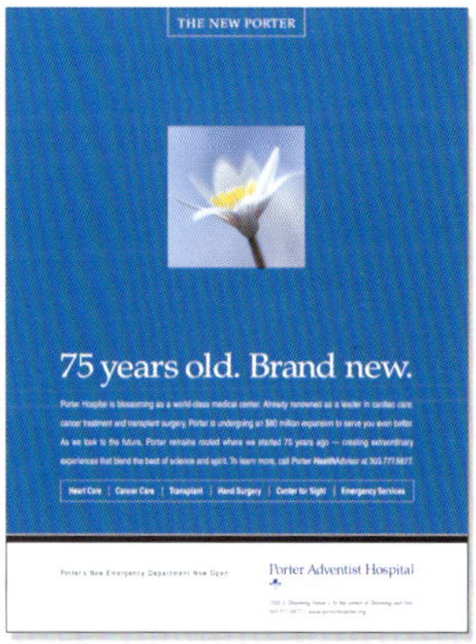
THE NEW PORTER
75 years old. Brand new.
Porter Adventist Hospital

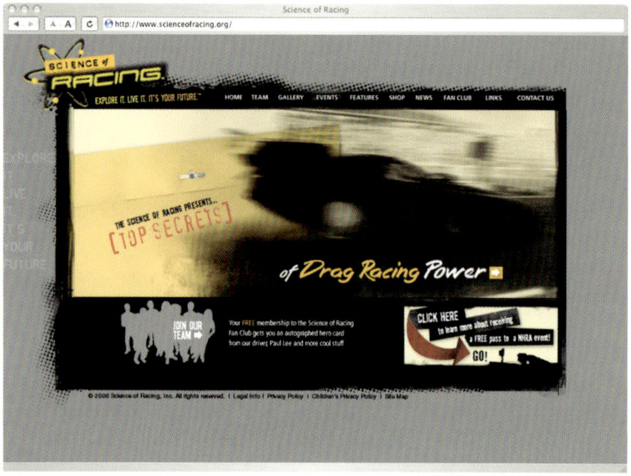

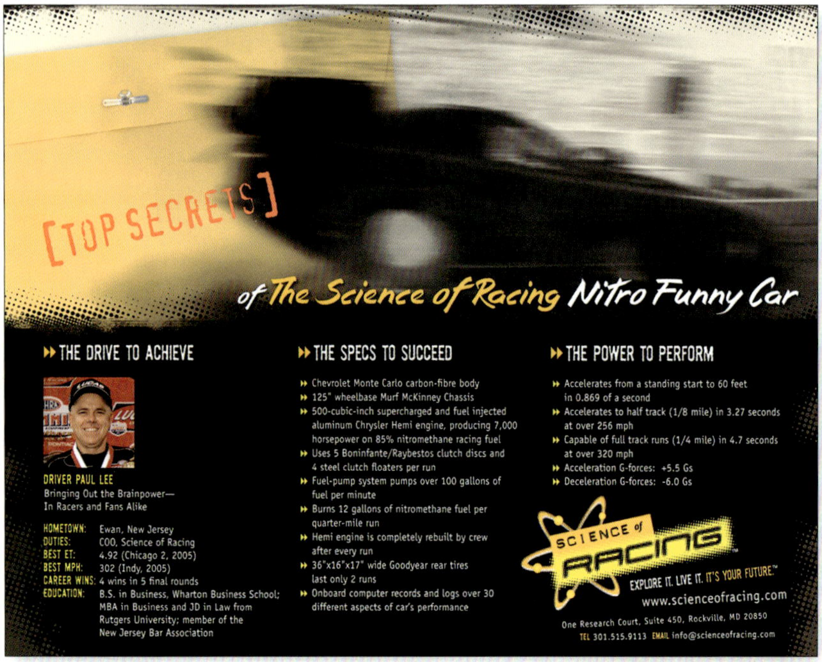

client
Science of Racing
design firm
Jill Tanenbaum Graphic Design & Advertising Inc.
www.jtdesign.com
designer
Jennifer Prophet

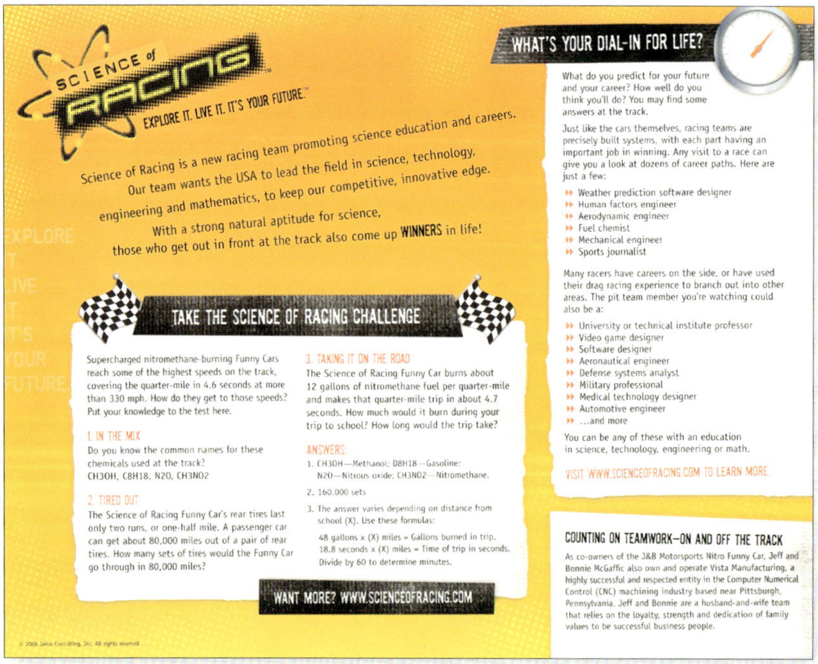

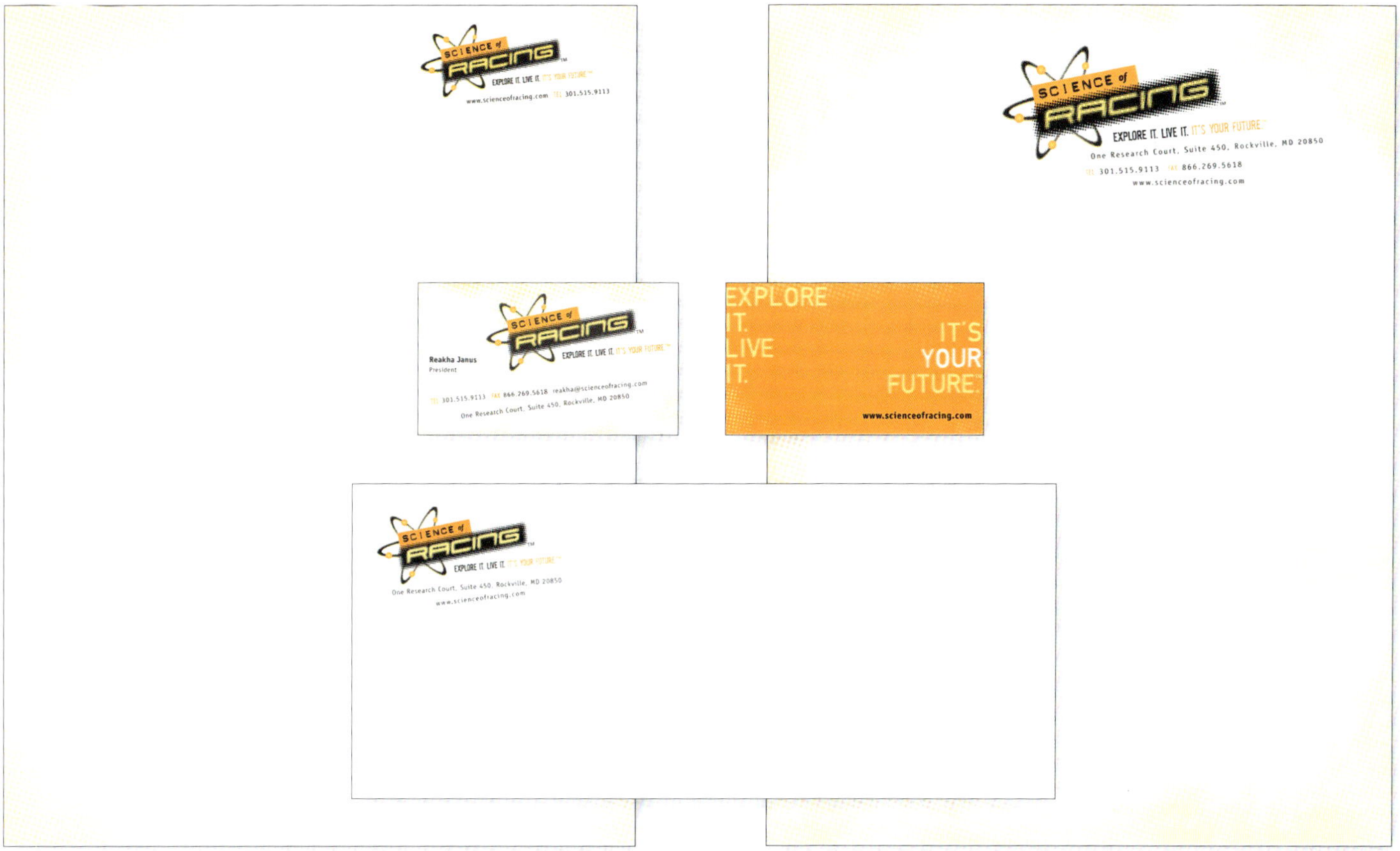
SCIENCE of RACING
EXPLORE IT. LIVE IT. IT'S YOUR FUTURE.
www.scienceofracing.com TEL 301.515.9113
One Research Court, Suite 450, Rockville, MD 20850
TEL 301.515.9113 FAX 866.269.5618
www.scienceofracing.com
Reakha Janus
President
TEL 301.515.9113 FAX 866.269.5618 reakha@scienceofracing.com
One Research Court, Suite 450, Rockville, MD 20850
EXPLORE IT. LIVE IT.
IT'S YOUR FUTURE.
www.scienceofracing.com

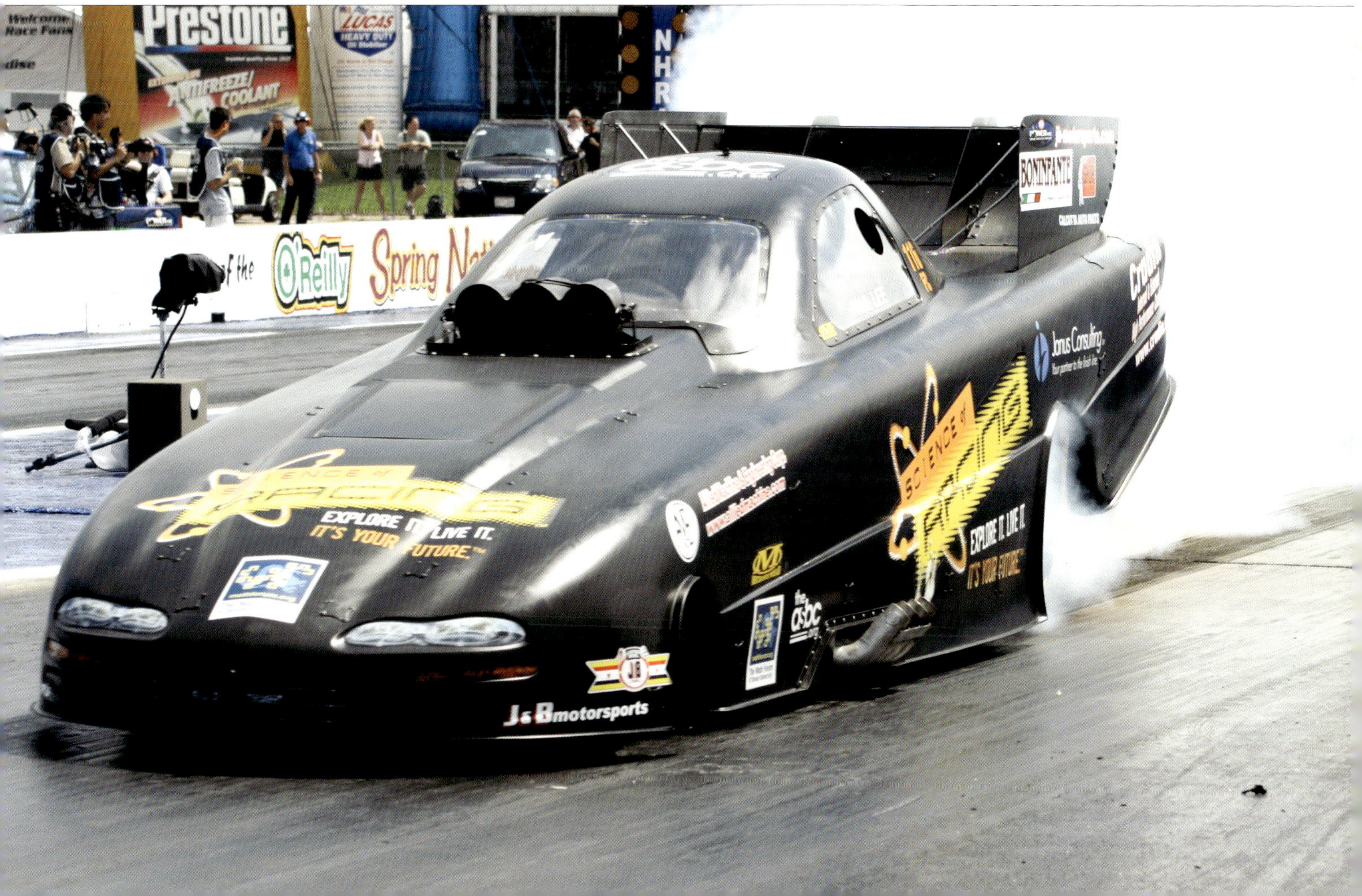
Prestone
LUCAS
ANTIFREEZE/COOLANT
O'Reilly
SCIENCE of RACING
EXPLORE IT. LIVE IT. IT'S YOUR FUTURE.
BONINFANTE
Janus Consulting
J&B motorsports

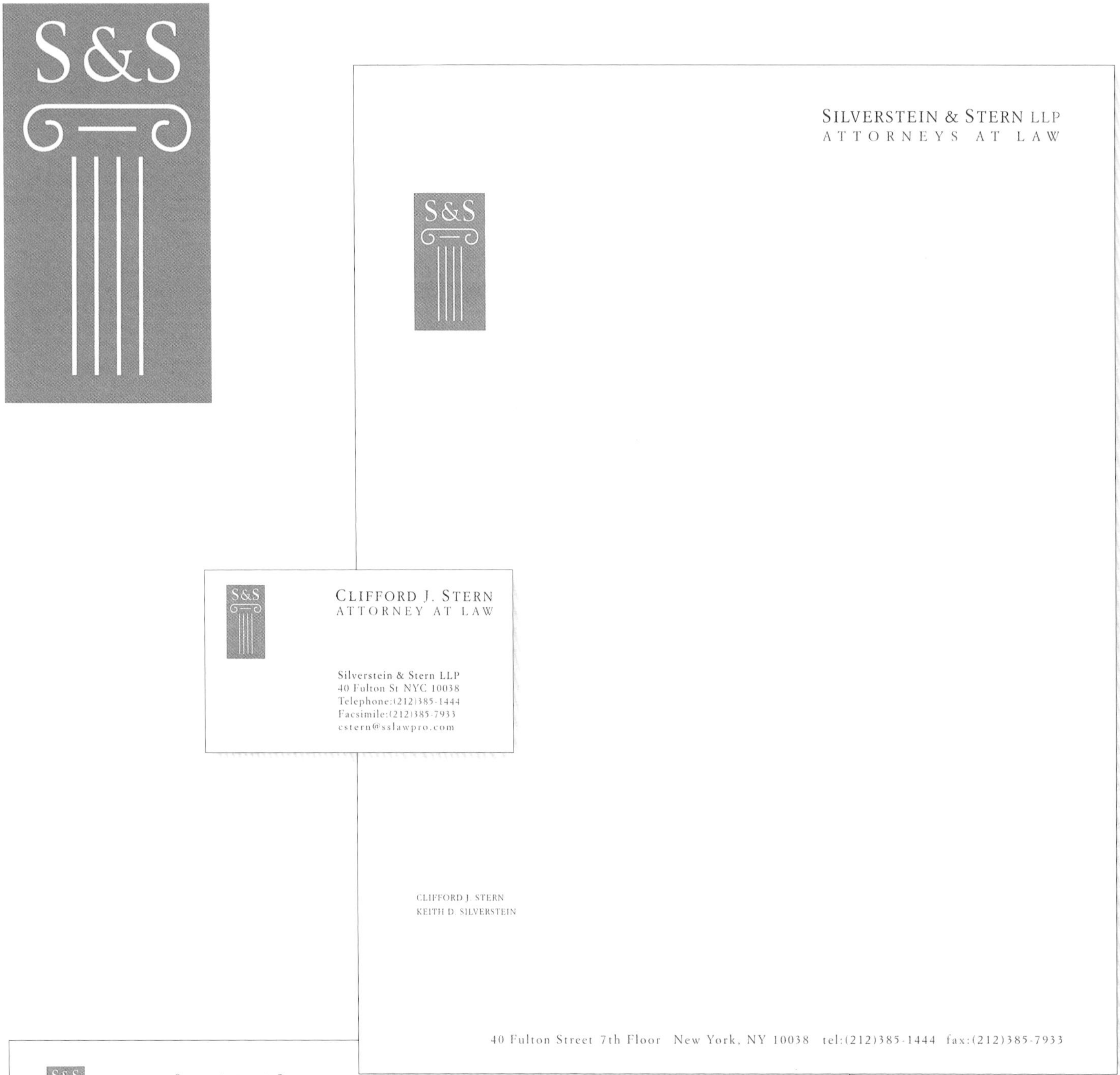

client
Silverstein & Stern LLP
design firm
Susan Meshberg Graphic Design
designers
Susan Meshberg, Rob Johnson

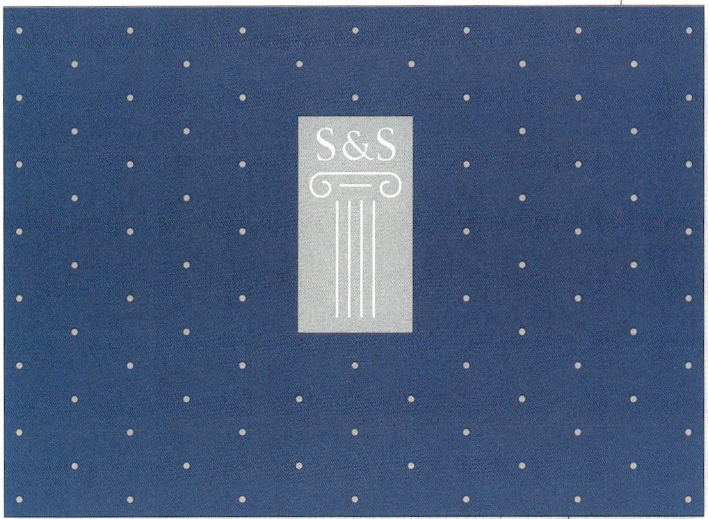
S&S

S&S
SILVERSTEIN & STERN LLP
ATTORNEYS AT LAW
40 Fulton St 7th fl NY, NY 10038

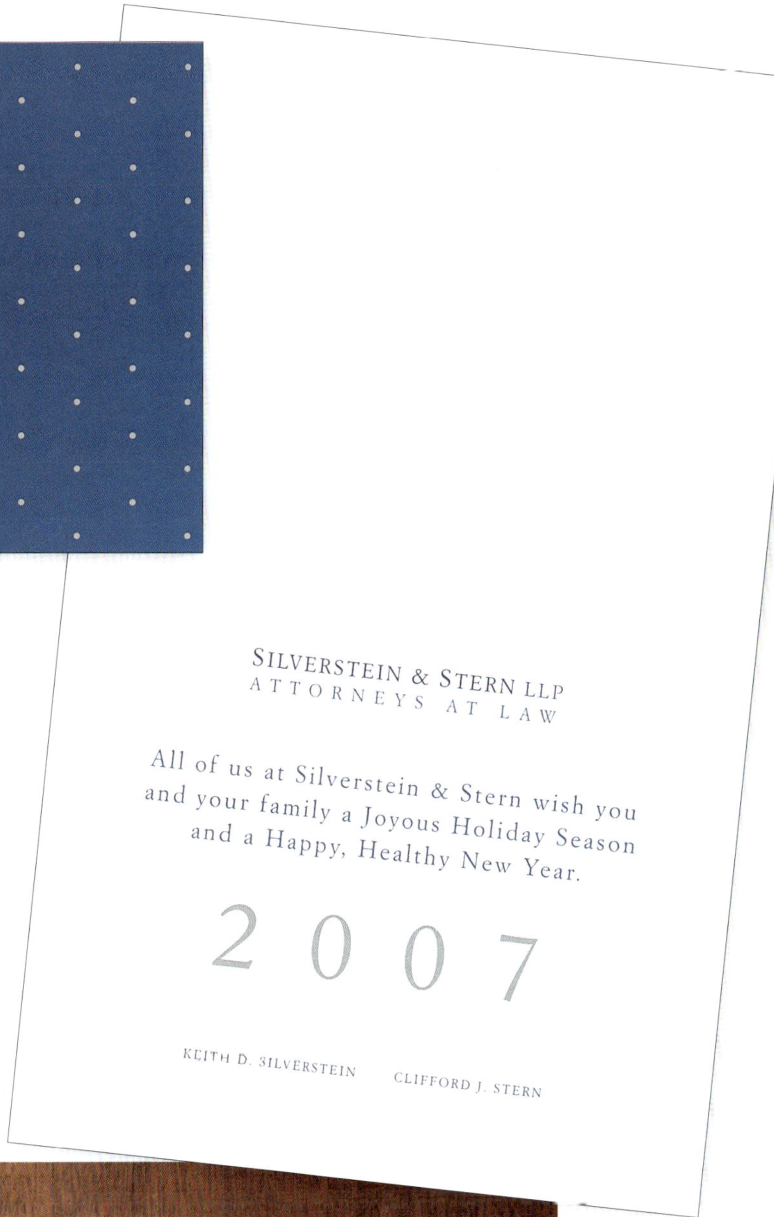
SILVERSTEIN & STERN LLP
ATTORNEYS AT LAW
All of us at Silverstein & Stern wish you
and your family a Joyous Holiday Season
and a Happy, Healthy New Year.
2007
KEITH D. SILVERSTEIN
CLIFFORD J. STERN

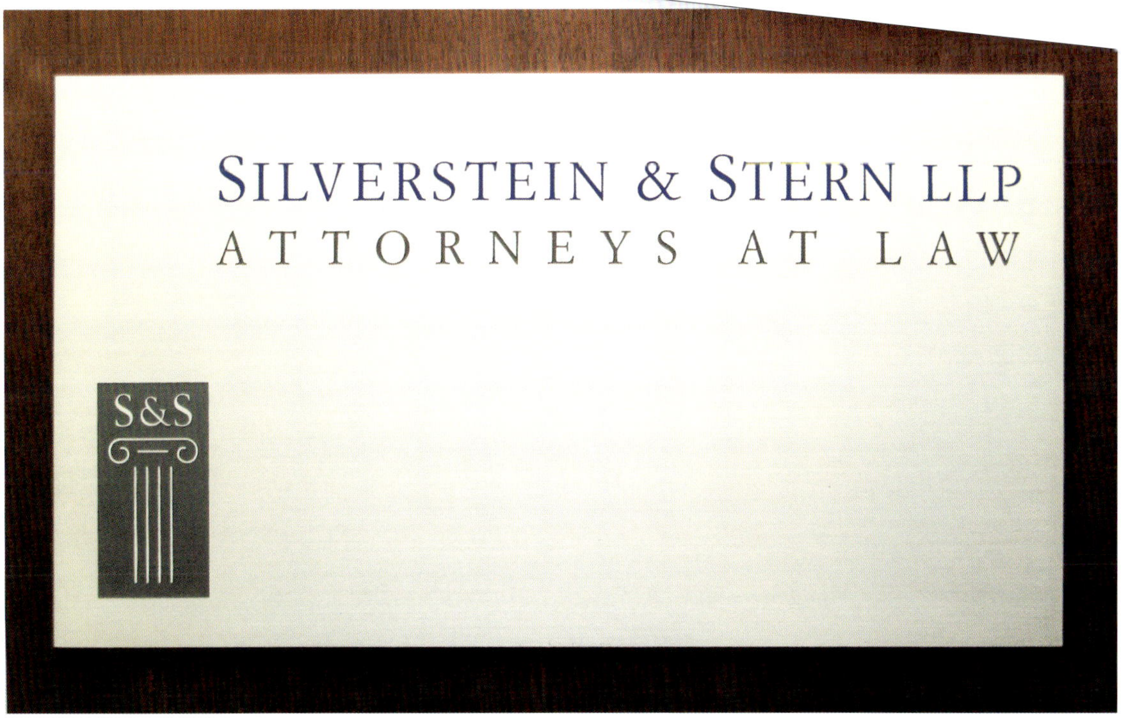
SILVERSTEIN & STERN LLP
ATTORNEYS AT LAW
S&S

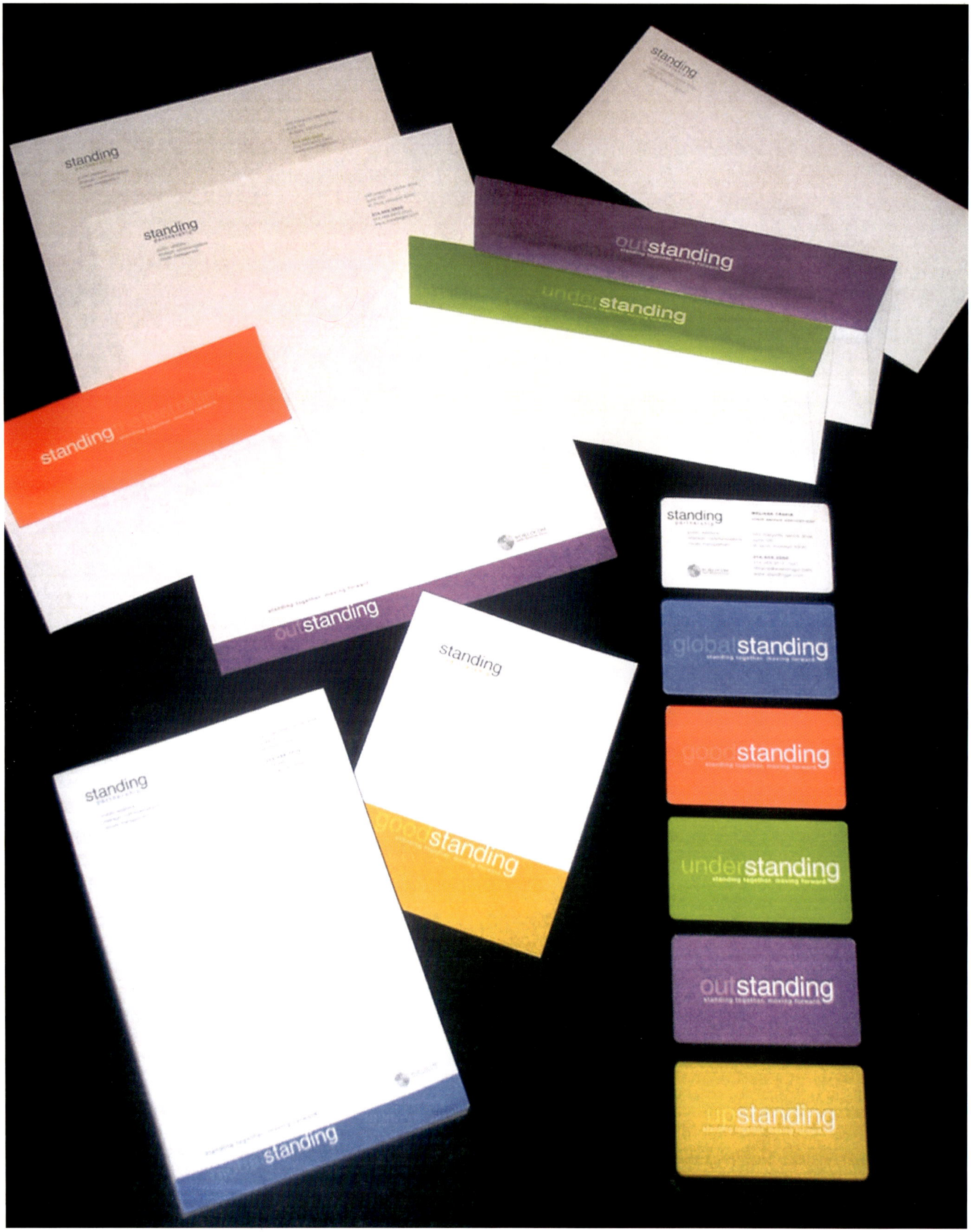

client
Standing Partnership
design firm
Paradowski Creative
www.paradowski.com

creative director
Alex Paradowski
designers
Steve Cox, Dennis Bland, Jeff Skubic, Jerry Gennaria

account manager
Nila Paradowski

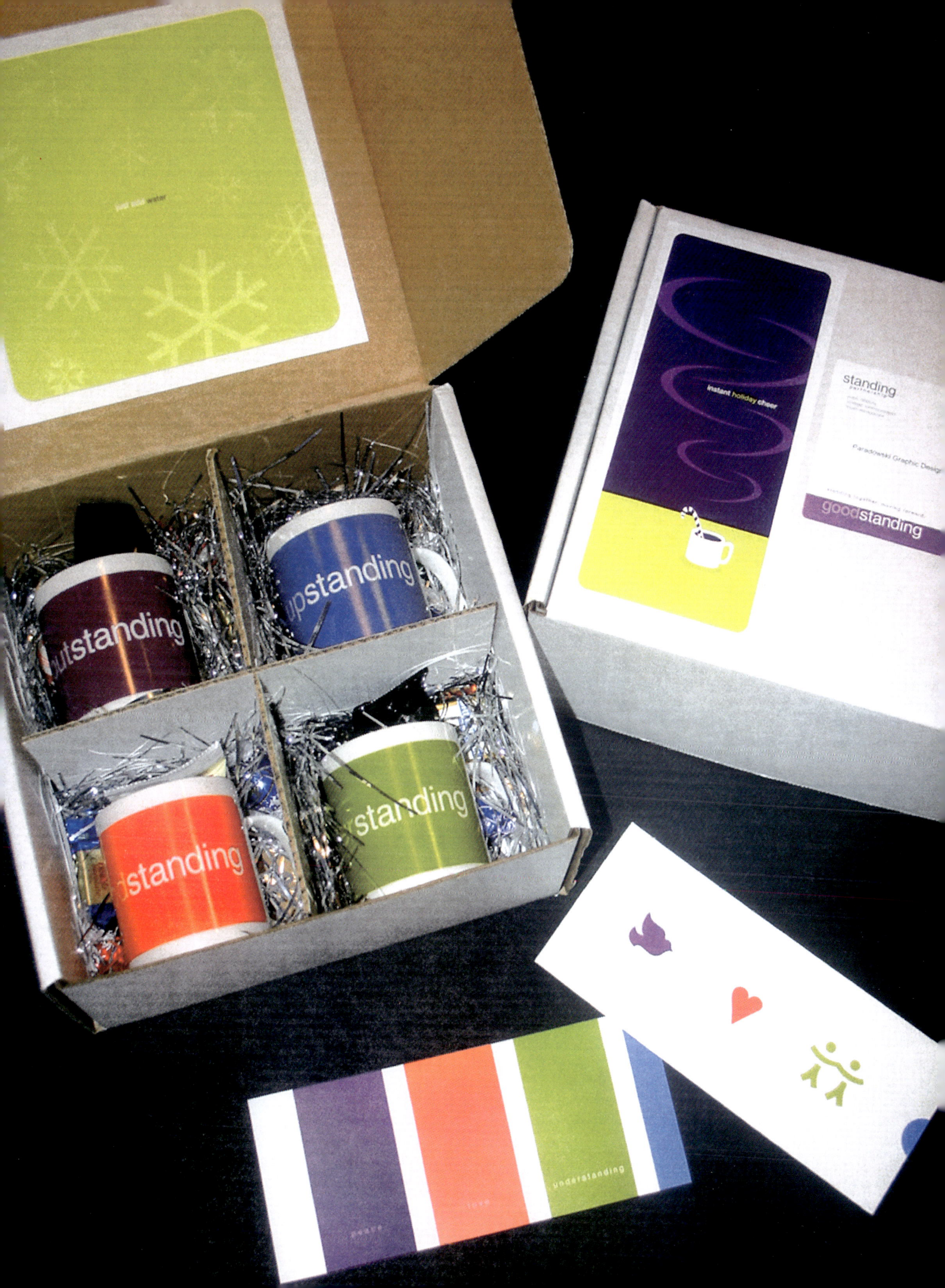
upstanding
standing
standing
standing
instant holiday cheer
standing
Paradowski Graphic Desig
goodstanding
understanding

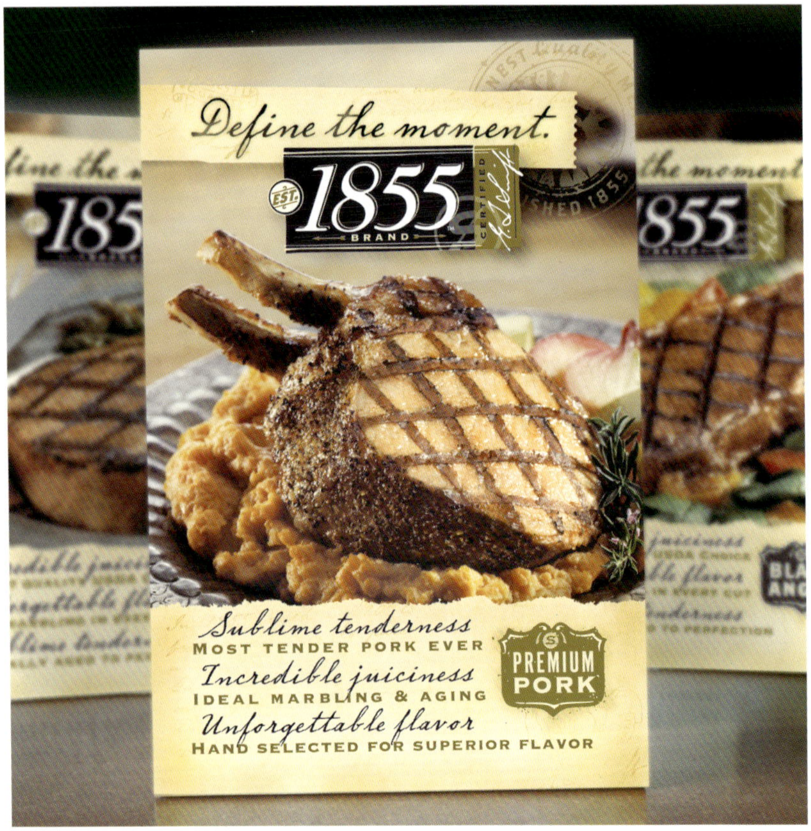

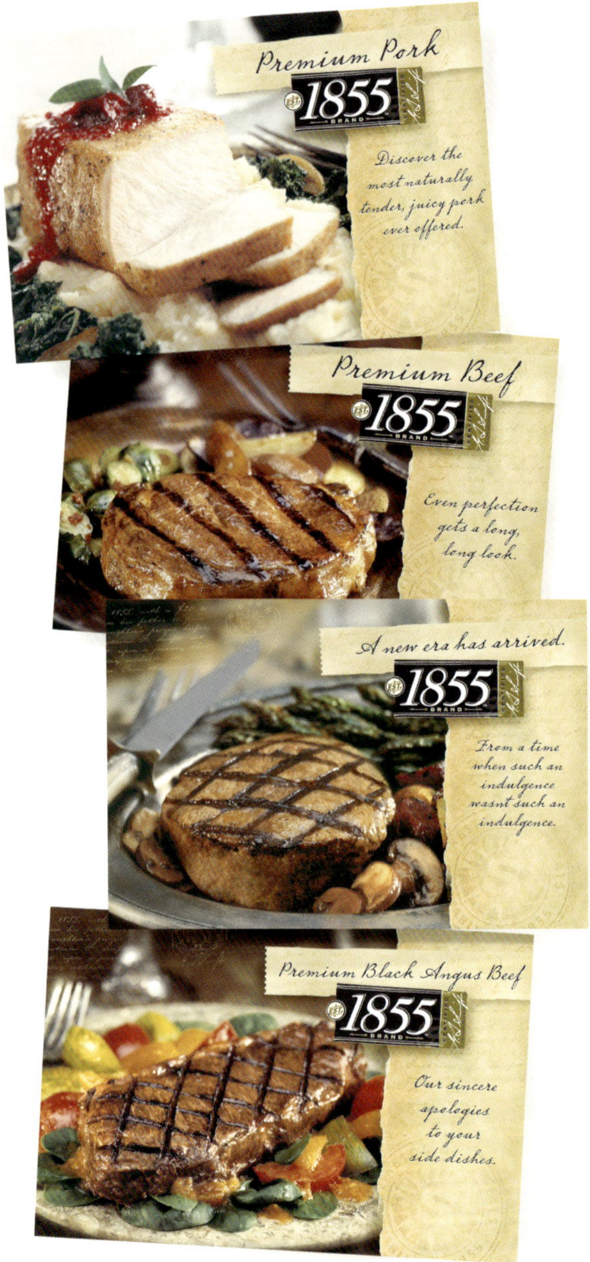

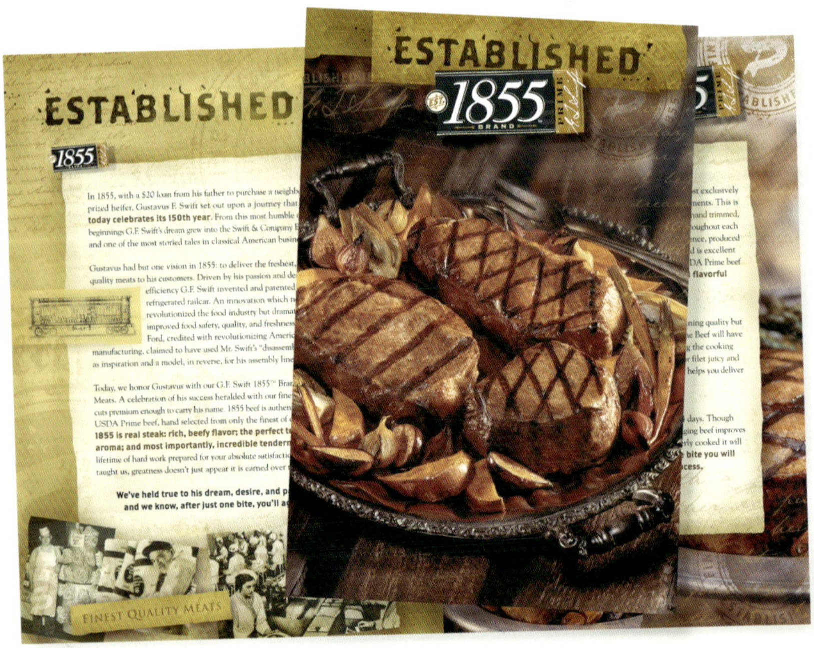

client
Swift & Company
design firm
Insight Design Communications
and Schafer Condon Carter
insightdesign.com
sccadv.com
designers
Greg Menefee, Tracy Holdeman,
Ron Sone, Fran D'Amico, Paul Chauncey

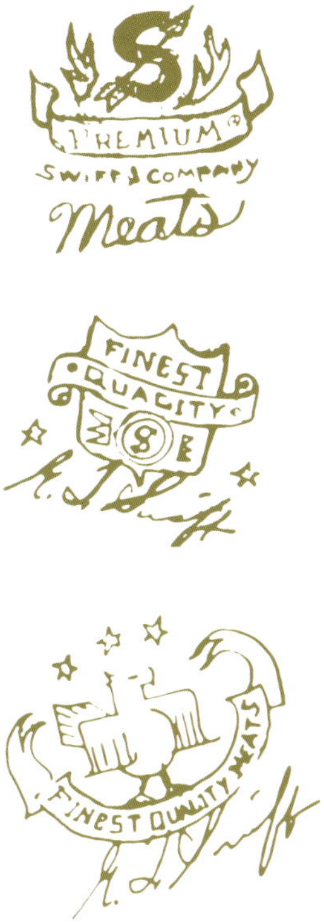
PREMIUM
SWIFT & COMPANY
Meats
FINEST
QUALITY
FINEST QUALITY MEATS

EST.
1855
BRAND
CERTIFIED
FINEST QUALITY MEATS
Director of Marketing
Greg Menefee
970.506.7759 office
970.346.4735 fax
970.381.1041 cell
Swift & Company
1770 Promontory Circle
Greeley, CO 80634-9038
1855brand.com
STABLISH
Swift & Company • 1770 Promontory Circle • Greeley, CO 80634-9038
Telephone: 800-727-2333 Website: 1855brand.com

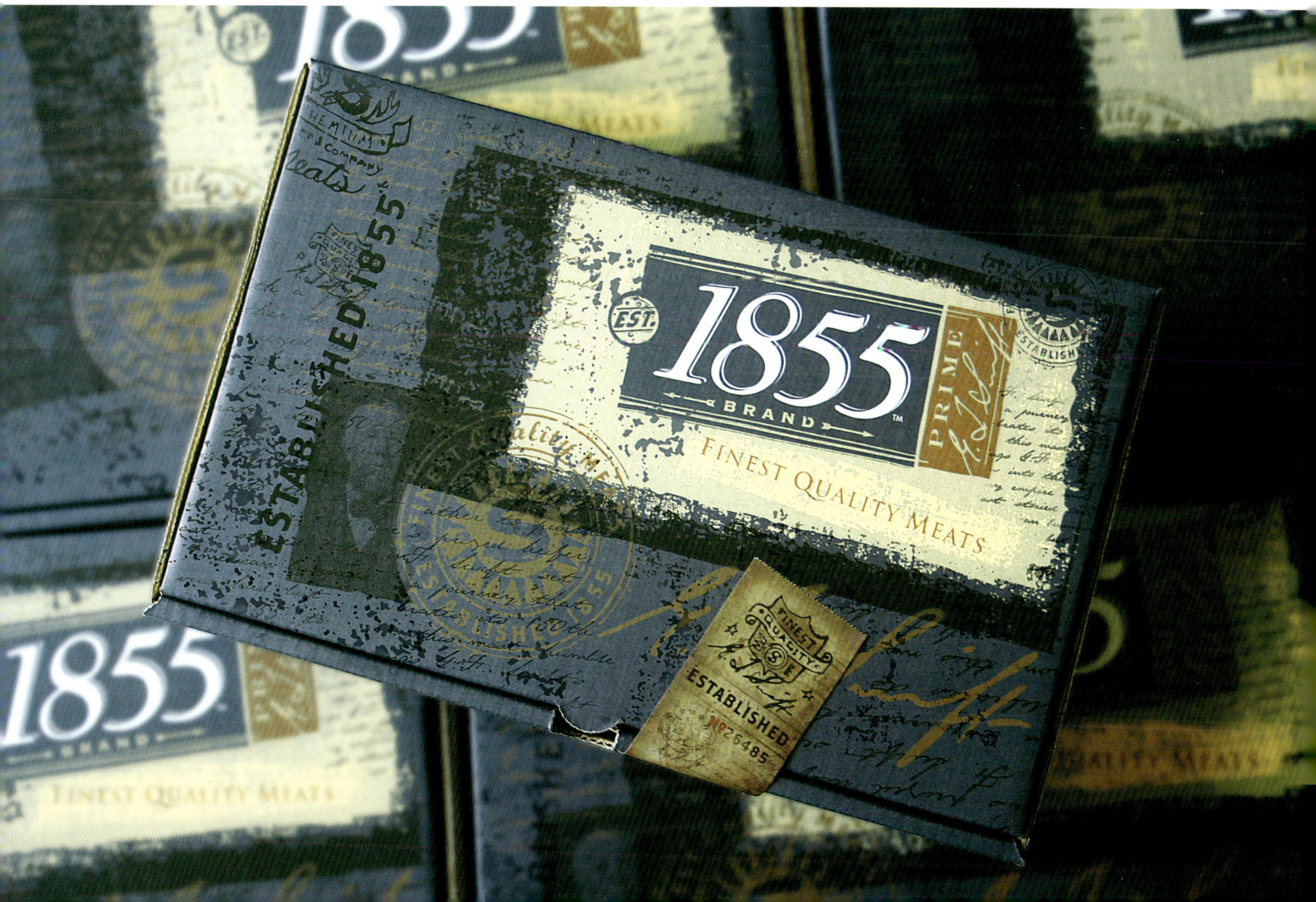
EST.
1855
BRAND
PRIME
FINEST QUALITY MEATS
ESTABLISHED 1855
FINEST
QUALITY
ESTABLISHED
№26485

ViewPoint Bank

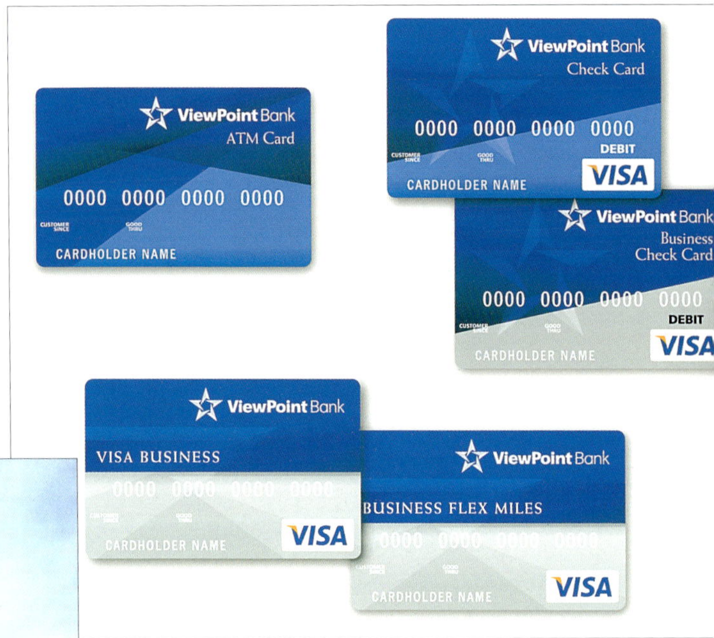

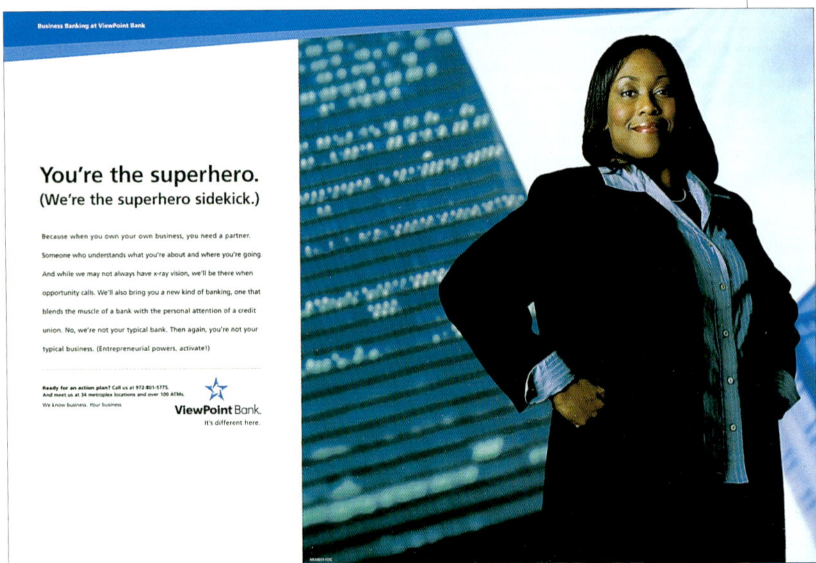

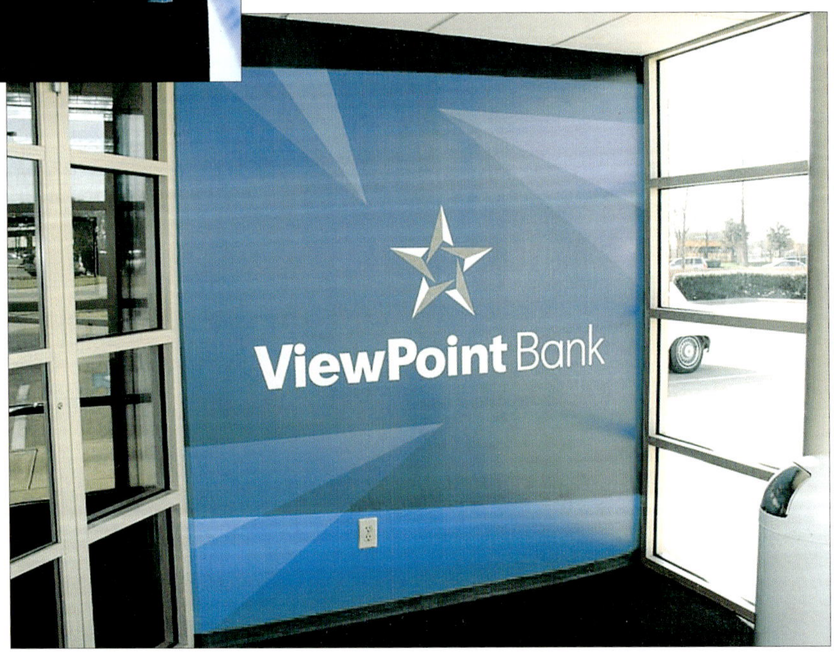

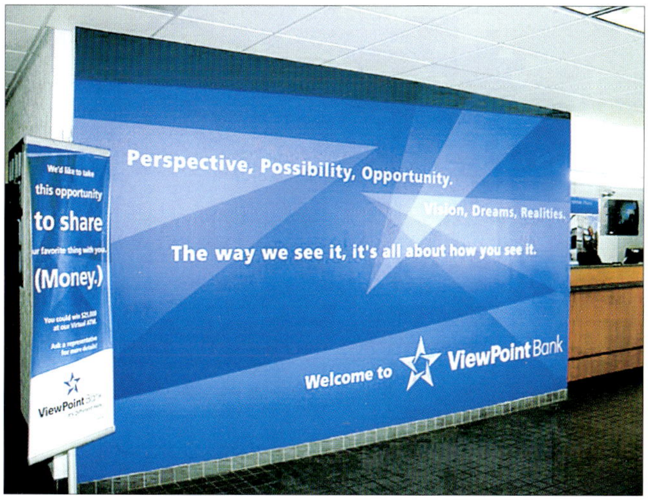

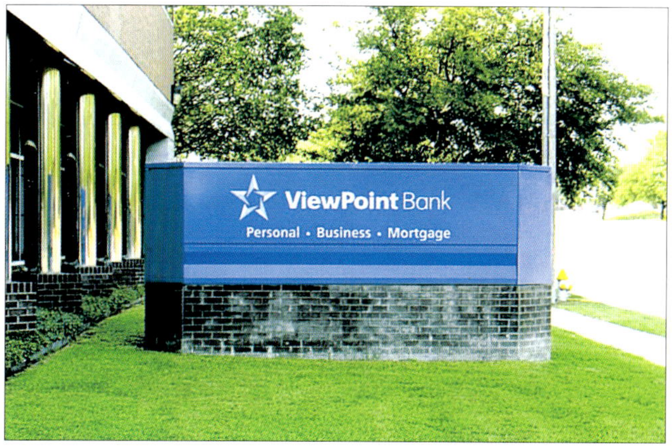

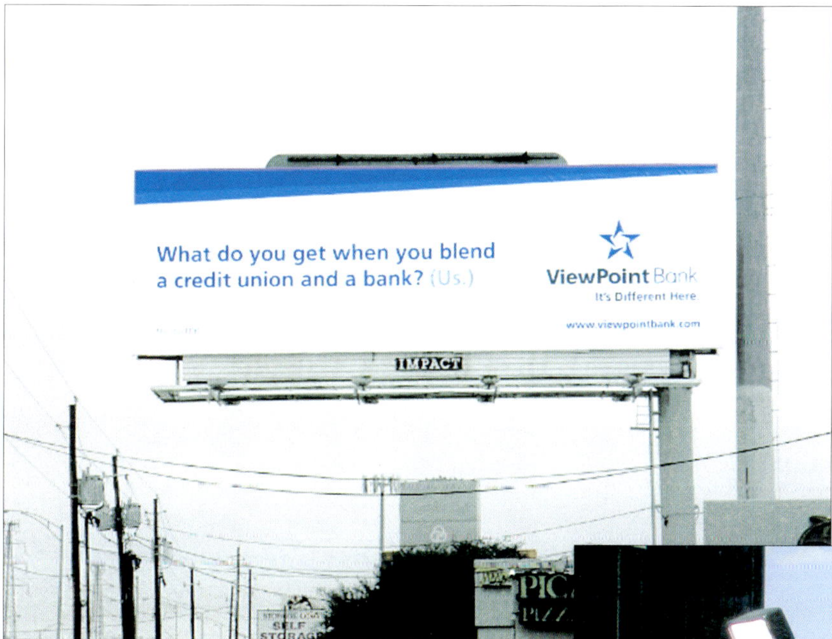

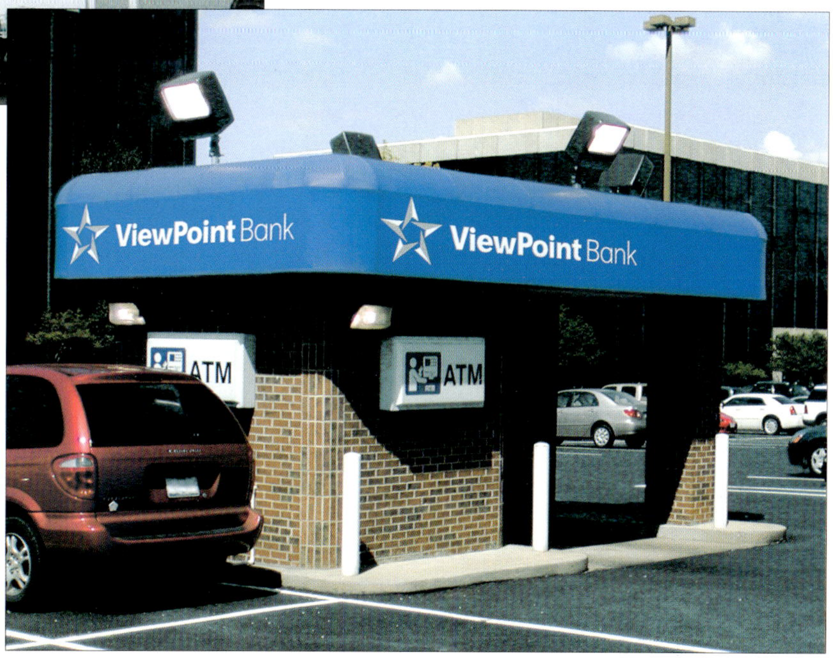

client
ViewPoint Bank
design firm
Marcantel | Crouch | LeBlanc
www.mcl-usa.com
designers
Richard LeBlanc, Tom Marcantel

VISION SCIENCES

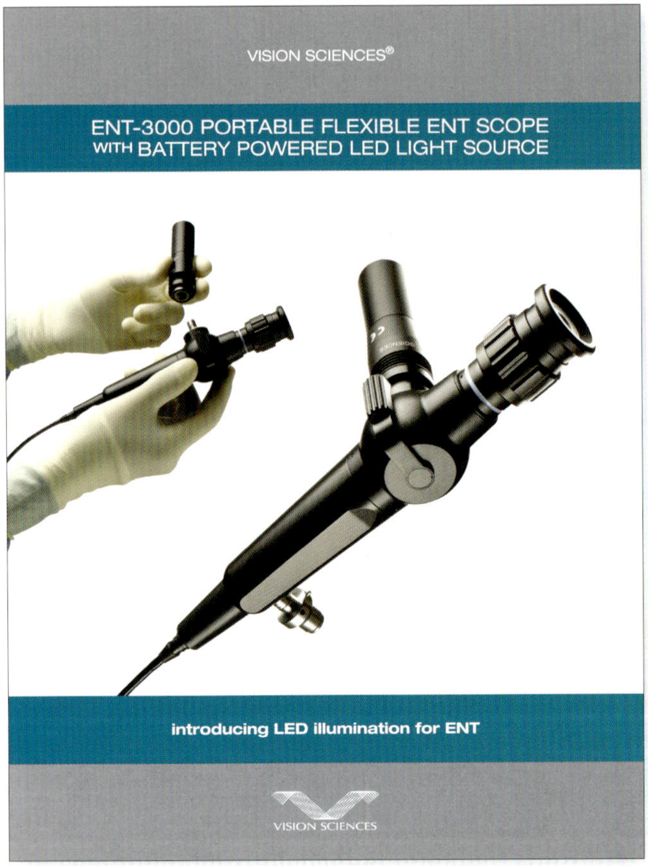

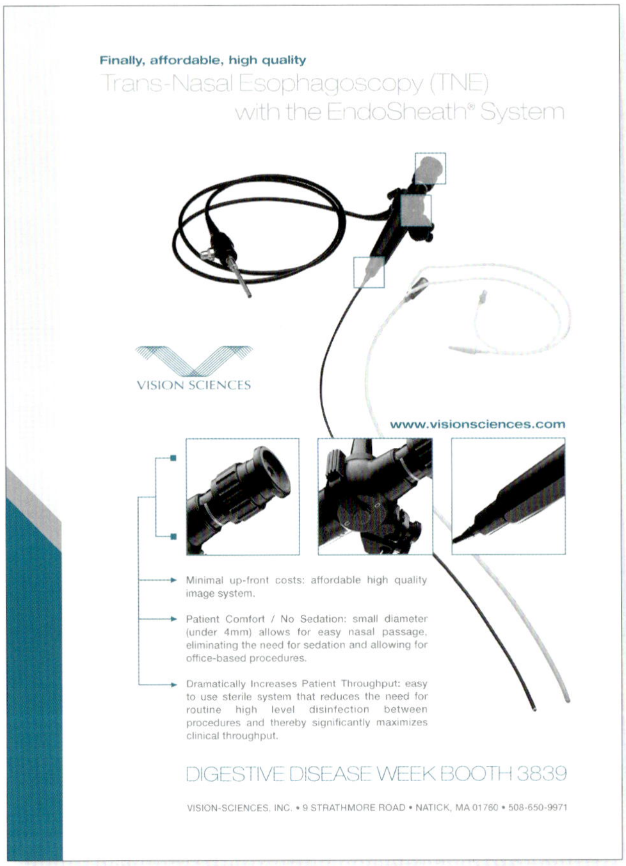

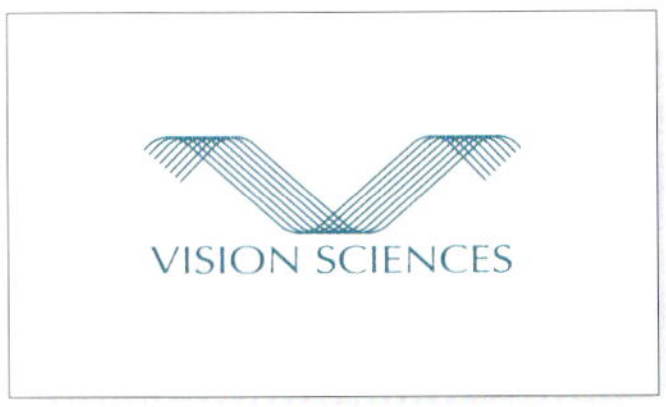

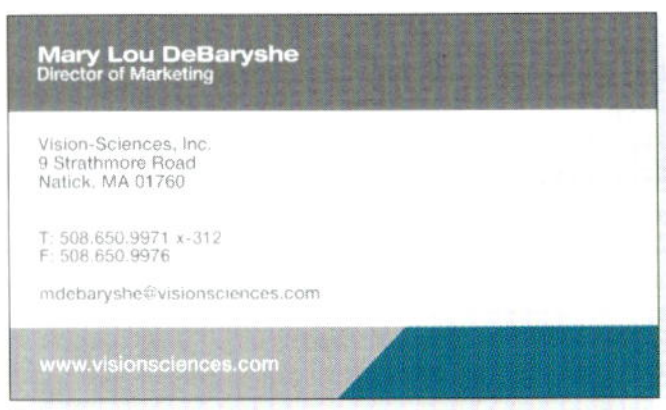

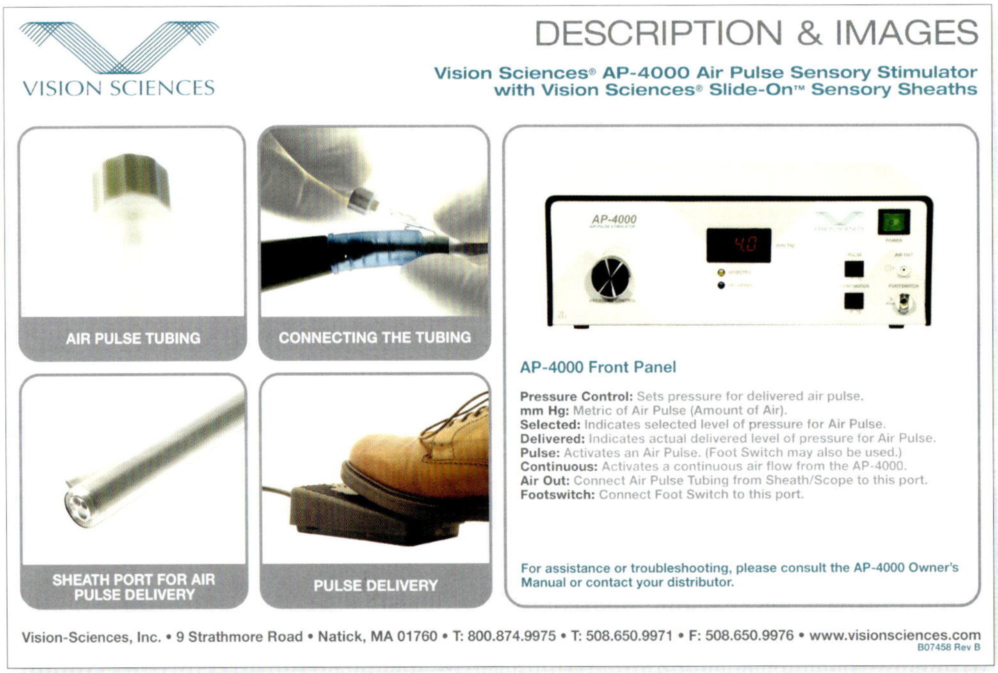

client
Vision Sciences
design firm
Graphic Advance
www.graphicadvance.com
designer
Avaid Stark

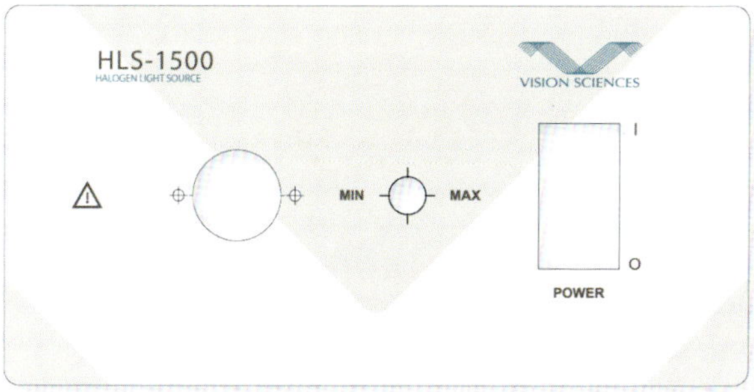

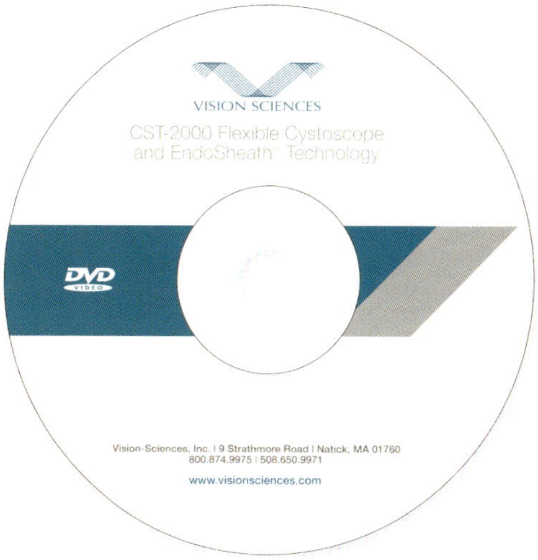

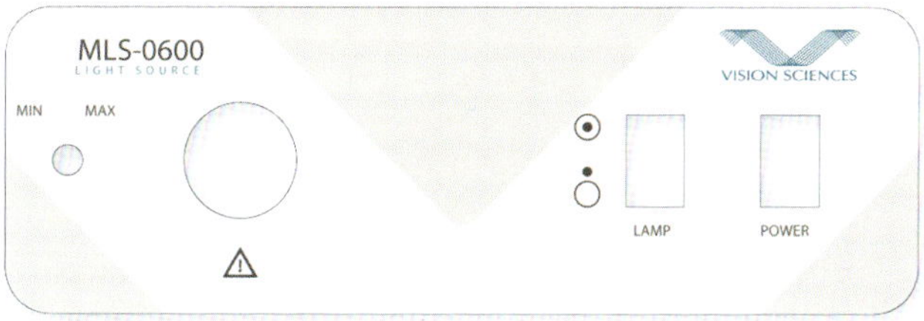

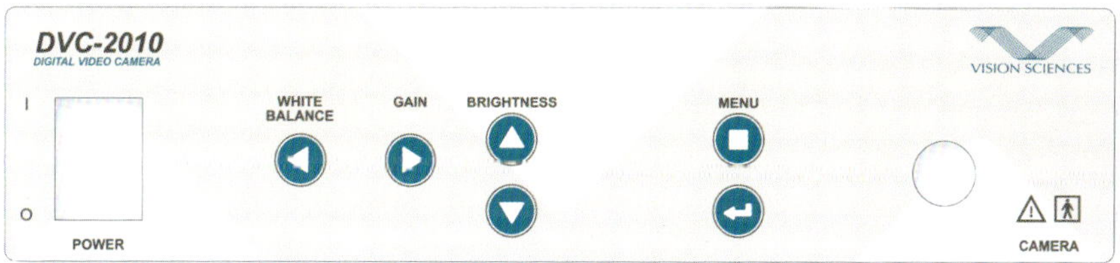

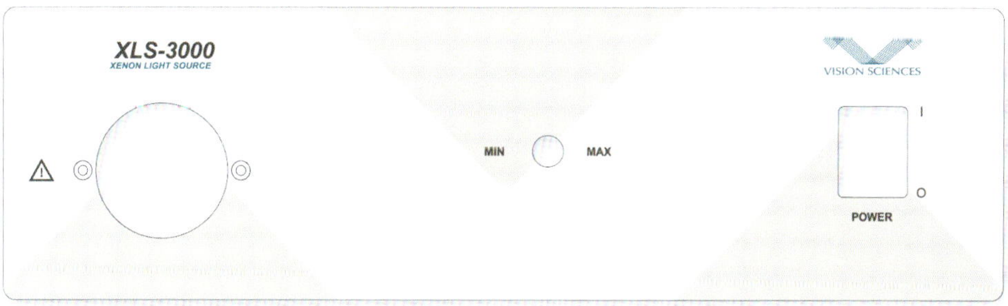

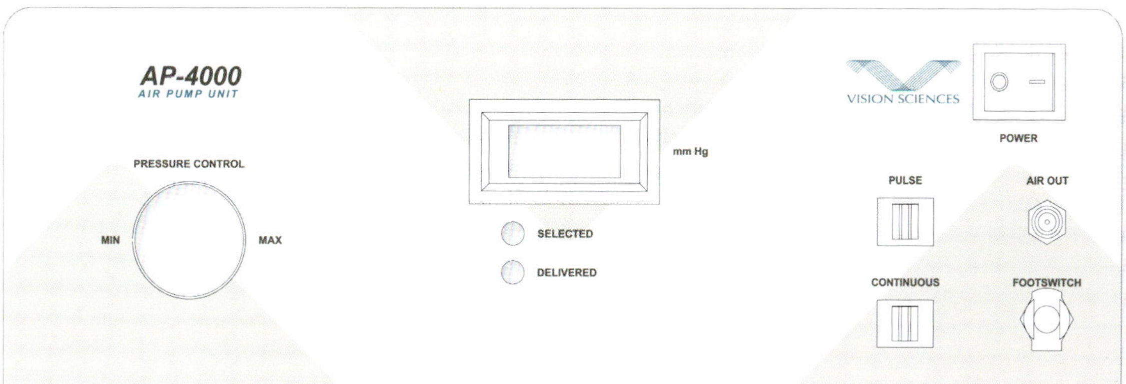

Water World
America's Biggest. America's Best.

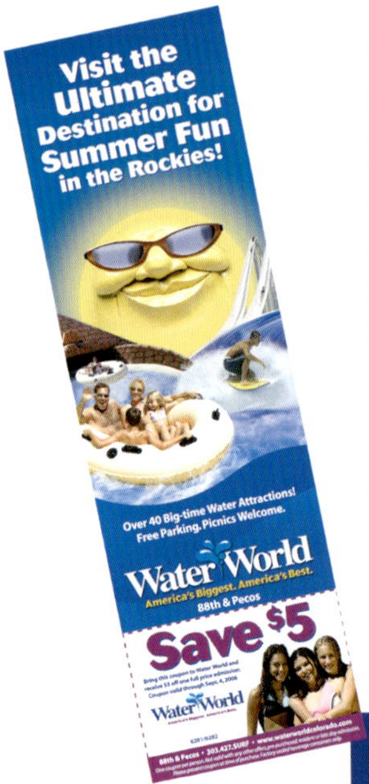

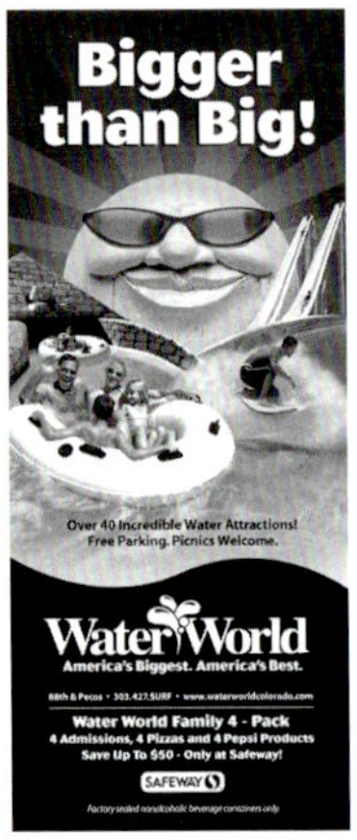

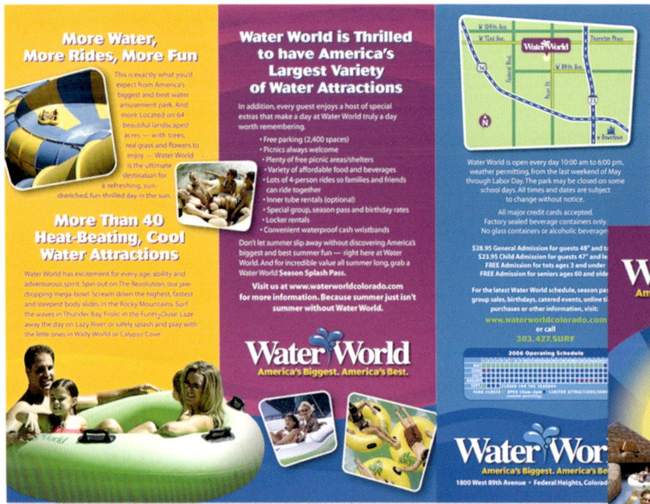

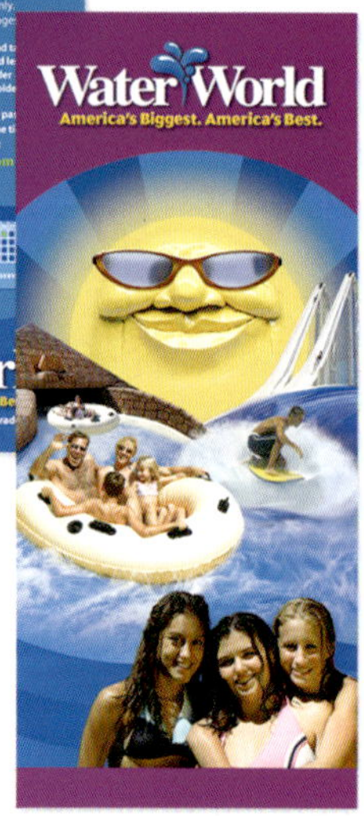

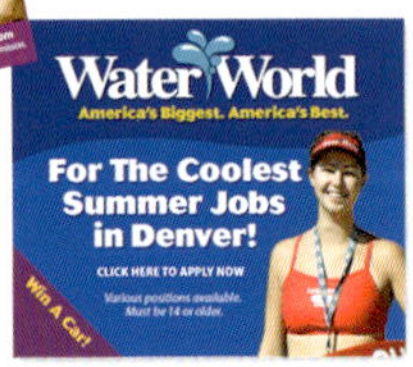

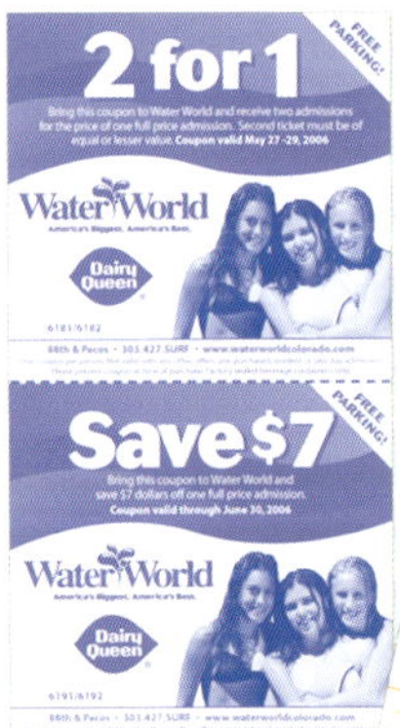

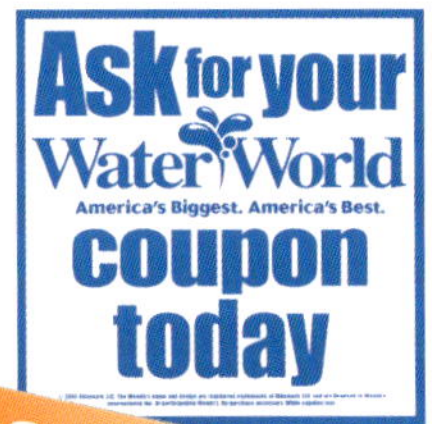

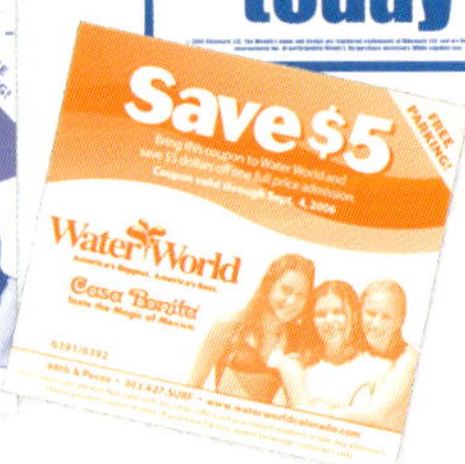

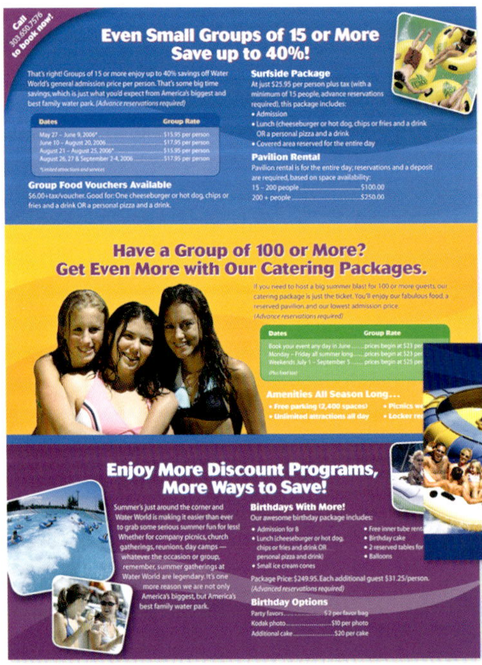

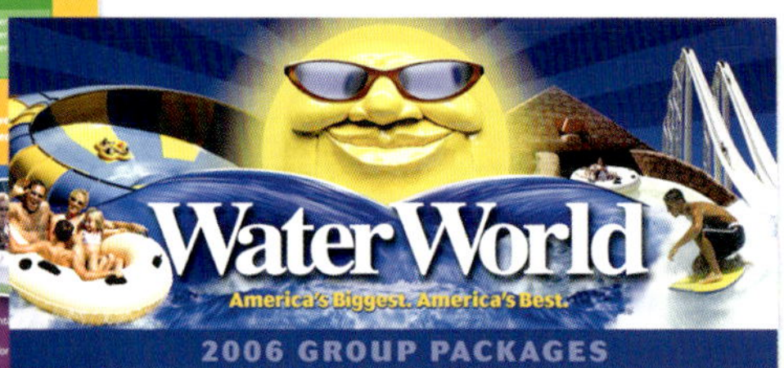

client
Water World
design firm
Rassman Design
www.rassmandesign.com
designers
John Rassman, Jennifer Harlow

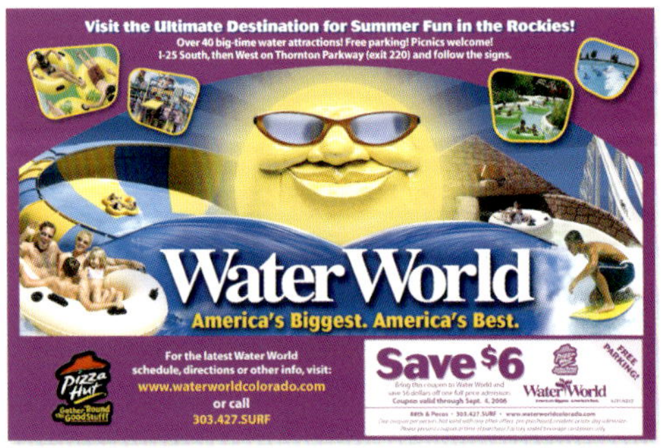

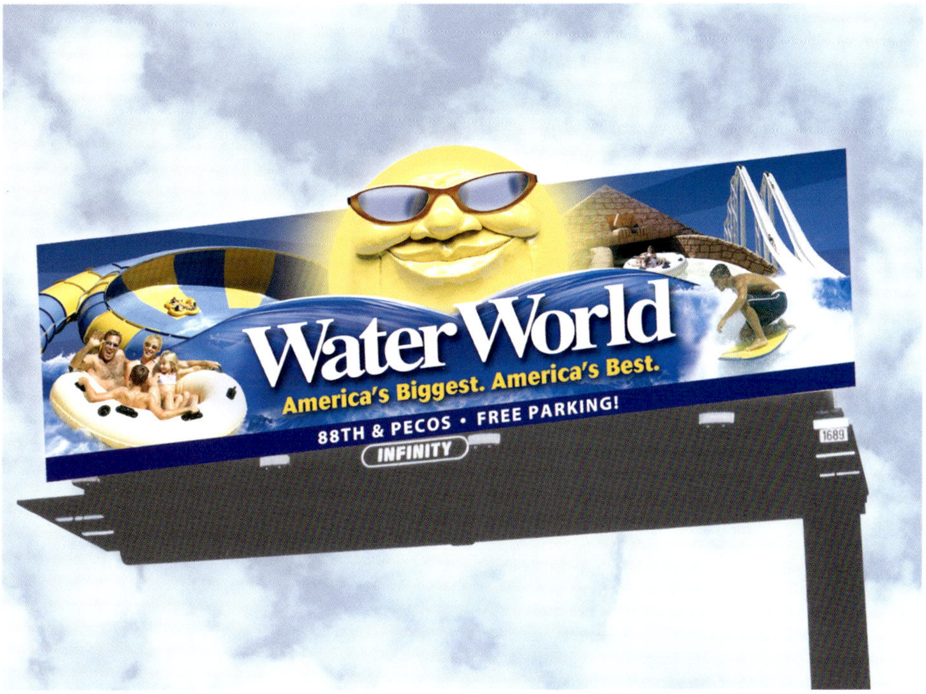
Water World
America's Biggest. America's Best.
88TH & PECOS • FREE PARKING!
INFINITY
1689

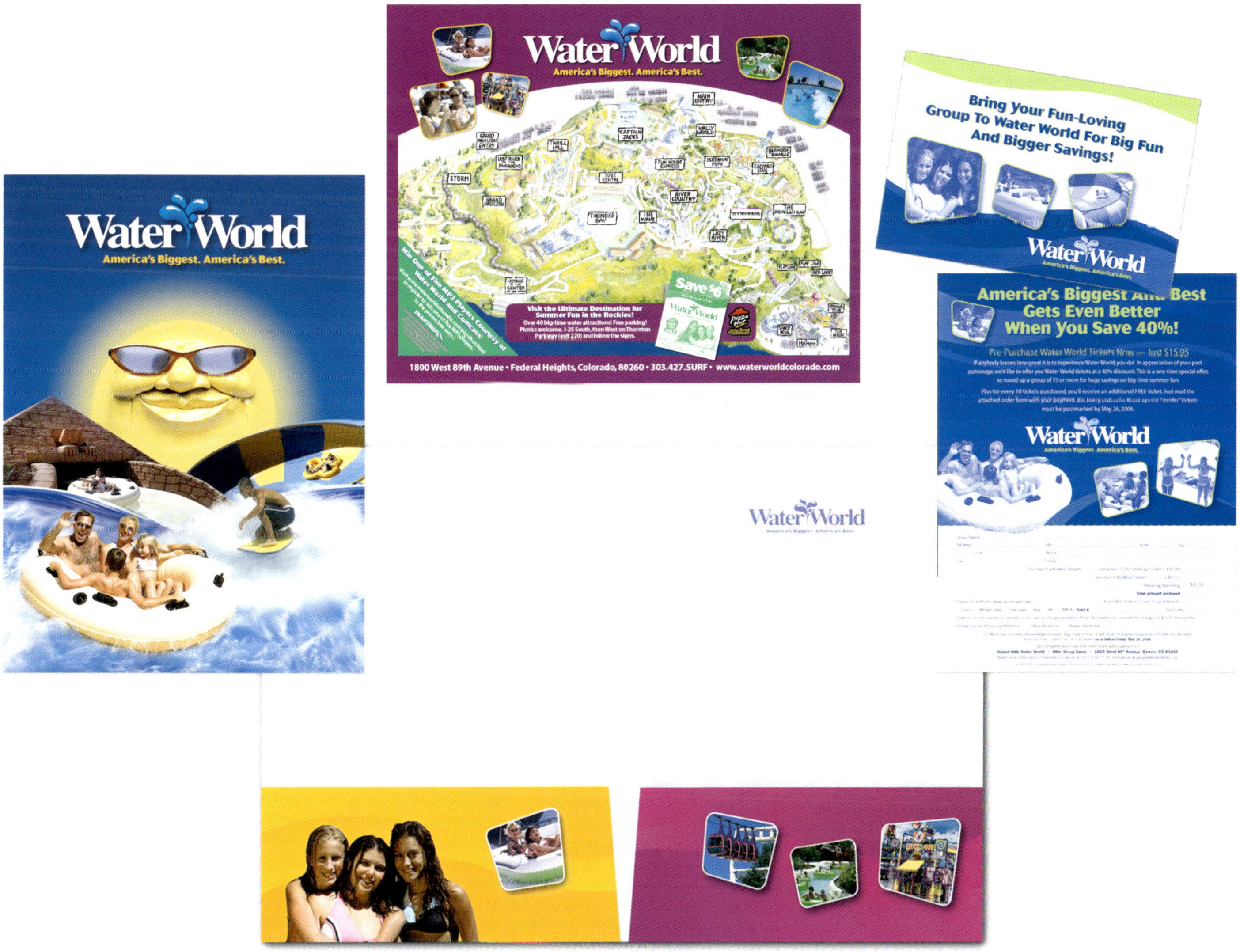
Water World
America's Biggest. America's Best.
Visit the Ultimate Destination for Summer Fun in the Rockies!
Save $6
1800 West 89th Avenue • Federal Heights, Colorado, 80260 • 303.427.SURF • www.waterworldcolorado.com
Bring Your Fun-Loving Group To Water World For Big Fun And Bigger Savings!
Water World
America's Biggest And Best Gets Even Better When You Save 40%!
Pre-Purchase Water World Tickets Now — Just $15.95
Water World
America's Biggest. America's Best.
Water World
Water World
America's Biggest. America's Best.

The WAVE

TRANSIT SYSTEM

Ride the Wave

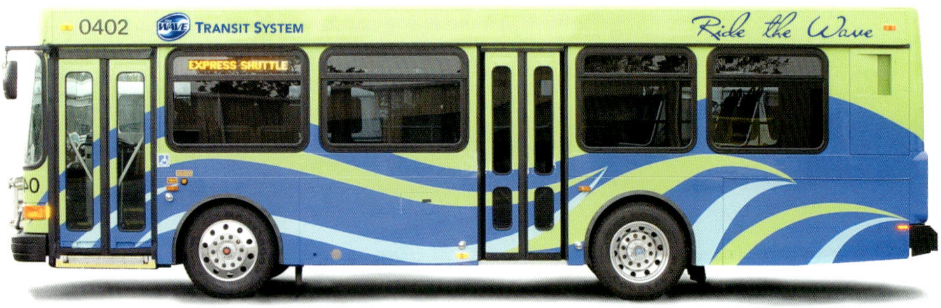

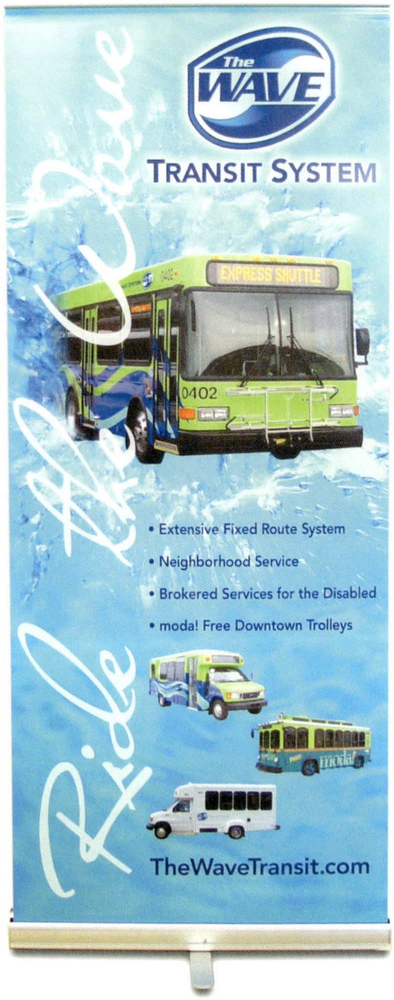

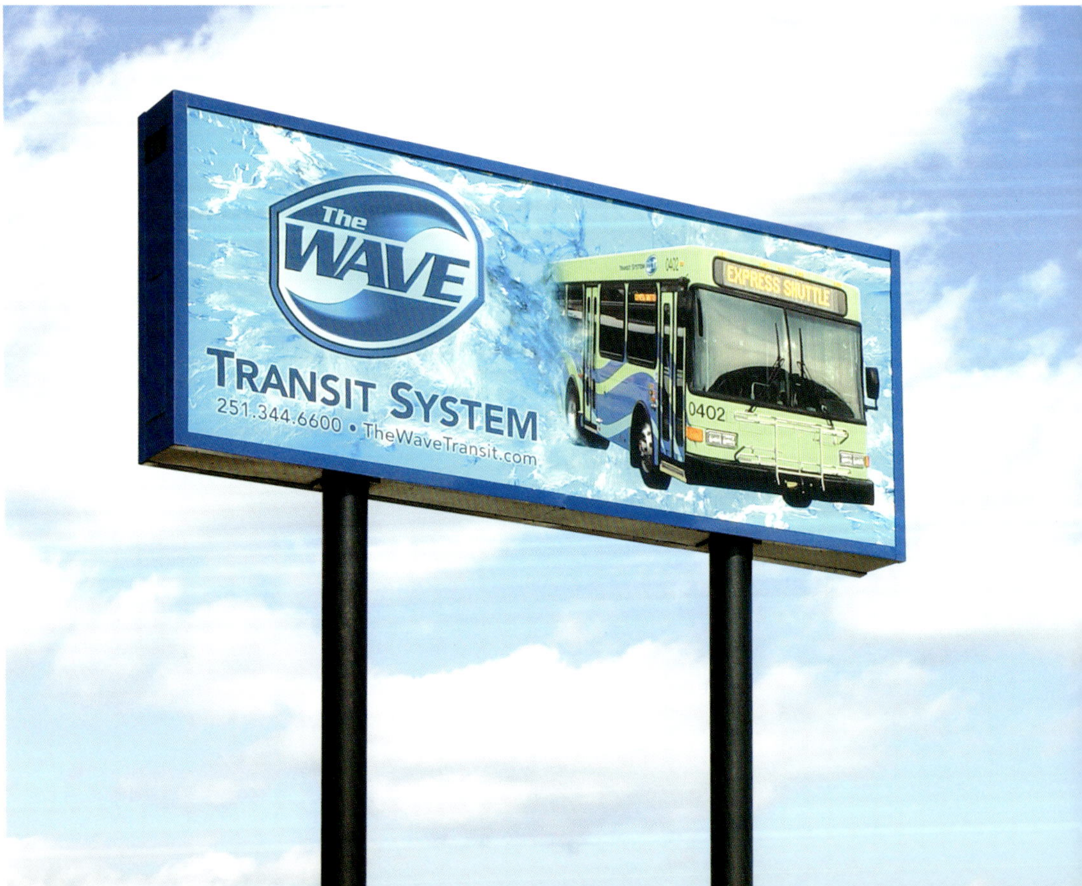

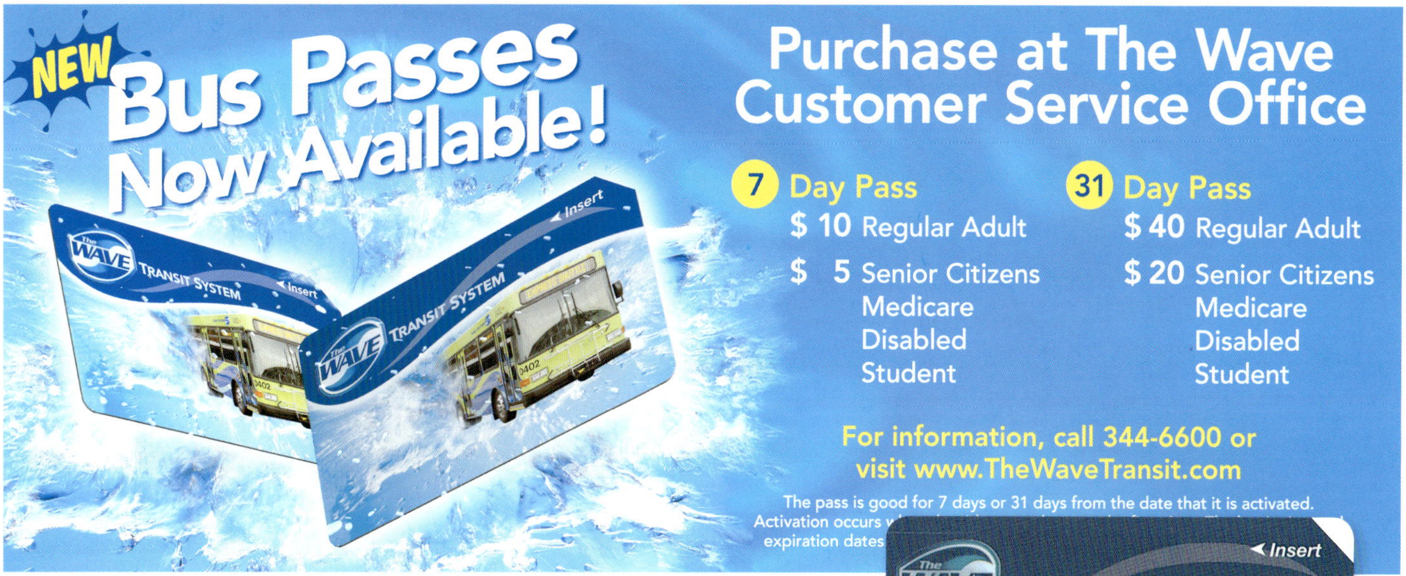

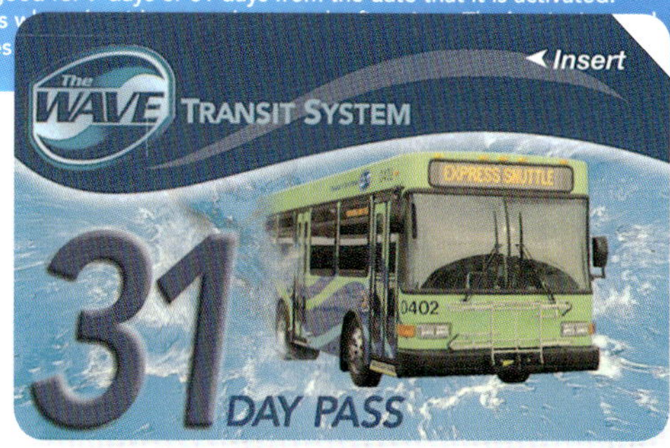

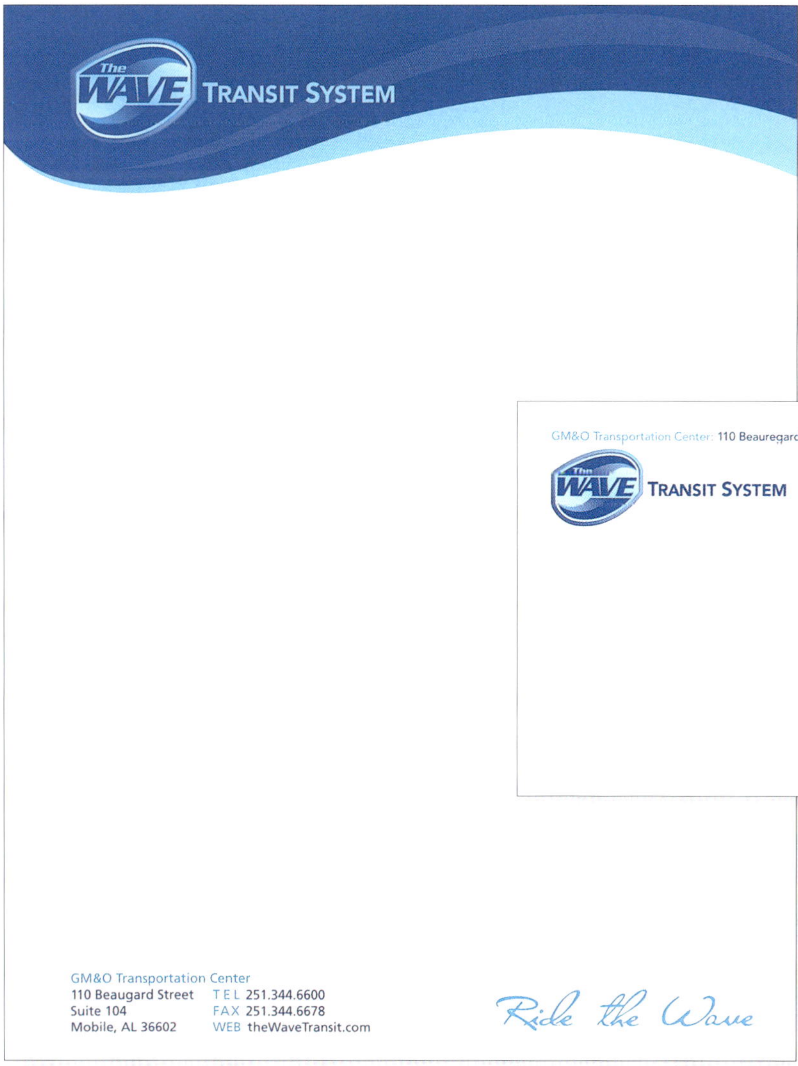

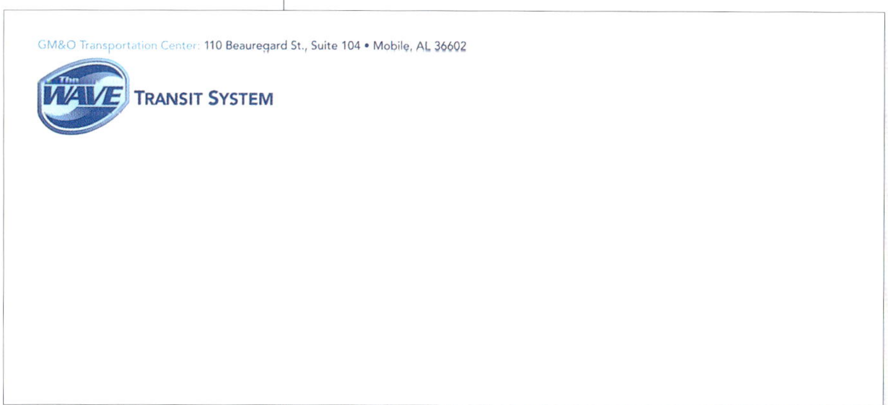

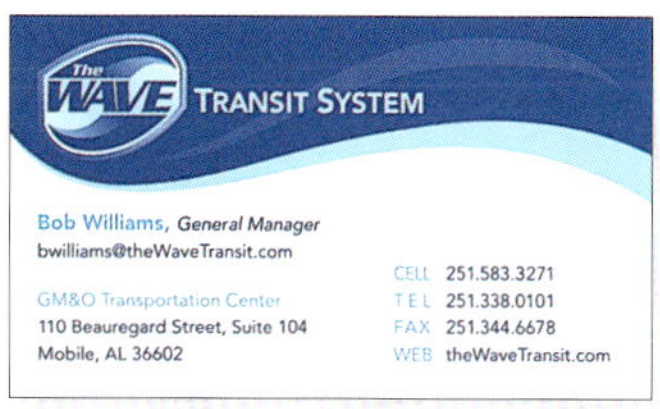

client
The Wave Transit System
design firm
Pixallure Design
pixallure.com
designers
Terry Edeker, Steven Lutz

WILSONS LEATHER

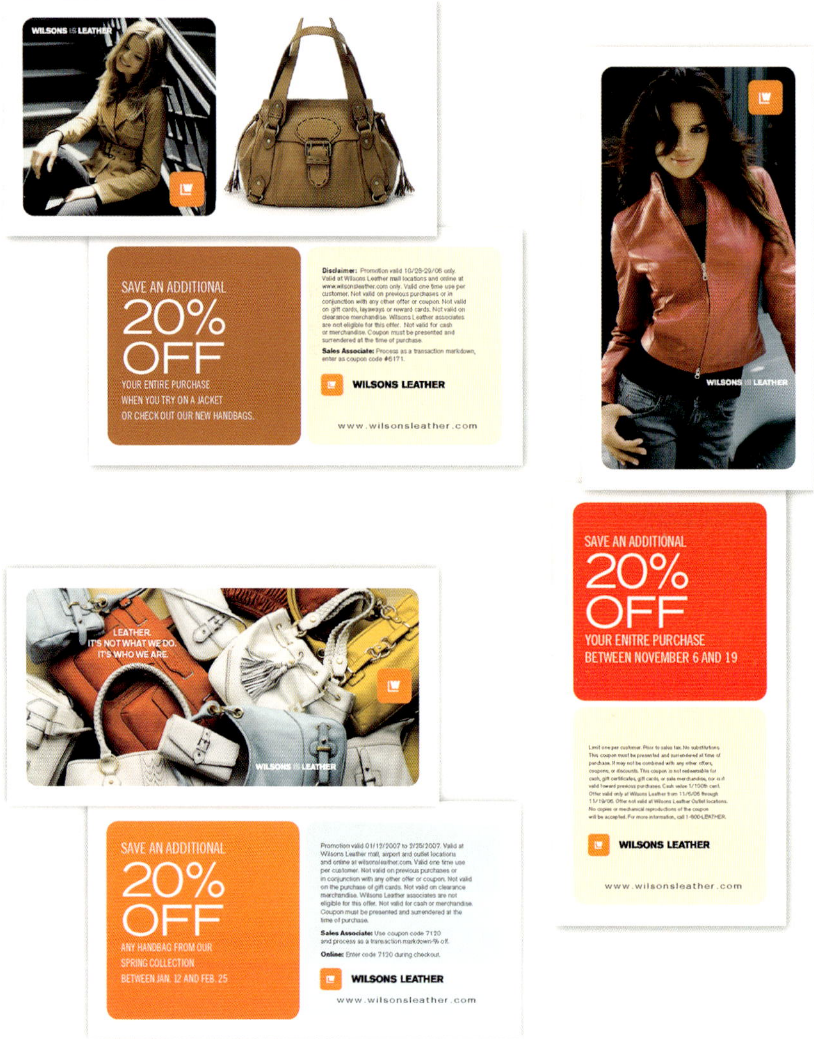

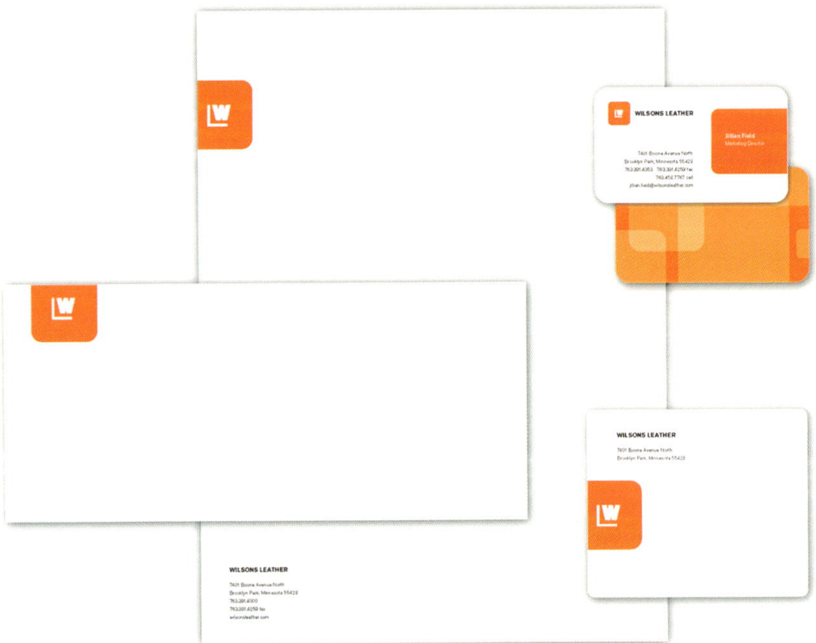

client
Wilsons Leather
design firm
Marcantel | Crouch | LeBlanc
www.mcl-usa.com
designers
Richard LeBlanc, Tom Marcantel, Julie Crouch

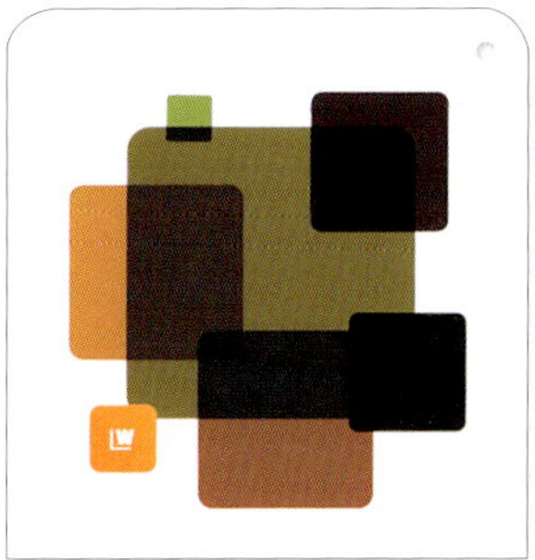

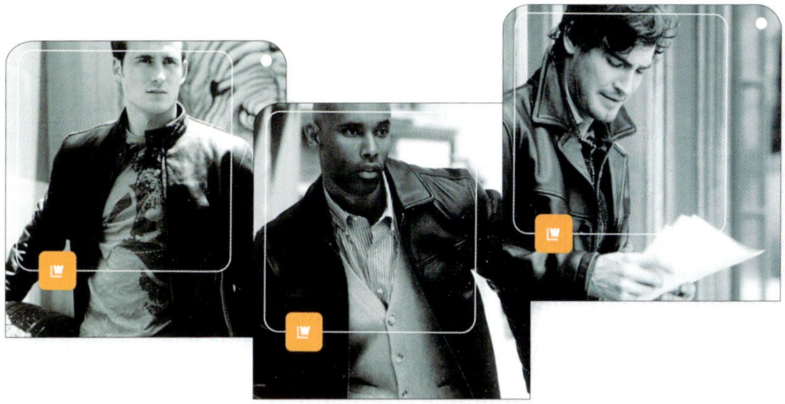

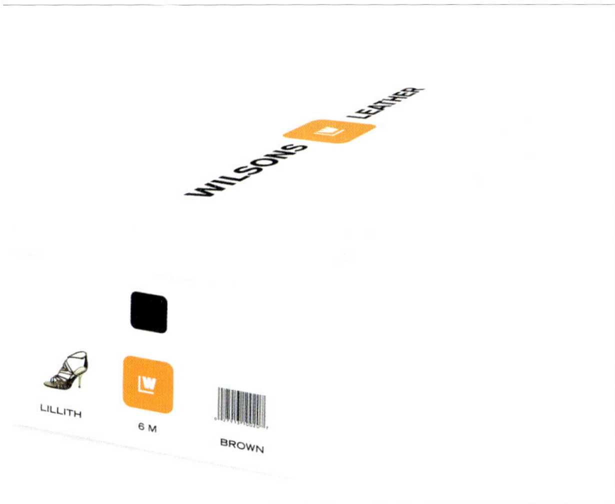
WILSONS LEATHER
LILLITH
6 M
BROWN

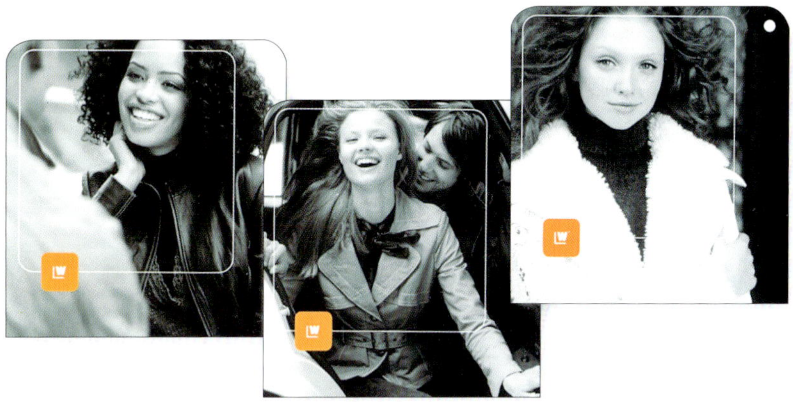

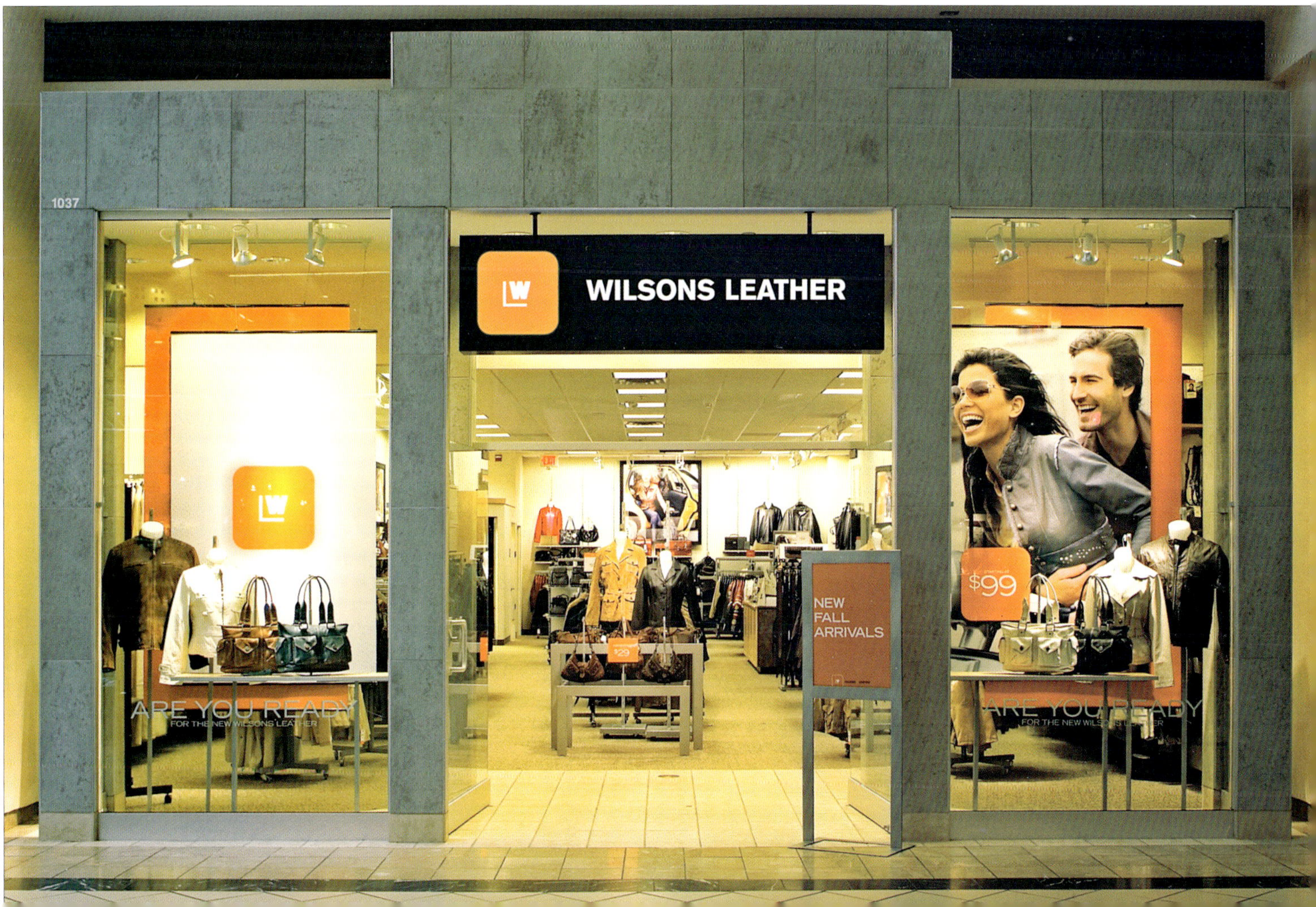
1037
WILSONS LEATHER
NEW
FALL
ARRIVALS
$99
ARE YOU READY
FOR THE NEW WILSONS LEATHER

WINDHAM
MOUNTAIN

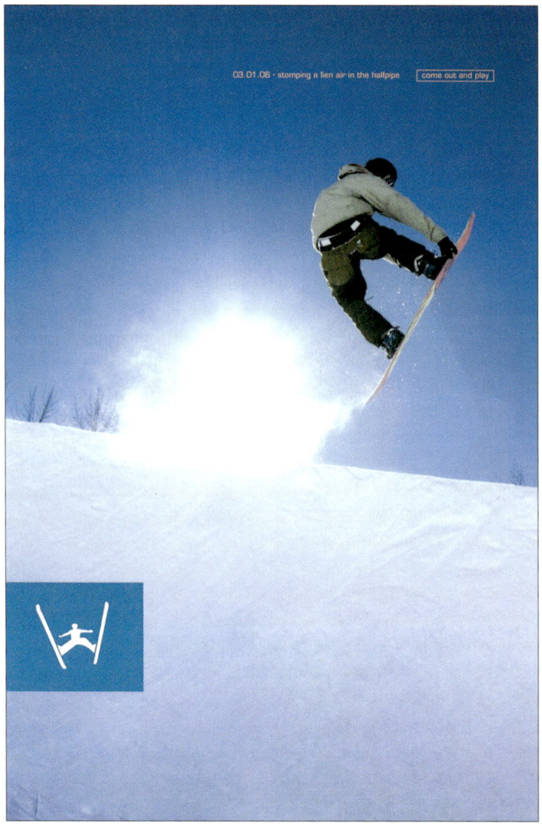

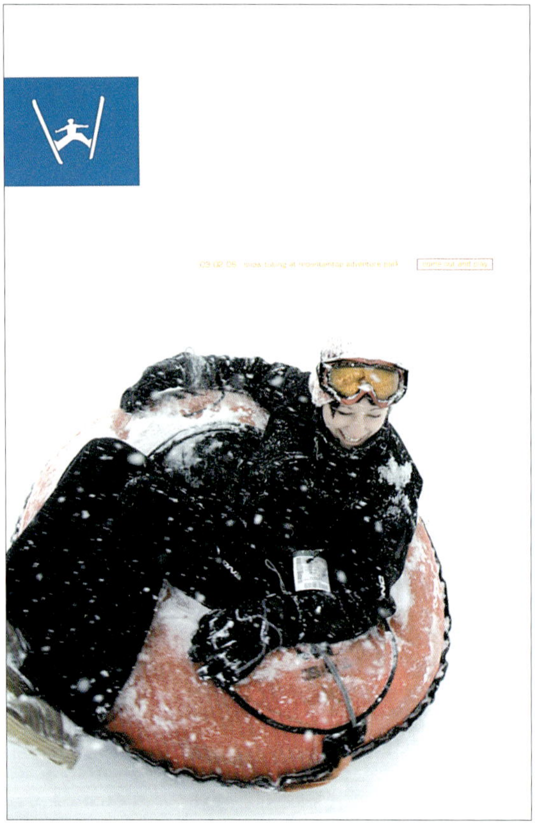

client
Windham Mountain
design firm
Smith & Jones
www.smithandjones.com
designer
Sara Tack

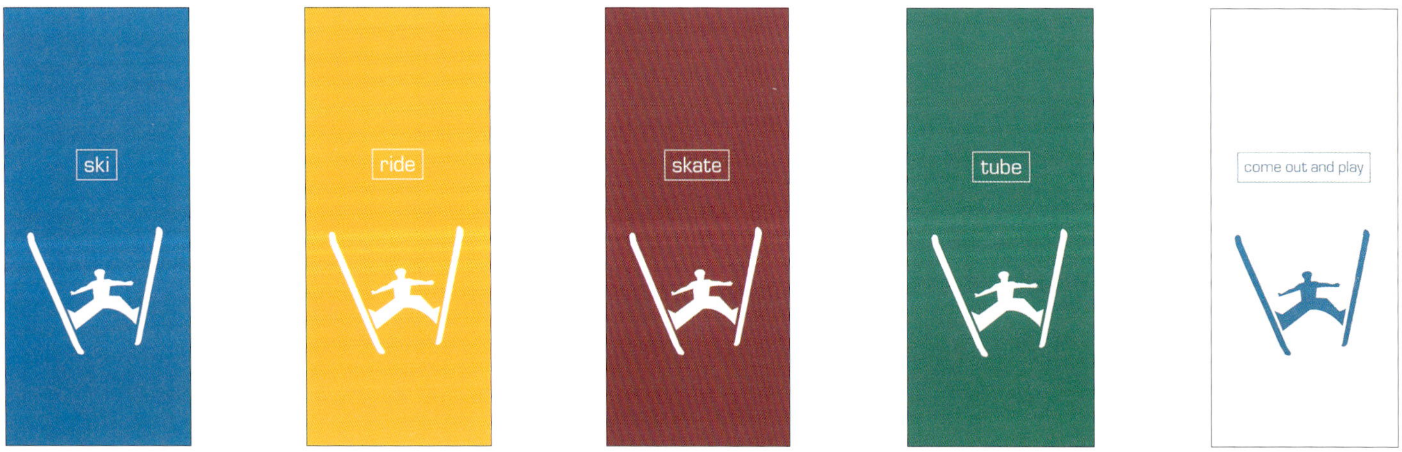

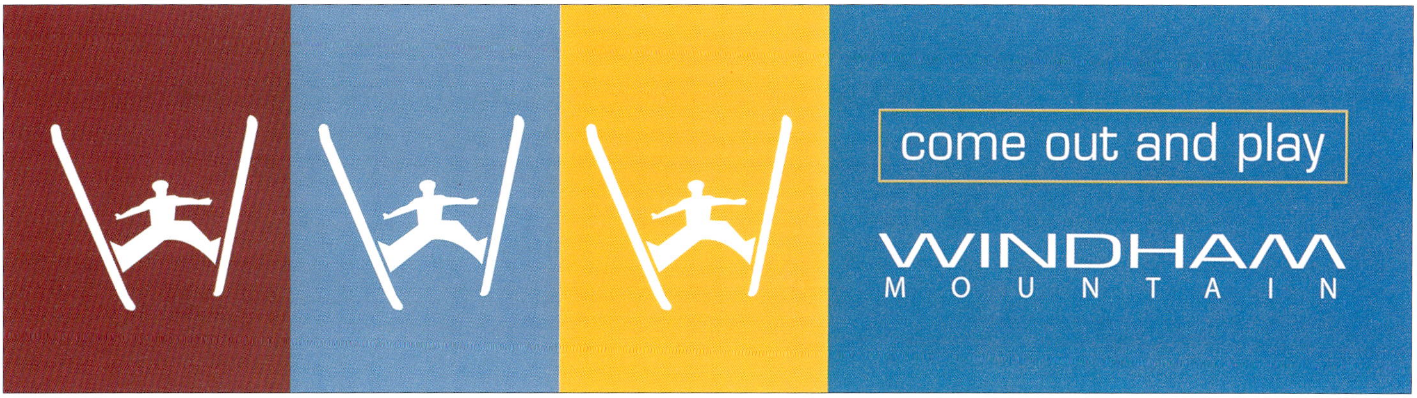
come out and play
WINDHAM
MOUNTAIN

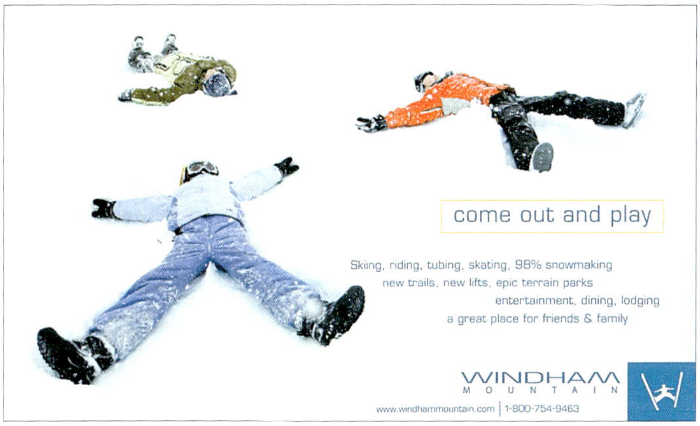
come out and play
Skiing, riding, tubing, skating, 98% snowmaking
new trails, new lifts, epic terrain parks
entertainment, dining, lodging
a great place for friends & family
WINDHAM
MOUNTAIN
www.windhammountain.com | 1-800-754-9463

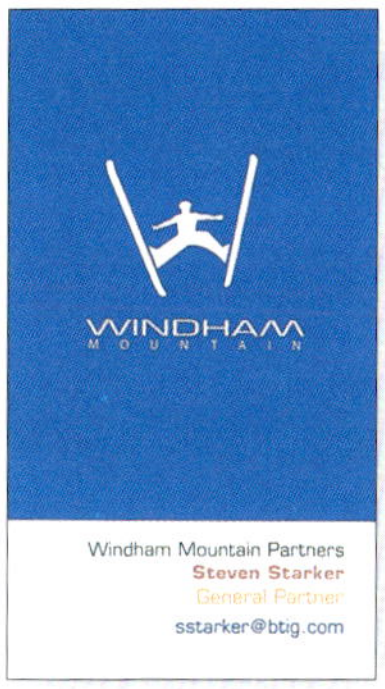
WINDHAM
MOUNTAIN
Windham Mountain Partners
Steven Starker
General Partner
sstarker@btig.com

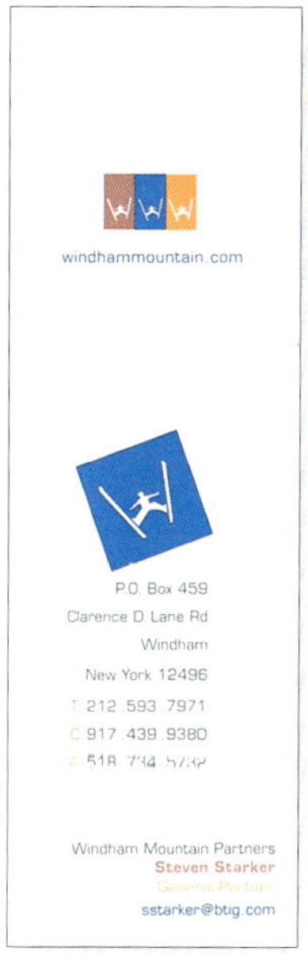
windhammountain.com
P.O. Box 459
Clarence D. Lane Rd
Windham
New York 12496
T 212 593 7971
C 917 439 9380
Windham Mountain Partners
Steven Starker
General Partner
sstarker@btig.com

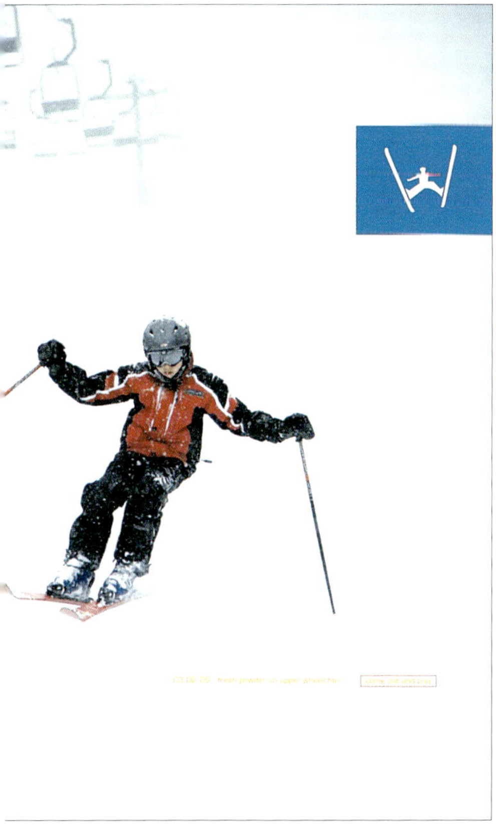

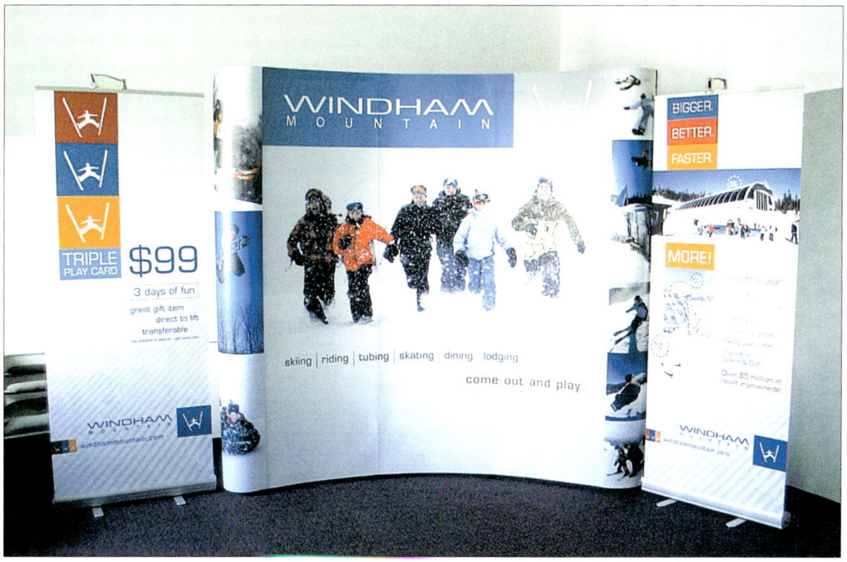
TRIPLE PLAY CARD
$99
3 days of fun
WINDHAM
MOUNTAIN
skiing | riding | tubing | skating | dining | lodging
come out and play
BIGGER.
BETTER.
FASTER.
MORE!

XTREME SCENTS®
SILVER
XP™

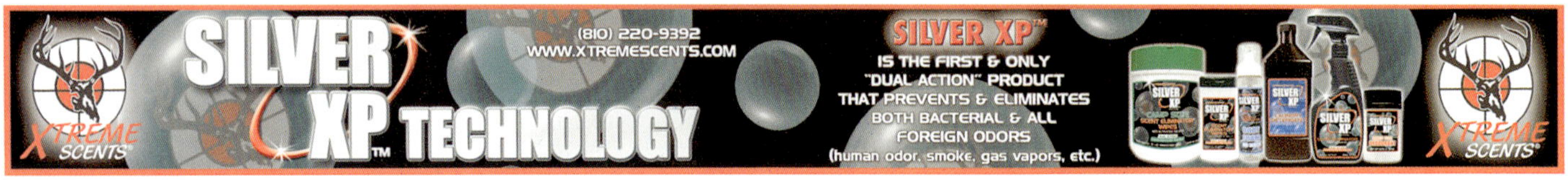

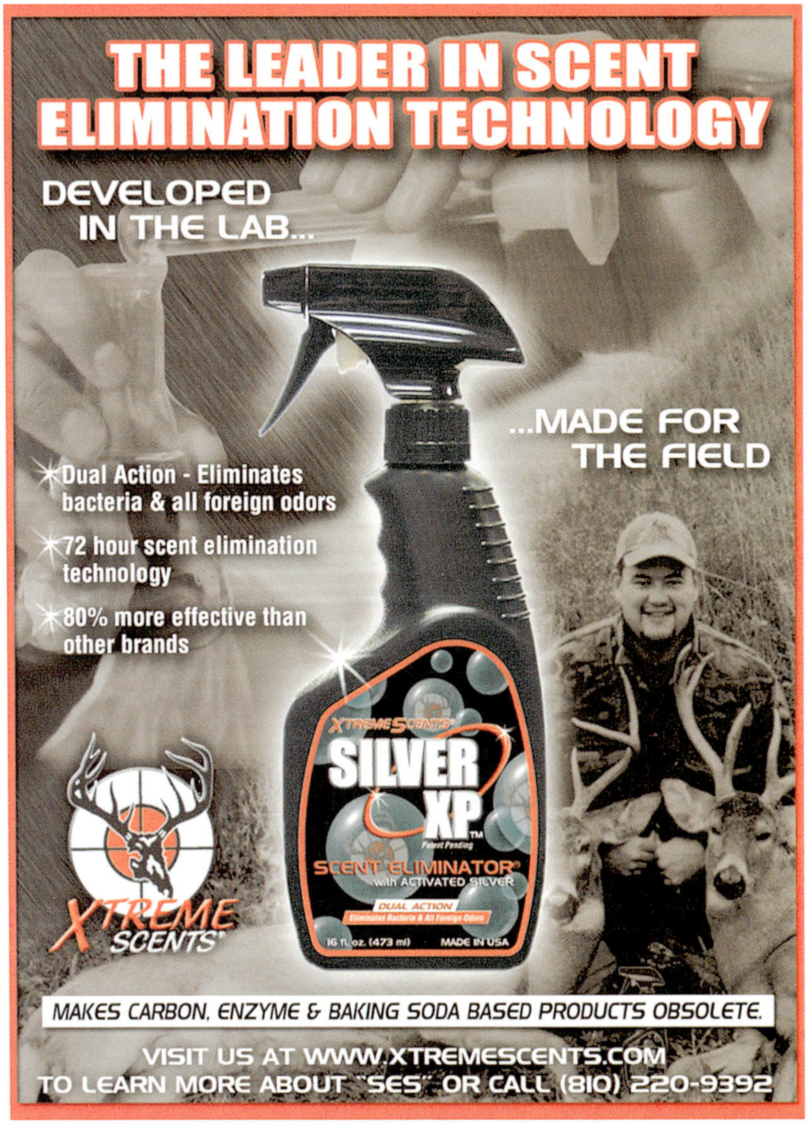

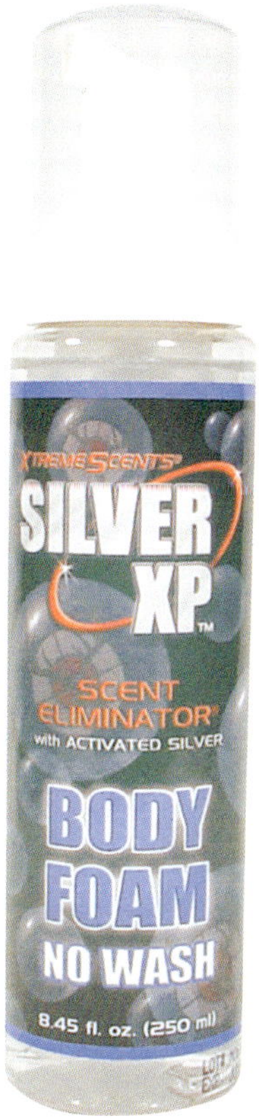

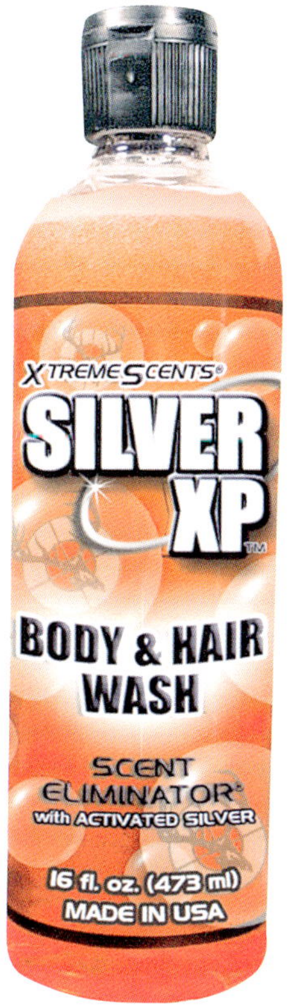

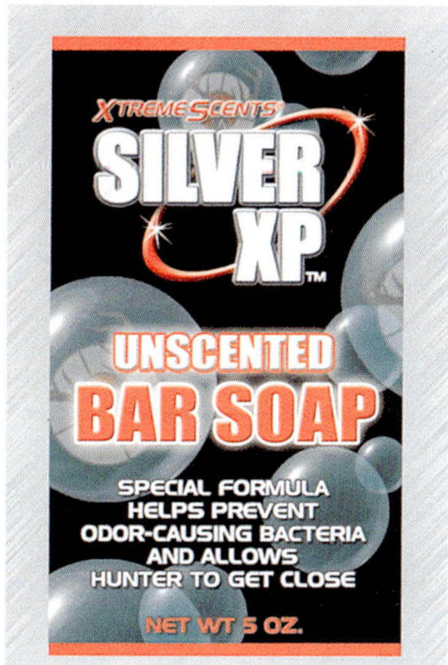

client
Xtreme Scents
design firm
Excelda Manufacturing
designer
Melissa Tigner

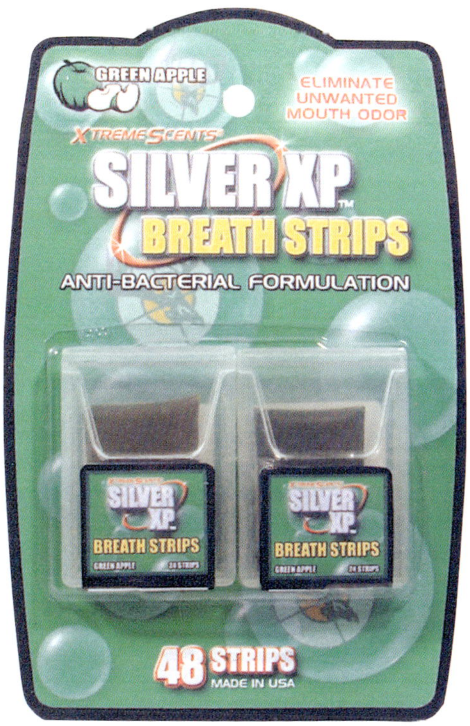

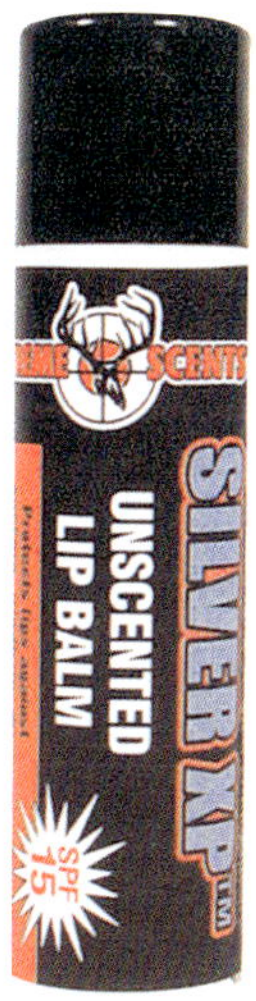

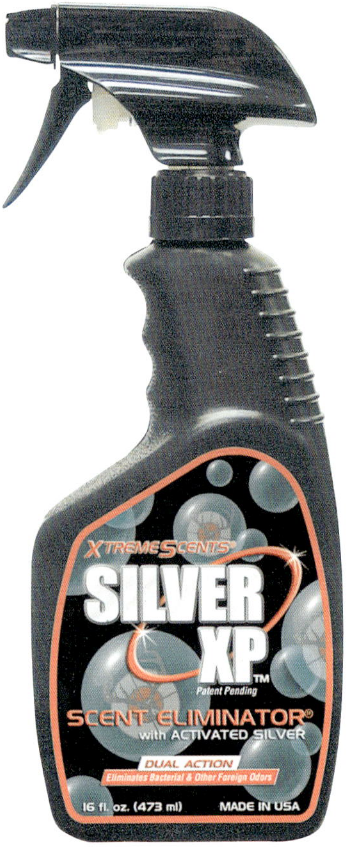

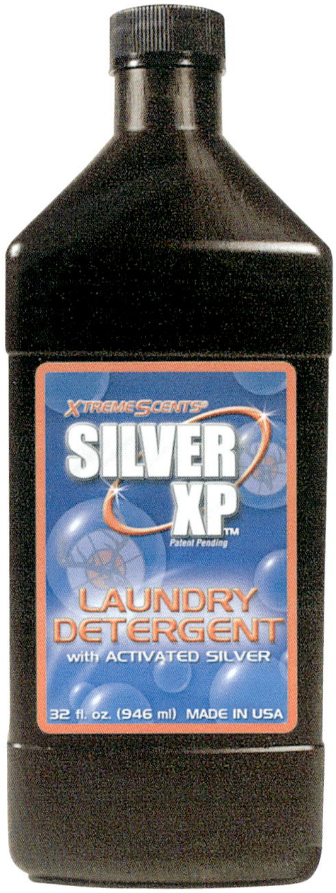

(continued from pages 46 - 47)
client
Xtreme Scents
design firm
Excelda Manufacturing

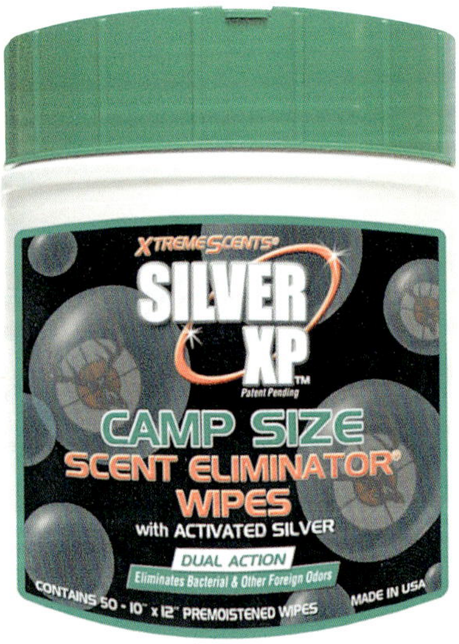

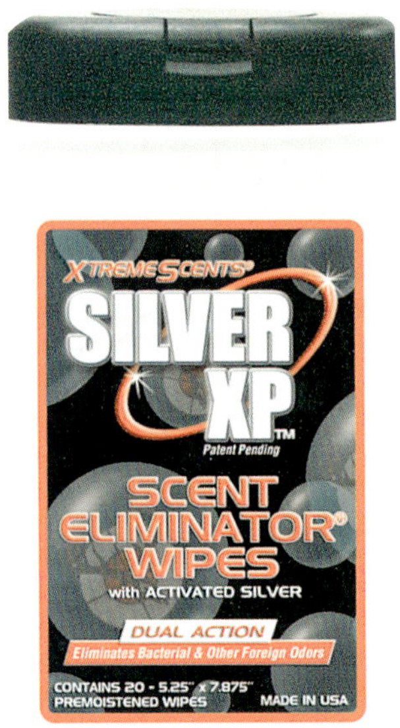

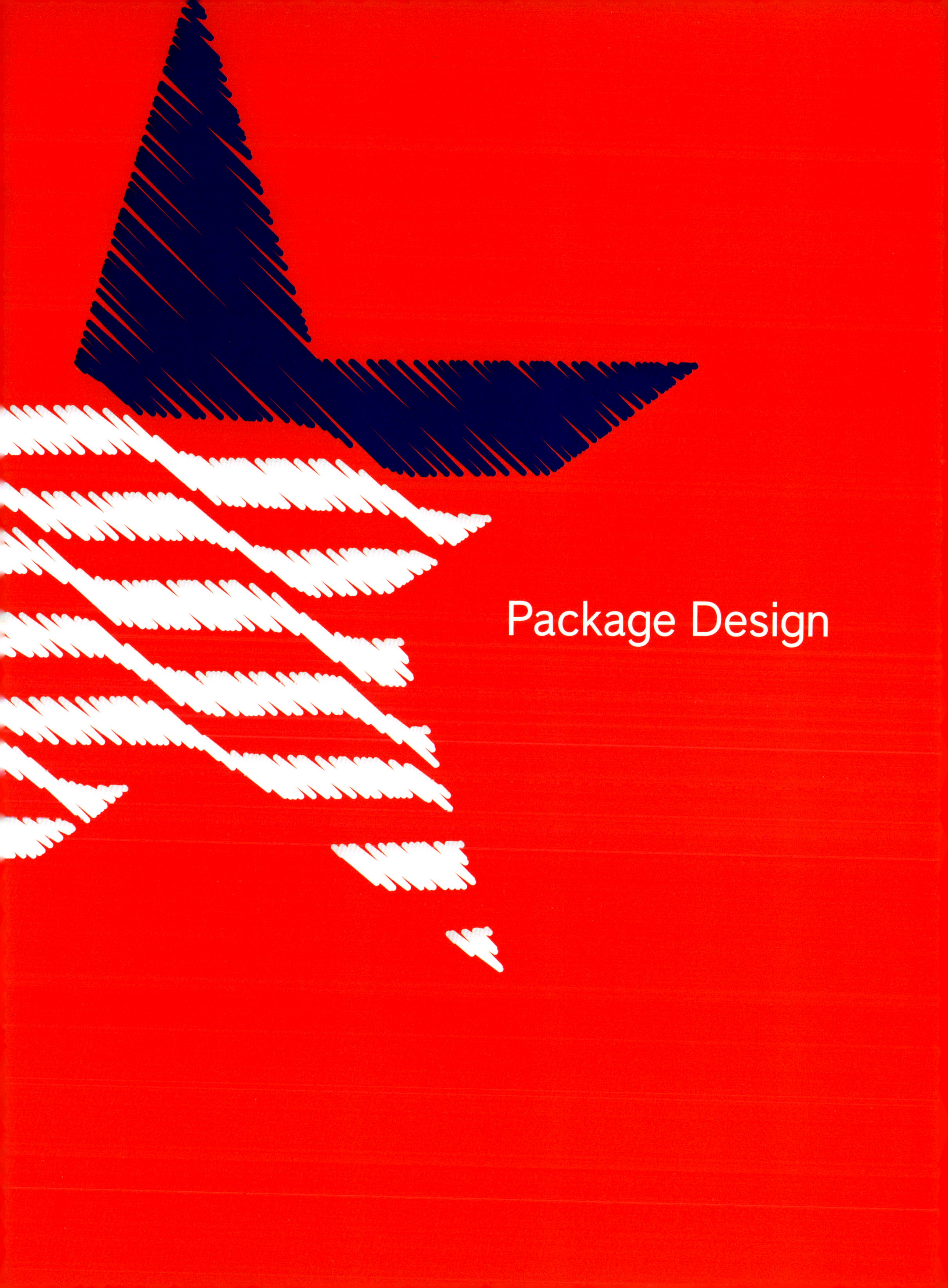
Package Design

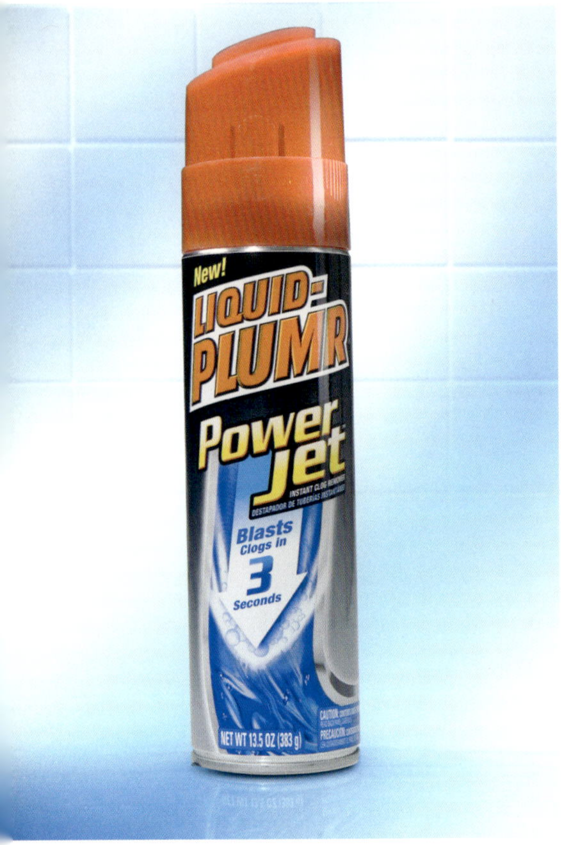

client
Mega Brands
design firm
Smith Design
smithdesign.com
designers
Carol Konkowski, Ken Kiger, Angel Sonto

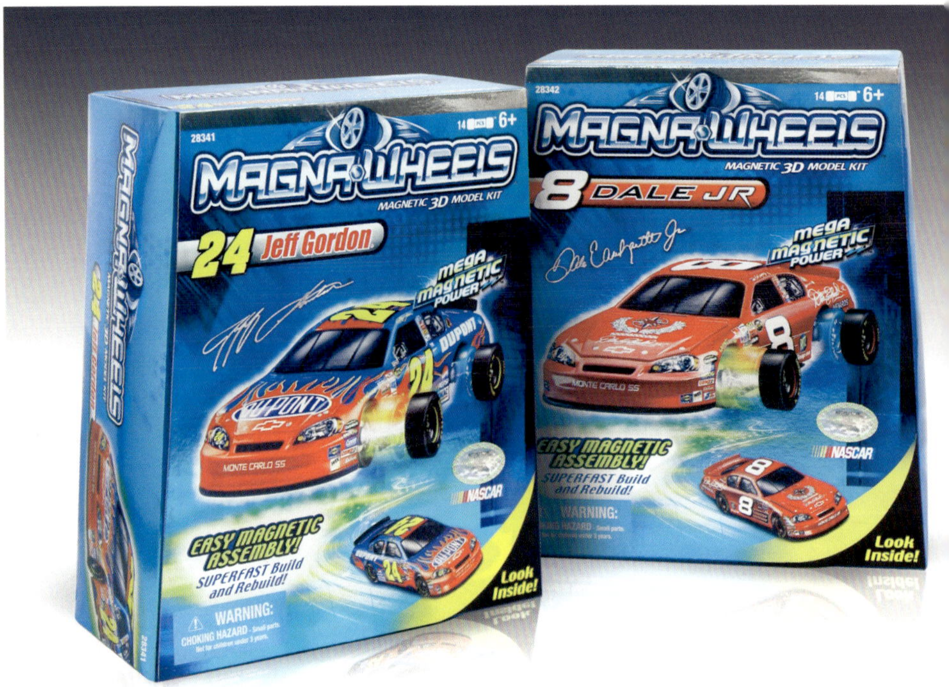

client
The Clorox Company
design firm
Clorox Creative Services
art director
Chris Twilling
designer
Anthony Luk

client
Acme United Corporation
design firm
Tom Fowler, Inc.
www.tomfowlerinc.com
art directors
Mary Ellen Butkus, Elizabeth P. Ball
designer
Mary Ellen Butkus

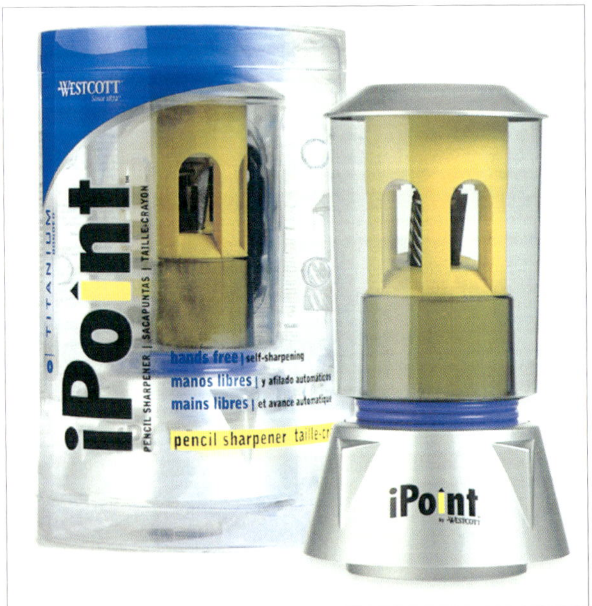

client
Interdynamics, Inc.
design firm
Tom Fowler, Inc.
www.tomfowlerinc.com
designer
Mary Ellen Butkus

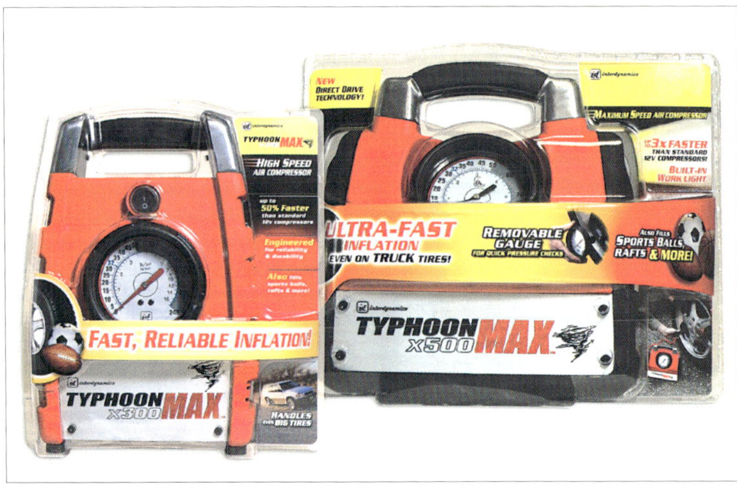

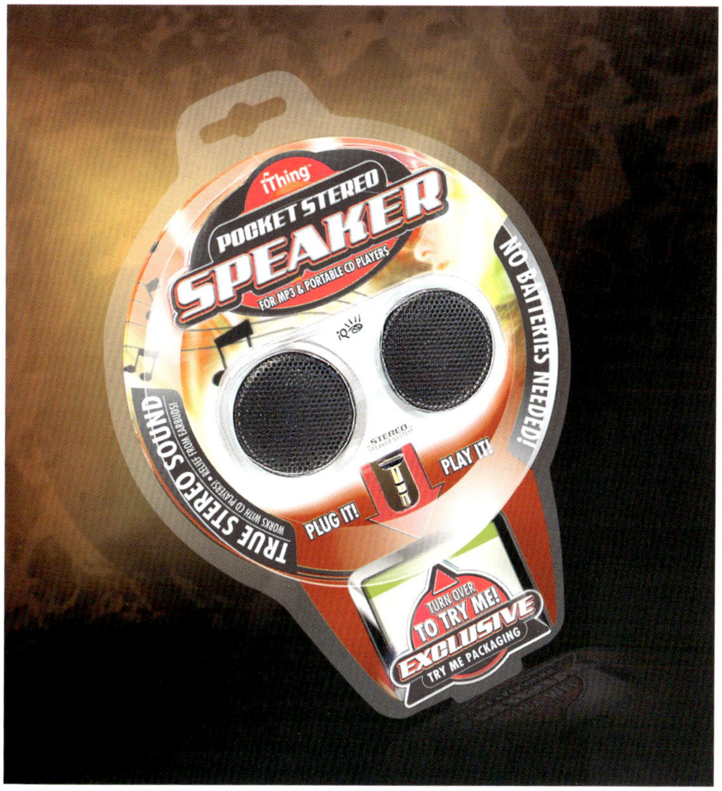

client
IQ Hong Kong
design firm
Zen Design Group
www.zendesigngroup.com
designers
Matt Chapman, David Perrin

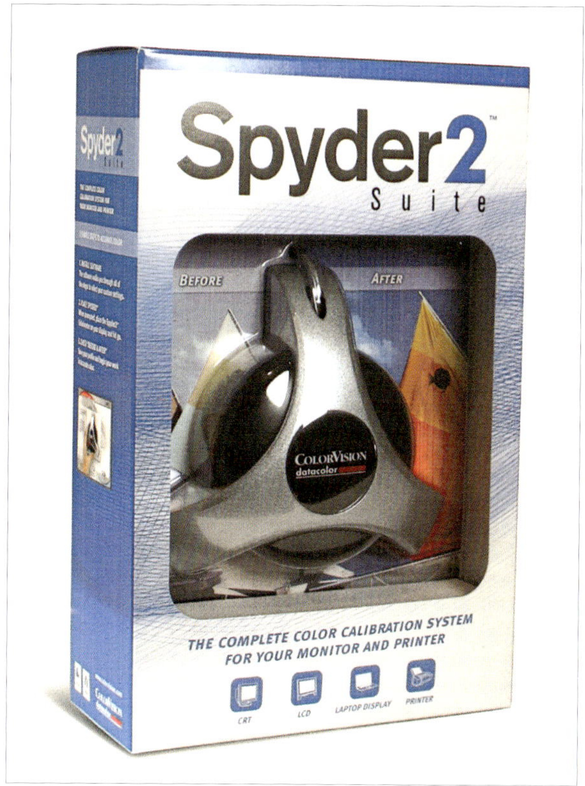

client
Datacolor
design firm
Jensen Design Assoc., Inc.
designers
Dean Kojima, David Jensen

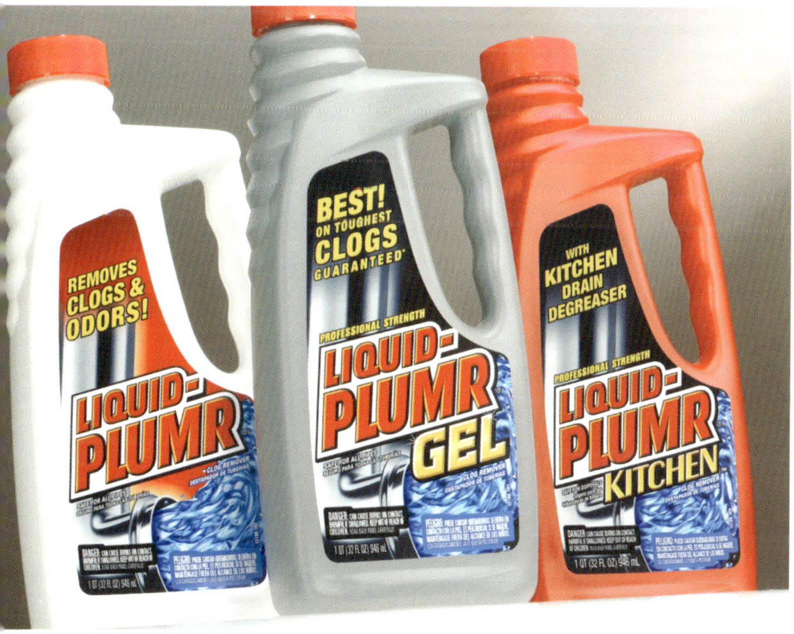

client
The Clorox Company
design firm
Clorox Creative Services
art director
Chris Twilling
designer, illustrator
Tim Ferdun

client
Microgravity Enterprises
design firm
Lightspeed Commercial Arts
www.lightspeedca.net
designer
Michael J. Hamers

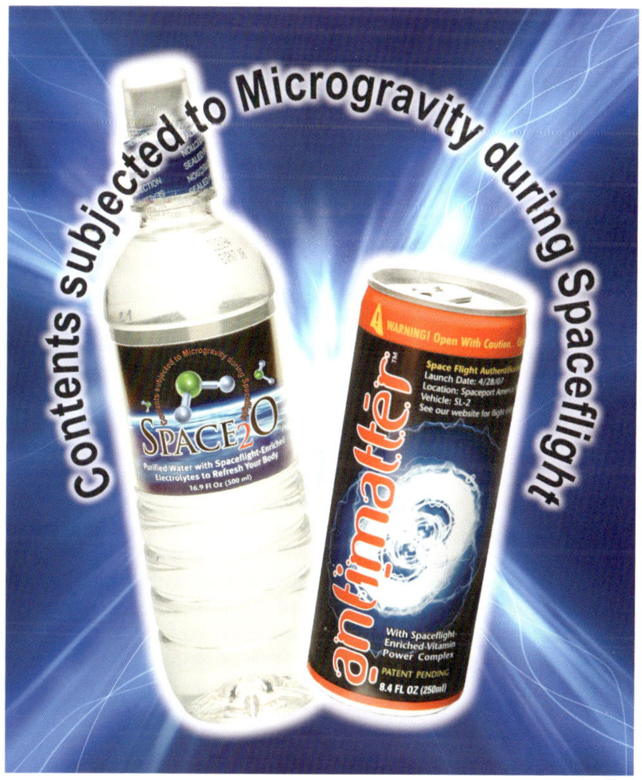

client
AMES International
design firm
Hornall Anderson Design Works
www.hadw.com
designers
Jack Anderson, Kathy Saito,
Sonja Max, Henry Yiu, Yuri Shvets

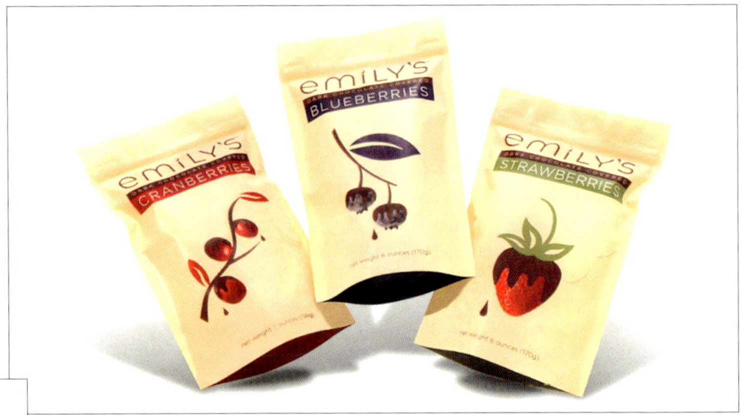

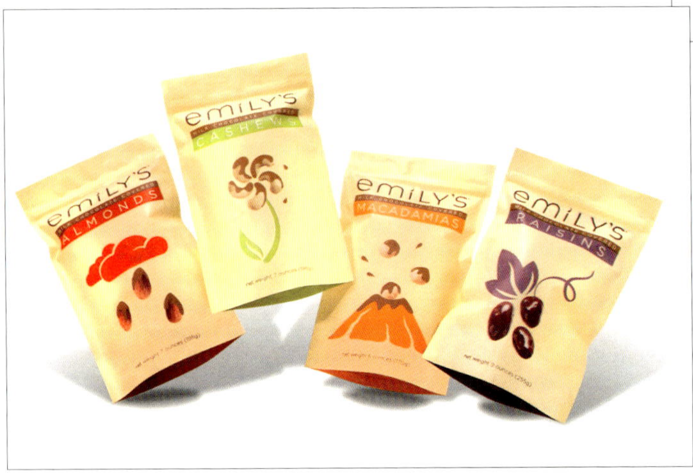

client
The Kingsford Product Company
design firm
Clorox Creative Services
designer
Tim Ferdun

client
Unilever
design firm
Smith Design
smithdesign.com
designers
Laura Markley,
Angel Sonto, Ivan Angelic

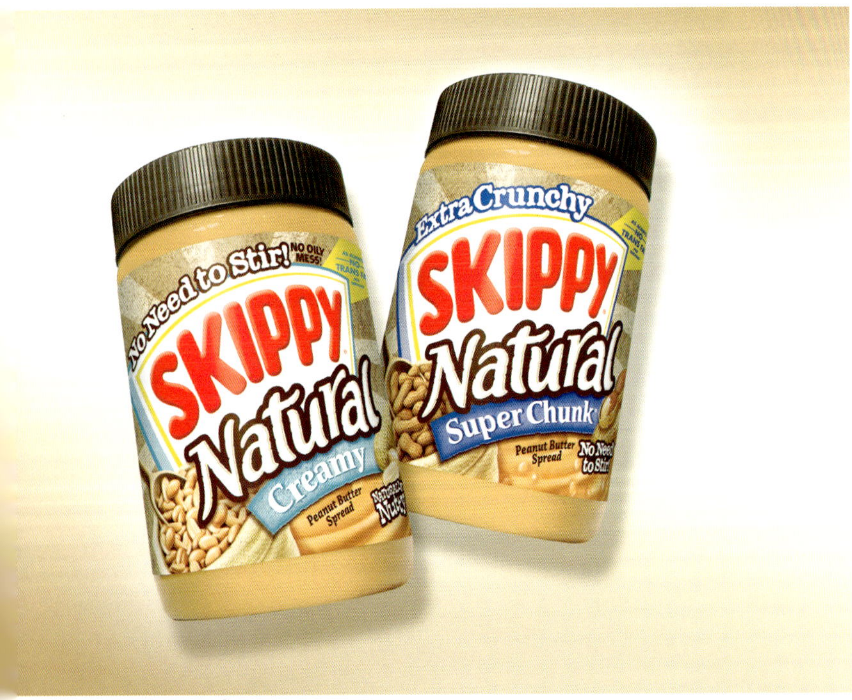

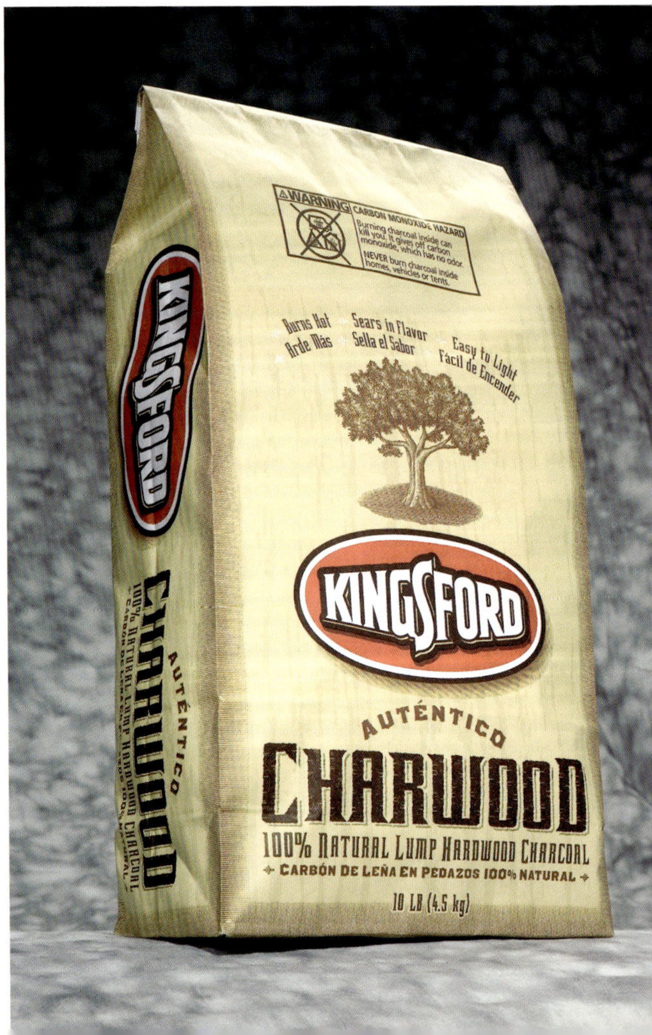

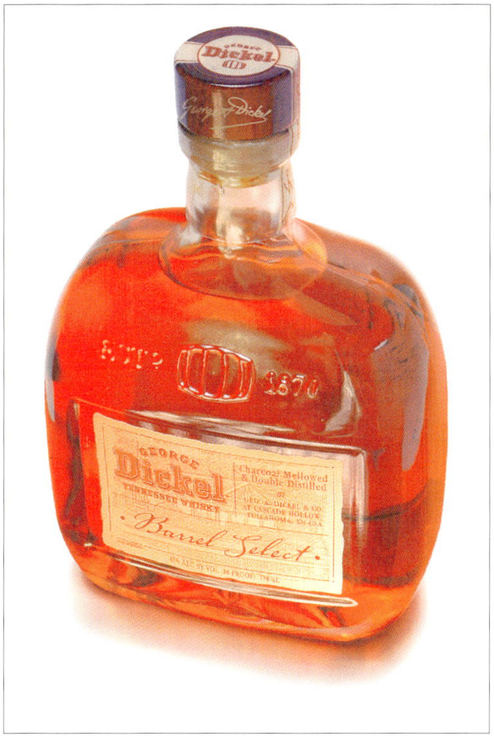

client
Diageo
design firm
PMthree Branding
www.pmthree.com
designer
Jessica Annunziato

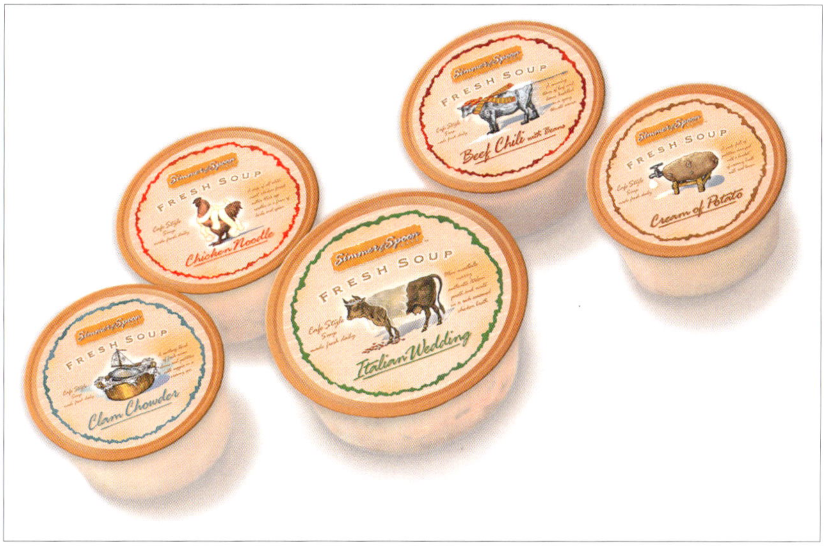

client
Sandridge Foods
design firm
PMthree Branding
www.pmthree.com
designer
Paul Port

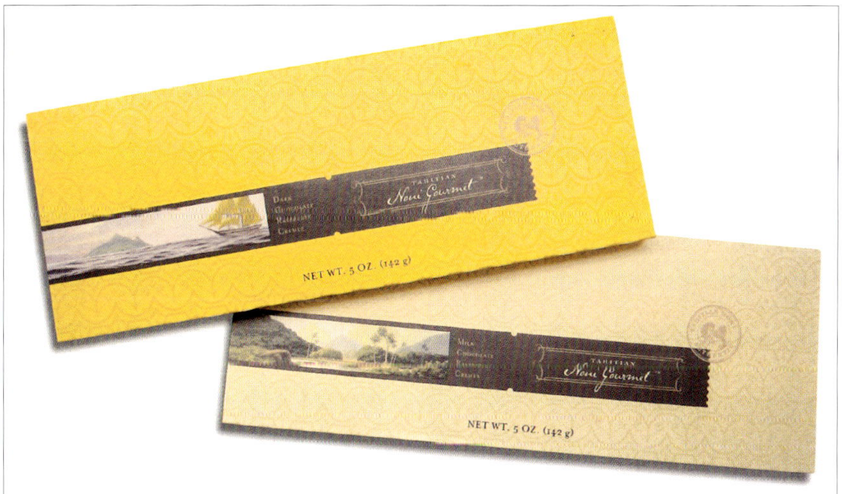

client
Tahitian Noni
design firm
Hornall Anderson Design Works
www.hadw.com
designers
Lisa Cerveny, Sonja Max,
Belinda Bowling, Ensi Mofasser,
Kathy Saito, Beth Grimm,
Julie Jacobson

client
Millennium
design firm
Hornall Anderson Design Works
www.hadw.com
designers
Lisa Cerveny, Mary Hermes, Tiffany Place,
Hillary Radbill, Elmer dela Cruz, Beckon Wyld

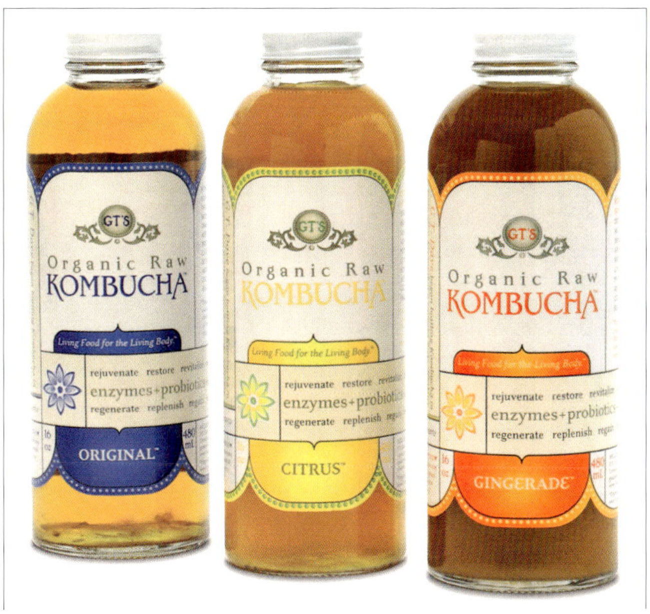

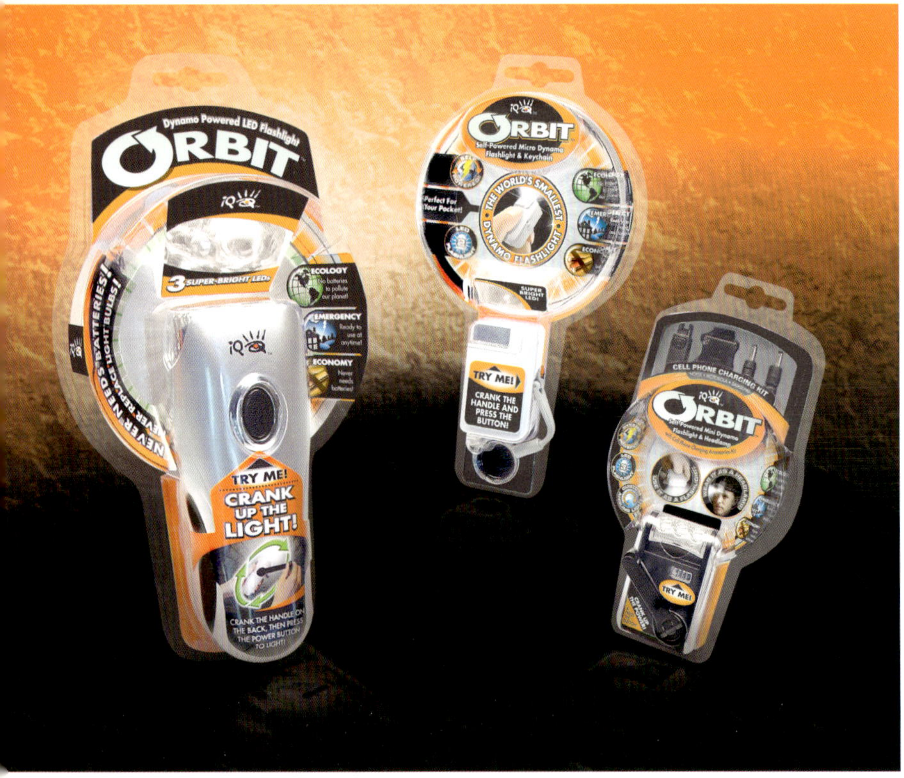

client
IQ Hong Kong
design firm
Zen Design Group
www.zendesigngroup.com
designers
Matt Chapman, David Perrin

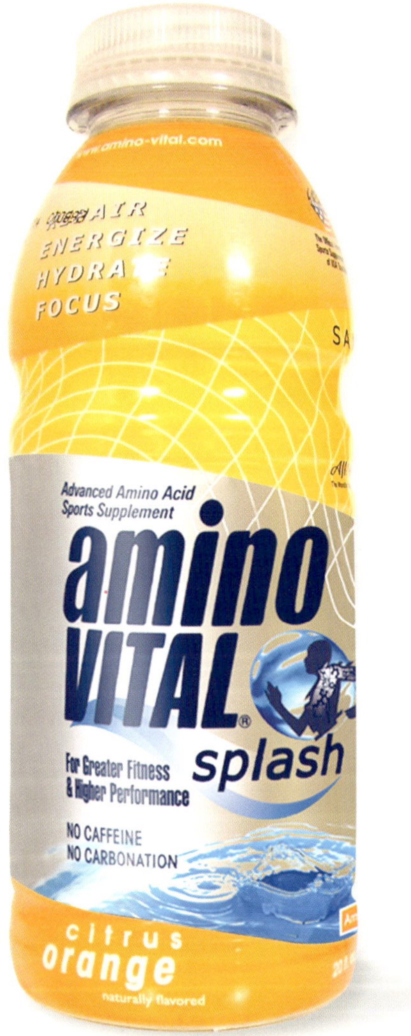

client
Ajinomoto
design firm
silver creative group
silvercreativegroup.com
designers
Nikolaos Niarhos, Tracy Waxenberg,
Margaret Singsen, Donna Bonato

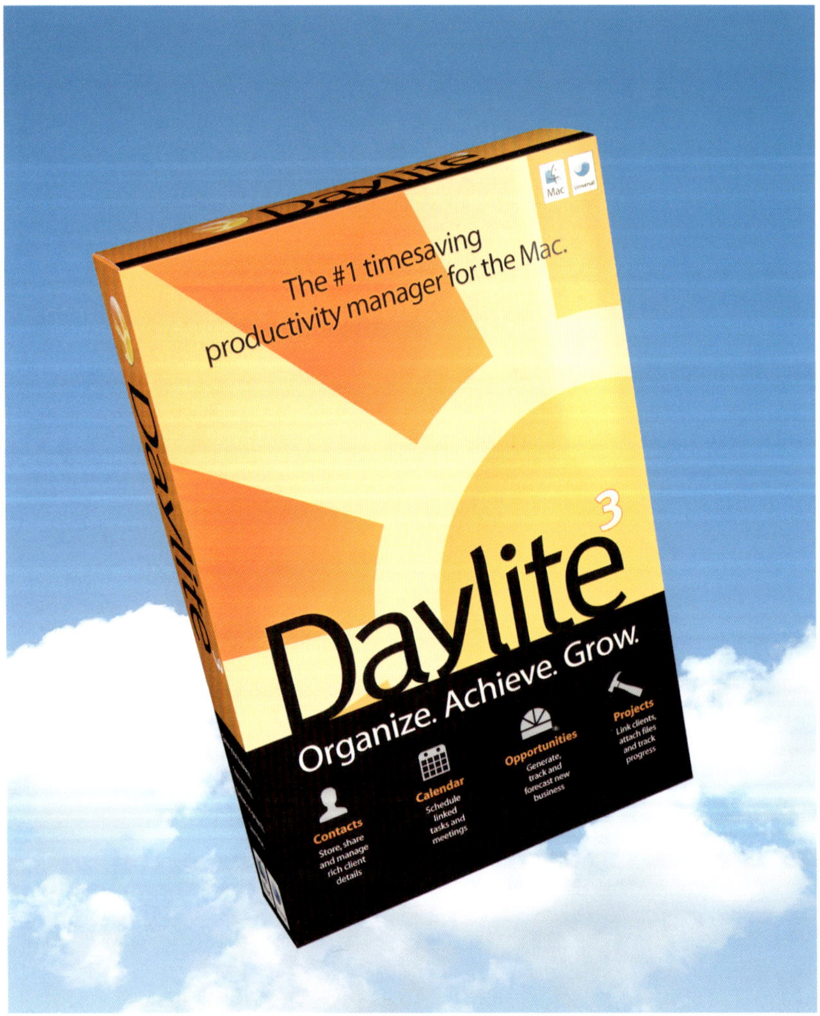

client
Market Circle
design firm
R. Bird
www.rbird.com
designers
Joseph Favata, Richard Bird

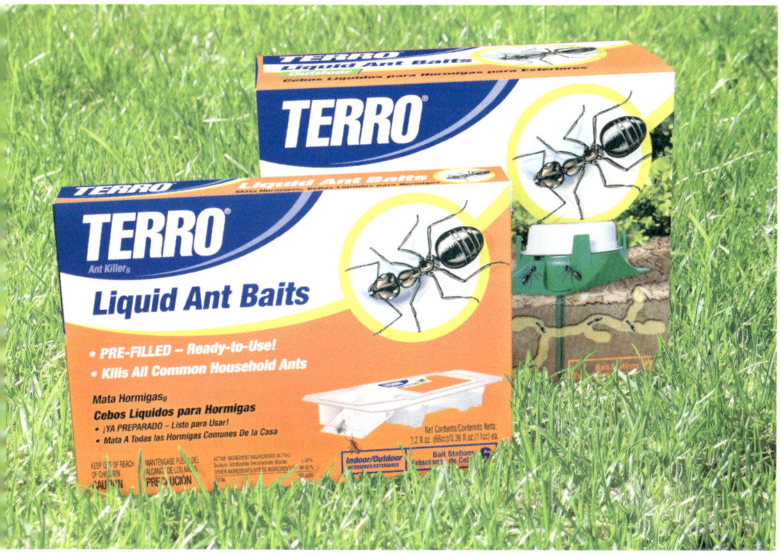

client
Senoret
design firm
R. Bird
www.rbird.com
designers
R. Bird Design Team

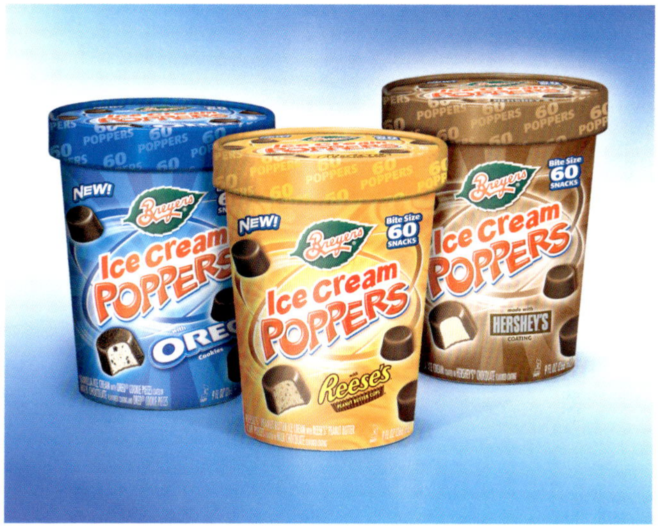

client
Unilever Foods North America
design firm
Smith Design
smithdesign.com
designers
Laura Markley, Angel Souto

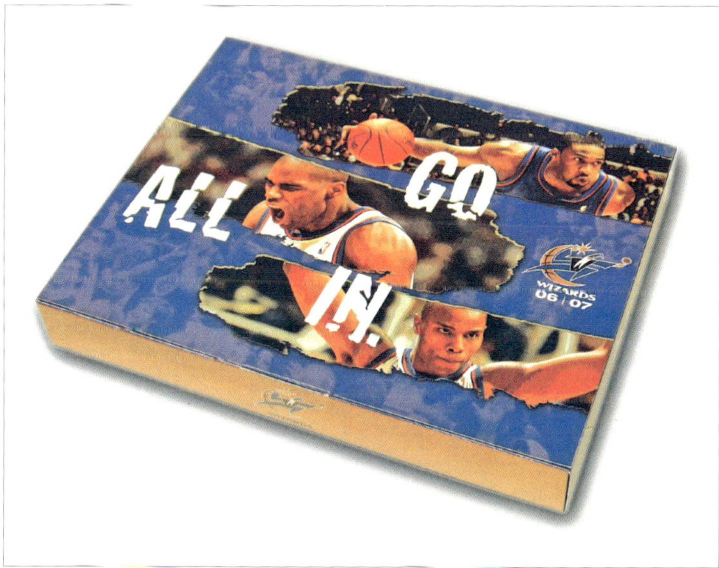

client
Washington Sports & Entertainment
design firm
Fixation Marketing
www.fixation.com
designers
Bruce E. Morgan, Elizabeth Ellen

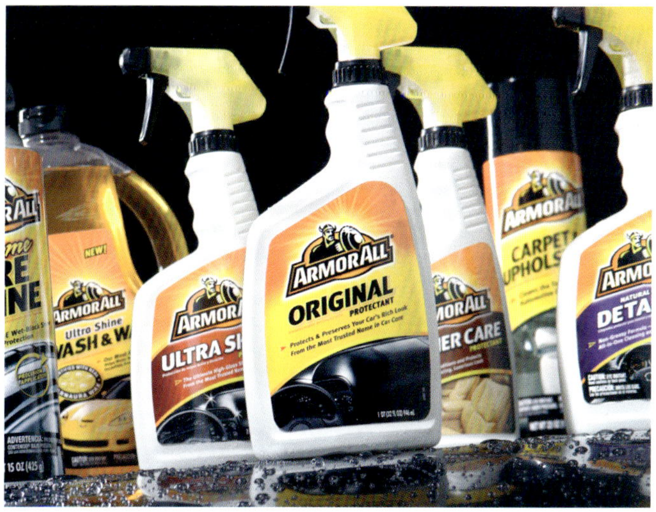

client
The Armor All Products Company
design firm
Clorox Creative Services
art director
Chris Twilling
designers
Tim Ferdun, Anthony Luk,
Jose Rodriguez

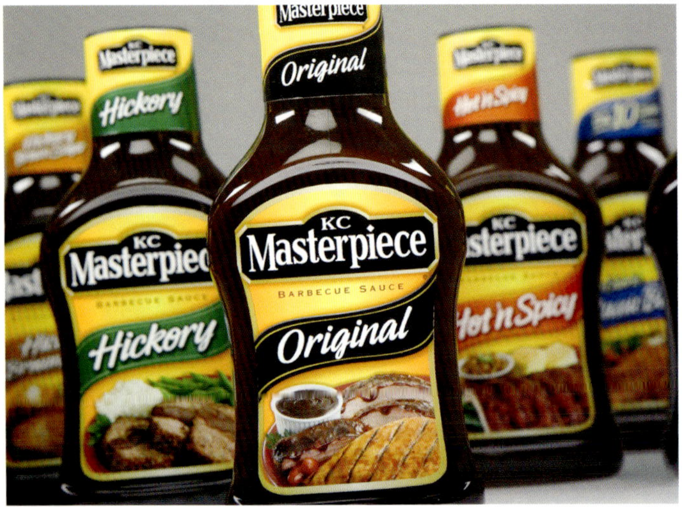

client
The HV Food Products Company
design firm
Clorox Creative Services
art director
Liliana Barbieri
designer
Tim Ferdun

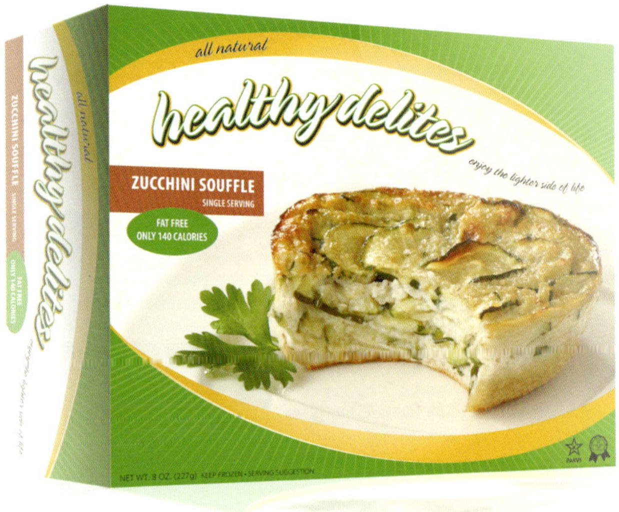

client
Classic Cooking
design firm
Zero Gravity Design Group
www.zerogny.com
designers
Zero Gravity Design Group

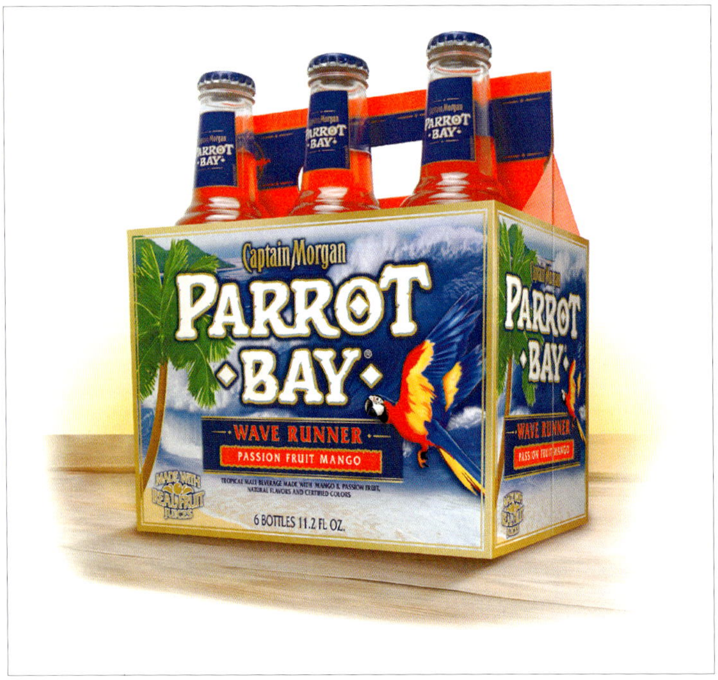

client
Diageo
design firm
PMthree Branding
www.pmthree.com
designer
Paul Port

client
Unilever
design firm
Tom Fowler, Inc.
www.tomfowlerinc.com
creative director
Elizabeth P. Ball
art director, designer
Mary Ellen Butkus

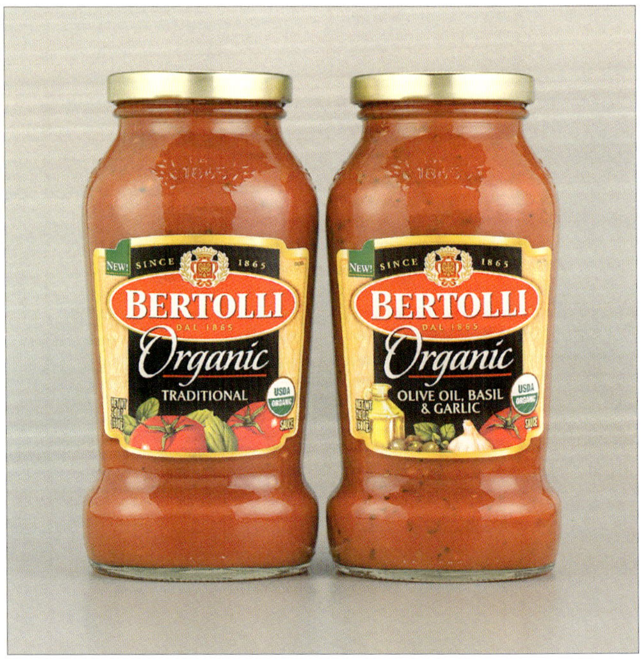

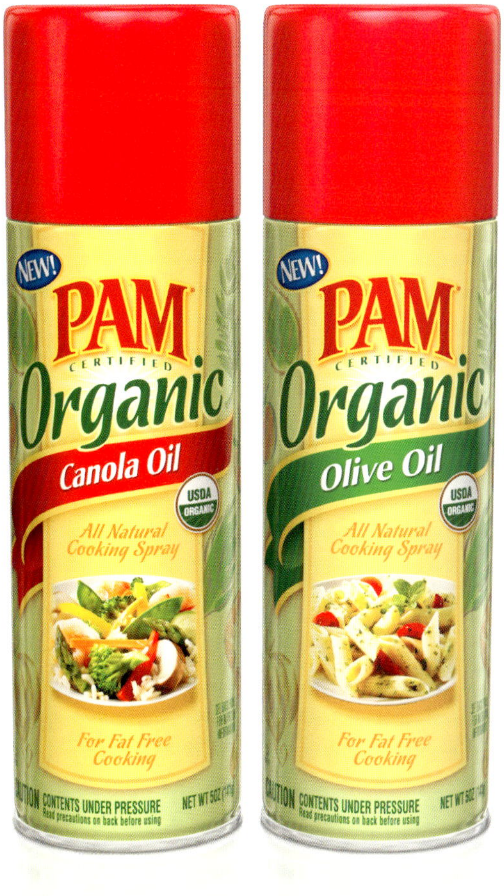

client
ConAgra Foods Company, Inc.
design firm
Thompson Design Group
www.ttdg.com
designers
Thompson Design Group

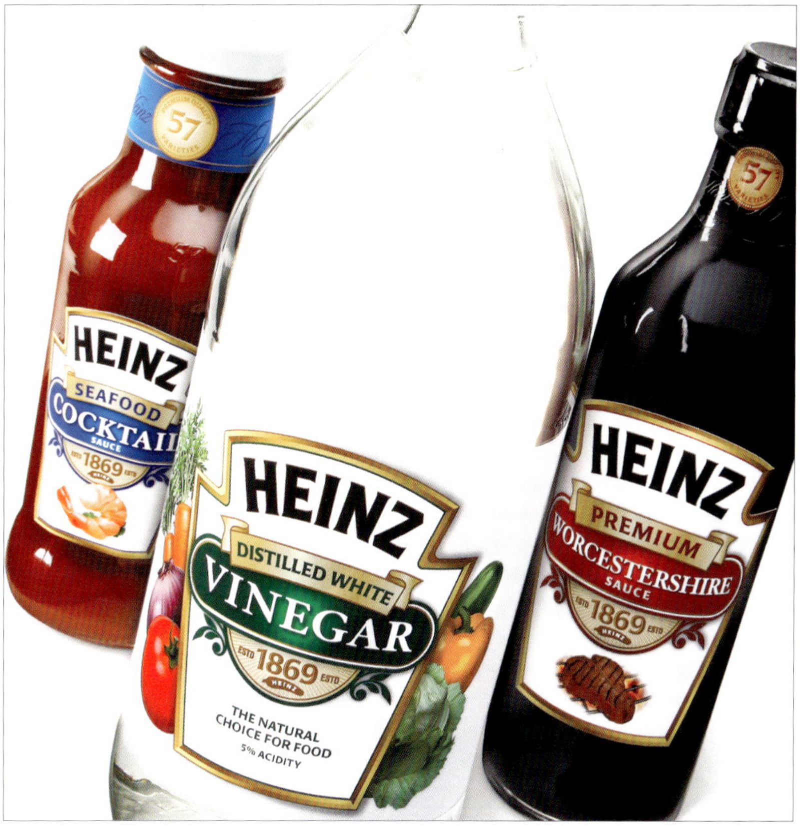

client
H.J. Heinz
design firm
Wallace Church, Inc.
www.wallacechurch.com
creative director
Stan Church
designer
Heather Allen

client
Gerber
design firm
PMthree Branding
www.pmthree.com
designers
Jessica Annunziato,
Ralph Miolla

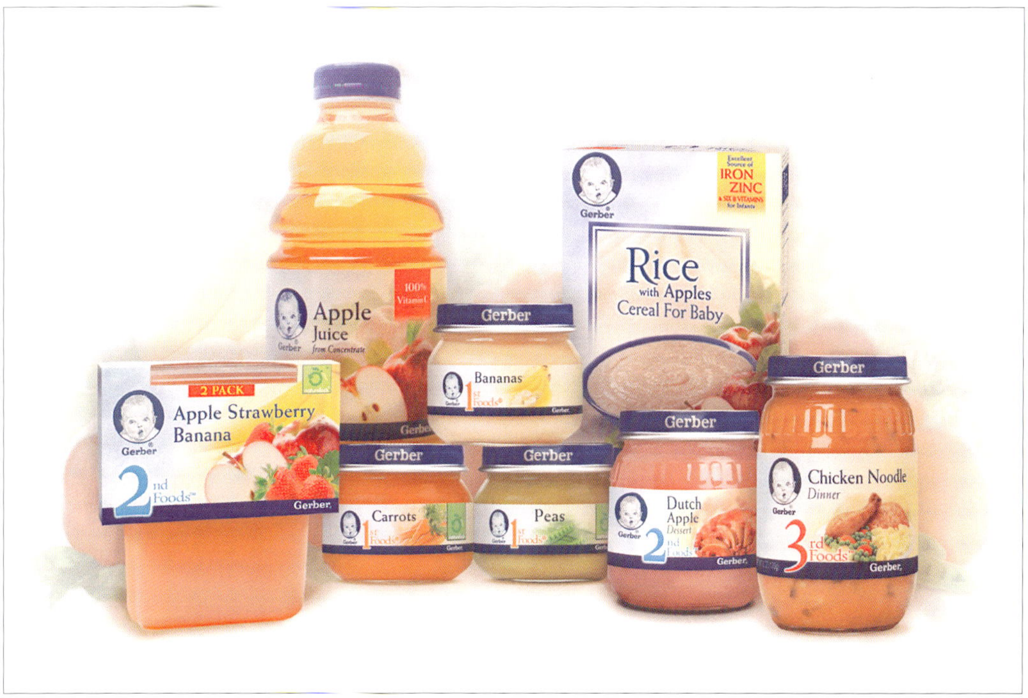

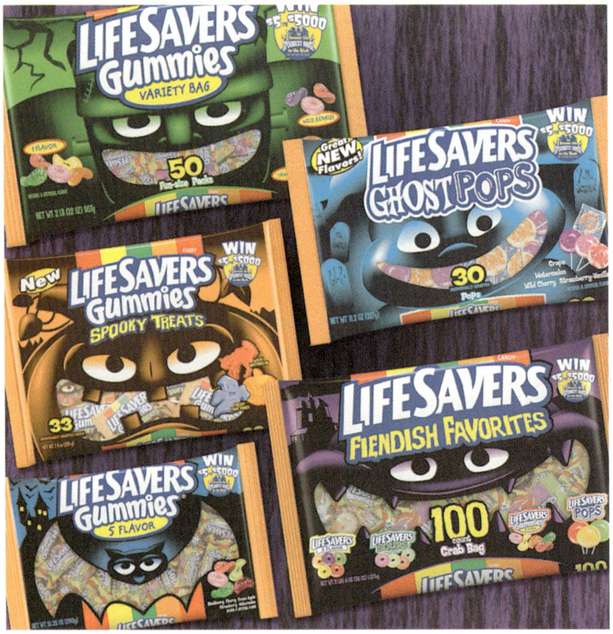

client
Wm. Wrigley Jr. Company
design firm
Cassata & Associates
cassata.net
designer
James Miskeyics

client
The Clorox Pet Products Company
design firm
Clorox Creative Services
designers
Tim Ferdun, Anthony Luk

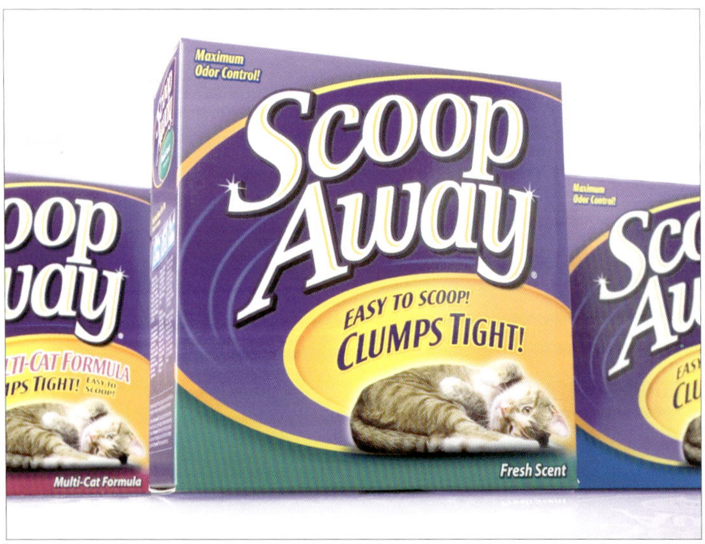

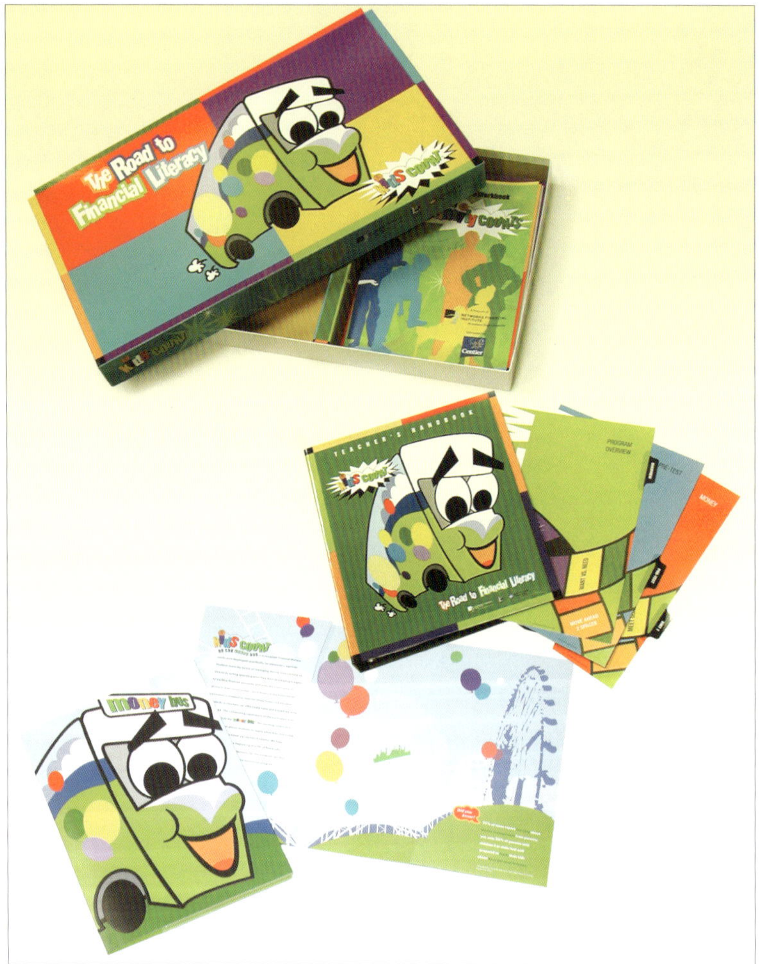

client
Networks Financial Institute
design firm
Gibson Group
www.gibsongrp.com
designer
Diane McGuire

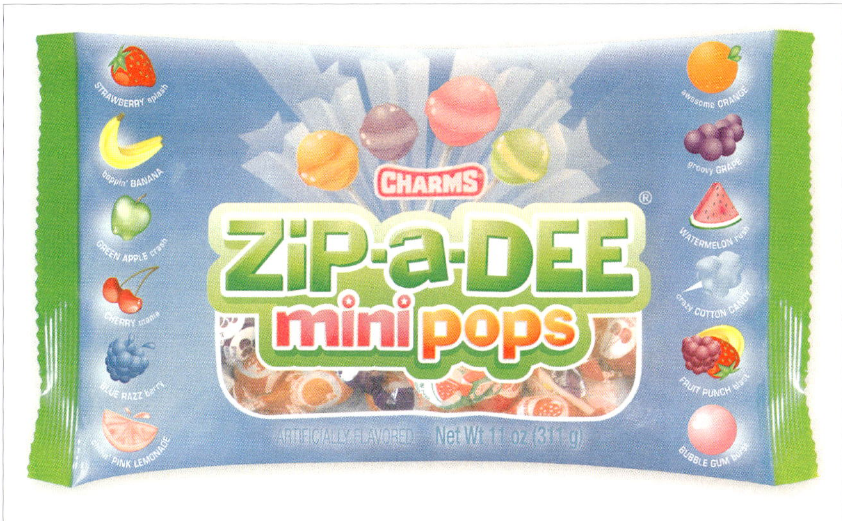

client
Charms Marketing Company
design firm
Design Resource Center
www.drcchicago.com
designers
John Norman, Melanie Gibb

client
The Dannon Company, Inc.
design firm
Zunda Group, LLC
www.zundagroup.com
art directors
Charles Zunda, Gary Esposito
designers
Daniel Price, Amy Dresner-Yules

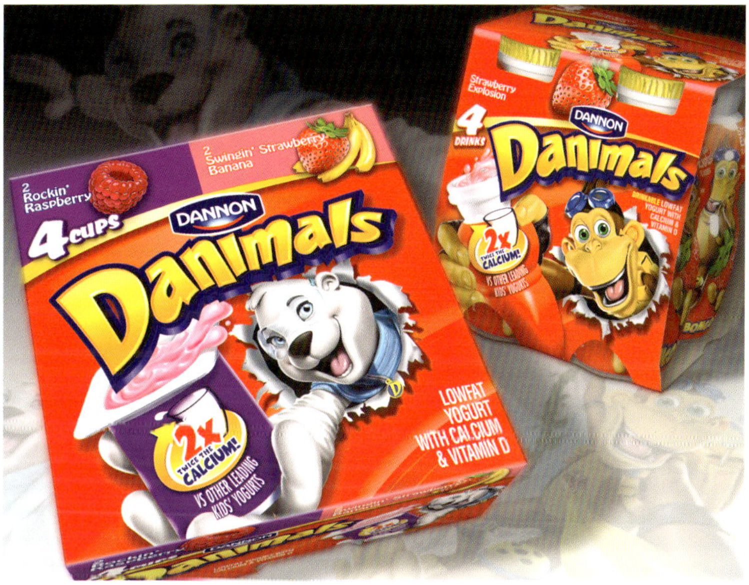

client
Borden (American Dairy Brands)
design firm
Smith Design
smithdesign.com
designers
Carol Konkowski, Eileen Berezni,
Lynn Vaughan, Angel Sonto

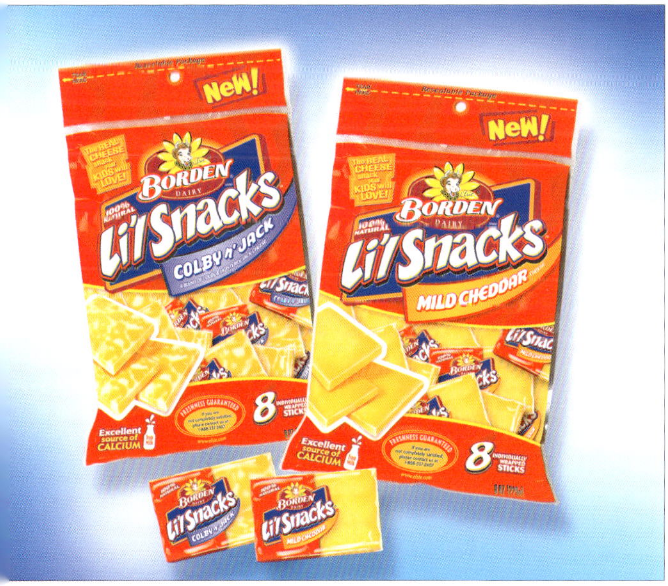

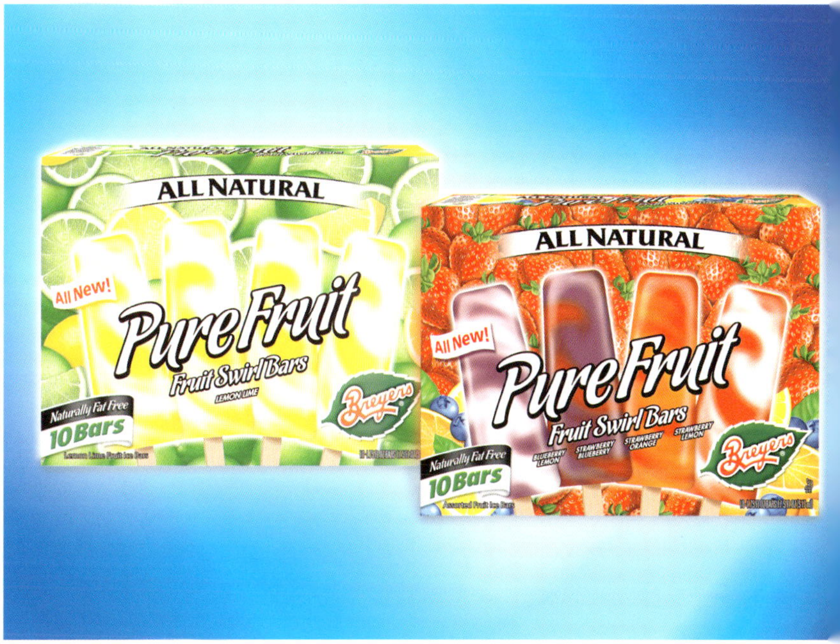

client
Unilever Foods North America
design firm
Smith Design
smithdesign.com
designers
Eileen Berezni, Angel Sonto

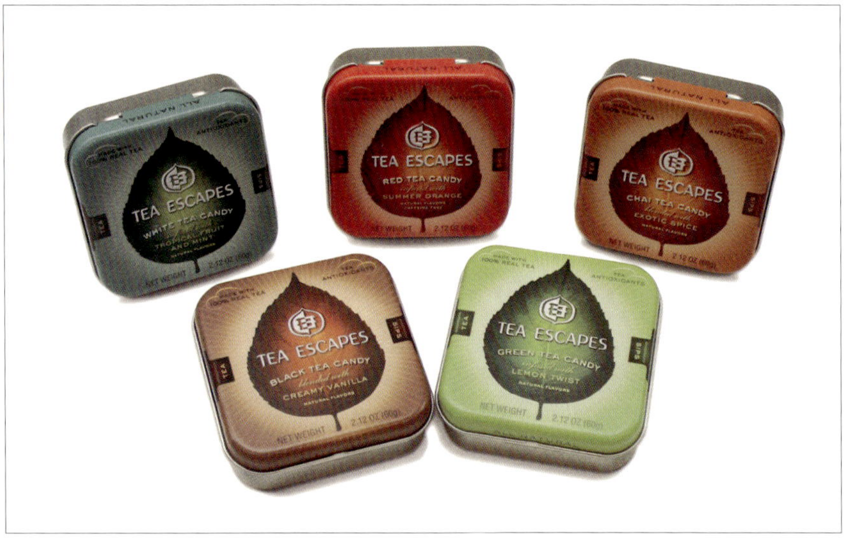

client
Tea Escapes
design firm
Hornall Anderson Design Works
www.hadw.com
designers
Jack Anderson, David Bates, Beth Grimm, Kathleen Gibson, Jacob Carter

client
Frederick Cellars
design firm
Octavo Designs
designers
Sue Hough, Mark Burrier

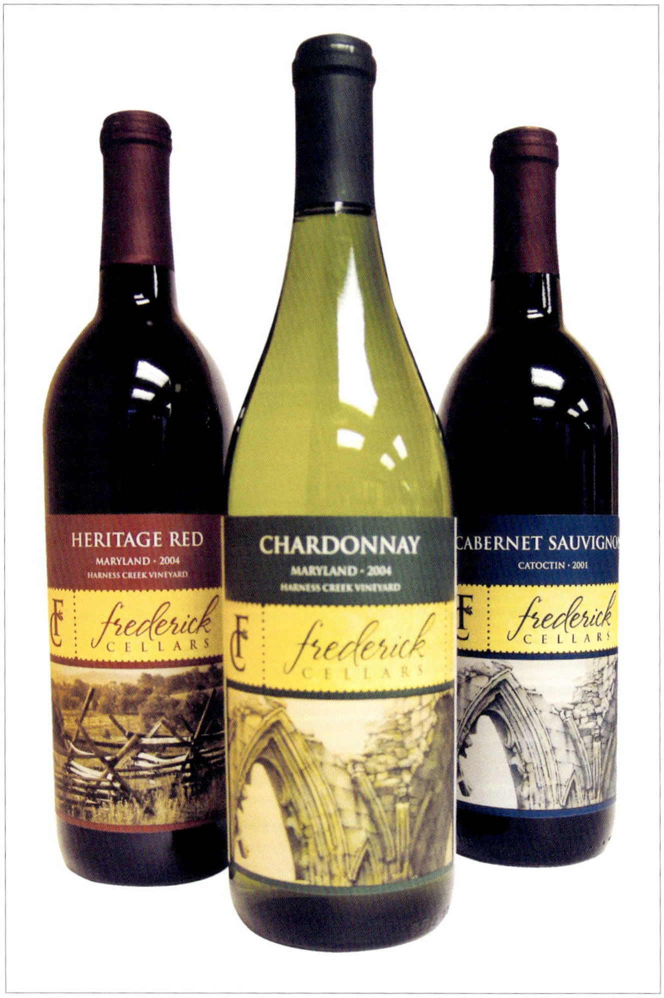

client
Widmer Brothers Brewery
design firm
Hornall Anderson Design Works
www.hadw.com
designers
Jack Anderson, Larry Anderson, Jay Hilburn, Bruce Stigler, Elmer dela Cruz, Hayden Schoen, Daymon Bruck

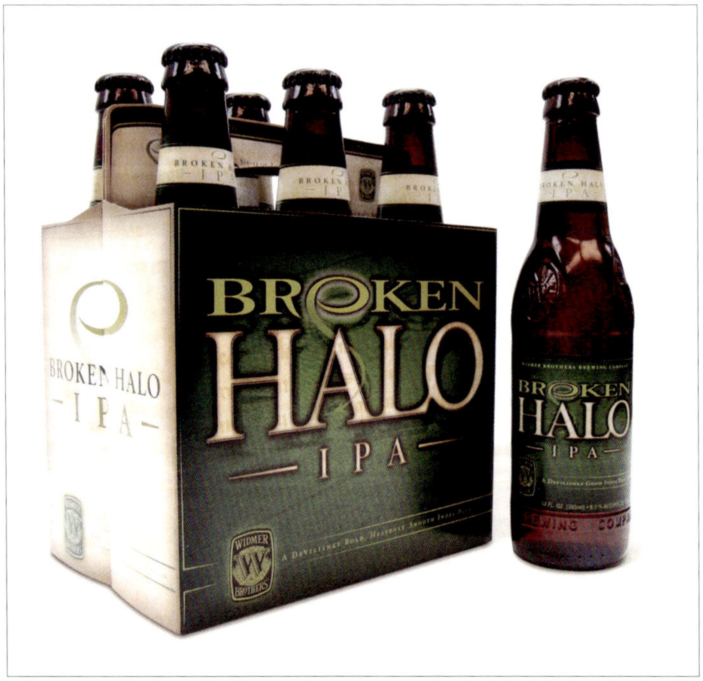

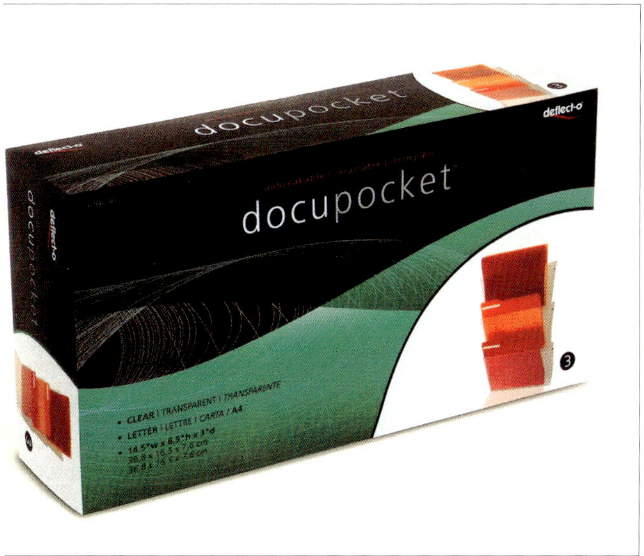

client
Deflecto Corporation

design firm
Design Resource Center
www.drcchicago.com

designers
John Norman,
Melanie Gibb

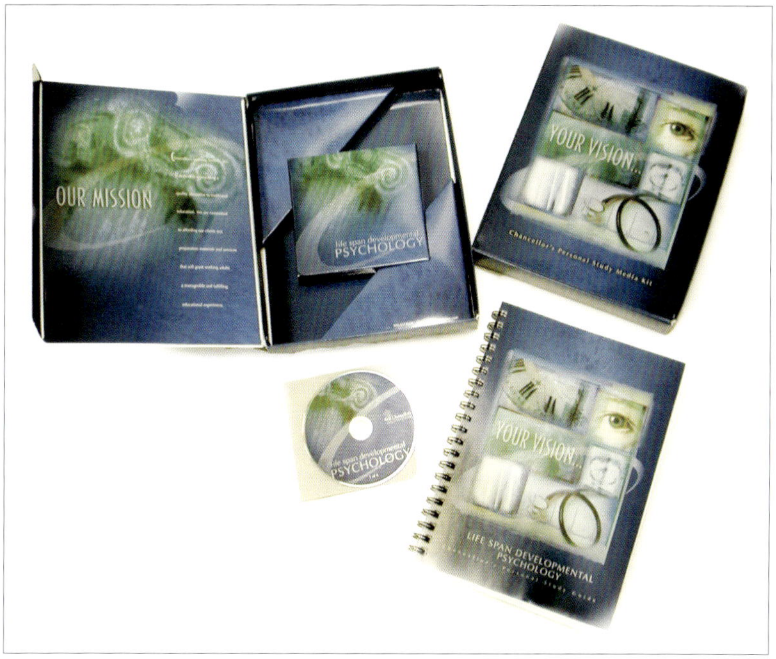

client
Chancellor's Learning Systems

design firm
Gibson Group
www.gibsongrp.com

designer
Diane McGuire

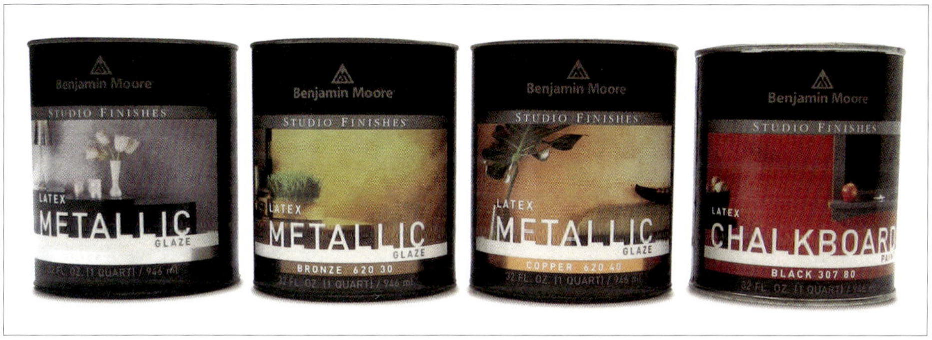

client
Benjamin Moore

design firm
Hornall Anderson Design Works
www.hadw.com

designers
Lisa Cerveny, Mary Hermes, Holly Craven,
Belinda Bowling, Mary Chin Hutchison, Tiffany Place

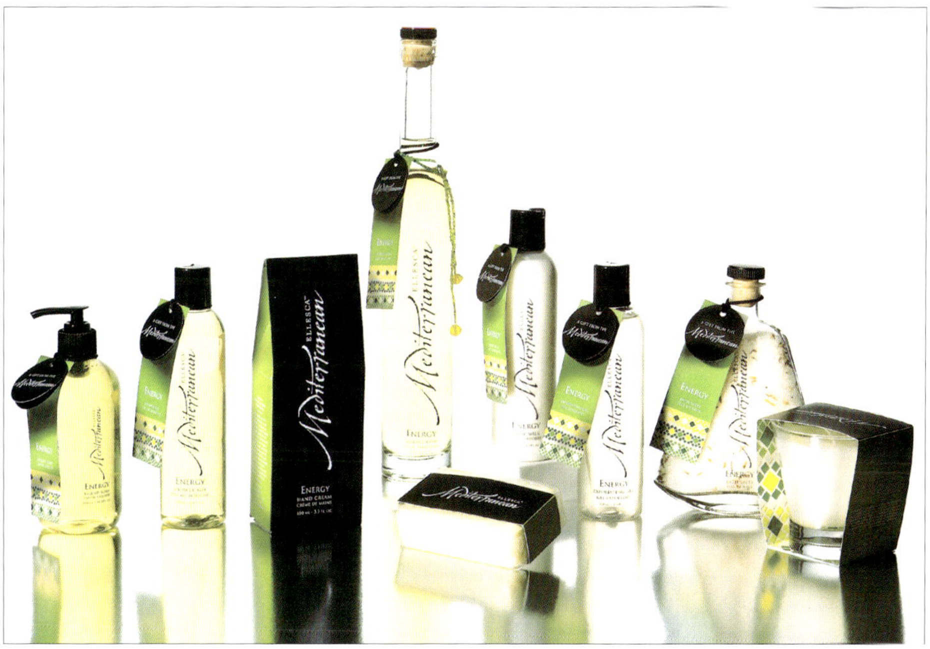

client
Ellesca

design firm
viadesign
www.viadesign.com

designer
Theresa Vandenberg

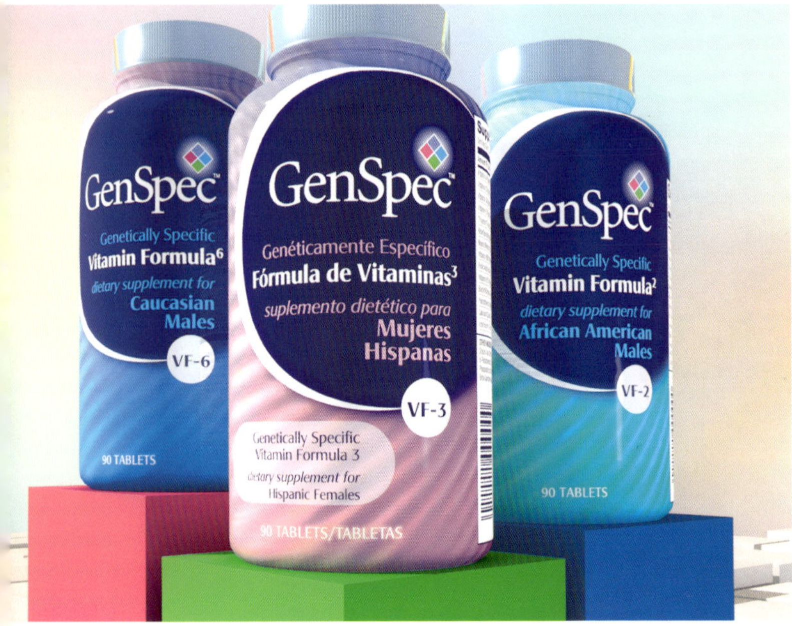

client
Ethnicor
design firm
R. Bird
www.rbird.com
designers
R. Bird Design Team

client
Johnson & Johnson
design firm
The Bailey Group
www.baileygp.com
designers
Steve Perry, Christian Williamson

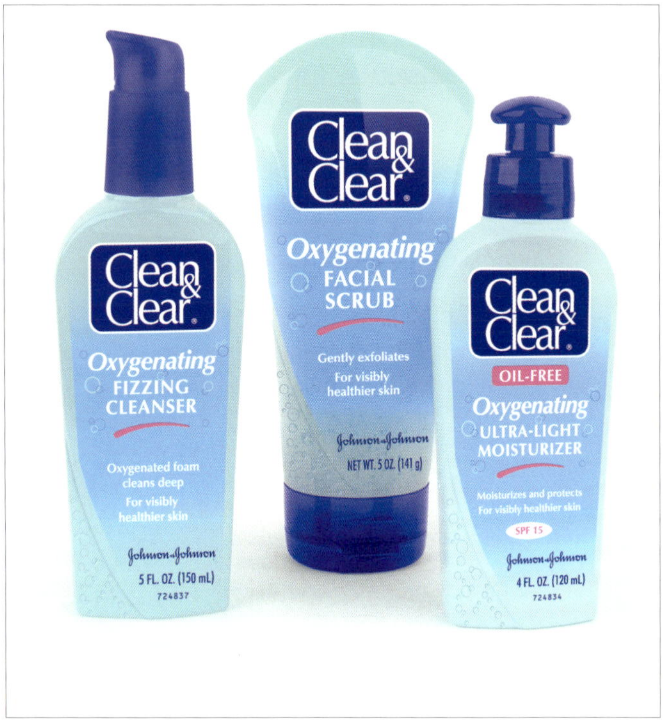

client
Prestige Brands, Inc.
design firm
Zunda Group, LLC
www.zundagroup.com
art director
Charles Zunda
designer
Siri Korsgren

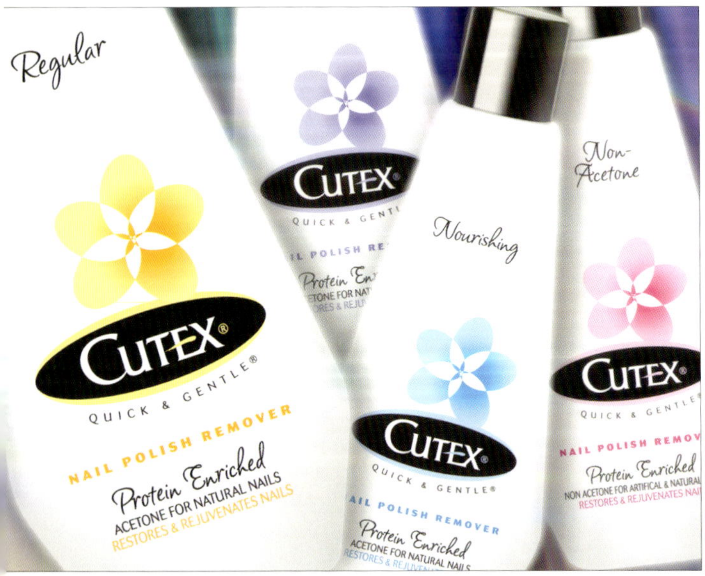

client
Solstice Medicine Co.
design firm
R. Bird
www.rbird.com
designers
R. Bird Design Team

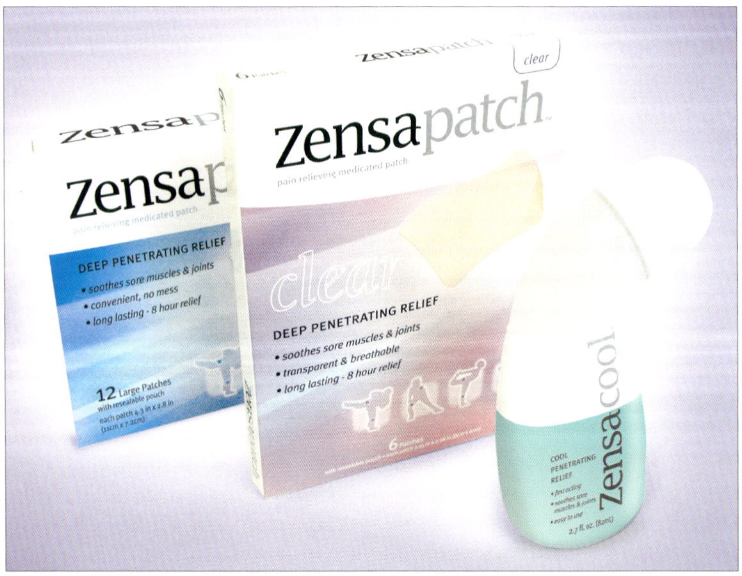

client
P.I.N.K. Vodka
—David Mandell
design firm
The Bailey Group
www.baileygp.com
designers
Steve Perry, Christian Williamson

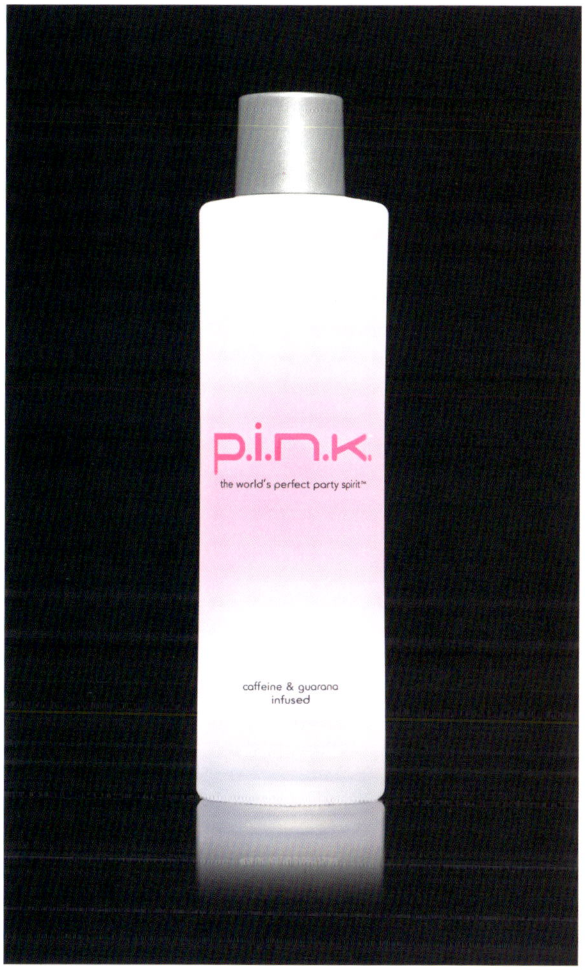

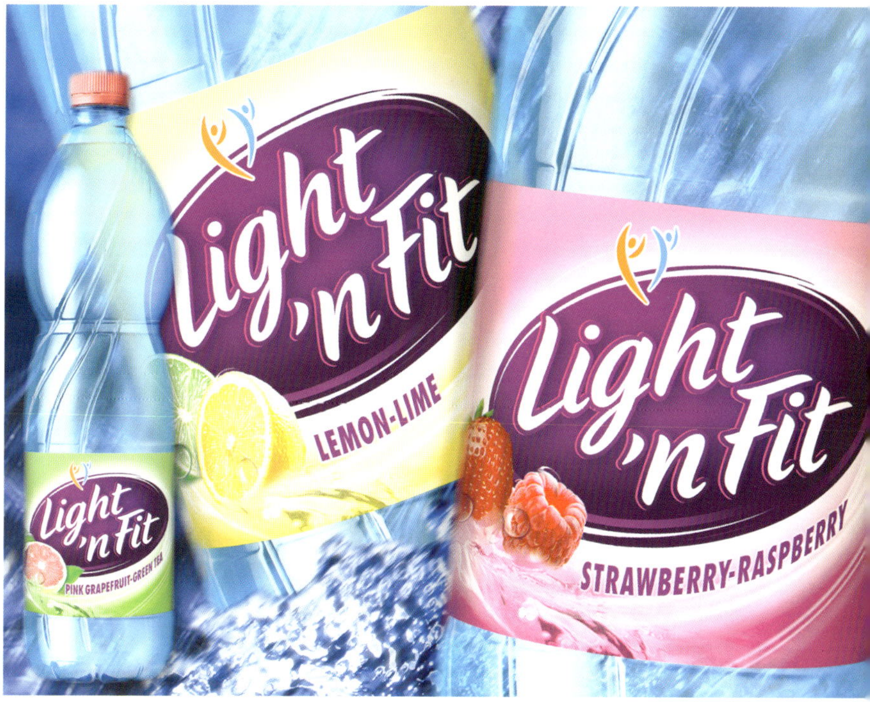

client
Great Brands of Europe, Inc.
design firm
Zunda Group, LLC
www.zundagroup.com
art directors
Charles Zunda, Gary Esposito
designers
Daniel Price, Jean Legros

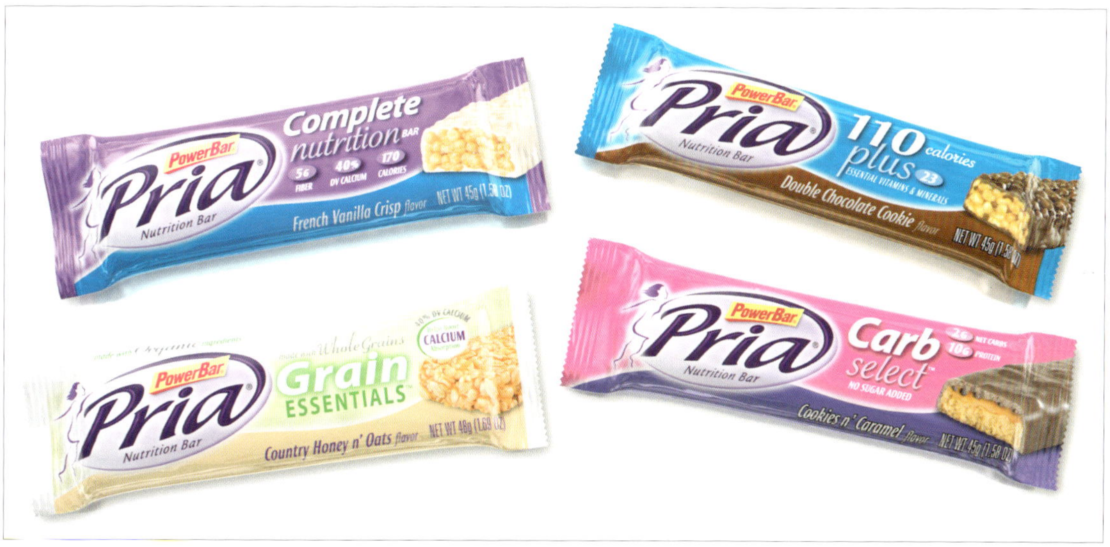

client
powerBar, Inc.
design firm
Thompson Design Group
www.ttdg.com
designers
Thompson Design Group

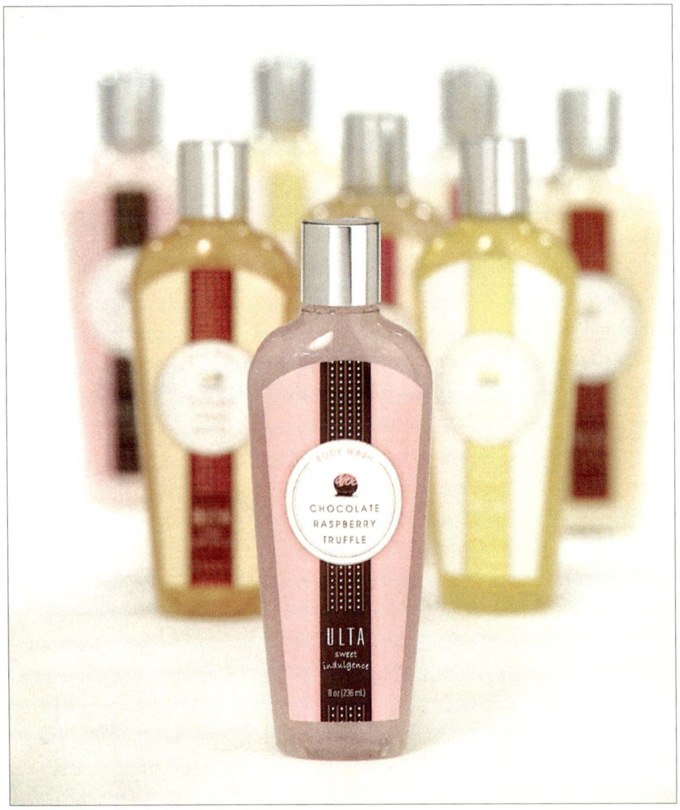

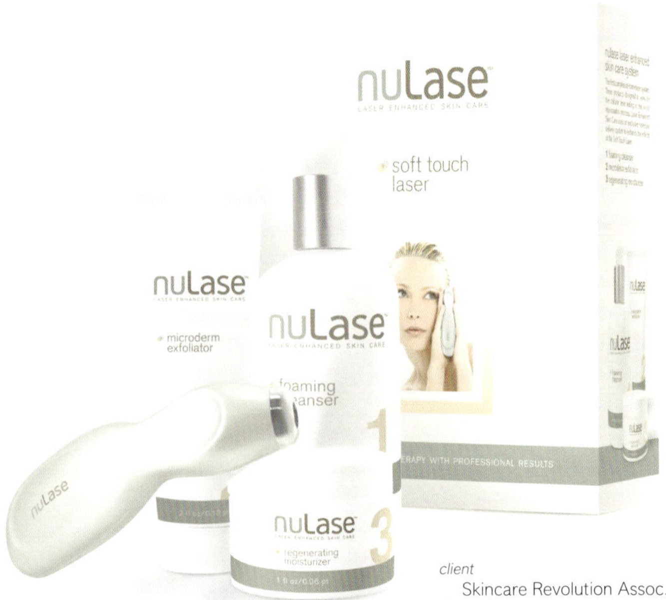

client
Skincare Revolution Assoc.
design firm
Jensen Design Assoc., Inc.
designers
Alyssa Igawa, Dave Jensen

client
Ulta Corporation
design firm
Design Resource Center
www.drcchicago.com
designers
John Norman,
Melanie Gibb

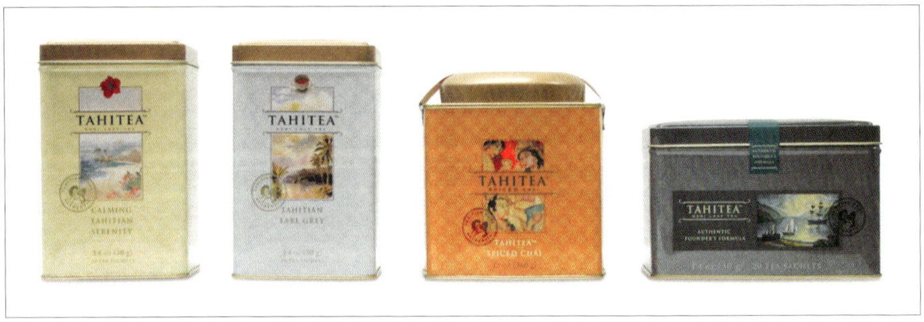

client
Tahitian Noni
design firm
Hornall Anderson
Design Works
www.hadw.com
designers
Lisa Cerveny,
Sonja Max,
Beth Grimm,
Belinda Bowling,
Ensi Mofasser,
Kathy Saito,
Julie Jacobson

client
Kelly's Spa
design firm
Winter Ad Agency
www.winteradagency.com
designers
Mary Winter,
Michelle Fournier

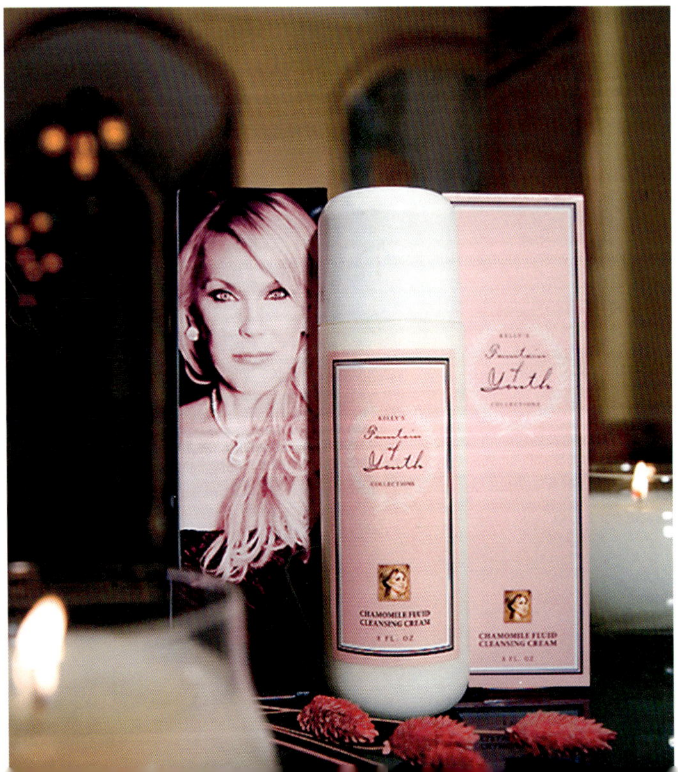

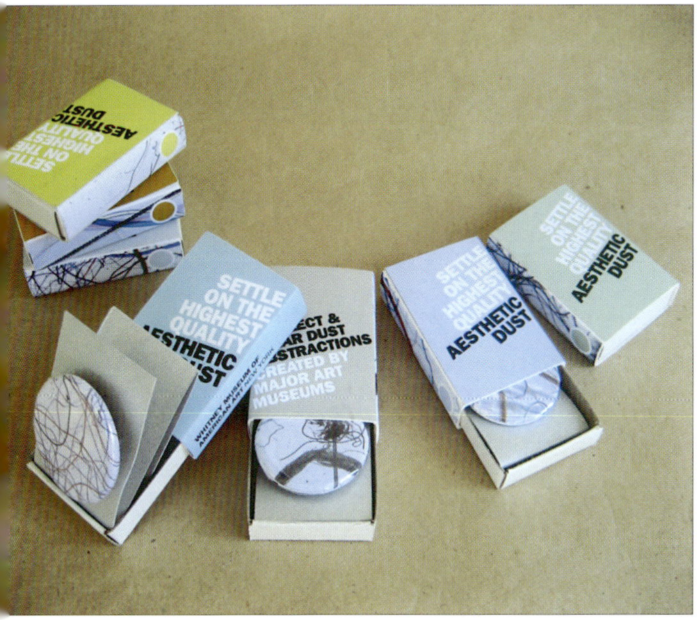

client
Sean Miller
design firm
Connie Hwang Design
www.conniehwangdesign.com
designer
Connie Hwang

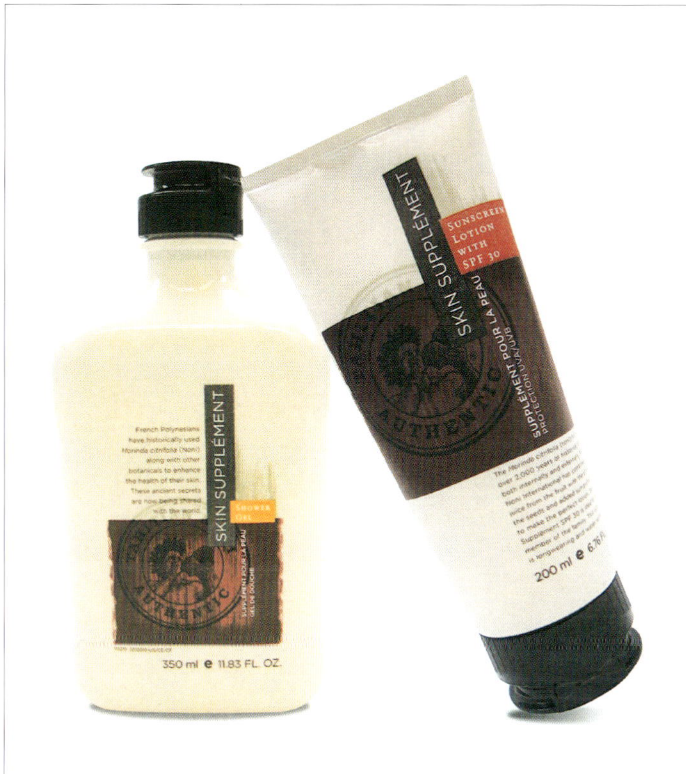

client
Tahitian Noni
design firm
Hornall Anderson Design Works
www.hadw.com
designers
Lisa Cerveny, Sonja Max,
Belinda Bowling, Ensi Mofasser,
Kathy Saito, Julie Jacobson,
Beth Grimm

client
Ulta Corporation
design firm
Design Resource Center
www.drcchicago.com
designers
John Norman, Melanie Gibb

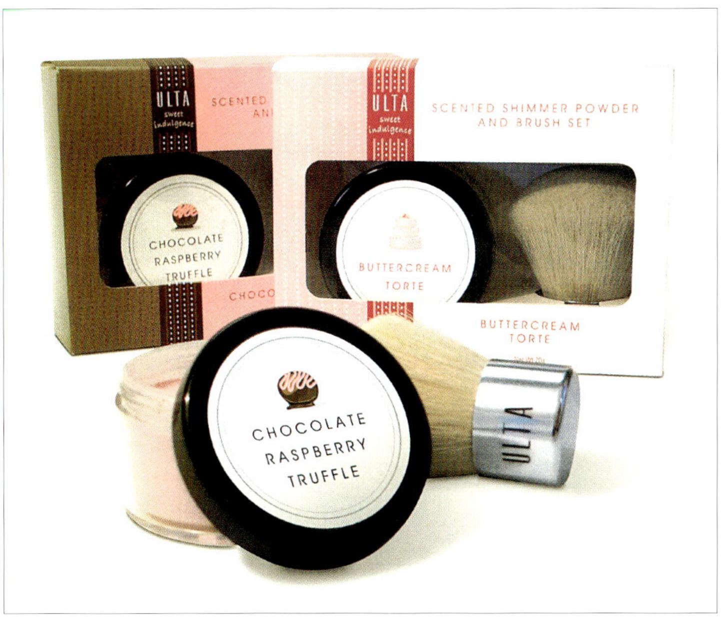

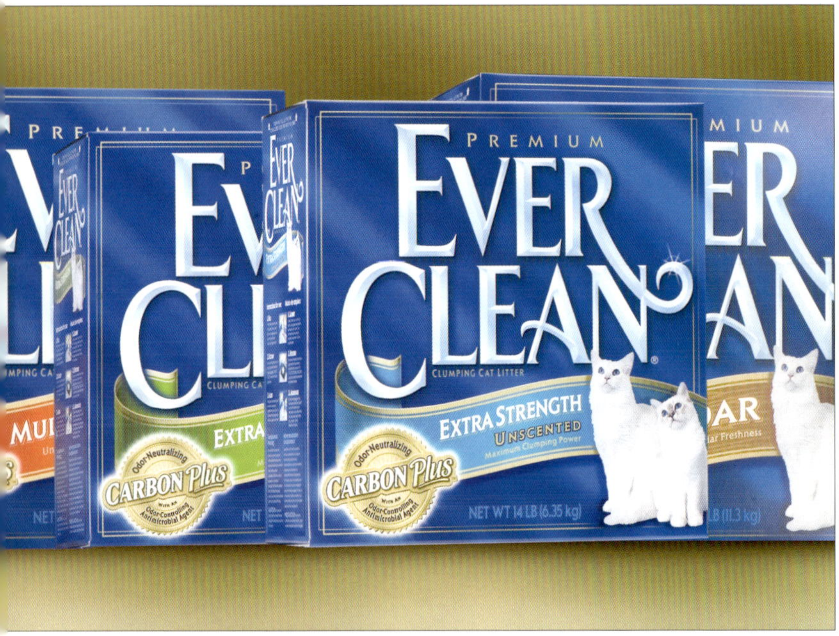

client
The Clorox Pet Products Company
design firm
Clorox Creative Services
art director
Liliana Barbieri
designer
Tim Ferdun

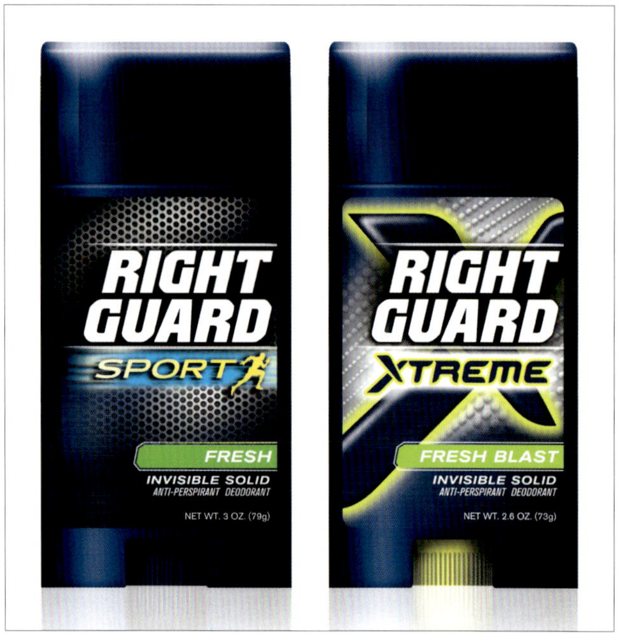

client
The Dial Corp.
design firm
Wallace Church, Inc.
www.wallacechurch.com
creative director
Stan Church
designer
John Bruno

client
foneGEAR
design firm
Zen Design Group
www.zendesigngroup.com
designers
Kok Hwa Chung, David Perrin, Matt Chapman, Julie Yu

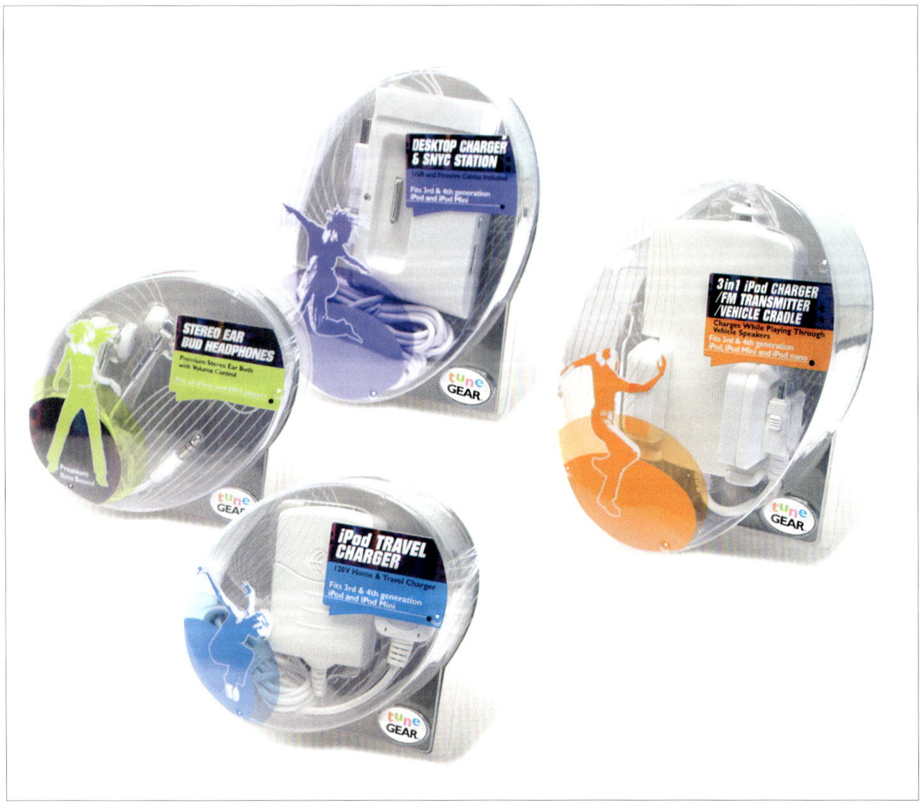

client
The Clorox Company
design firm
Clorox Creative Services
art director
Chris Twilling
designers
Tim Ferdun, Sunnie Moon

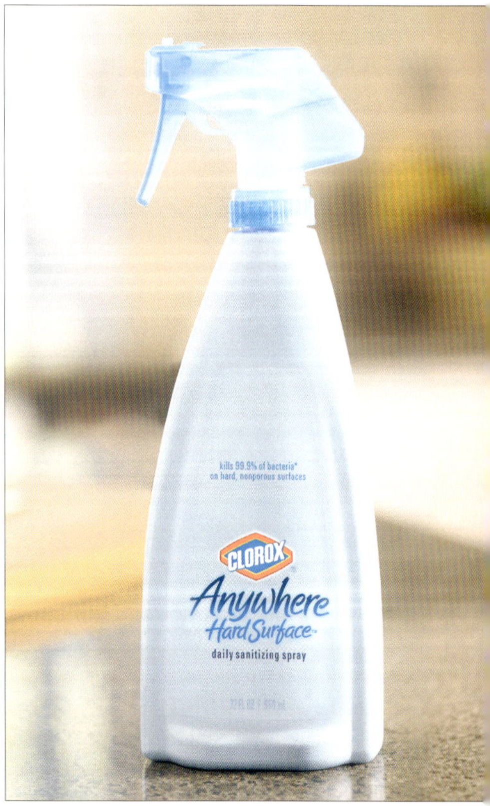

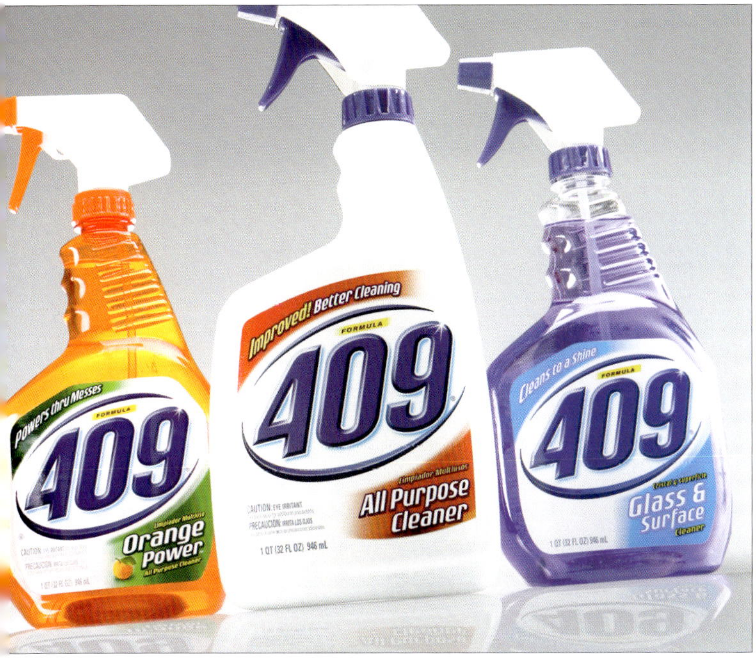

client
The Clorox Company
design firm
Clorox Creative Services
art director
Chris Twilling
designers
Tim Ferdun, Anthony Luk

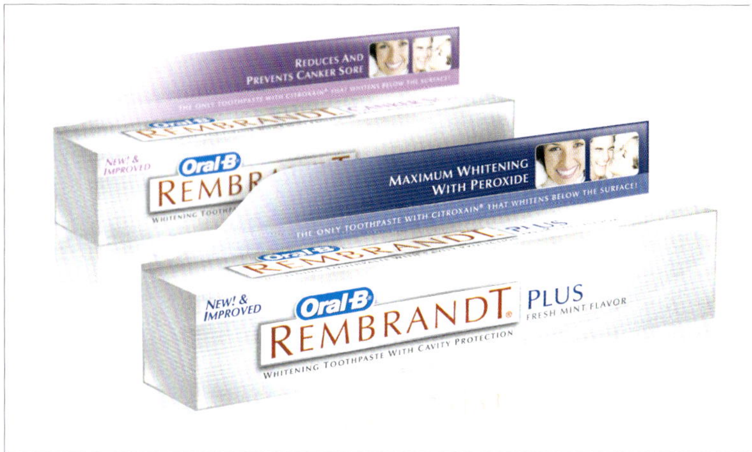

client
The Gillette Company
design firm
Wallace Church, Inc.
www.wallacechurch.com
creative director
Stan Church
designer
John Bruno

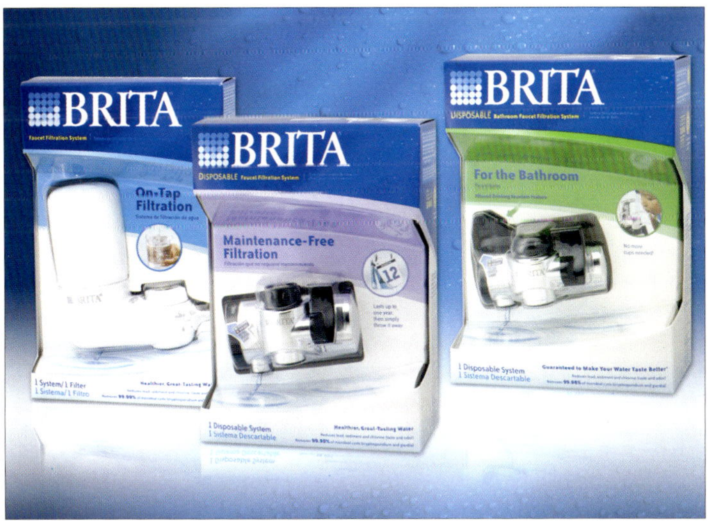

client
The Brita Products Company
design firm
Clorox Creative Services
art director
Liliana Barbieri
designer
Anthony Luk
photographer
Kevin Ng

client
The Clorox Company
design firm
Clorox Creative Services
art director
Chris Twilling
designers
Christine Darnell, Sunnie Moon

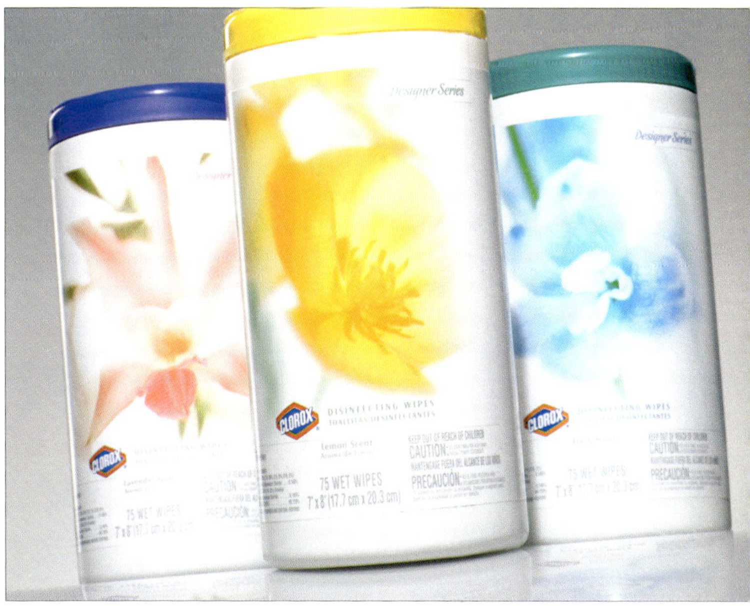

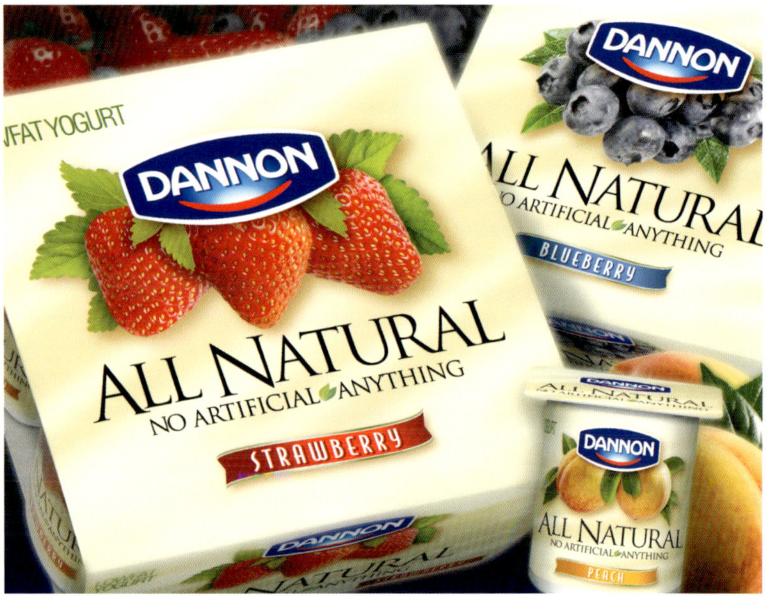

client
The Dannon Company, Inc.
design firm
Zunda Group, LLC
www.zundagroup.com
art directors
Charles Zunda, Gary Esposito
designers
Charles Zunda, Amy Dresner-Yules

client
Millennium
design firm
Hornall Anderson Design Works
www.hadw.com
designers
Lisa Cerveny, Mary Hermes,
Tiffany Place, Hillary Radbill,
Elmer de la Cruz, Beckon Wyld

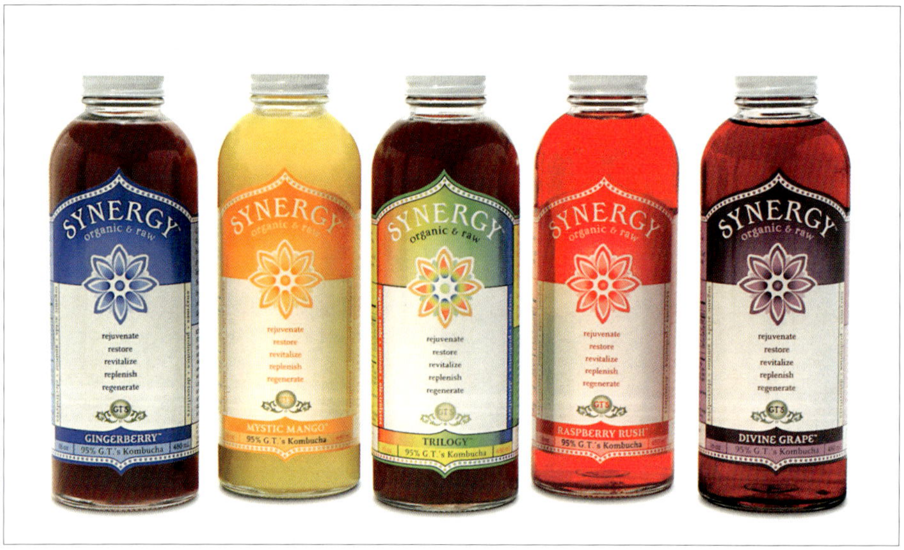

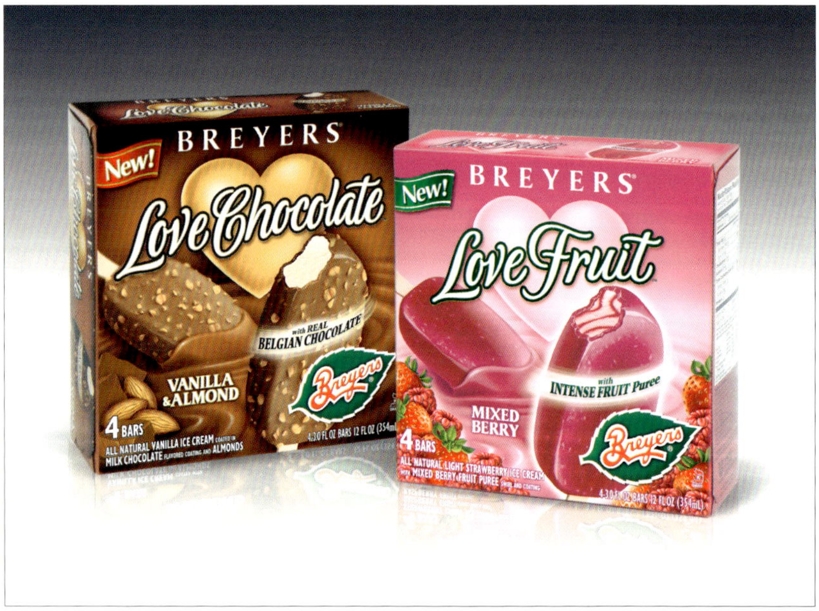

client
Unilever Foods North America
design firm
Smith Design
smithdesign.com
designers
Glenn Hagen, Lyn Vaughan,
Angel Souto, Brian Sheridan

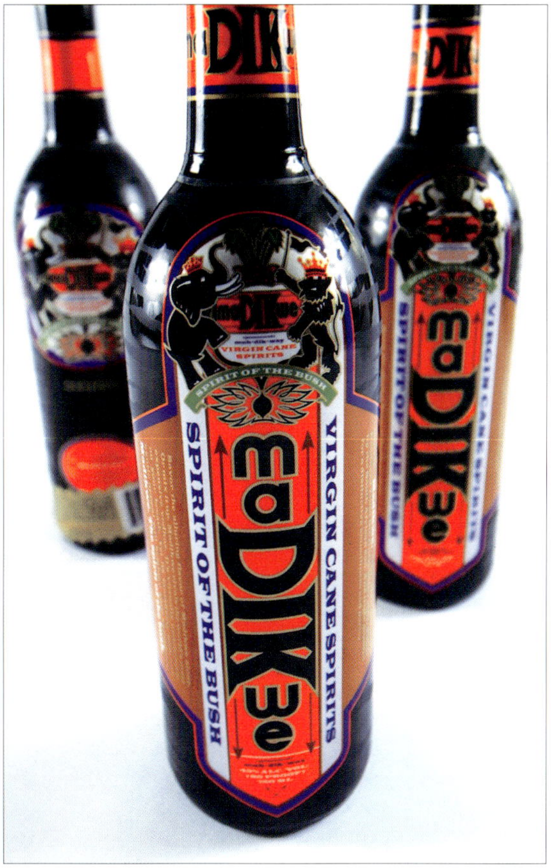

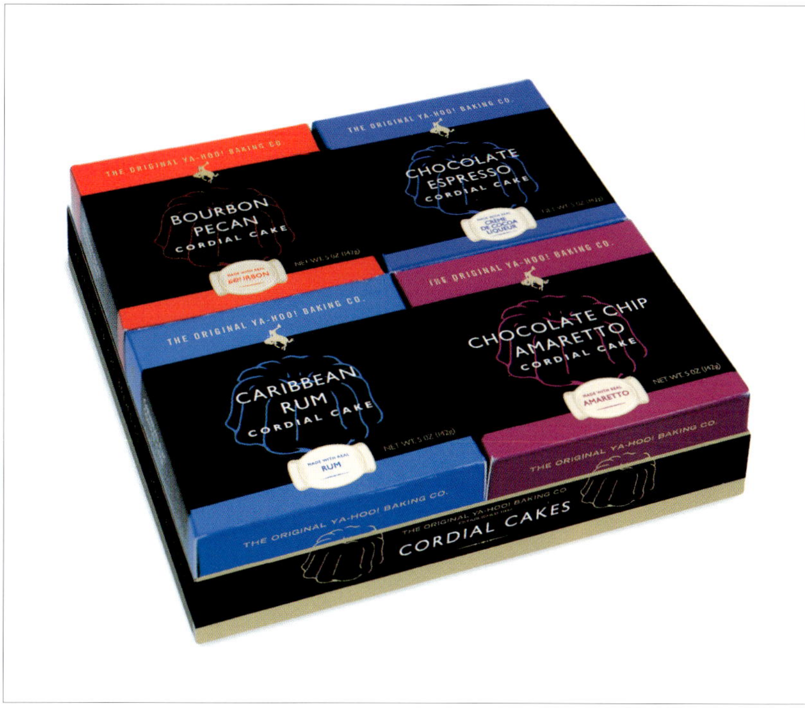

client
The Original Ya-Hoo! Baking Co.
design firm
Marcante | Crouch | LeBlanc
www.mcl-usa.com
designer
Richard LeBlanc

client
maDIKwe
design firm
Sayles Graphic Design
www.saylesdesign.com
designers
John Sayles, Jessi O'Brien

client
Herip Design Associates, Inc.
design firm
Herip Design Associates, Inc.
www.heripassociates.com
designers
Walter M. Herip,
Jen Hollo Crabtree,
John R. Menter

client
Welch's
design firm
The Bailey Group
www.baileygp.com
designers
Dave Fiedler, Gary LaCroix

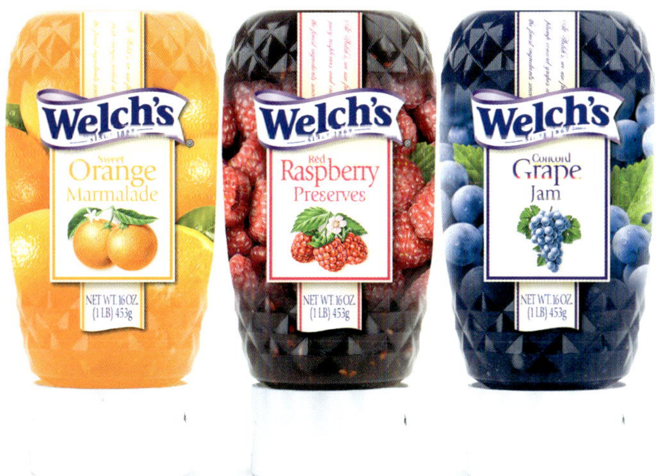

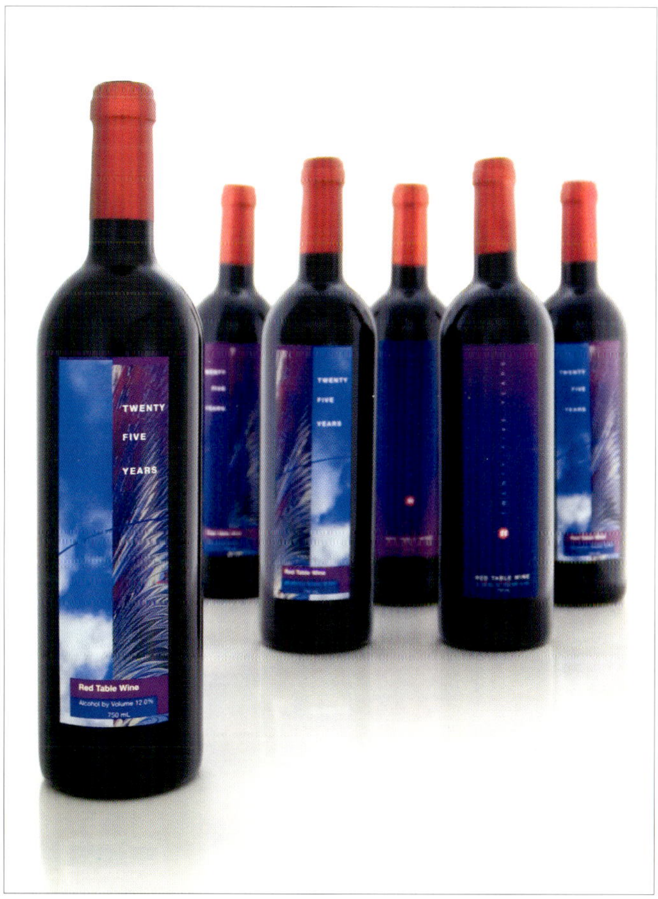

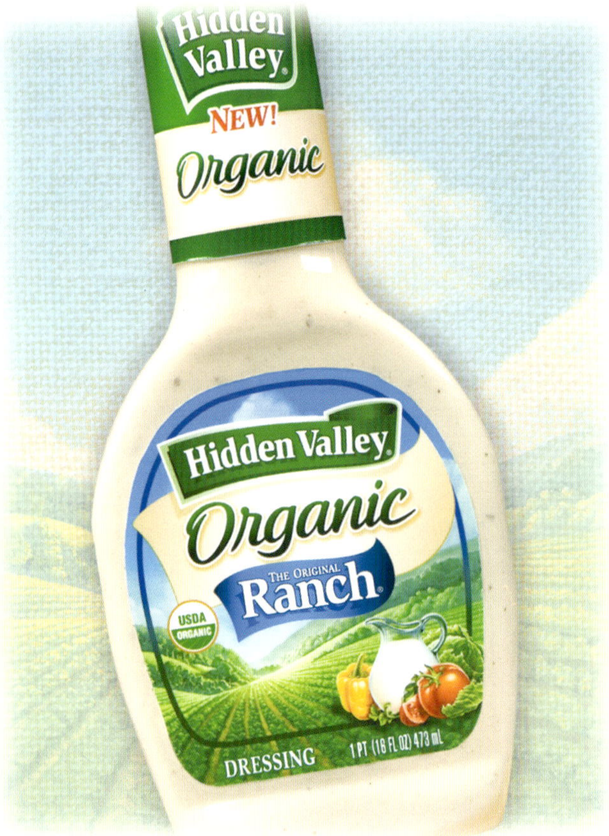

client
The HV Food Products Company
design firm
Clorox Creative Services
art director
Liliana Barbieri
designer
Tim Ferdun

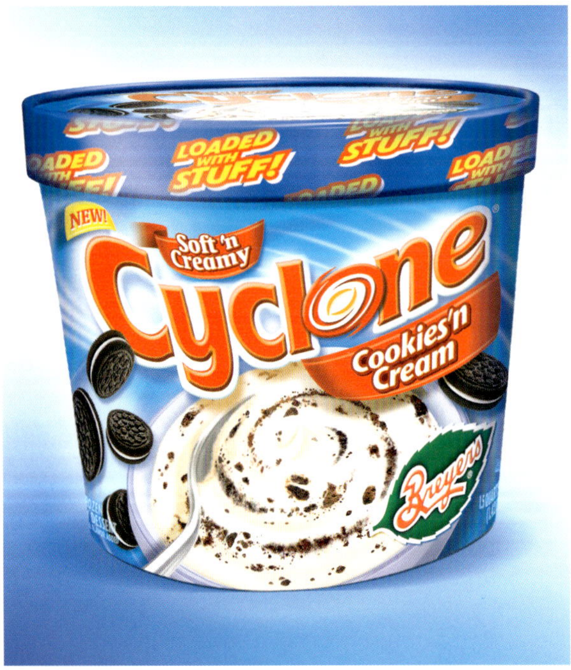

client
Unilever Foods
North America
design firm
Smith Design
smithdesign.com
designers
Carol Konkowski,
Angel Souto

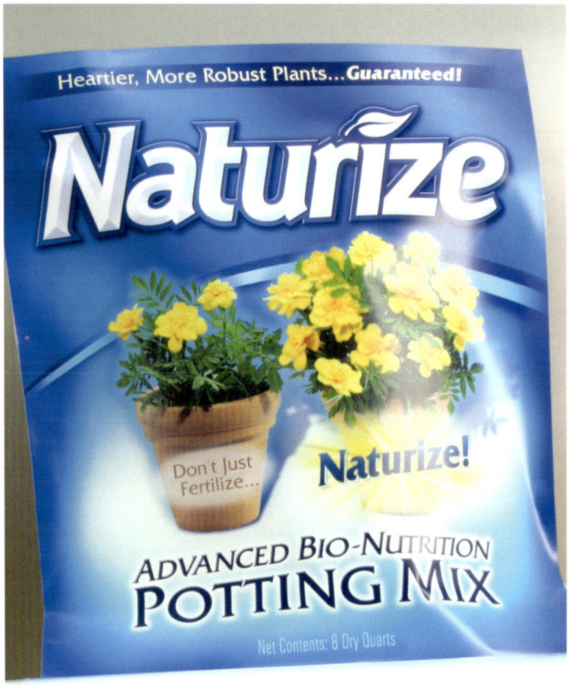

client
BioSciences LLC
design firm
Clorox Creative Services
art director
Bruce Willardson
designer, illustrator
Tim Ferdun

client
The Clorox Pet Products Company
design firm
Clorox Creative Services
designer
Tim Ferdun

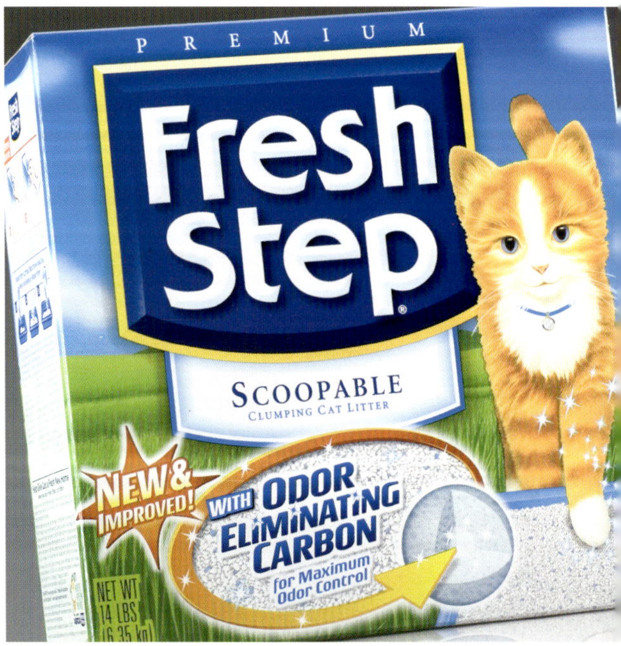

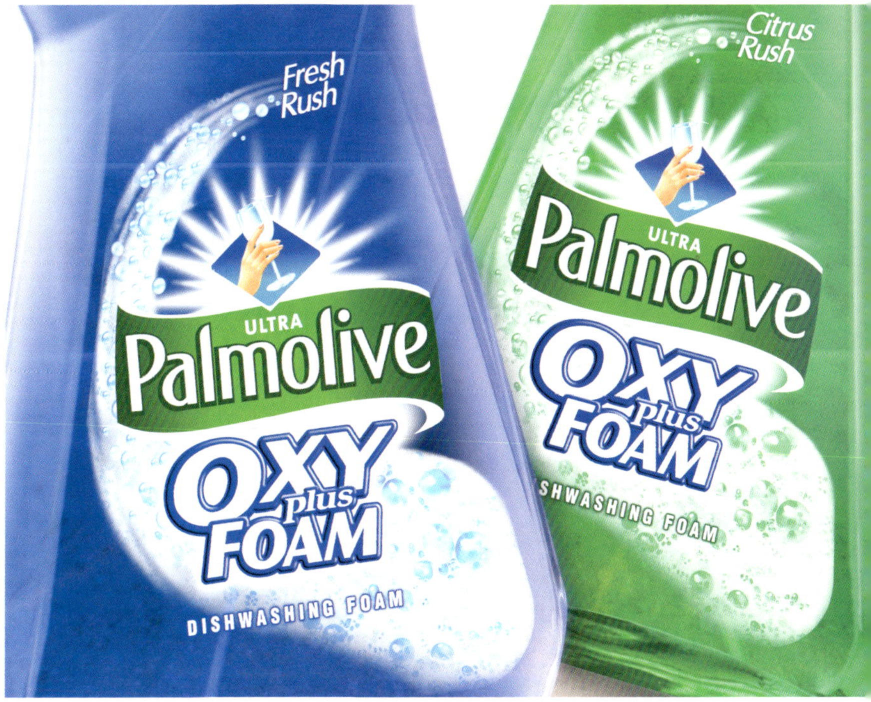

client
Colgate-Palmolive Company
design firm
Zunda Group, LLC
www.zundagroup.com
art directors
Charles Zunda, Gary Esposito
designers
Daniel Price, Lorraine Casscles

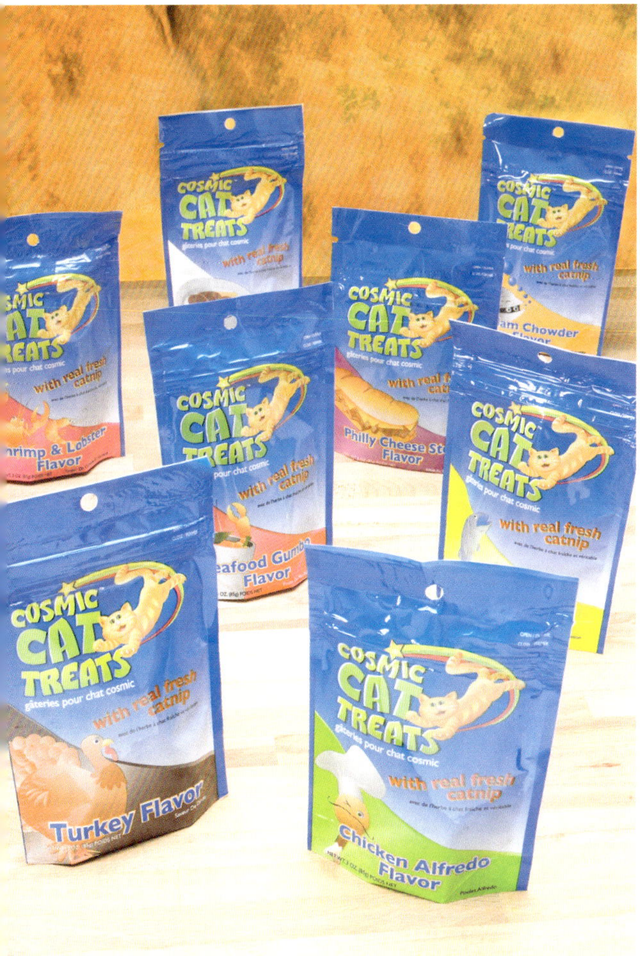

client
Cosmic Pet Products
design firm
Catalpha Advertising and Design
www.catalpha.com
designers
Karen Kerski, Michael Garlitz

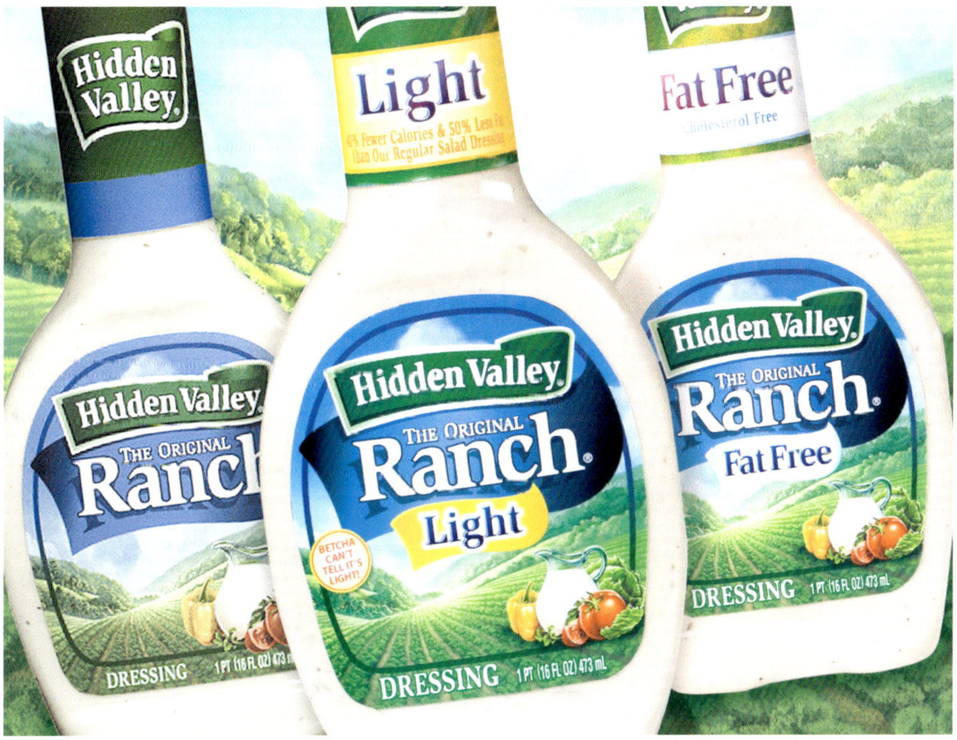

client
The HV Food Products Company
design firm
Clorox Creative Services
art director
Liliana Barbieri
designer
Tim Ferdun

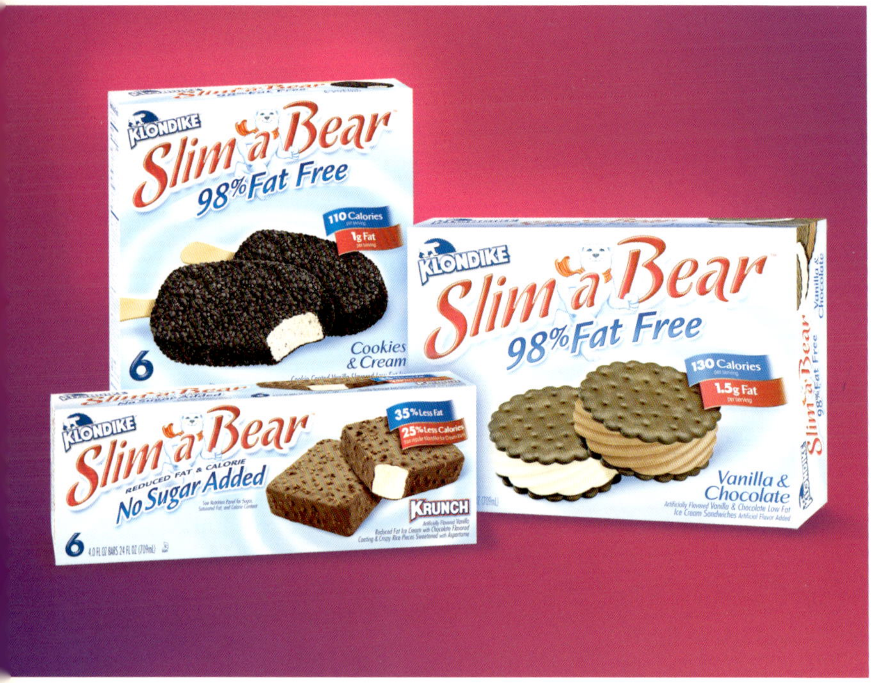

client
Unilever Foods North America
design firm
Smith Design
smithdesign.com
designers
Laura Markley,
Angel Souto

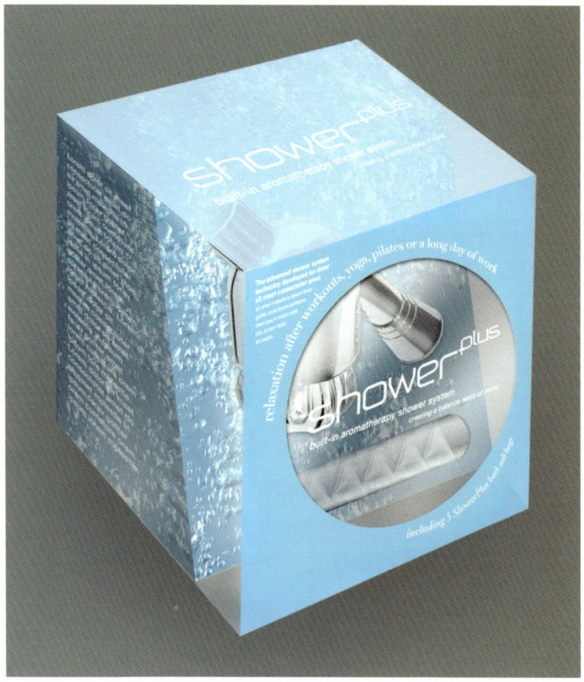

client
The Showerball Corp.
design firm
Creasia, LLC
creasiadesign.com
designer
Carmen Li

client
The Gillette Company
design firm
Wallace Church, Inc.
www.wallacechurch.com
creative director
Stan Church
designer
John Bruno

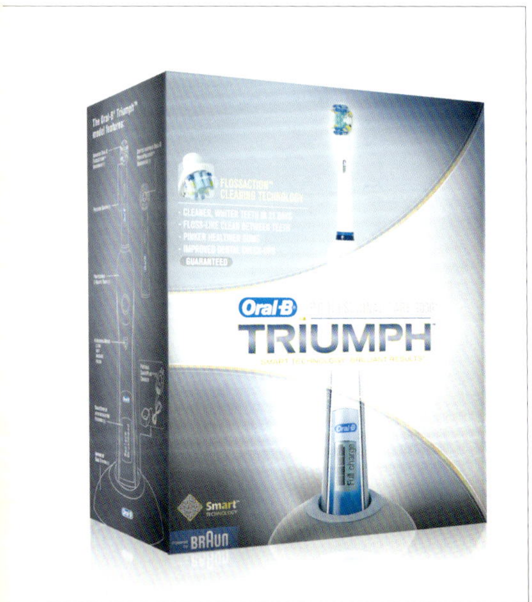

client
TDK Electronics Corp
design firm
Interrobang Design Collaborative
www.interrobangdesign.com
designer
Mark D. Sylvester

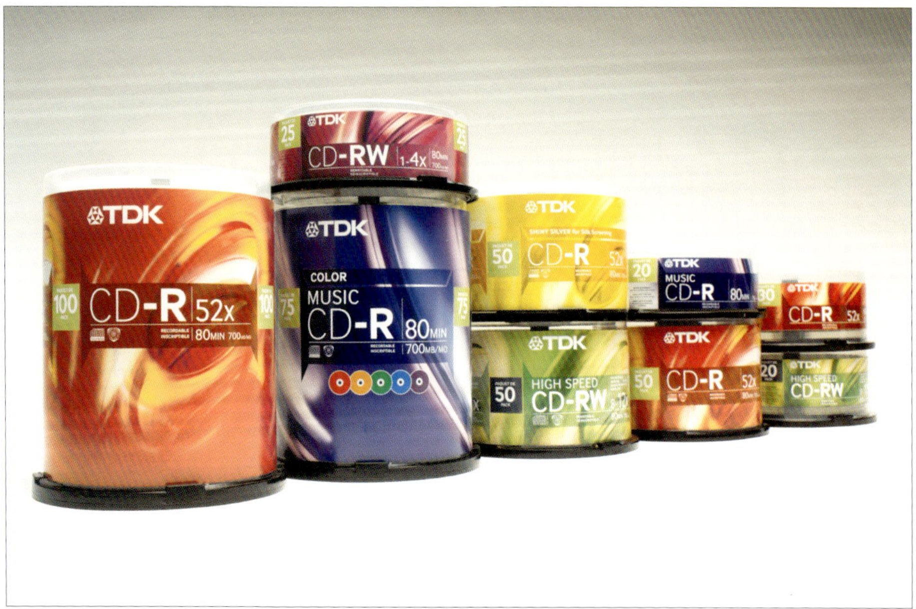

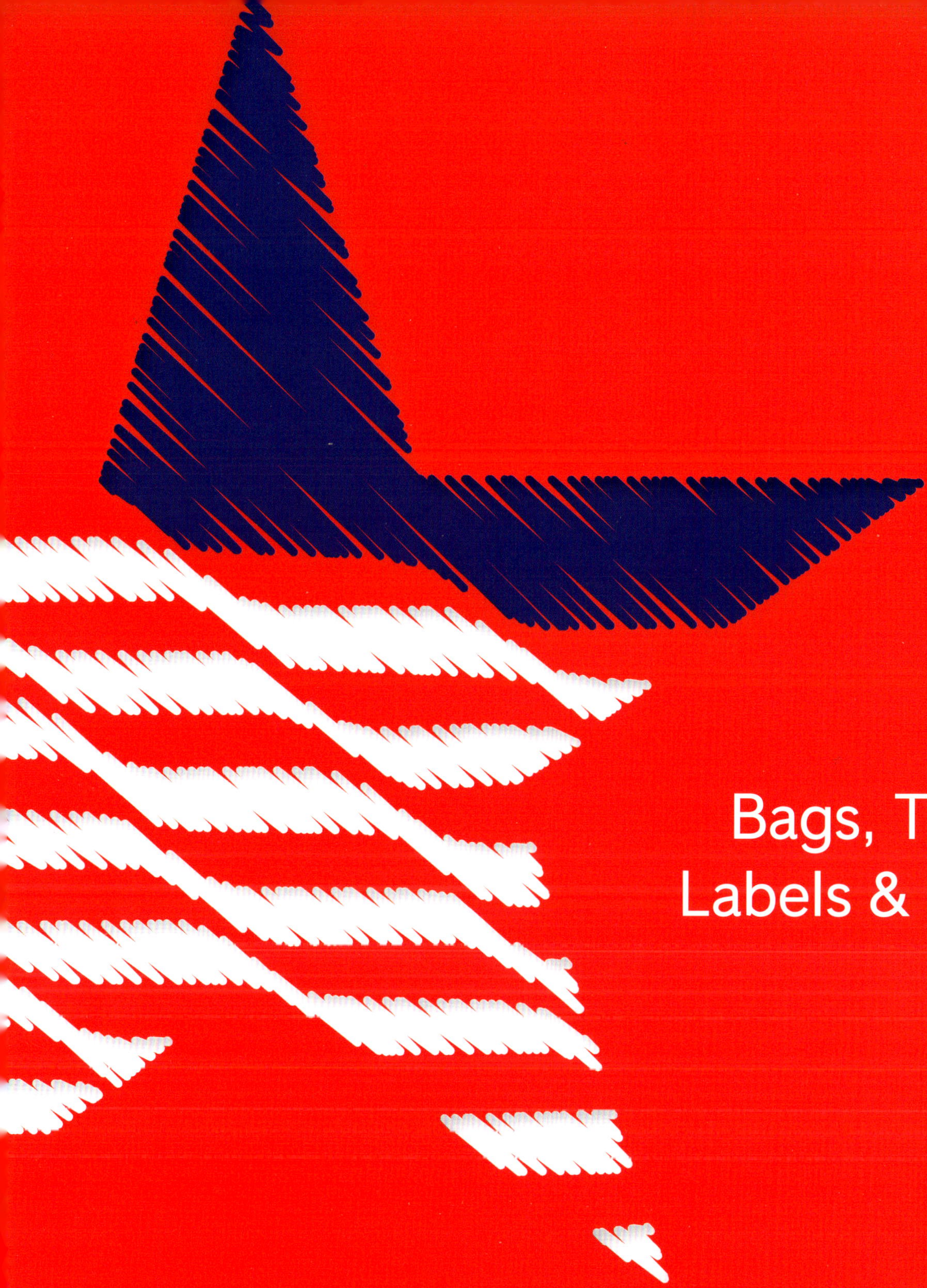

Bags, Tags, Labels & Boxes

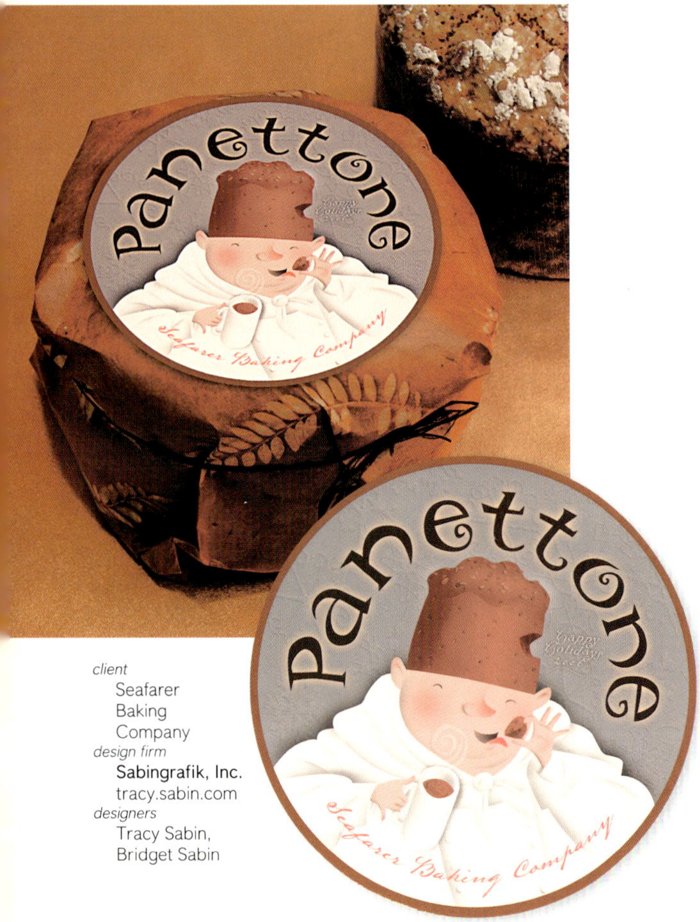

client
Seafarer Baking Company
design firm
Sabingrafik, Inc.
tracy.sabin.com
designers
Tracy Sabin, Bridget Sabin

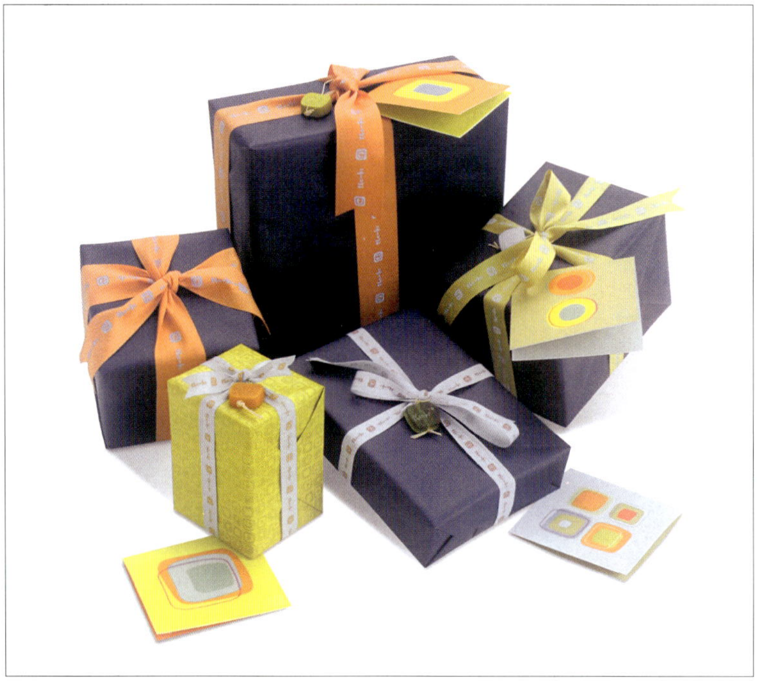

client
O.C. Tanner
design firm
Hornall Anderson Design Works
www.hadw.com
designers
Lisa Cerveny, Mary Hermes, Julia LaPine, Jana Nishi, Belinda Bowling, Lauren DiRusso, Elmer dela Cruz

client
eurie creative
design firm
eurie creative
designers
Victor Rodriguez, Carri Hall, Patty Mar, Tom Simmons

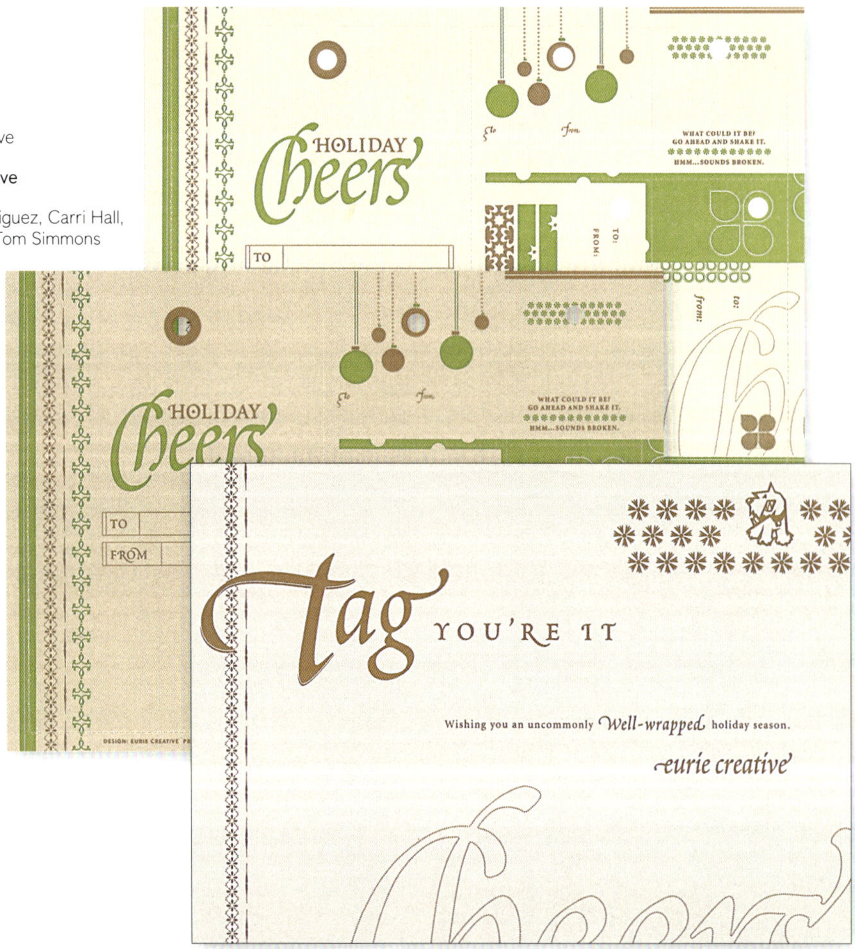

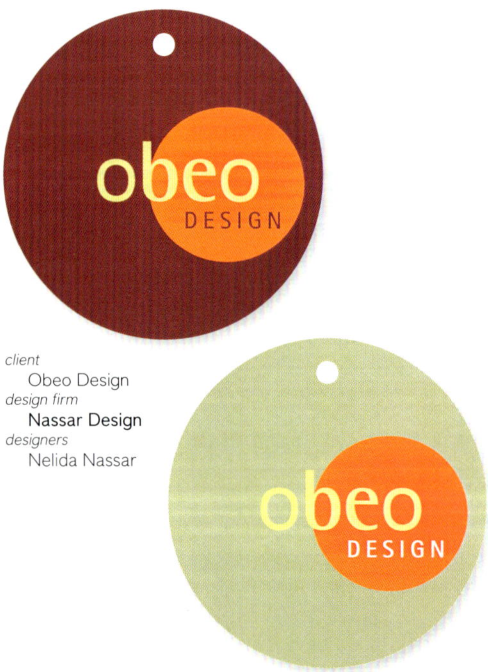

client
Obeo Design
design firm
Nassar Design
designers
Nelida Nassar

Stationery Design

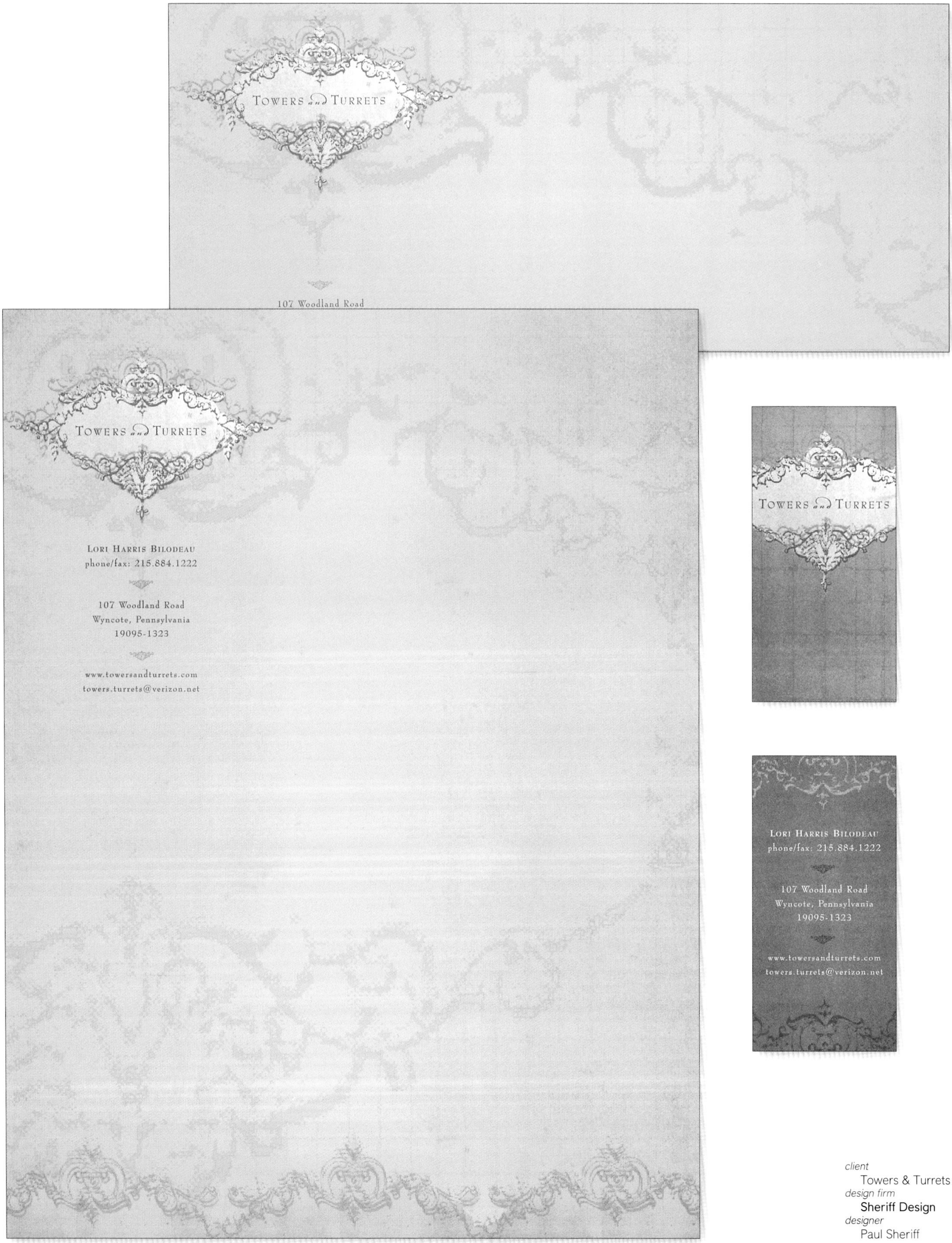

client
Towers & Turrets
design firm
Sheriff Design
designer
Paul Sheriff

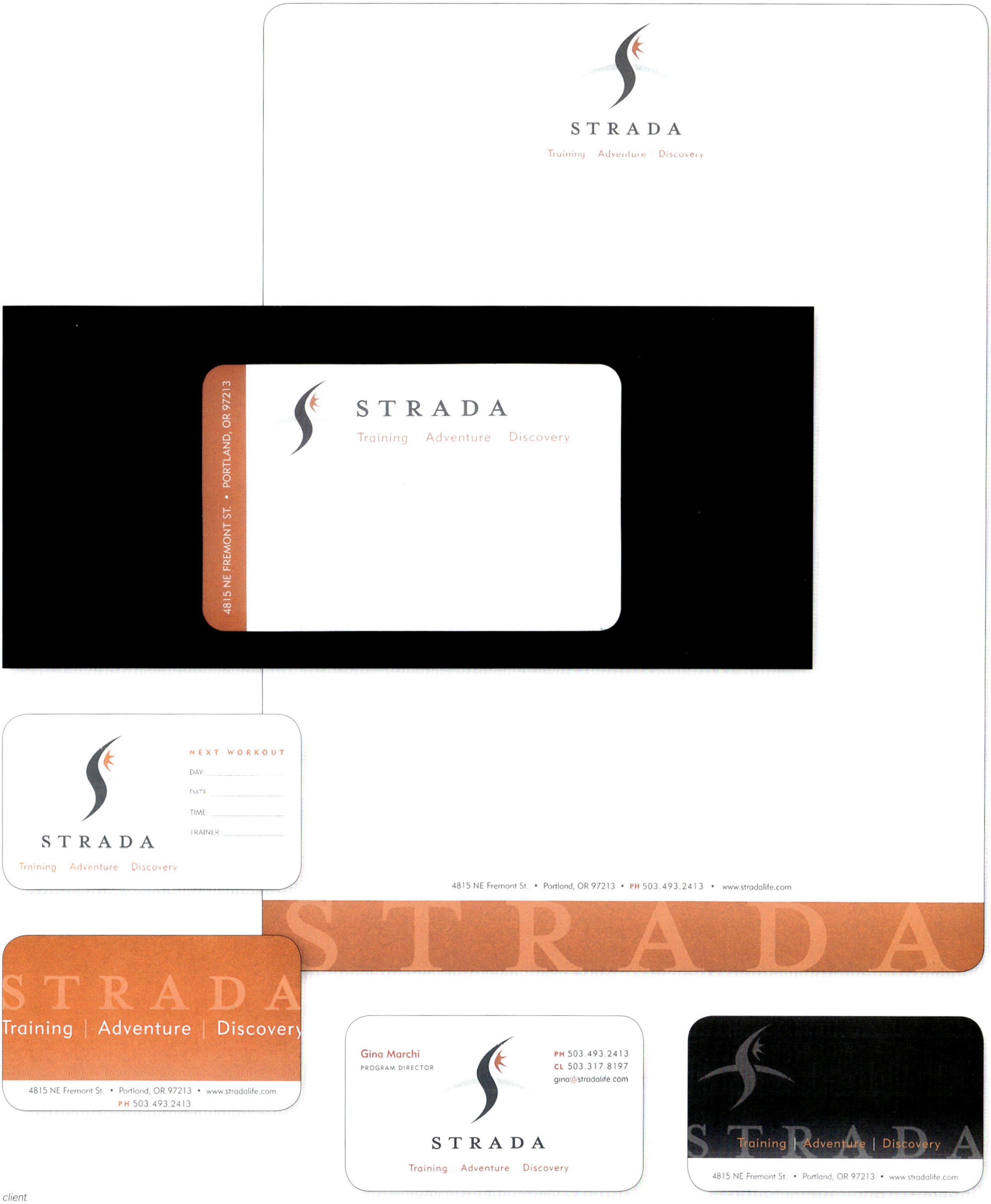

client
Strada
design firm
Defteling Design
www.defteling.com
designer
Alex Wijnen

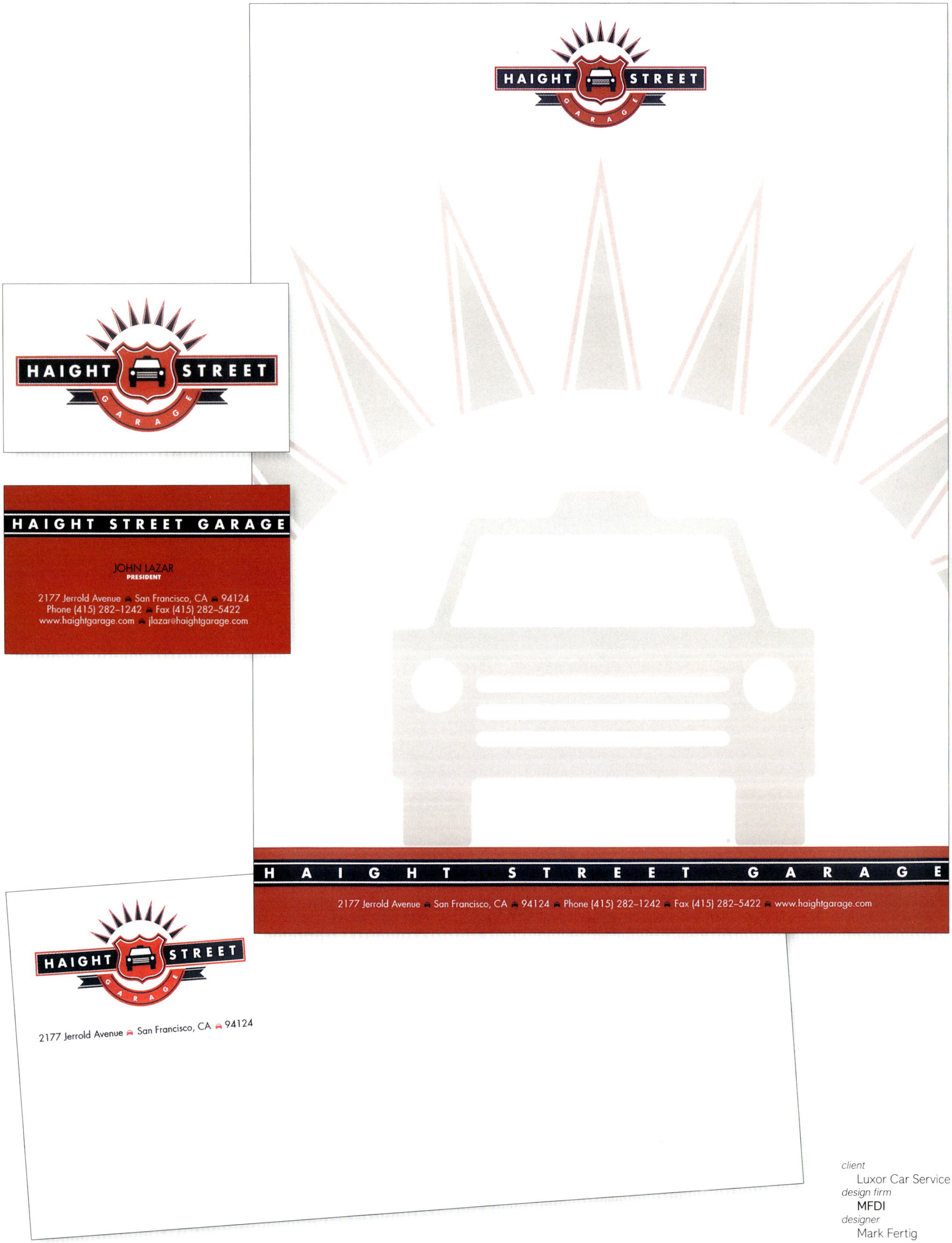

client
Luxor Car Service
design firm
MFDI
designer
Mark Fertig

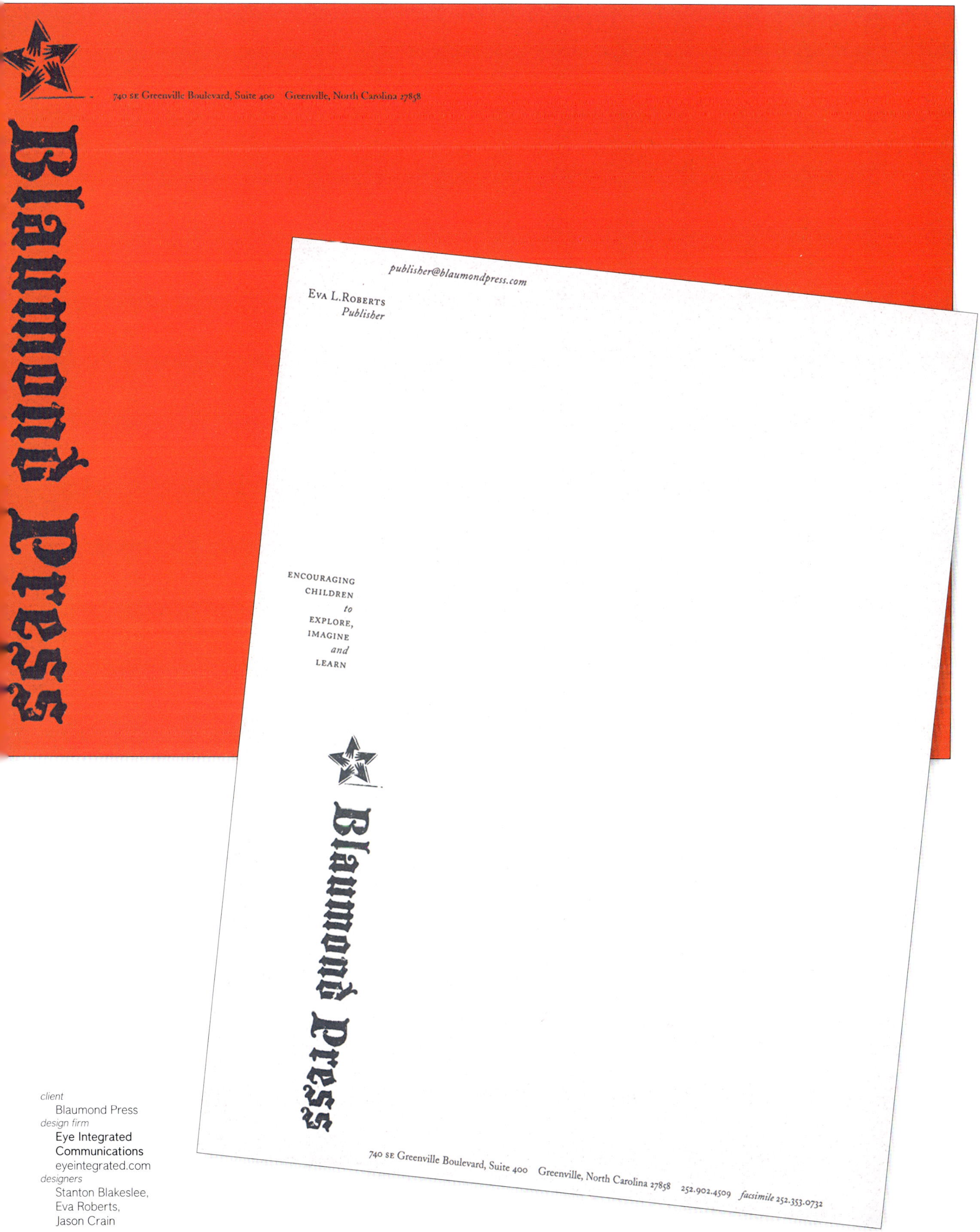

client
Blaumond Press
design firm
Eye Integrated Communications
eyeintegrated.com
designers
Stanton Blakeslee, Eva Roberts, Jason Crain

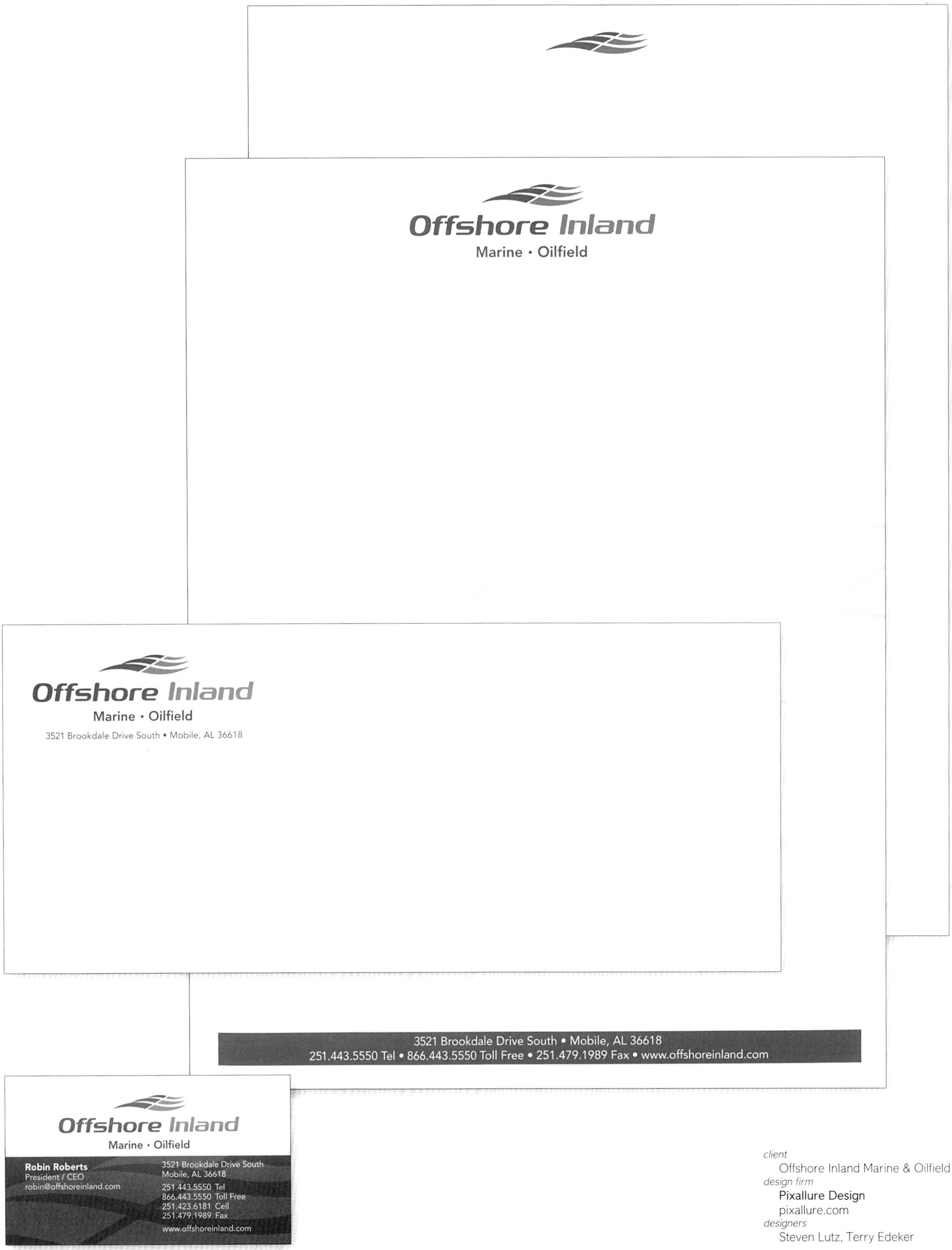

client
Offshore Inland Marine & Oilfield
design firm
Pixallure Design
pixallure.com
designers
Steven Lutz, Terry Edeker

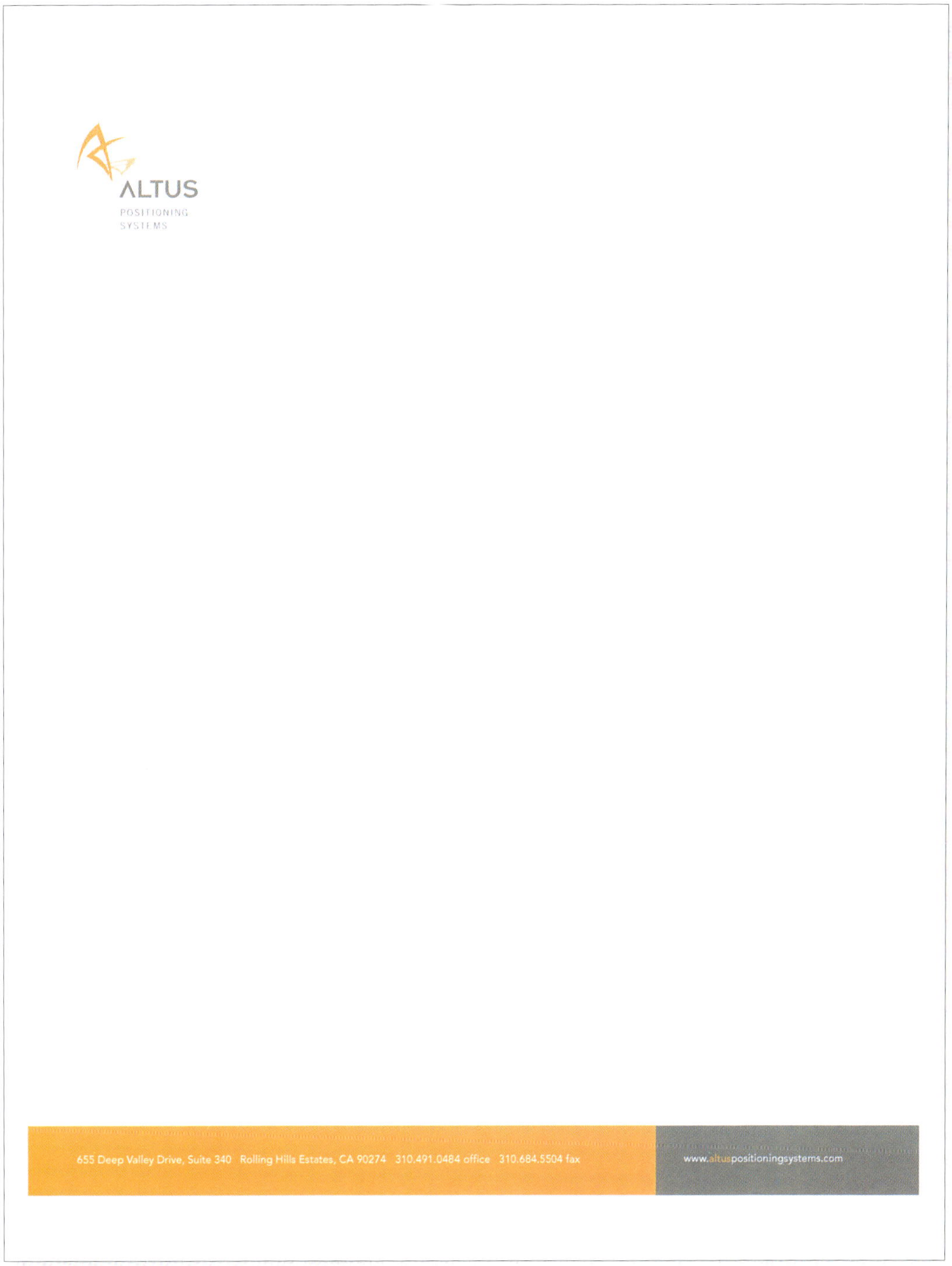

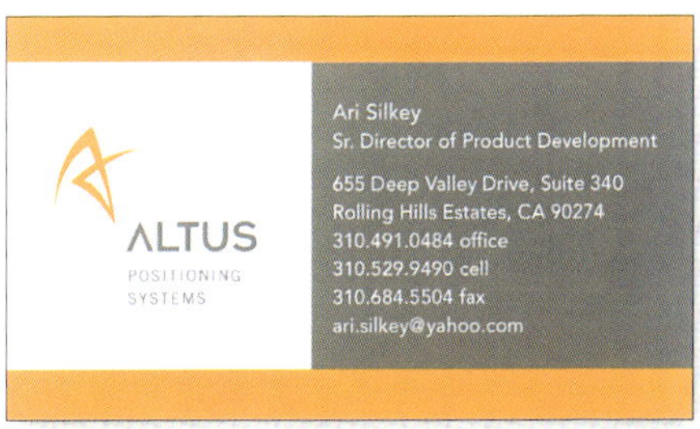

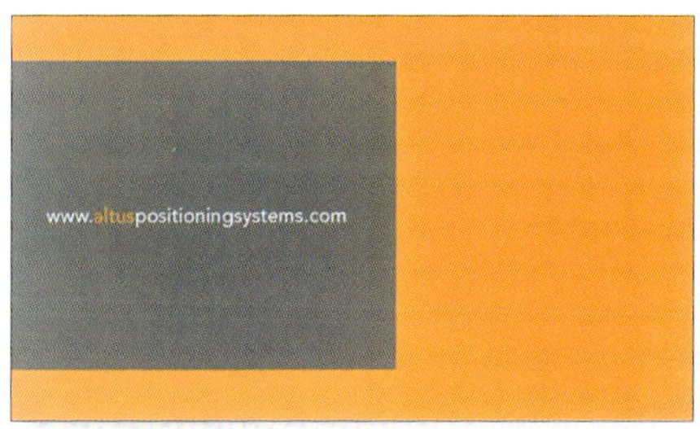

client
Altus Positioning Systems
design firm
IE Design + Communications
www.iedesign.net
creative director
Marcie Carson
designers
Jane Lee, Christine Kenney

client
Columbus Zoo
design firm
V.M.A., Inc.
vmai.com
designers
Doug Knopp,
Amritha Ward

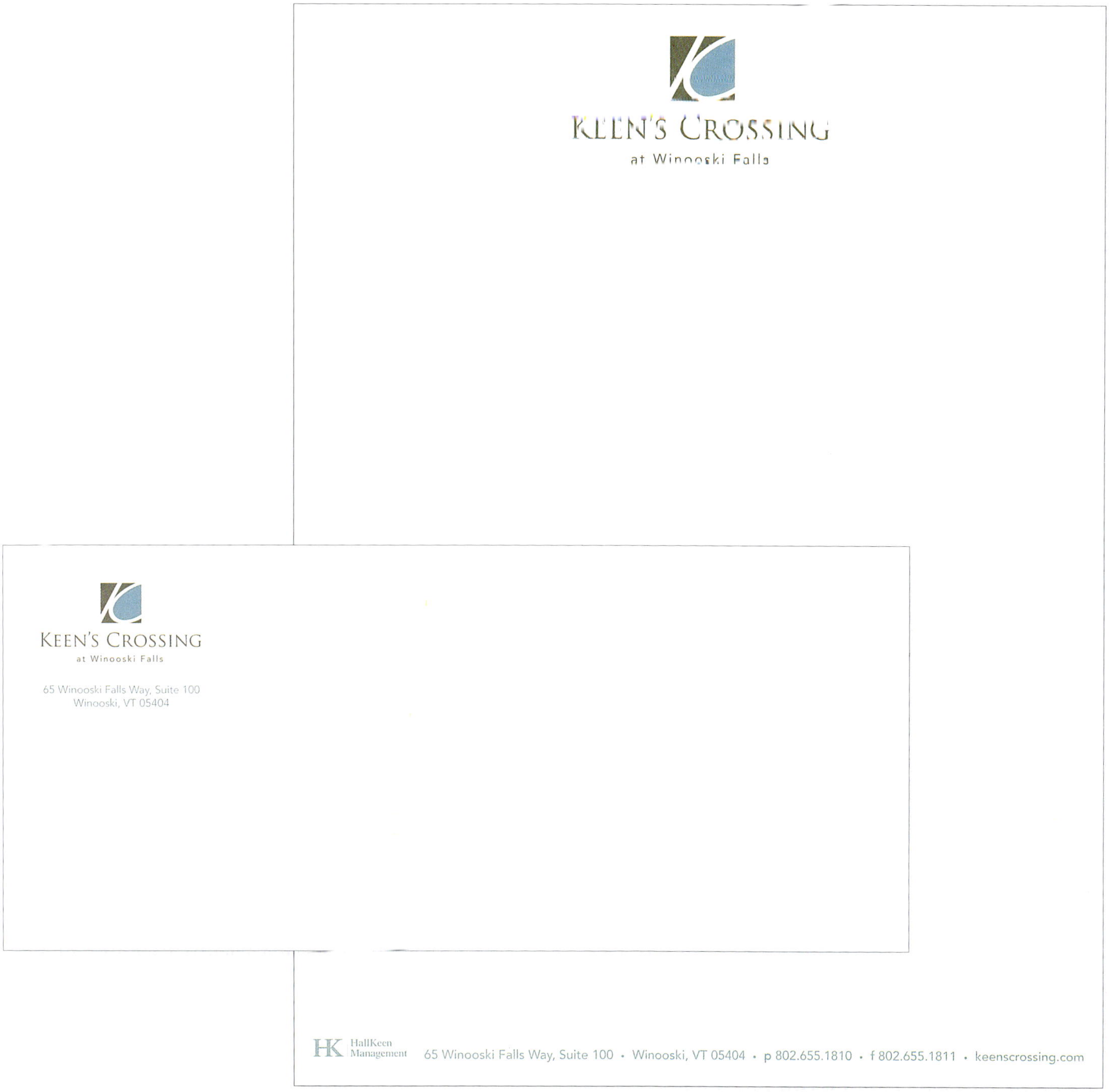

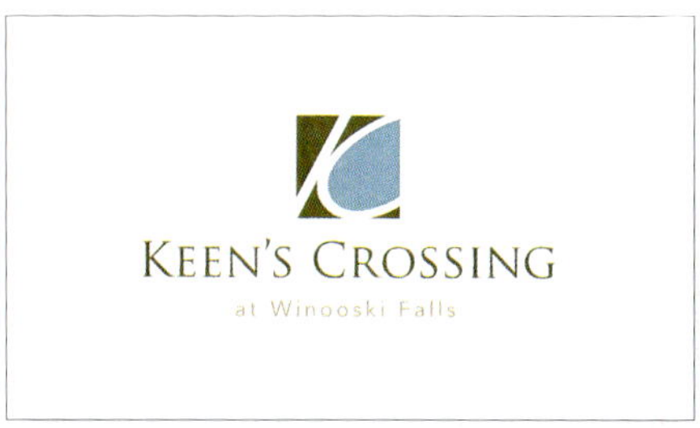

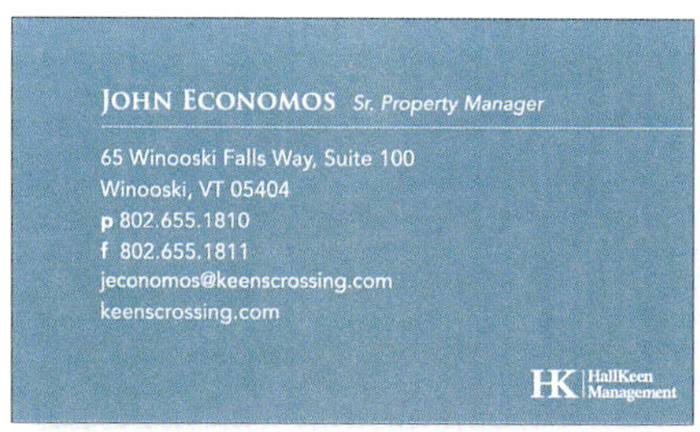

client
Keen's Crossing
design firm
Paul Kaza Associates
www.paulkaza.com
designer
Carissa Butler

client
Angara, Inc.
design firm
Helena Seo Design
www.helenaseo.com
designer
Helena Seo

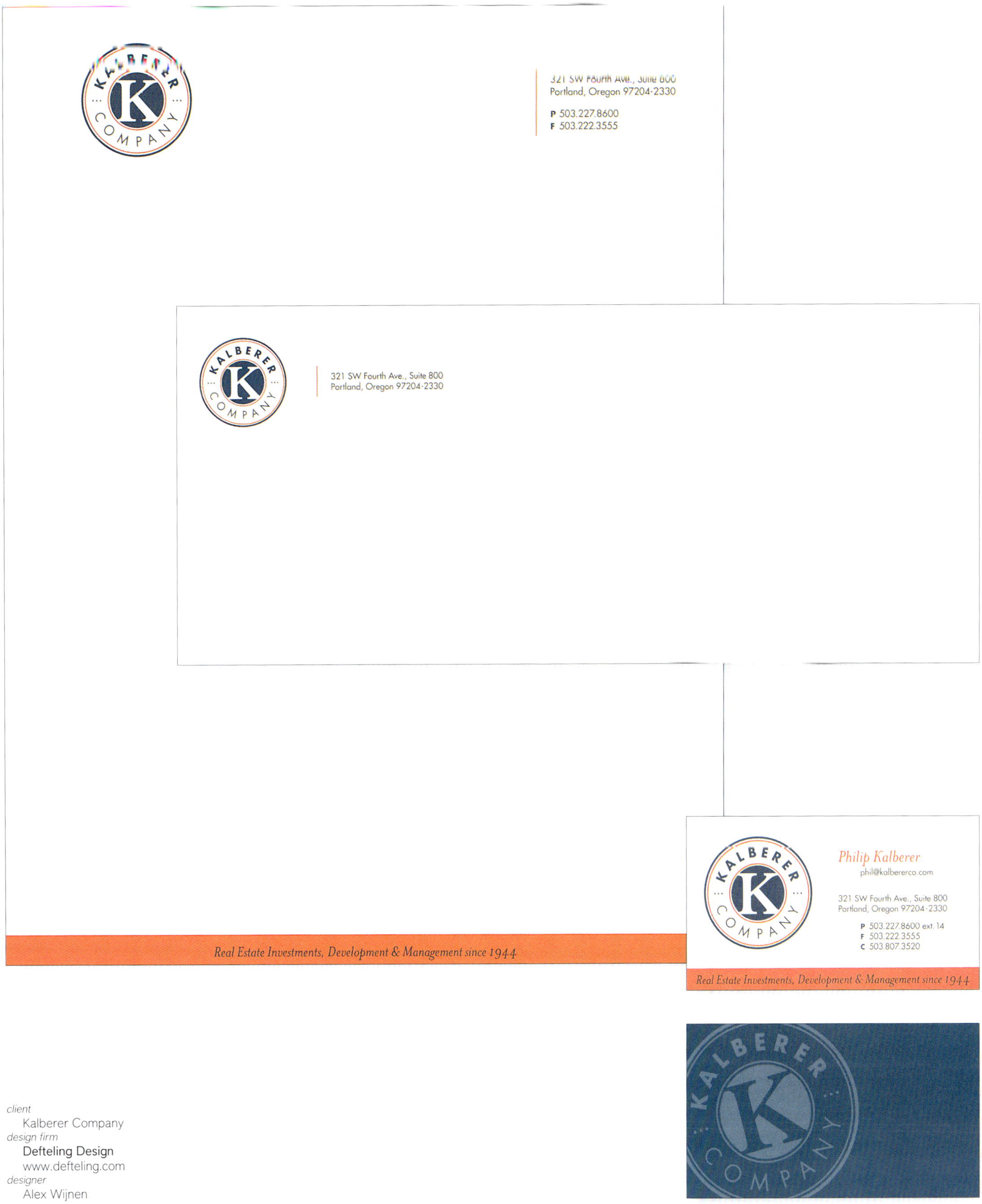

client
Kalberer Company
design firm
Defteling Design
www.defteling.com
designer
Alex Wijnen

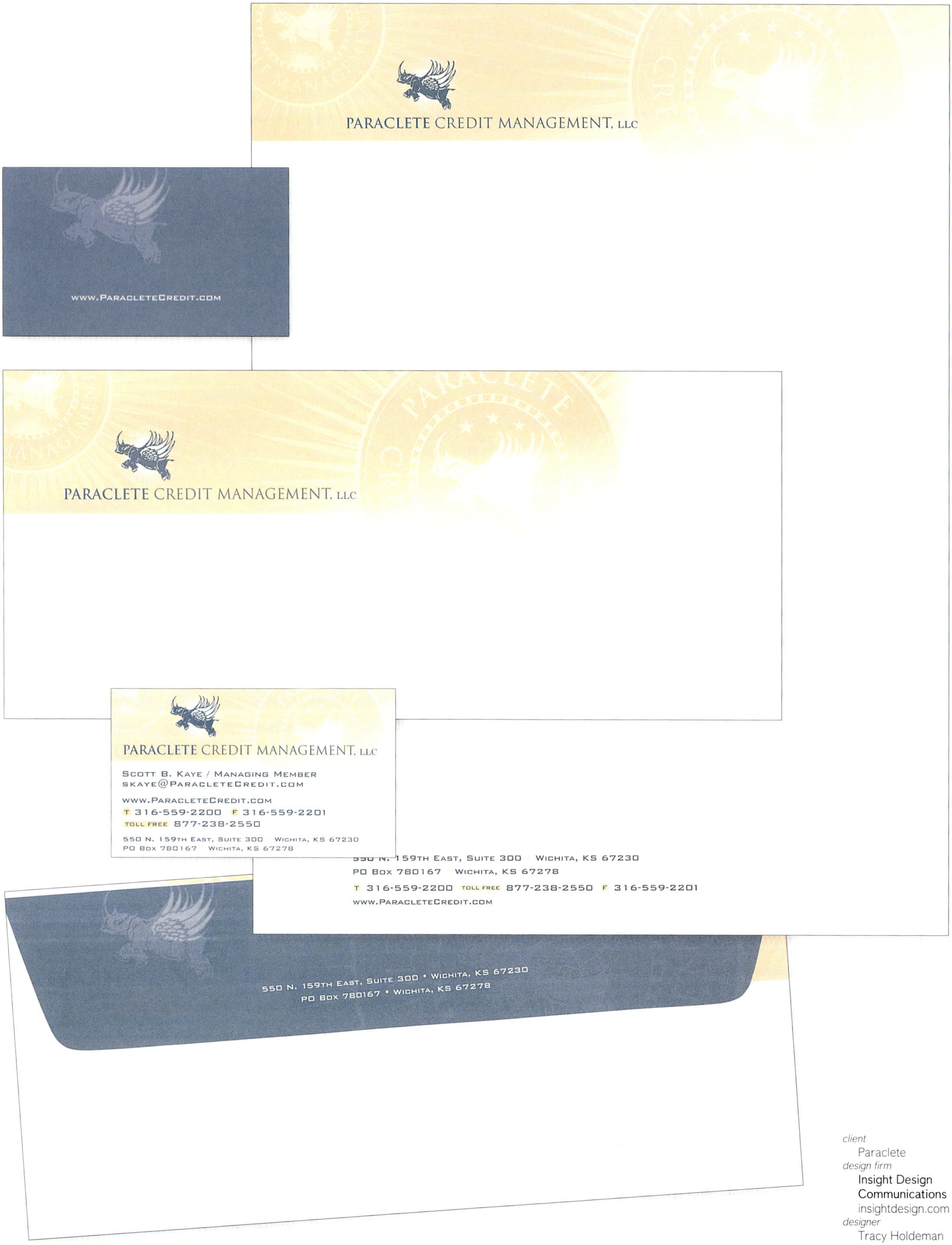

client
Paraclete
design firm
Insight Design Communications
insightdesign.com
designer
Tracy Holdeman

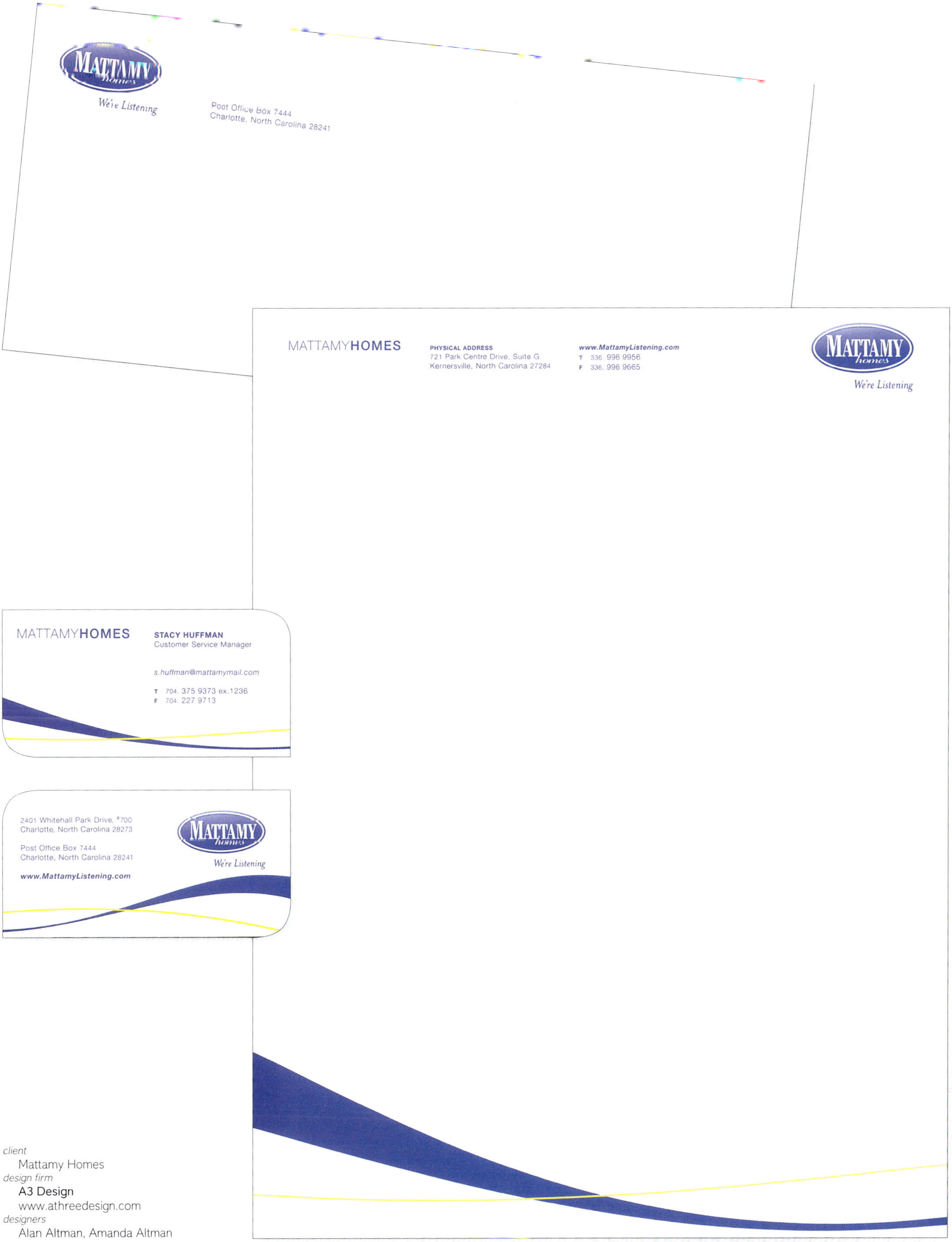

client
Mattamy Homes
design firm
A3 Design
www.athreedesign.com
designers
Alan Altman, Amanda Altman

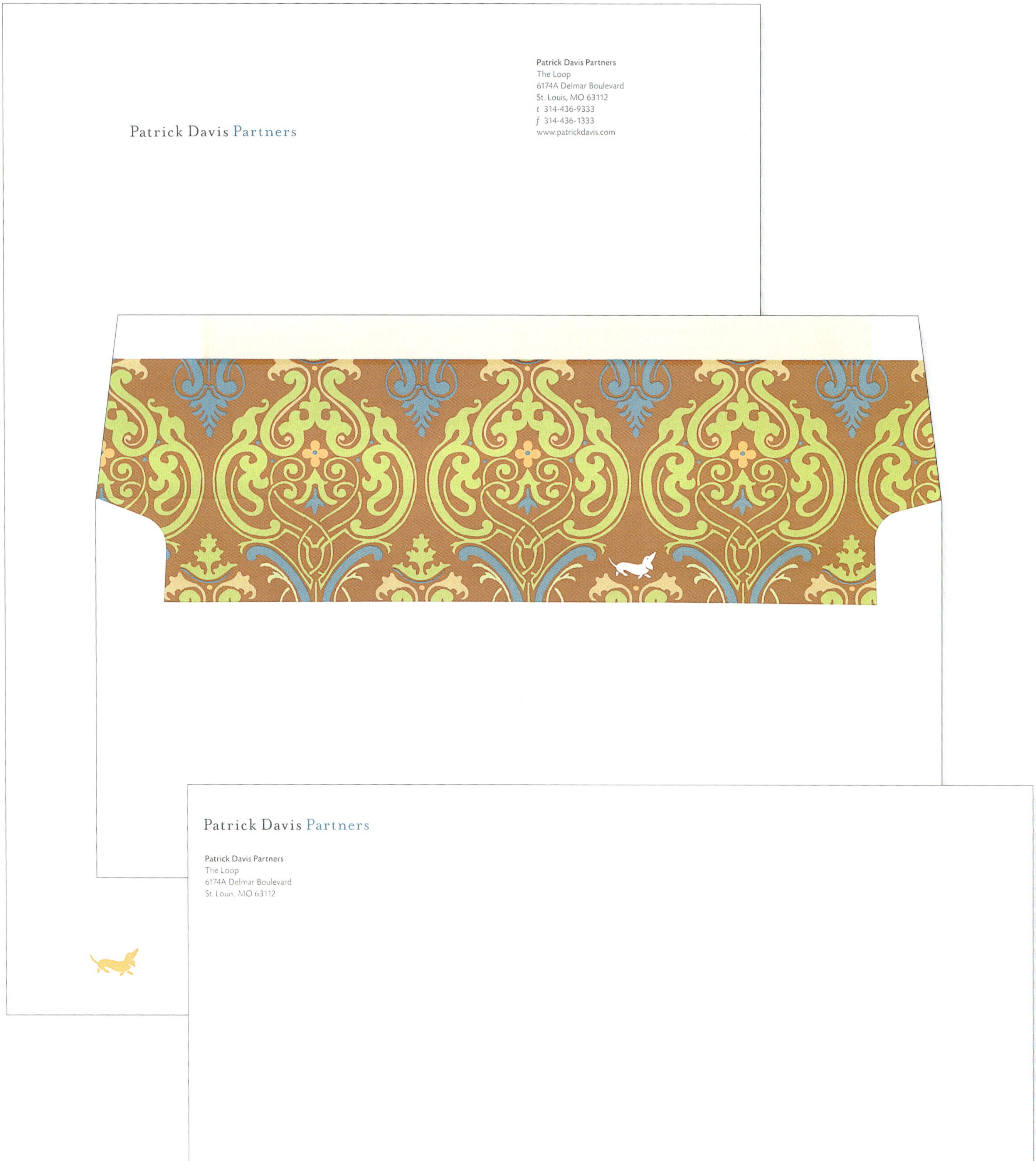

client
Patrick Davis Partners
design firm
Kiku Obata & Company
designers
Joe Floresca, Eleanor Safe

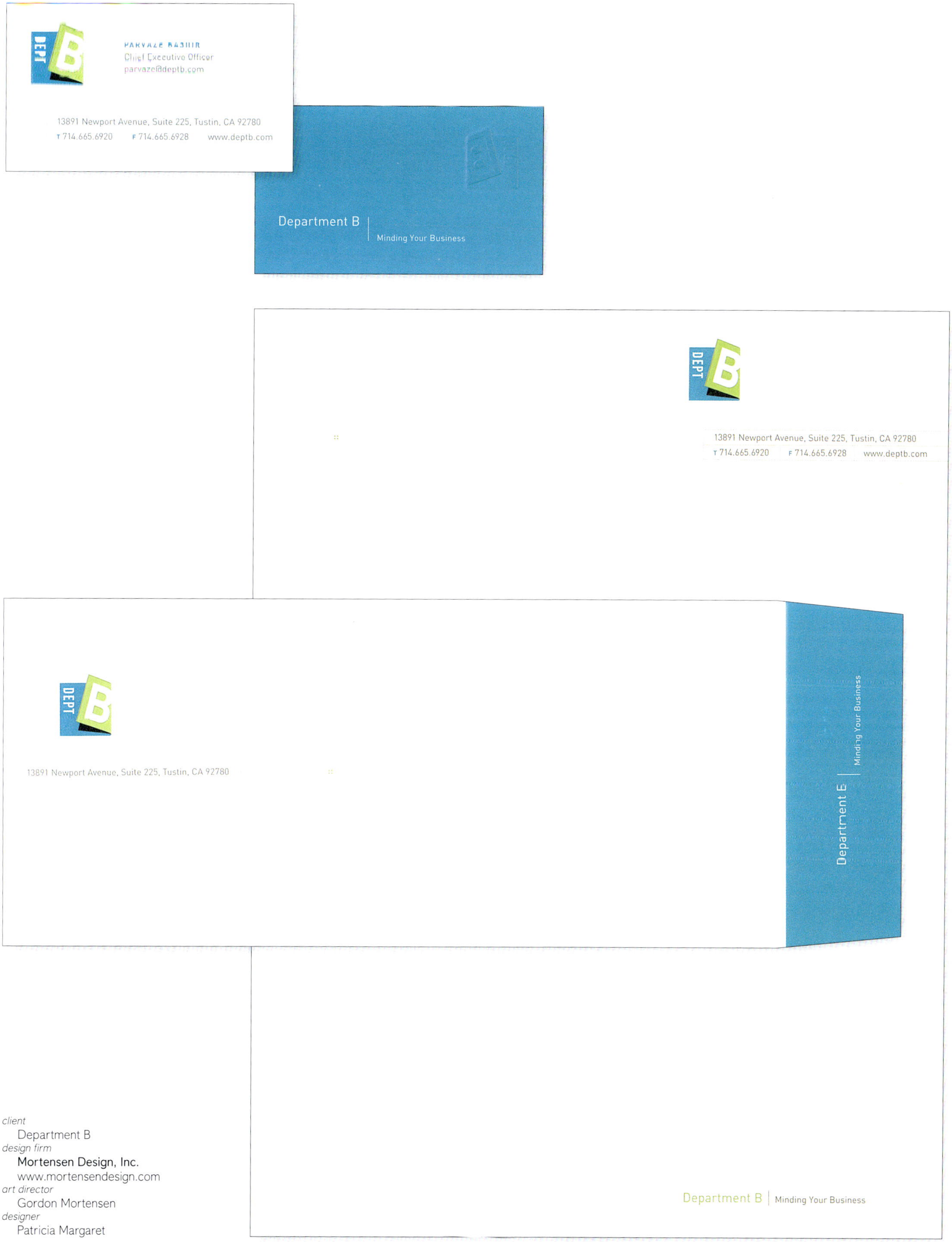

client
Department B
design firm
Mortensen Design, Inc.
www.mortensendesign.com
art director
Gordon Mortensen
designer
Patricia Margaret

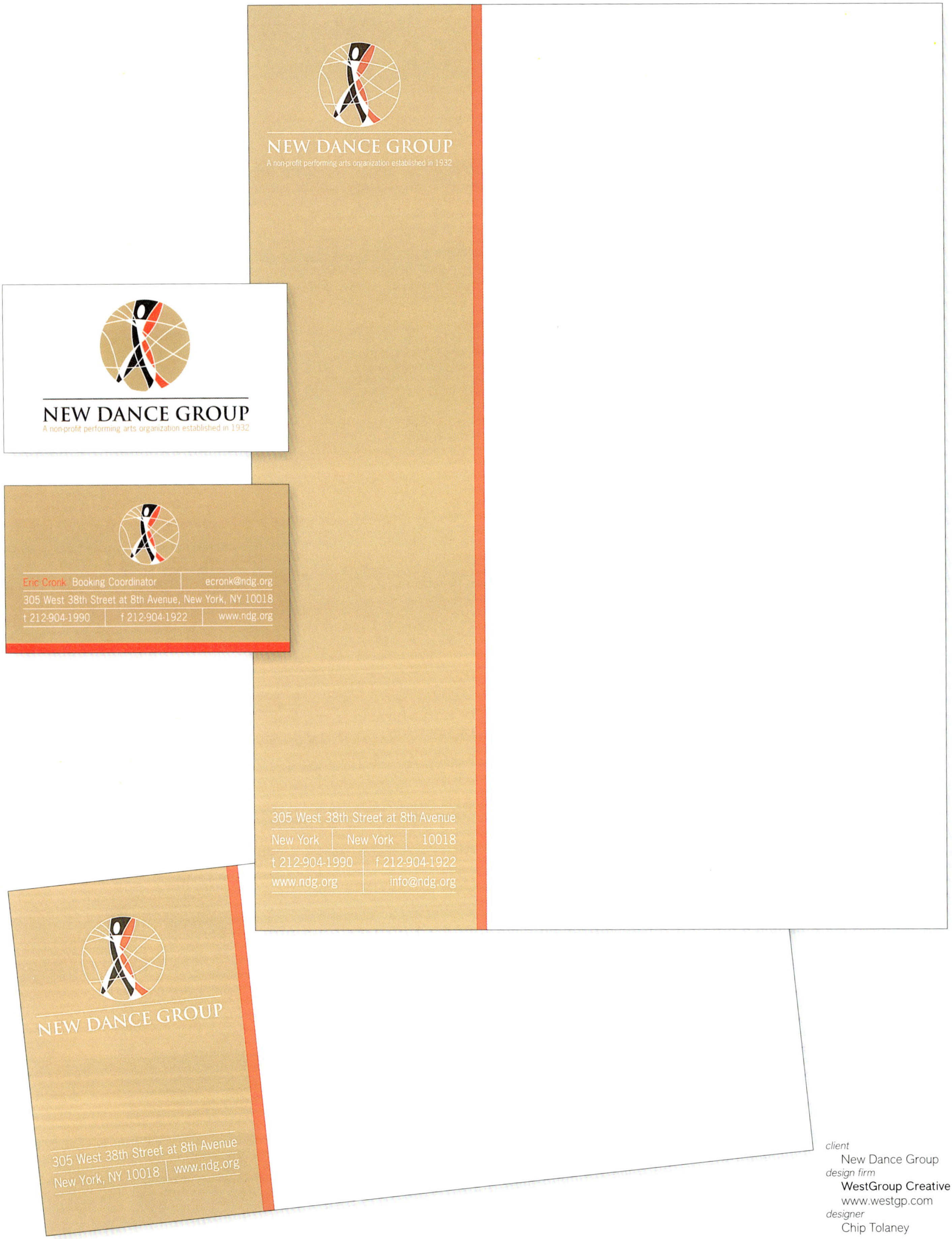

client
New Dance Group
design firm
WestGroup Creative
www.westgp.com
designer
Chip Tolaney

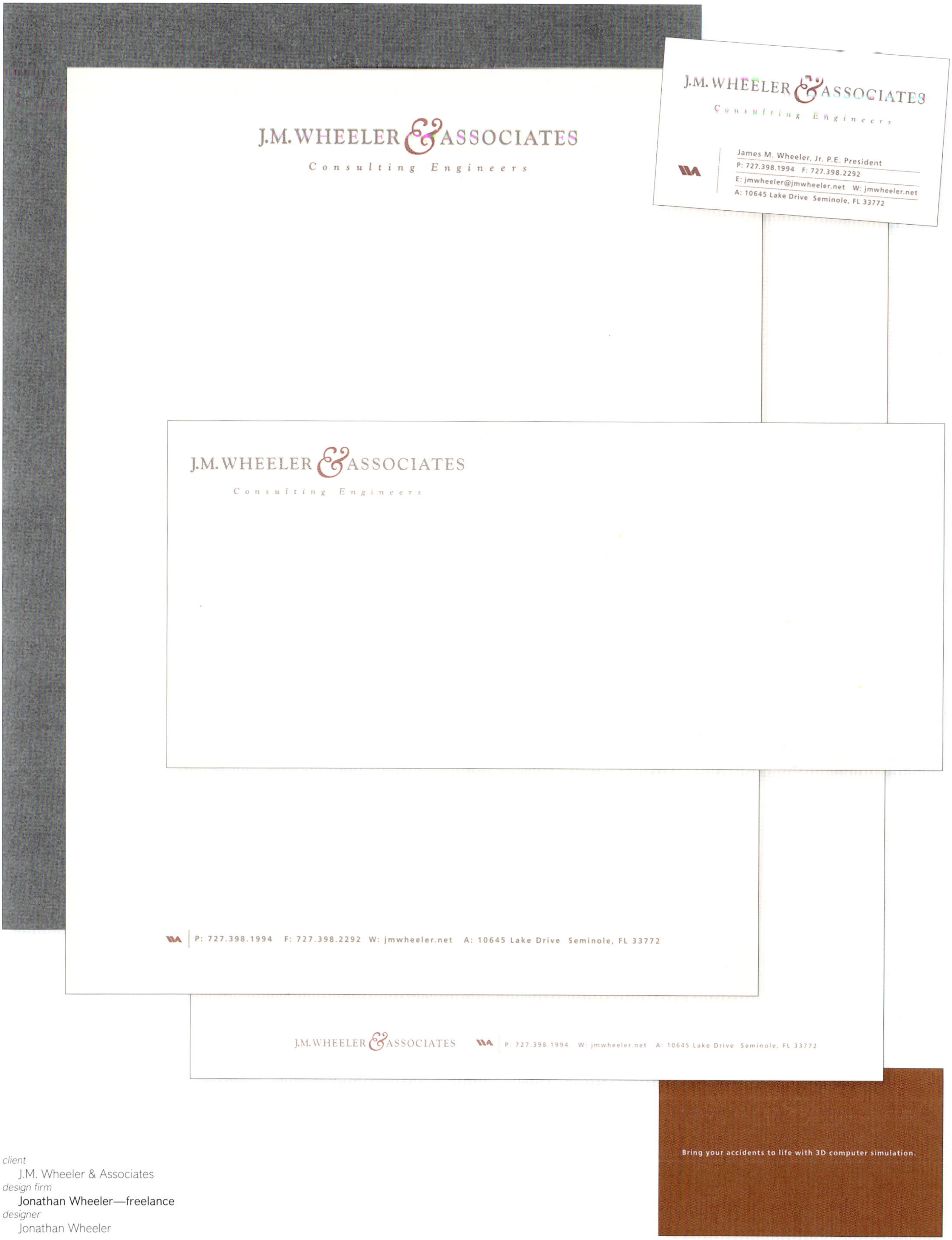

client
J.M. Wheeler & Associates
design firm
Jonathan Wheeler—freelance
designer
Jonathan Wheeler

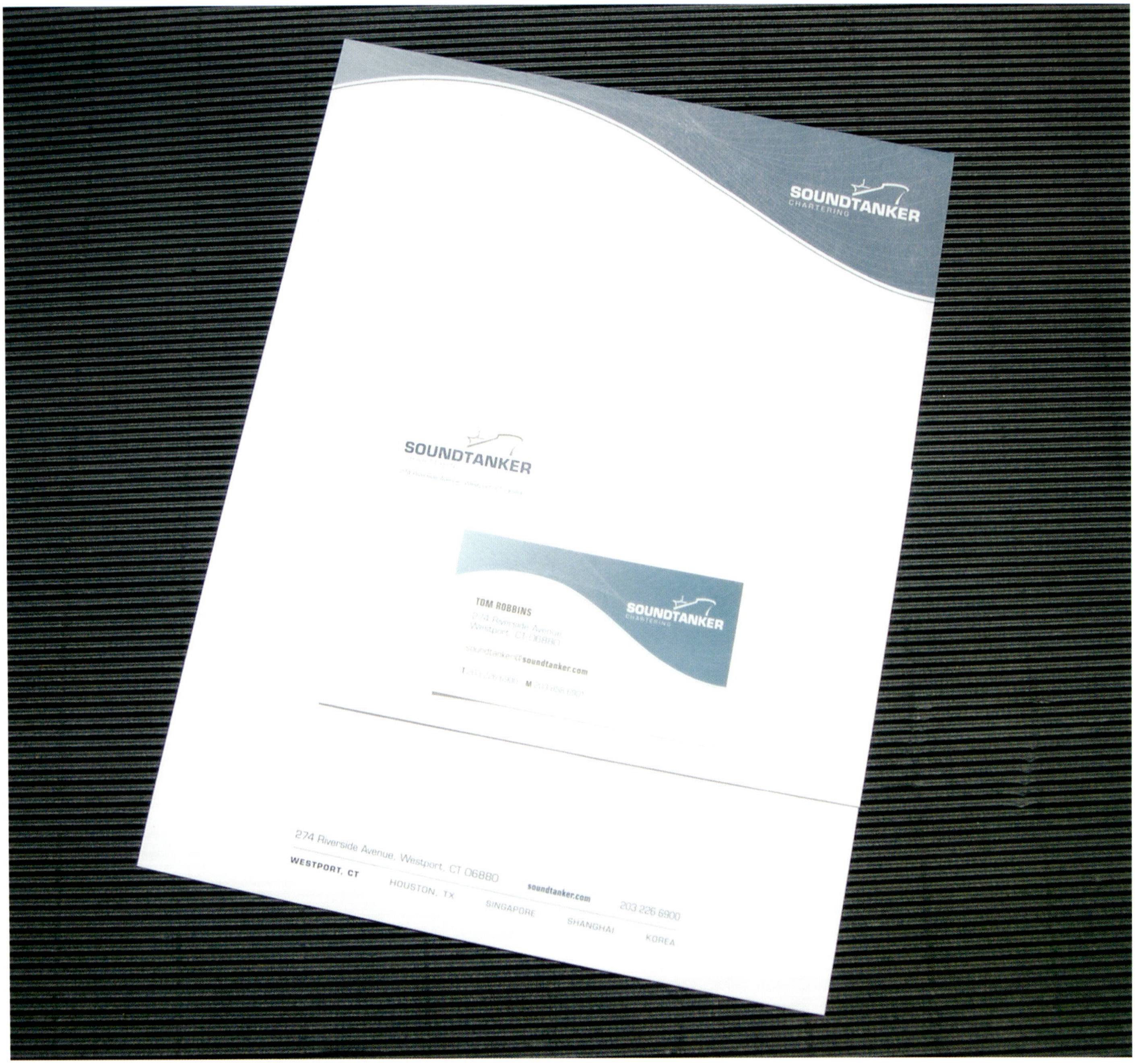

client
Soundtanker
design firm
silver creative group
silvercreativegroup.com
designer
Suzanne Petrow

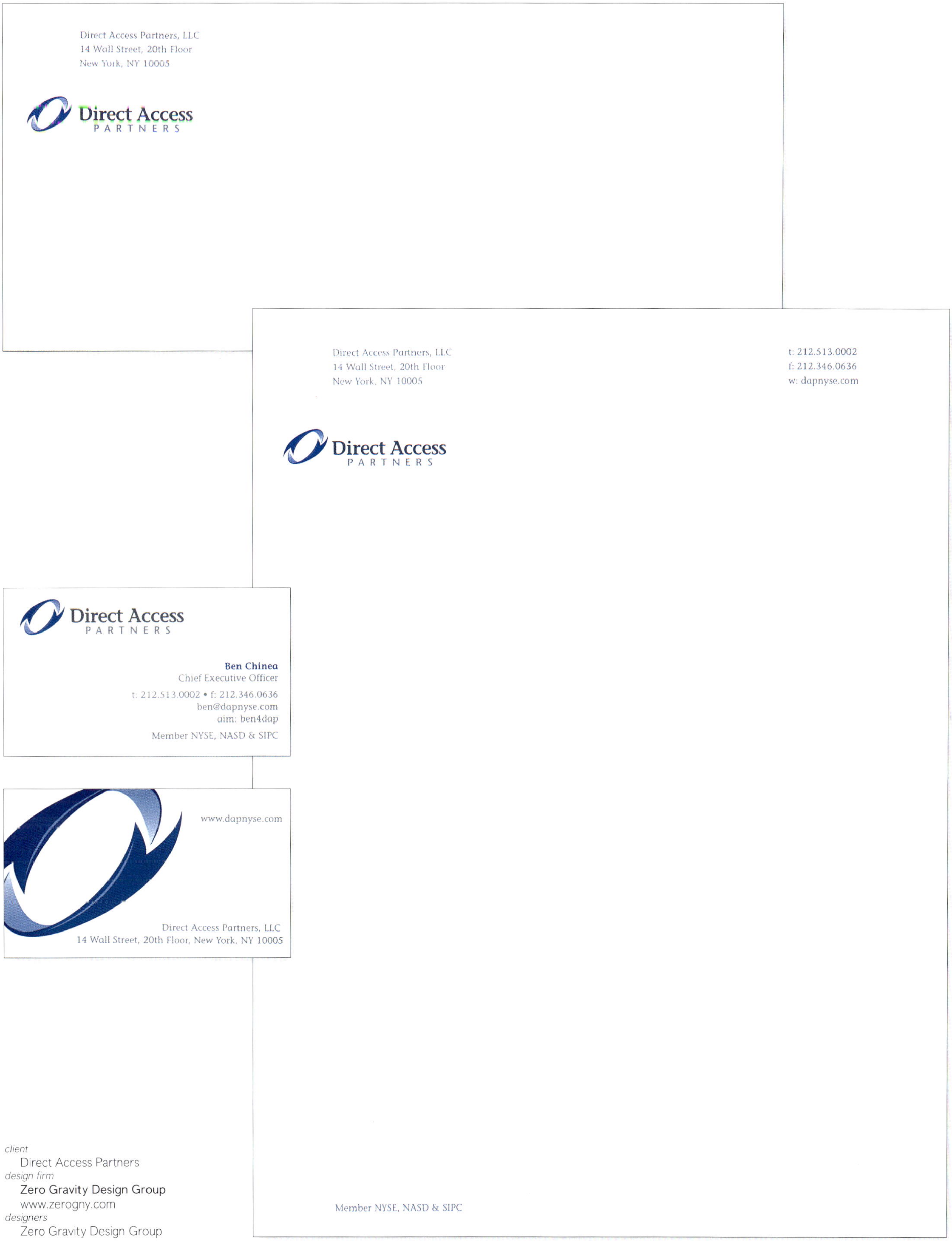

client
Direct Access Partners
design firm
Zero Gravity Design Group
www.zerogny.com
designers
Zero Gravity Design Group

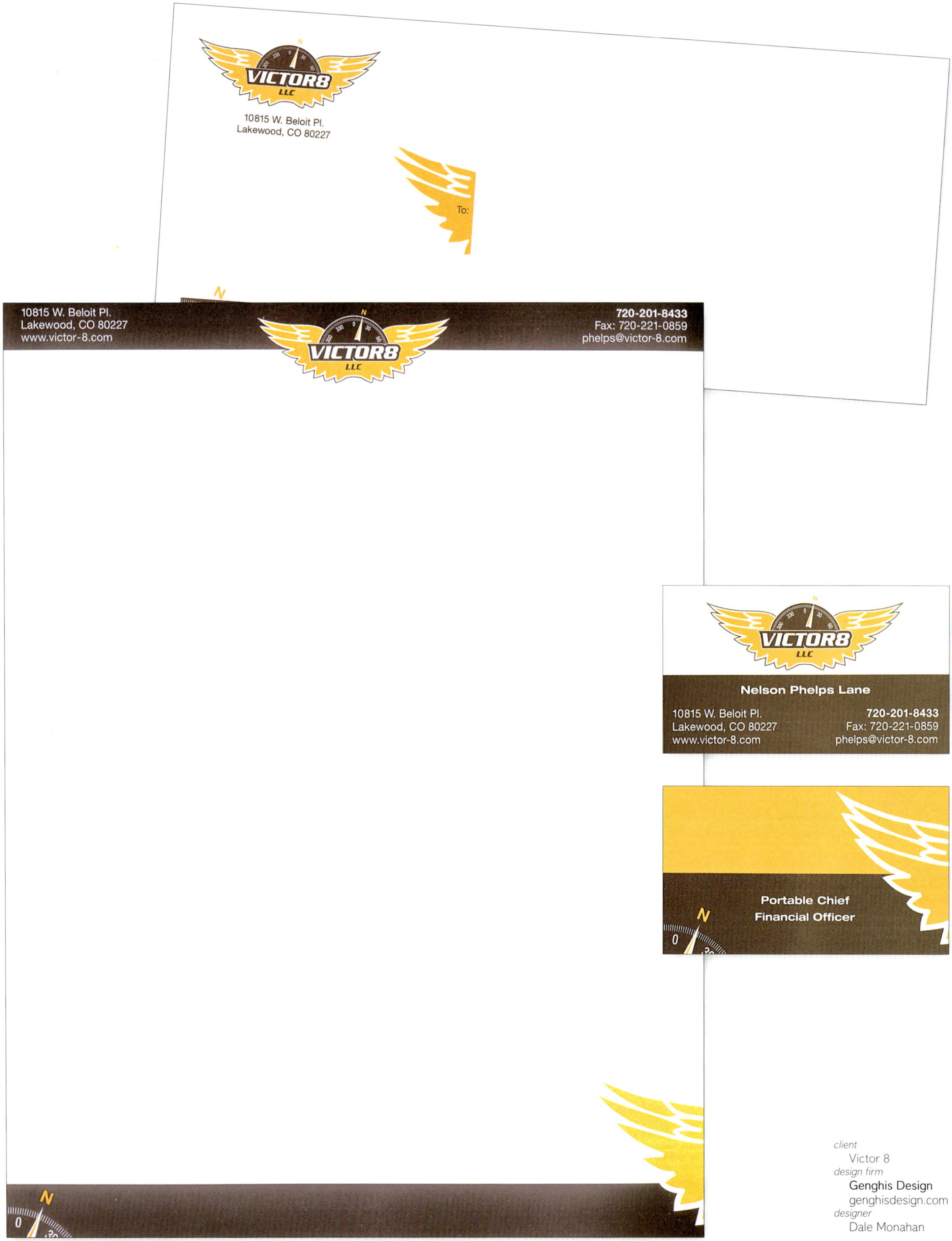

client
Victor 8
design firm
Genghis Design
genghisdesign.com
designer
Dale Monahan

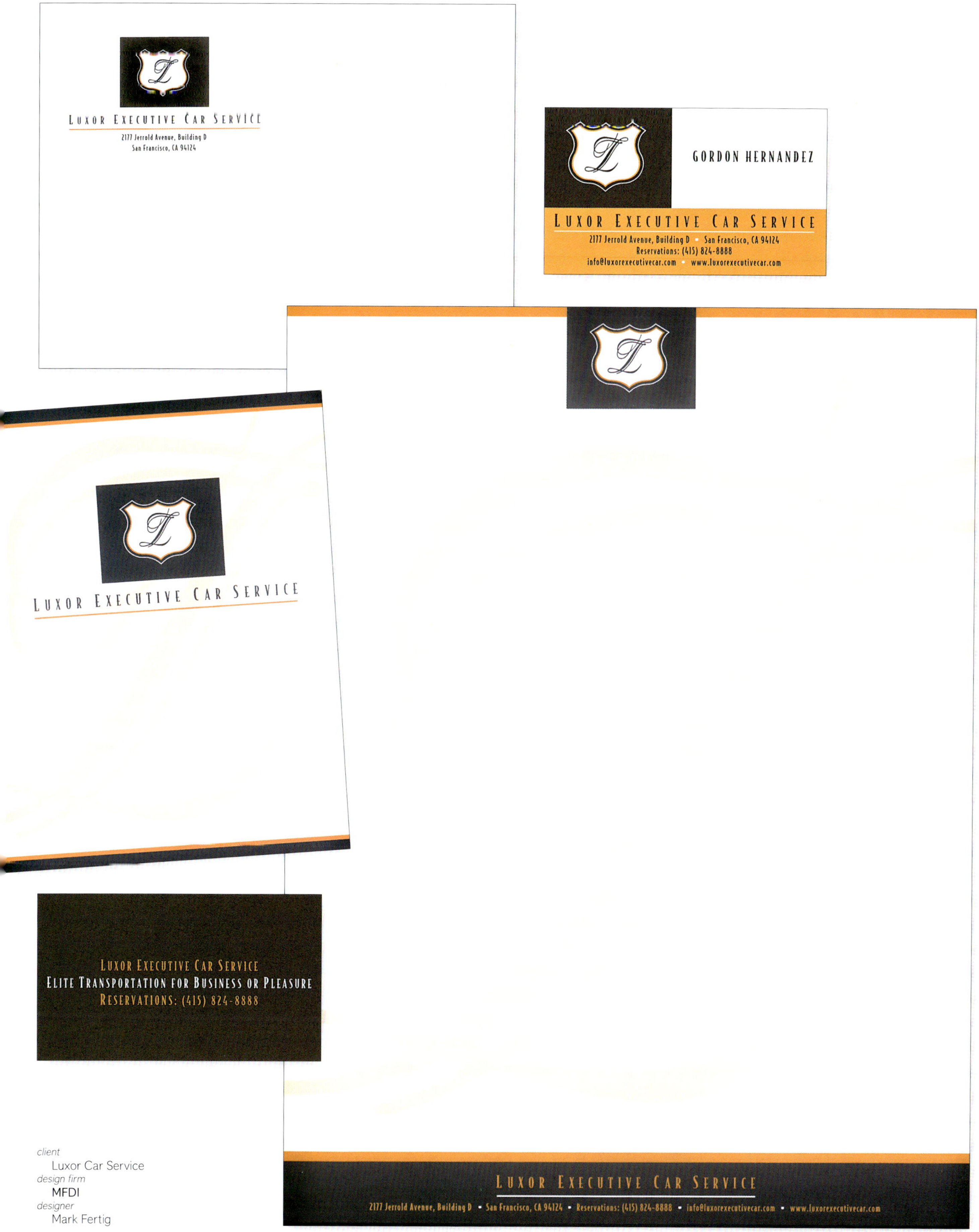

client
Luxor Car Service
design firm
MFDI
designer
Mark Fertig

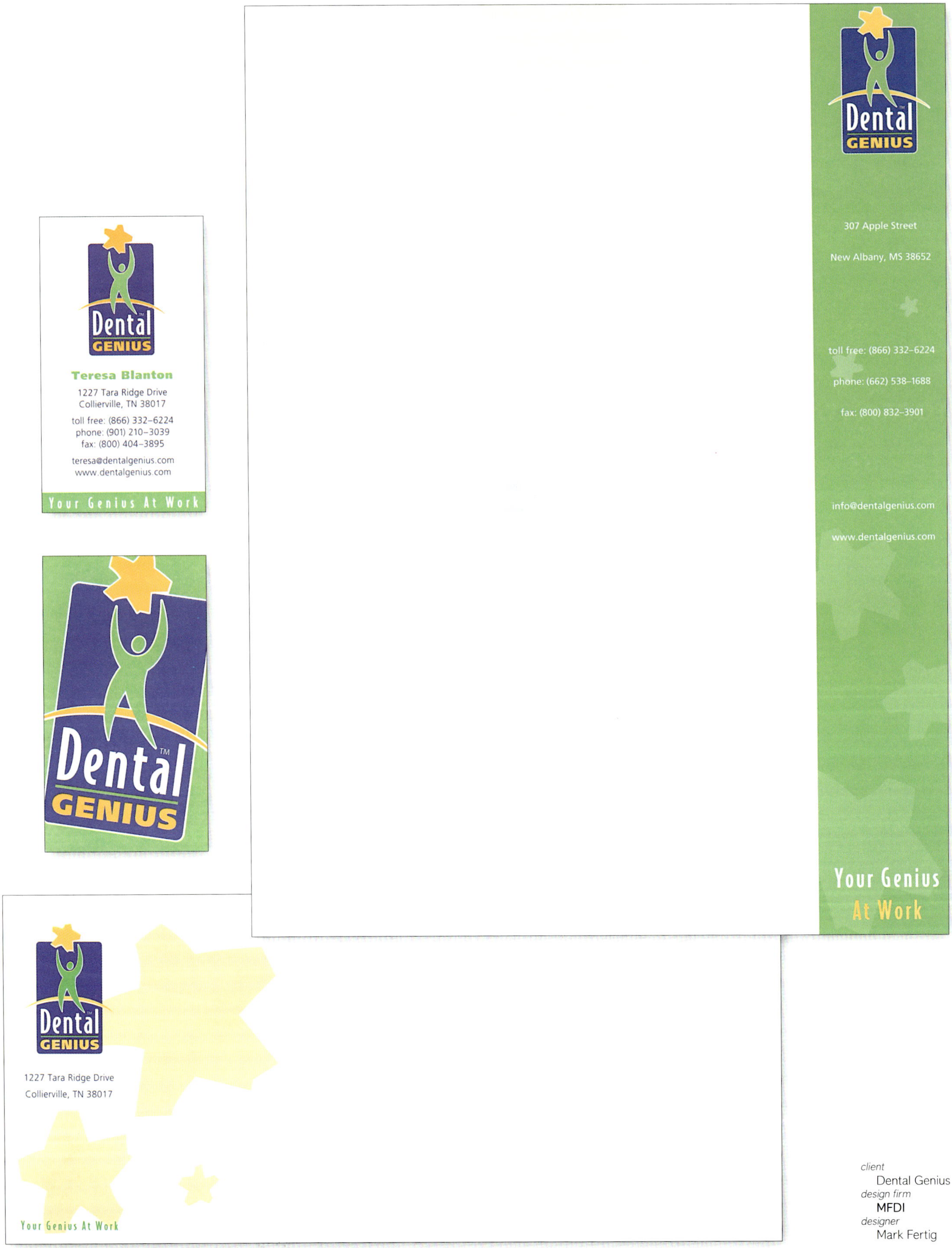

client
Dental Genius
design firm
MFDI
designer
Mark Fertig

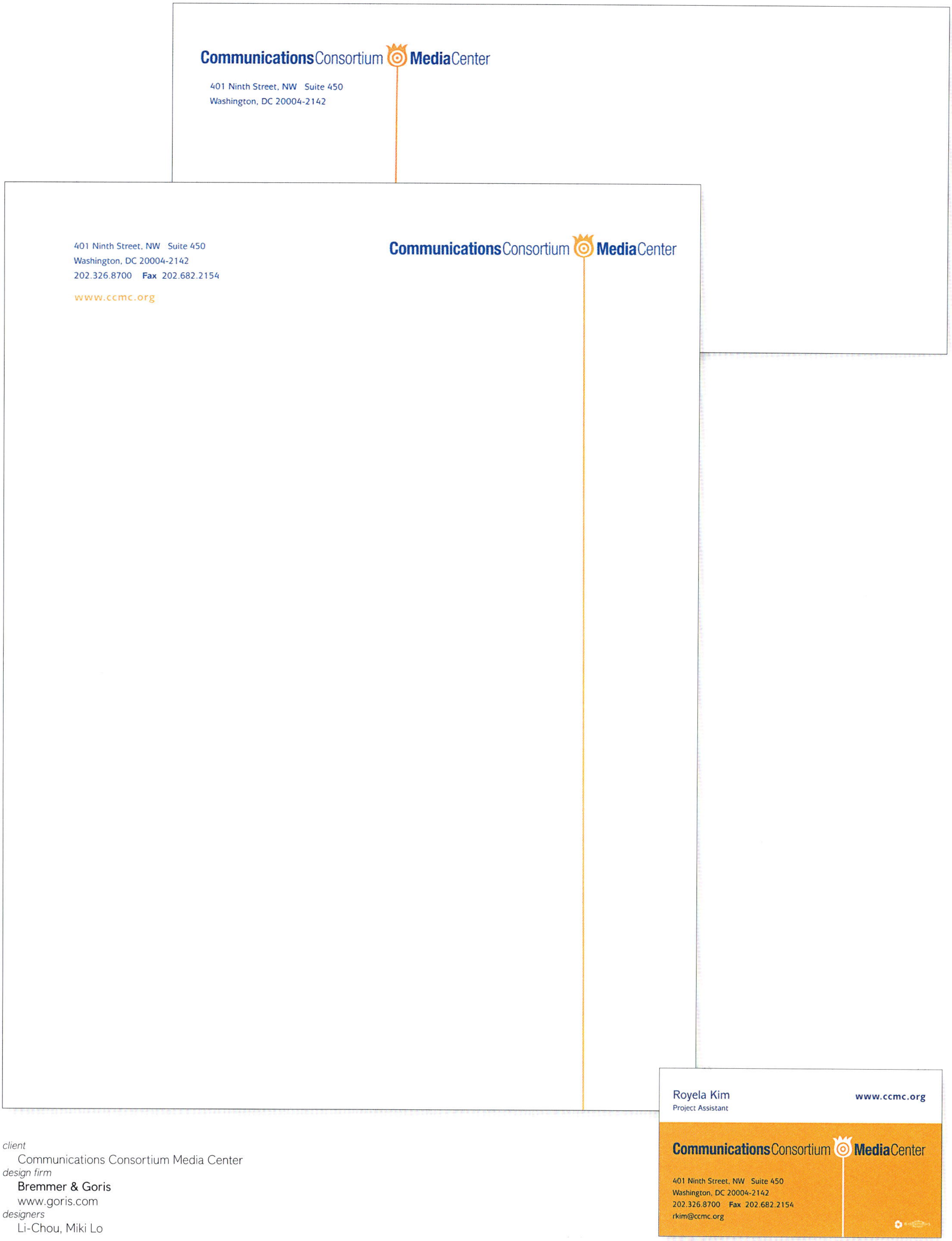

client
Communications Consortium Media Center
design firm
Bremmer & Goris
www.goris.com
designers
Li-Chou, Miki Lo

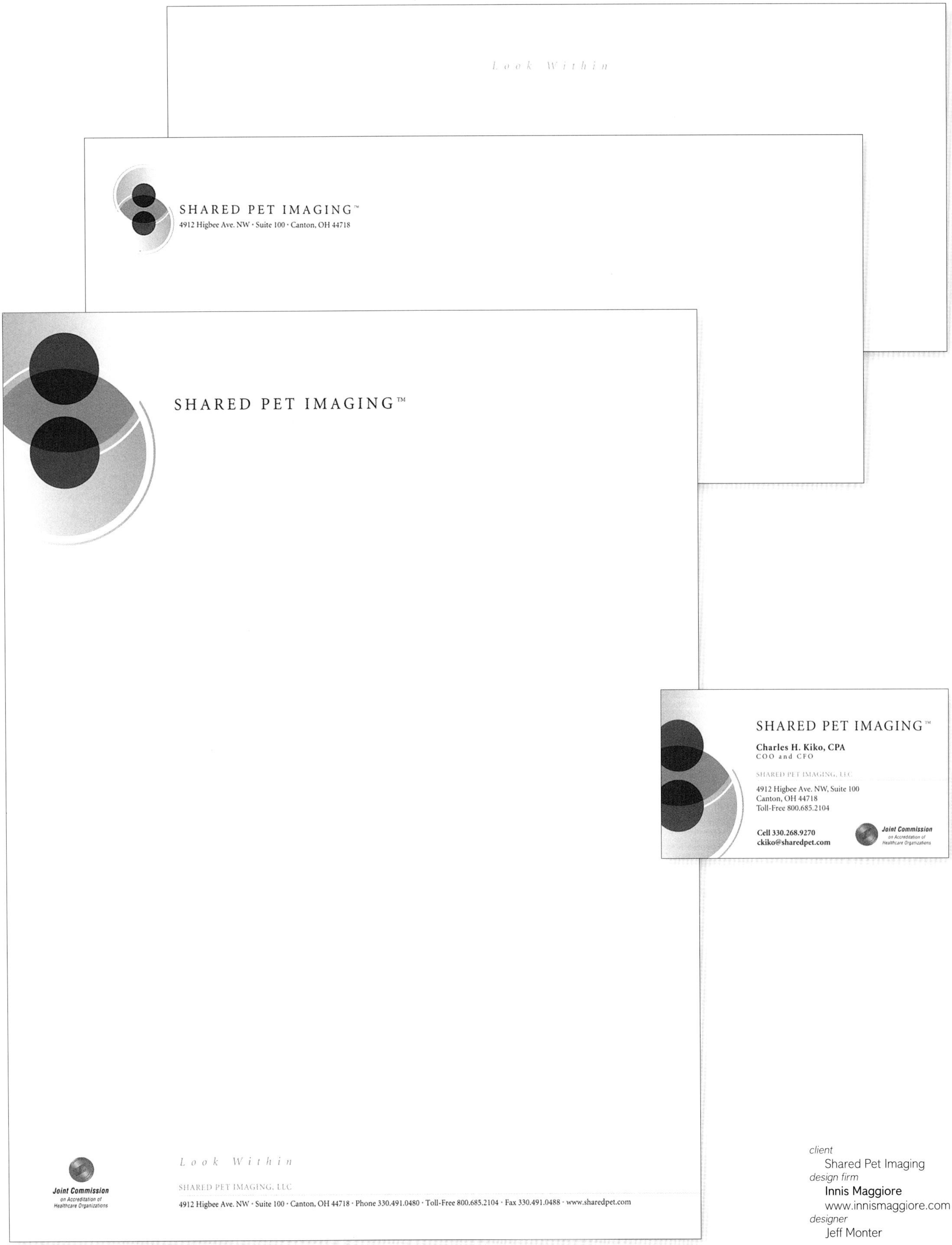

client
Shared Pet Imaging
design firm
Innis Maggiore
www.innismaggiore.com
designer
Jeff Monter

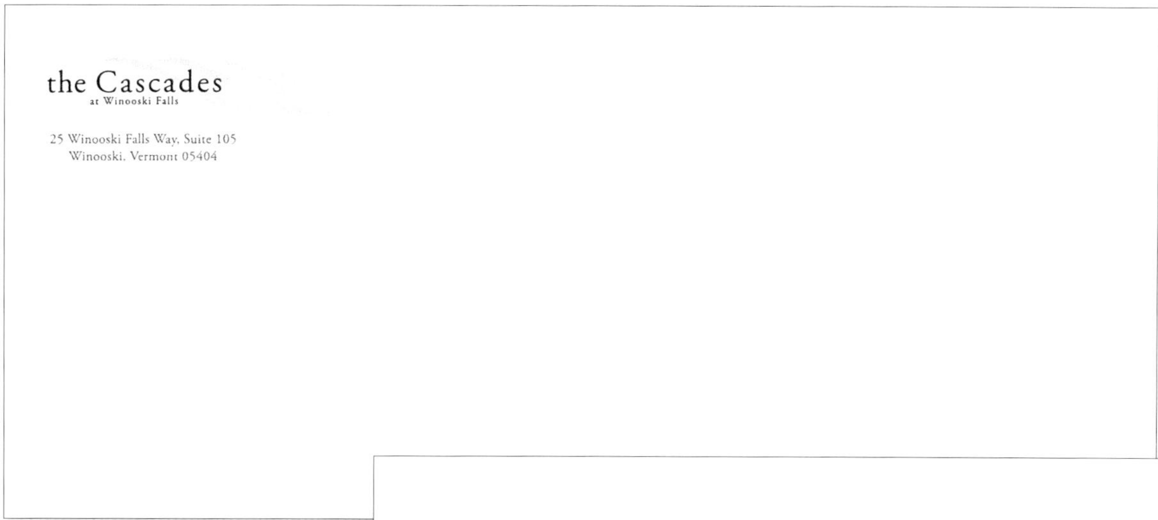

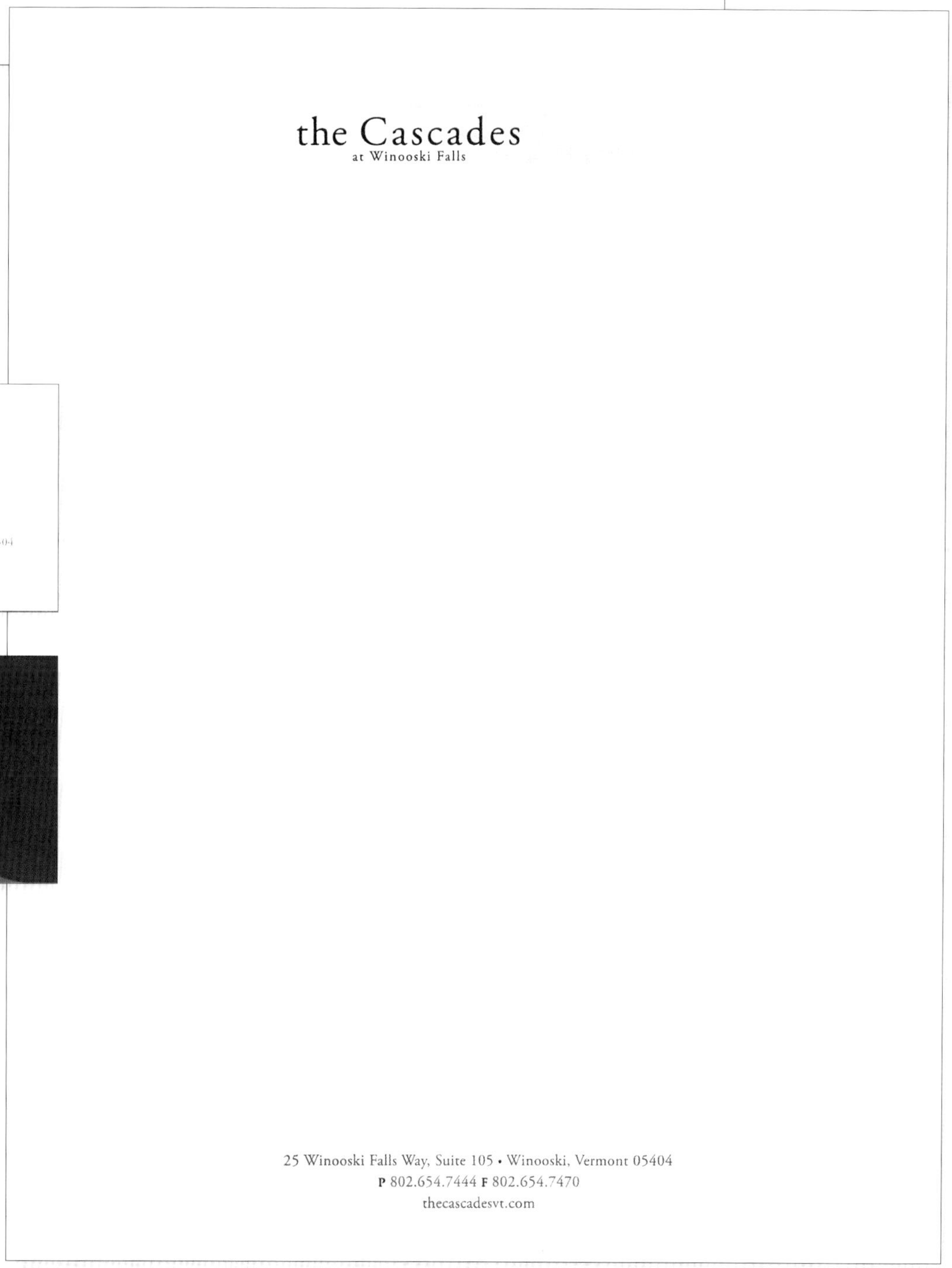

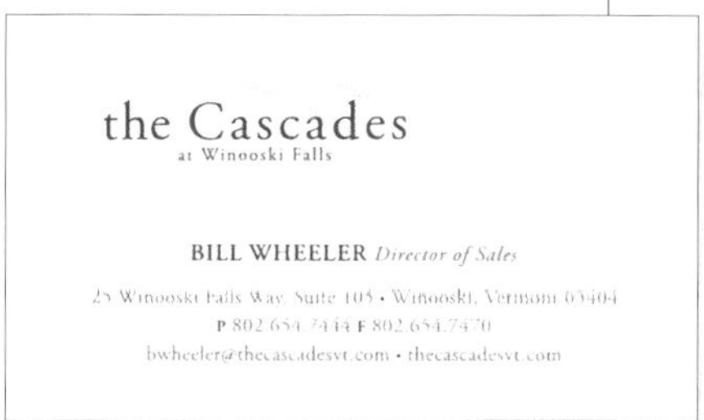

client
The Cascades
design firm
Paul Kaza Associates
www.paulkaza.com
designers
Donda Thibault, Carissa Butler

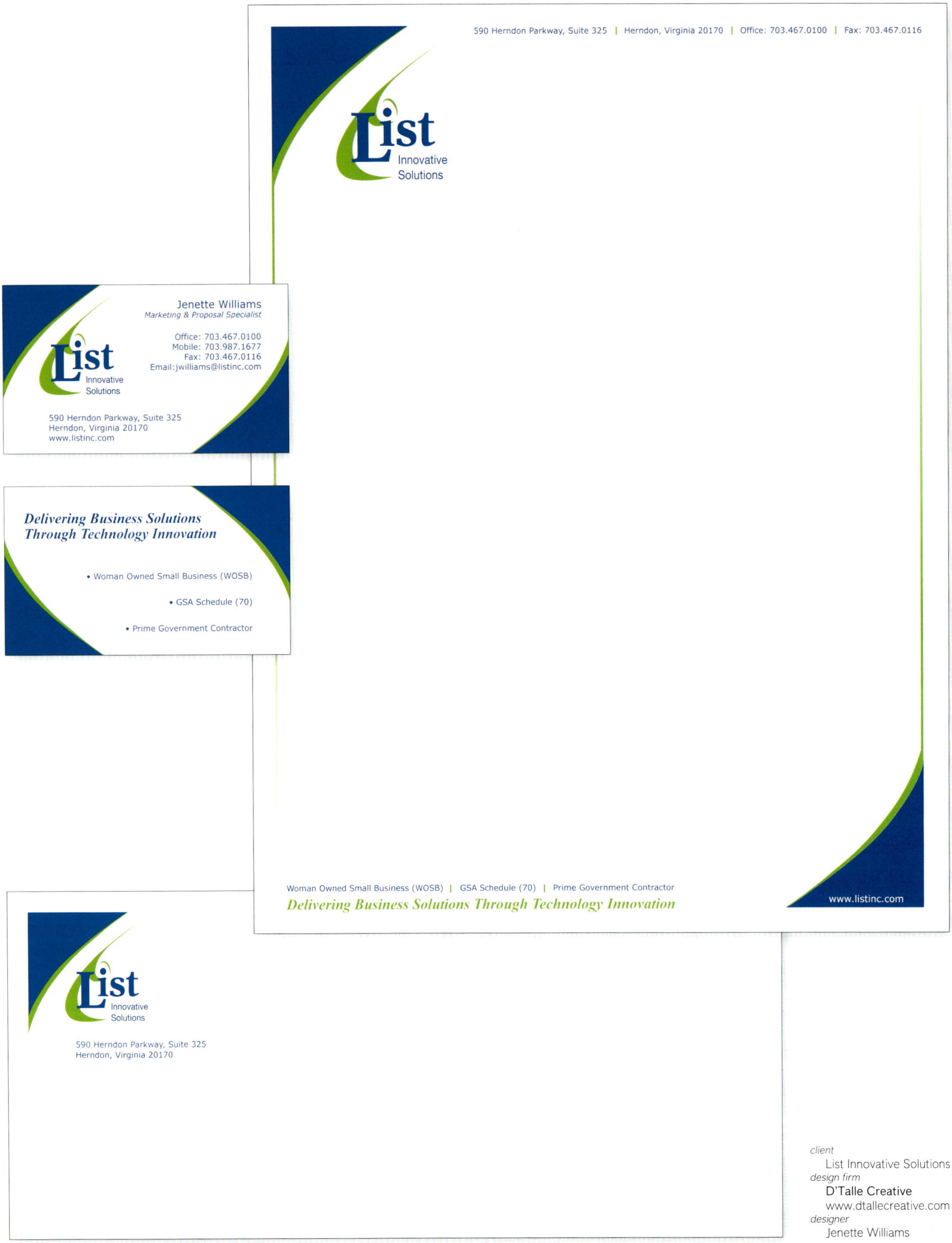

client
List Innovative Solutions
design firm
D'Talle Creative
www.dtallecreative.com
designer
Jenette Williams

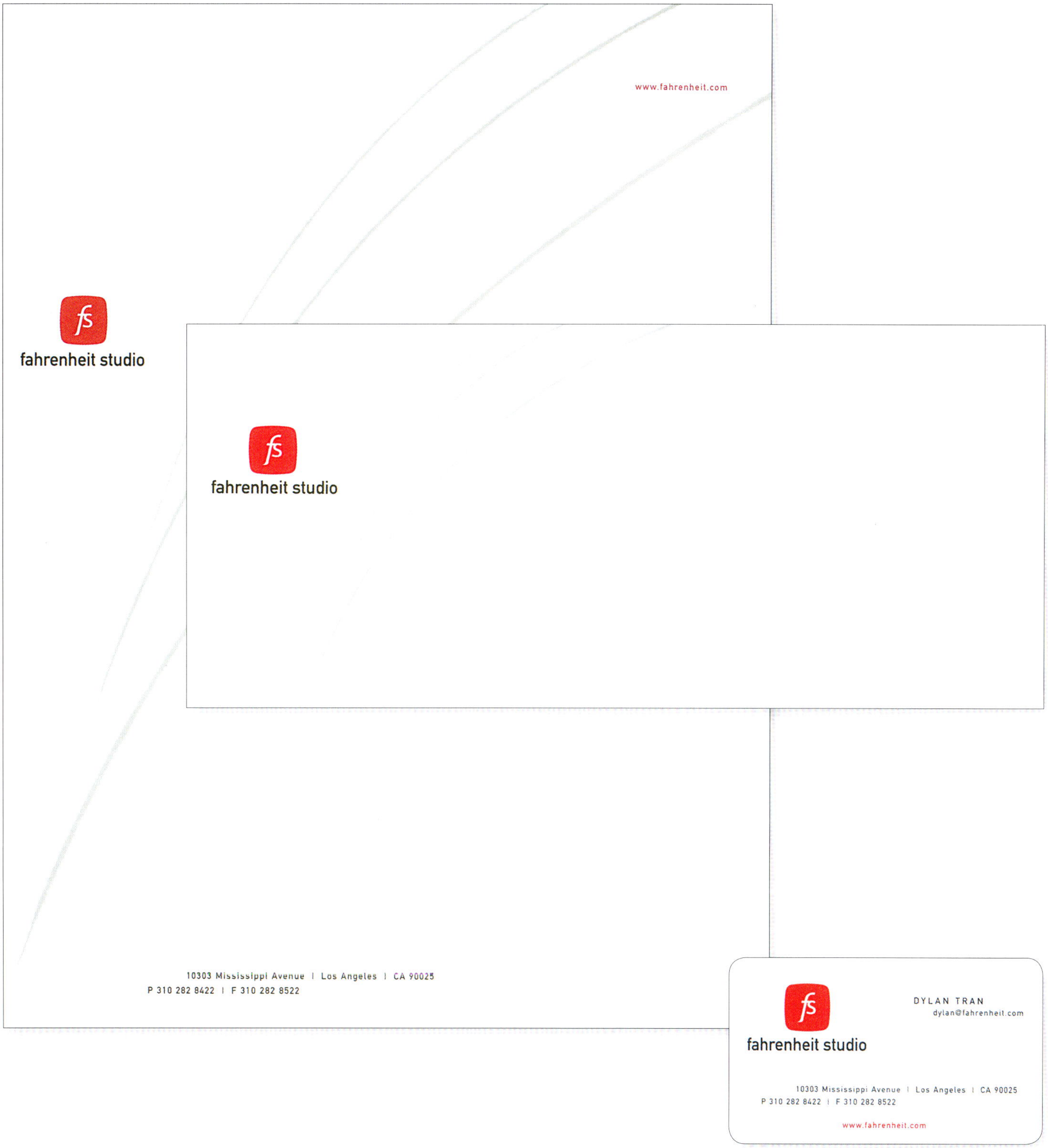

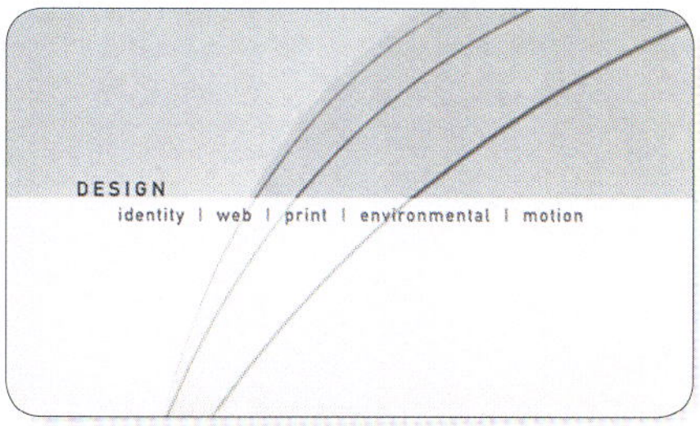

client
Fahrenheit Studio
design firm
Fahrenheit Studio
www.fahrenheit.com
designers
Fahrenheit Studio

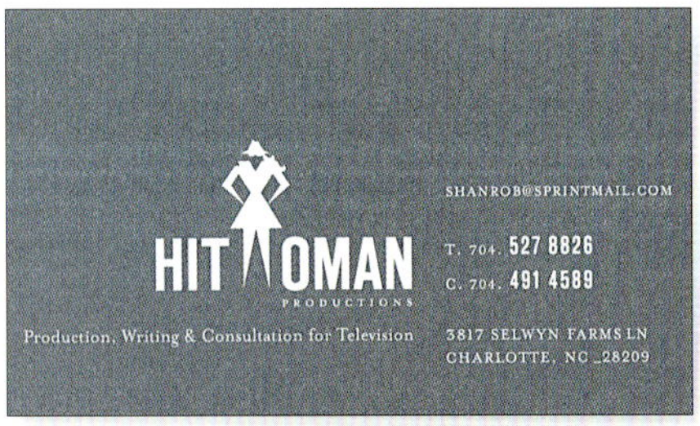

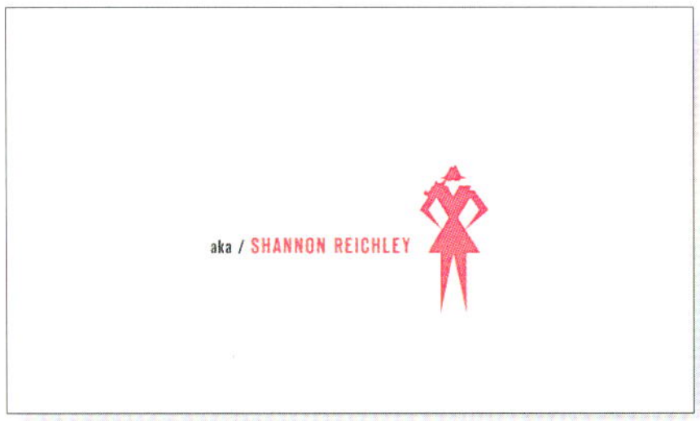

client
Hit Woman Productions
design firm
A3 Design
www.athreedesign.com
designers
Alan Altman, Amanda Altman

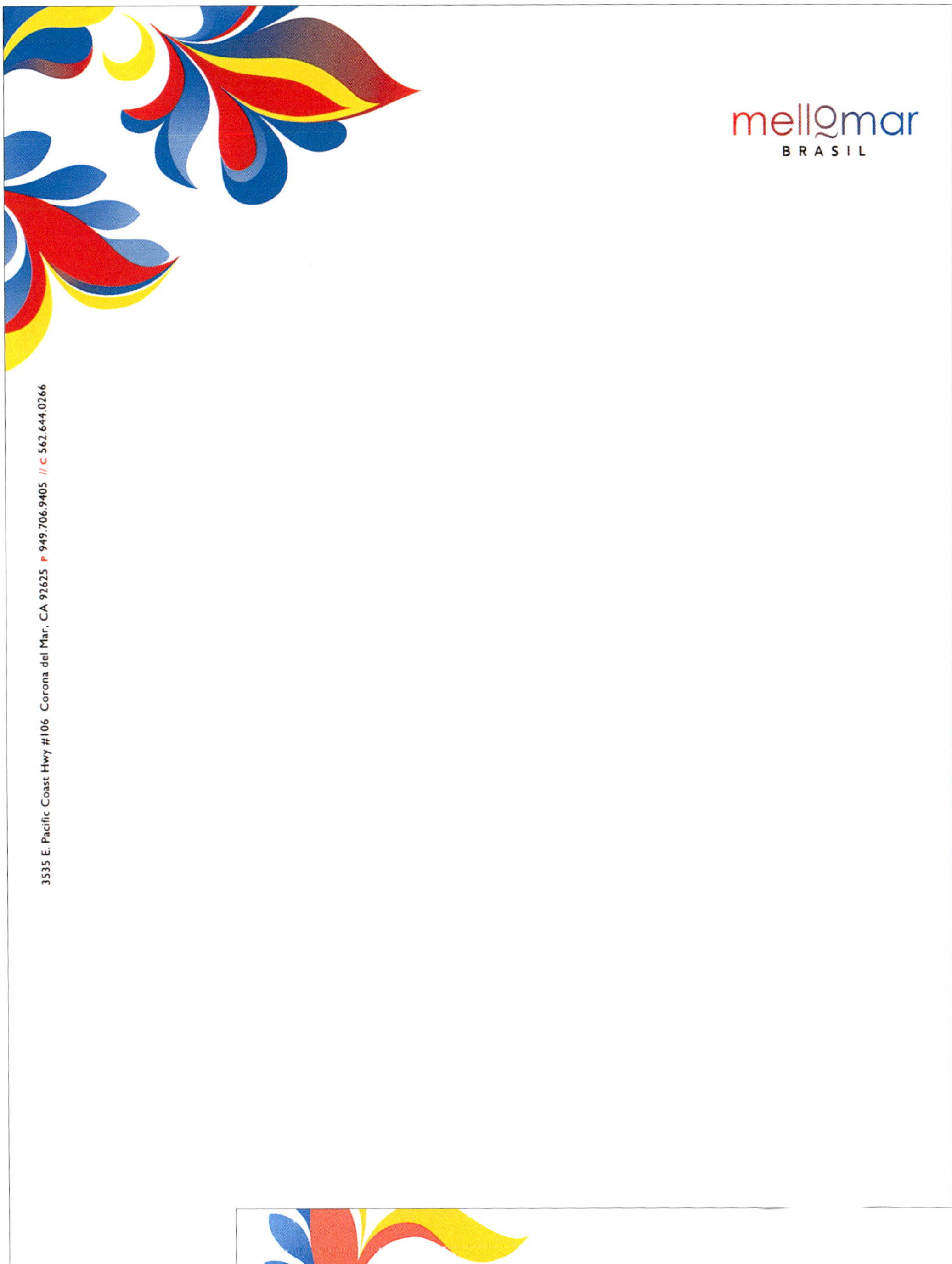

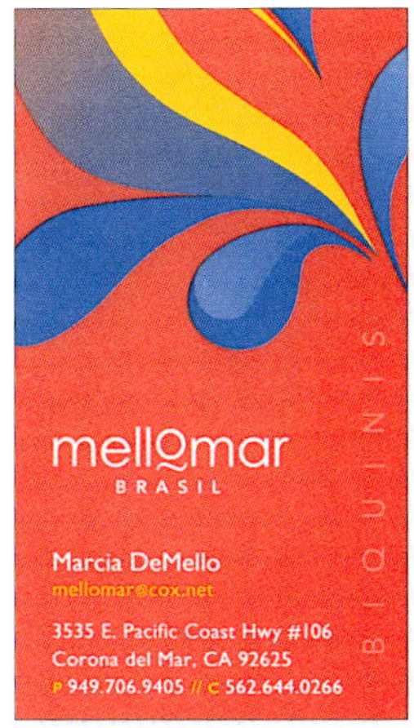

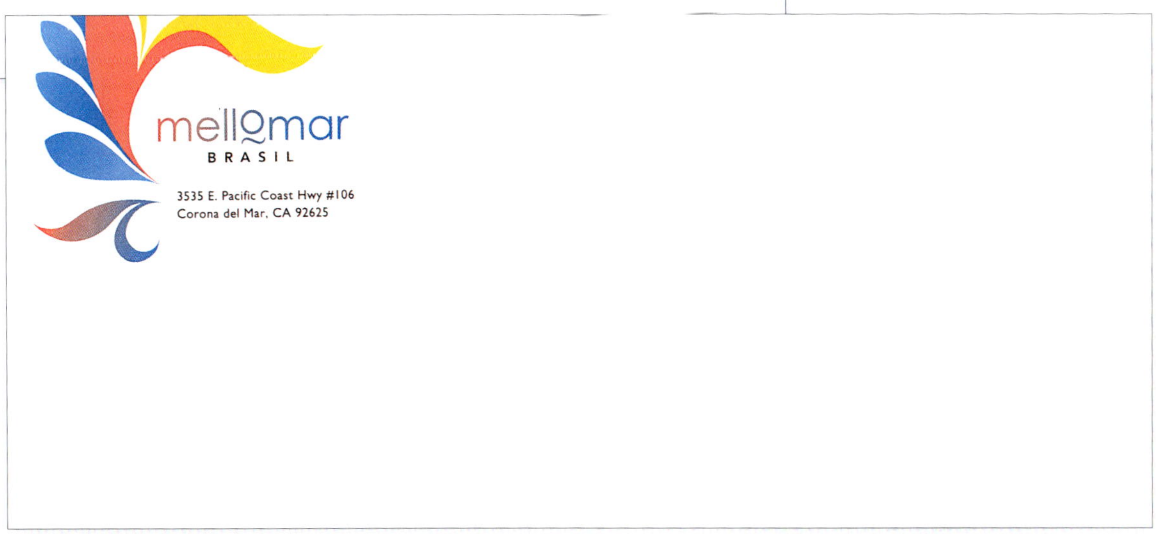

client
Mellomar
design firm
IE Design +
Communications
www.iedesign.net
creative director
Marcie Carson
designer
Christine Kenney

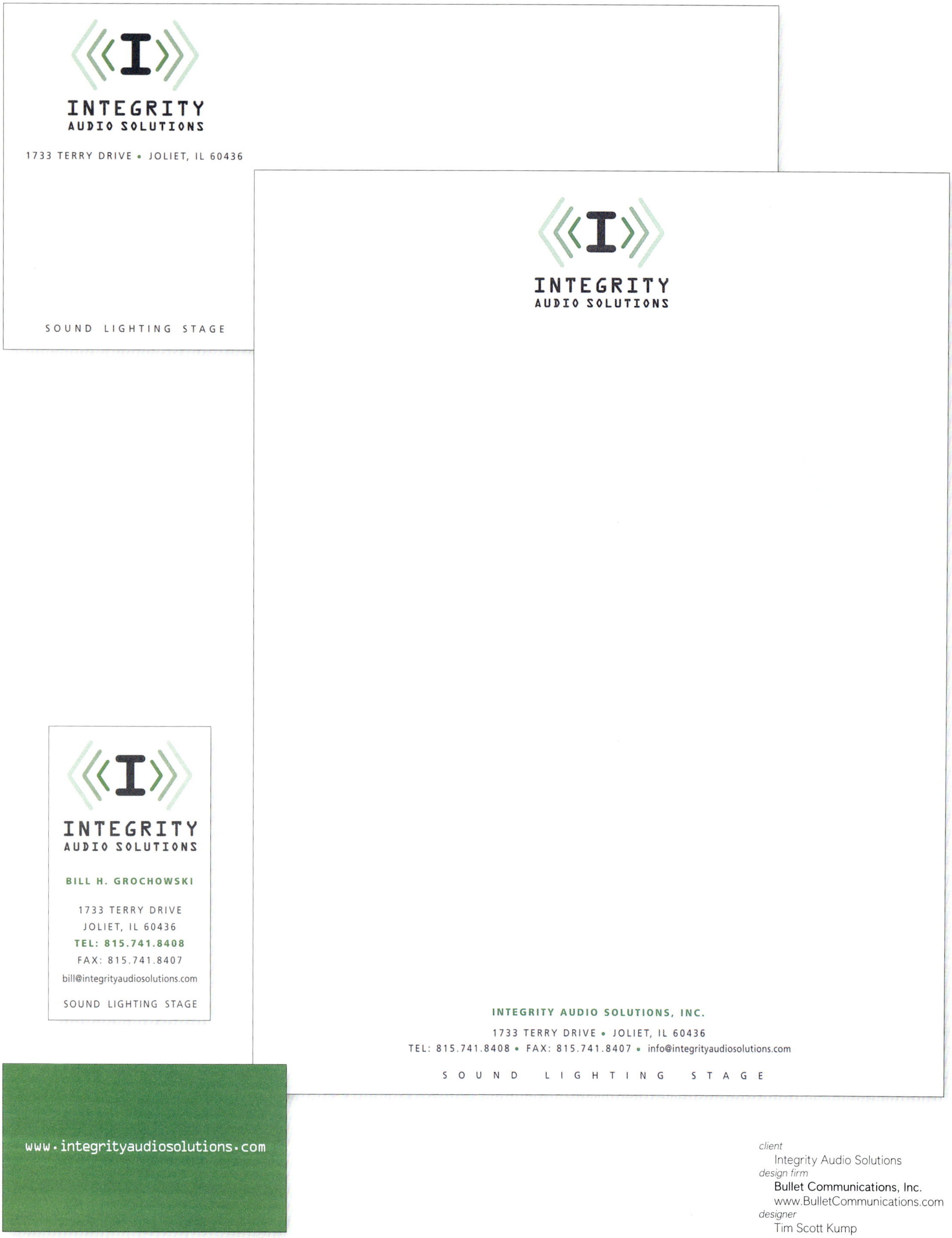

client
Integrity Audio Solutions
design firm
Bullet Communications, Inc.
www.BulletCommunications.com
designer
Tim Scott Kump

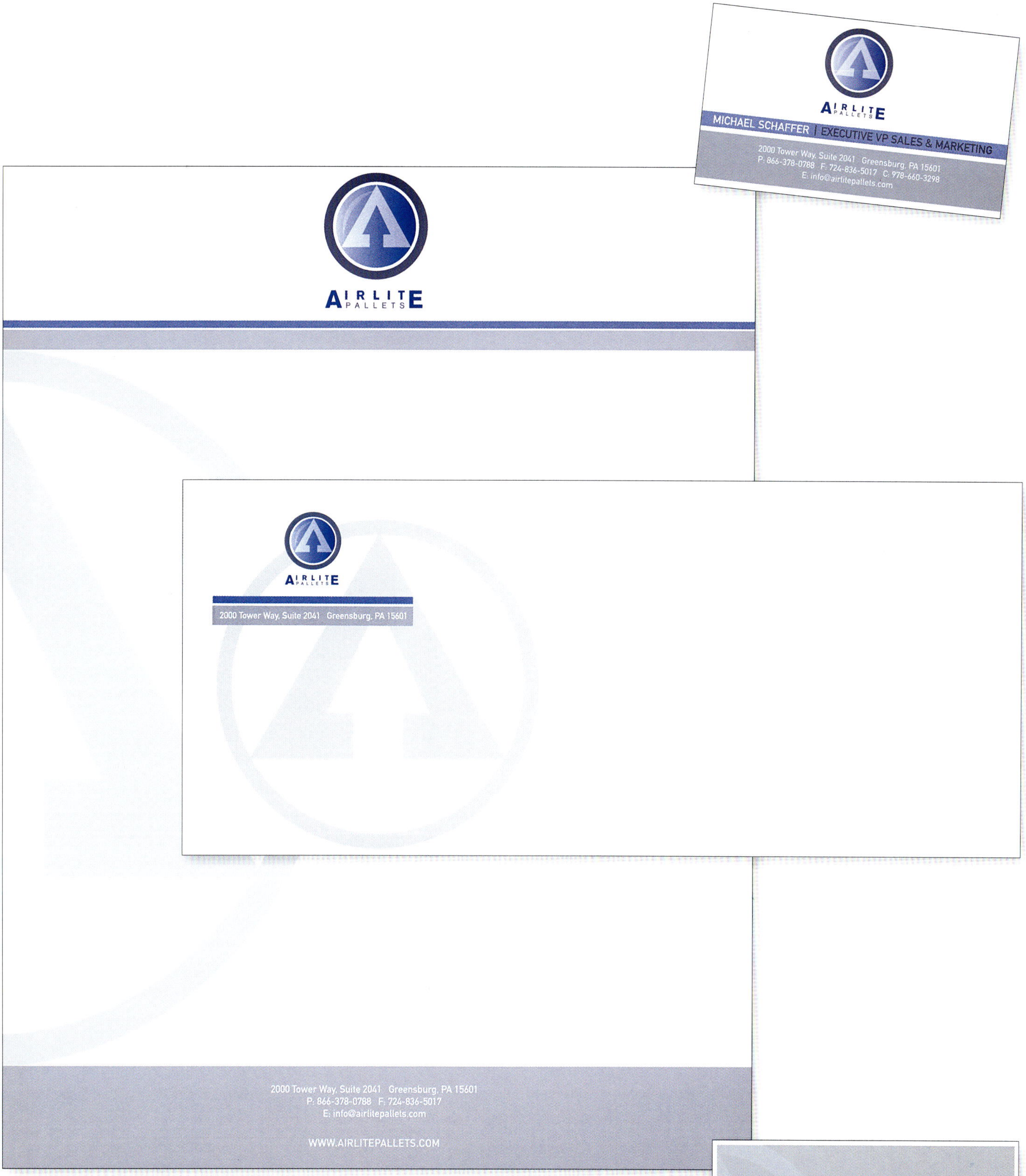

client
Airlite Pallets
design firm
Reinnov8 Design Group
www.reinnov8.com
designer
Richard A. Hooper

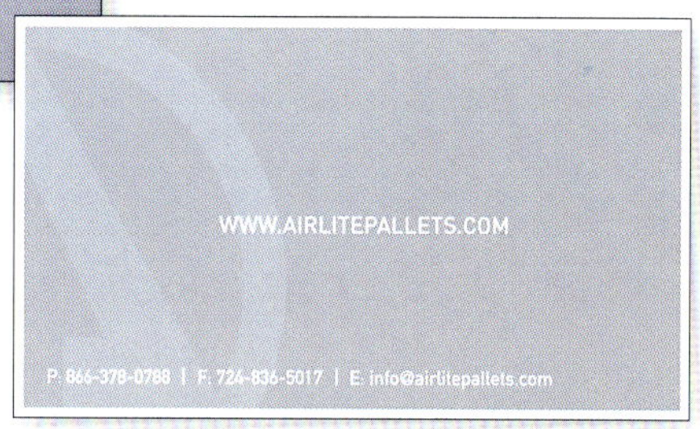

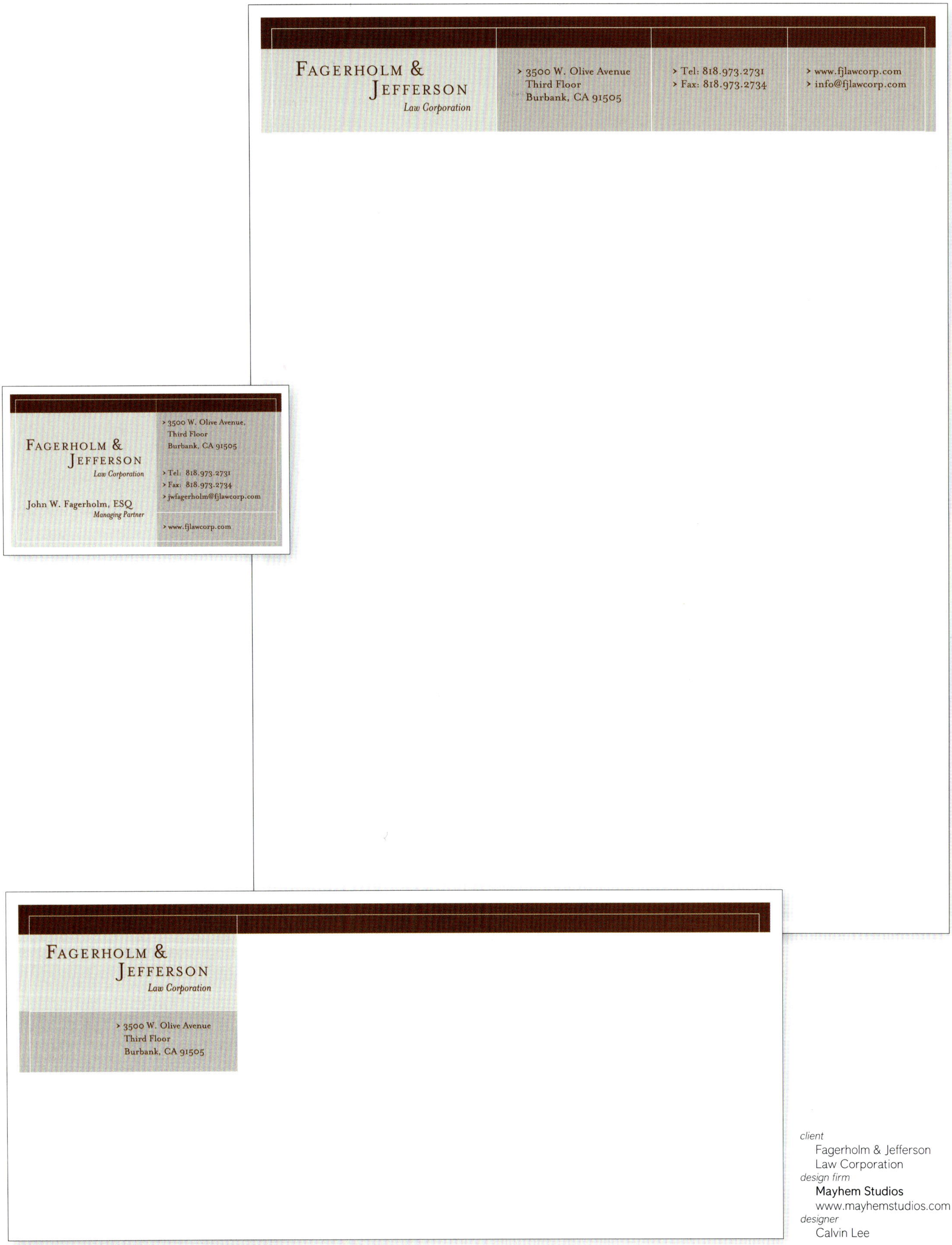

client
Fagerholm & Jefferson
Law Corporation
design firm
Mayhem Studios
www.mayhemstudios.com
designer
Calvin Lee

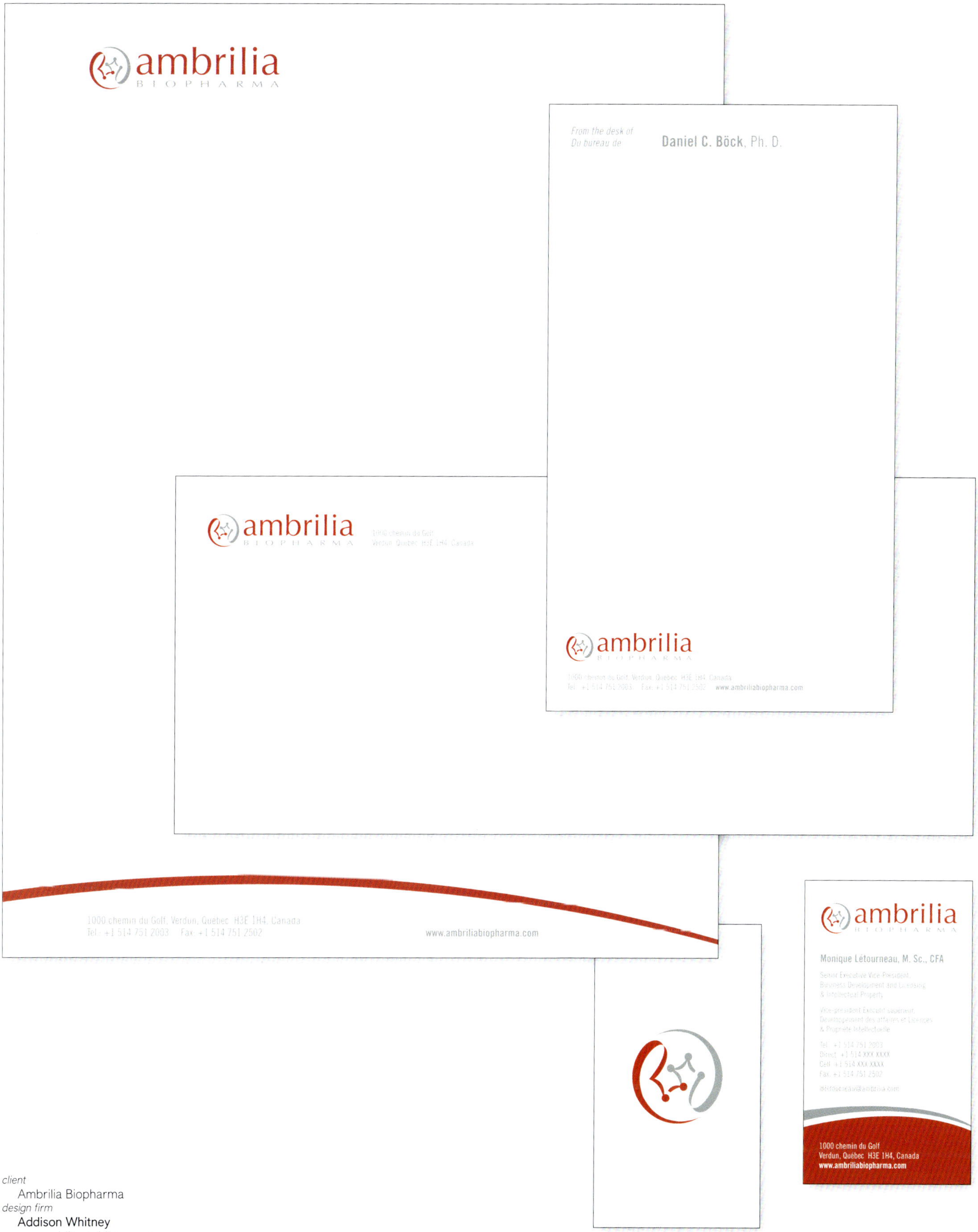

client
Ambrilia Biopharma
design firm
Addison Whitney
www.addisonwhitney.com
designers
Trey Walsh, Kristin Hager, Kimberlee Davis

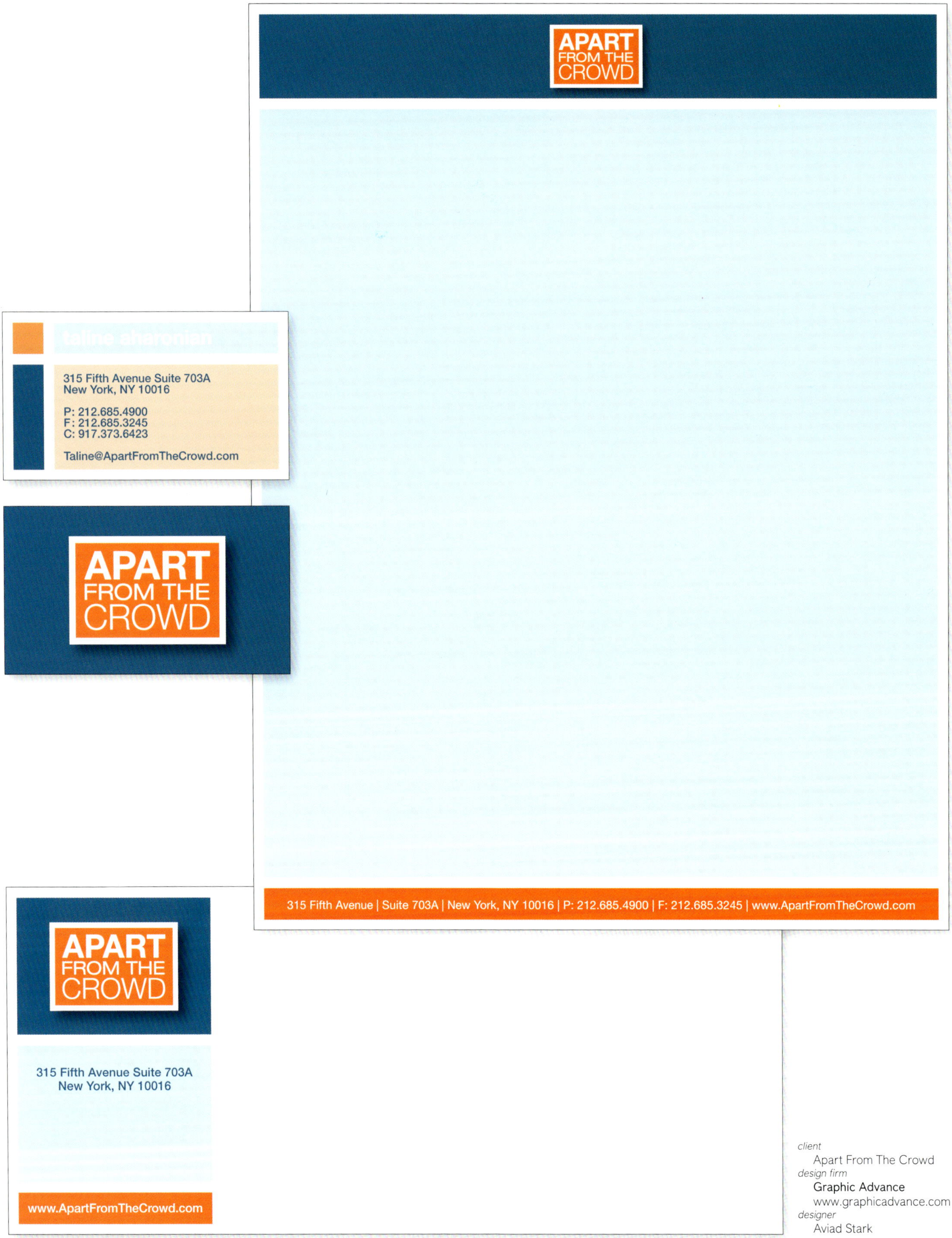

client
Apart From The Crowd
design firm
Graphic Advance
www.graphicadvance.com
designer
Aviad Stark

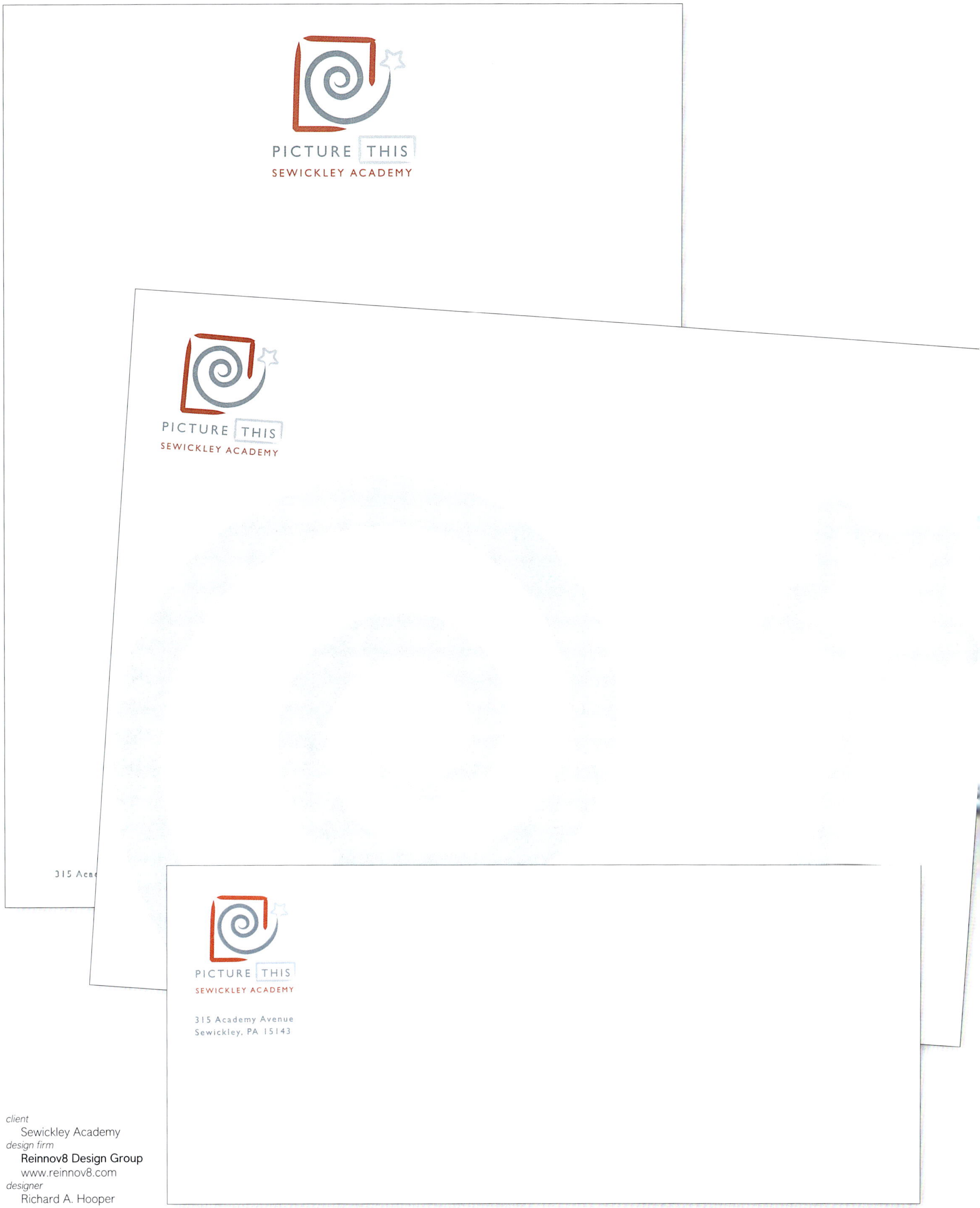

client
Sewickley Academy
design firm
Reinnov8 Design Group
www.reinnov8.com
designer
Richard A. Hooper

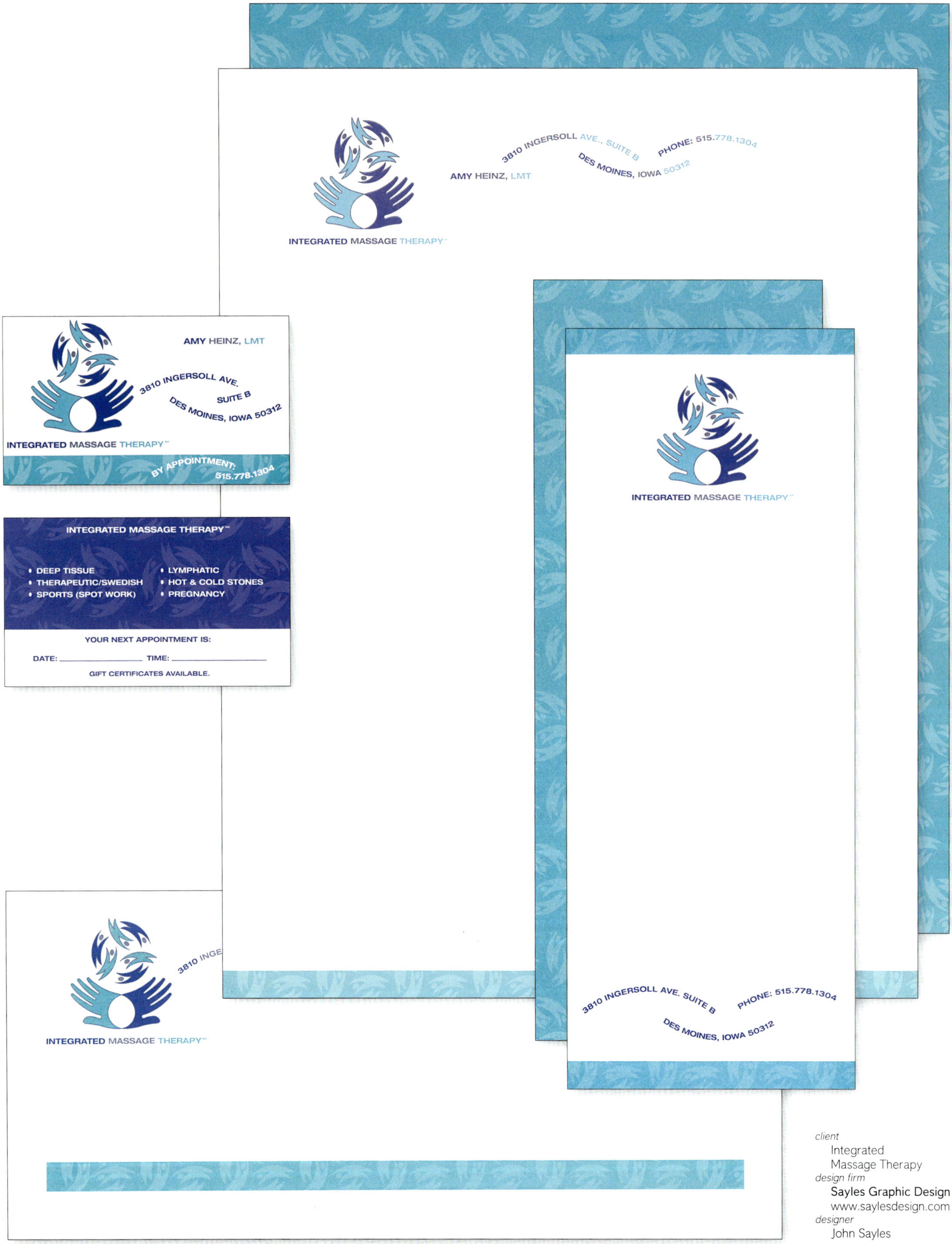

client
Integrated
Massage Therapy
design firm
Sayles Graphic Design
www.saylesdesign.com
designer
John Sayles

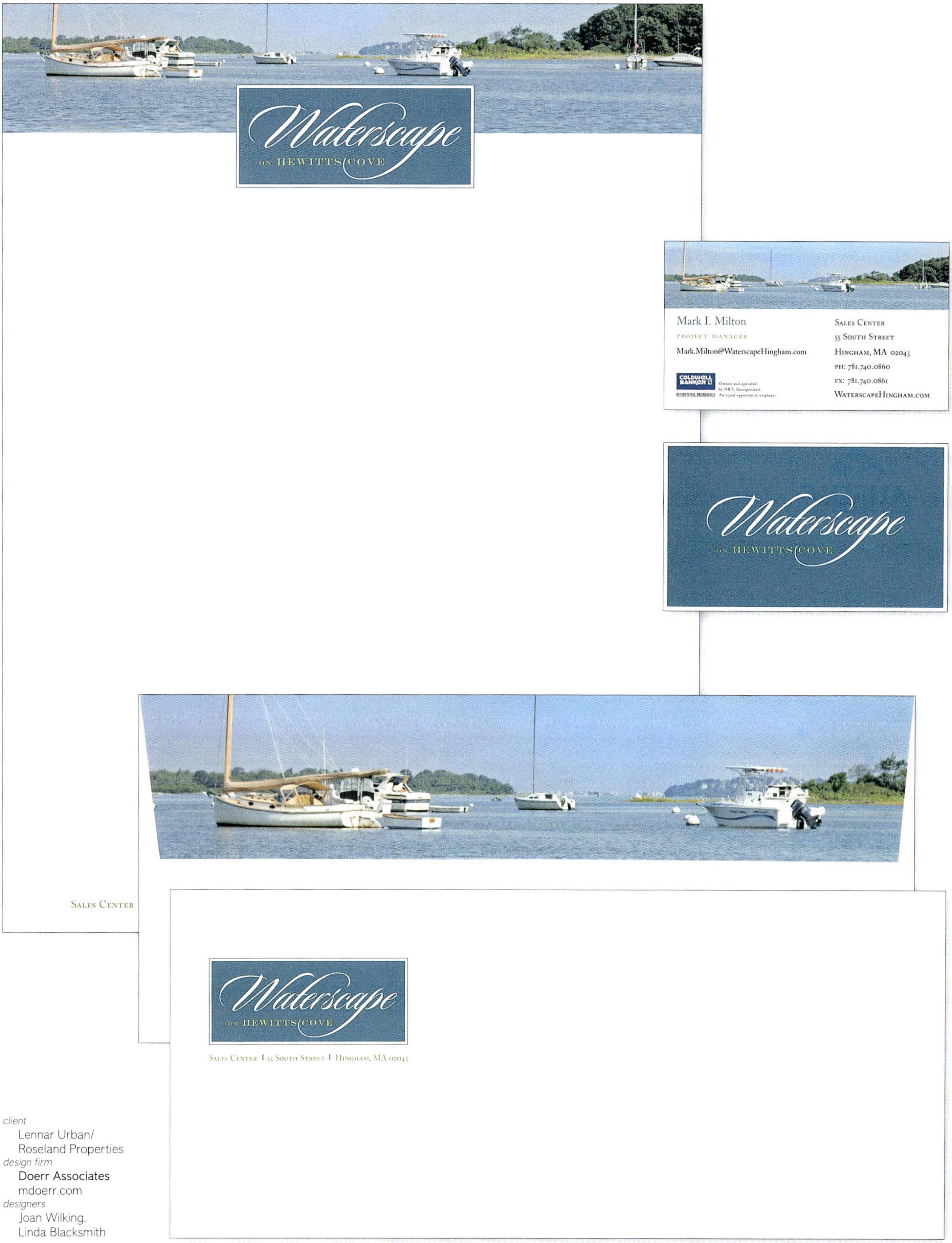

client
Lennar Urban/
Roseland Properties
design firm
Doerr Associates
mdoerr.com
designers
Joan Wilking,
Linda Blacksmith

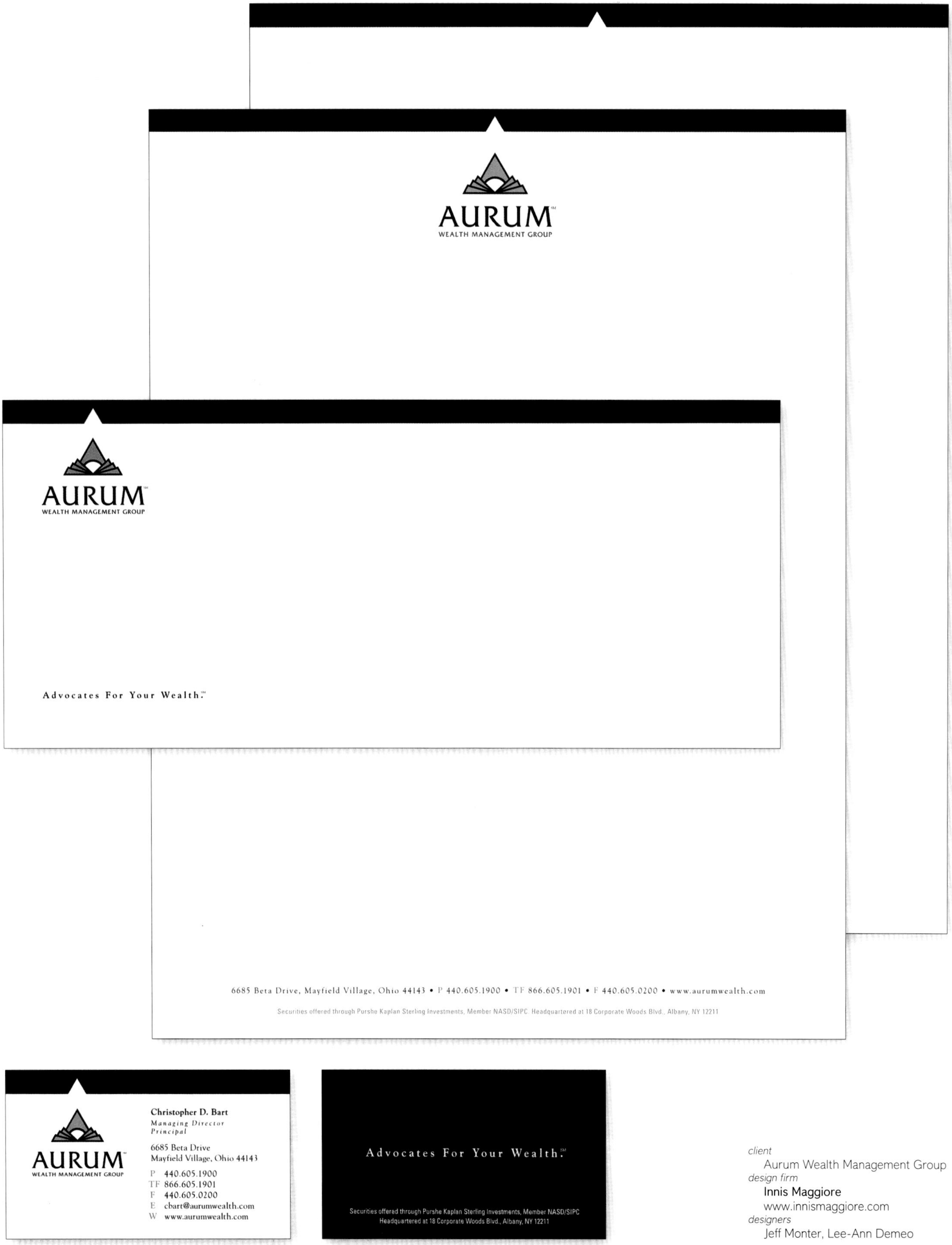

client
Aurum Wealth Management Group
design firm
Innis Maggiore
www.innismaggiore.com
designers
Jeff Monter, Lee-Ann Demeo

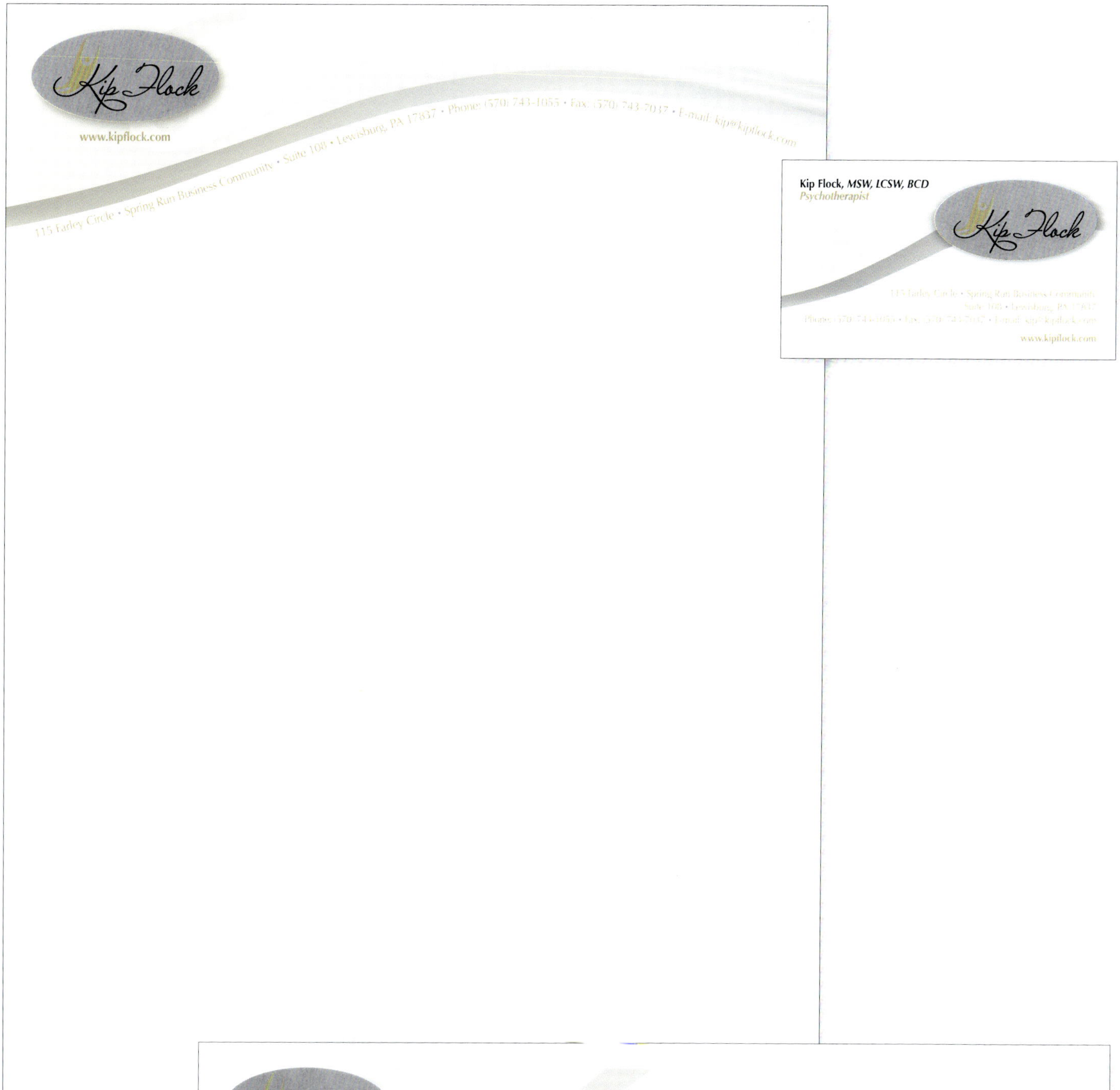

client
Kip Flock
design firm
Sire Advertising
www.sireadvertising.com
creative director
Shawn Felty
designer
Jessica Varner

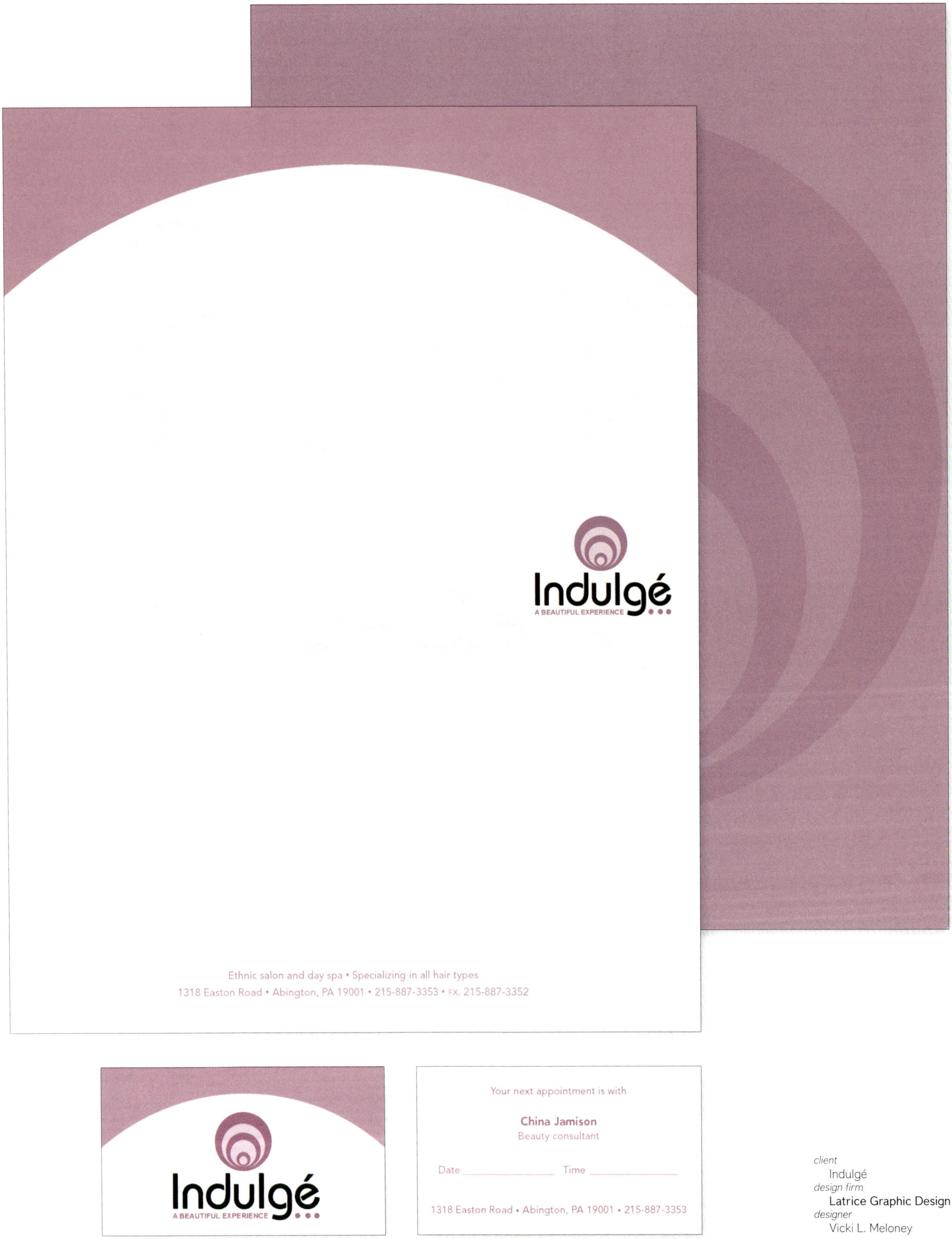

client
Indulgé
design firm
Latrice Graphic Design
designer
Vicki L. Meloney

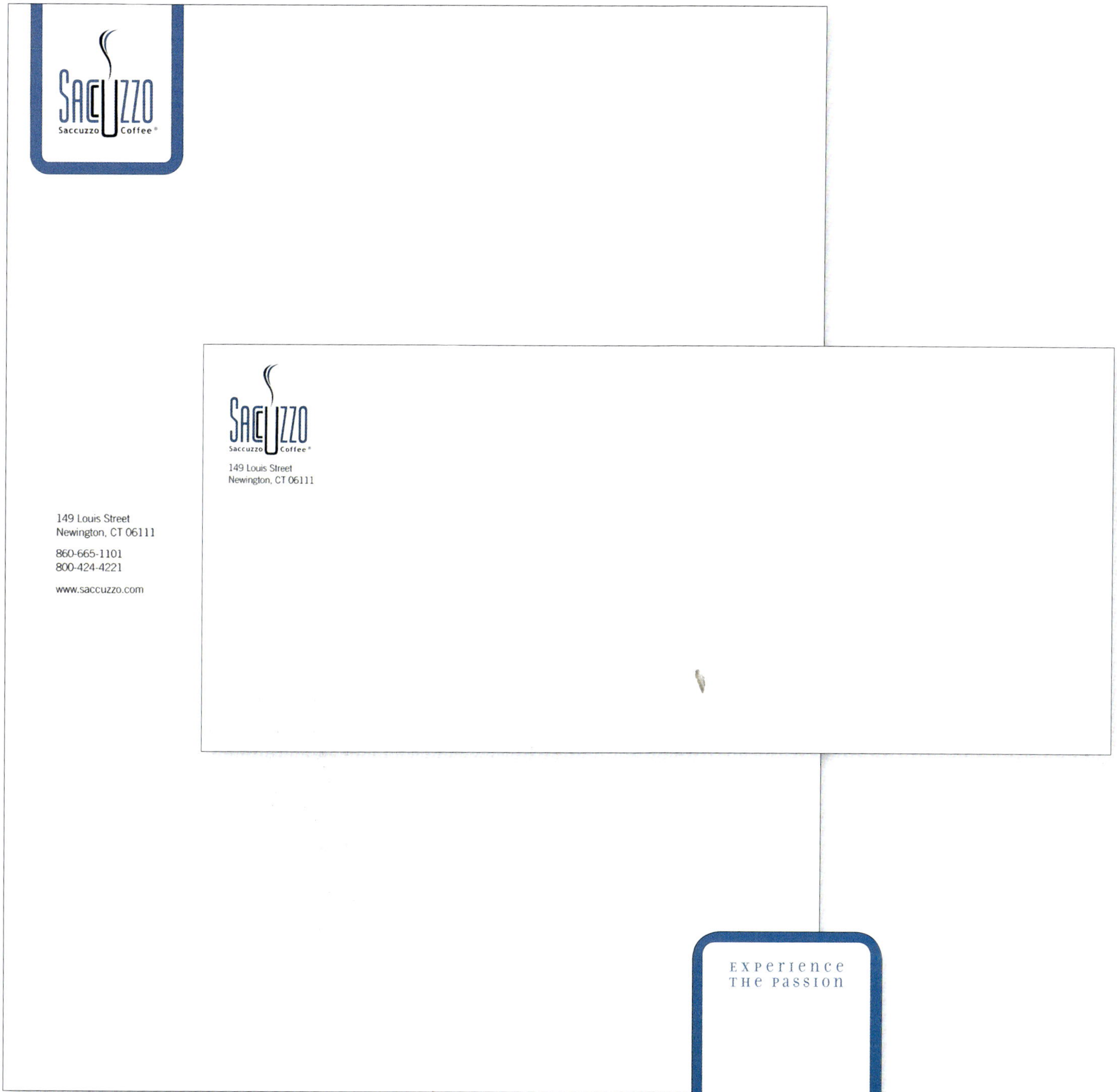

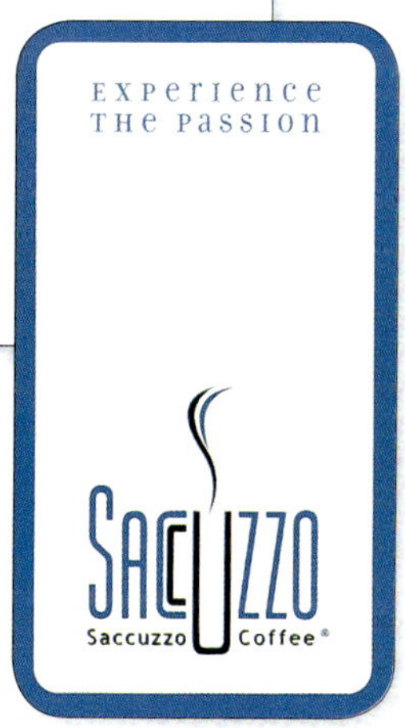

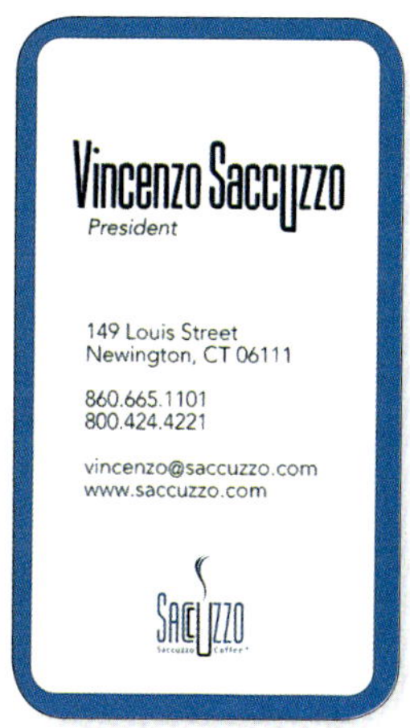

client
Saccuzzo Coffee
design firm
Fathom Applied Strategy
designer
Joe Philippon

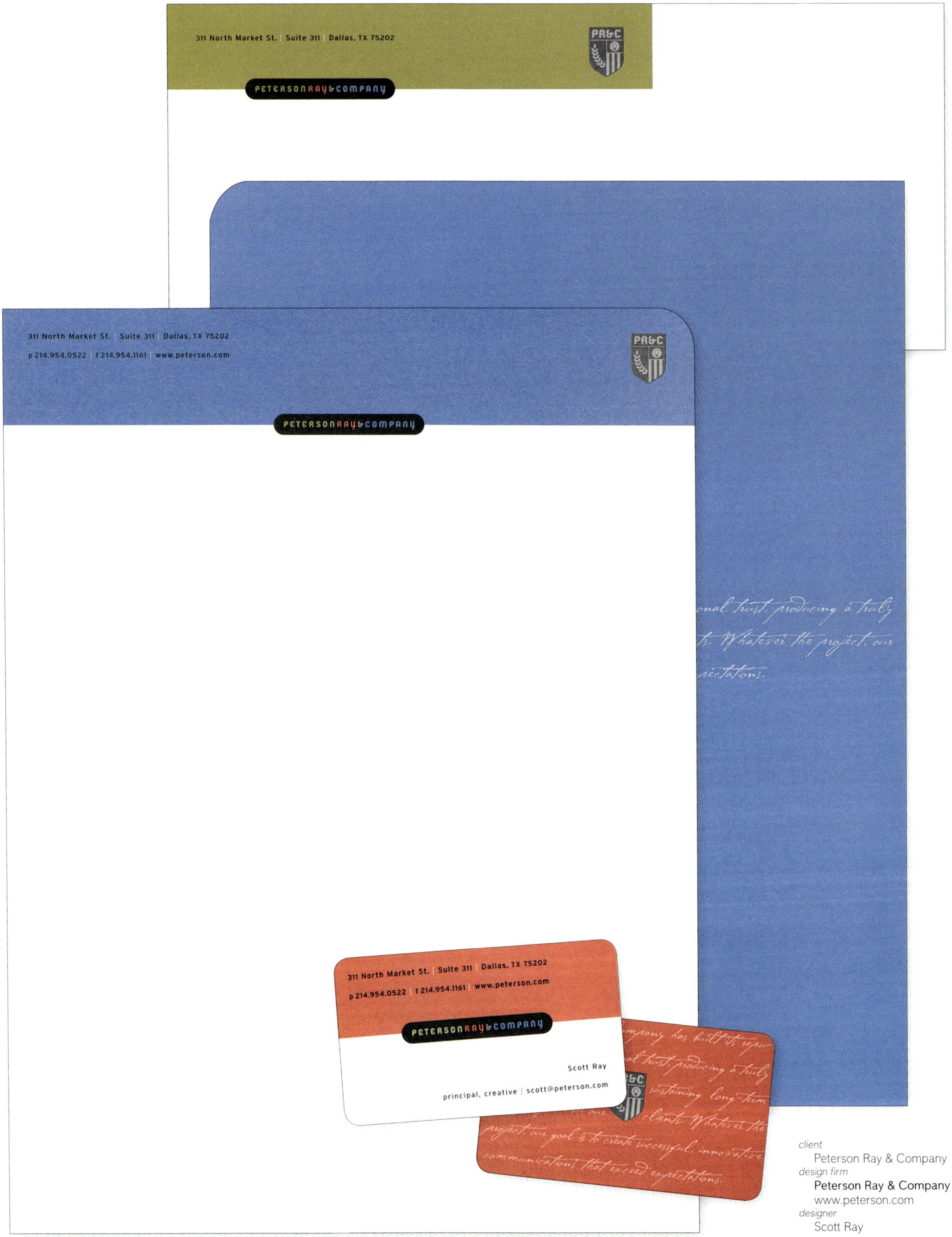

client
Peterson Ray & Company
design firm
Peterson Ray & Company
www.peterson.com
designer
Scott Ray

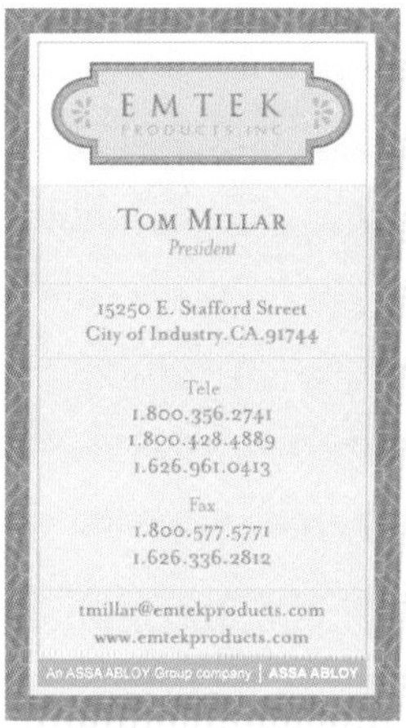

client
Emtek Products
design firm
Mayhem Studios
www.mayhemstudios.com
designer
Calvin Lee

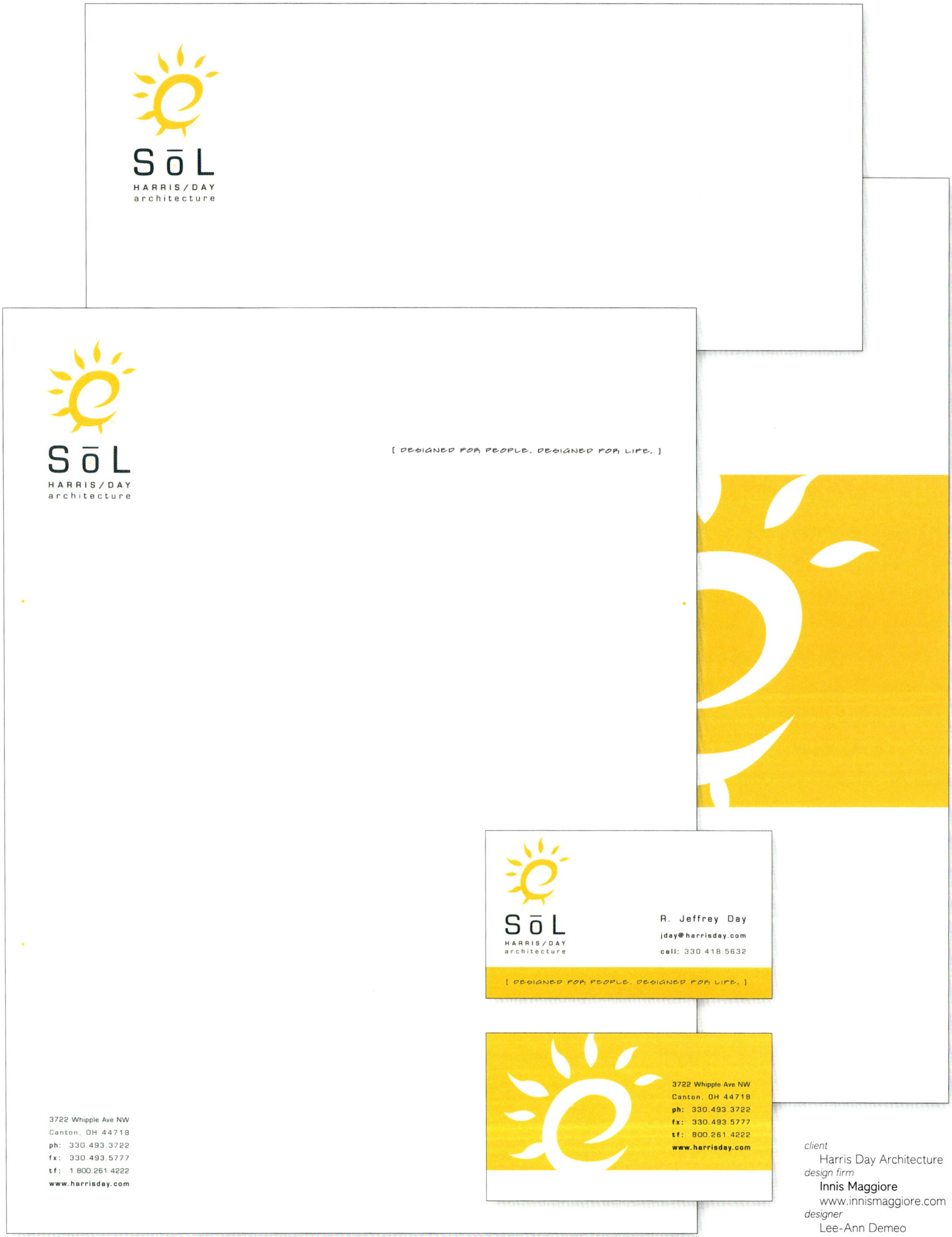

client
Harris Day Architecture
design firm
Innis Maggiore
www.innismaggiore.com
designer
Lee-Ann Demeo

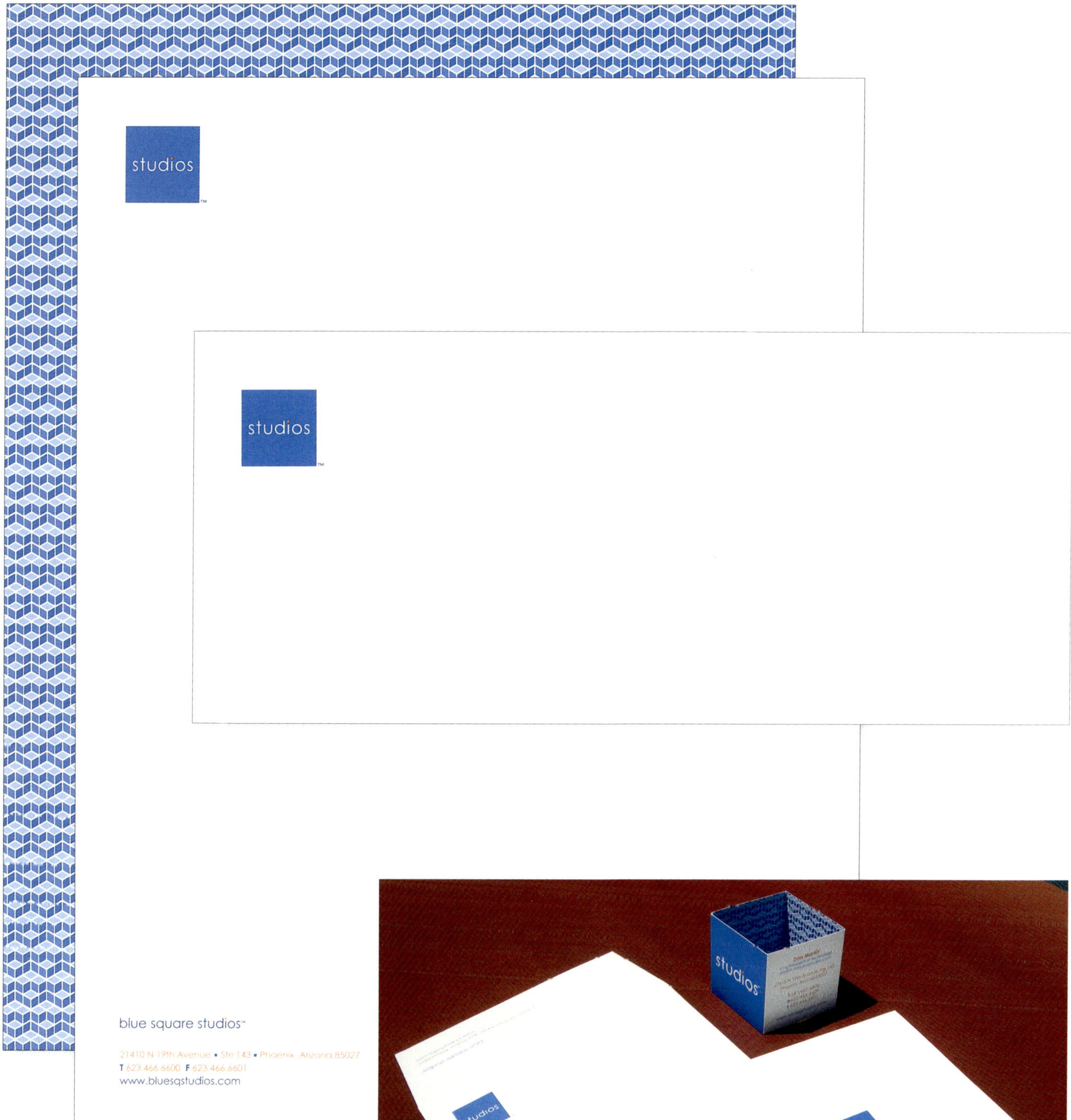

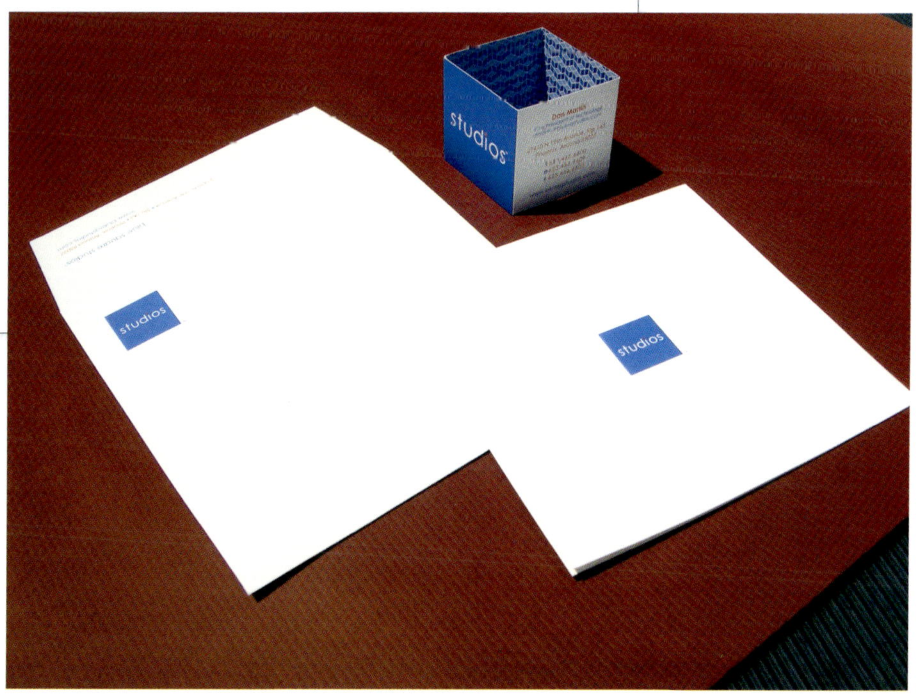

client
Blue Square Studios
design firm
Rule29 Creative
www.rule29.com
designers
Justin Ahrens, Josh Jensen

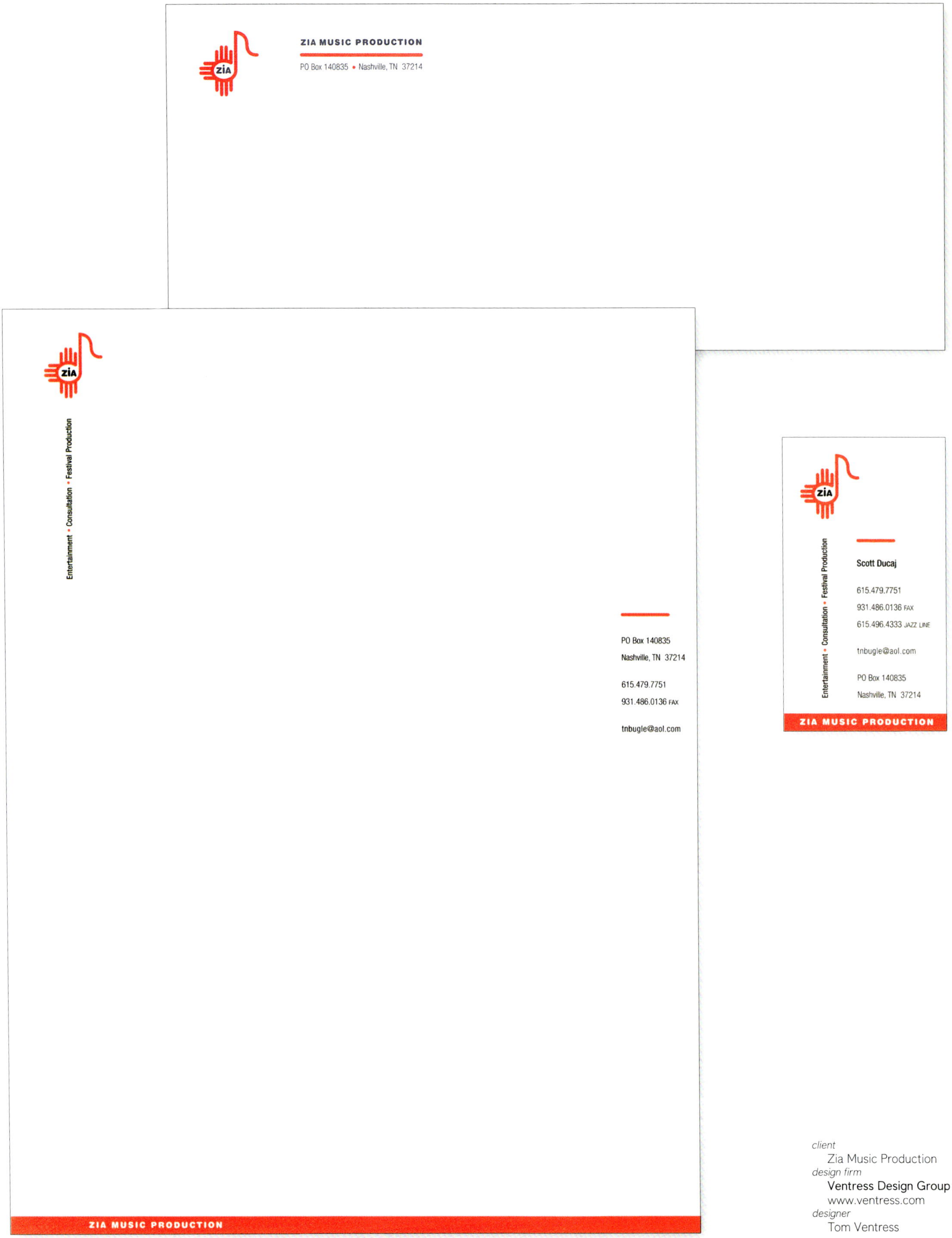

client
Zia Music Production
design firm
Ventress Design Group
www.ventress.com
designer
Tom Ventress

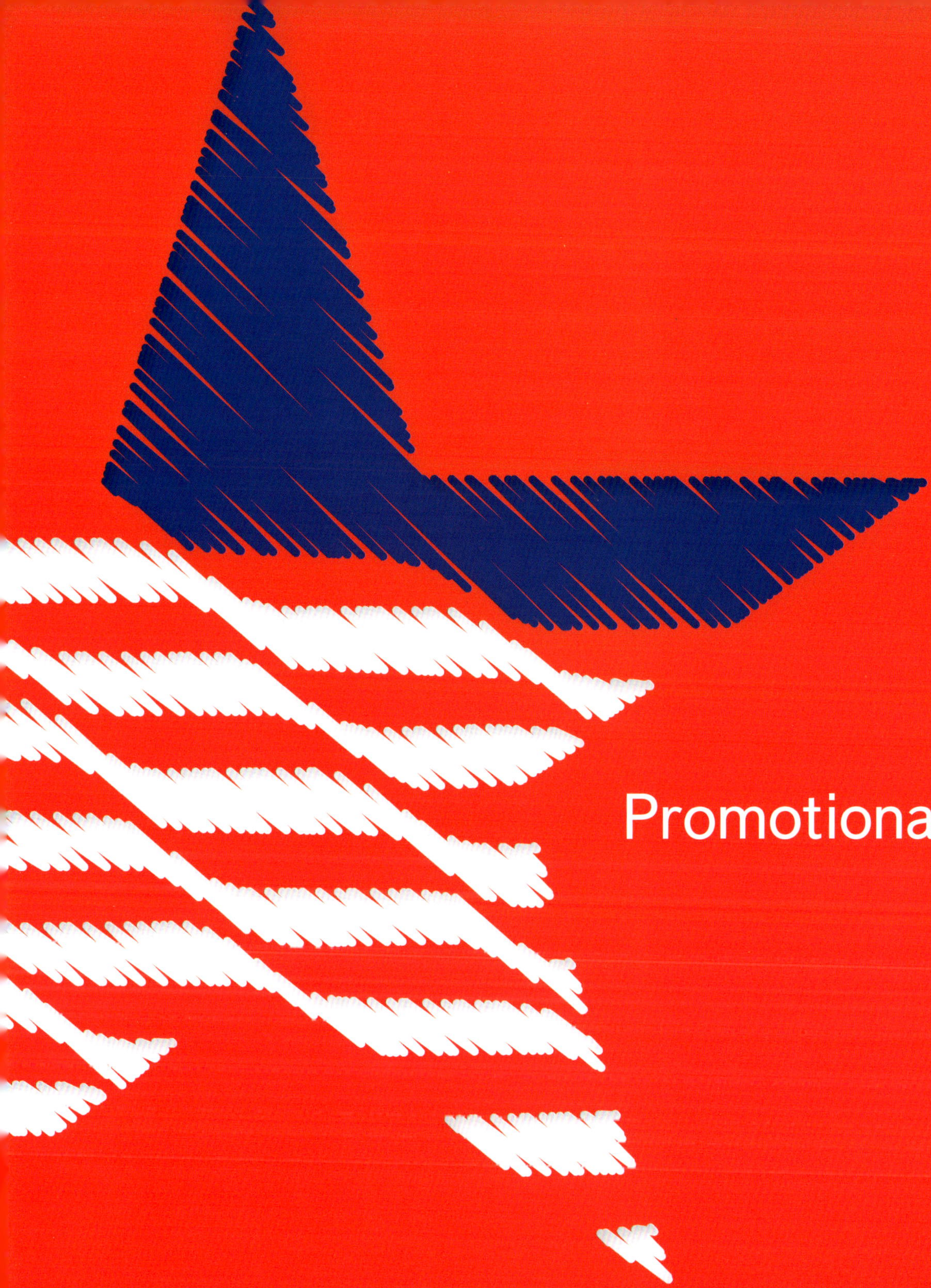

Promotional Design

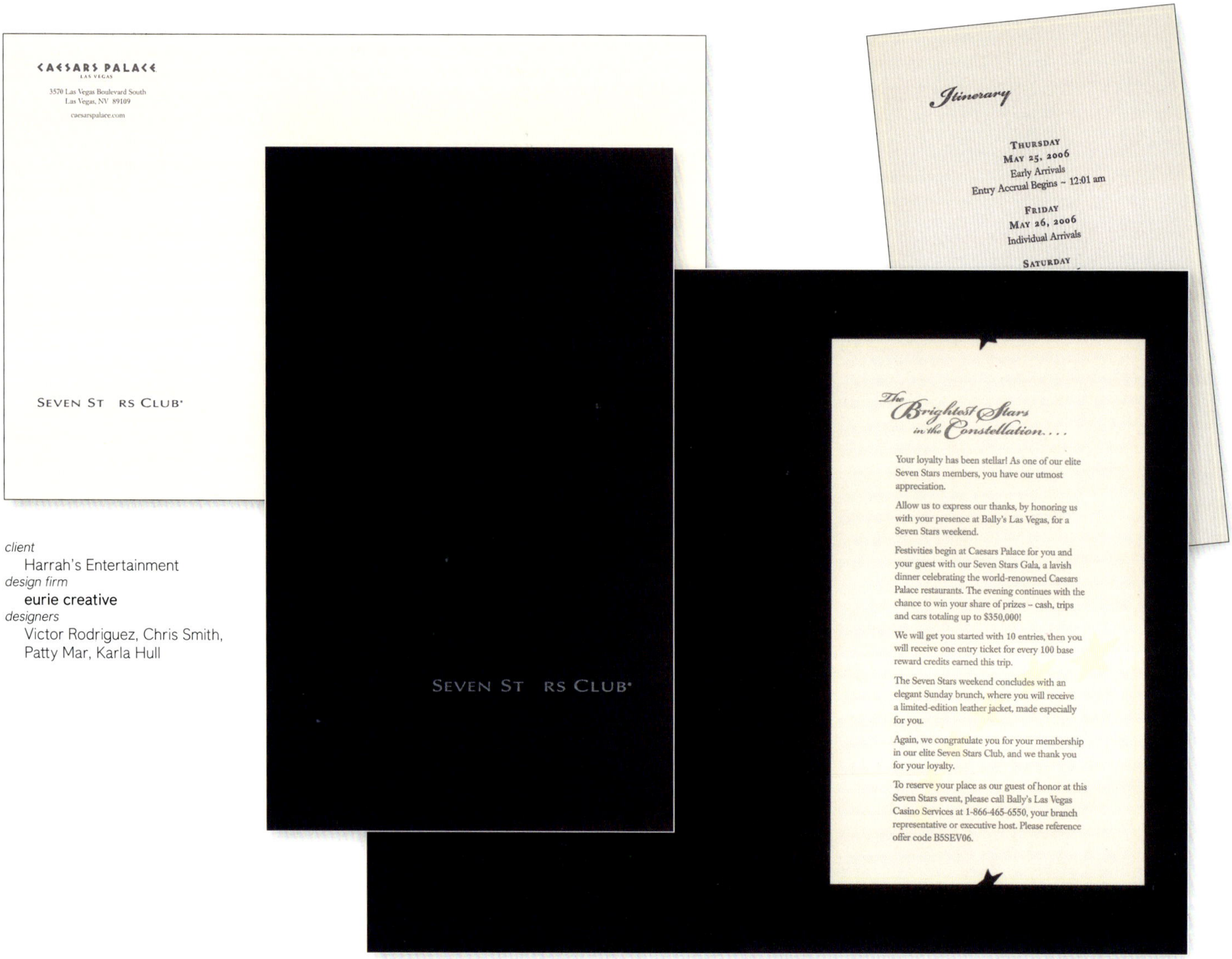

client
Harrah's Entertainment
design firm
eurie creative
designers
Victor Rodriguez, Chris Smith, Patty Mar, Karla Hull

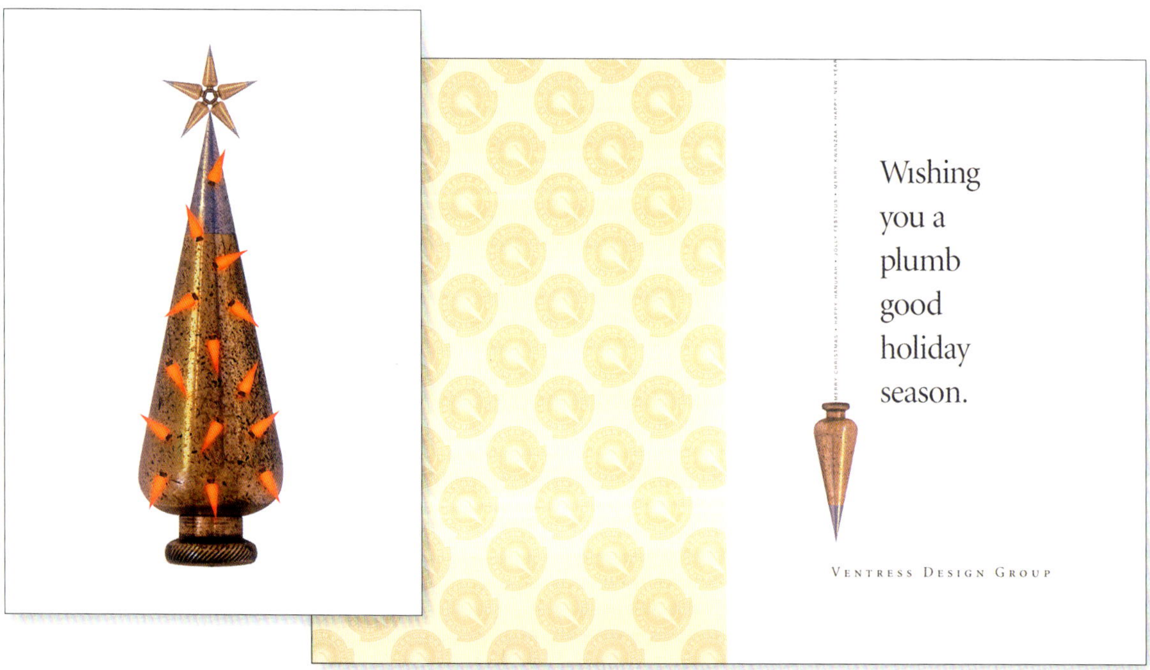

client
Ventress Design Group
design firm
Ventress Design Group
www.ventress.com
designer
Tom Ventress

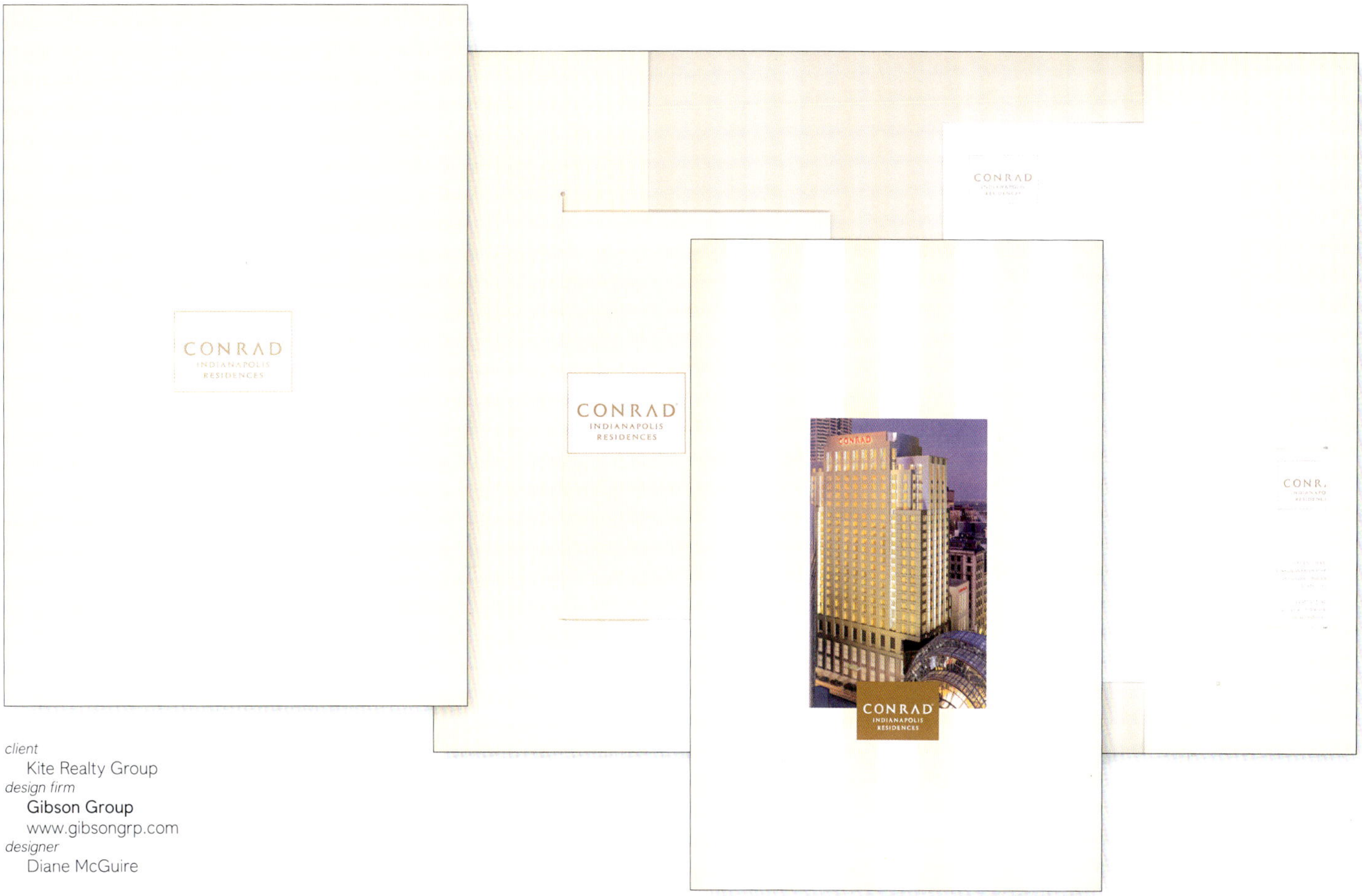

client
Kite Realty Group
design firm
Gibson Group
www.gibsongrp.com
designer
Diane McGuire

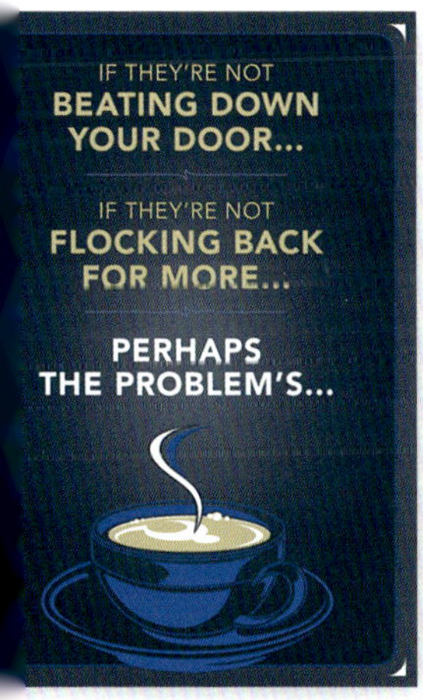

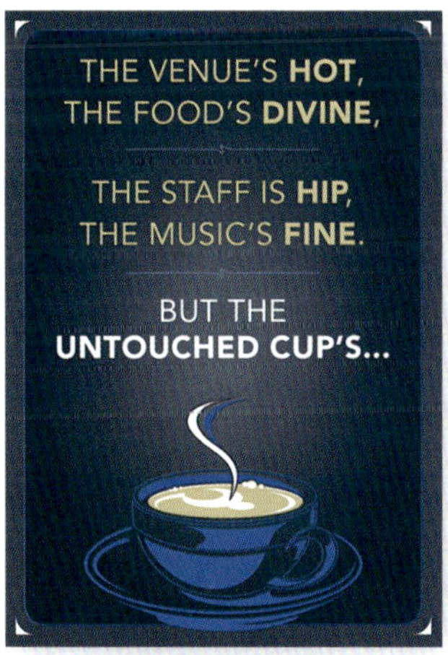

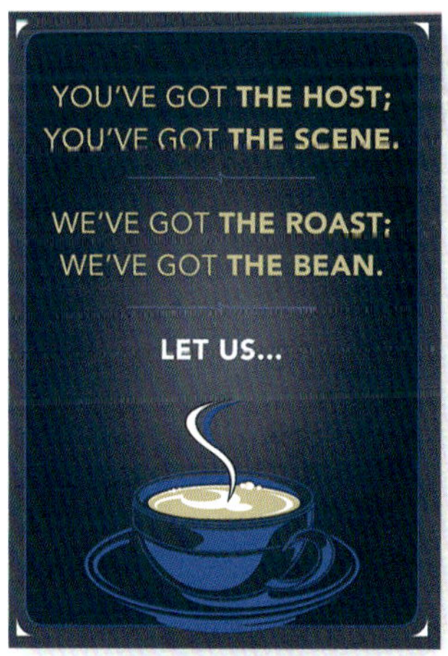

client
Saccuzzo Coffee
design firm
Fathom
Applied Strategy
www.fathom.net
designers
Bil Jenak,
Michelle Guilmette

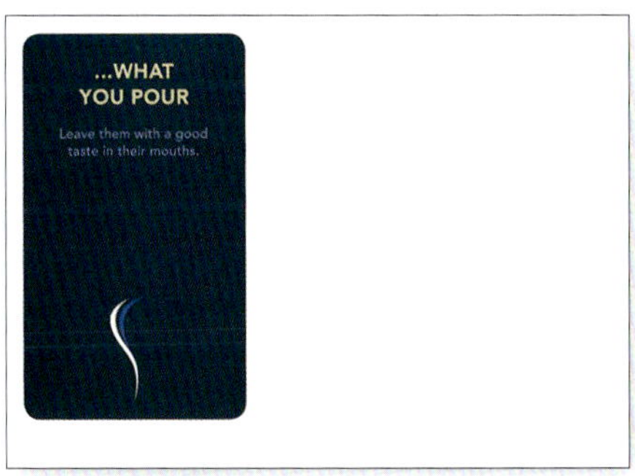

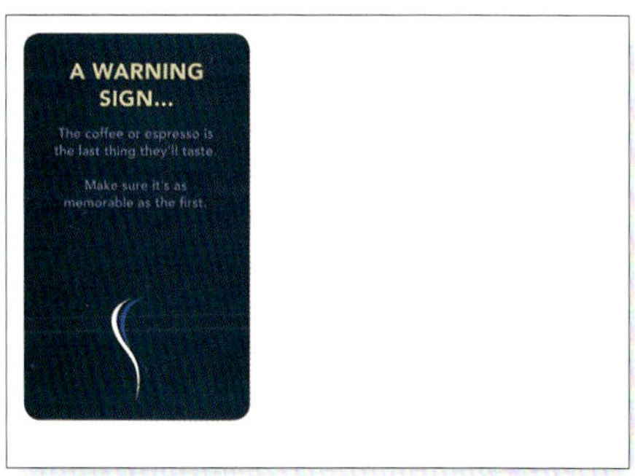

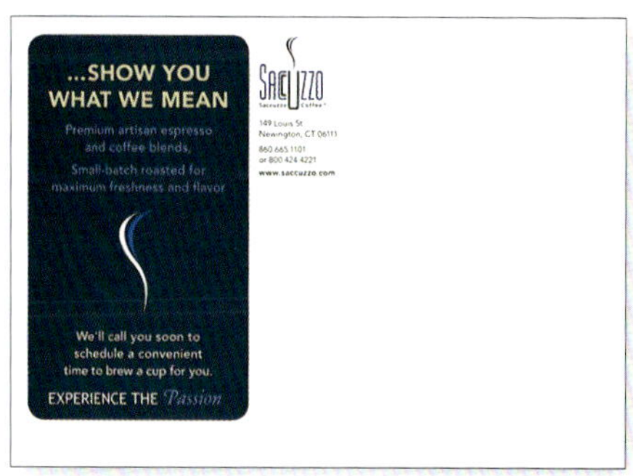

client
Wallace Church, Inc.
design firm
Wallace Church, Inc.
www.wallacechurch.com
creative director
Stan Church
designer
Maritess Manaluz

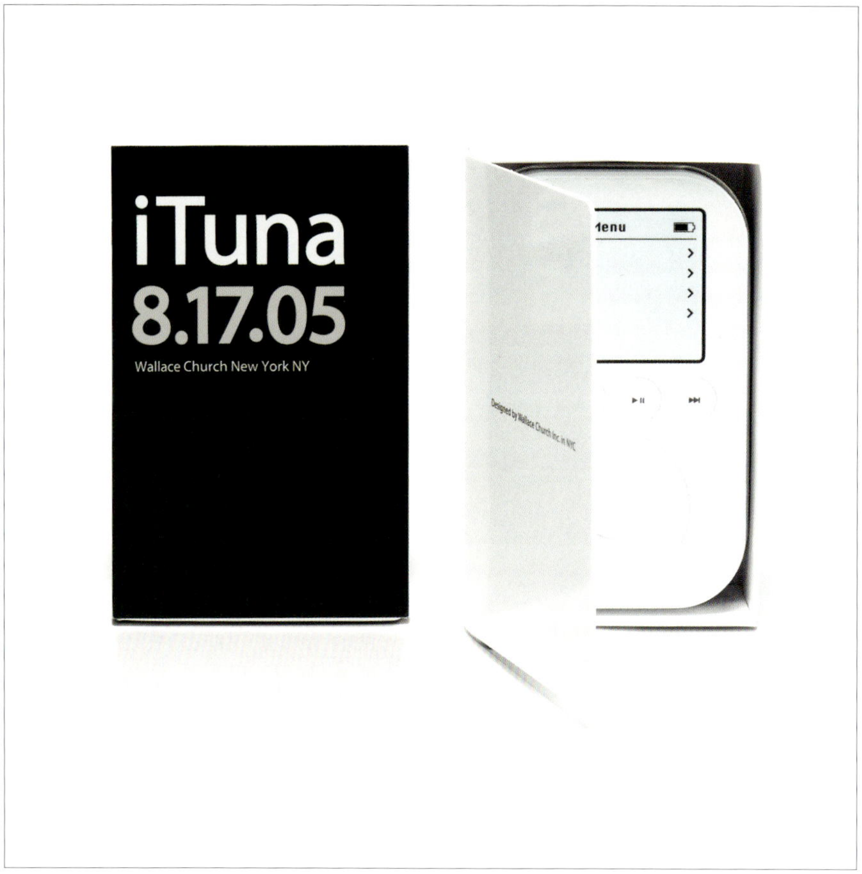

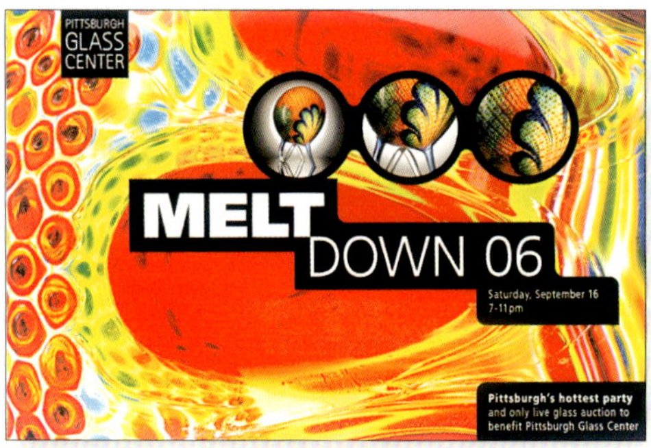

client
Pittsburgh Glass Center
design firm
Robert Meyers Design
www.robertmeyersdesign.com
designer
Robert Meyers

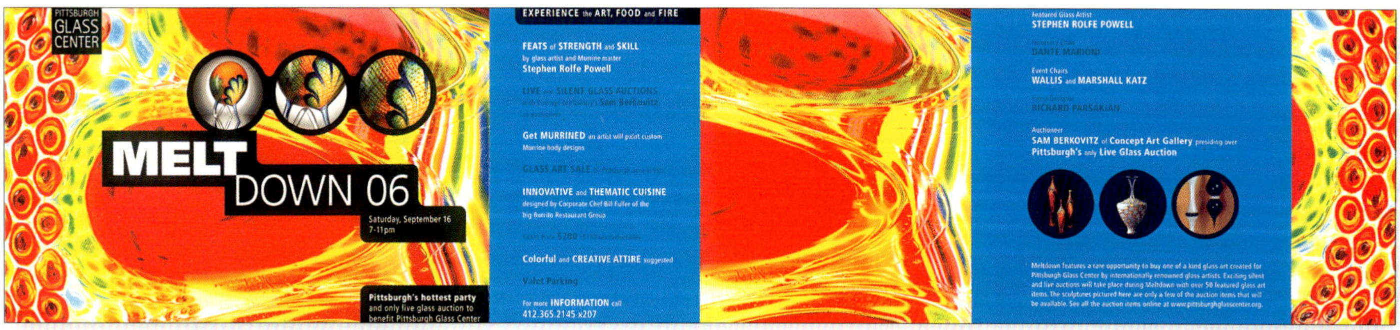

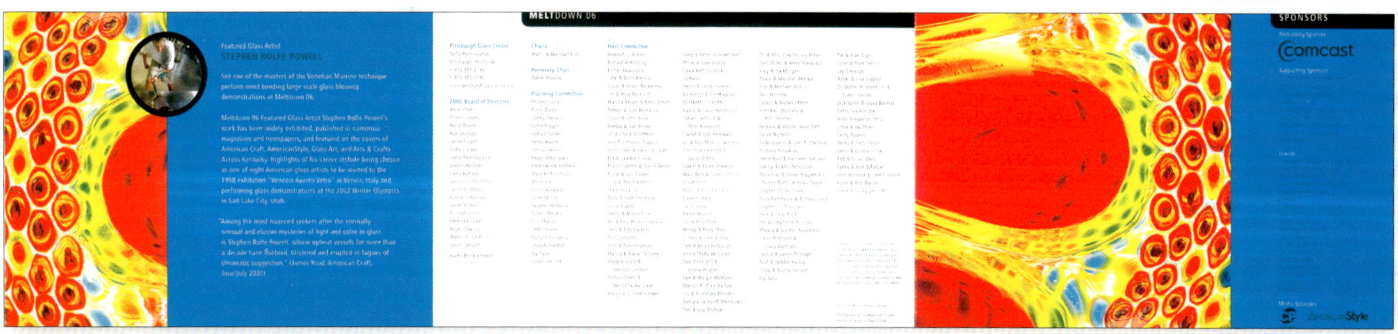

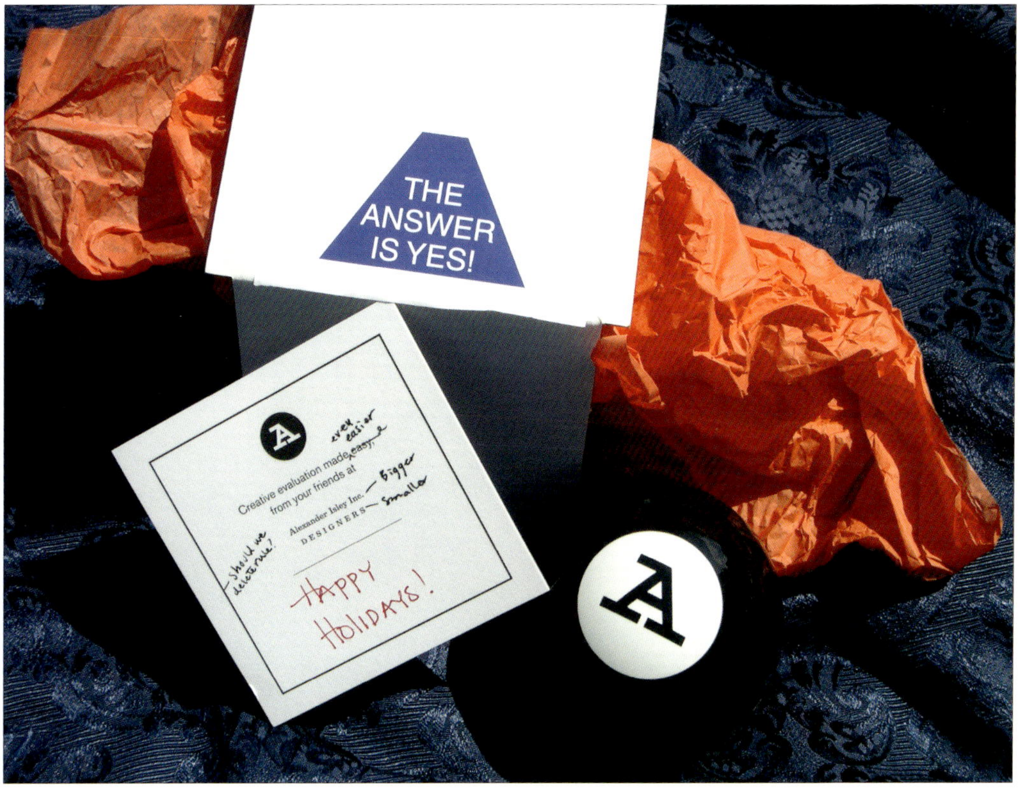

client
Alexander Isley inc.
design firm
Alexander Isley inc.
www.AlexanderIsley.com
designers
Alexander Isley,
Cherith Victorino,
George Kokkinidis

client
Mortensen Design, Inc.
design firm
Mortensen Design, Inc.
www.mortensendesign.com
art director
Gordon Mortensen
designer
Patricia Margaret

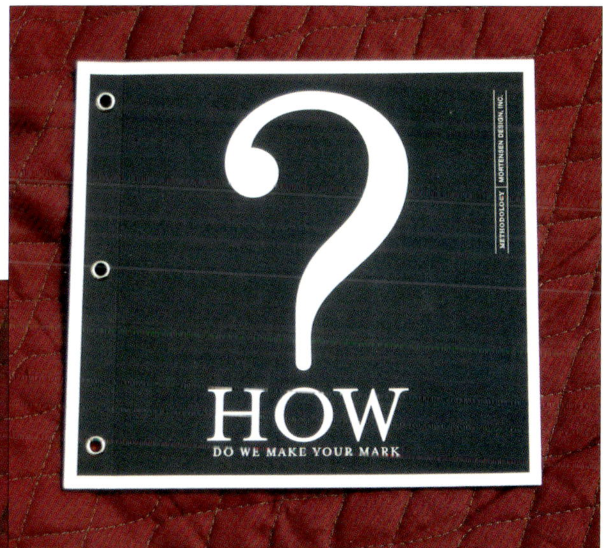

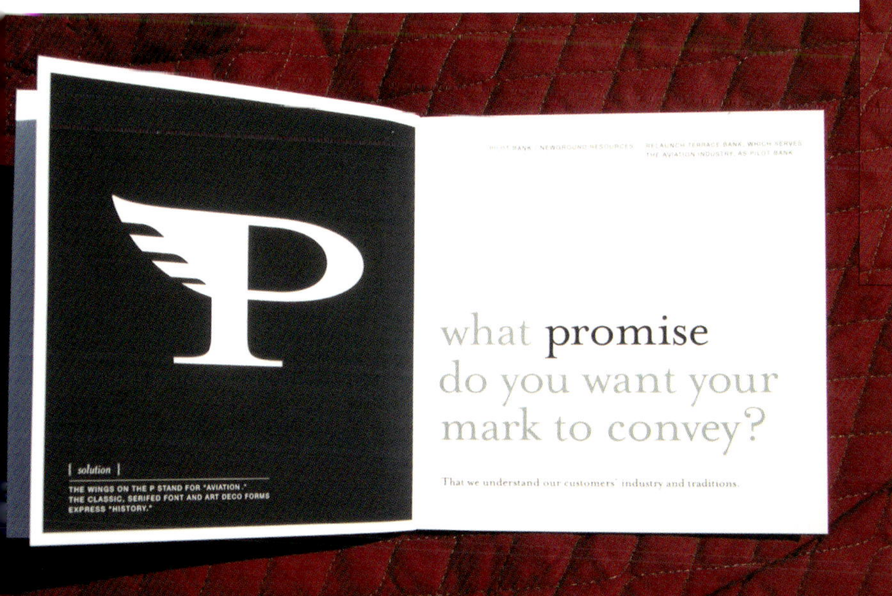

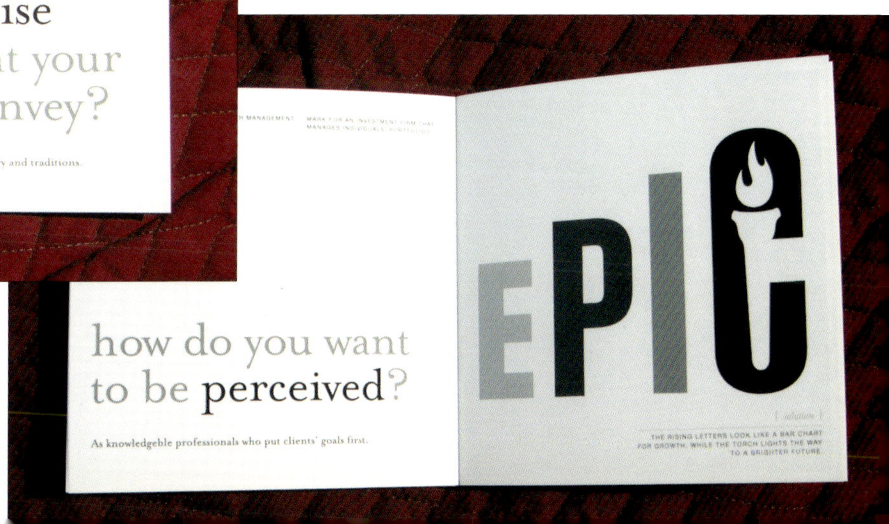

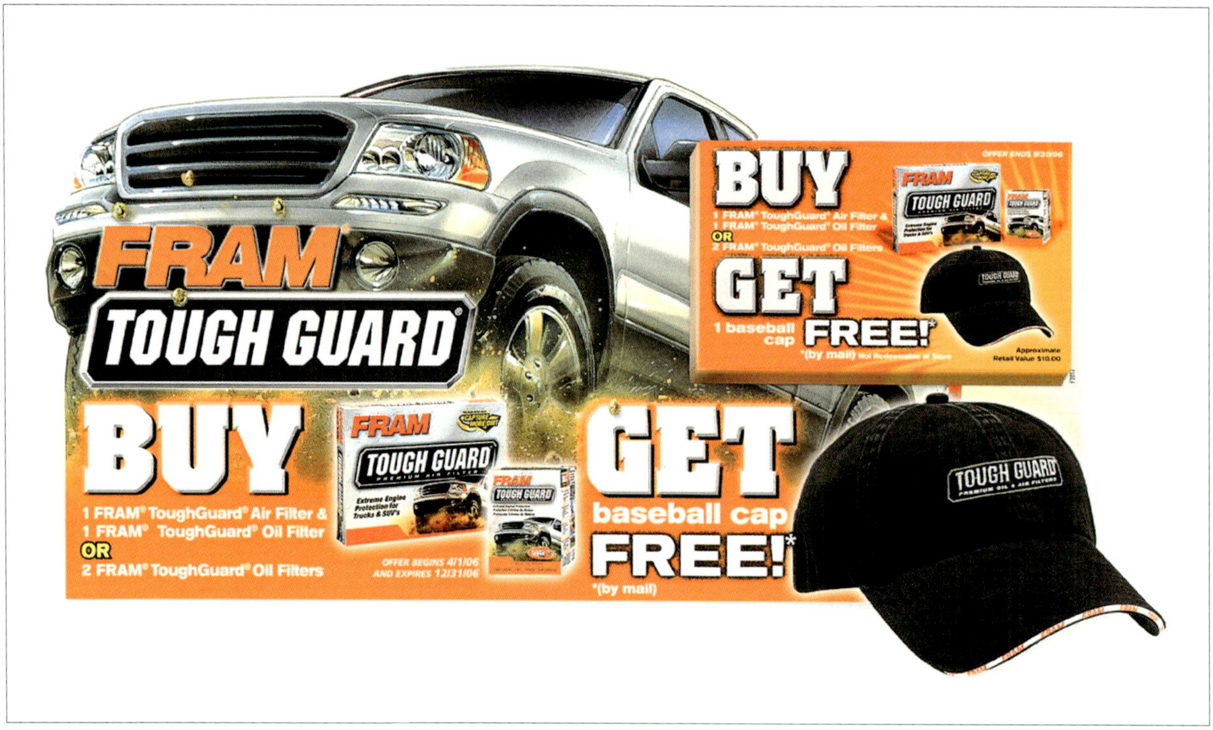

client
Honeywell Consumer Products
design firm
Tom Fowler, Inc.
www.tomfowlerinc.com
art director
Mary Ellen Butkus
designer
Brien O'Reilly

client
DeWALT
design firm
Catalpha Advertising and Design
www.catalpha.com
designers
Karen Kerski, Michael Garlitz

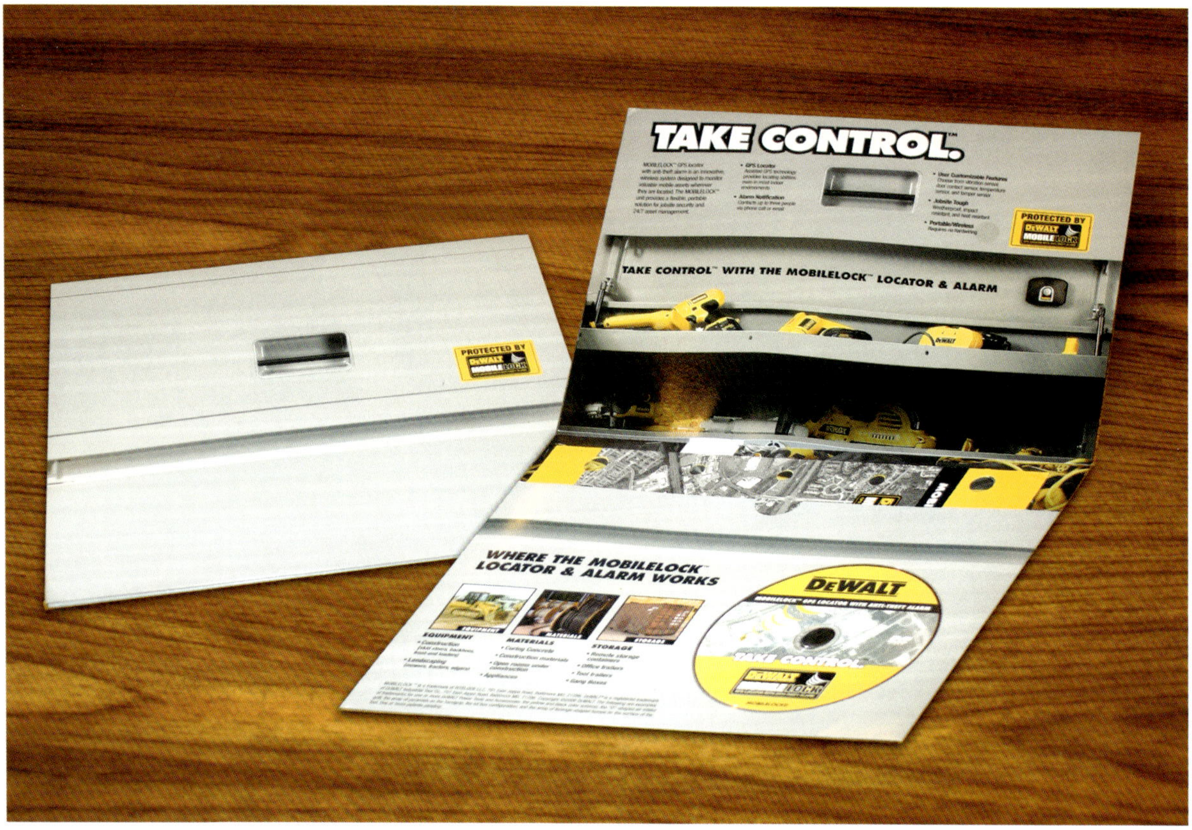

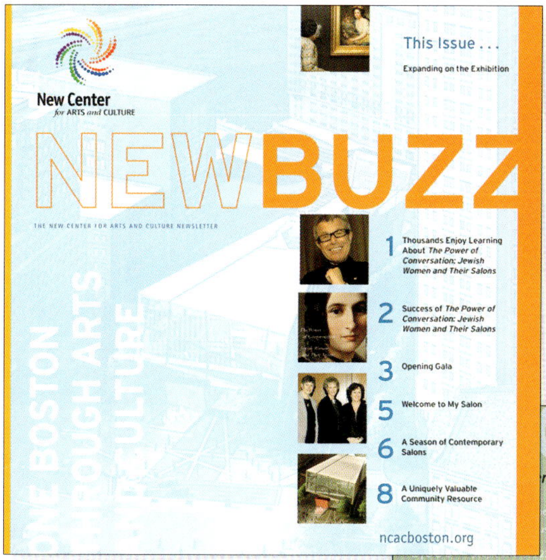

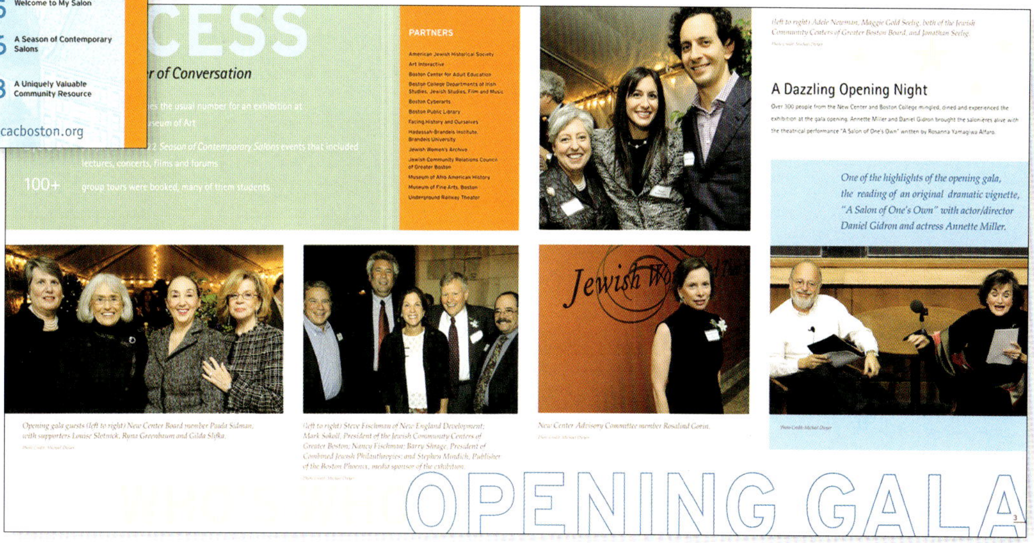

client
New Center
design firm
Gill Fishman Associates
www.gillfishmandesign.com
designer
Alicia Ozyjowski

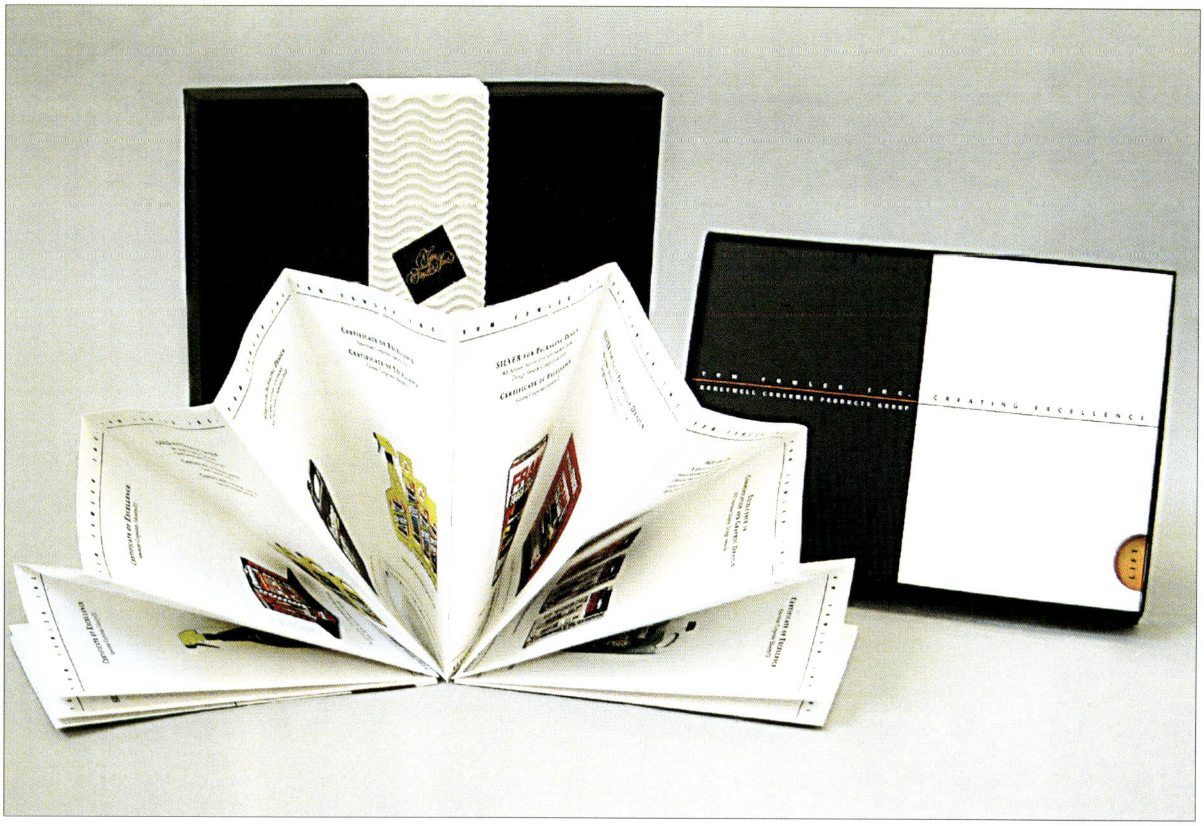

client
Tom Fowler, Inc.
design firm
Tom Fowler, Inc.
www.tomfowlerinc.com
designer
Mary Ellen Butkus

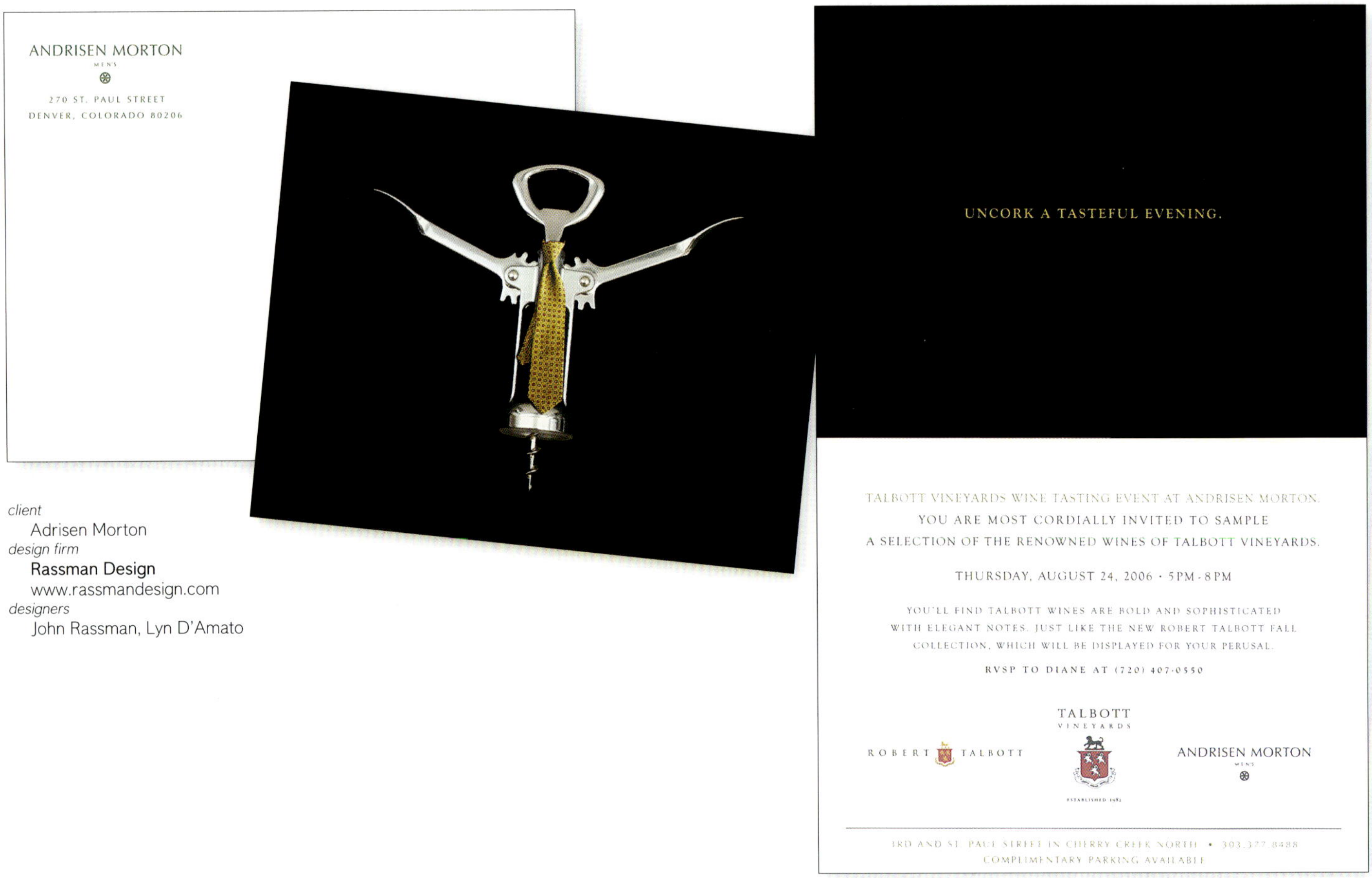

client
Adrisen Morton
design firm
Rassman Design
www.rassmandesign.com
designers
John Rassman, Lyn D'Amato

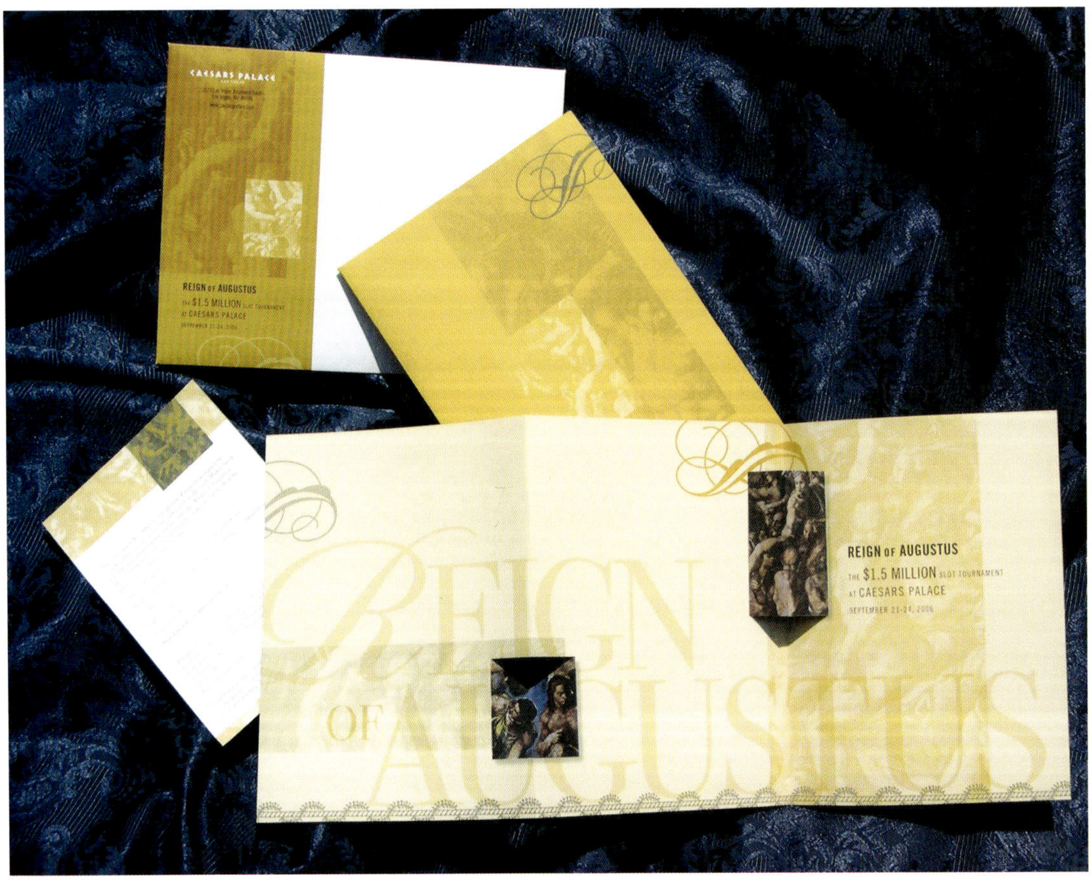

client
Caesars Palace Las Vegas
design firm
eurie creative
designers
Victor Rodriguez,
Chris Smith, Mike Enriquez

client
JDRF—Las Vegas Chapter
design firm
eurie creative
designer
Victor Rodriguez

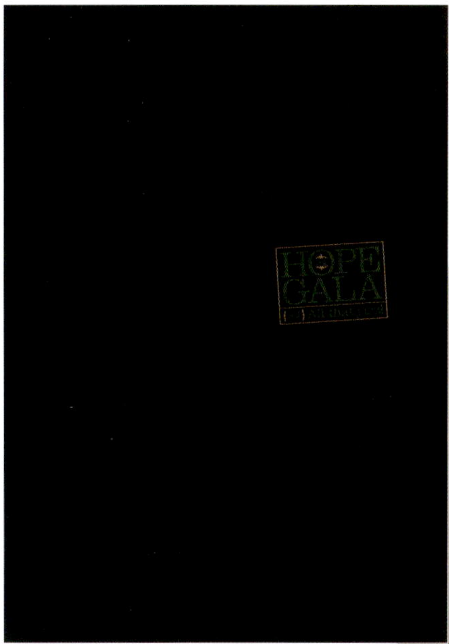

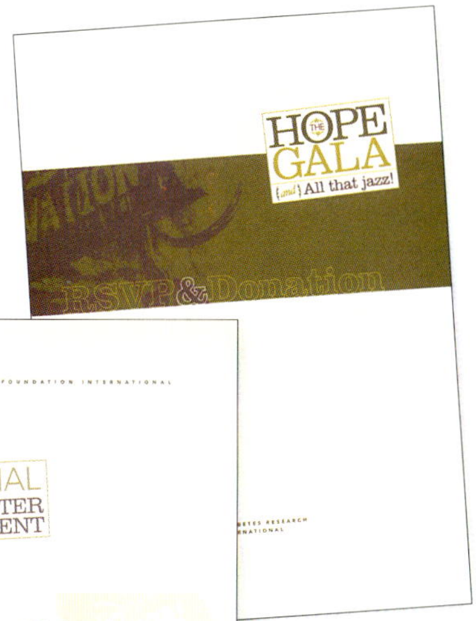

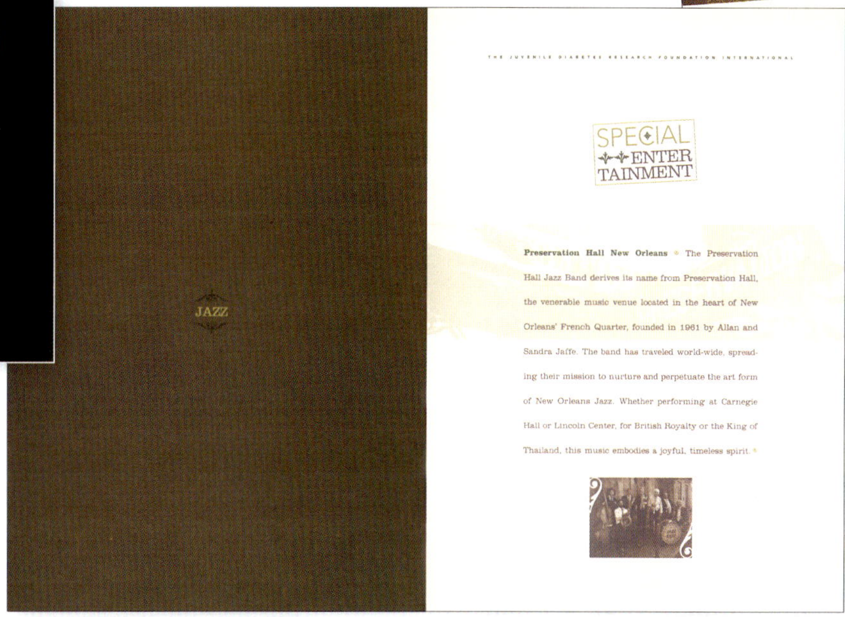

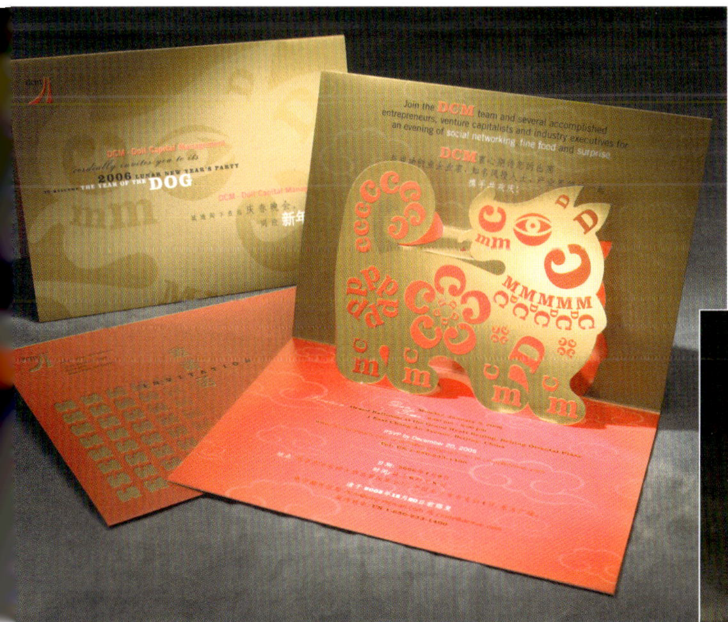

client
DCM
design firm
Gee + Chung Design
www.geechungdesign.com
designers
Earl Gee, Fani Chung

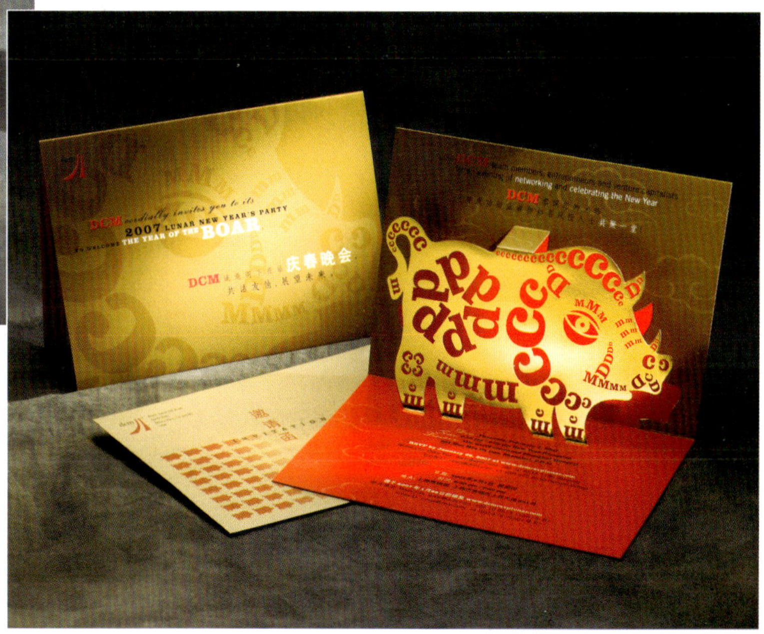

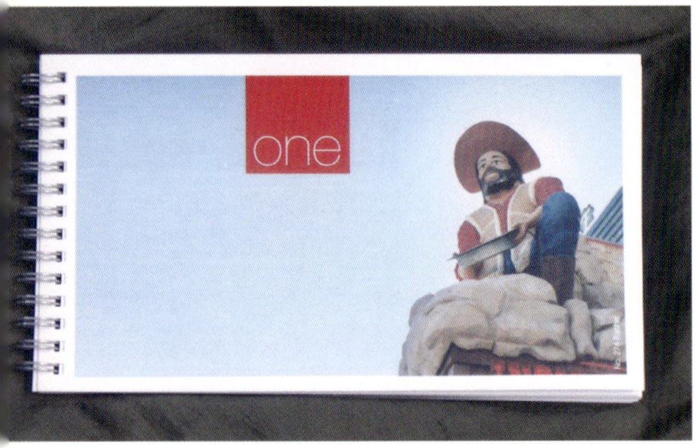

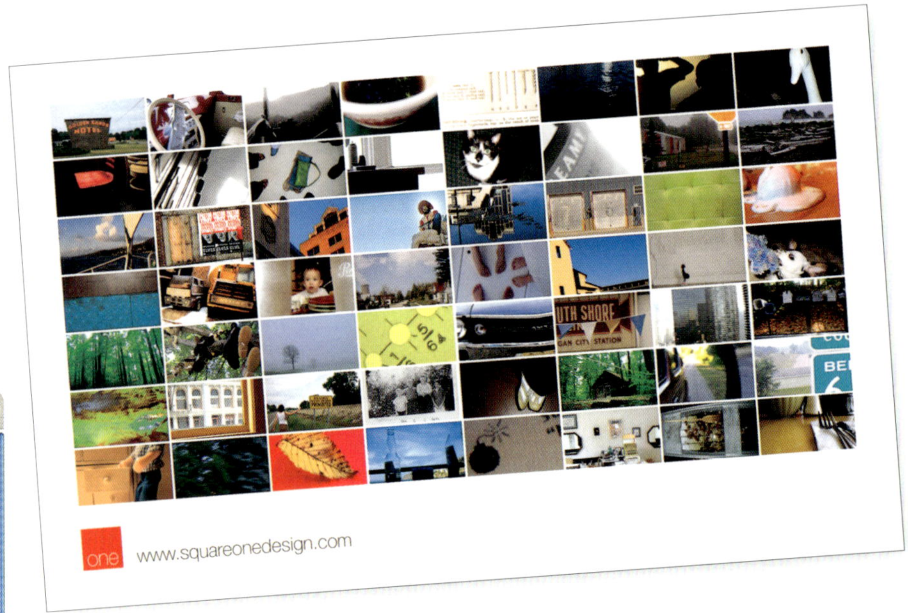

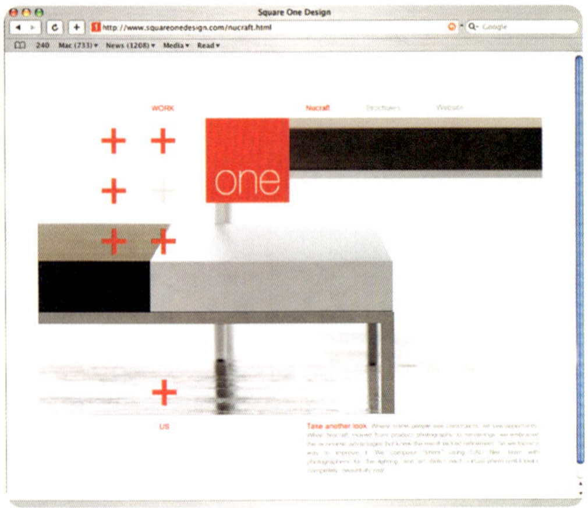

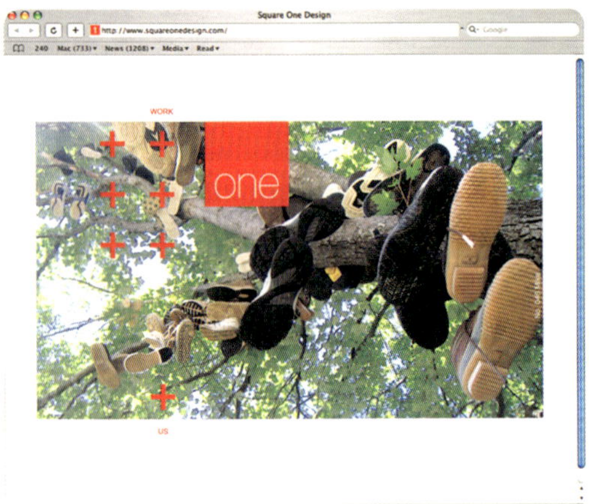

client
Square One Design
design firm
Square One Design
www.wordencompany.com
designers
Anna Huddleston, John Totten,
Lin Ver Meulen, Mike Gorman

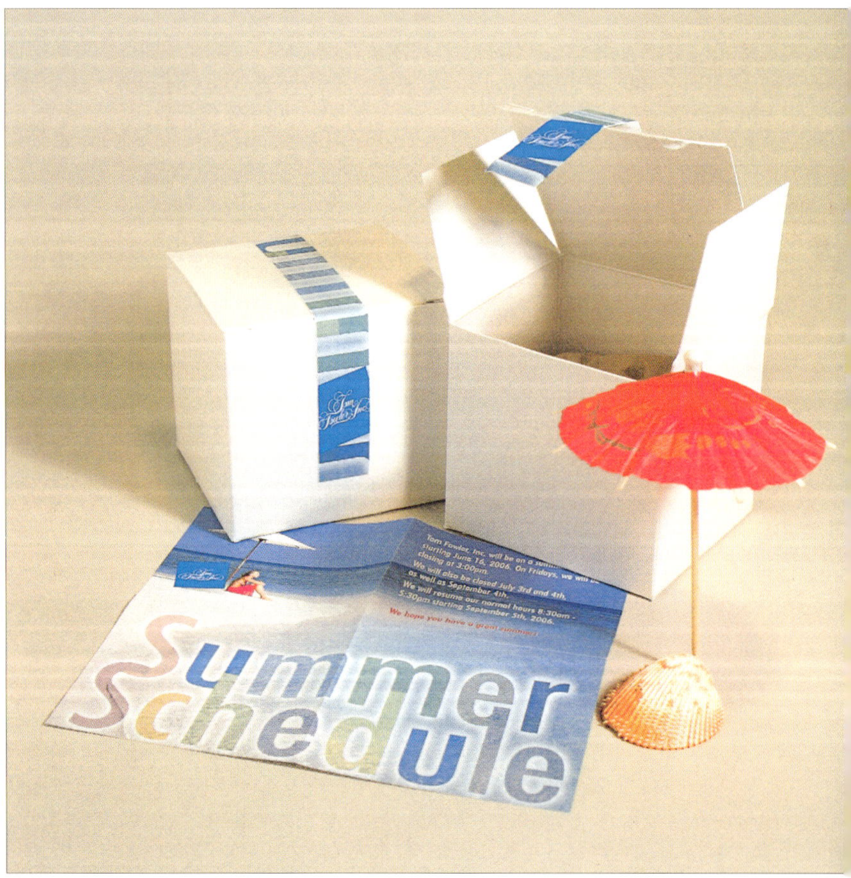

client
Tom Fowler, Inc.
design firm
Tom Fowler, Inc.
www.tomfowlerinc.com
designer
Elizabeth P. Ball

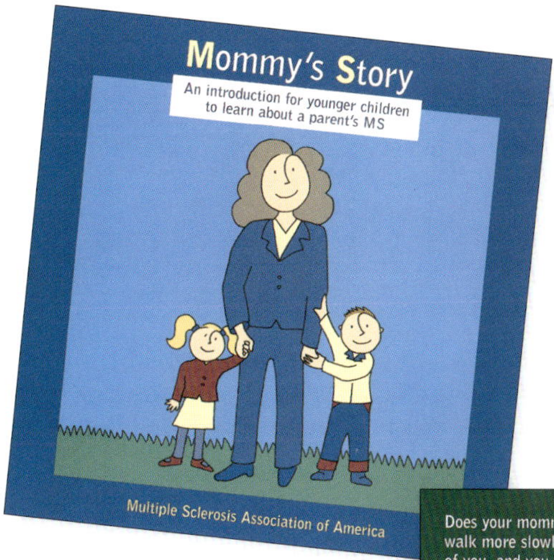

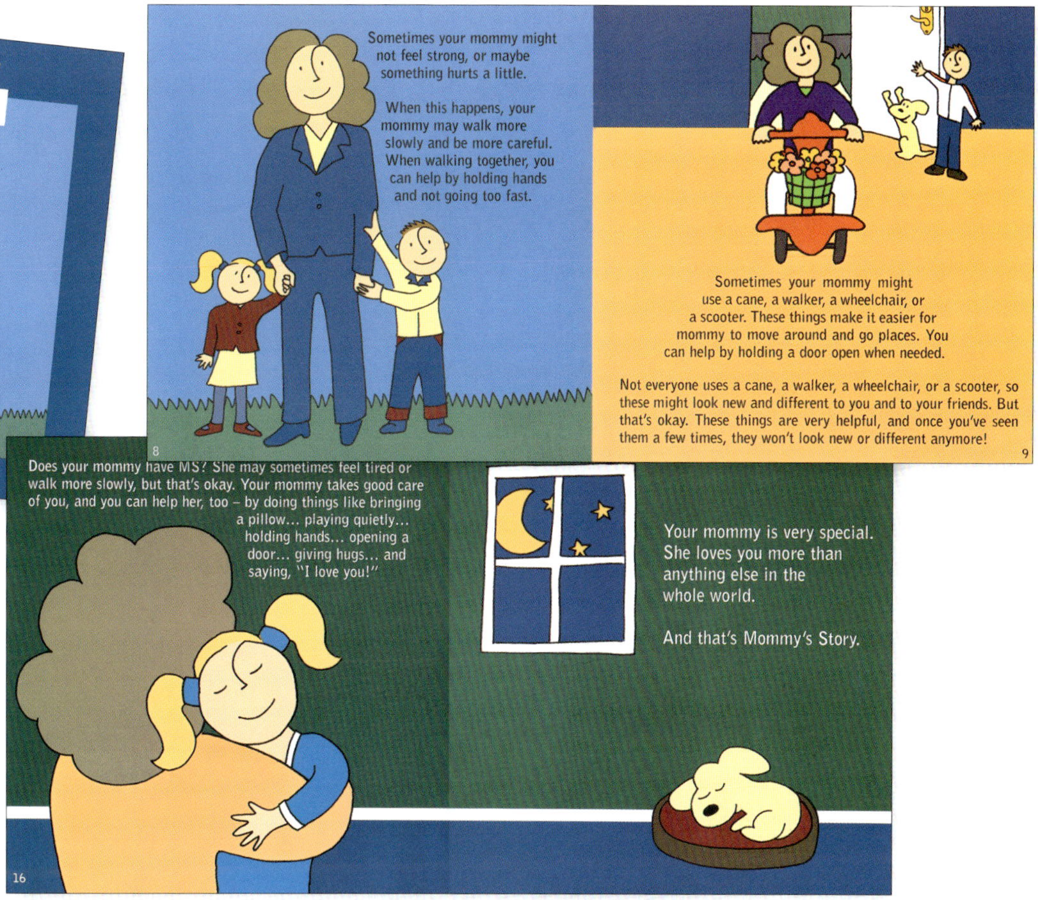

client
Multiple Sclerosis Association of America
design firm
Speedy Motorcycle Studio
www.speedymotorcycle.com
designer
E. June Roberts-Lunn

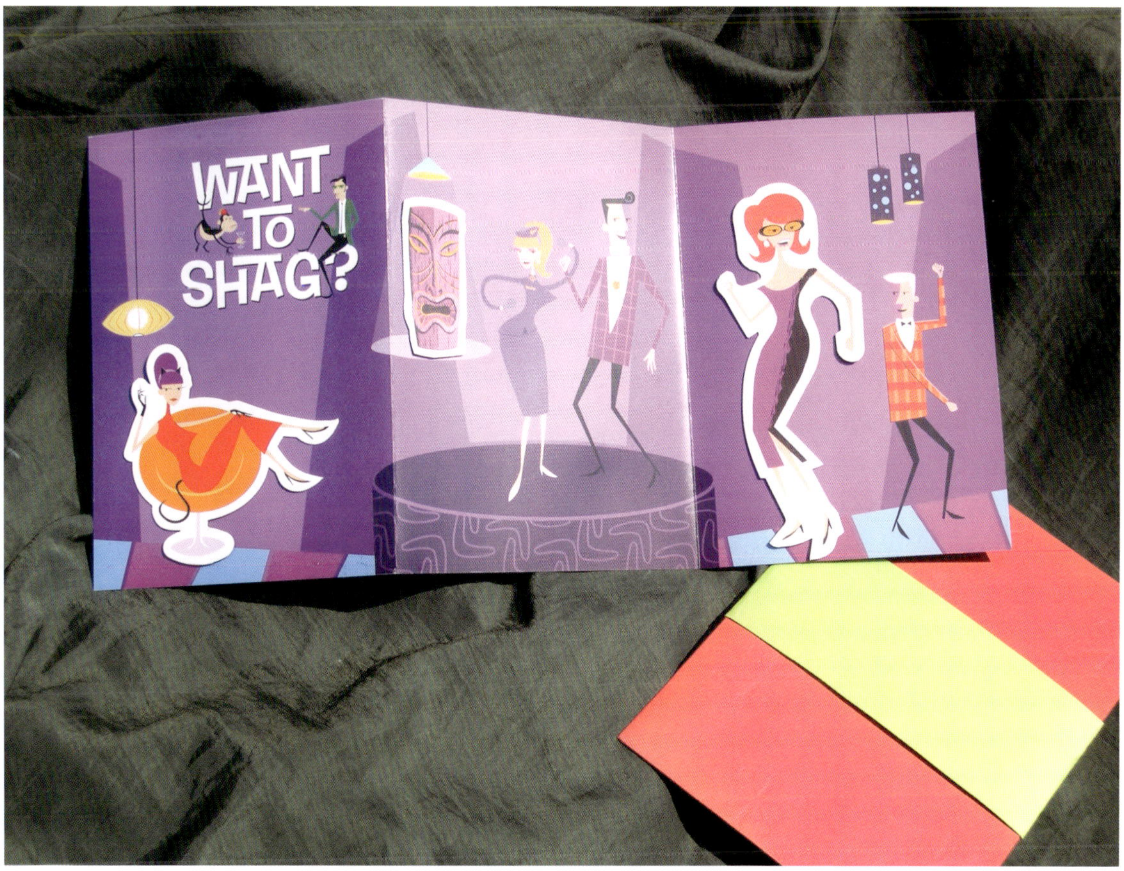

client
AIGA Las Vegas
design firm
eurie creative
designers
Victor Rodriguez,
Chris Smith,
Patty Mar,
Jan Jonas

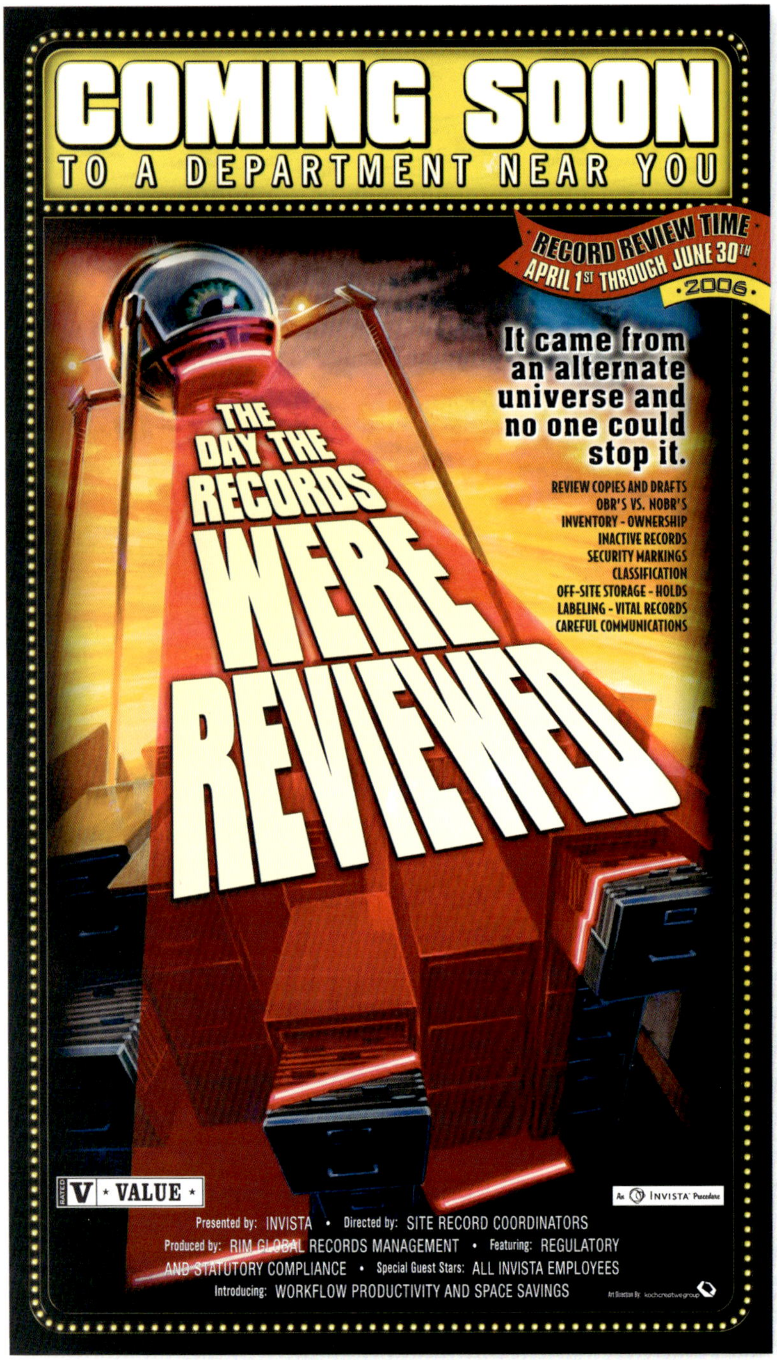

client
Invista
design firm
Koch Creative Group
www.kochcreativegroup.com
creative director
Kay Davis
art director
Dustin Commer
illustrator
Scott Dawson
copywriter
Jason Fortune

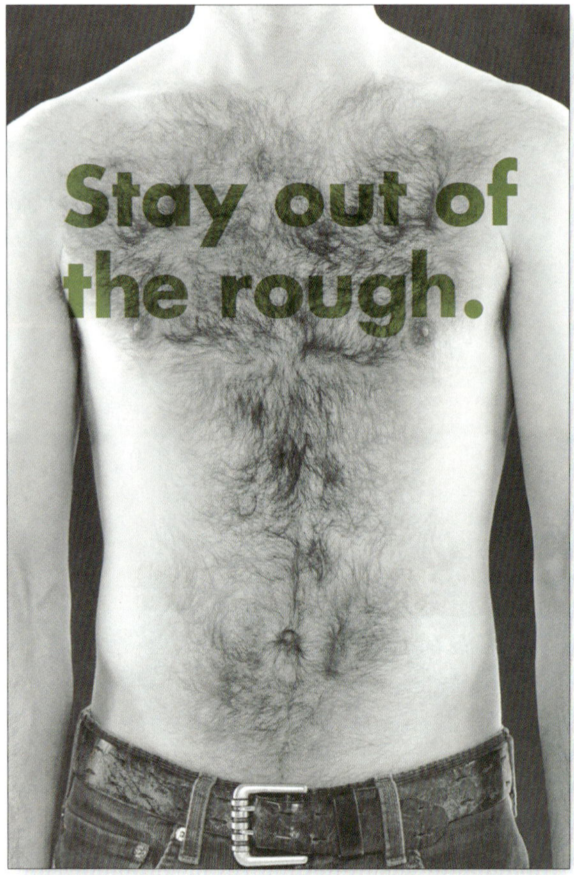

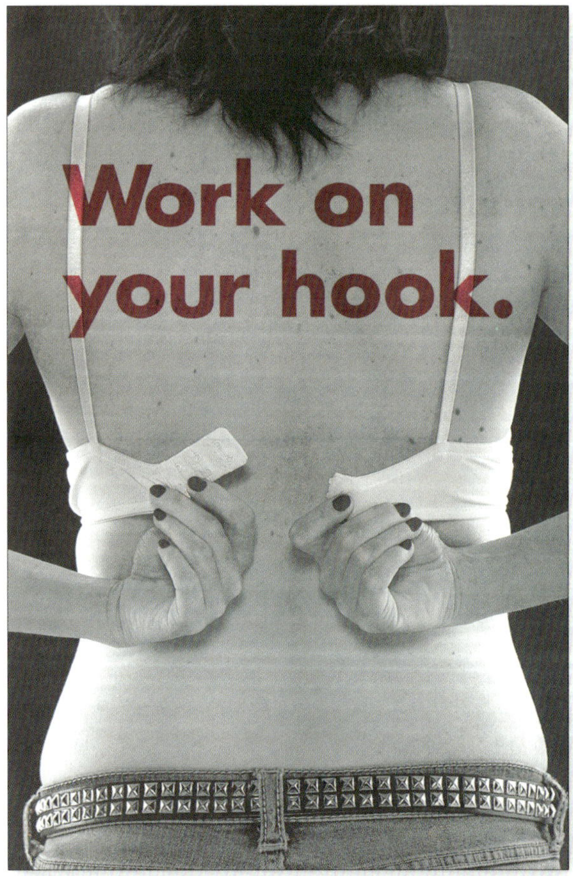

client
Ad Club of West Michigan
design firm
Square One Design
designers
Martin Schoenborn,
Mike Gorman

client
University Galleries
design firm
Connie Hwang Design
www.conniehwangdesign.com
designer
Connie Hwang

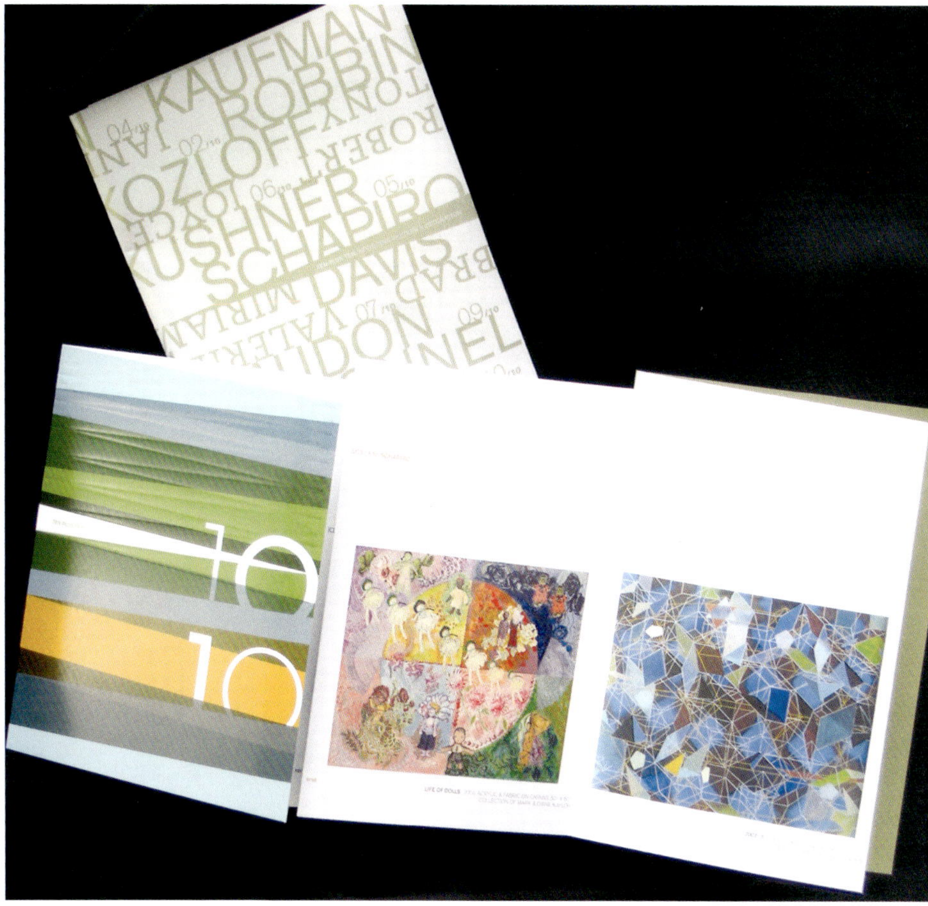

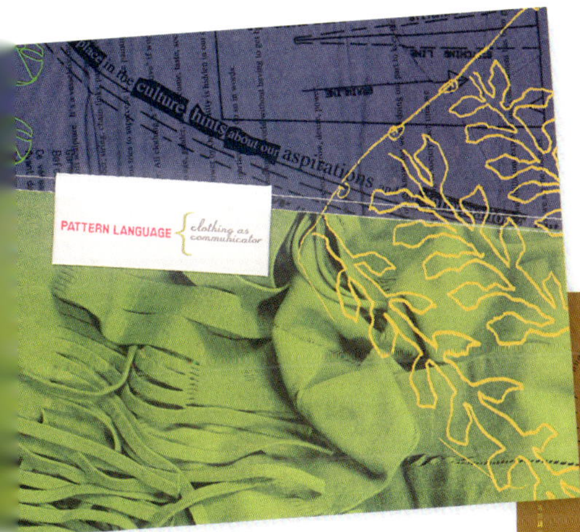

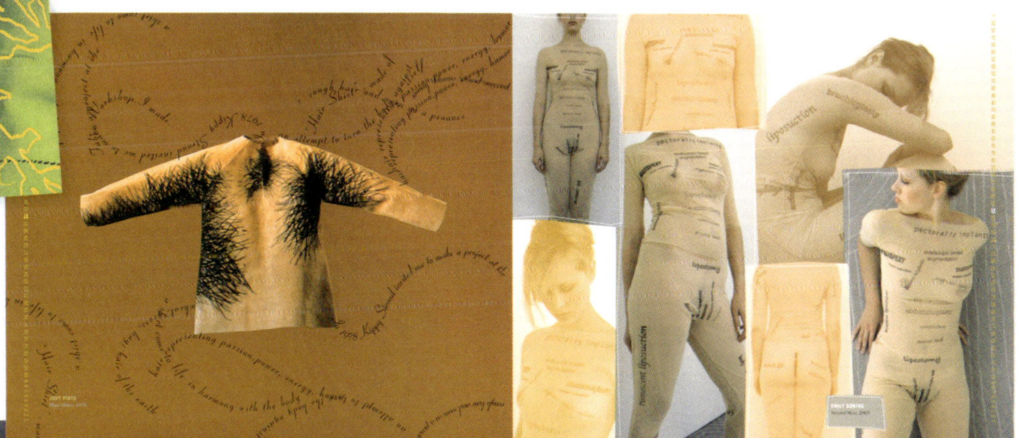

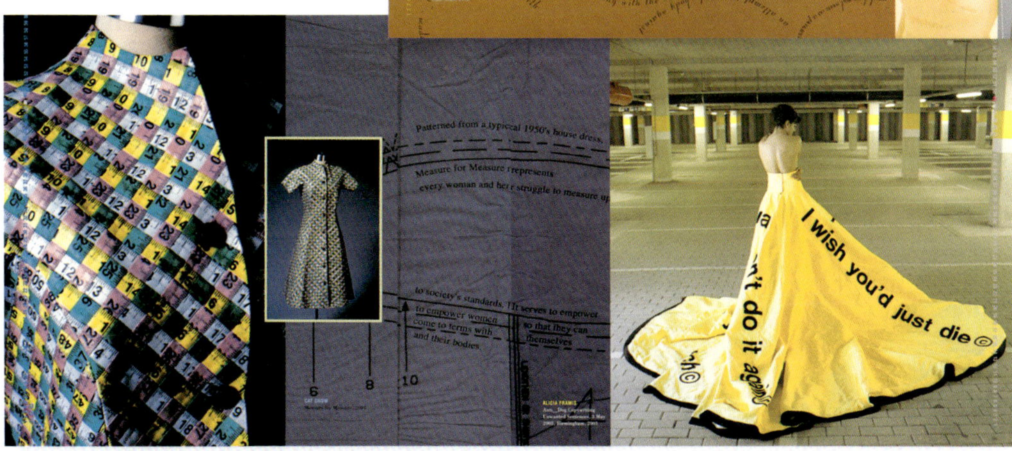

client
Tufts University
design firm
Sheriff Design
designer
Paul Sheriff

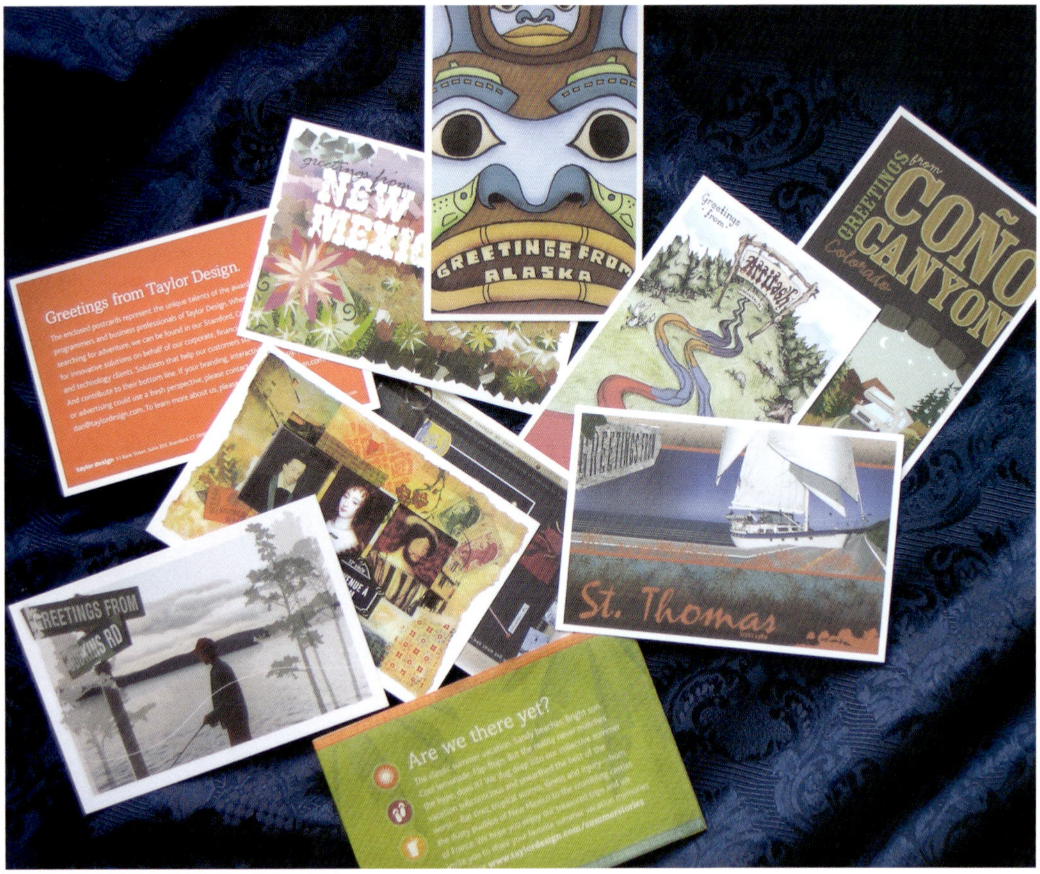

client
Taylor Design
design firm
Taylor Design
www.taylordesign.com
designers
Suzy Reusch, Hannah Fichaualer

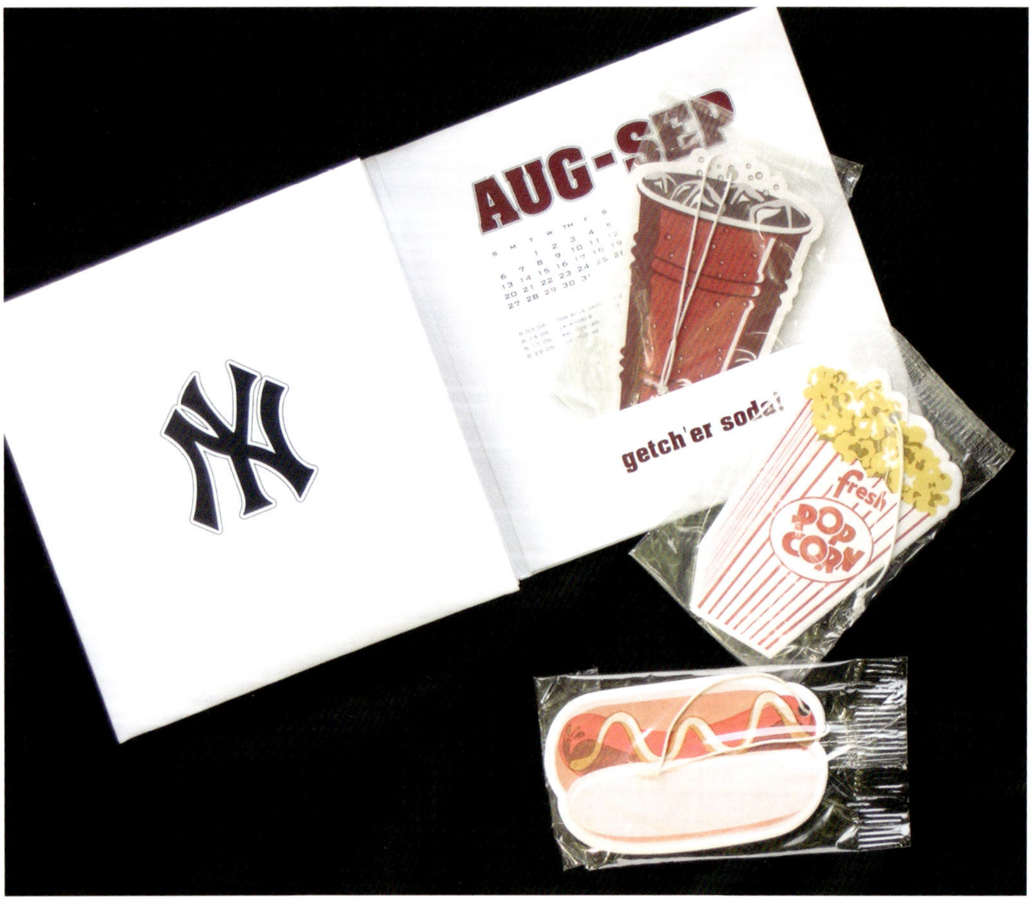

client
Wallace Church, Inc.
design firm
Wallace Church, Inc.
www.wallacechurch.com
creative director
Stan Church
designer
Jhomy Irrazaba

client
Invista
design firm
Koch Creative Group
www.kochcreativegroup.com
creative director
Kay Davis
art director
Dustin Commer
illustrator
Scott Dawson
copywriter
Jason Fortune

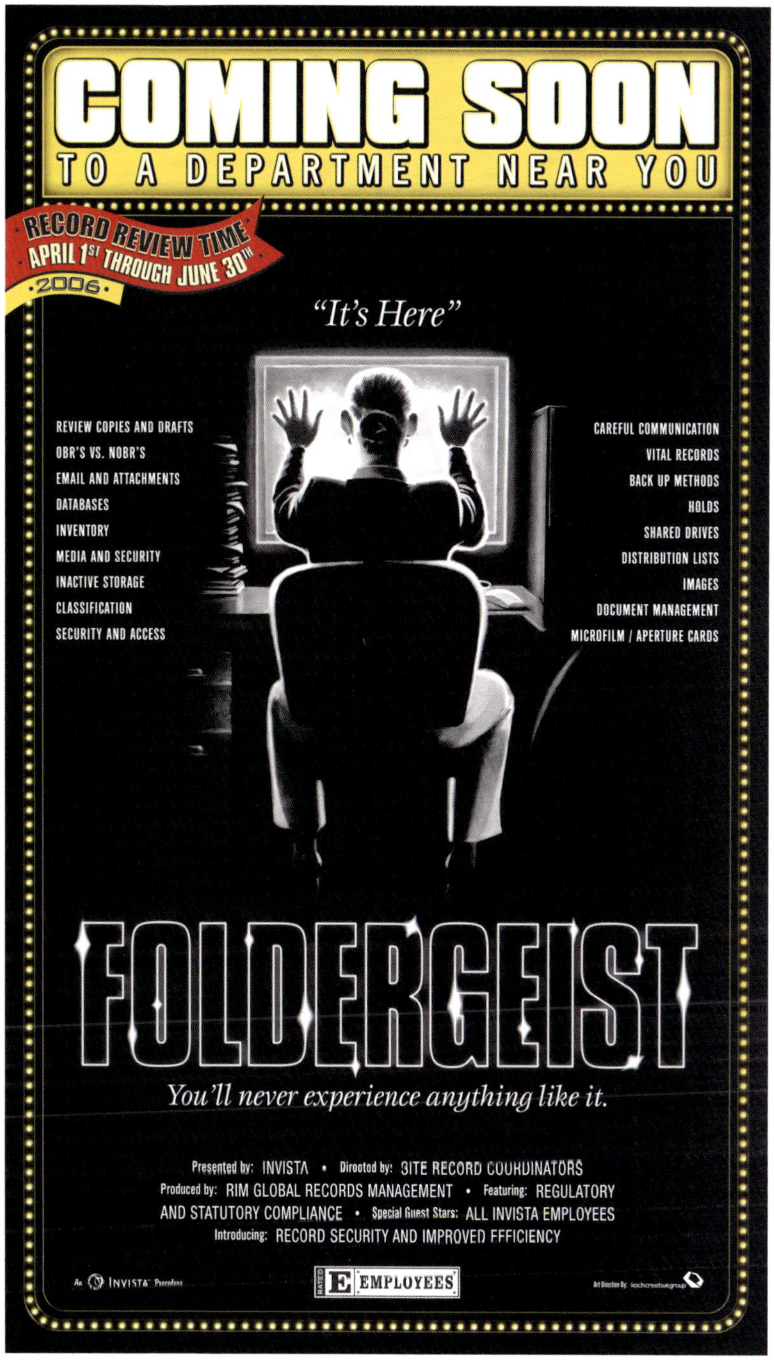

client
Paris Las Vegas
design firm
eurie creative
designers
Victor Rodriguez, Karla Hull

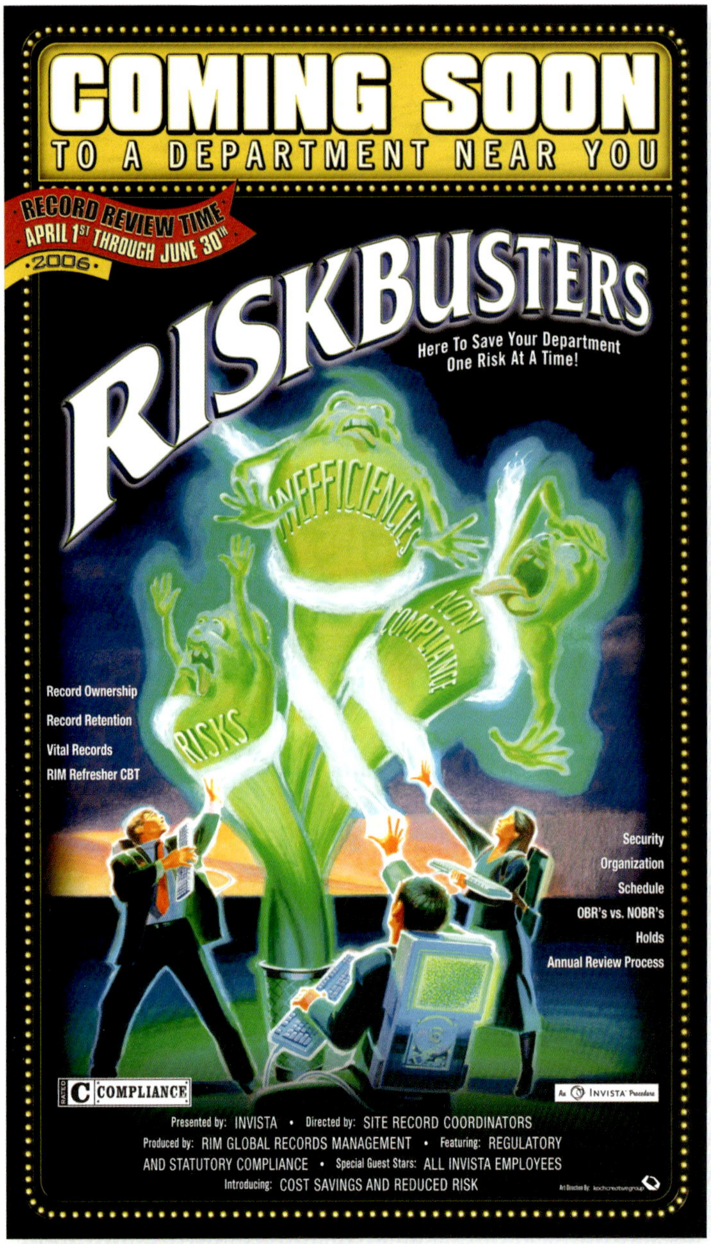

client
Invista
design firm
Koch Creative Group
www.kochcreativegroup.com
creative director
Kay Davis
art director
Dustin Commer
illustrator
Scott Dawson
copywriter
Jason Fortune

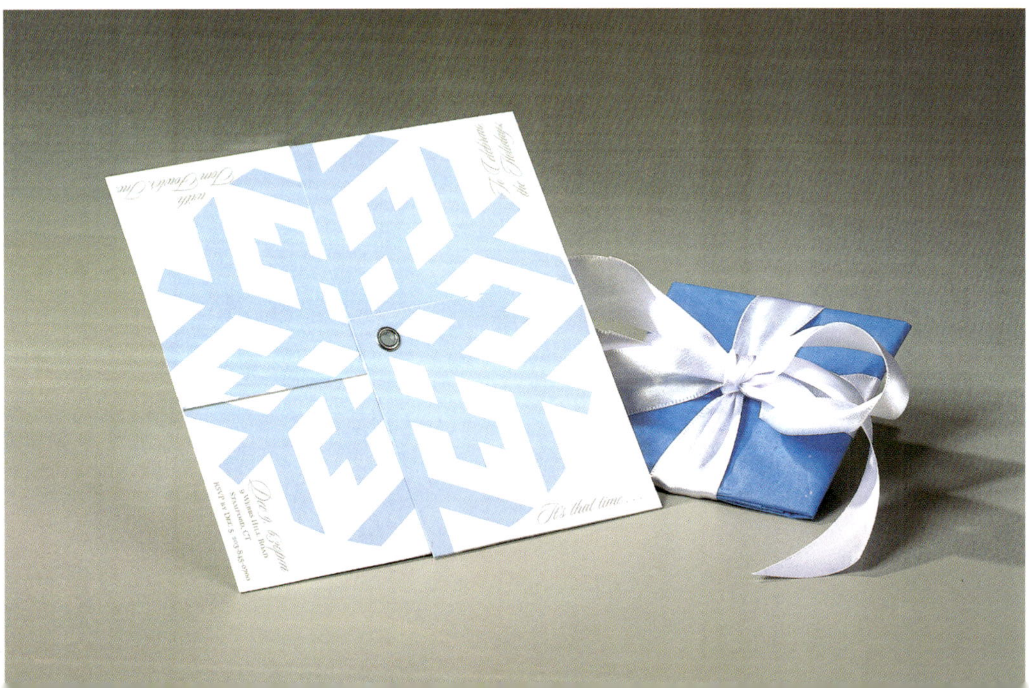

client
Tom Fowler, Inc.
design firm
Tom Fowler, Inc.
www.tomfowlerinc.com
designers
Elizabeth P. Ball,
Brien O'Reilly

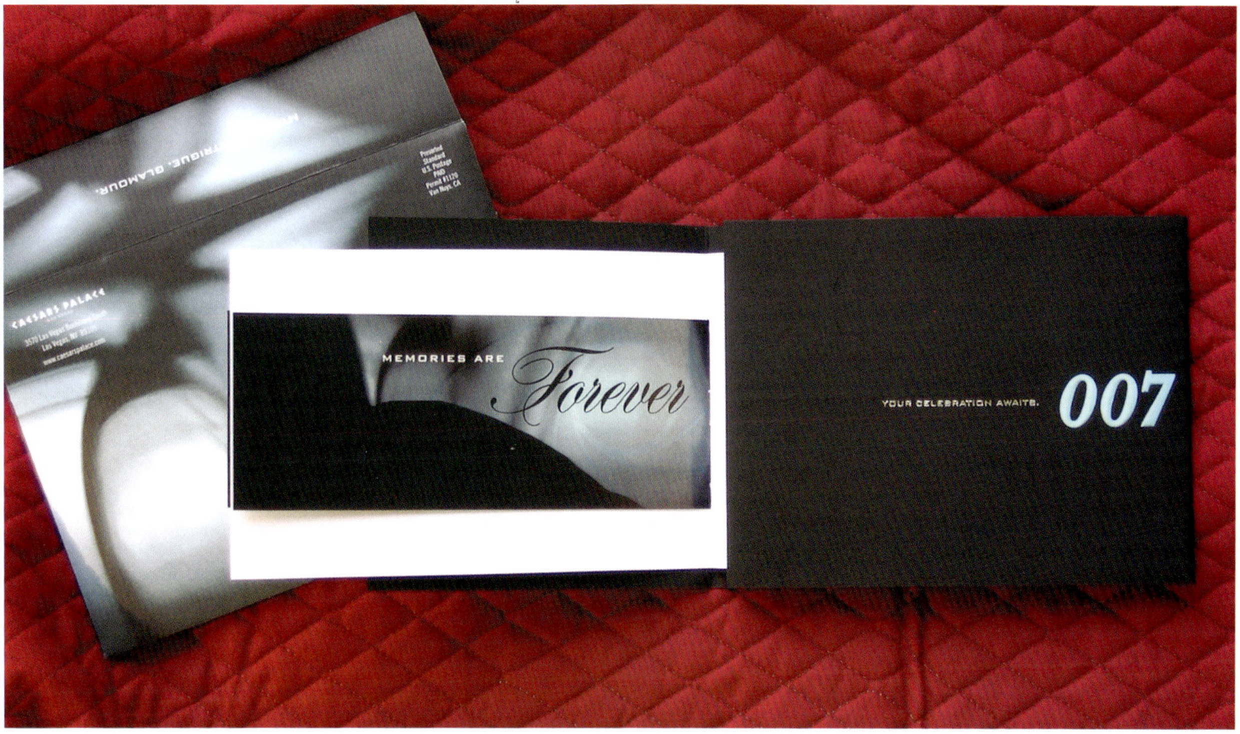

client
Caesars Palace Las Vegas
design firm
eurie creative
designers
Victor Rodriguez, Chris Smith, Mike Enriquez, Karla Hull

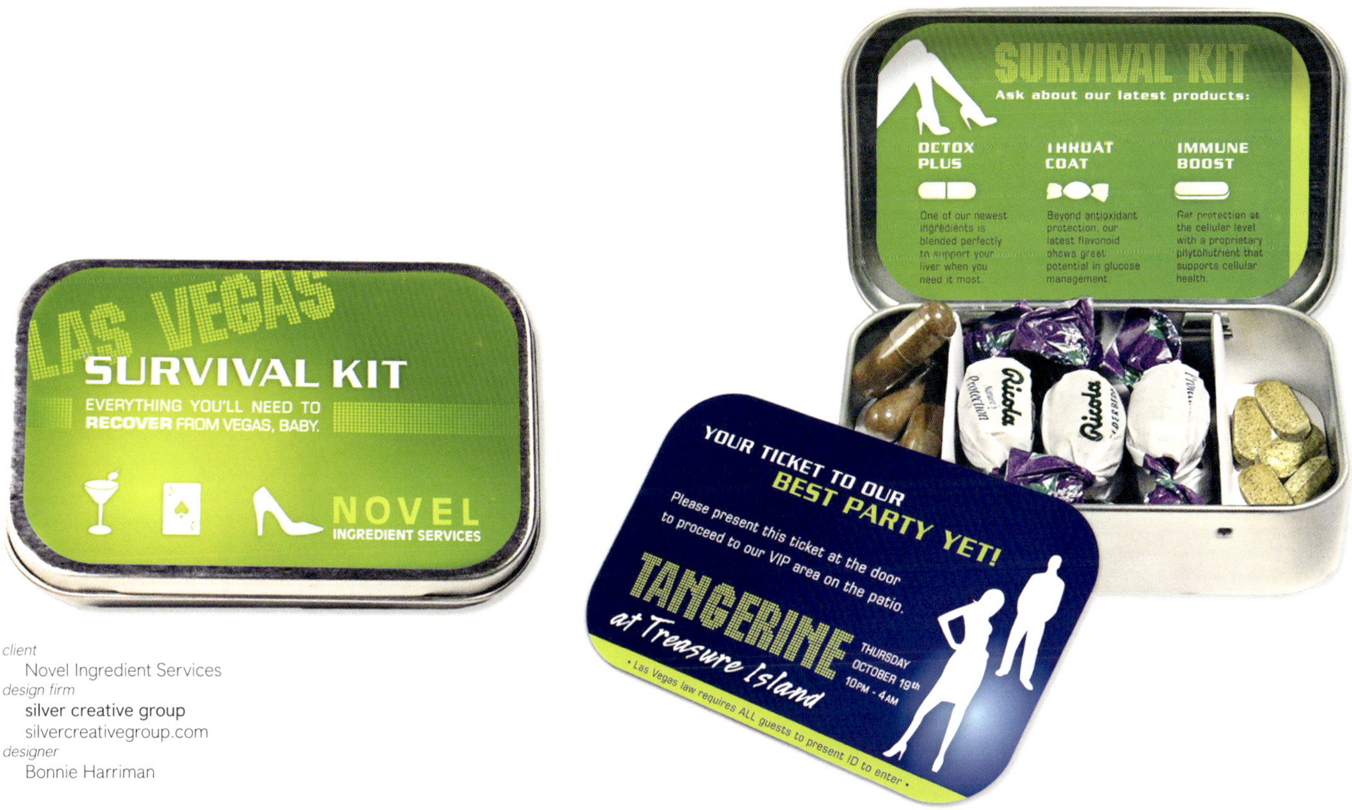

client
Novel Ingredient Services
design firm
silver creative group
silvercreativegroup.com
designer
Bonnie Harriman

client
Levine & Associates
design firm
Levine & Associates
www.levinedc.com
designers
Greg Sitzmann,
Lena Markley,
Megan Riordan

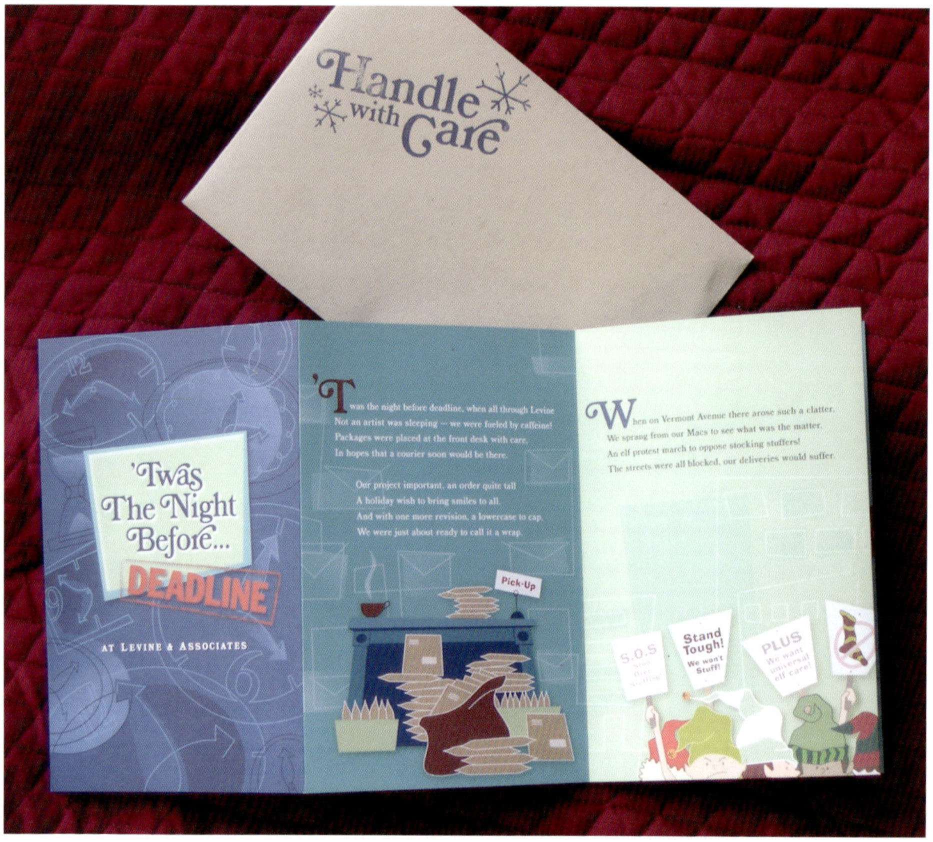

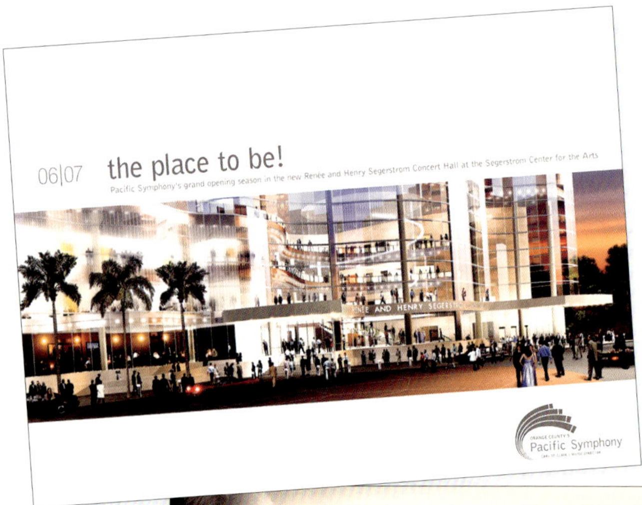

client
Orange County Pacific Symphony
design firm
Jensen Design Assoc. Inc.
www.jensendesign.com
designer
Alyssa Igawa

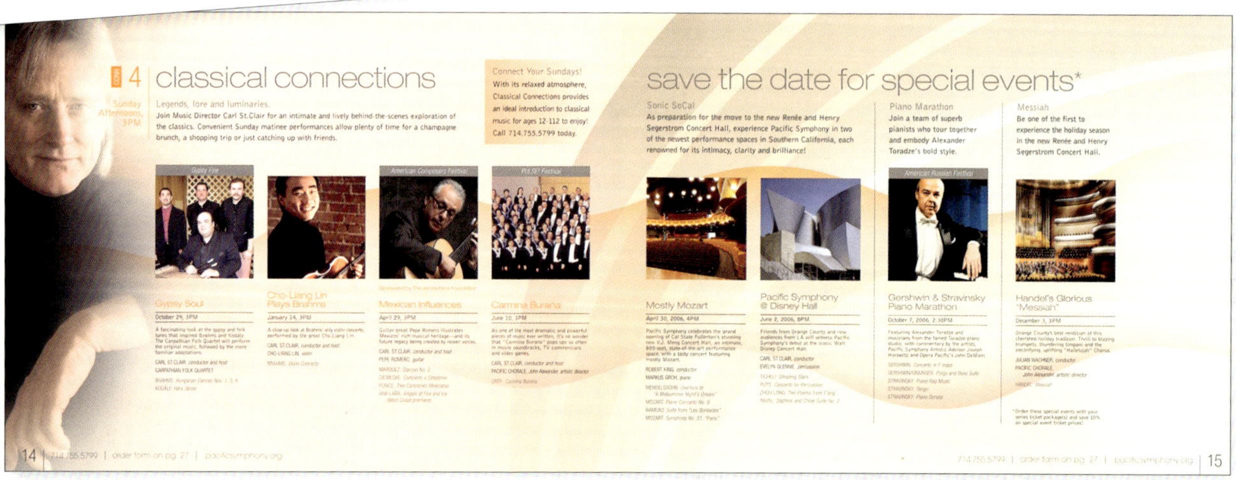

client
Jensen Design Assoc. Inc.
design firm
Jensen Design Assoc. Inc.
www.jensendesign.com
designers
Steph Windham, Jerome Calleja,
Joel Penos, David Jensen,
Alyssa Igawa

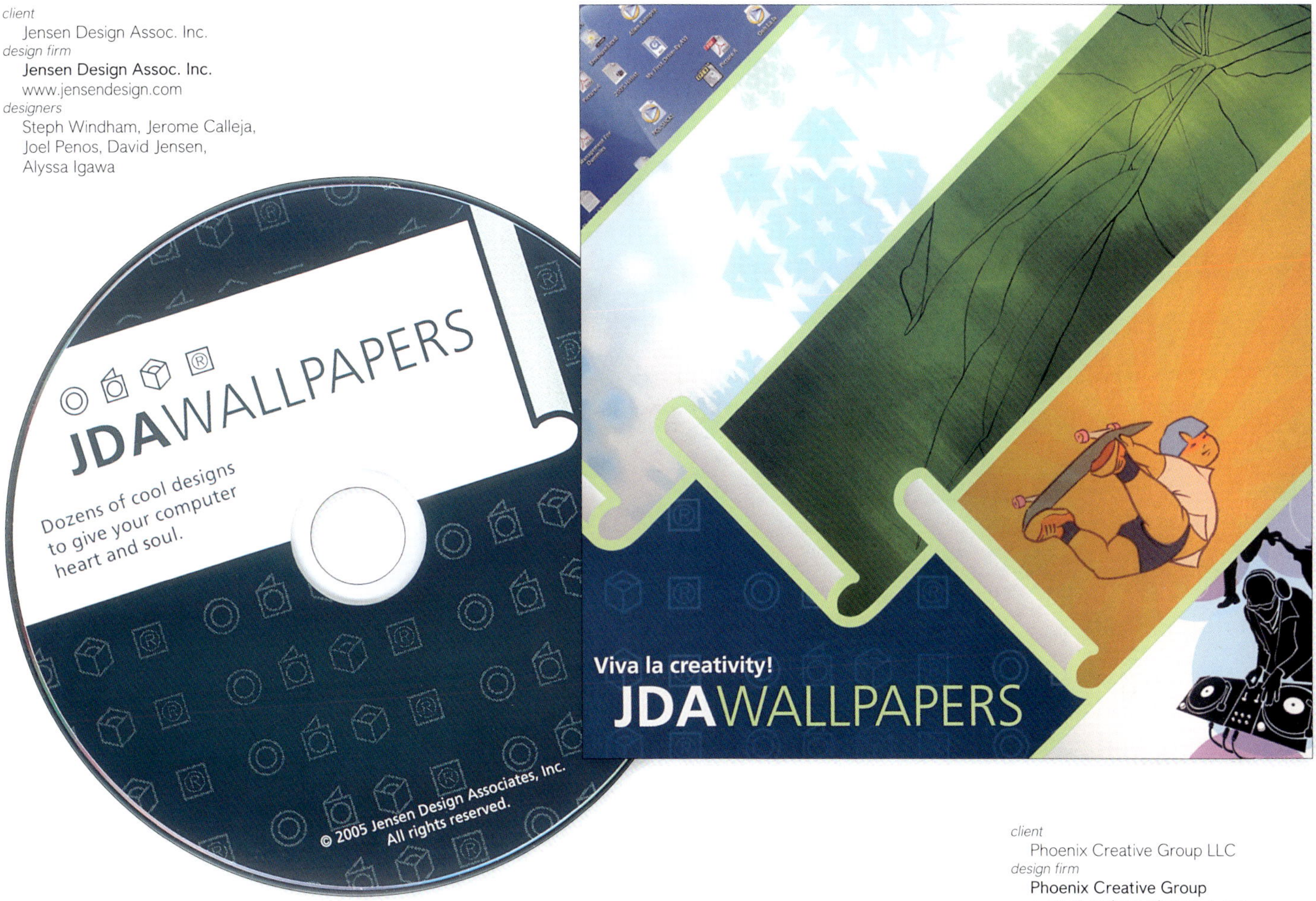

client
Phoenix Creative Group LLC
design firm
Phoenix Creative Group
www.phoenixcreativegroup.com
senior art director
Nicole Kassolis
art director
Sean Mullins
photographer
Nick Lutkins

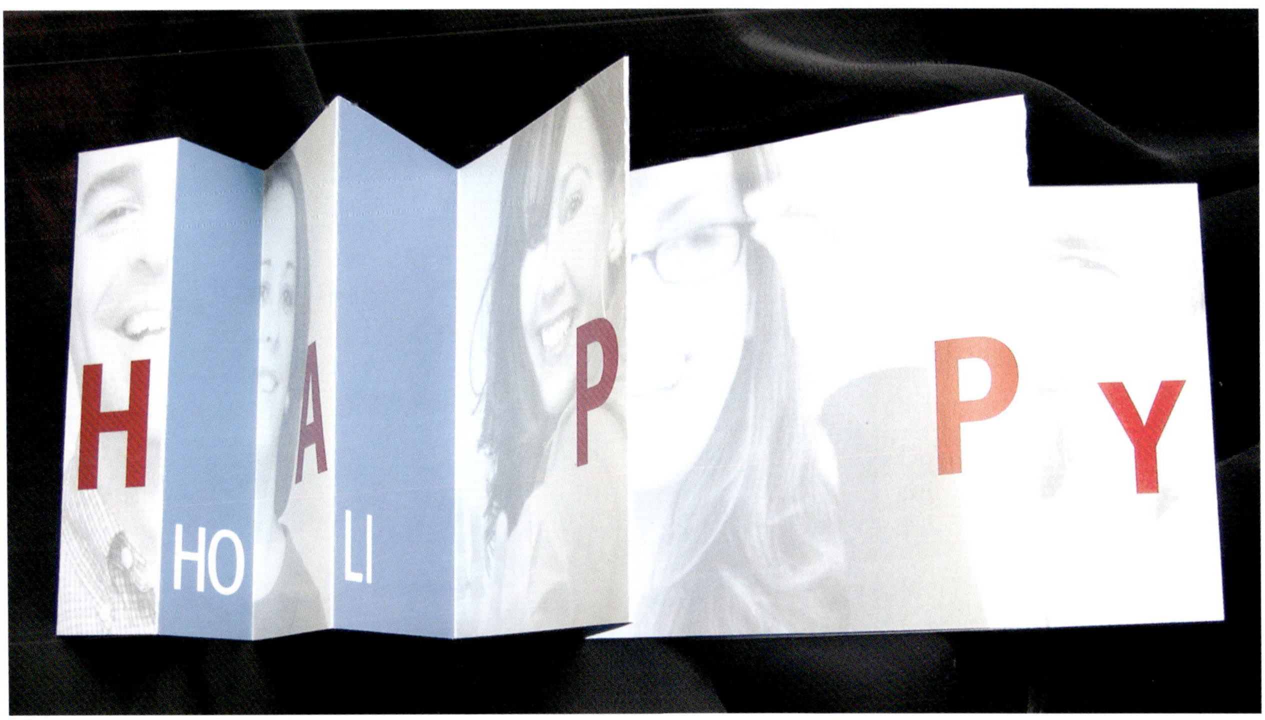

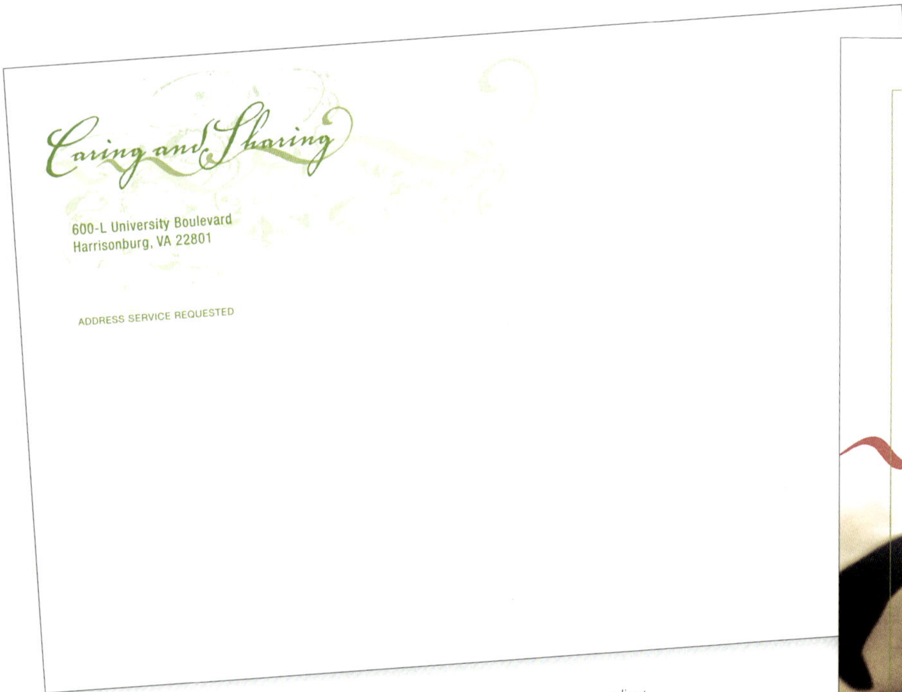

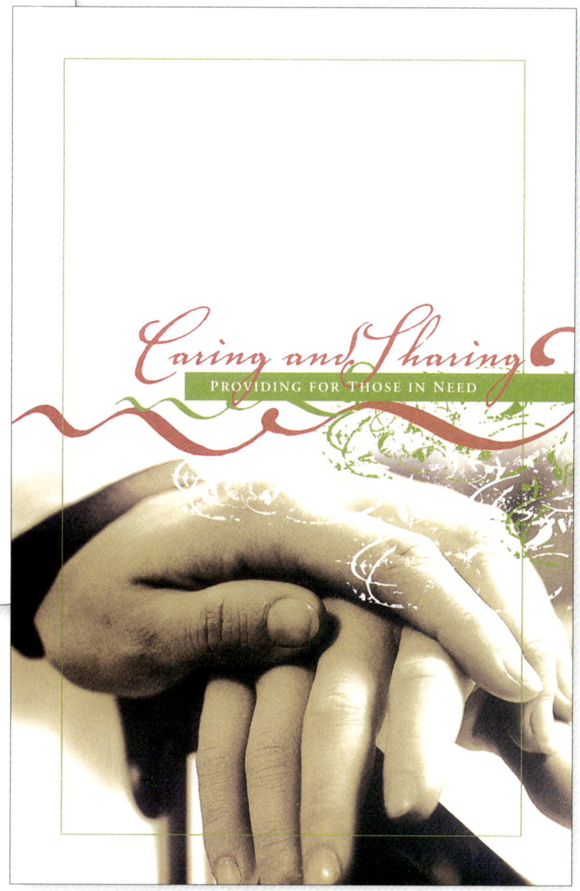

client
Sunnyside Communities
design firm
Grafix Dezine
www.grafixdezine.com
designer
Oleg Yagolnikov

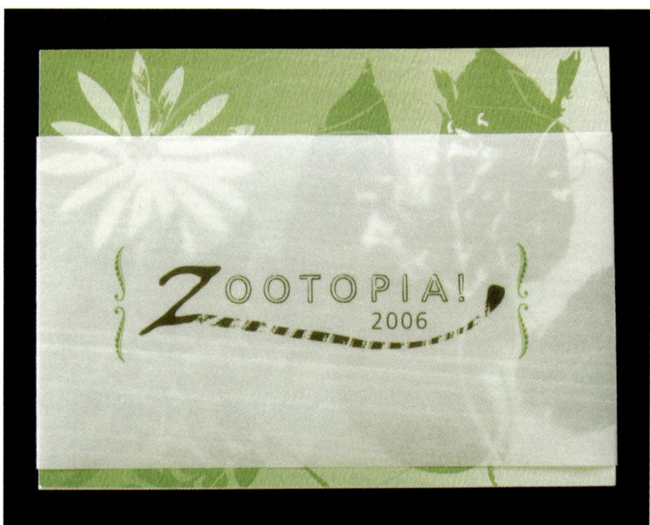

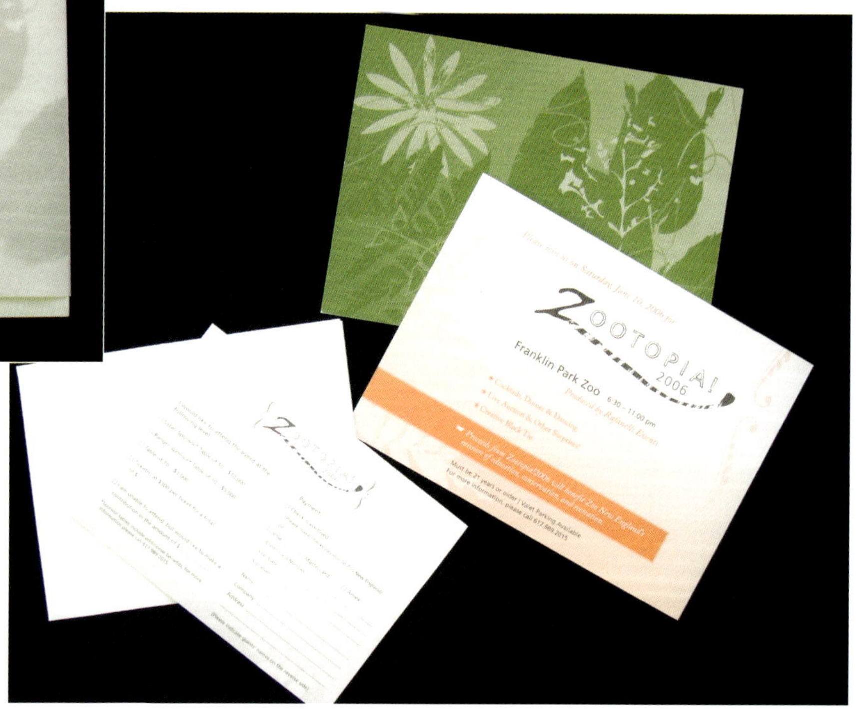

client
Zoo New England
design firm
kor group
www.kor.com
designers
Karen Dendy Smith,
Brigitte Ting

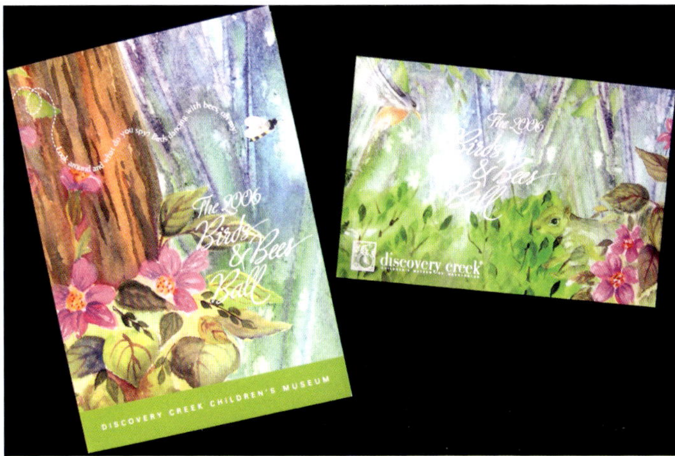

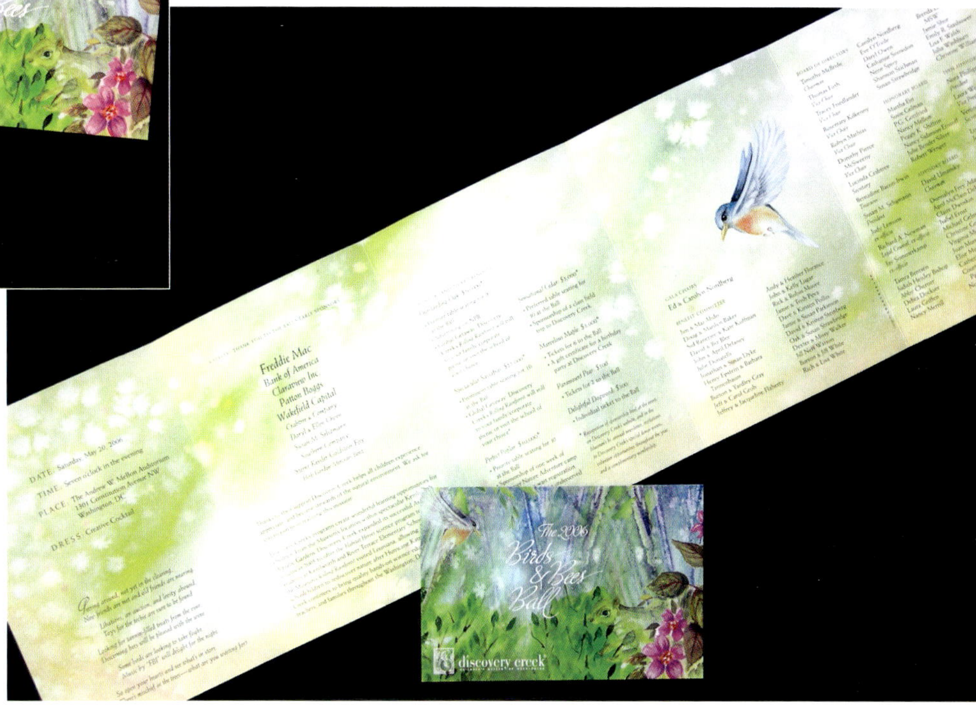

client
Discovery Creek
design firm
Crabtree + Company
designers
Susan Angrisani,
Tamara Finn

client
Caesars Palace Las Vegas
design firm
eurie creative
designers
Victor Rodriguez, Chris Smith,
Mike Enriquez
cover designers
CDI Studios

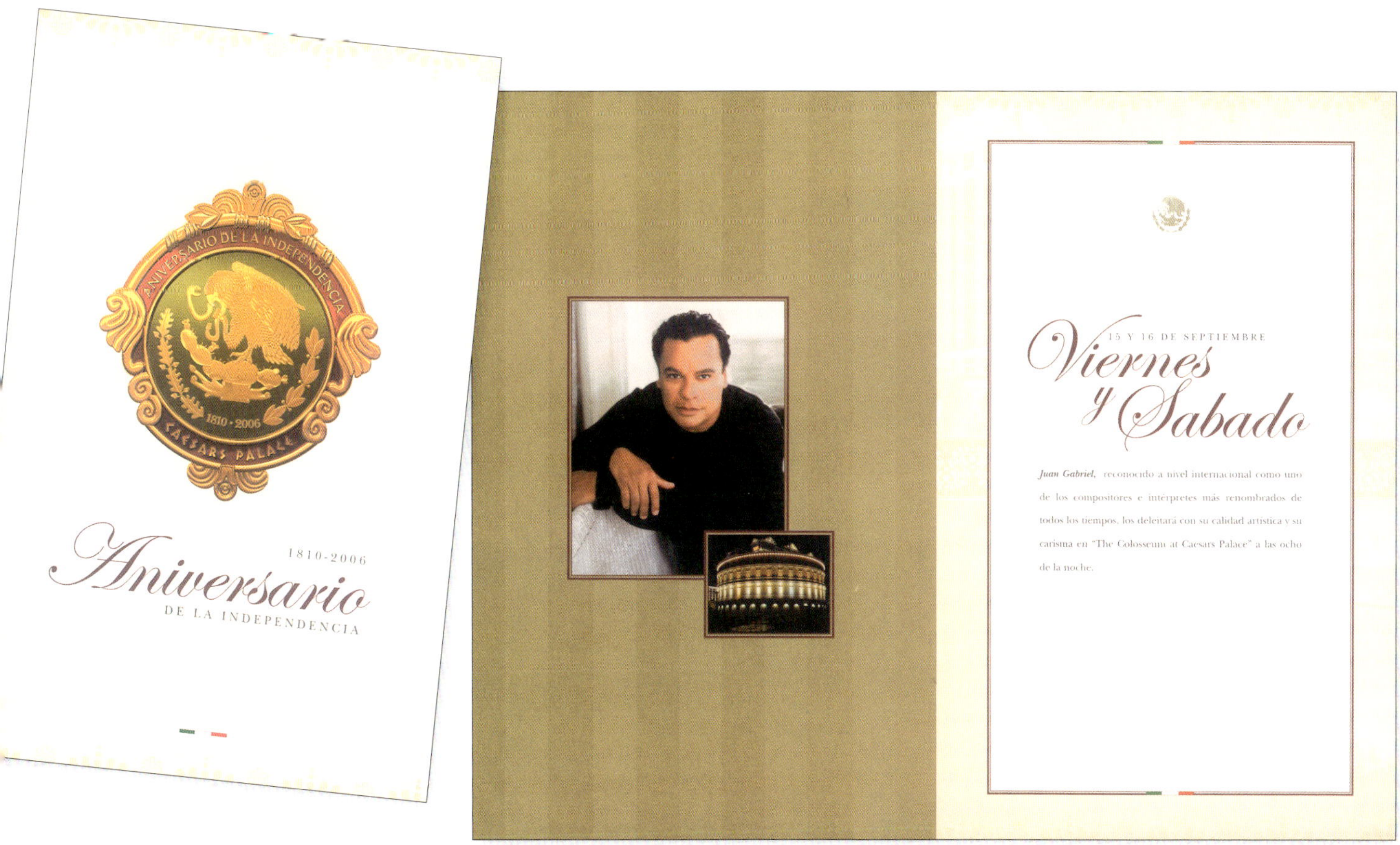

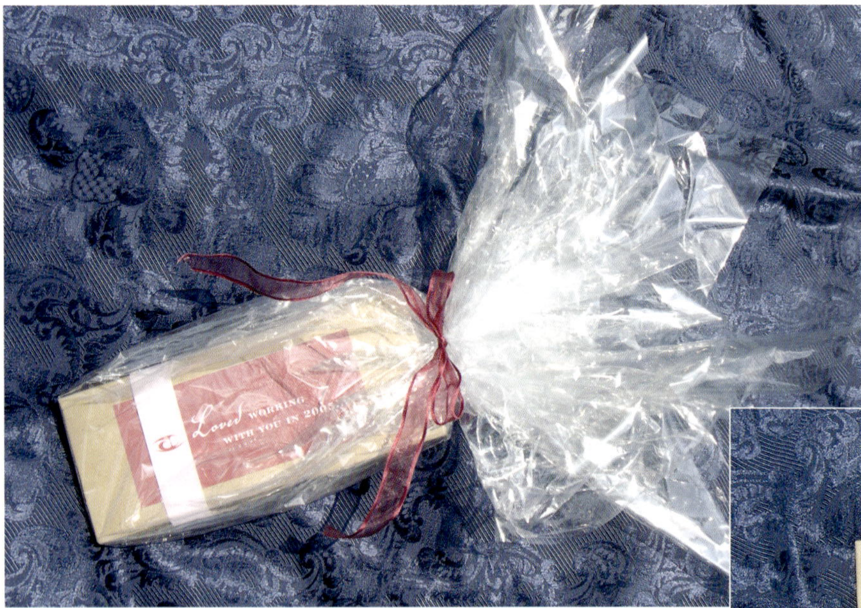

client
Alchemy Consulting & Design LLC
design firm
Alchemy Consulting & Design LLC
www.alchemize.com

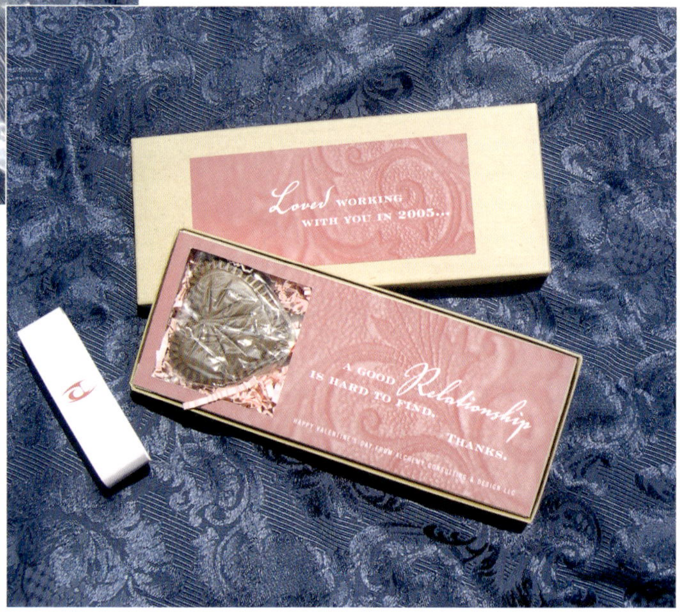

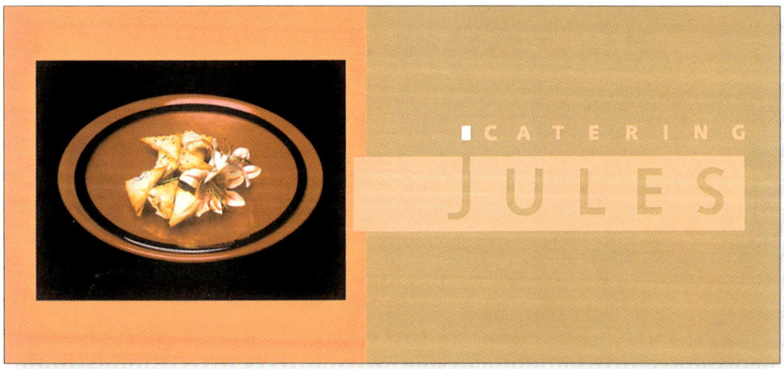

client
Jules Catering
design firm
Mastrogiannis Design, Inc.
designer
Peter Mastrogiannis

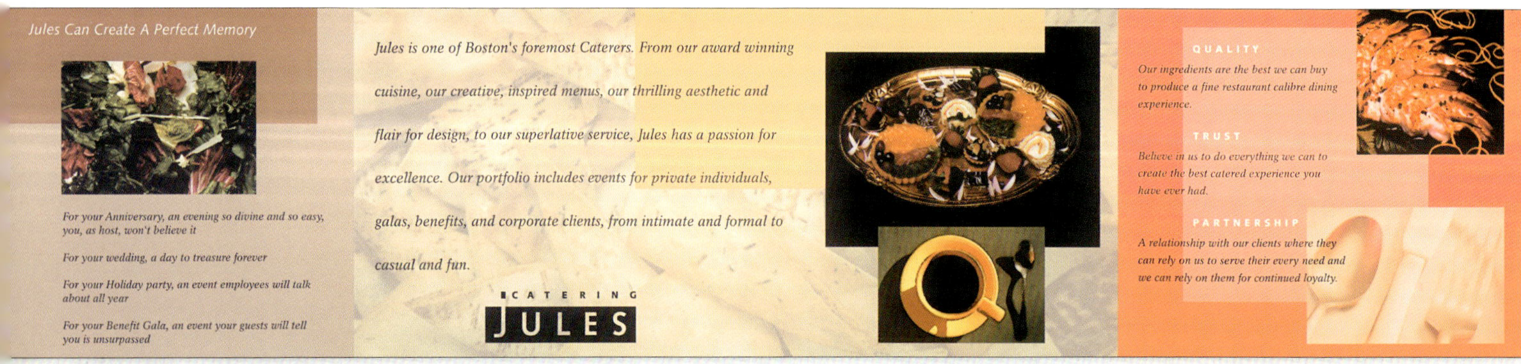

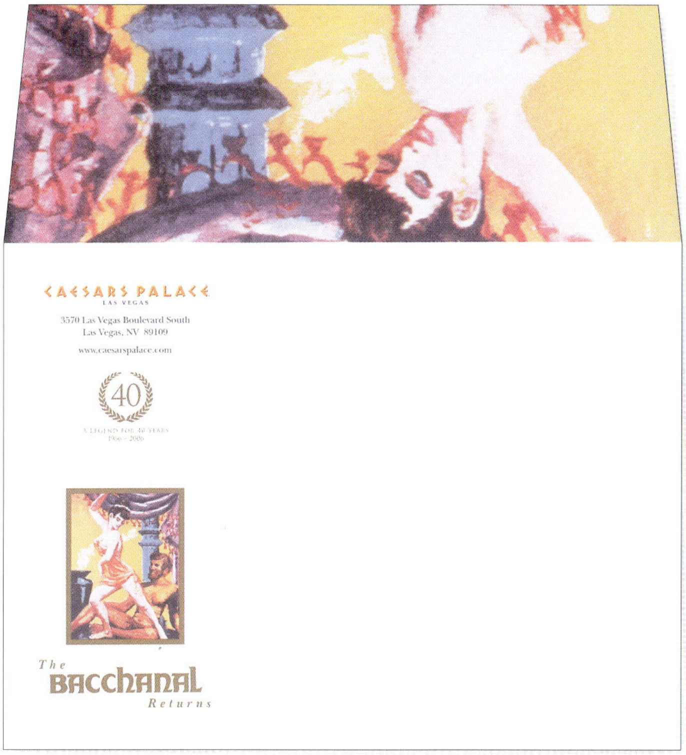

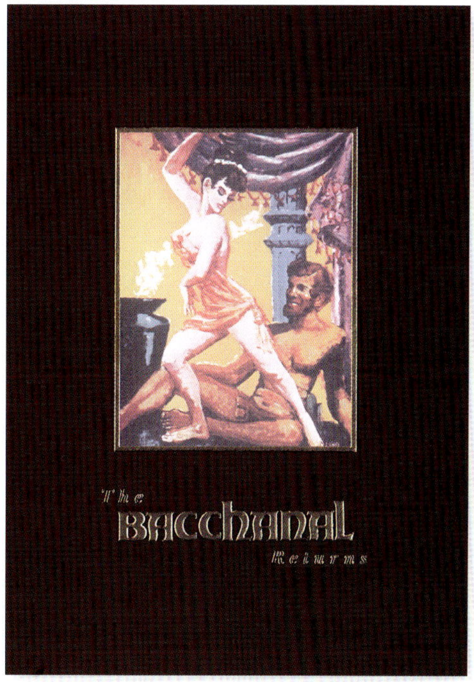

client
Caesars Palace
Las Vegas
design firm
eurie creative
designers
Victor Rodriguez,
Chris Smith,
Mike Enriquez

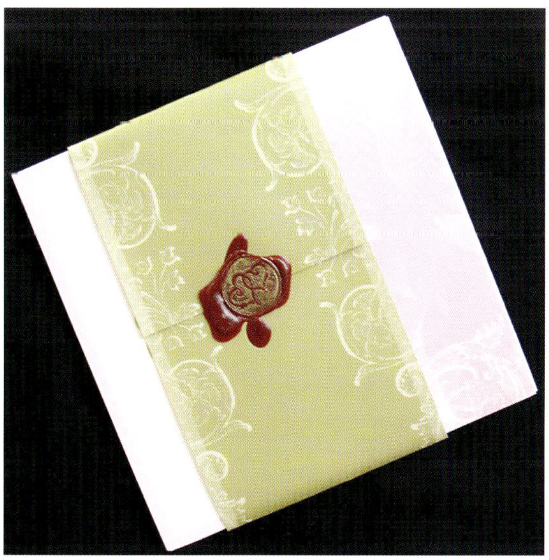

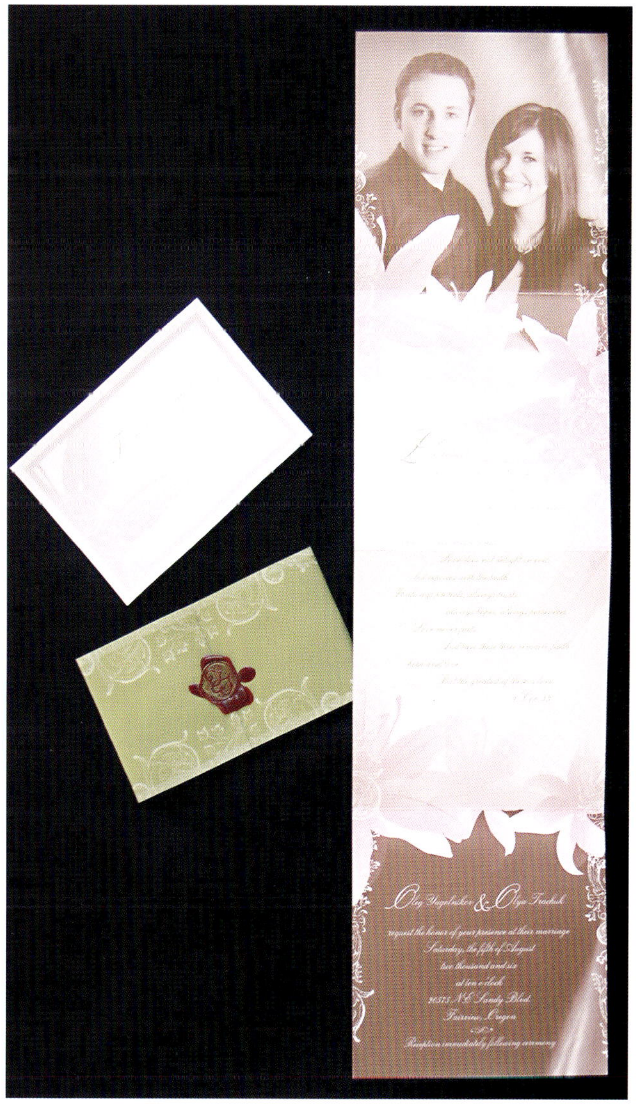

client
Oleg Yagolnikov, Olya Trachuk
design firm
Grafix Dezine
www.grafixdezine.com
designer
Oleg Yagolnikov

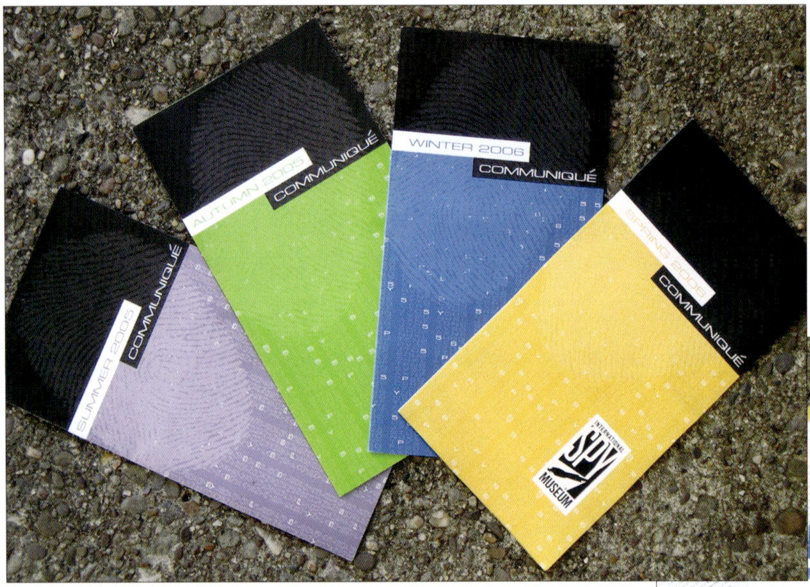

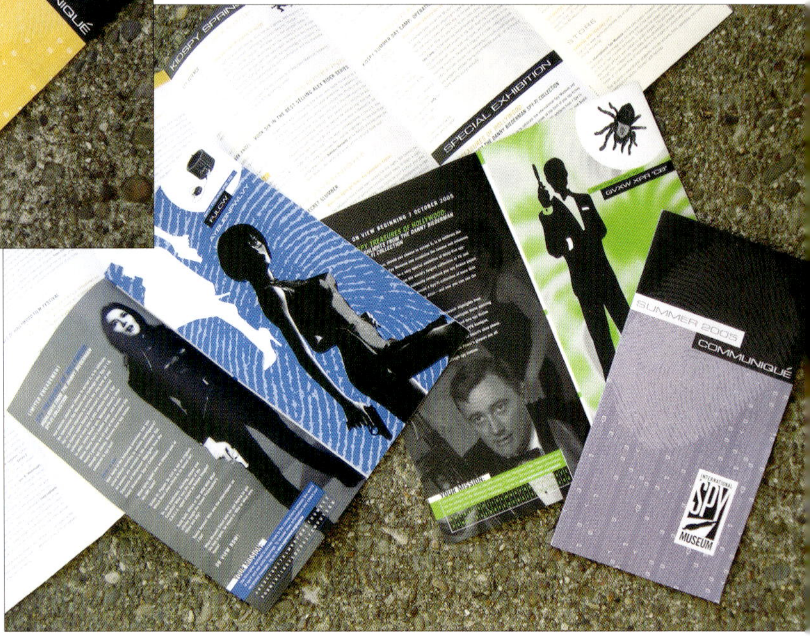

client
Spy Museum
design firm
Crabtree + Company
designers
Susan Angrisani,
Joe Velasquez

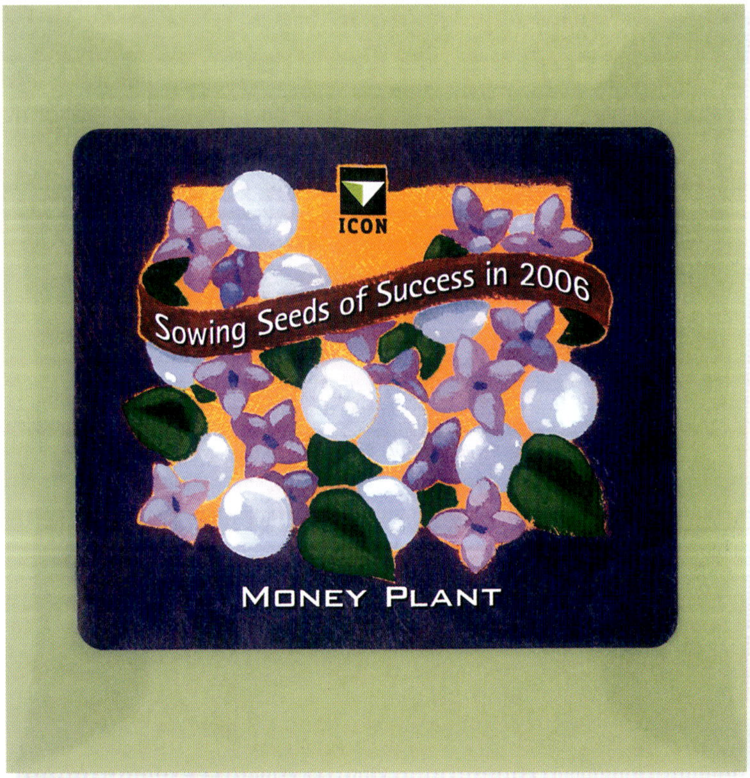

client
Icon Graphics Inc.
design firm
Icon Graphics Inc.
thinkfeelchoose.com
designers
Icon Graphics Inc.

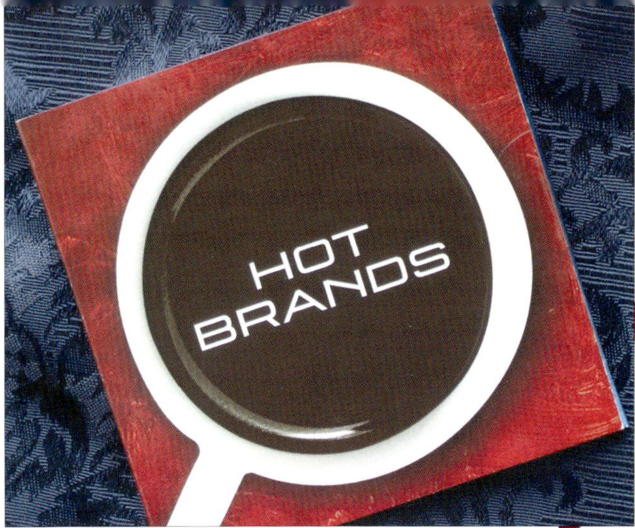

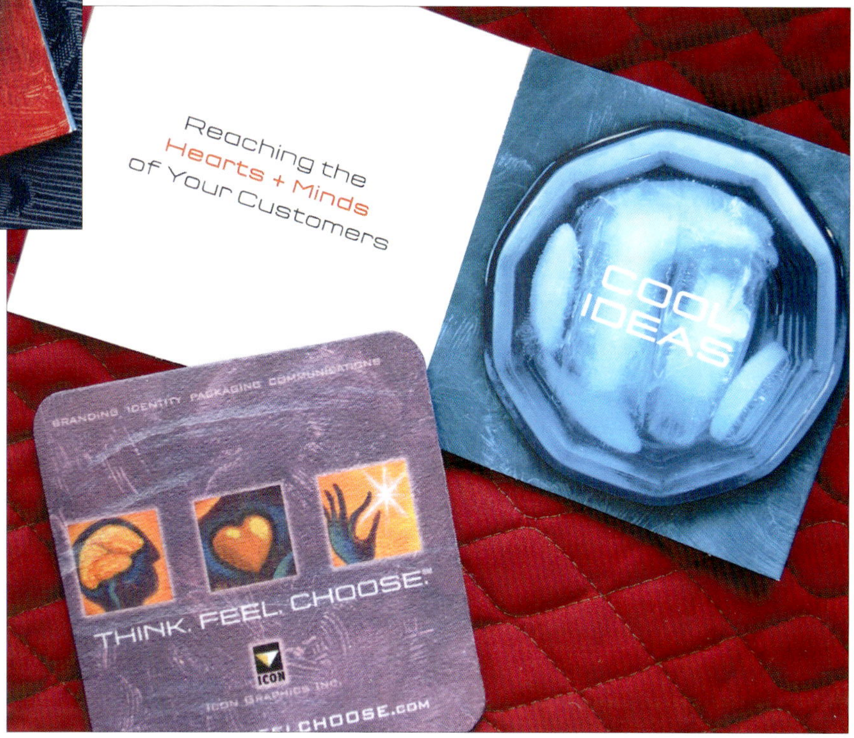

client
Icon Graphics Inc.
design firm
Icon Graphics Inc.
thinkfeelchoose.com
designers
Icon Graphics Inc.

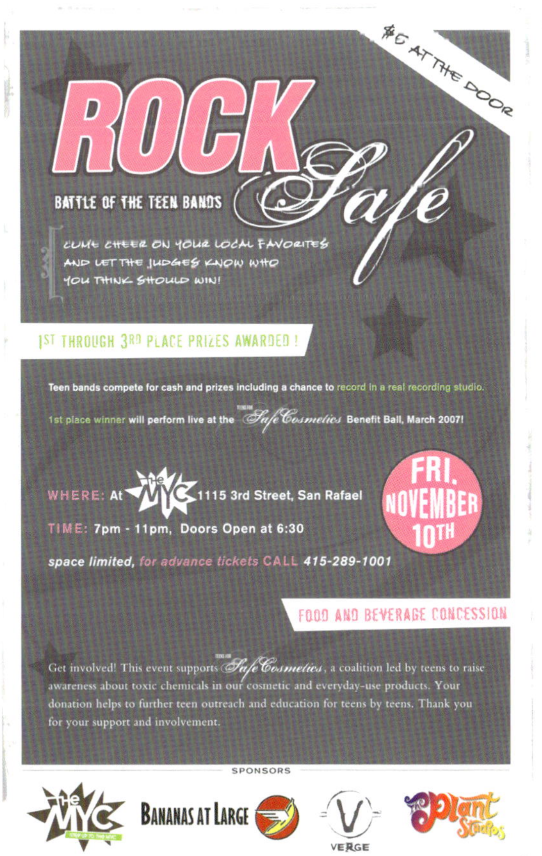

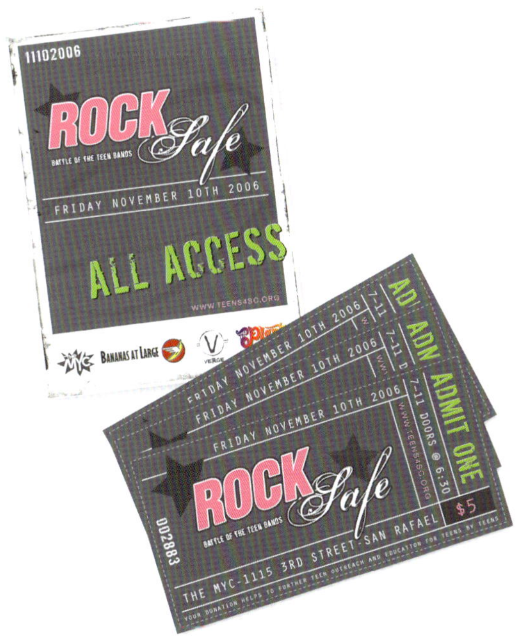

client
Teens for Safe Cosmetics
design firm
Axion Design
axiondesign.com

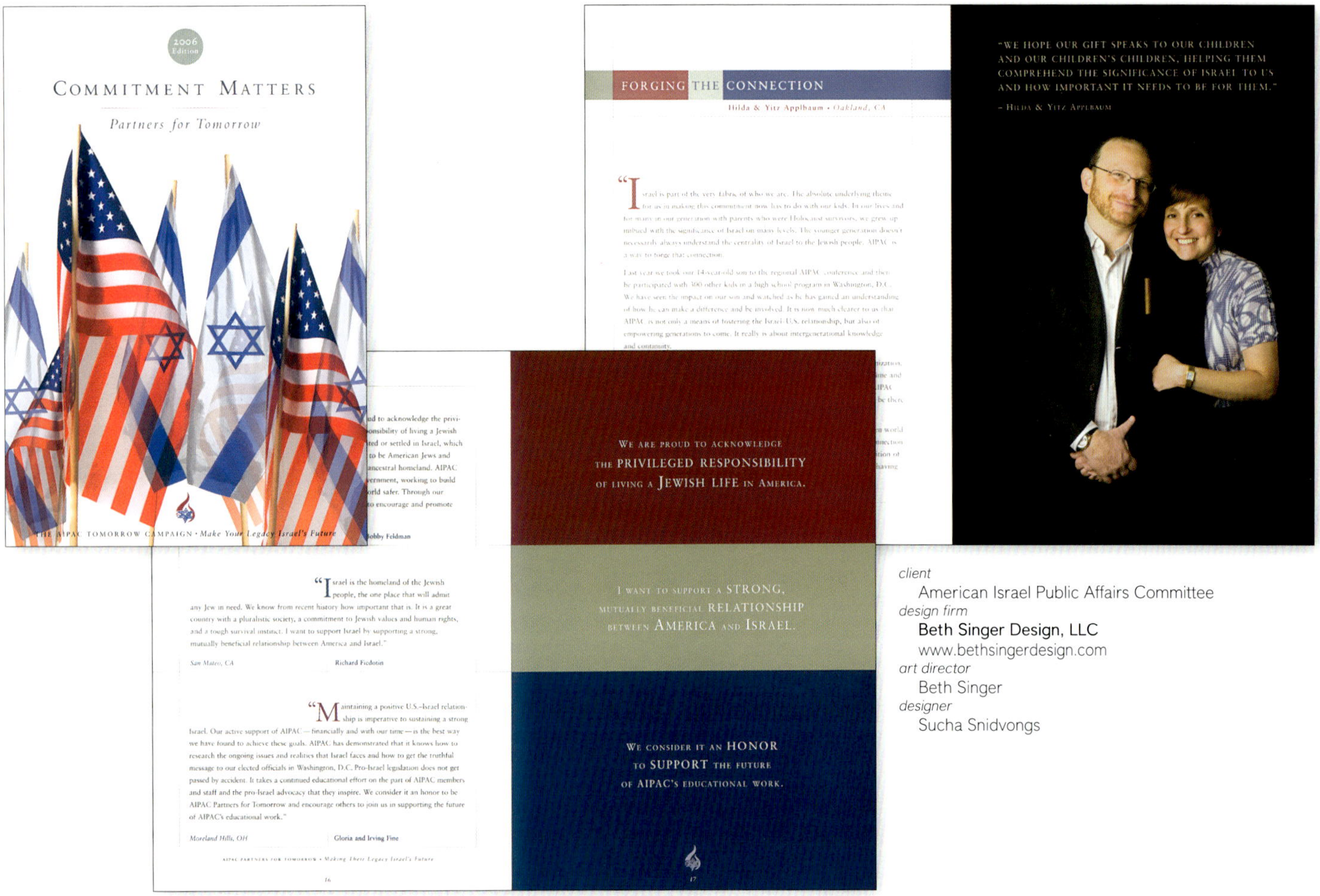

client
American Israel Public Affairs Committee
design firm
Beth Singer Design, LLC
www.bethsingerdesign.com
art director
Beth Singer
designer
Sucha Snidvongs

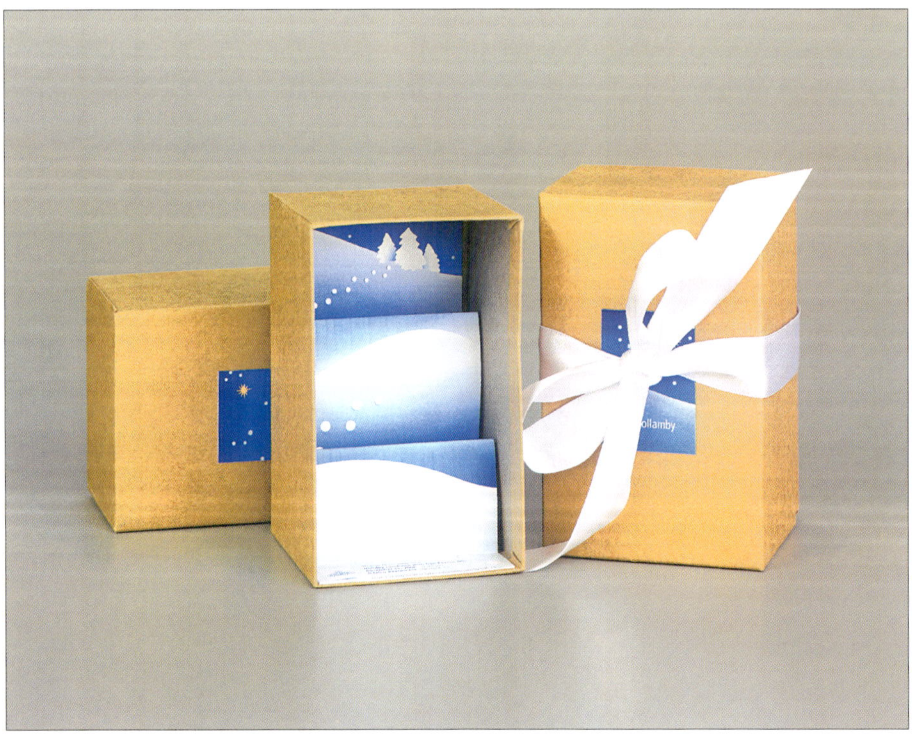

client
Tom Fowler, Inc.
design firm
Tom Fowler Inc.
www.tomfowlerinc.com
designer
Elizabeth P. Ball

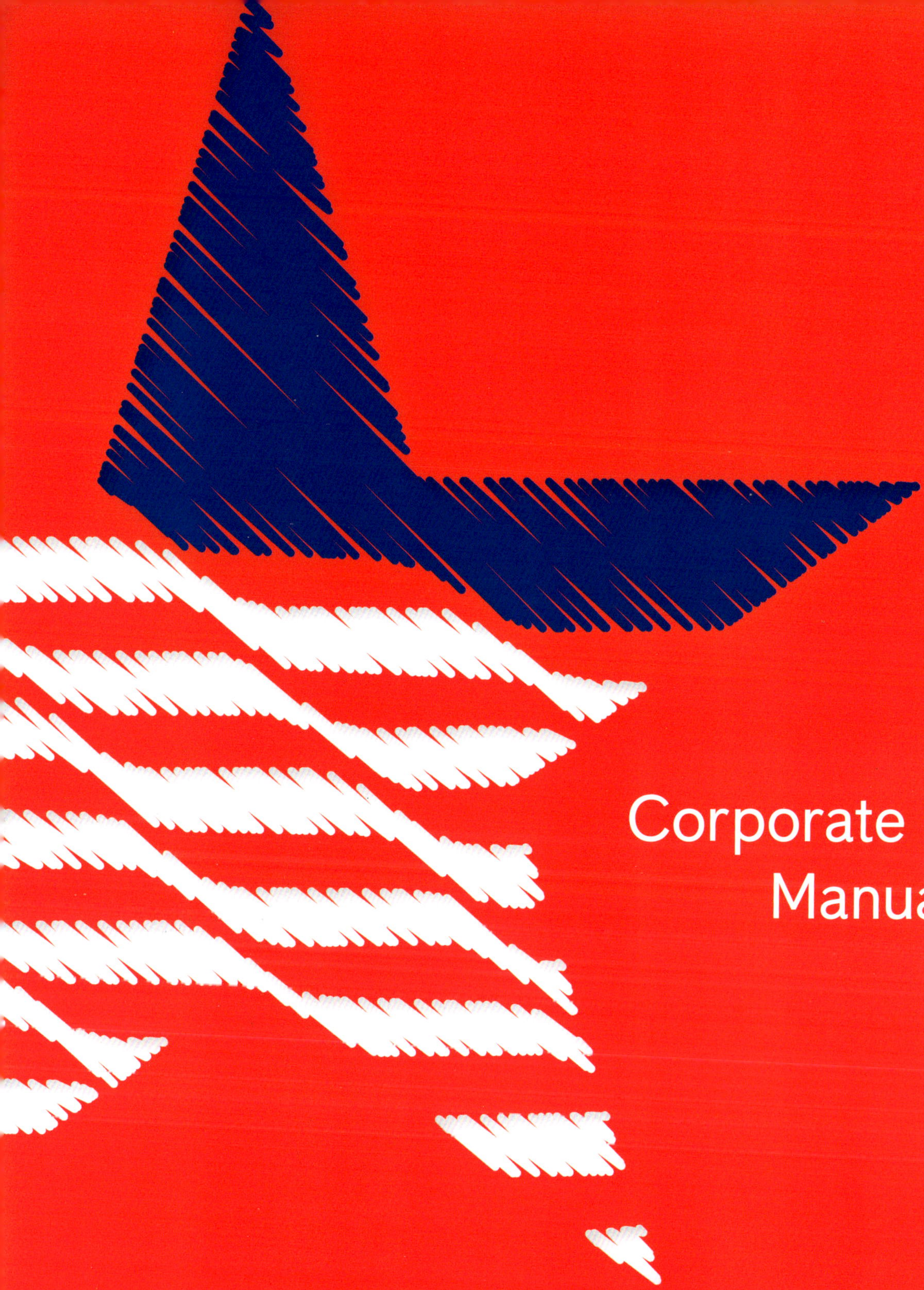

Corporate Identity Manuals

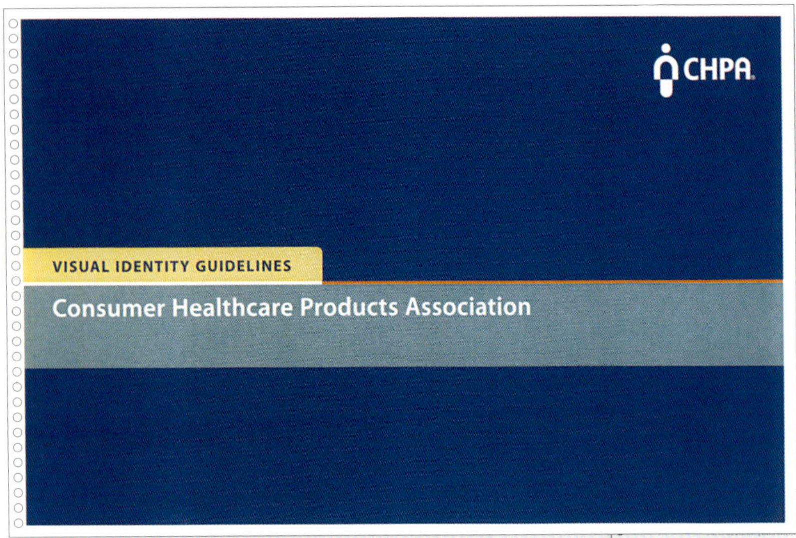

client
Consumer Healthcare Products Assoc.
design firm
Grafik Marketing Communications
www.grafik.com
designers
Melissa Wilets, Michelle Mar Collins

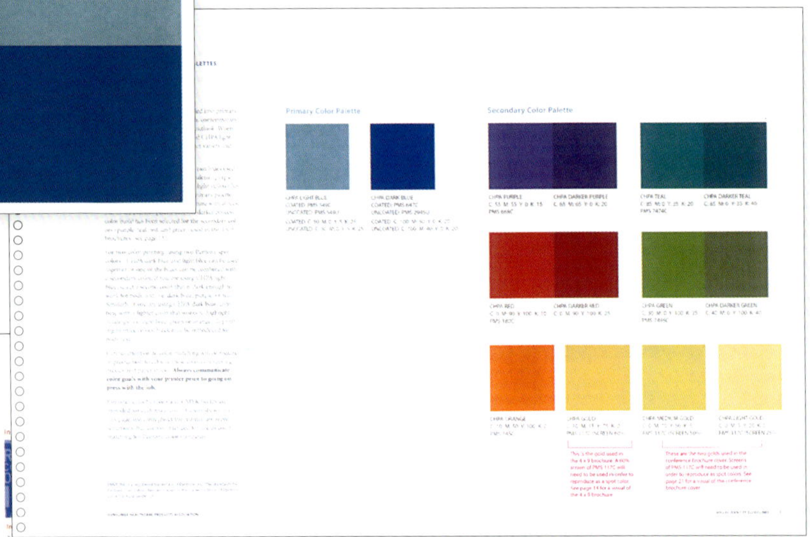

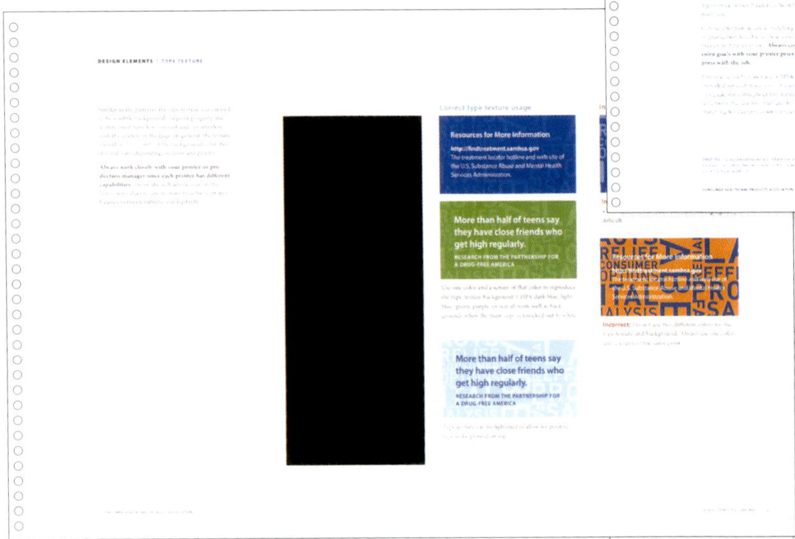

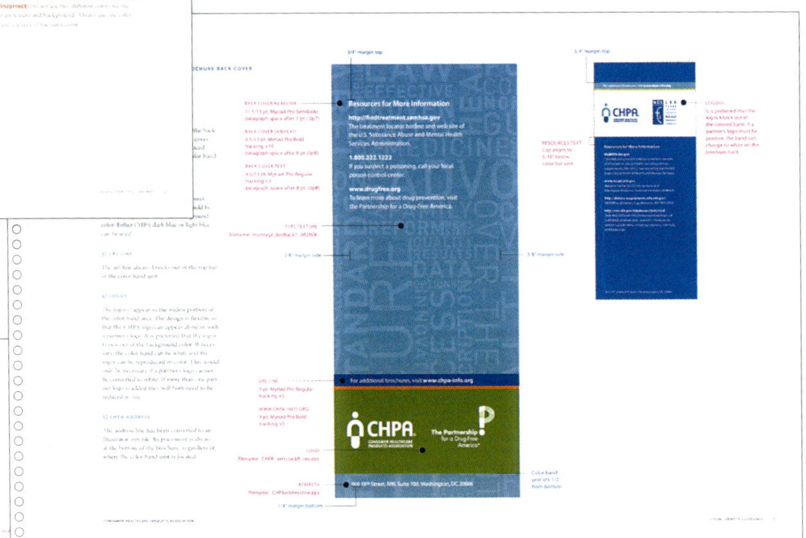

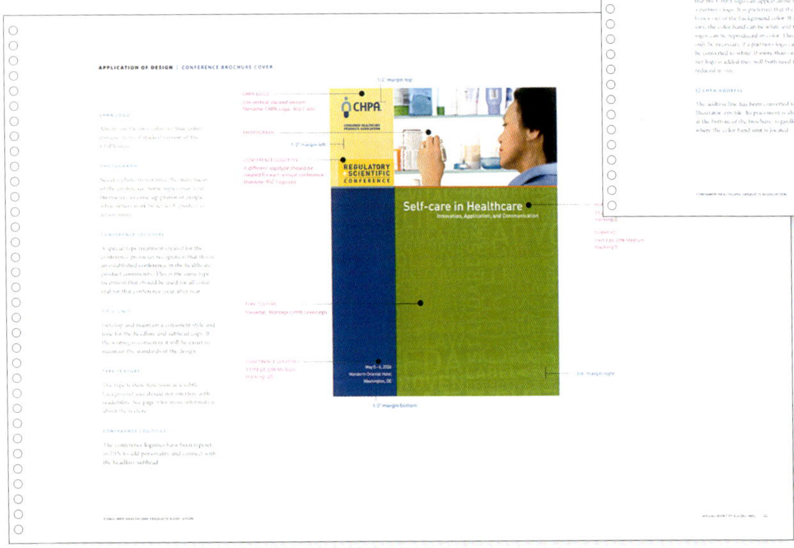

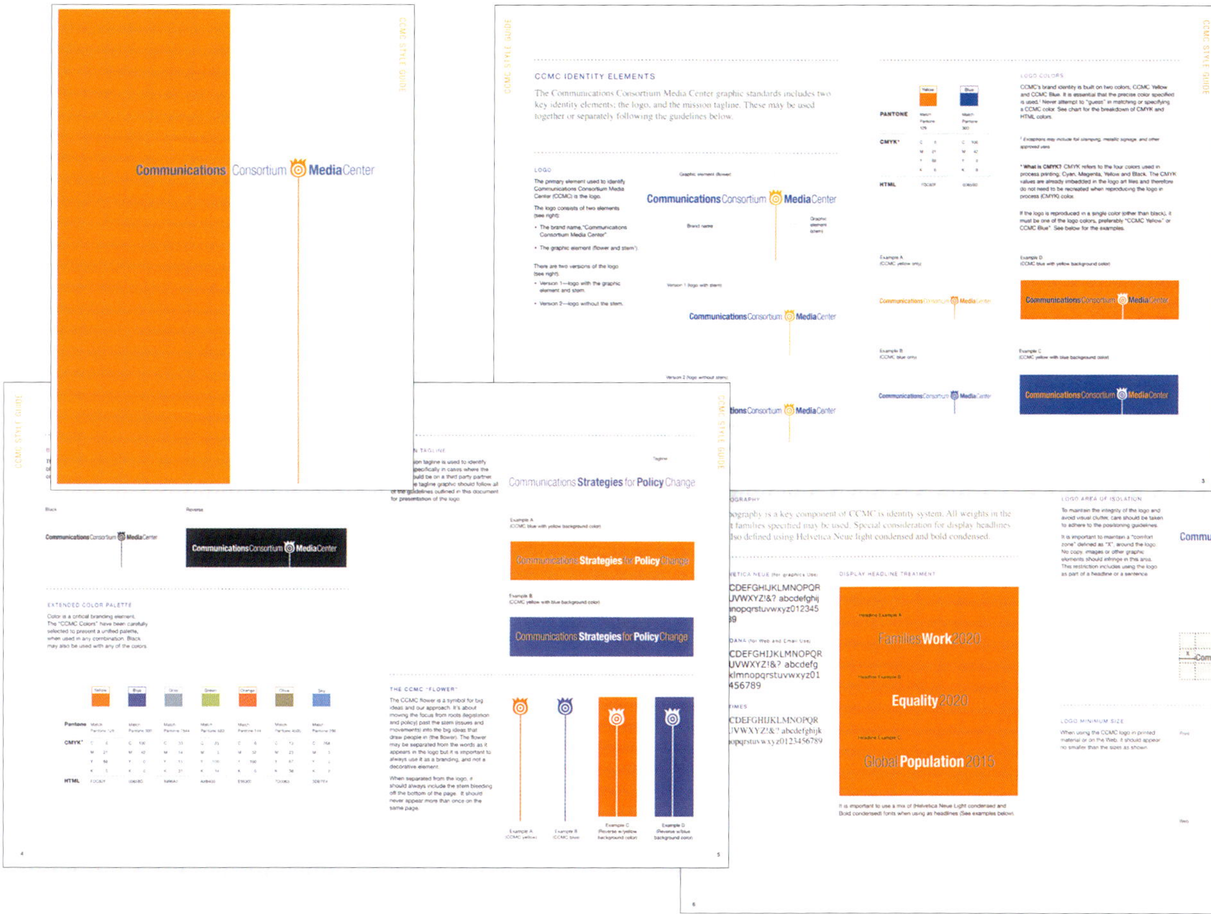

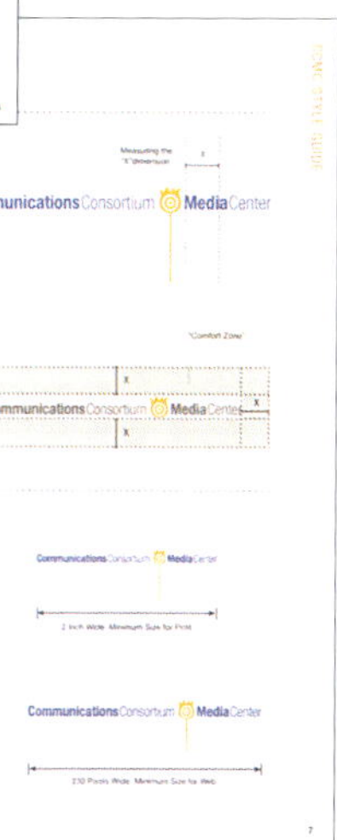

client
Communications Consortium Media Center
design firm
Bremmer & Goris
www.goris.com
designers
Li-Chow, Miki Lo

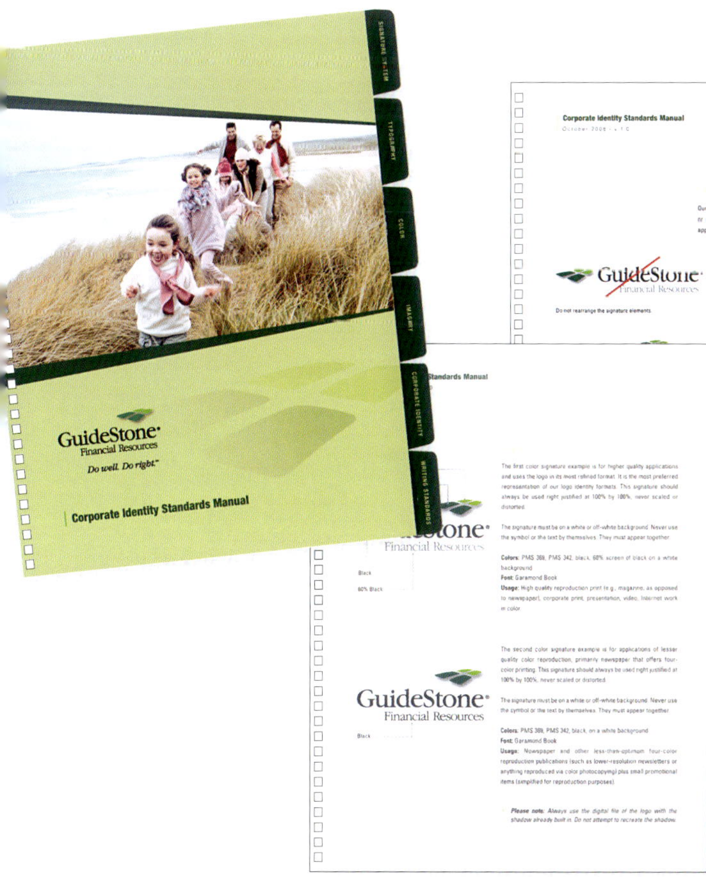

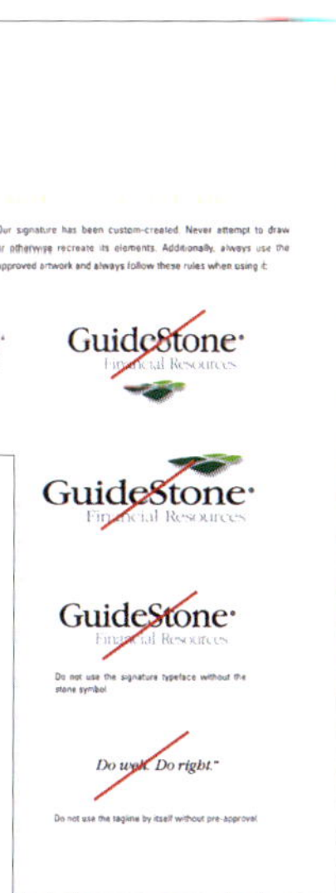

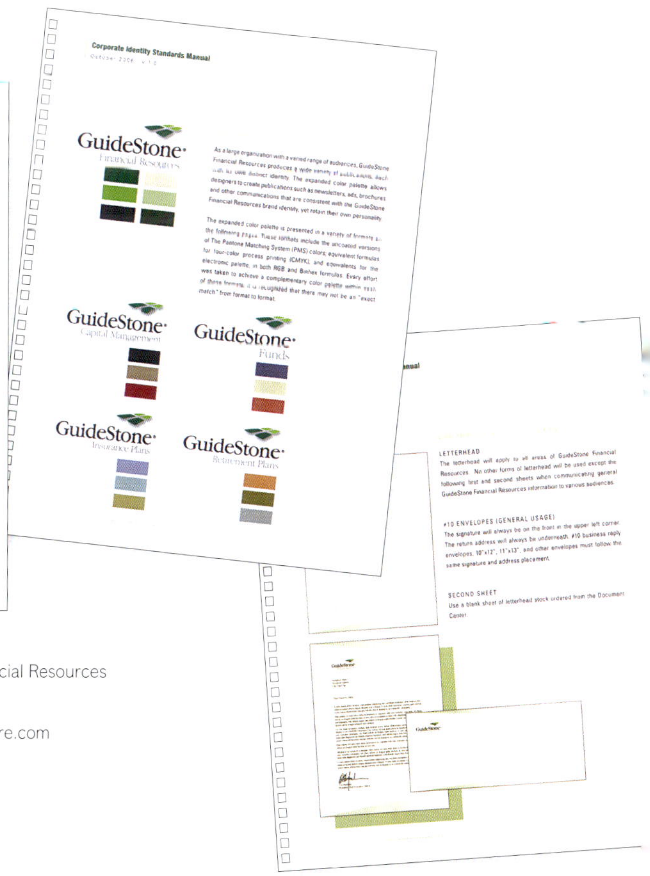

client
Guidestone Financial Resources
design firm
Innis Maggiore
www.innismaggiore.com
designer
Laura Speakman

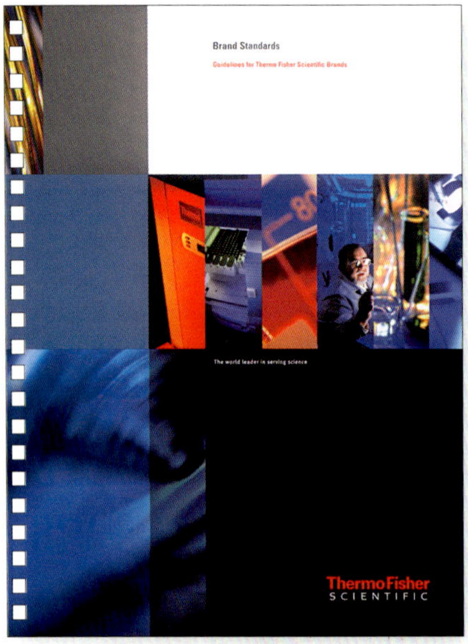

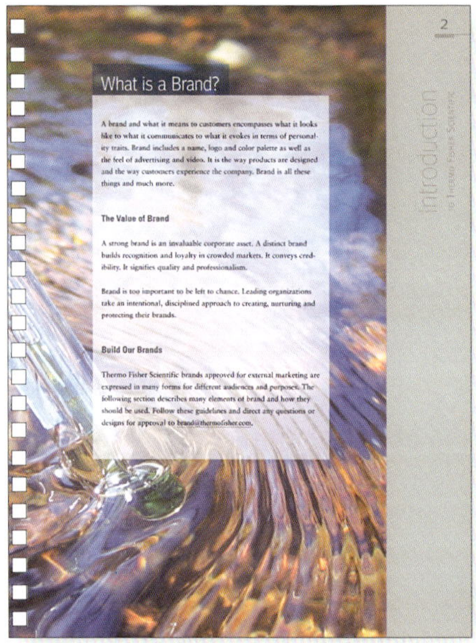

client
ThermoFisher Scientific
design firm
O'Brien & Neville, Inc.
www.oandn.com
designers
Kathleen O'Brien,
Paul Neville,
Bill Covino

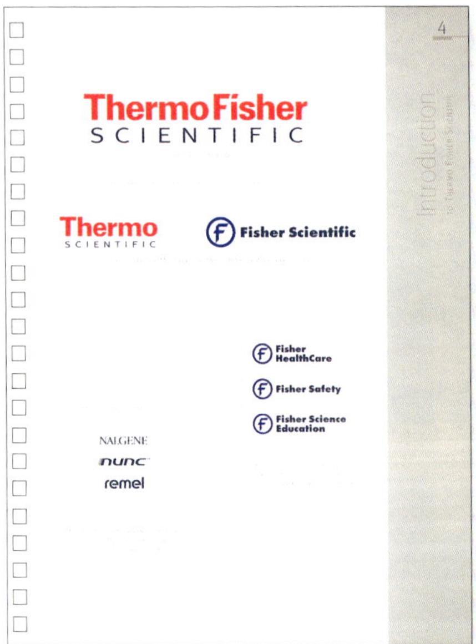

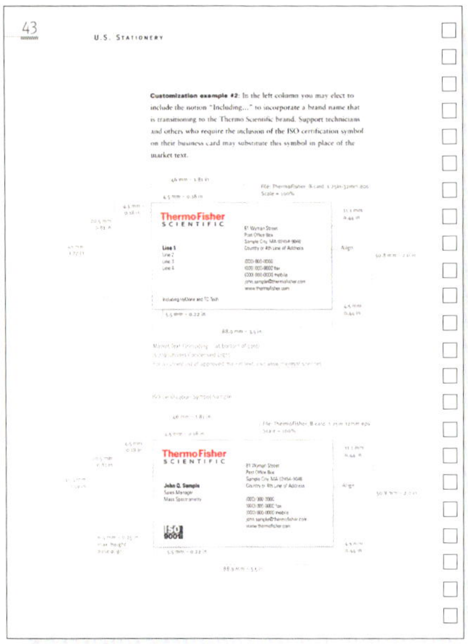

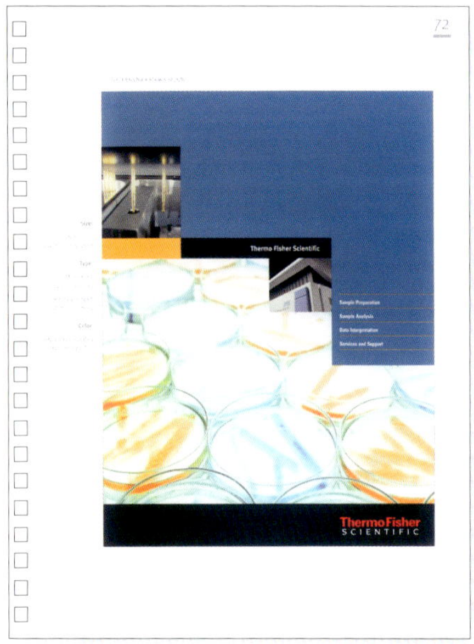

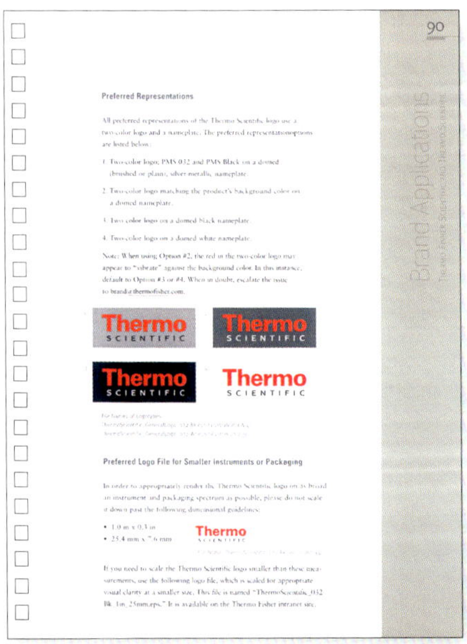

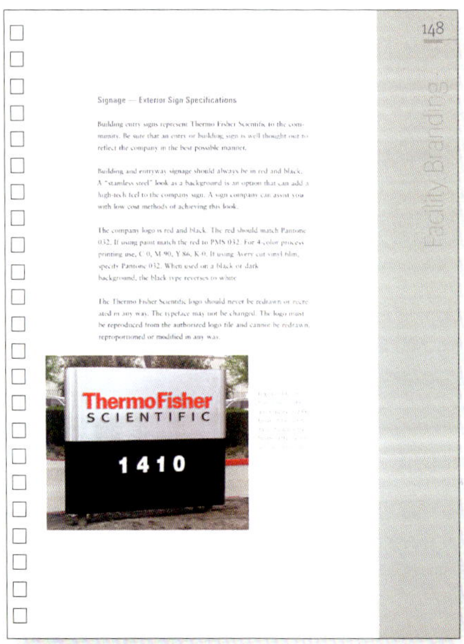

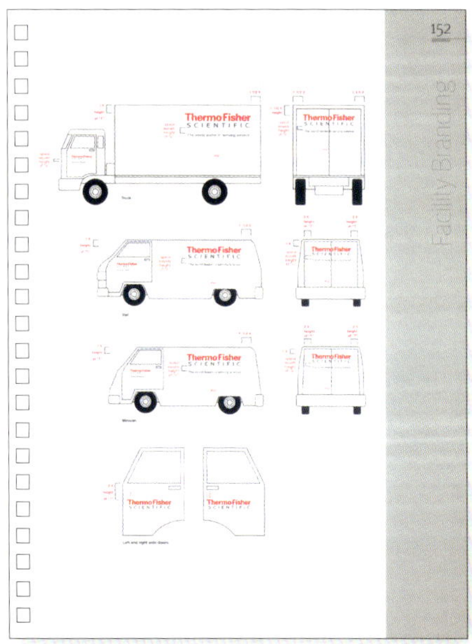

Signage
& Environmental
Graphics

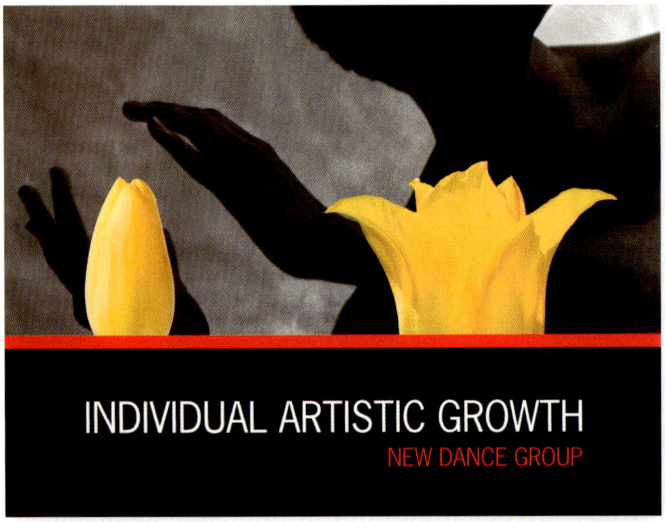

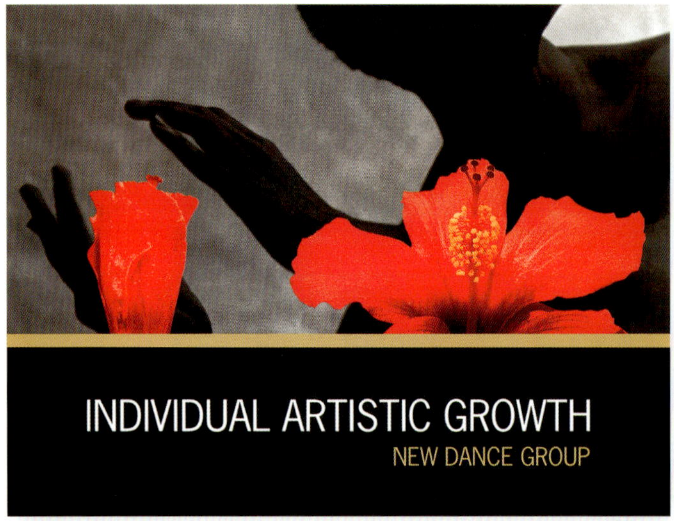

client
New Dance Group
design firm
WestGroup Creative
www.westgp.com
designer
Chip Tolaney

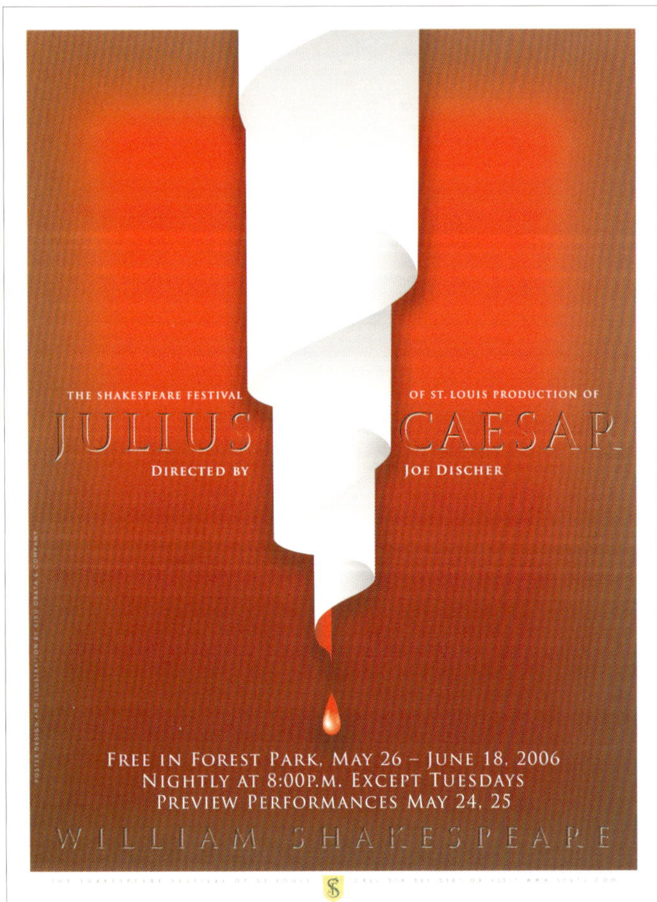

client
The Shakespeare Festival of St. Louis
design firm
Kiku Obata & Company
designer
Rich Nelson

client
Tahitian Noni Café
design firm
Hornall Anderson Design Works
www.hadw.com
designers
Lisa Cerveny, James Tee, Sonja Max,
Tiffany Place, Elmer dela Cruz, Leo Raymundo

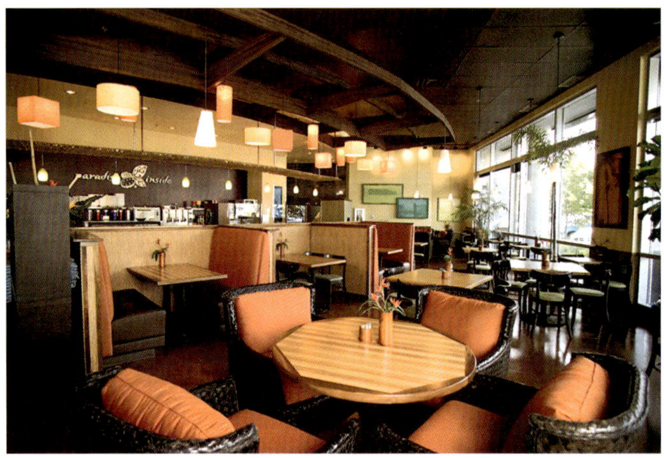

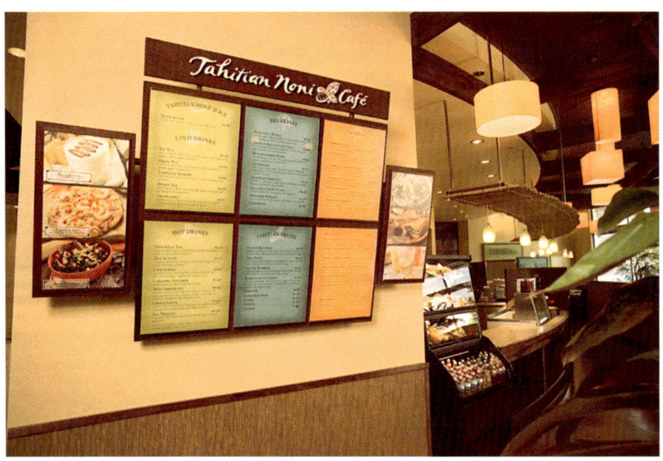

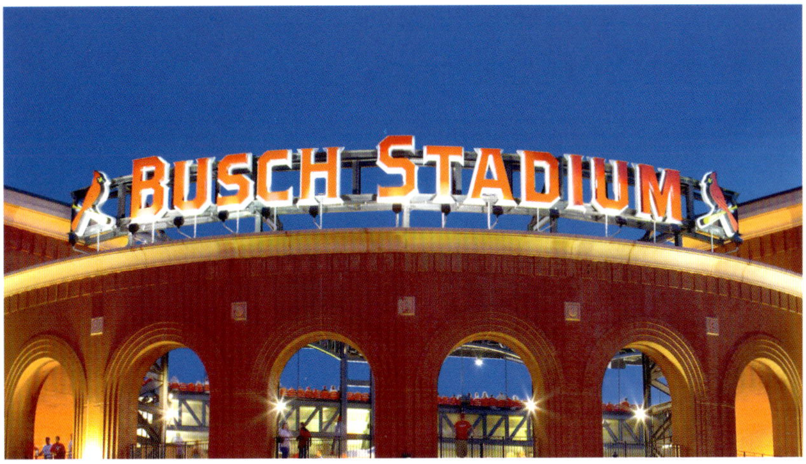

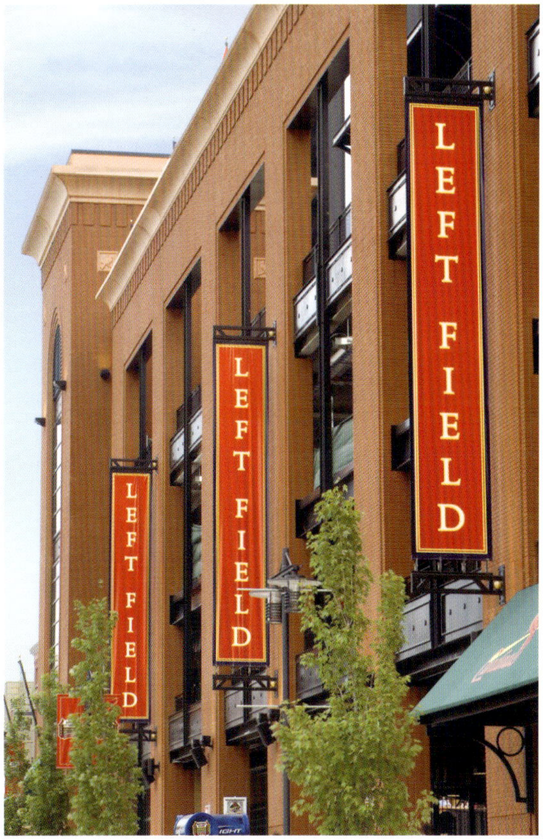

client
St. Louis Cardinals
design firm
Kiku Obata & Company
designers
Kiku Obata, Laura McCanna, Rich Nelson, Carole Jerome, Russell Buchanan, Jr., David Leavey, Todd Mayberry, Jef Ebers, Denise Fuehne

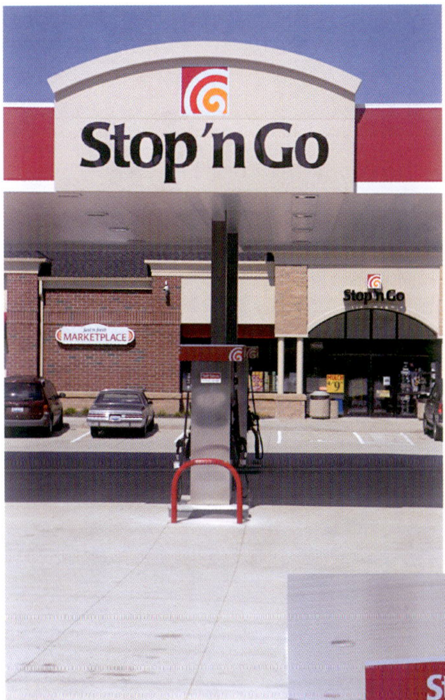

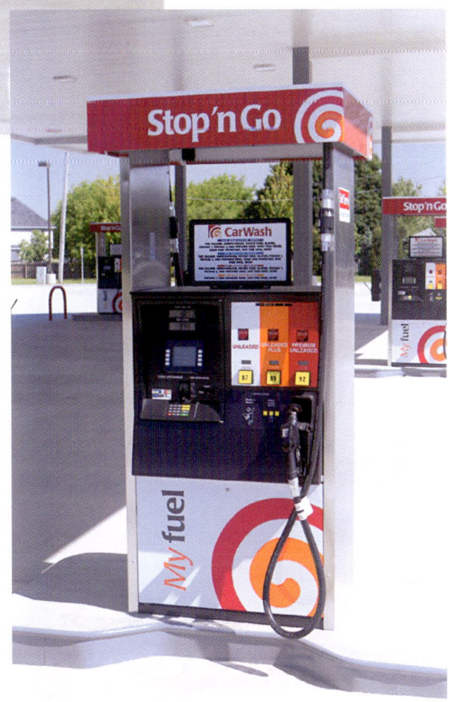

client
Stop 'N Go
design firm
Innis Maggiore
www.innismaggiore.com
designer
Lee-Ann Demeo

client
New Dance Group
design firm
WestGroup Creative
www.westgp.com
designer
Chip Tolaney

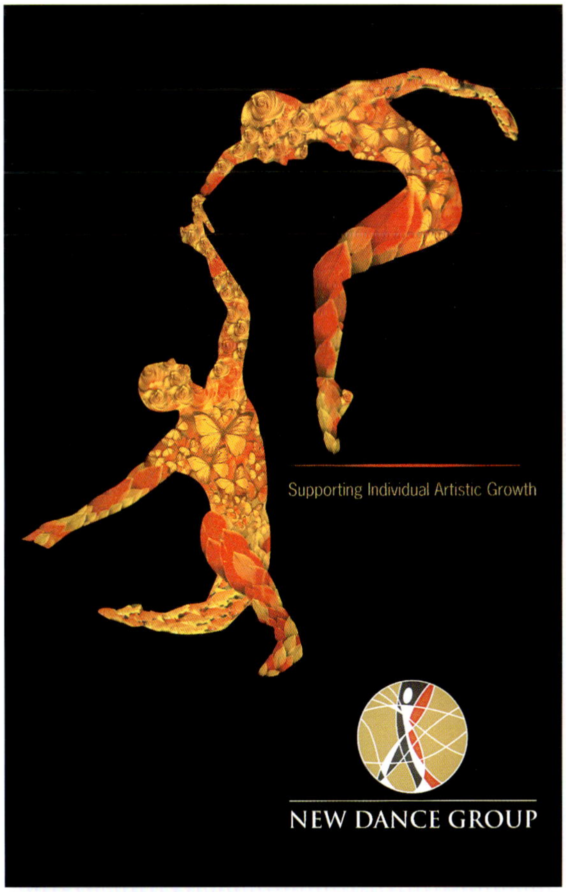

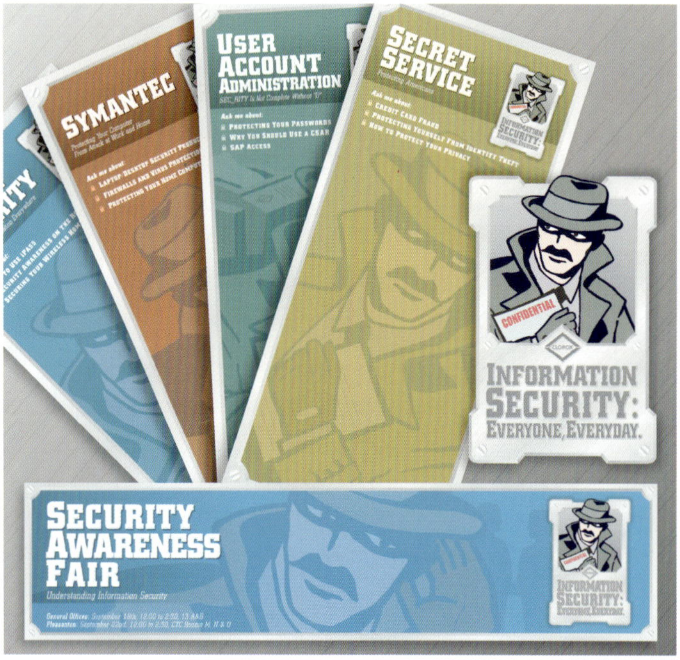

client
The Clorox Company
design firm
Clorox Creative Services
designer
Tim Ferdun
illustrator
Skip Morrow

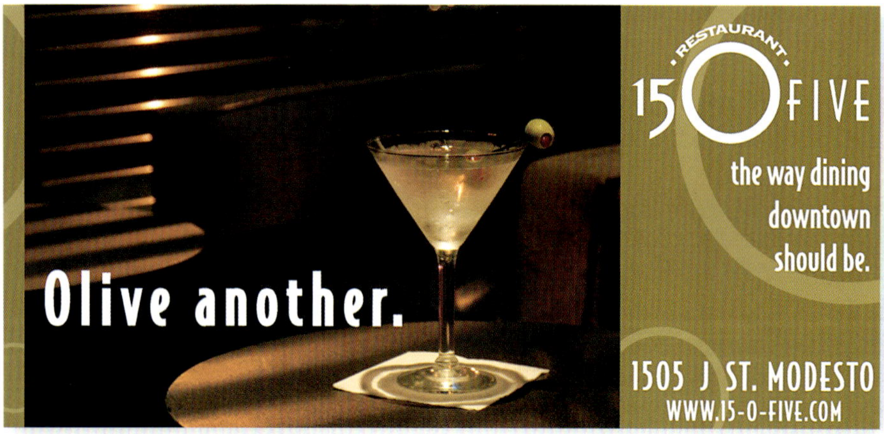

client
15-0-Five
design firm
Never Boring Design Assoc.
www.neverboring.com
designer
Shawna Bayers

client
Washington Sports & Entertainment
design firm
Fixation Marketing
www.fixation.com
designers
Bruce E. Morgan, Elizabeth Ellen

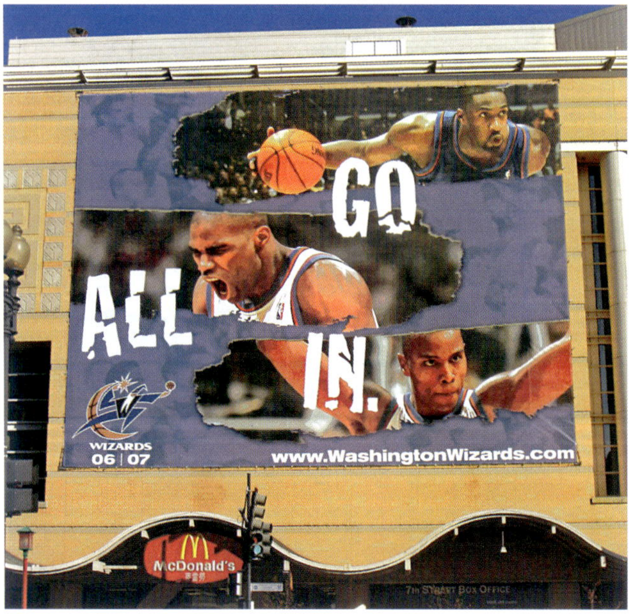

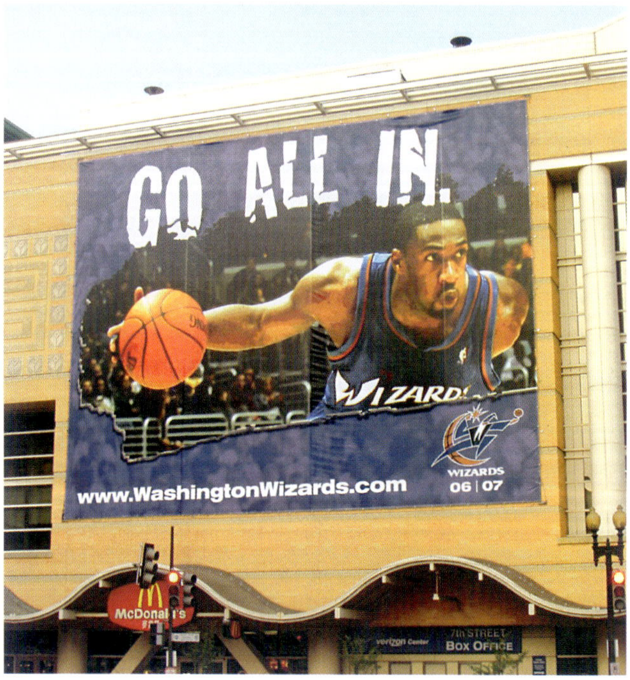

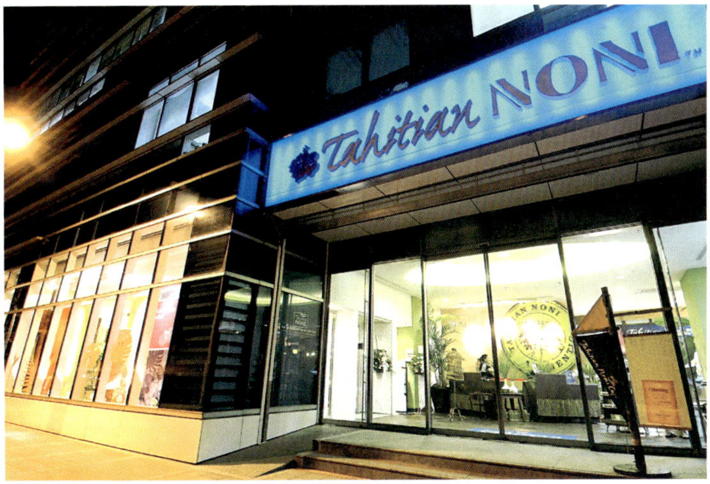

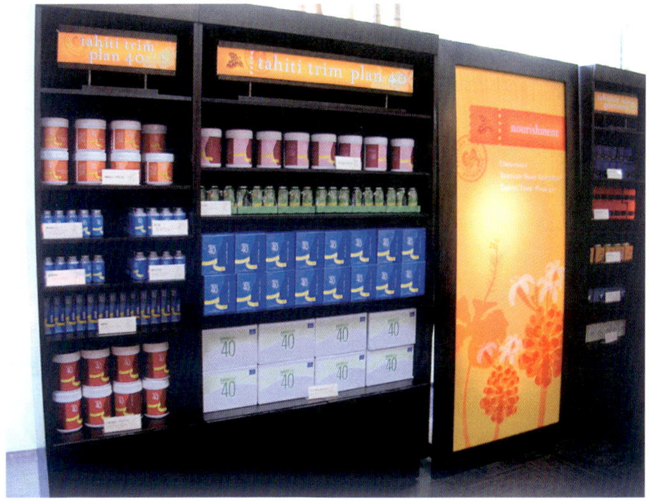

client
Tahitian Noni
design firm
Hornall Anderson Design Works
www.hadw.com
designers
Lisa Cerveny, James Tee, Tiffany Place, Sonja Max, Elmer dela Cruz, Leo Raymundo

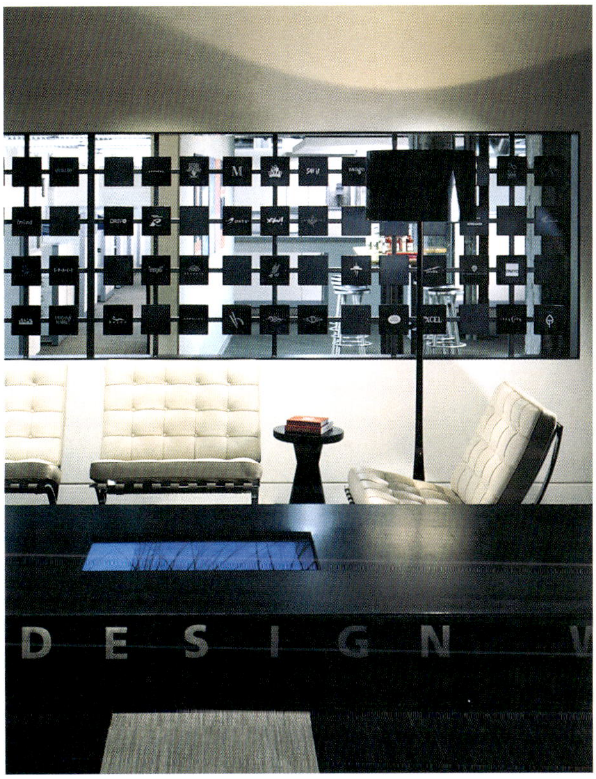

client
Hornall Anderson Design Works
design firm
Hornall Anderson Design Works
www.hadw.com
designers
Jack Anderson, SKB Architects

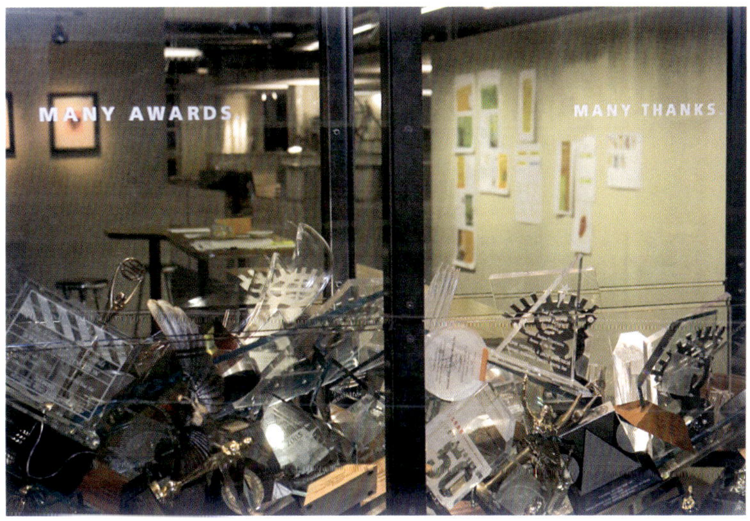

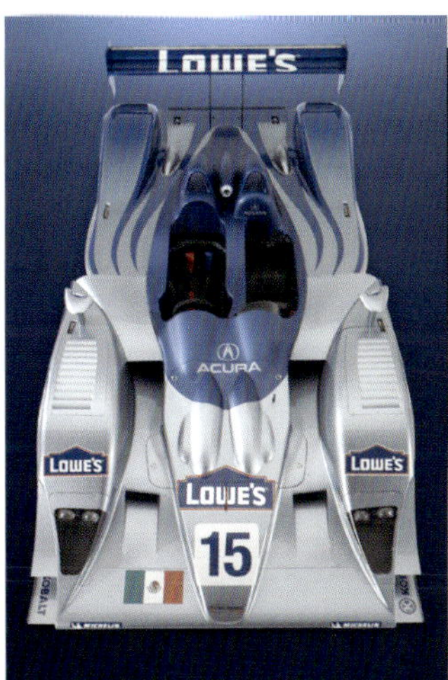

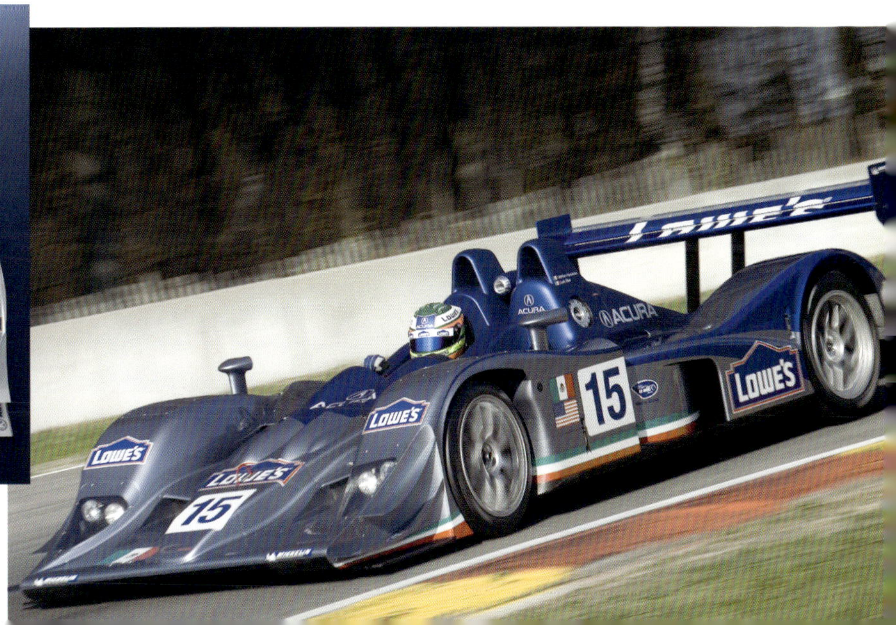

client
Fernandez Racing
design firm
SiMPLE DESIGN
simpledesigninc.com
designer
Robert Mitchell

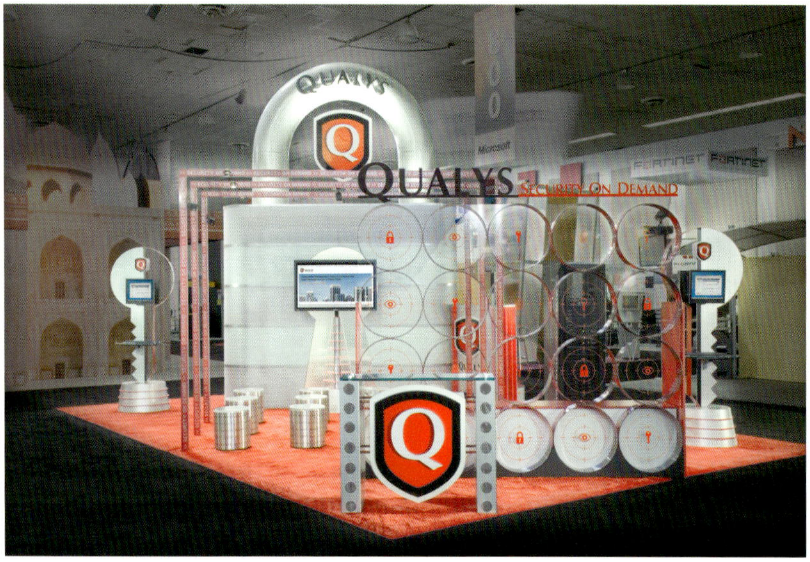

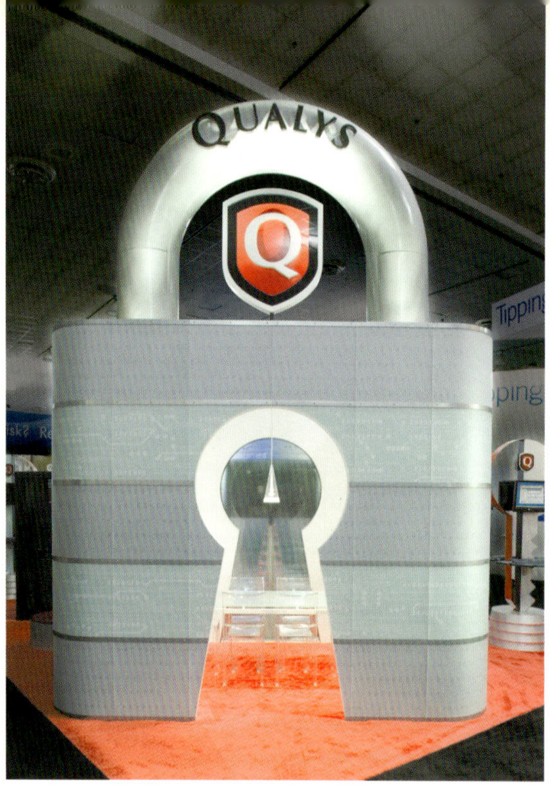

client
Qualys, Inc.
design firm
Gee & Chung Design
www.geechungdesign.com
designer
Earl Gee

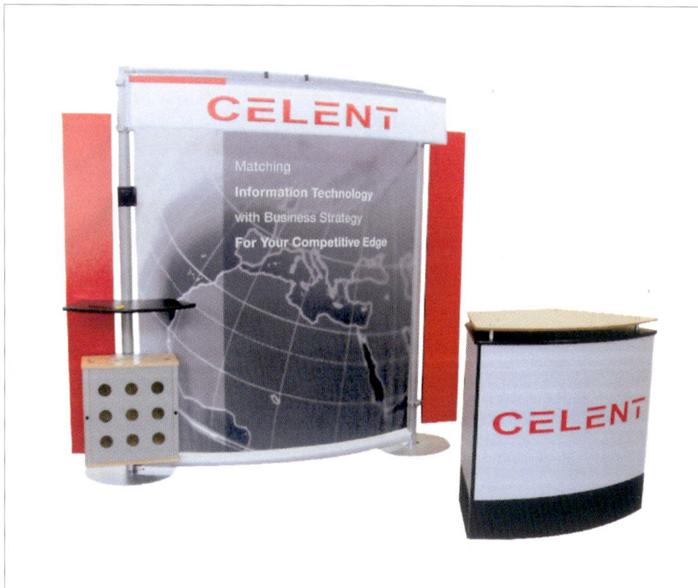

client
Celent
design firm
Cullinane
www.cullinane.com
designer
Jia Kang Sung

client
American Israel Public Affairs Committee
design firm
Beth Singer Design, LLC
www.bethsingerdesign.com
art director
Beth Singer
designers
Sucha Snidvongs, Sandra Audia, Viva Productions

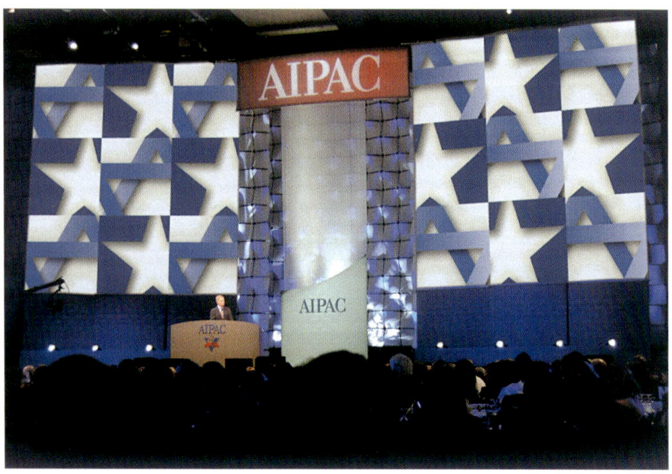

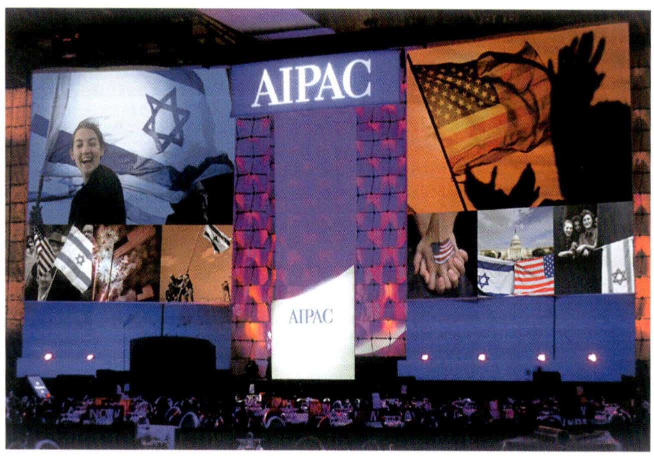

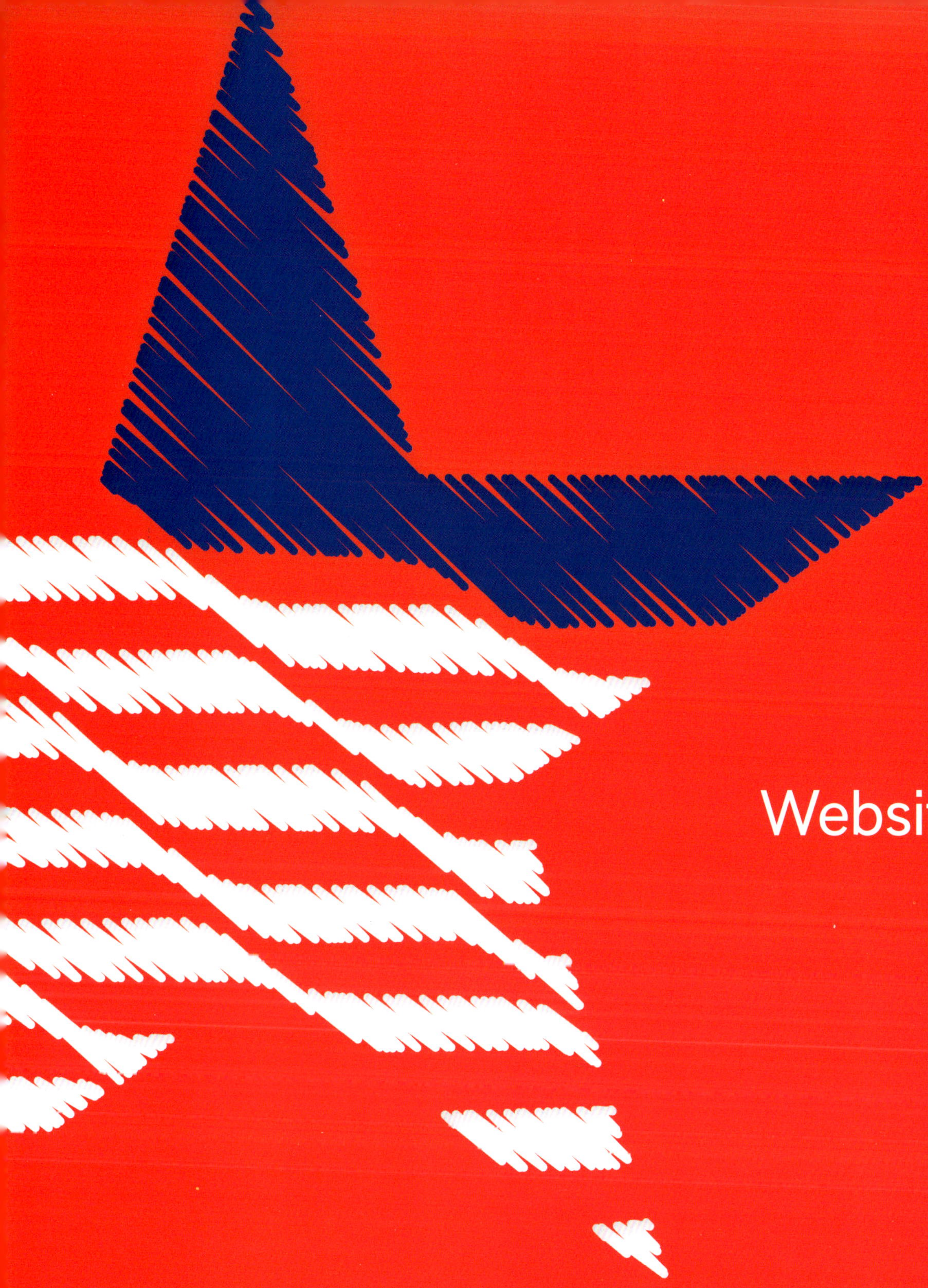

Websites

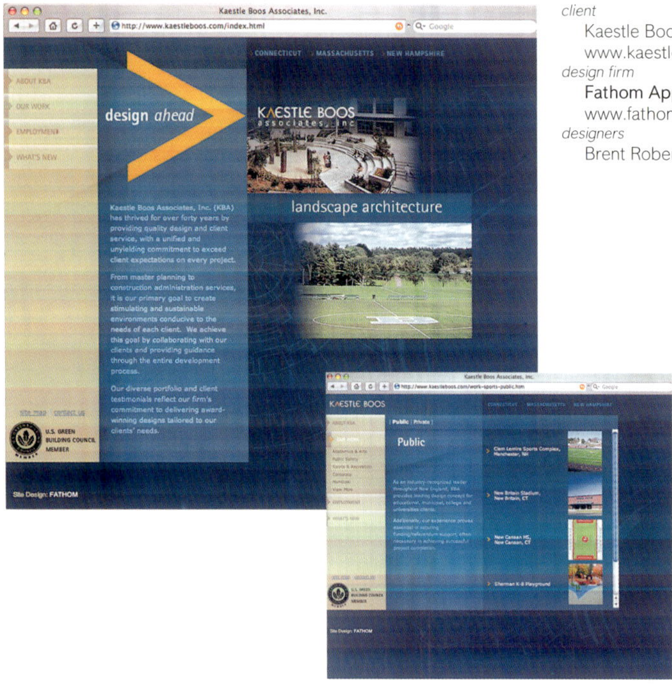

client
Kaestle Boos Associates, Inc.
www.kaestleboos.com
design firm
Fathom Applied Strategy
www.fathom.net
designers
Brent Robertson, Adrain Kecki, Bil Jenak

client
Wölffer Estate Vineyard & Stables
wolfferstables.com
design firm
Zero Gravity Design Group
www.zerogny.com
designers
Zero Gravity Design Group

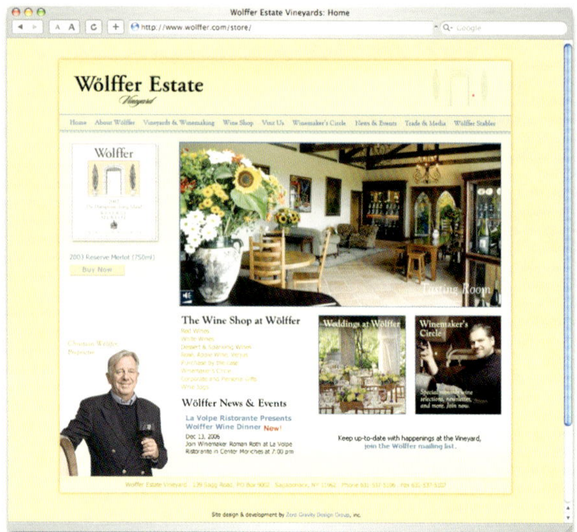

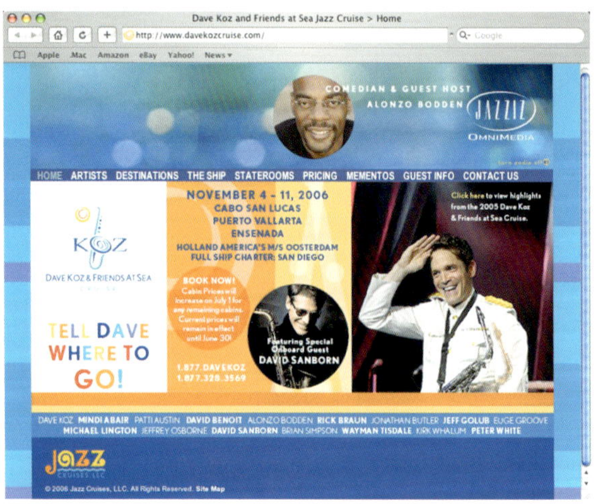

client
Jazz Cruises, LLC
www.davekozcruise.com
design firm
Kiku Obata & Company
designers
Rich Nelson, Carlos Zamora, Todd Owyoung,
Troy Guzman, Teresa Norton-Young

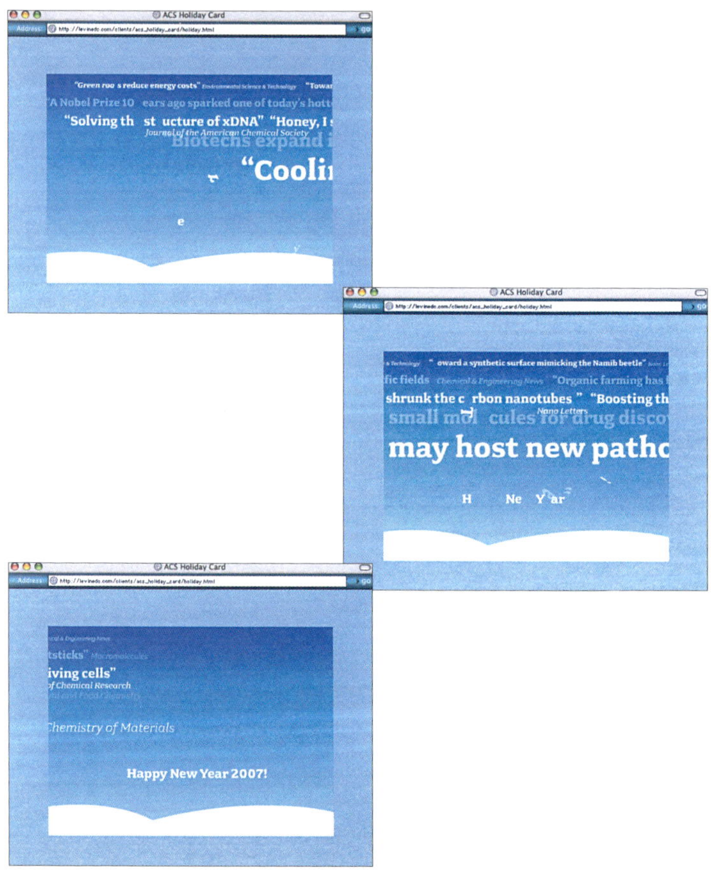

client
American Chemical Society
www.levinedc.com/clients/
acs_holidaycard/holiday.html
design firm
Levine & Associates
www.levinedc.com
designer
Megan Riordan

client
Brodart Furniture
www.brodartfurniture.com
design firm
Sire Advertising
www.sireadvertising.com
creative directors
Shawn Felty, Sumer Buttorff
web designer
Bob Henninger

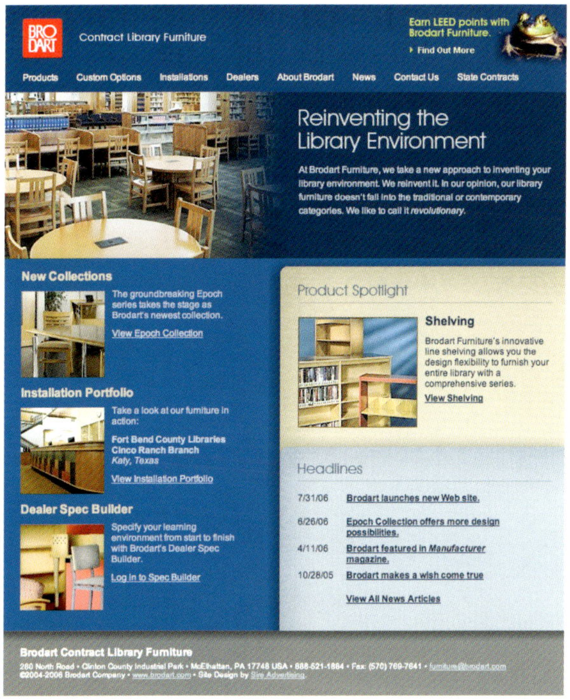

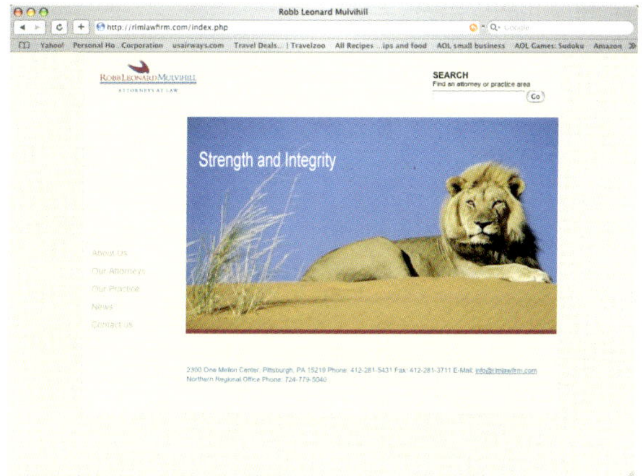

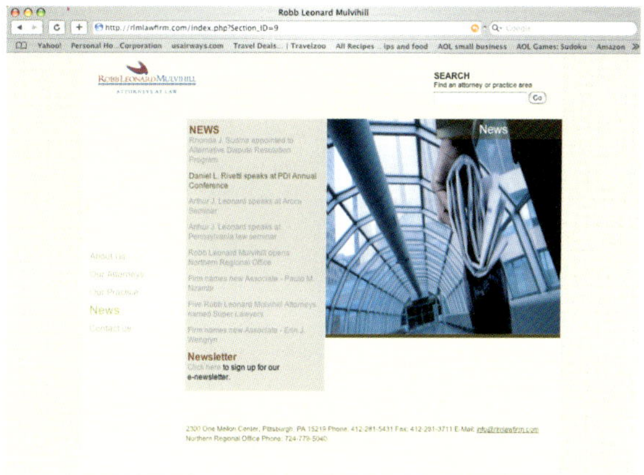

client
Robb Leonard Mulvihill
rlmlawfirm.com
design firm
Erisa Creative, LLC
designers
Erin May, Lisa Liptak

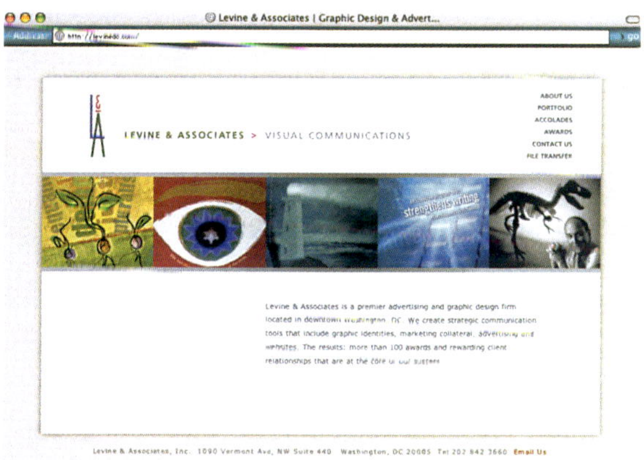

client
Levine & Associates
www.levinedc.com
design firm
Levine & Associates
www.levinedc.com
designer
Greg Sitzmann

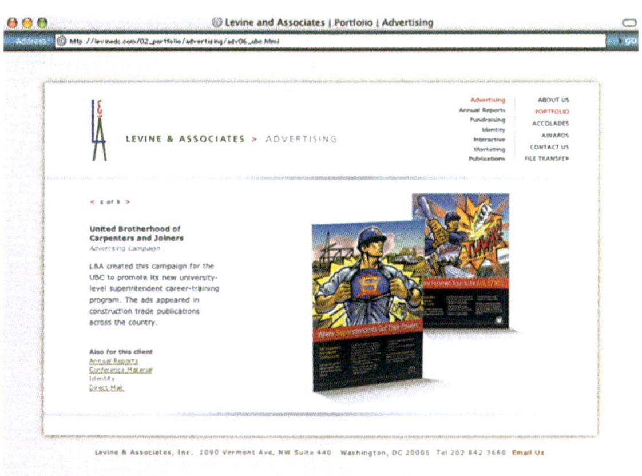

client
The Abbey Group
45province.com
design firm
Doerr Associates
mdoerr.com
designers
Joan Wilking, Linda Blacksmith

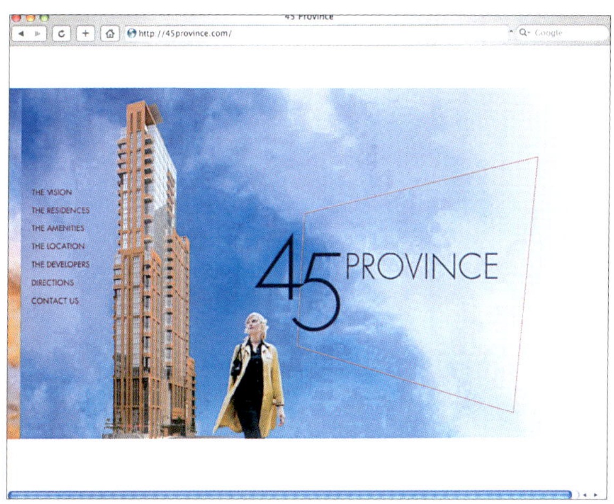

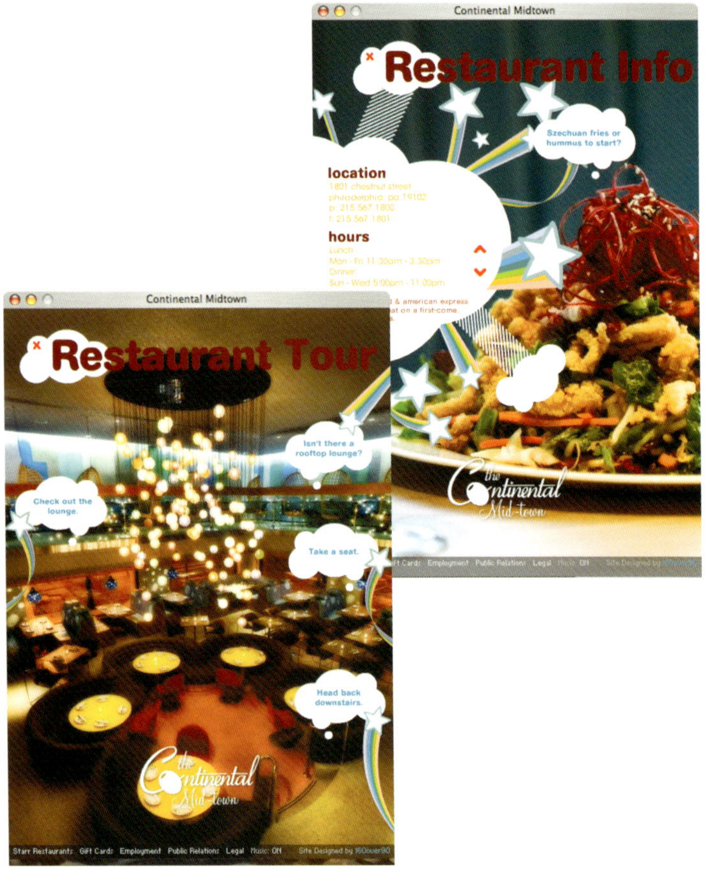

client
Starr Restaurants
continentalmidtown.com
design firm
160over90
www.160over90.com
designers
Ryan Blain, Giacomo Ciminello,
Jim Walls, Darryl Cilli

client
Jazz Cruises, LLC
www.jazzcruisesllc.com
design firm
Kiku Obata & Company
designers
Rich Nelson, Carlos Zamora,
Todd Owyoung, Troy Guzman,
Teresa Norton-Young

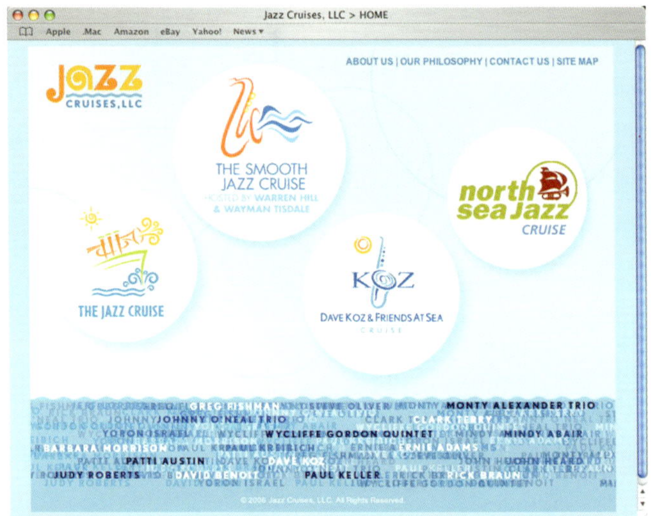

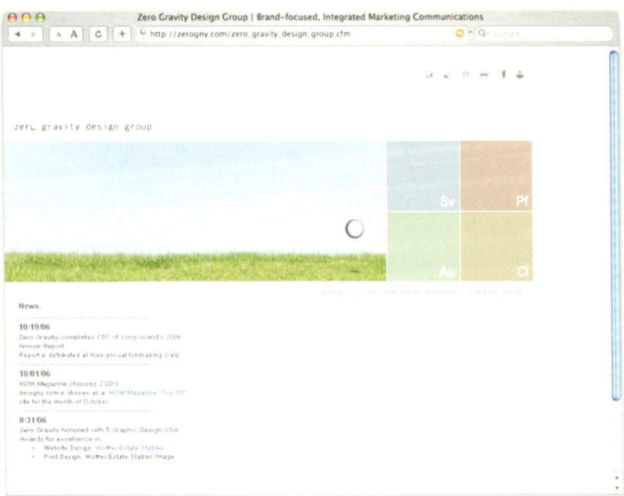

client
Zero Gravity Design Group
www.zerogny.com
design firm
Zero Gravity Design Group
www.zerogny.com
designers
Zero Gravity Design Group

client
Schottenstein Zox & Dunn Co.
www.szd.com
design firm
Greenfield/Belser Ltd.
www.gbltd.com
designers
Burkey Belser, Matt Mason
web team
Steve Gallagher, Paul Chang, David Rankin,
Fabrice Sarciaux, Jen Johnson, Dane Harrigan,
Annie Vastola

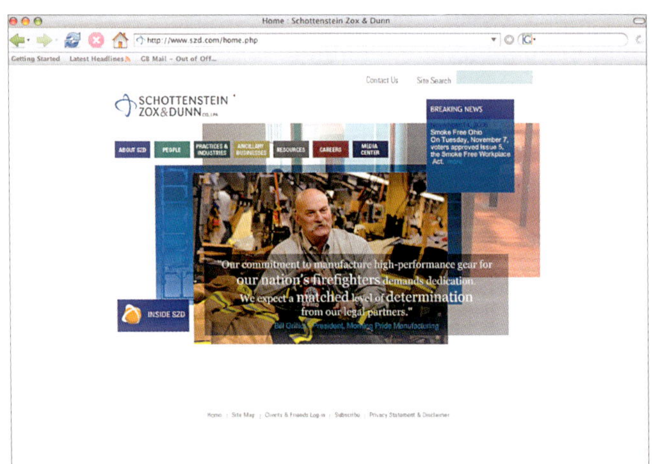

client
Rockrose Development Corp.
www.eastcoastlic.com
design firm
silver creative group
silvercreativegroup.com
designers
Suzanne Petrow, Travis Robie

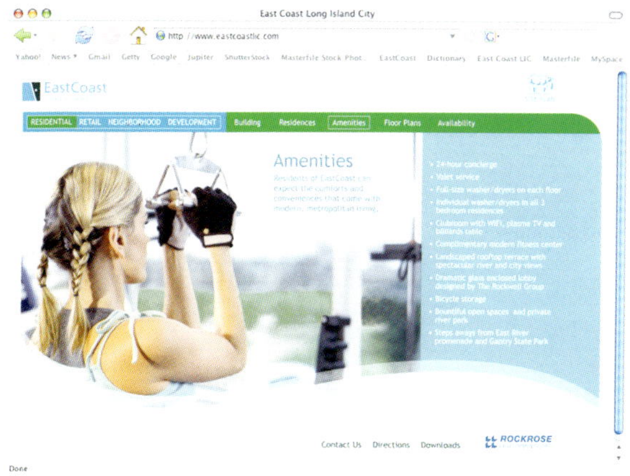

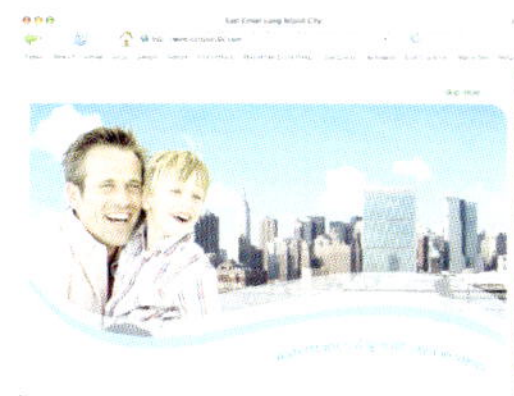

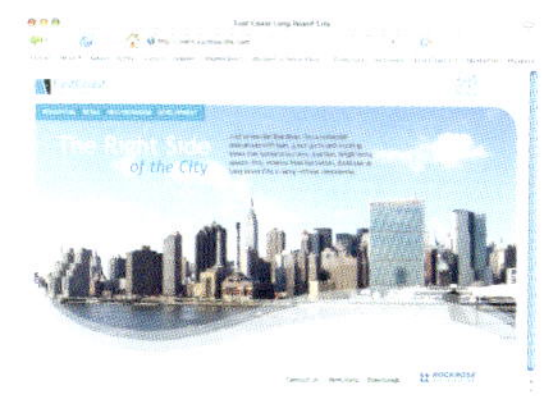

client
Fustolo Development LLC
liveatoceanclub.com
design firm
Doerr Associates
mdoerr.com
designer
Joan Wilking

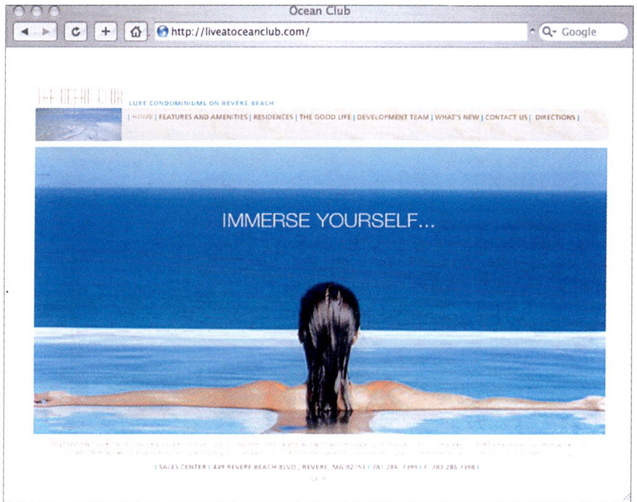

client
Starr Restaurants
www.morimotonyc.com
design firm
160over90
www.160over90.com
designers
Ryan Blain, Matt Bednavik, Giacomo Ciminello,
Cory McCall, Jim Walls, Darryl Cilli

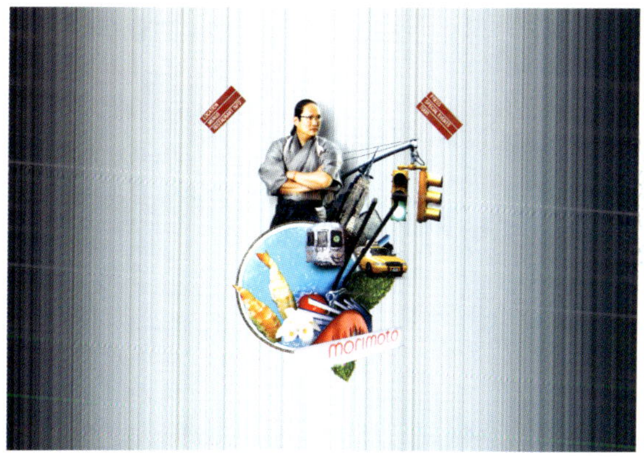

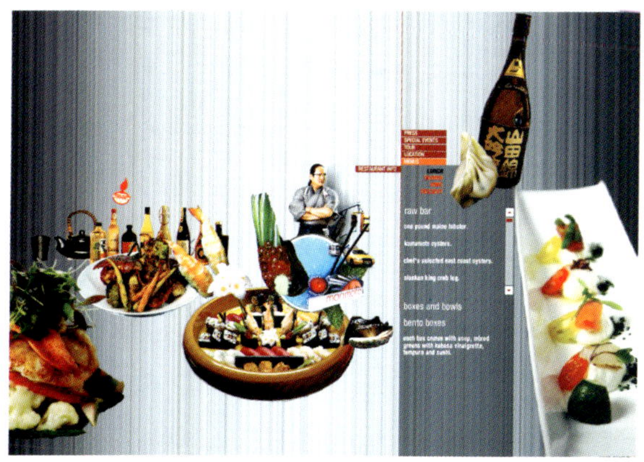

client
The Castleton Group
befree.castletongroup.com
design firm
Hummingbird Creative Group
www.hummingbird-creative.com
designer
Juli LaDuc

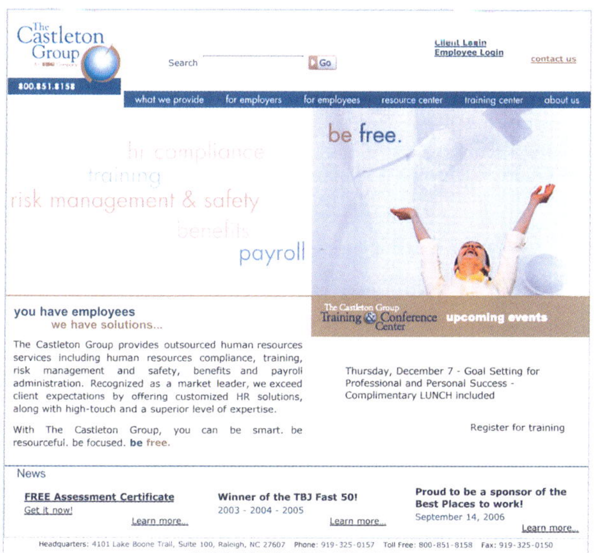

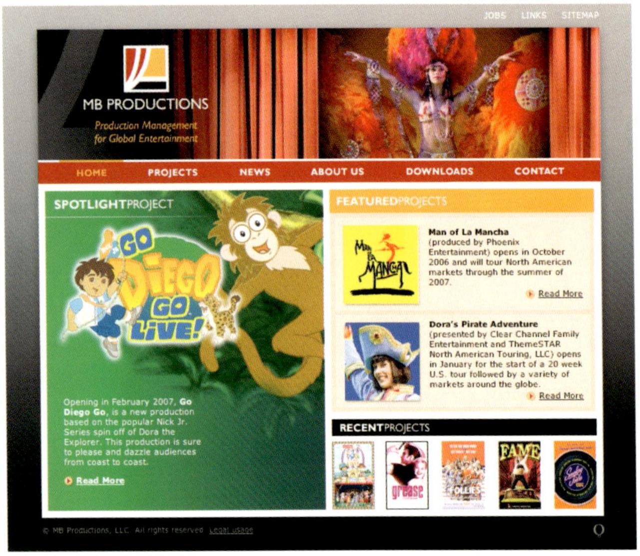

client
MB Productions, LLC
www.mbproductions.com
design firm
Octavo Designs
www.8vodesigns.com
designers
Mark Burrier, Sue Hough

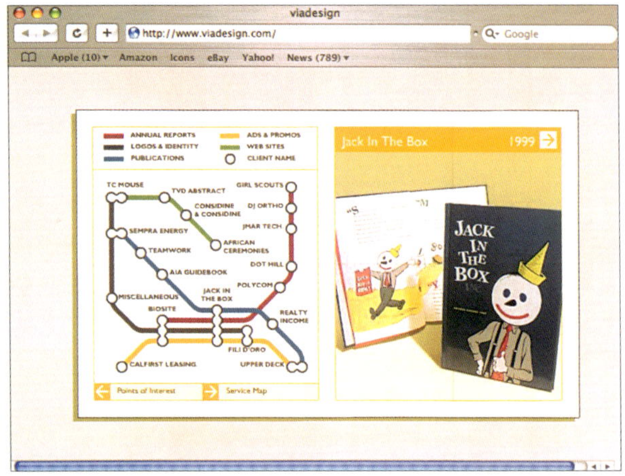

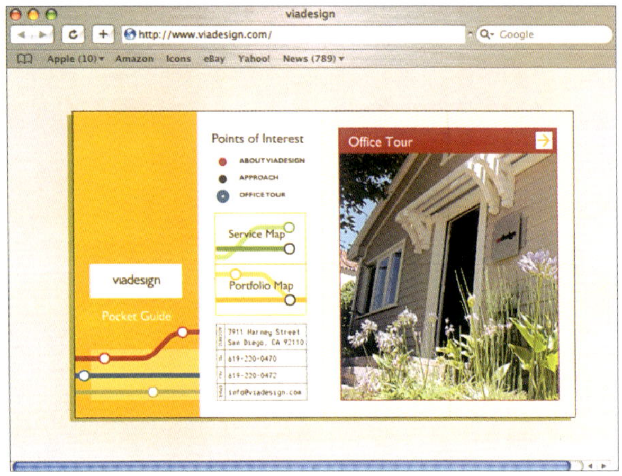

client
viadesign
www.viadesign.com
design firm
viadesign
www.viadesign.com
designer
Scott Pacheco

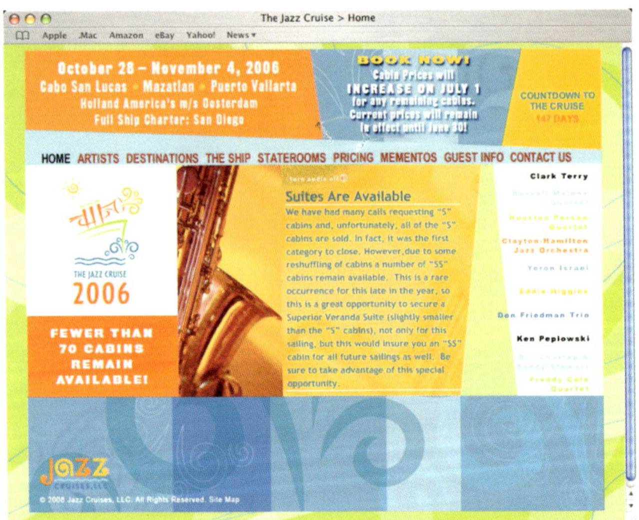

client
Jazz Cruises, LLC
www.thejazzcruise.com
design firm
Kiku Obata & Company
designers
Rich Nelson, Carlos Zamora, Todd Owyoung,
Troy Guzman, Teresa Norton-Young

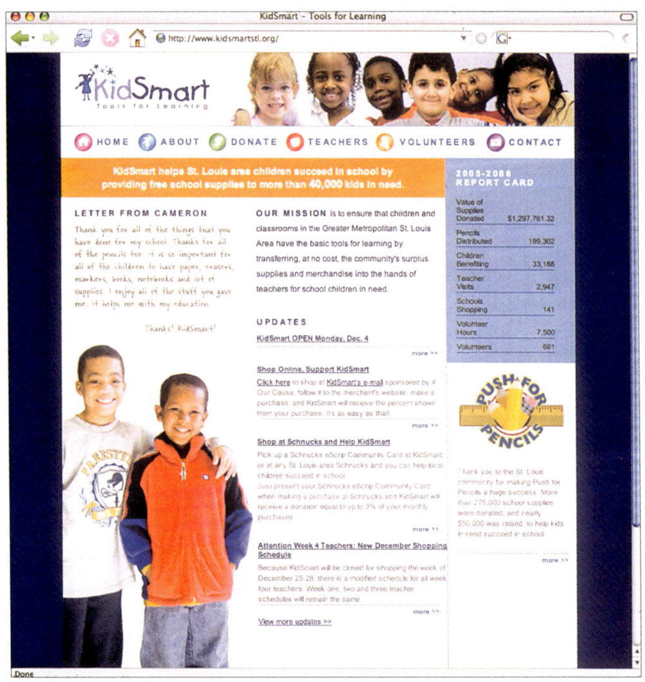

client
KidSmart—Tools for Learning
www.kidsmartstl.org
design firm
Paradowski Creative
www.paradowski.com
creative director
Alex Paradowski
designers
Jerry Gennaria, Dennis Bland,
Elizabeth Erickson

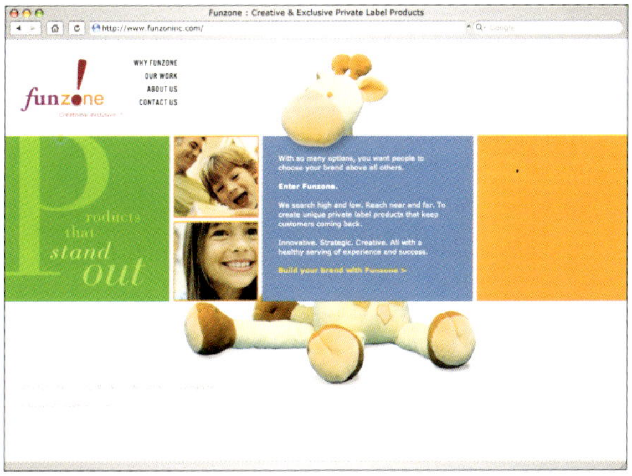

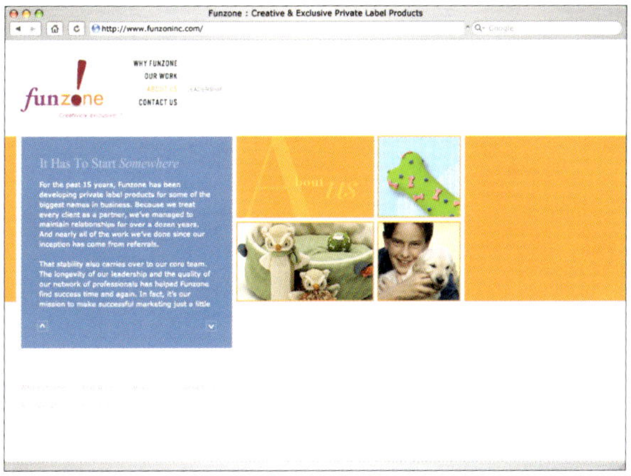

client
Funzone Flash Website
www.funzoneinc.com
design firm
IE Design + Communications
iedesign.com
designers
Kenny Goldstein, Mimi Lee, Tom Johson

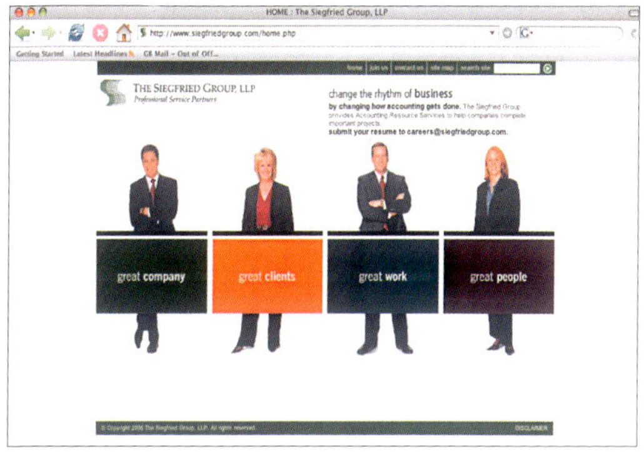

client
Siegfried Group
www.siegfriedgroup.com
design firm
Greenfield/Belser Ltd.
www.gbltd.com
designers
Siobhan Davis, Aaron Hansen, Burkey Belser
web team
Steve Gallagher, Paul Chang, David Rankin,
Fabrice Sarciaux, Jen Johnson, Dane Harrigan,
Annie Vastola

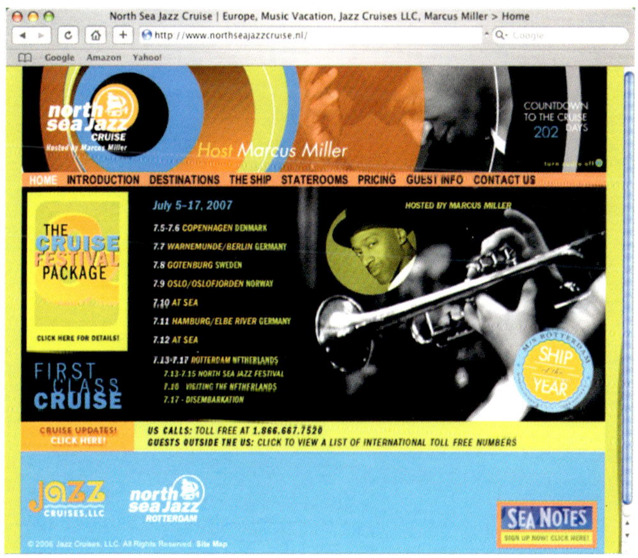

client
Jazz Cruises, LLC
www.northseajazzcruise.nl
design firm
Kiku Obata & Company
designers
Rich Nelson, Carlos Zamora,
Todd Owyoung, Troy Guzman,
Teresa Norton-Young

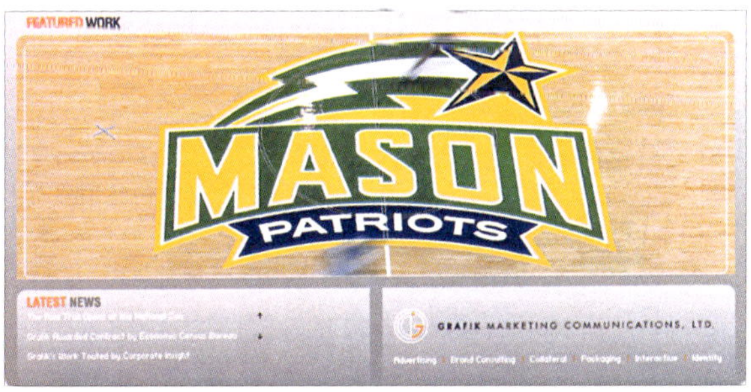

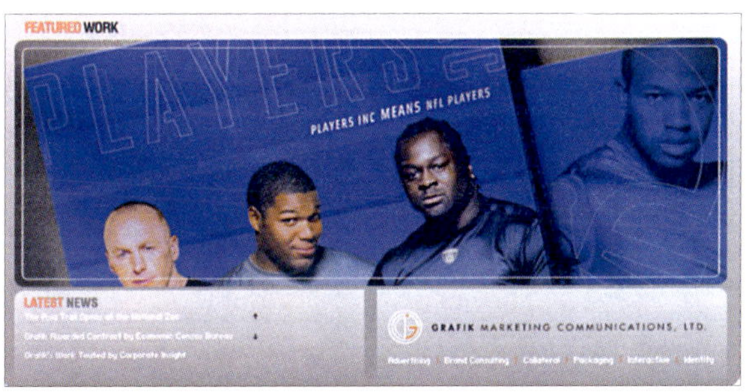

client
Grafik Marketing Communications
www.grafik.com
design firm
Grafik Marketing Communications
www.grafik.com
designers
James Smith, David Collins,
Greg Glaviano, Fabio Silva, Judy Kirpich

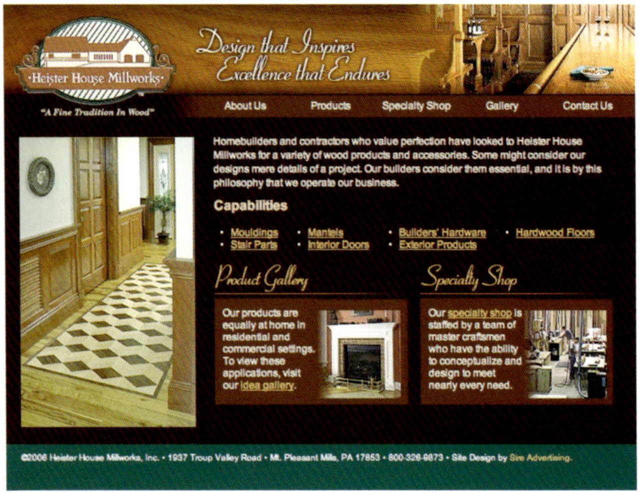

client
Heister House Millworks
www.hhmillworks.com
design firm
Sire Advertising
www.sireadvertising.com
creative director
Shawn Felty
web designer
Bob Henninger

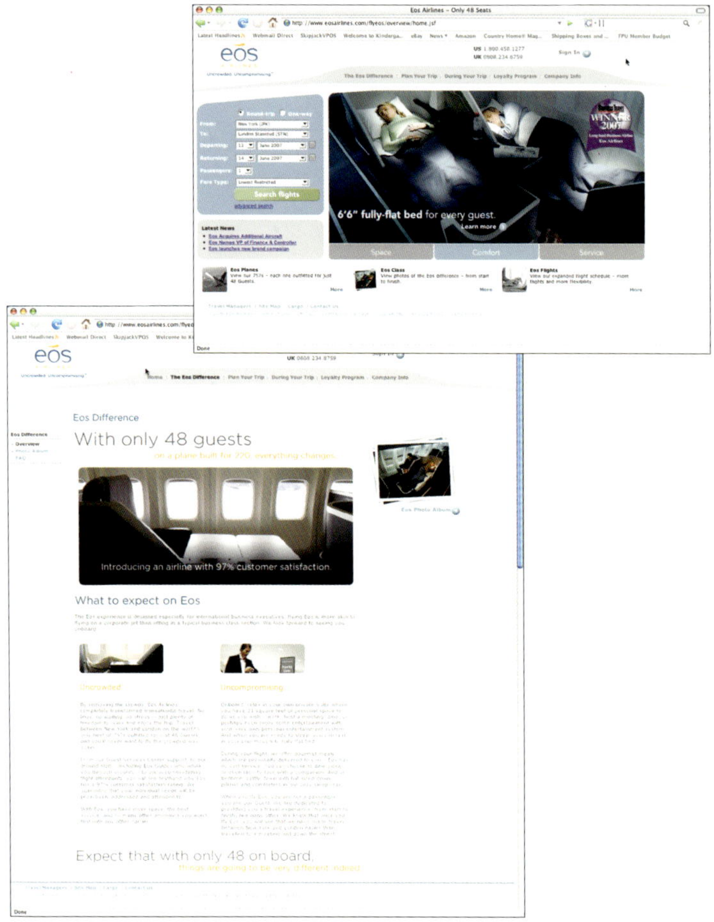

client
Eos Airlines
www.eosairlines.com
design firm
Hornall Anderson Design Works
www.hadw.com
designers
Jamie Monberg, Mark Popich,
Hans Krebs, Mobiam, Sally Bergesen

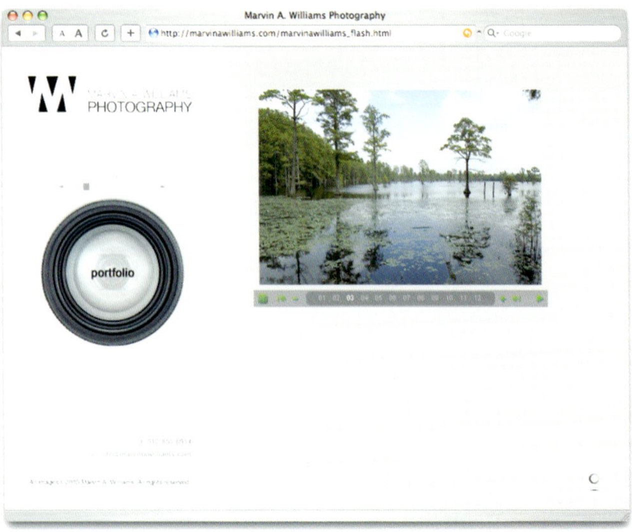

client
Marvin A. Williams Photography
marvinawilliams.com
design firm
Zero Gravity Design Group
www.zerogny.com
designers
Zero Gravity Design Group

client
Albright Care Services
www.albrightcare.org
design firm
Sire Advertising
www.sireadvertising.com
creative directors
Shawn Felty, Sumer Buttorff
web designers
Bob Henninger, Jessica Varner

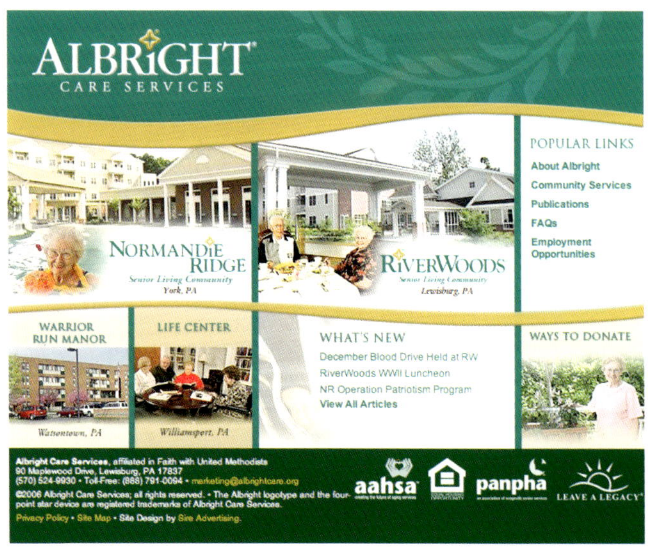

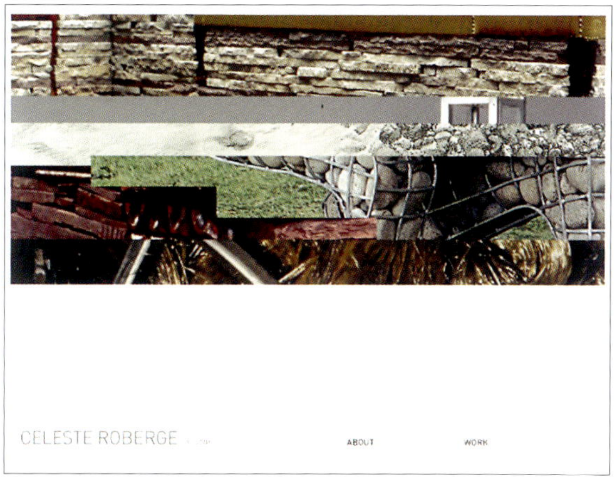

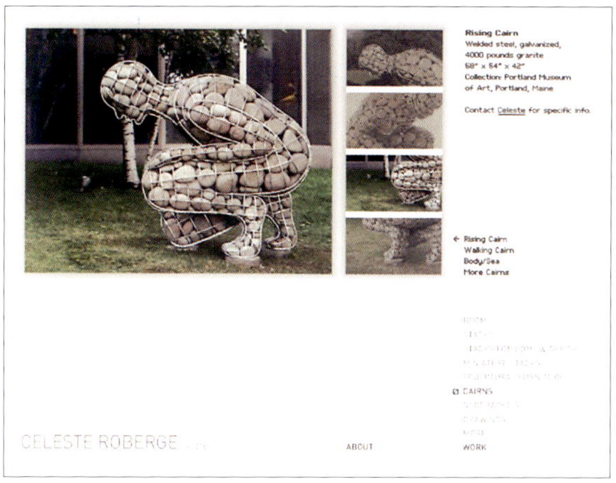

client
Celeste Roberge
www.celesteroberge.com
design firm
Connie Hwang Design
www.conniehwangdesign.com
designer
Connie Hwang

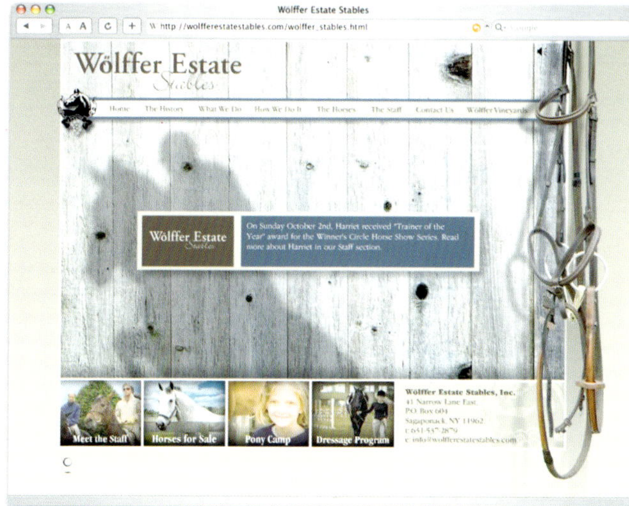

client
Wölffer Estate Vineyard & Stables
wolfferstables.com
design firm
Zero Gravity Design Group
www.zerogny.com
designers
Zero Gravity Design Group

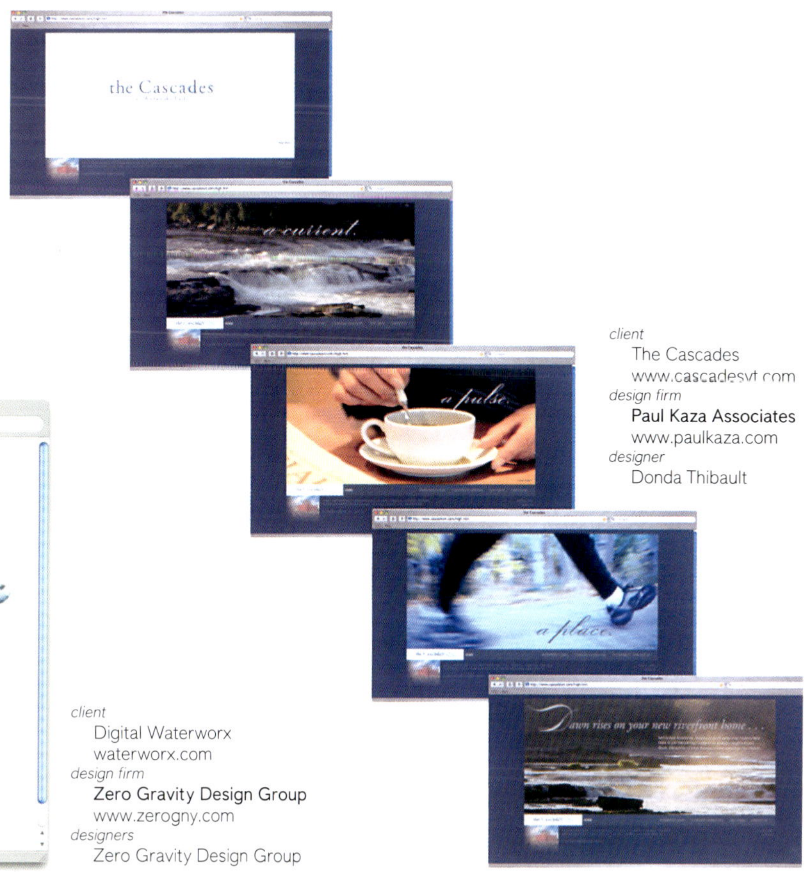

client
The Cascades
www.cascadesvt.com
design firm
Paul Kaza Associates
www.paulkaza.com
designer
Donda Thibault

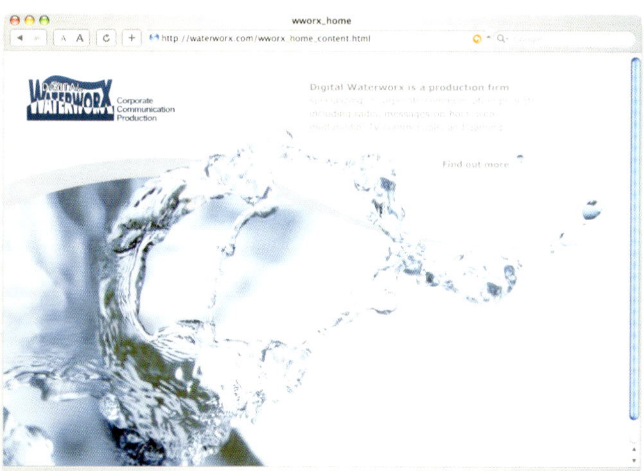

client
Digital Waterworx
waterworx.com
design firm
Zero Gravity Design Group
www.zerogny.com
designers
Zero Gravity Design Group

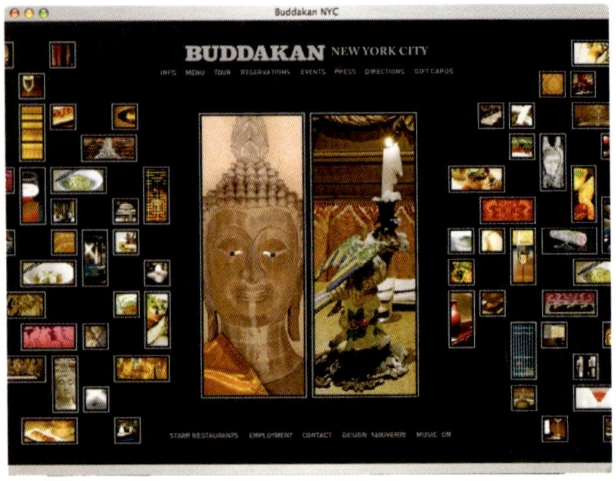

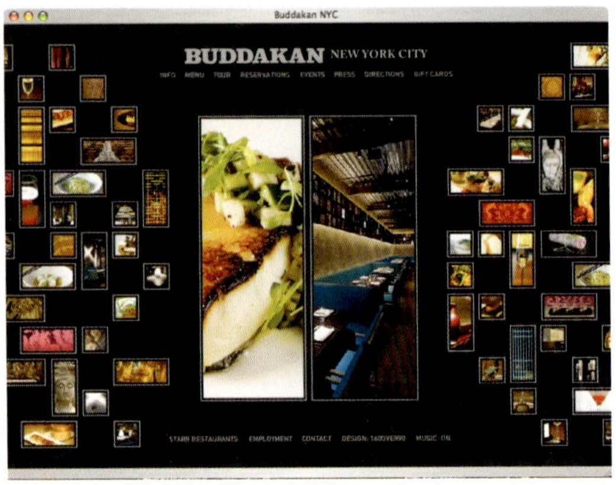

client
Starr Restaurants
www.buddakannyc.com
design firm
160over90
www.160over90.com
designers
Greg Ash, Ryan Blain,
Brendan Quinn, Jim Walls, Darryl Cilli

client
Mooreland Glen
www.mooreland glen.com
design firm
Fathom Applied Strategy
www.fathom.net
designer
Bil Jenak

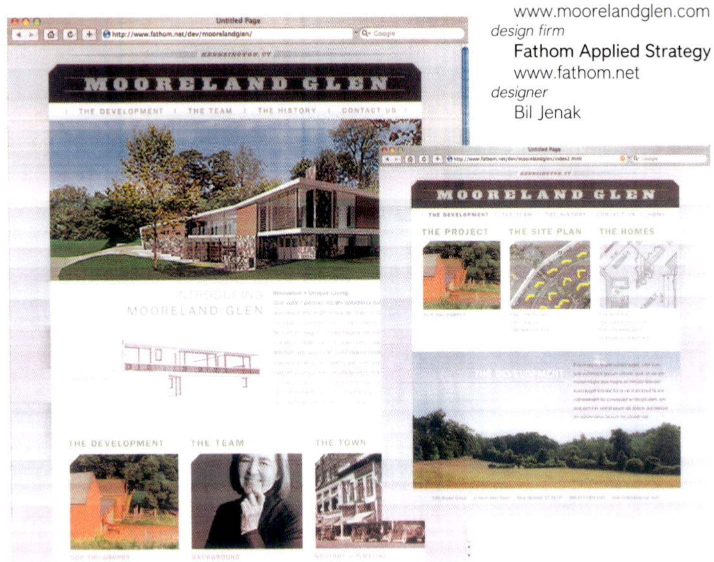

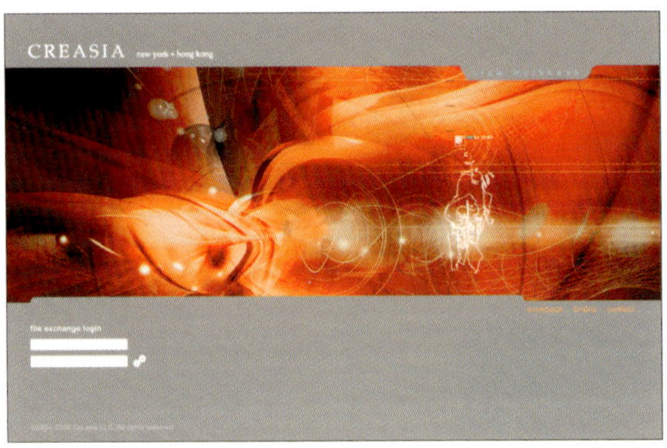

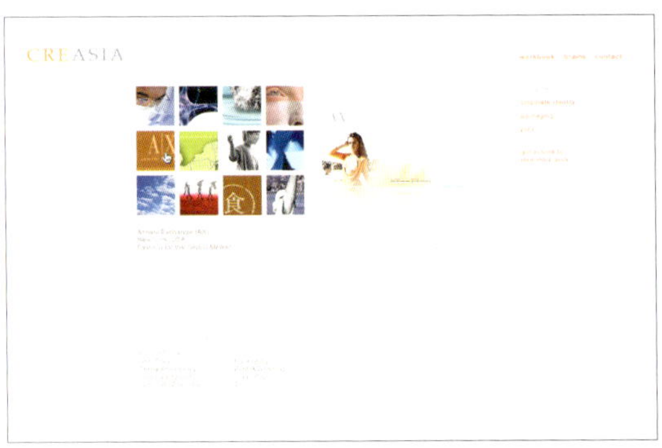

client
Creasia LLC
creasiadesign.com
design firm
Creasia LLC
creasiadesign.com
designer
Carmen Li

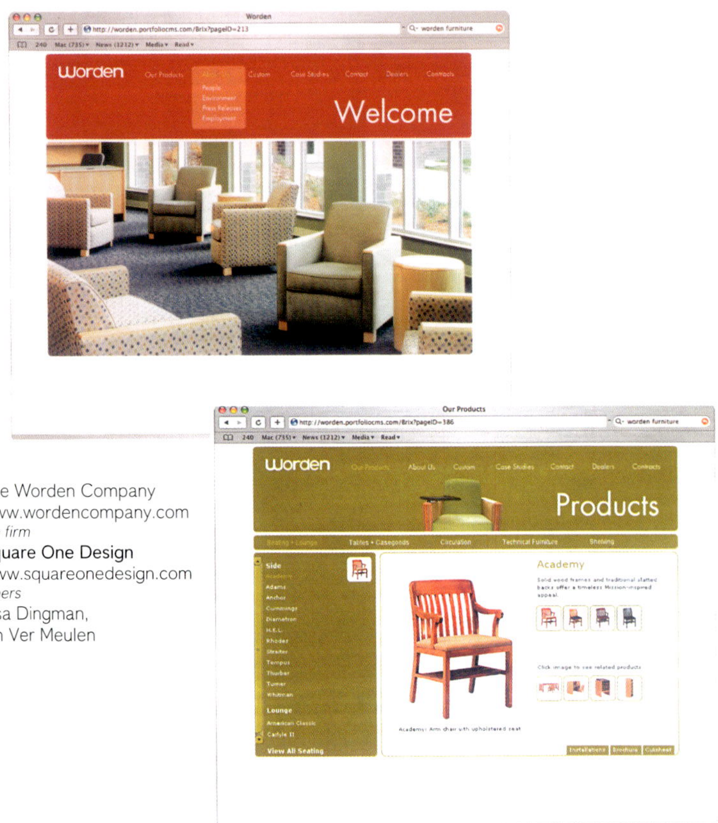

client
The Worden Company
www.wordencompany.com
design firm
Square One Design
www.squareonedesign.com
designers
Lisa Dingman,
Lin Ver Meulen

client
Collinsville Factory
www.collinsvillefactory.com
design firm
Fathom Applied Strategy
www.fathom.net
designers
Bil Jenak, Adrian Kecki

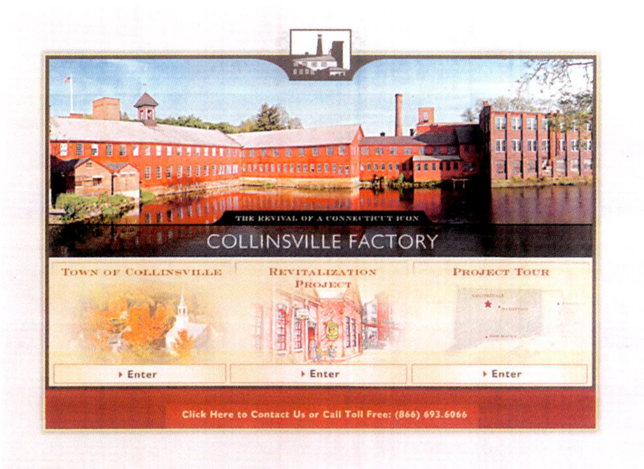

client
Jazz Cruises, LLC
www.thesmoothjazzcruise.com
design firm
Kiku Obata & Company
designers
Rich Nelson, Carlos Zamora, Todd Owyoung,
Troy Guzman, Teresa Norton-Young

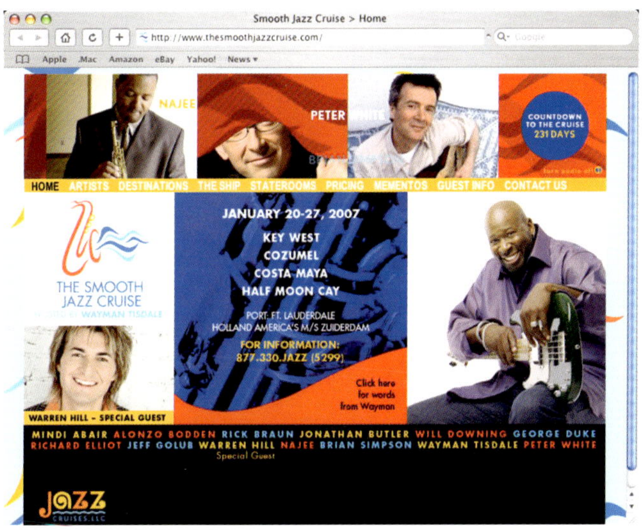

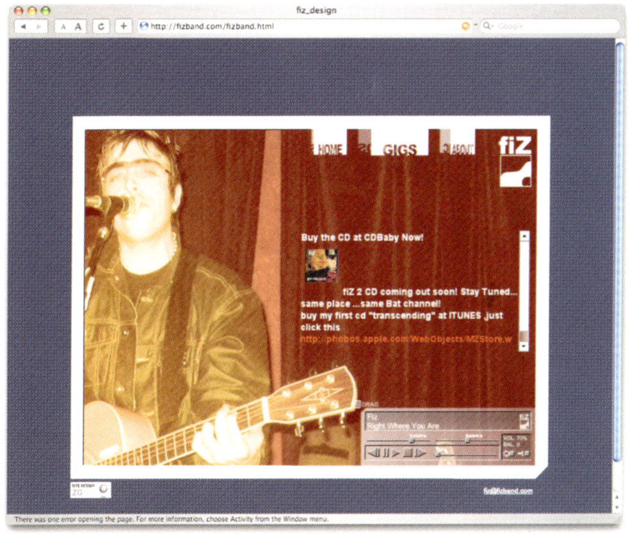

client
FiZ Band
fizband.com
design firm
Zero Gravity Design Group
www.zerogny.com
designers
Zero Gravity Design Group

client
IKKO Hibachi
Steakhouse & Sushi Bar
www.ikkosteakhouse.com
design firm
Jing Zhou Studio
www.jingzhoustudio.net
designer
Jing Zhou

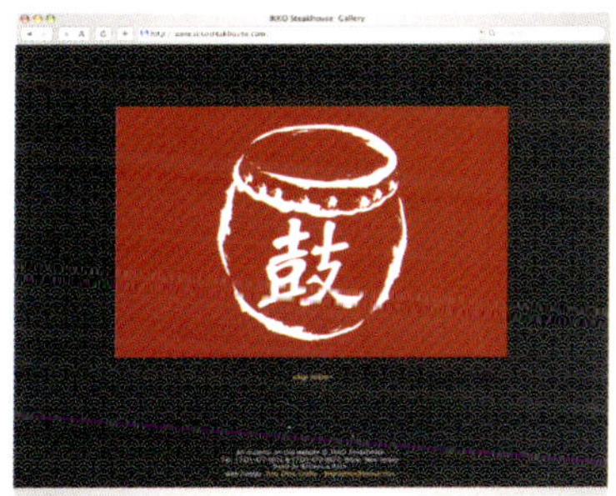

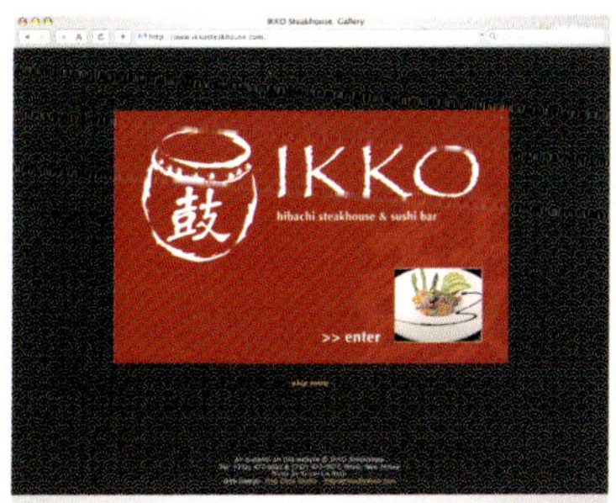

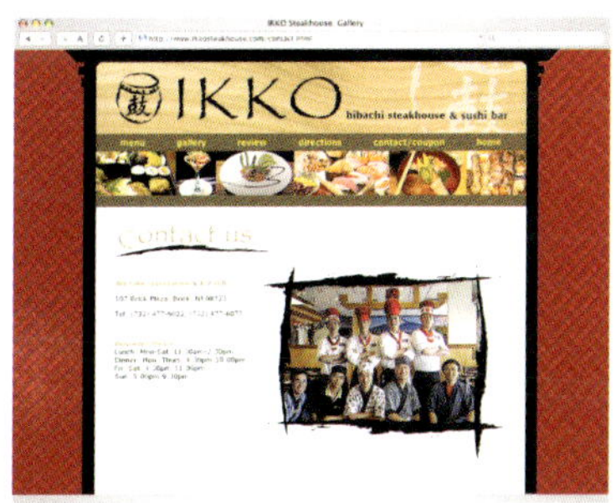

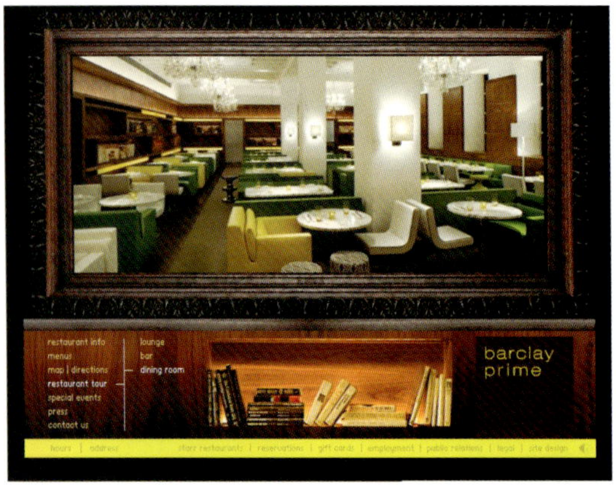

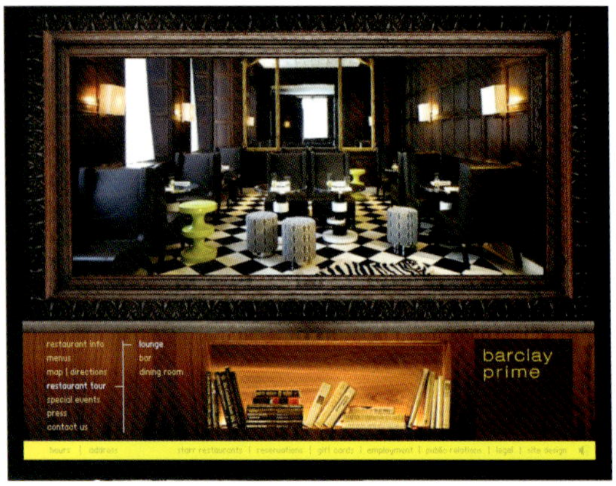

client
Starr Restaurants
www.barclayprime.com
design firm
160over90
www.160over90.com
designers
Darryl Cilli, Ryan Blain,
Greg Klein, Jim Walls,
Brendan Quinn

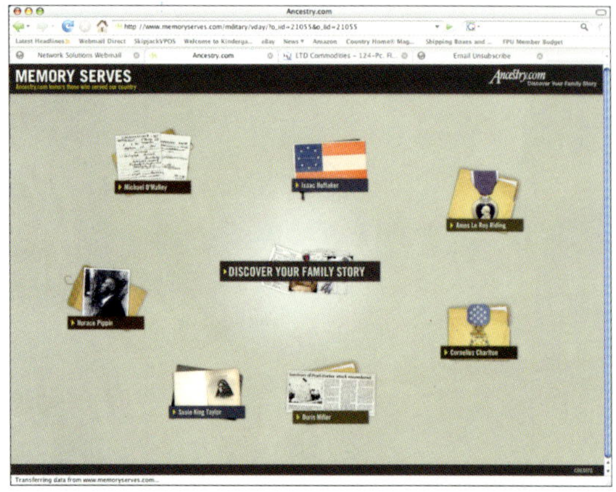

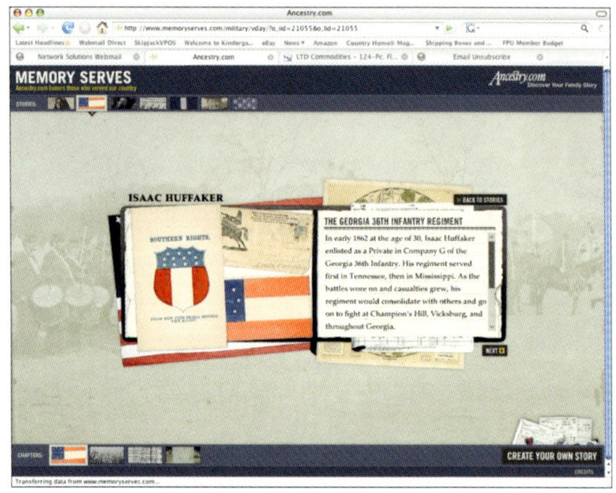

client
My Family
www.memoryserves.com
design firm
Hornall Anderson Design Works
www.hadw.com
designers
Jamie Monberg, Nathan Young,
Adrien Lo, John Close,
Roel Hava, Michele Godfrey

client
Silverhook Alaska Coffee
www.silverhookcoffee.com
design firm
IE Design +
Communications
iedesign.com
designer
Kenny Goldstein

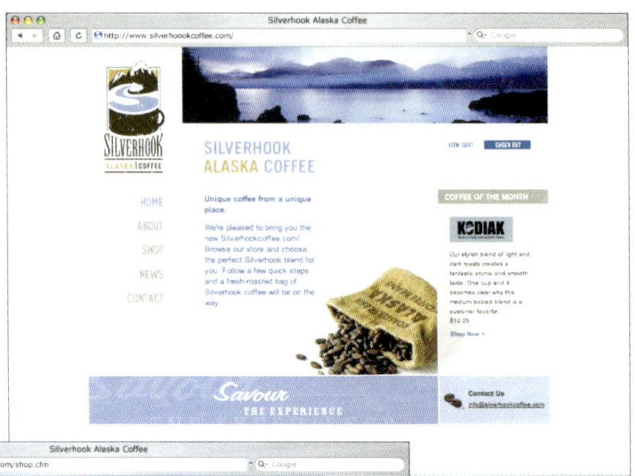

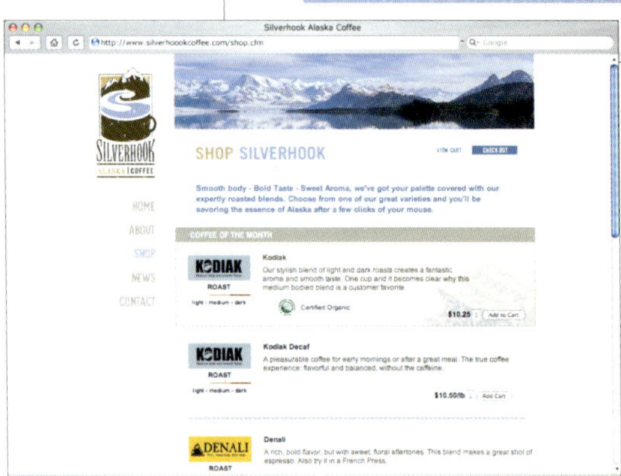

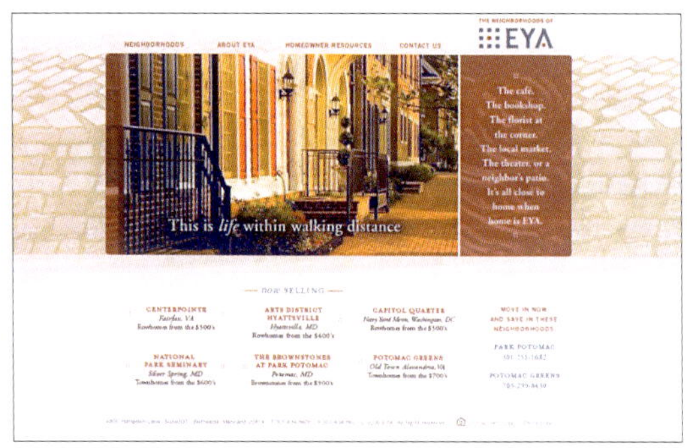

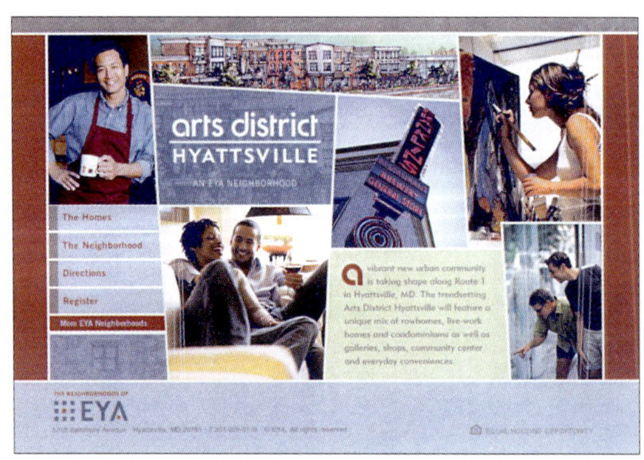

client
EYA
www.eya.com
design firm
Grafik Marketing
Communications
www.grafik.com
designers
Arthur Hsu,
Johnny Vitorovich,
Kathy Slack,
Hal Swetham,
Fabio Silva

client
USC Gould School of Law
weblaw.usc.edu
design firm
IE Design + Communications
iedesign.com
designer
Kenny Goldstein

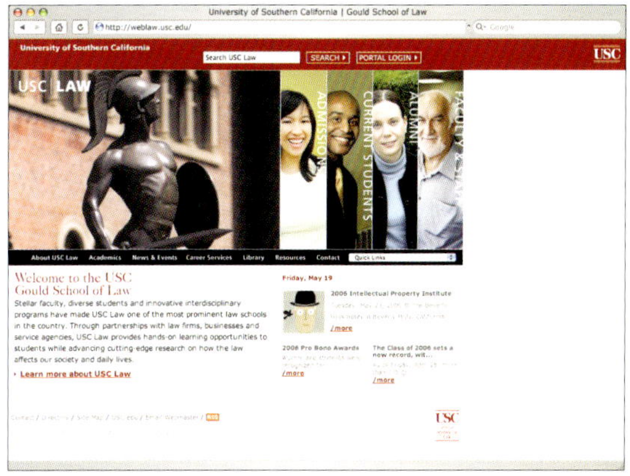

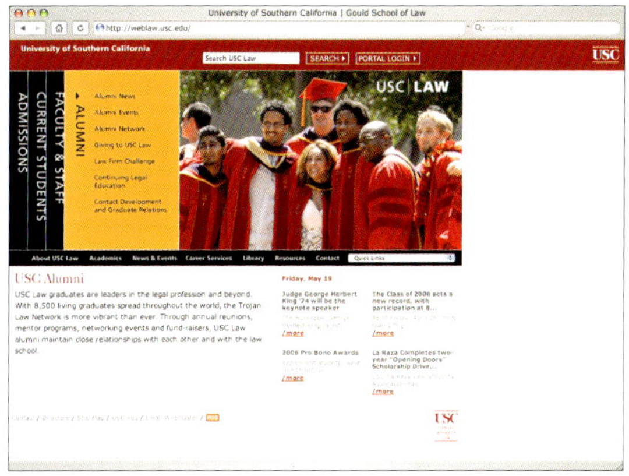

client
Slater's Home Furnishings
www.slatershome.com
design firm
Never Boring Design Assoc.
www.neverboring.com
designer
Shawna Bayers

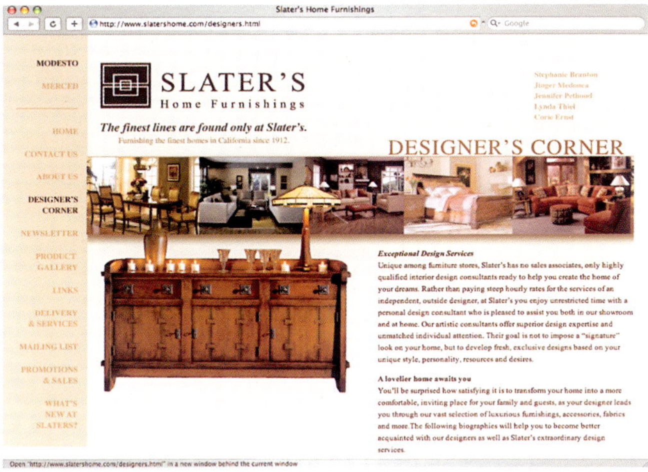

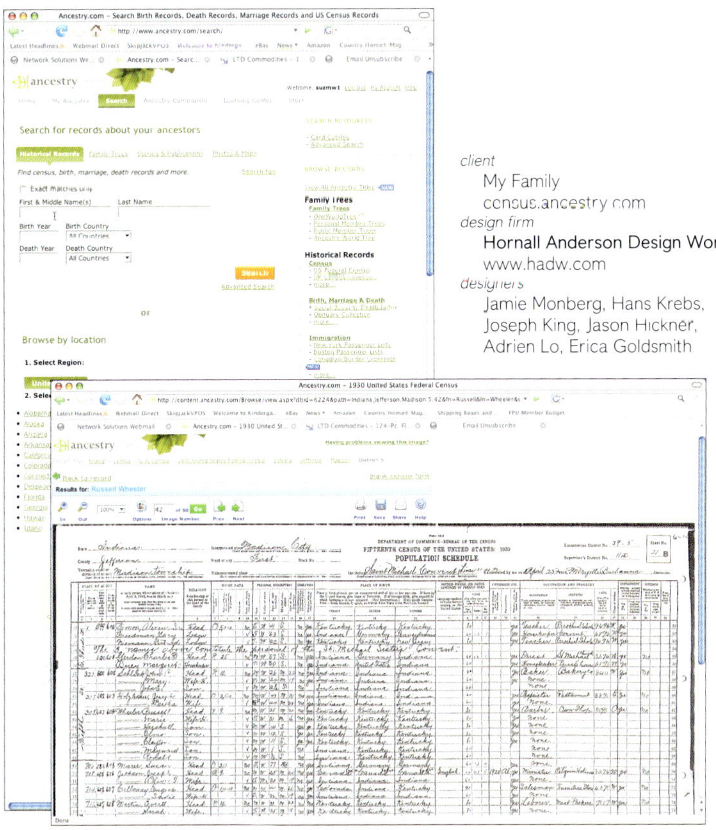

client
My Family
census.ancestry.com
design firm
Hornall Anderson Design Works
www.hadw.com
designers
Jamie Monberg, Hans Krebs,
Joseph King, Jason Hickner,
Adrien Lo, Erica Goldsmith

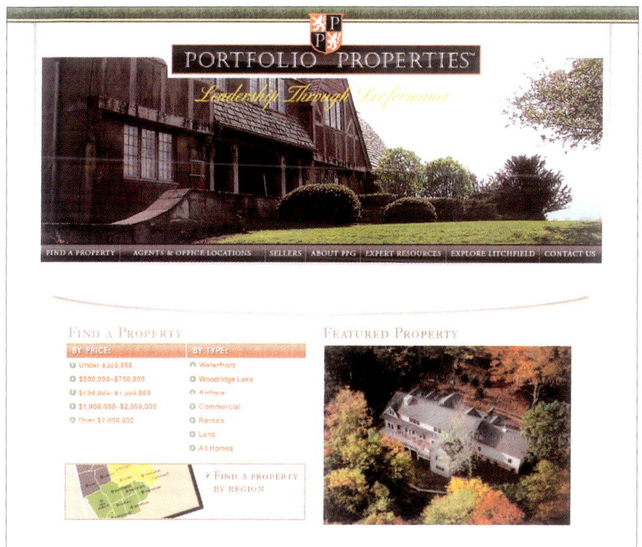

client
Portfolio Properties Group
www.ppgrealtors.com
design firm
Fathom Applied Strategy
www.fathom.net
designer
Adrian Kecki

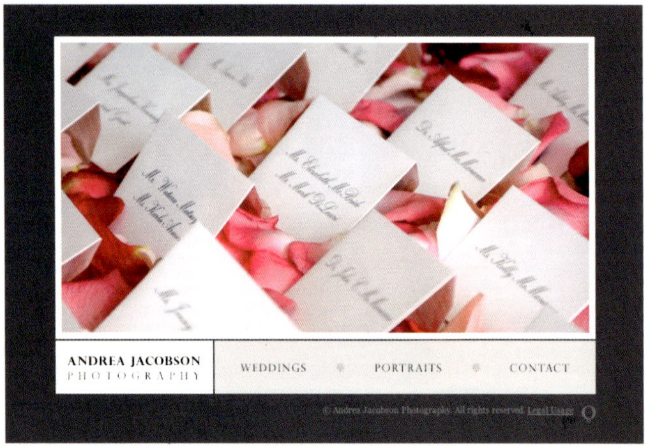

client
Andrea Jacobson Photography
www.andrea-jacobson.com
design firm
Octavo Designs
www.8vodesigns.com
designers
Mark Burrier, Sue Hough

client
Jazz Cruises, LLC
www.thelatinmusiccruise.com
design firm
Kiku Obata & Company
designers
Rich Nelson, Carlos Zamora, Todd Owyoung, Troy Guzman, Teresa Norton-Young

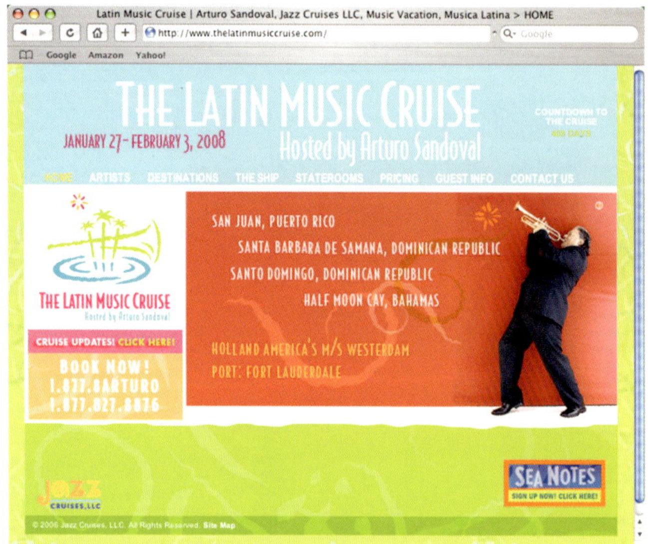

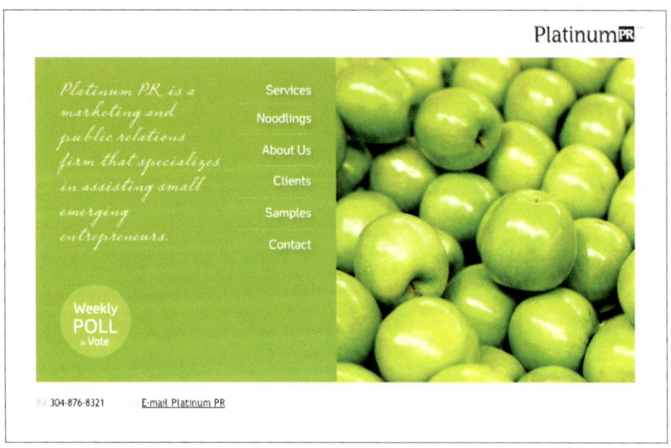

client
Platinum PR
www.platinumpublicrelations.com
design firm
Octavo Designs
www.8vodesigns.com
designers
Mark Burrier, Sue Hough

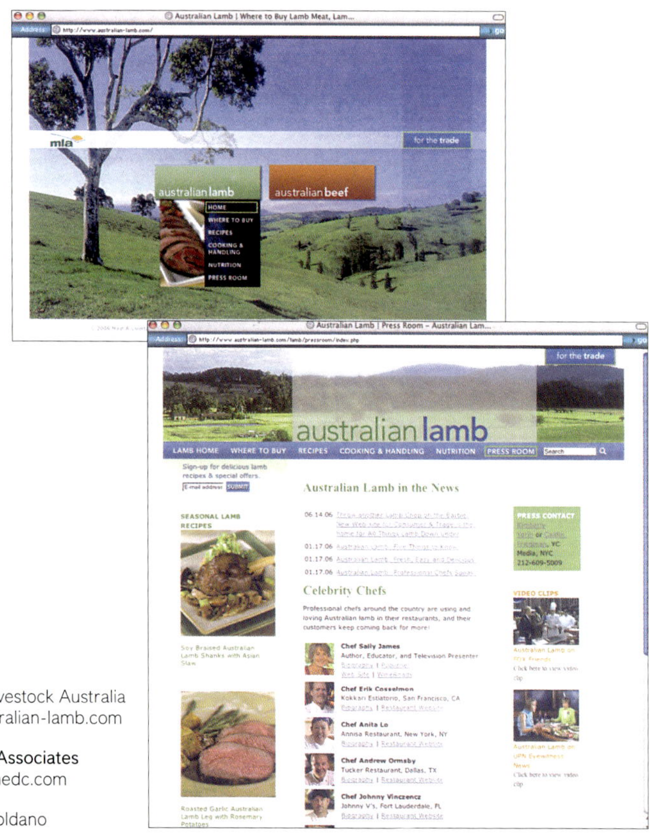

client
Meat & Livestock Australia
www.australian-lamb.com
design firm
Levine & Associates
www.levinedc.com
designer
Maggie Soldano

client
Make-a-Wish Connecticut Chapter
http://ctwish.org
design firm
Fathom Applied Strategy
www.fathom.net
designer
Adrian Kecki

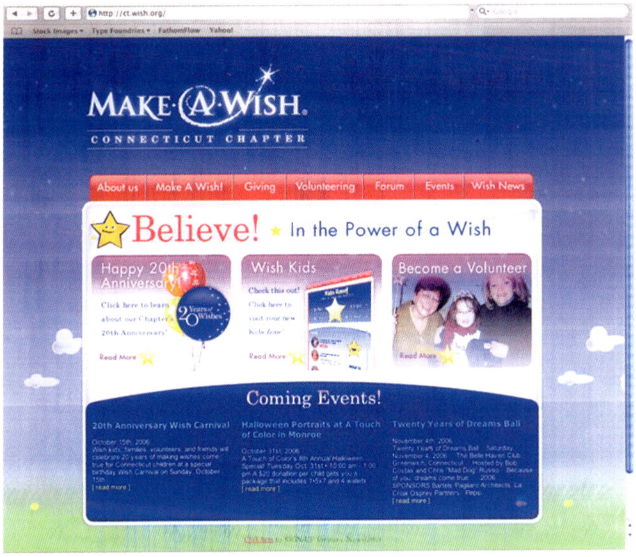

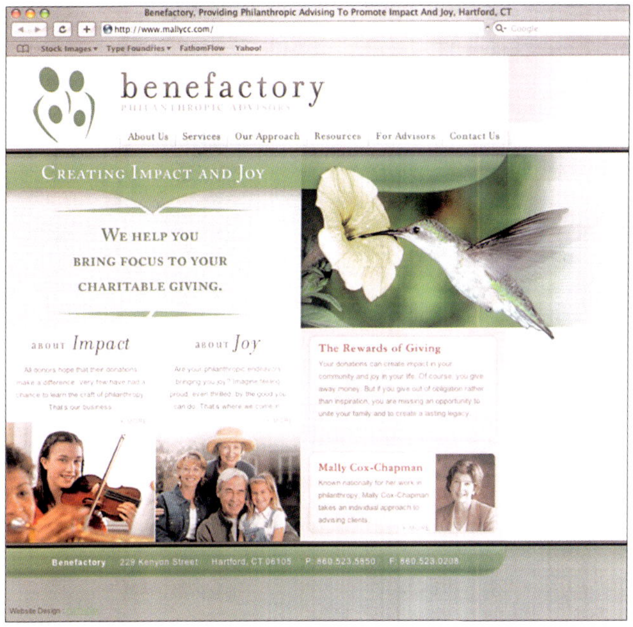

client
Benefactory Philanthropic Advisors
www.mallycc.com
design firm
Fathom Applied Strategy
www.fathom.net
designer
Bil Jenak

client
CETA—Institute for Life Support
design firm
Nordyke Design
designer
John Nordyke

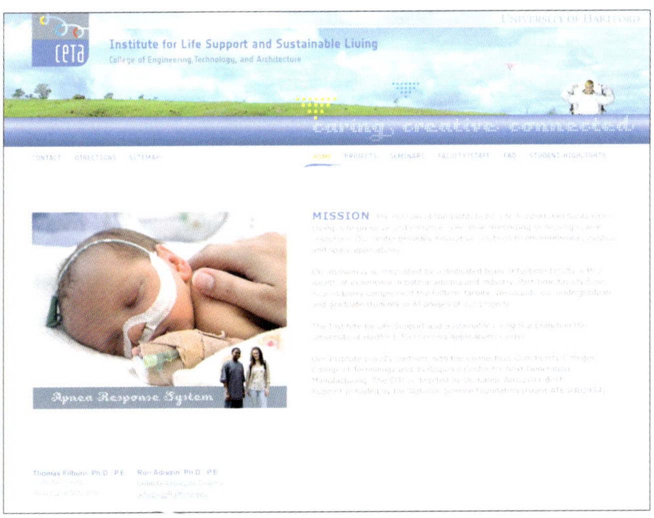

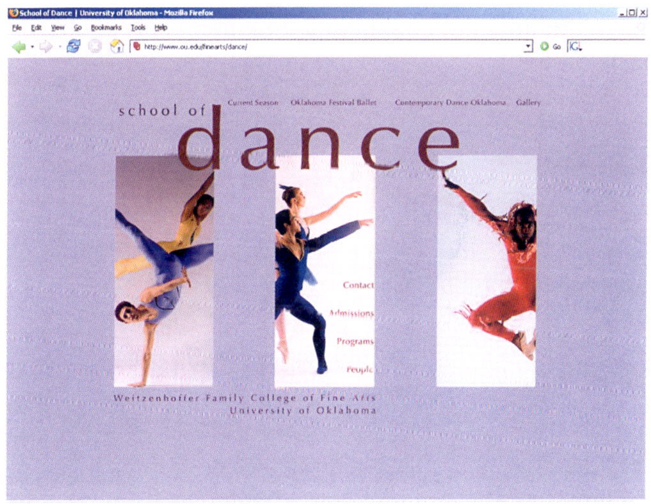

client
School of Dance, University of Oklahoma
www.ou.edu/finearts/dance
design firm
Larry Burditt
larryburditt.com
designer
Larry Burditt

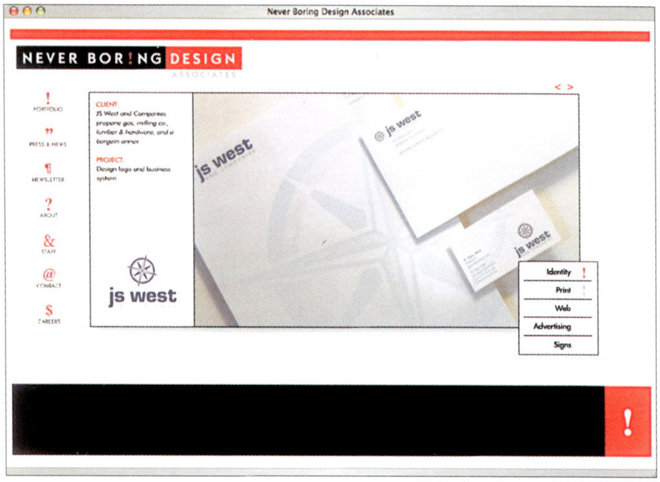

client
Never Boring Design
www.neverboring.com
design firm
Never Boring Design
www.neverboring.com
designer
Shawna Bayers

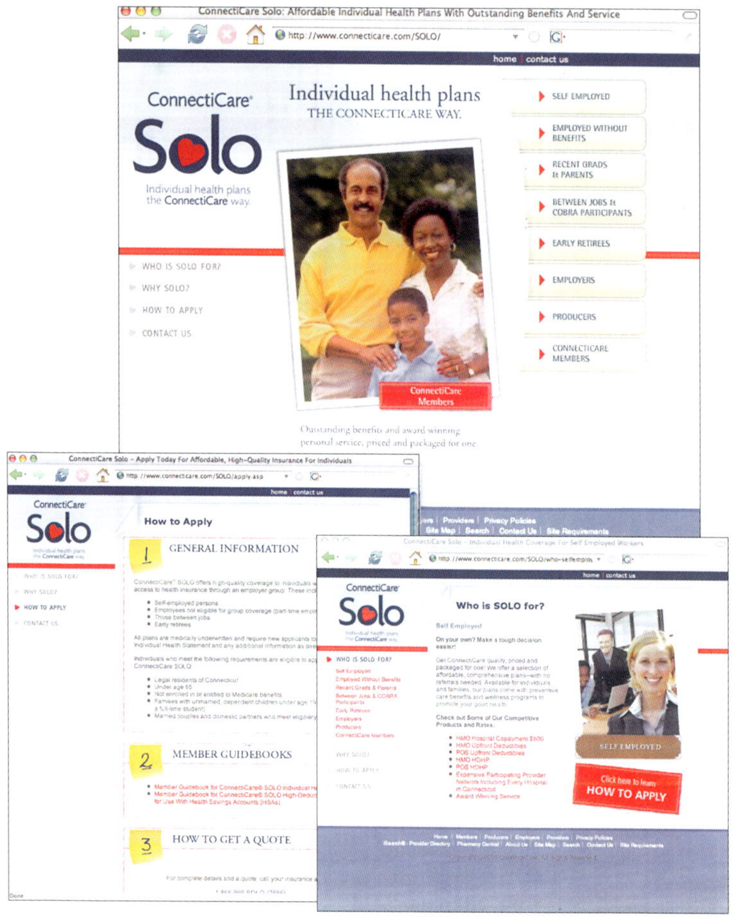

client
Connecticare Solo
www.connecticare.com/SOLO
design firm
Fathom Applied Strategy
www.fathom.net
designer
Adrian Kecki

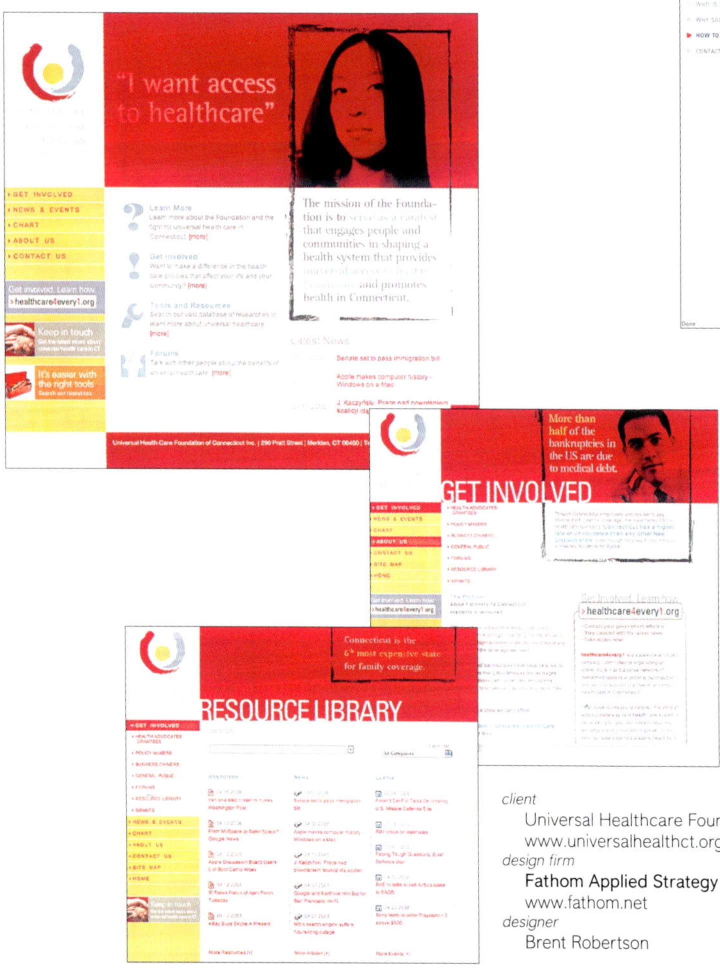

client
Universal Healthcare Foundation of Connecticut
www.universalhealthct.org
design firm
Fathom Applied Strategy
www.fathom.net
designer
Brent Robertson

Menus & Cups

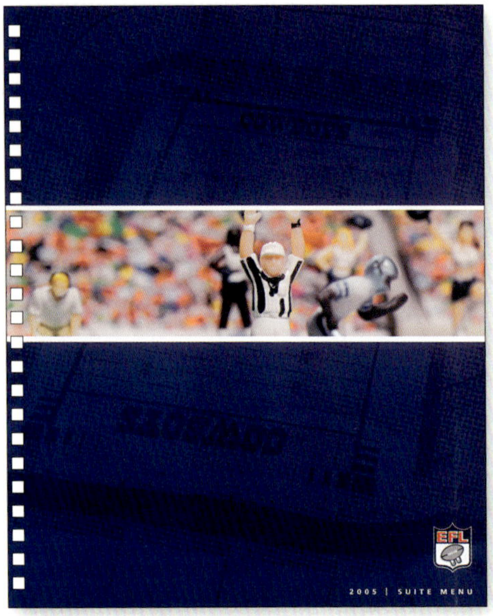

client
Dallas Cowboys
design firm
Kendall Creative Shop, Inc.
kendallcreative.com
designers
Tim Childress, Mark Platt

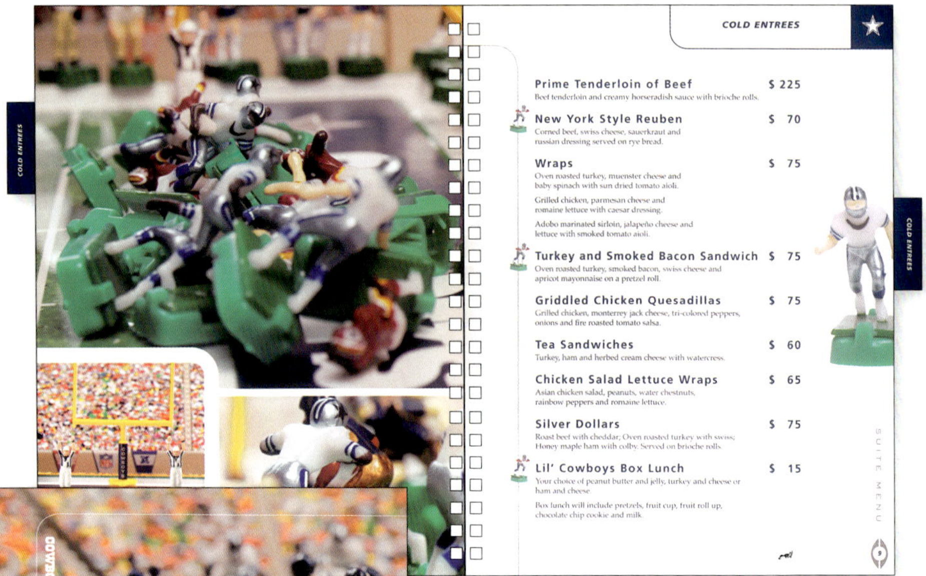

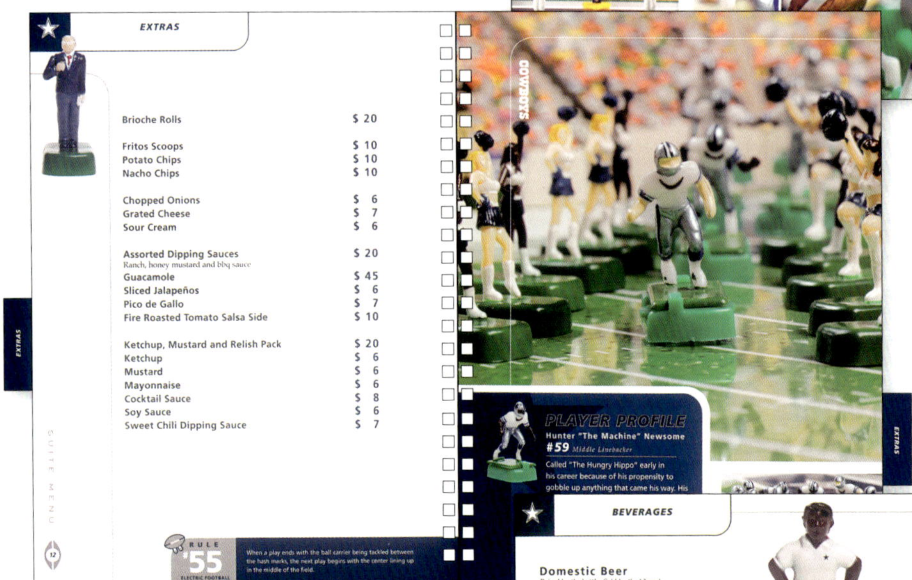

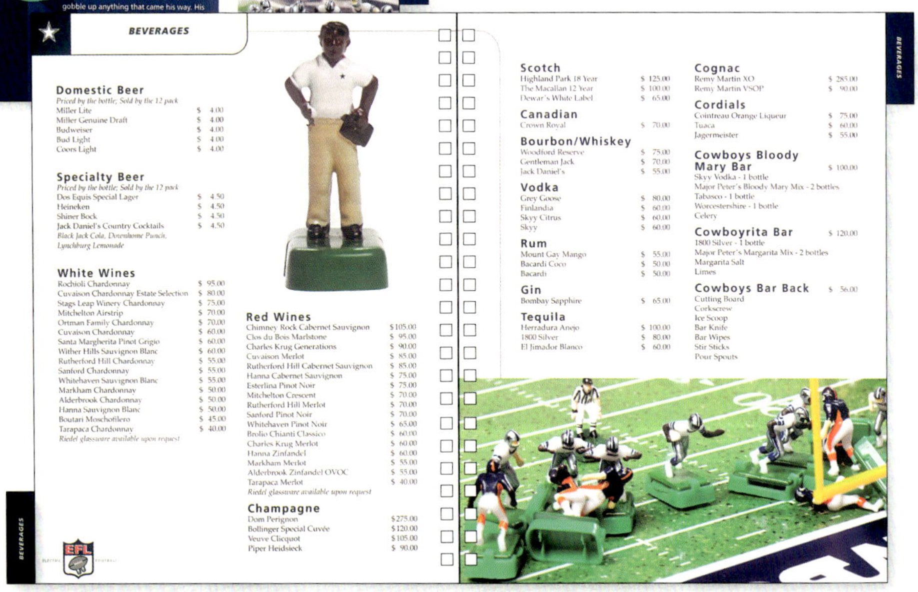

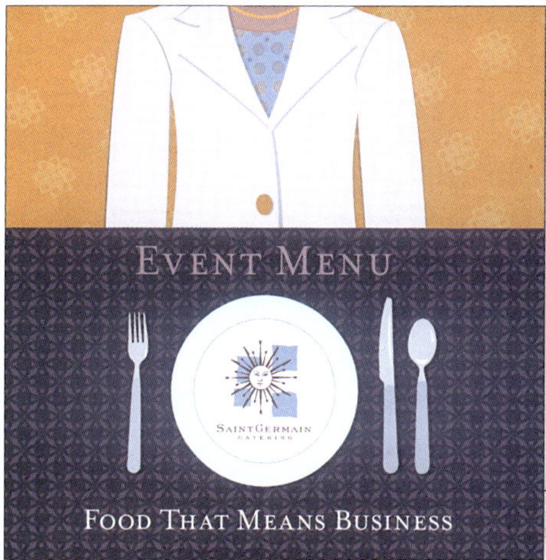

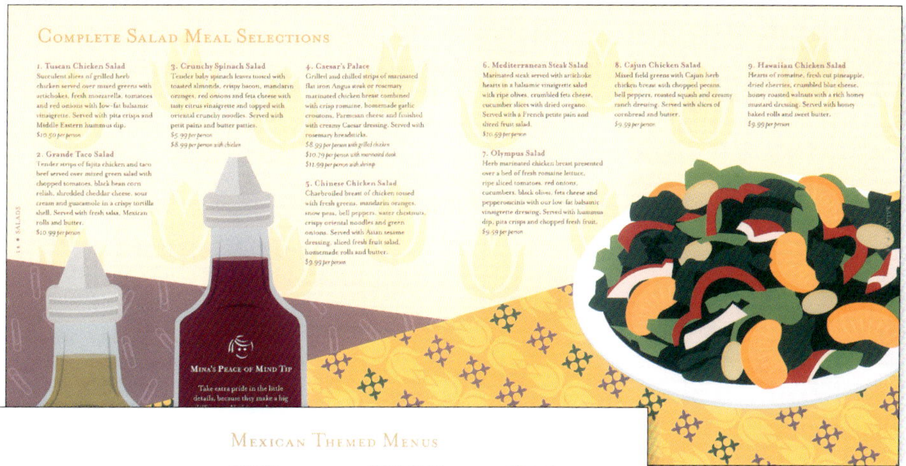

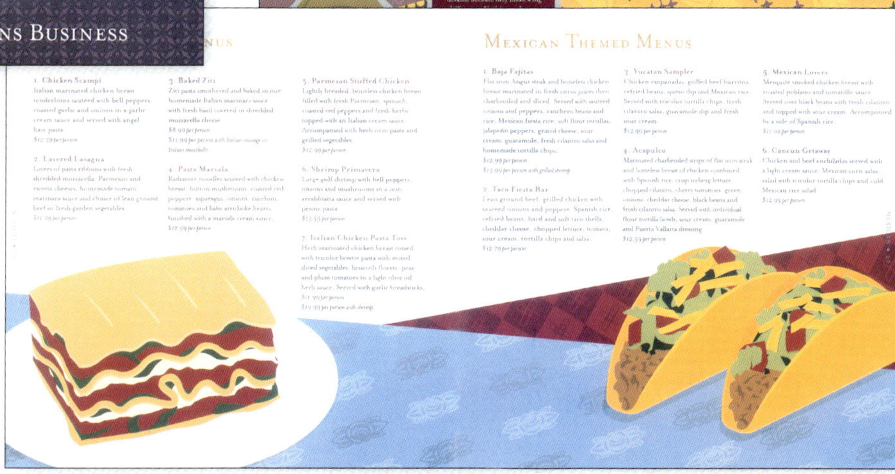

client
Saint Germain
design firm
Bremmer & Goris
www.goris.com
designer
Lara Dalinsky

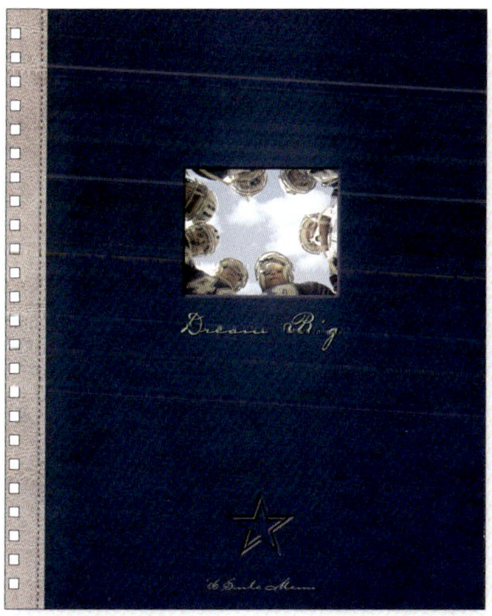

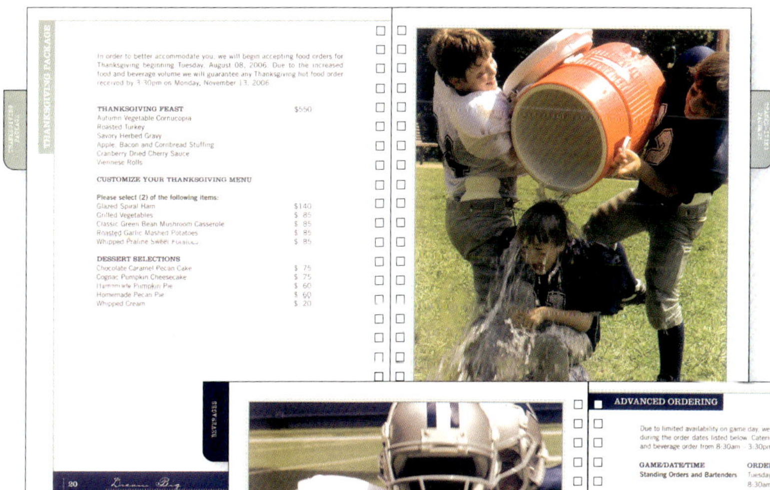

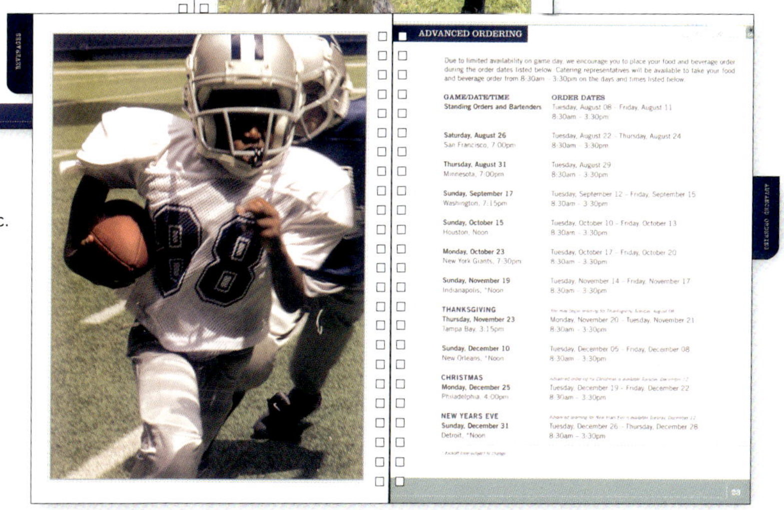

client
Dallas Cowboys
design firm
Kendall Creative Shop, Inc.
kendallcreative.com
designers
Ryan Briggs, Mark Platt

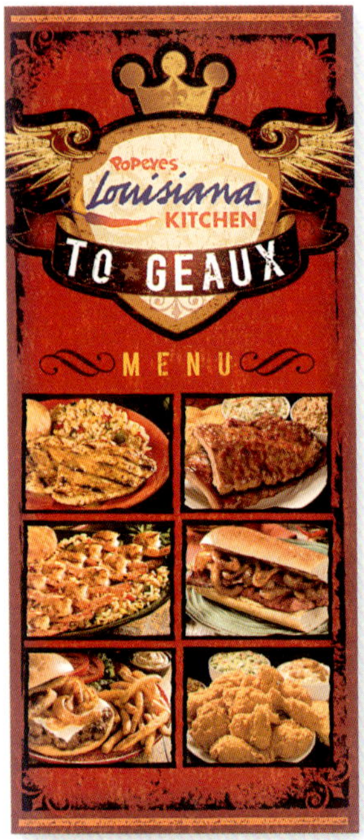

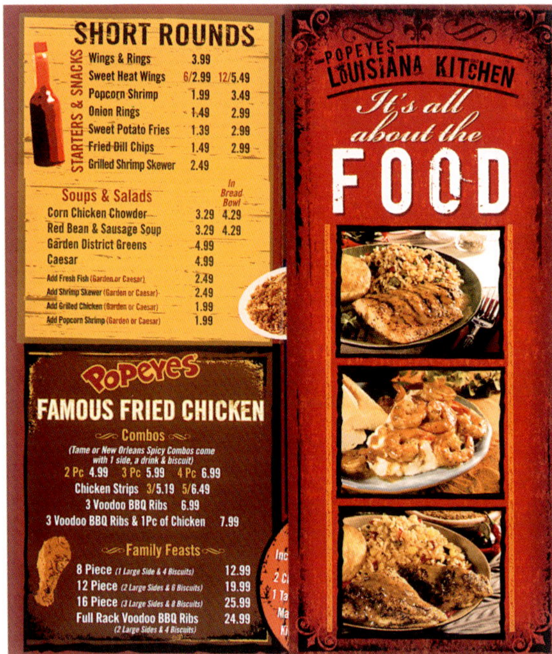

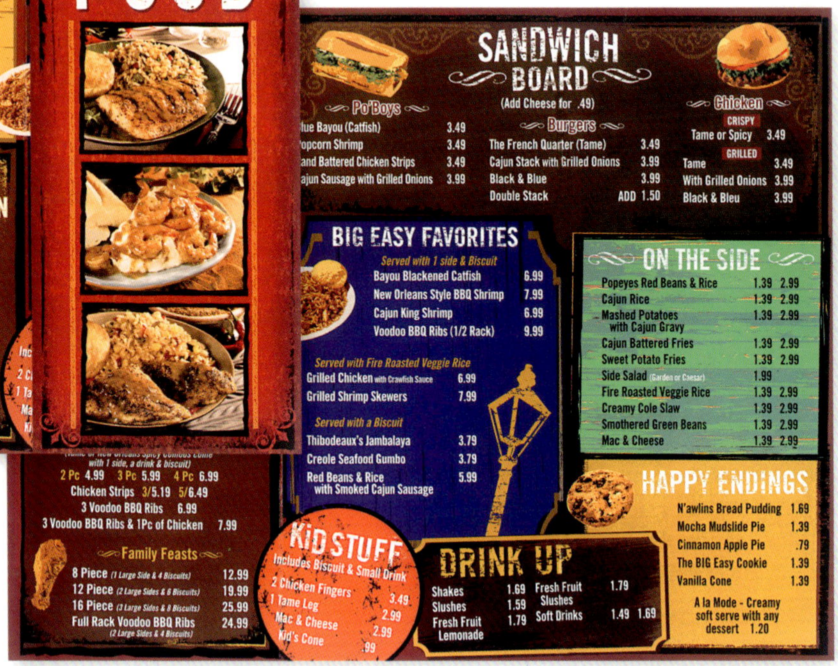

client
Popeyes Chicken & Biscuits
design firm
Berry Design Inc.
berrydesign.com
designers
Bob Berry, Chip Waller

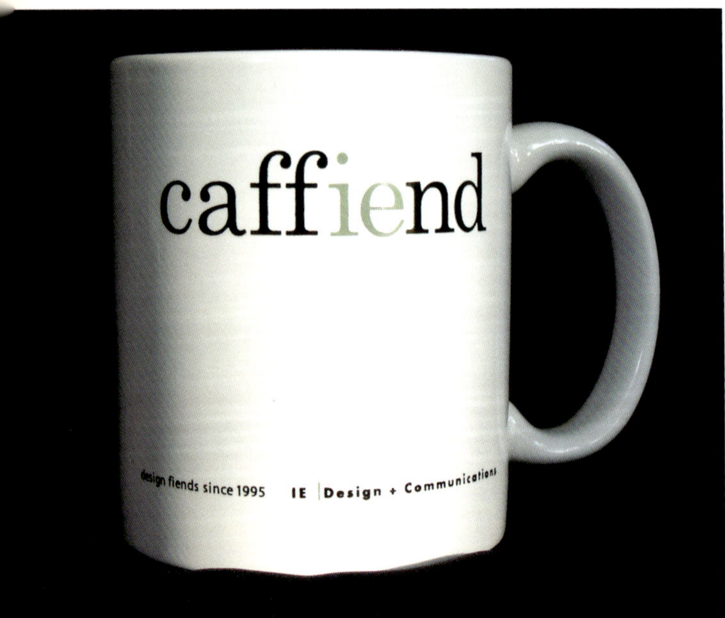

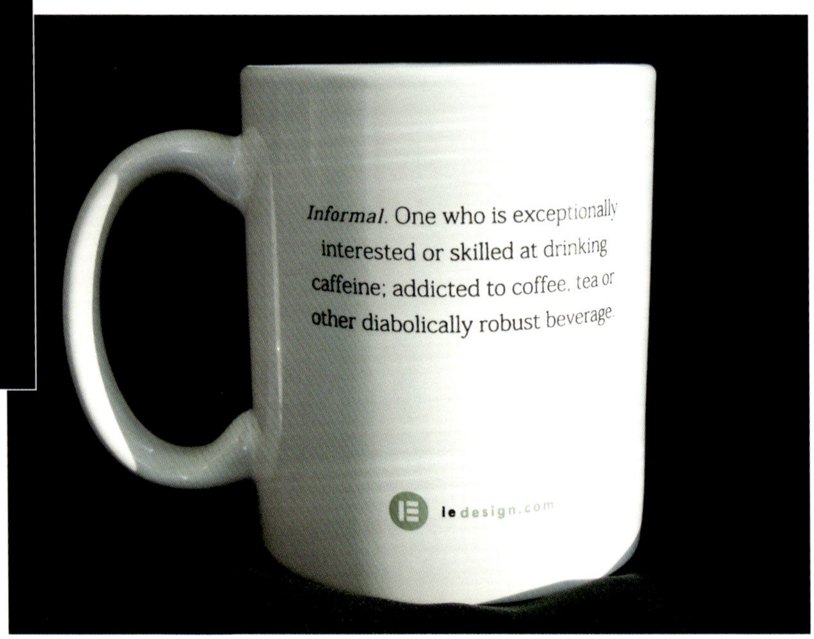

client
IE Design + Communications
design firm
IE Design + Communications
www.iedesign.net
designer
Marcie Carson

Apparel

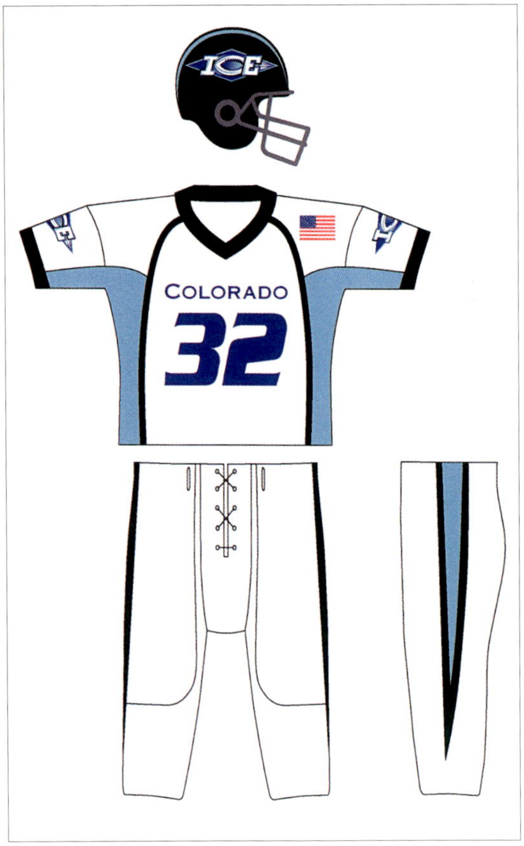

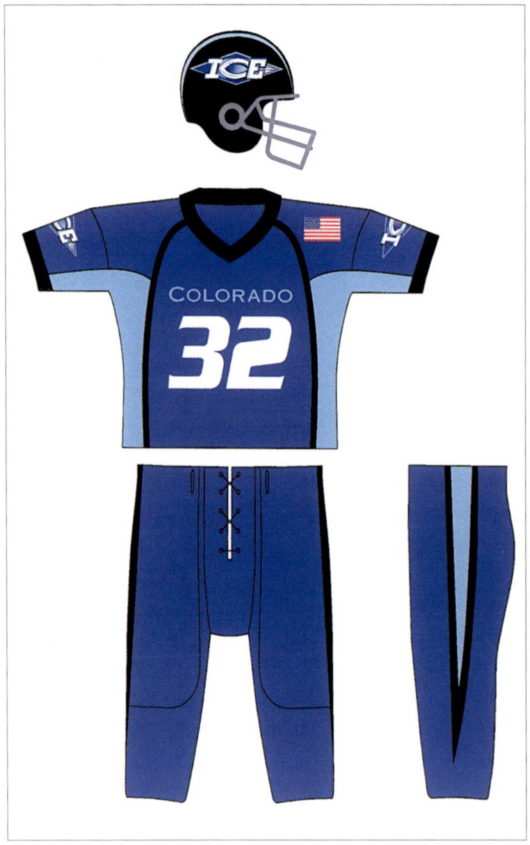

client
Colorado Ice Football
design firm
Ghengis Design
ghengisdesign.com
designer
Dale Monahan

client
HPC Cycling Team
design firm
D'Talle Creative
www.dtallecreative.com
designer
Jenette Williams

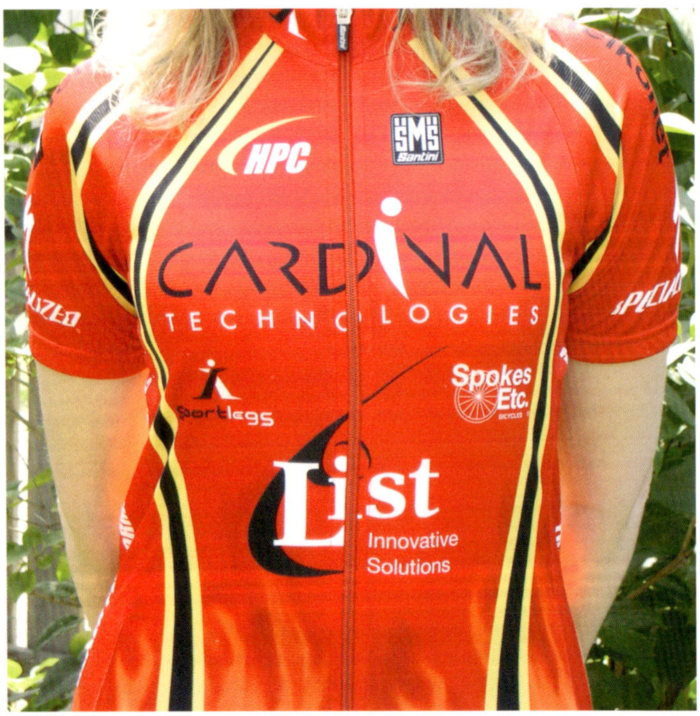

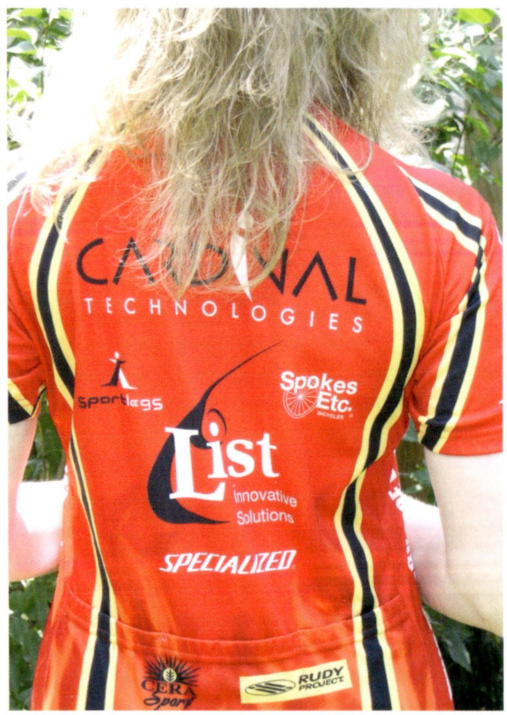

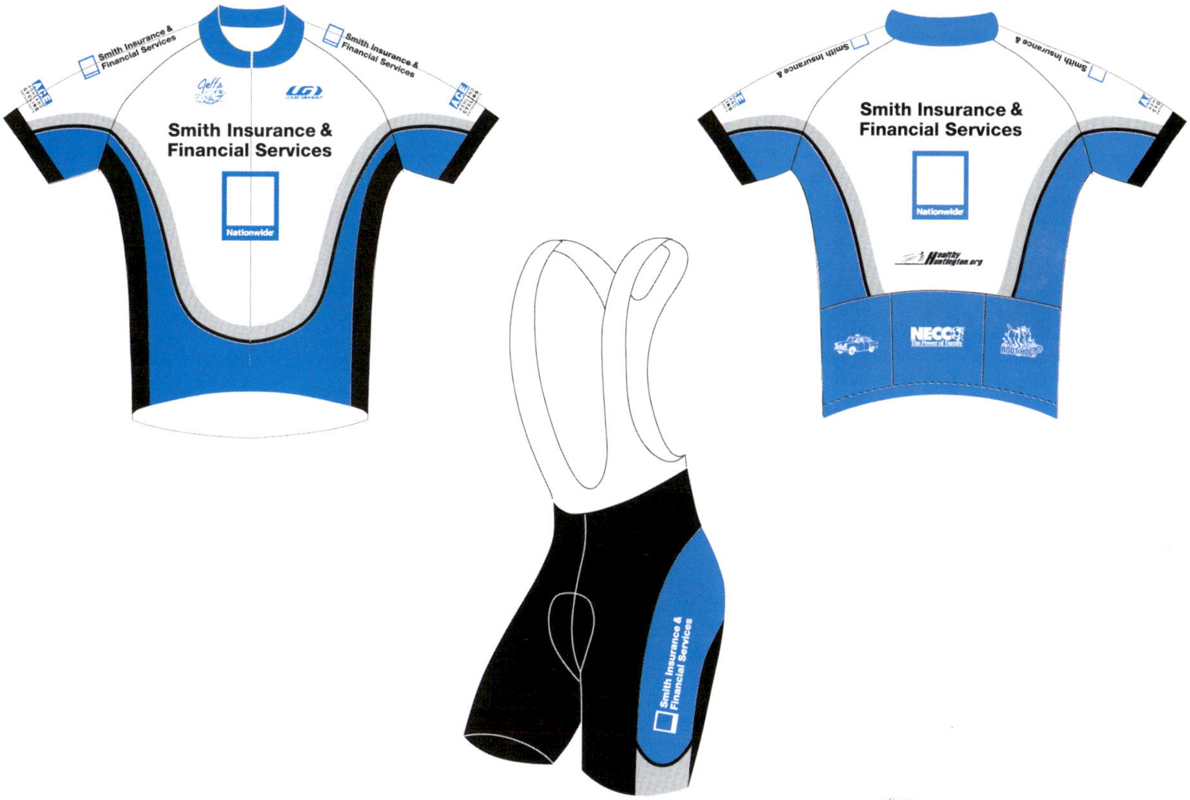

client
Smith Insurance & Financial Services
design firm
D'Talle Creative
www.dtallecreative.com
designer
Jenette Williams

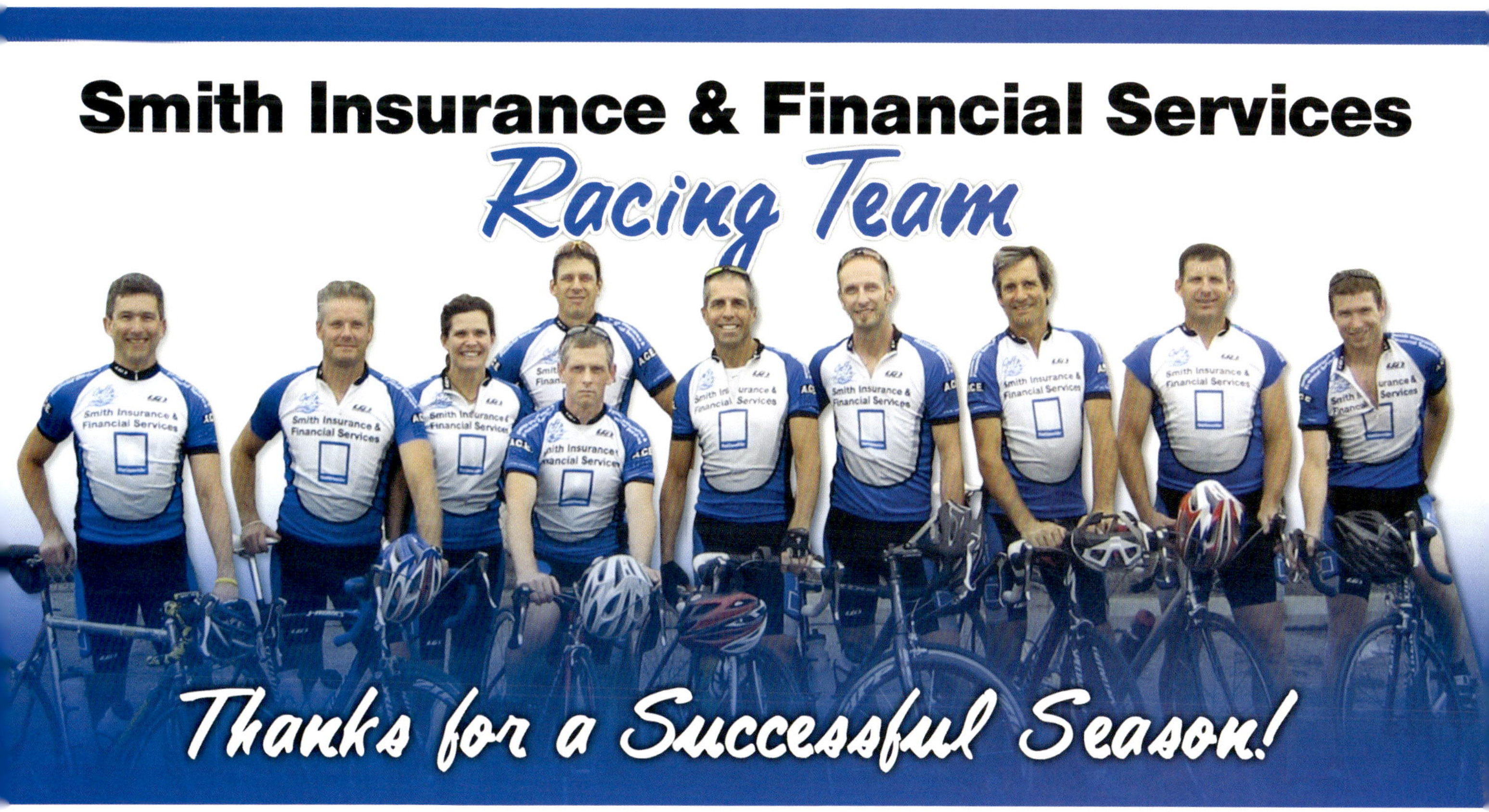

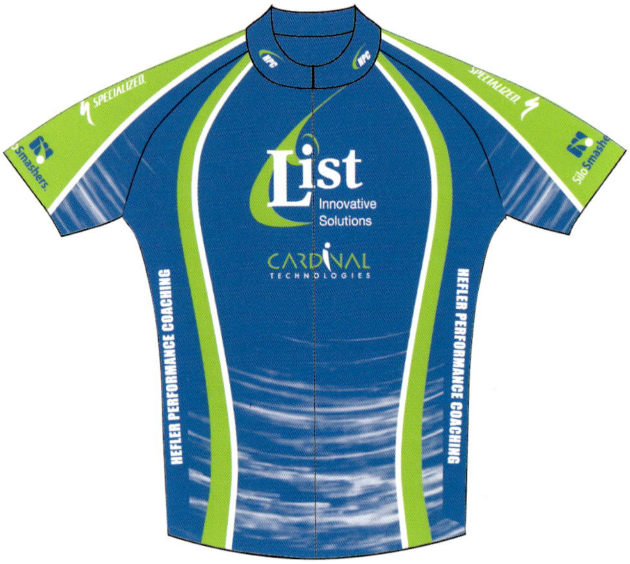

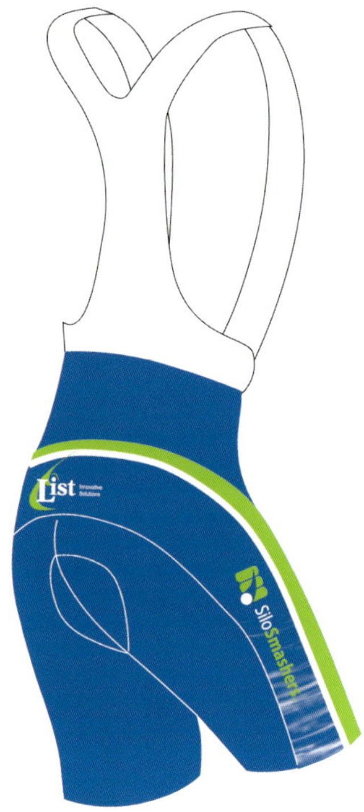

client
Hefler Performance Coaching
design firm
D'Talle Creative
www.dtallecreative.com
designer
Jenette Williams

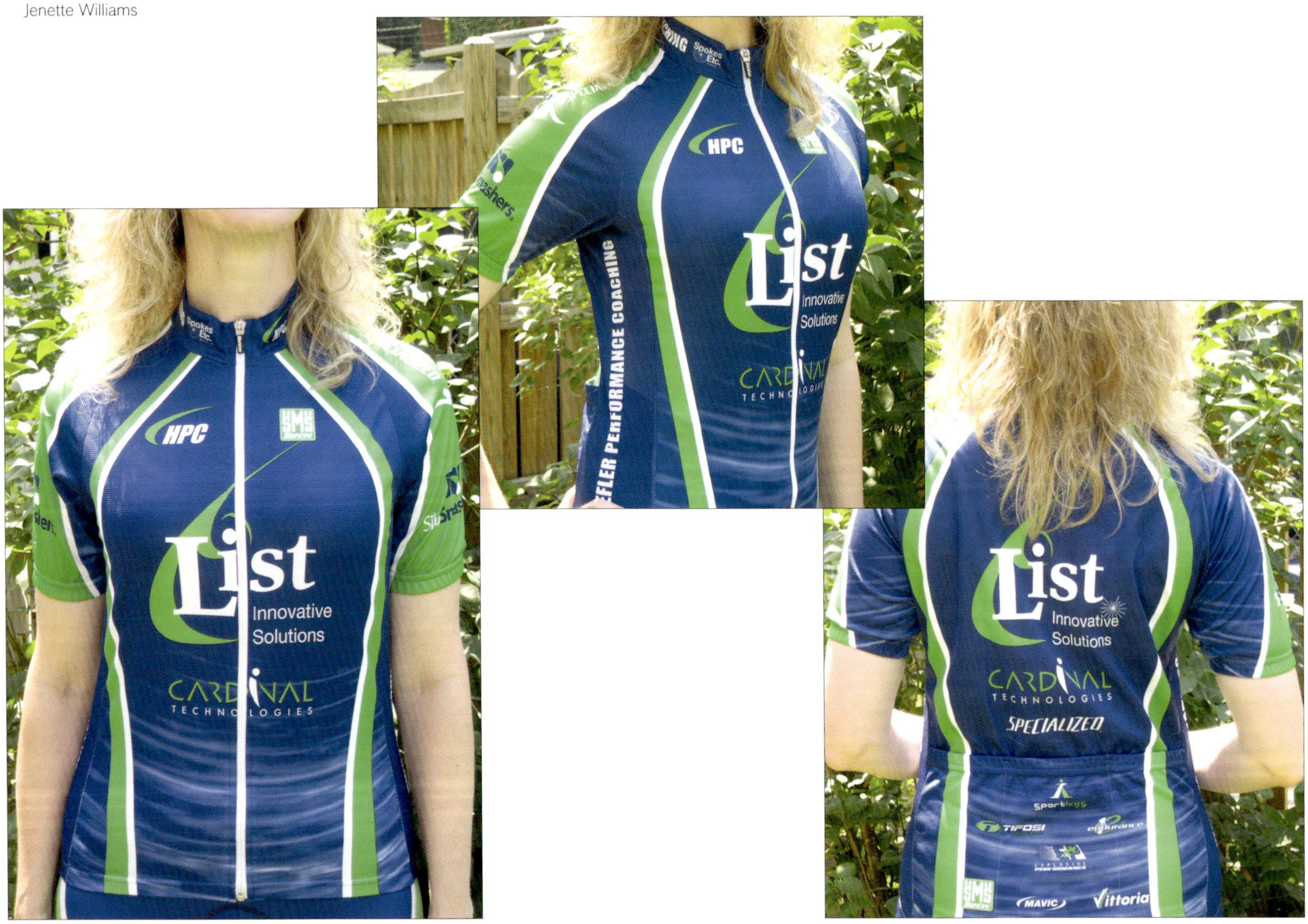

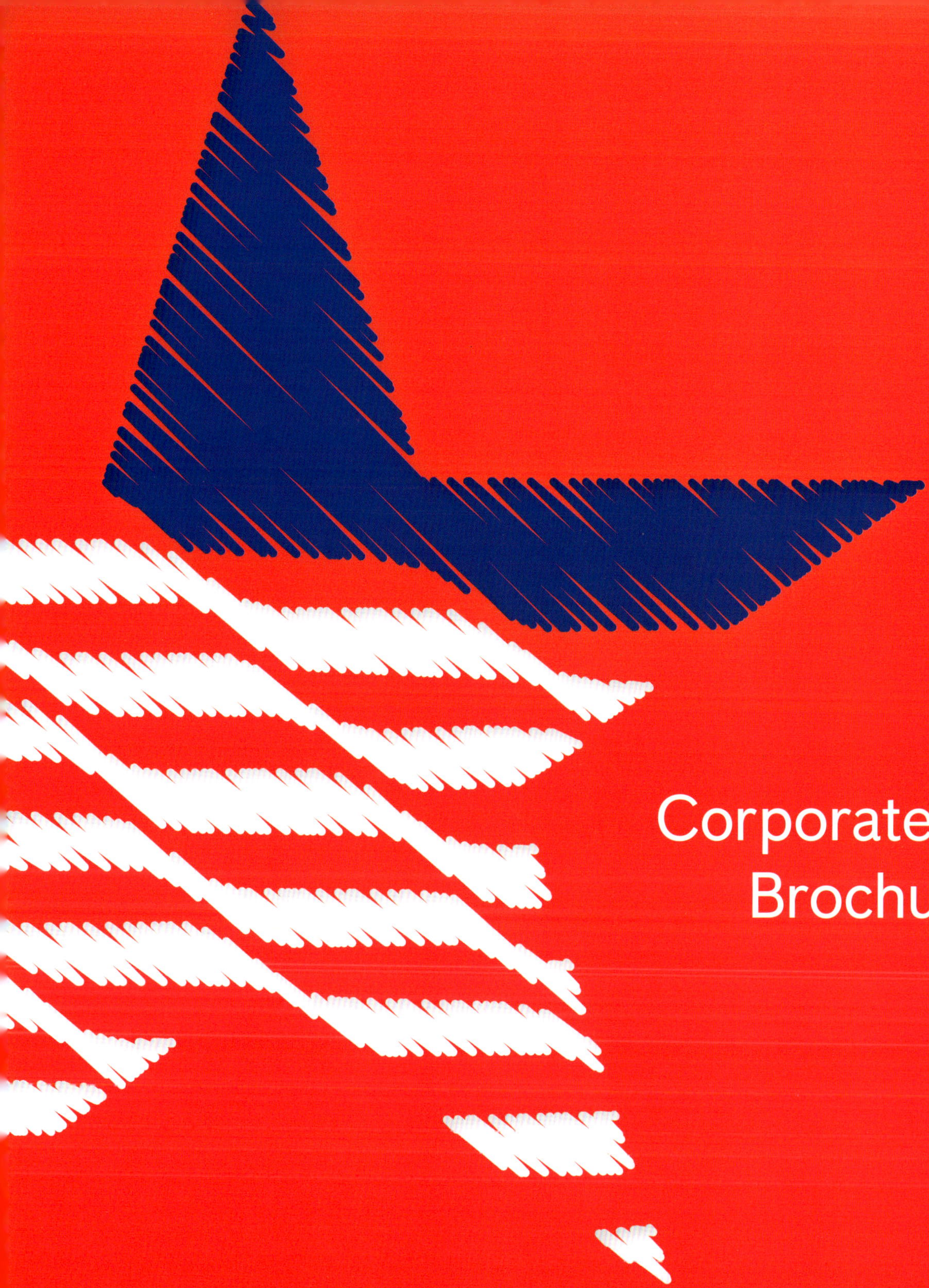

Corporate Image Brochures

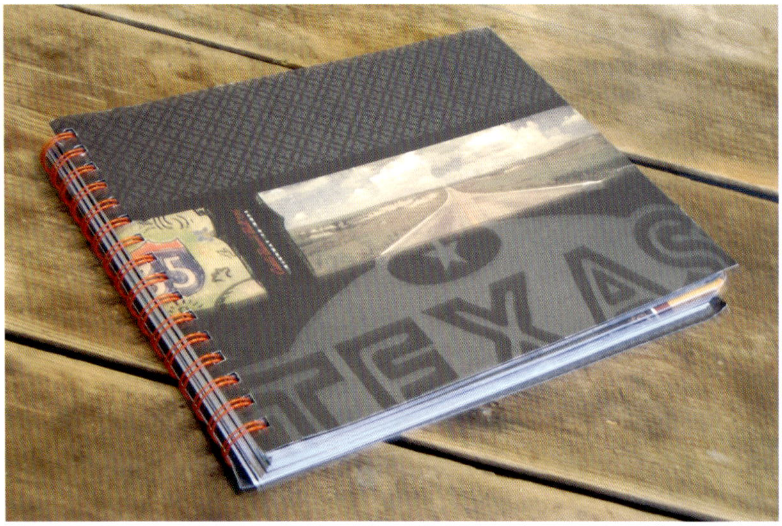

client
Cattle Baron's Ball '06
design firm
Kendall Creative Shop, Inc.
kendallcreative.com
designers
Ben Dolezal, Mark Platt

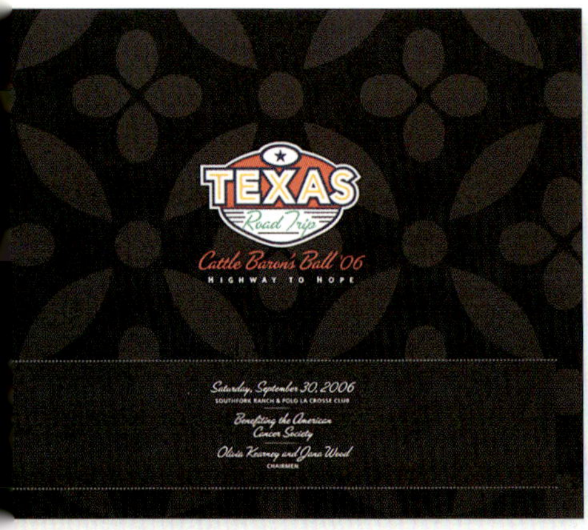

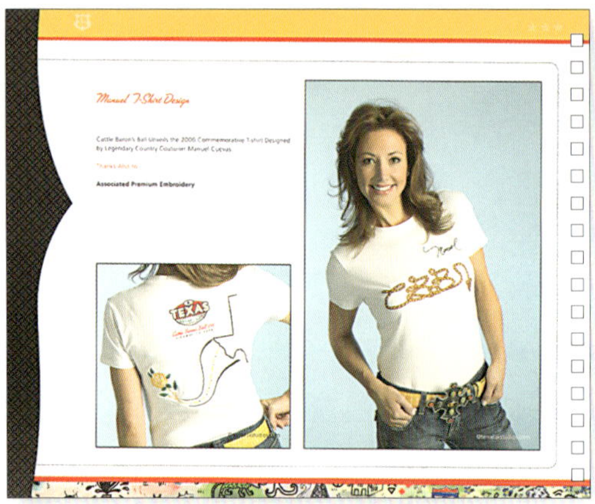

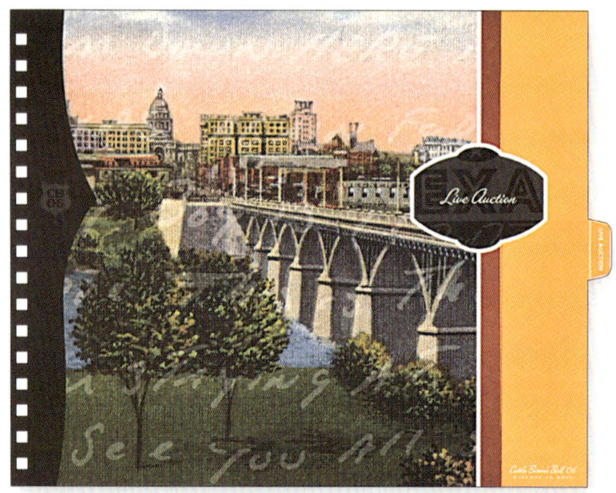

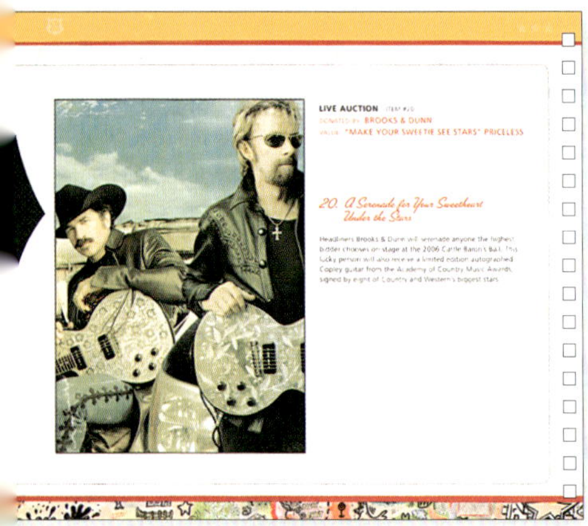

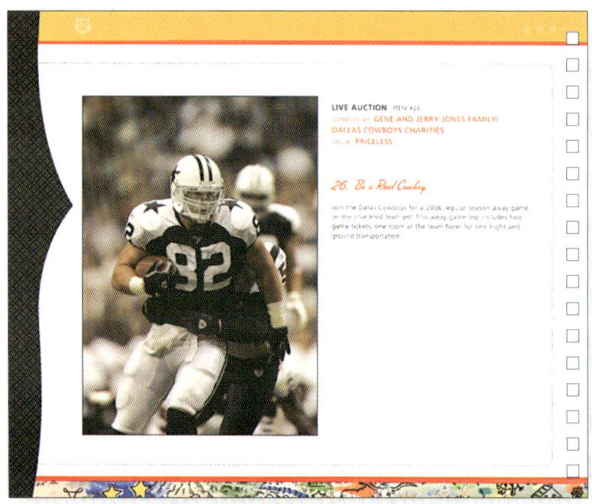

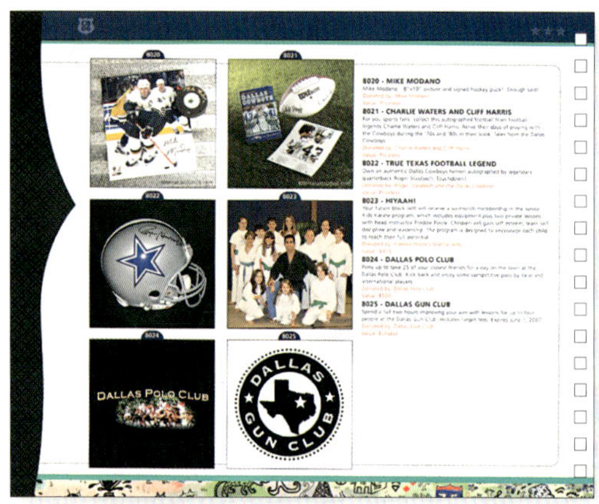

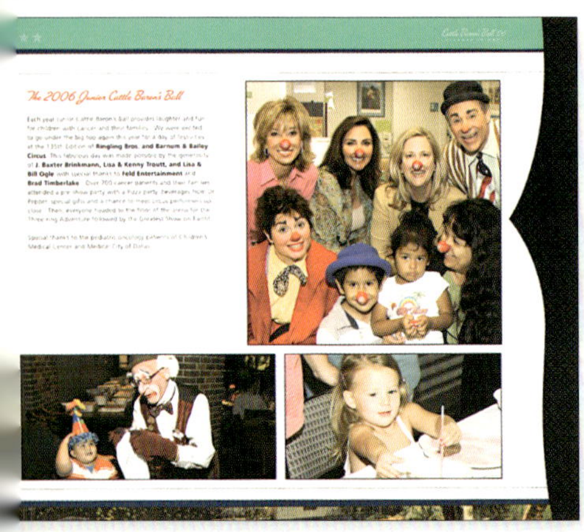

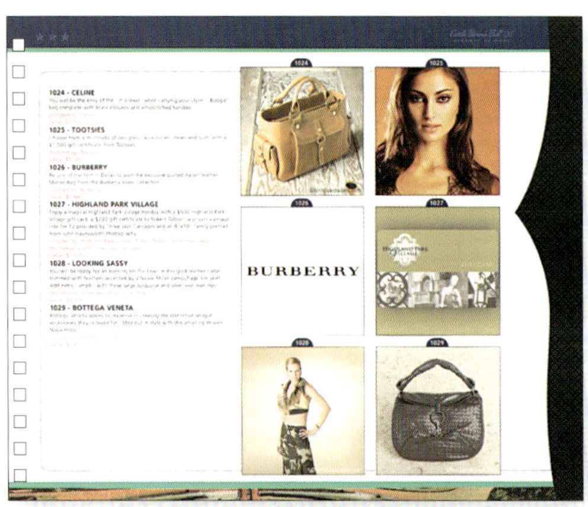

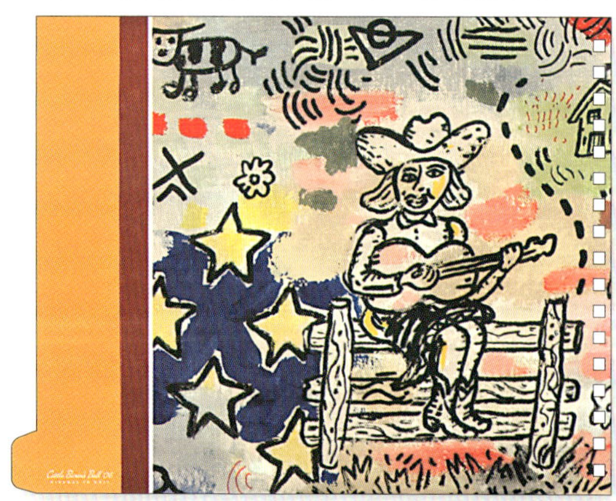

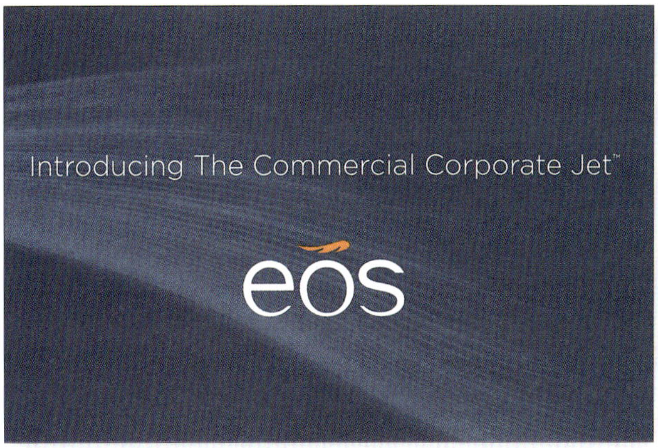

client
Eos Airlines
design firm
Hornall Anderson Design Works
www.hadw.com
designers
Jack Anderson, Julie Lock,
Laura Jakobsen, Beckon Wyld

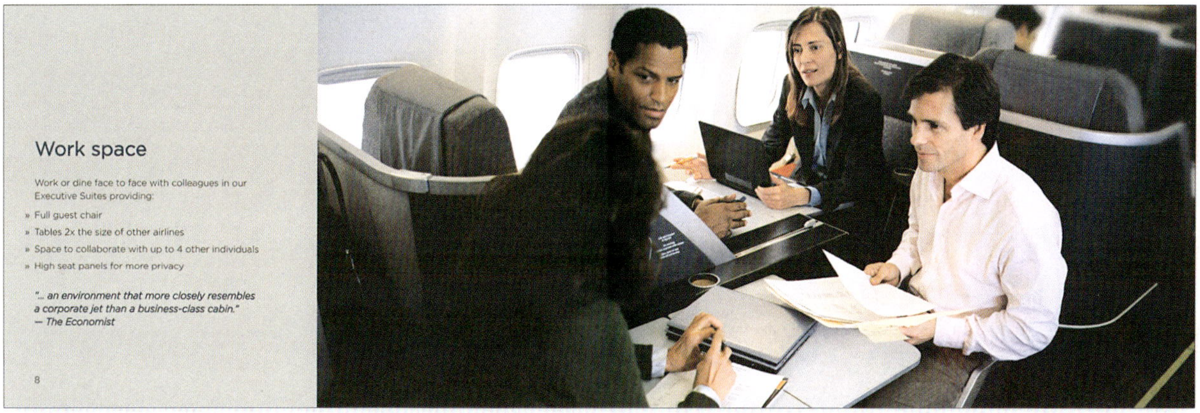

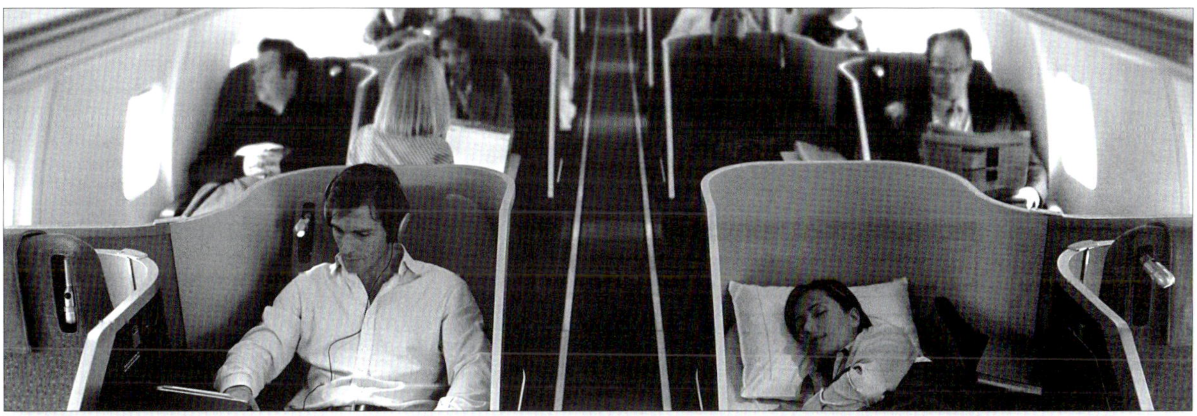

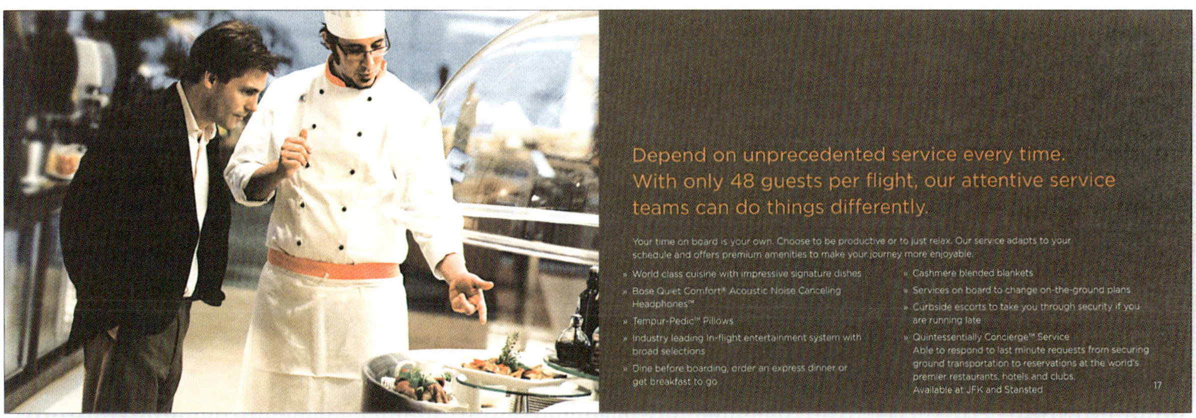

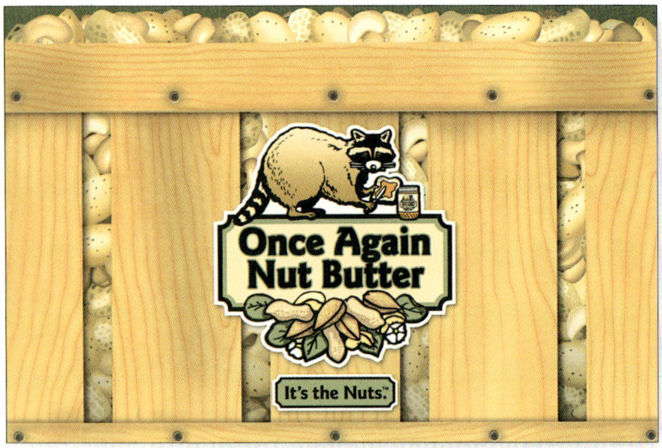

client
Once Again Nut Butter
design firm
Icon Graphics Inc.
thinkfeelchoose.com
designers
Icon Graphics Inc.

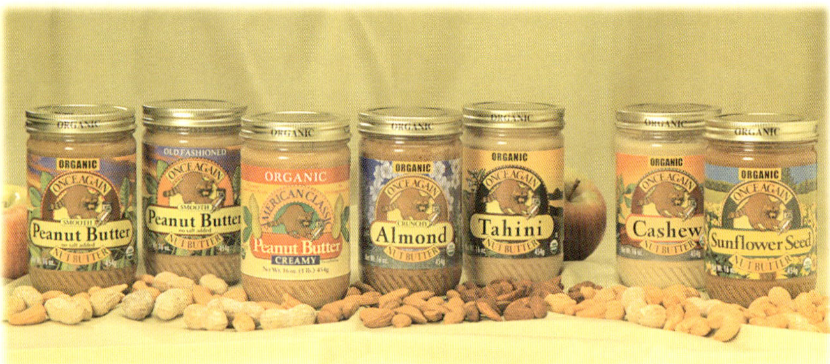

Our Once Again Nut Butter Full Product Line

The wholesome goodness of our nut butters keeps your customers coming back. Whether making a traditional PBJ, smearing on fruit or vegetables, or using in a recipe, Once Again products are a family favorite. The turnover of product on store shelves is certain to contribute to your success. Once Again—*It's the Nuts!*

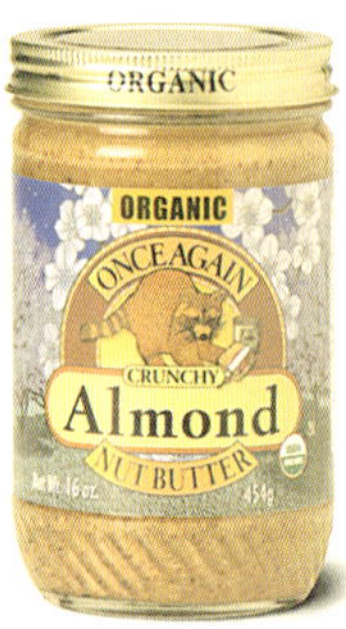

Almond Butter

Loaded with Vitamin E, magnesium, potassium, and protein, Once Again Almond Butter is a tasty alternative to traditional peanut butter with the rich, distinctive flavor that only the almond can deliver. Available in several varieties. Once Again Almond Butter is gluten free.

Almond Butter	12 (16 oz.) Jars	9 lb. Tub	35 lb. Tub
Smooth	•	•	
Crunchy	•	•	
Organic, Smooth	•	•	
Organic, Crunchy	•	•	
Raw, Smooth	•	•	
Raw, Crunchy	•	•	
Raw, Organic, Smooth	•	•	
Raw, Organic, Crunchy	•	•	

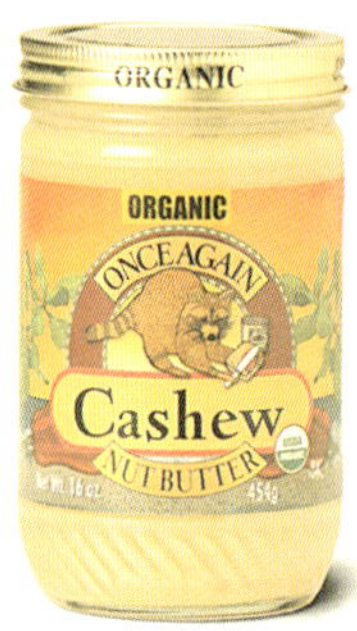

Cashew Butter

High in protein, vitamins, iron and fiber, the cashew is one of the most sought-after nuts in the world. The natural sweetness of the cashew only requires the addition of sunflower oil to make a spreadably-delicious nut butter. Once Again Cashew Butter is gluten free.

Cashew Butter	12 (16 oz.) Jars	9 lb. Tub	35 lb. Tub
Natural, Smooth	•	•	•
Organic, Smooth	•	•	

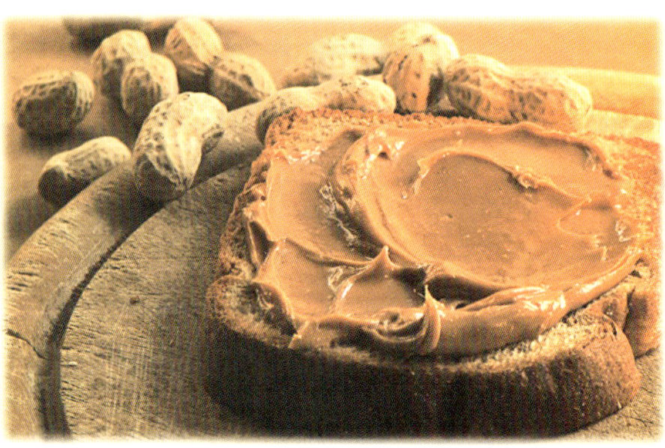

It's the Nuts.

Only the finest nuts and seeds are used to make Once Again products. What else could we use to make something so good, and so good for you? We have developed a worldwide network of suppliers that give us the reliability to meet demand. All of our products are natural, and do not contain any additives, extenders, hydrogenated oils, preservatives, or artificial coloring. It's the nuts that make it delicious! Many of our products are organically grown, without the use of artificial pesticides, herbicides, or genetically-modified organisms.

Contact us to find out how you can get our product on your shelves. As demand for natural and organically-grown food grows, be sure your nut butter offering is the best.

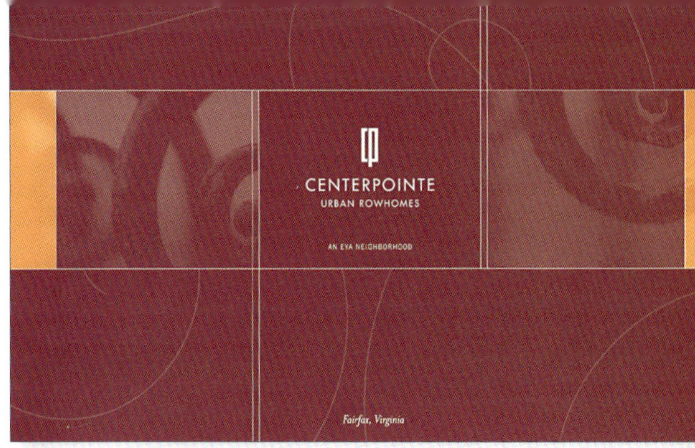

client
EYA
design firm
Grafik Marketing Communications
www.grafik.com
designers
Tom Kendzie, Johnny Vitorovich,
Hal Swetnam, Regina Esposito

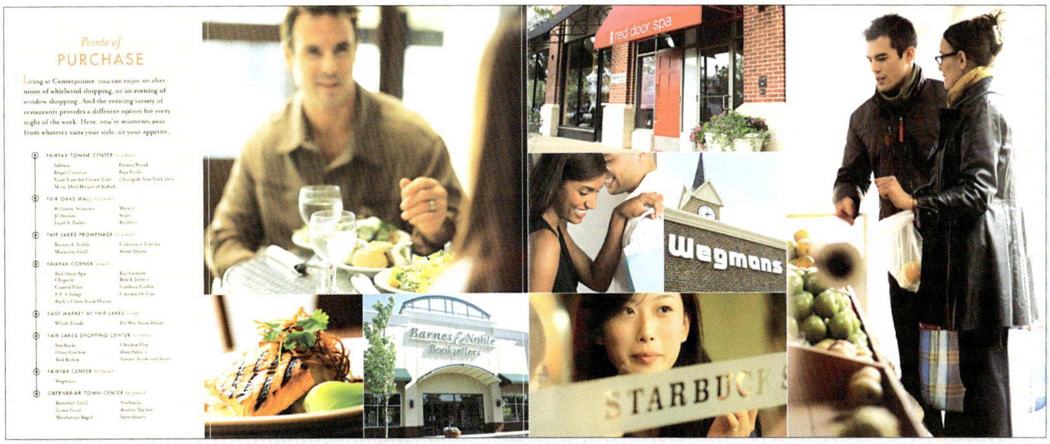

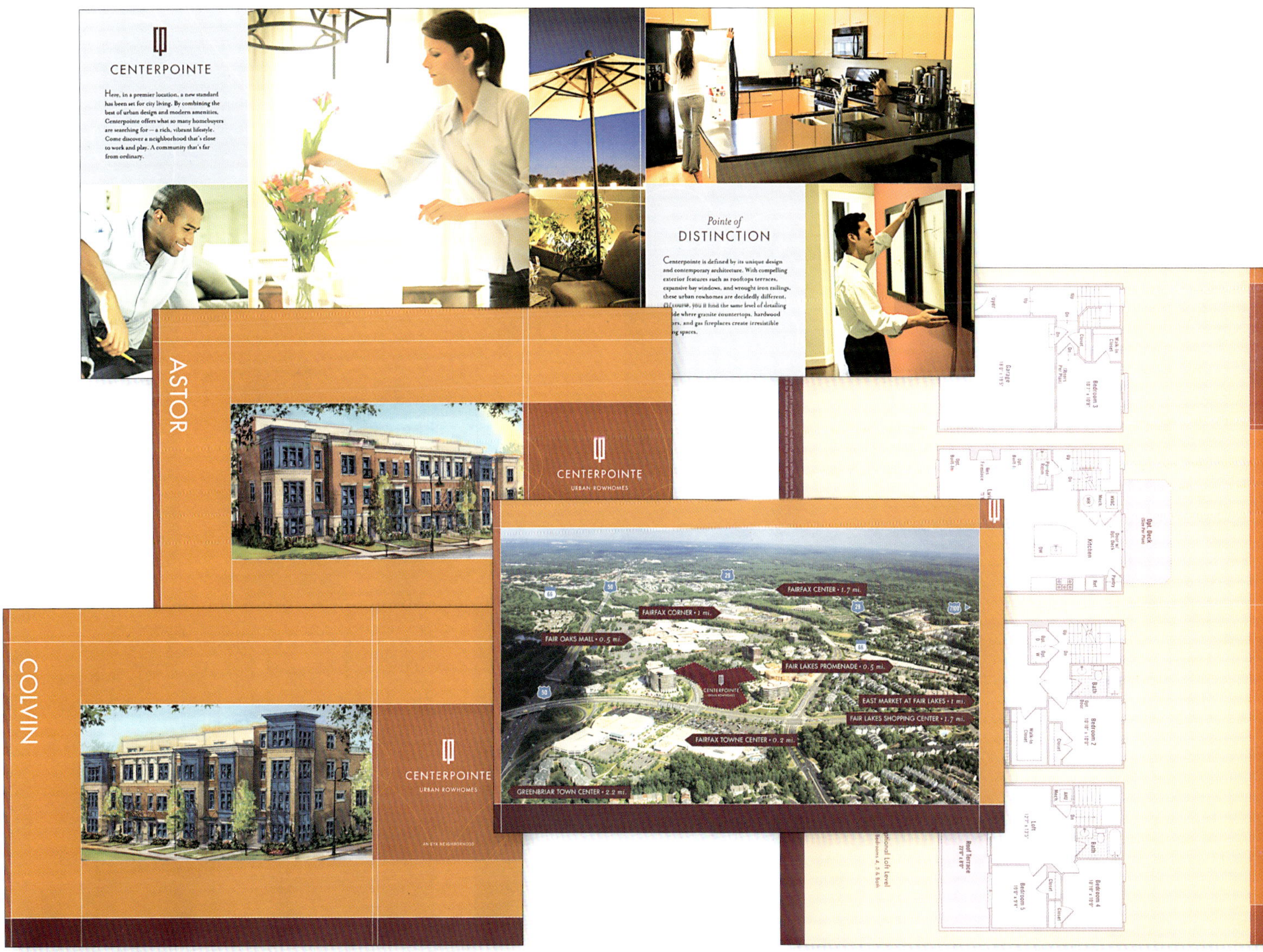

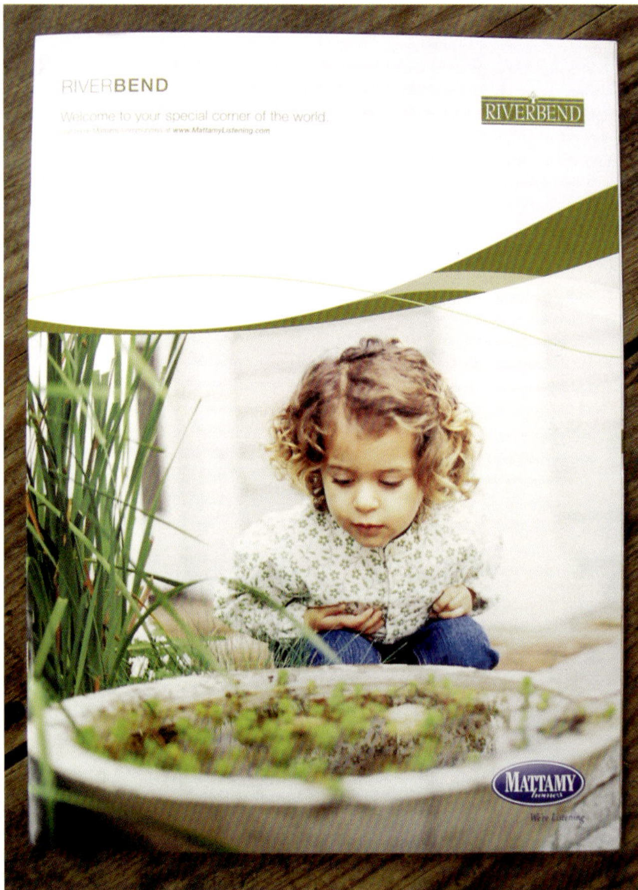

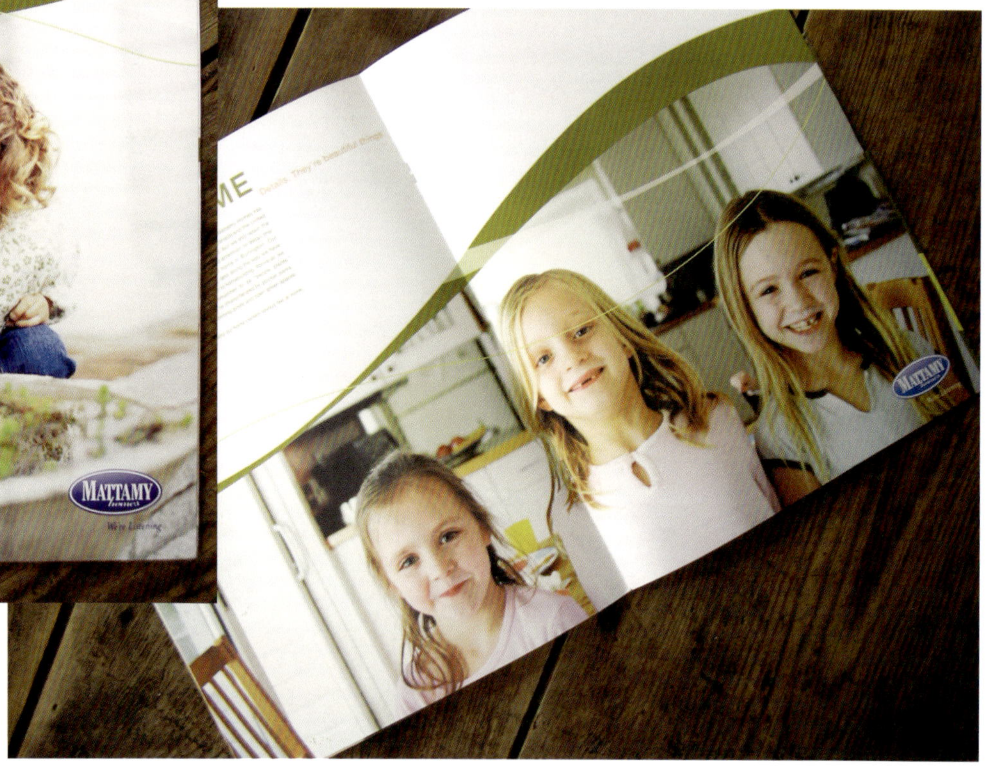

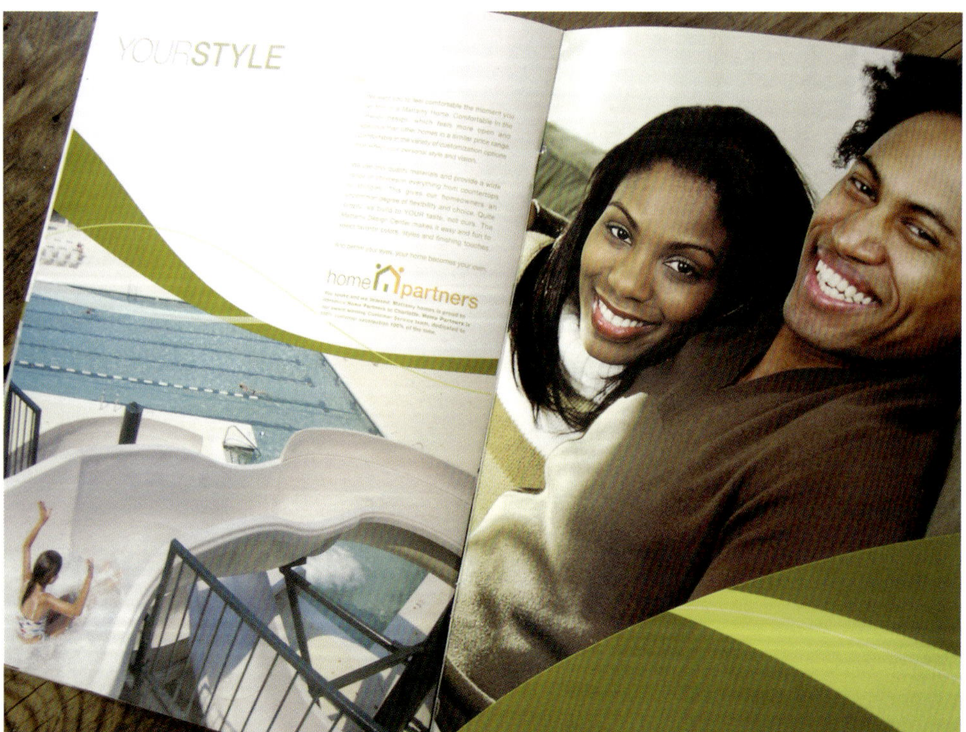

client
Mattamy Homes
design firm
A3 Design
www.athreedesign.com
designers
Alan Altman, Amanda Altman

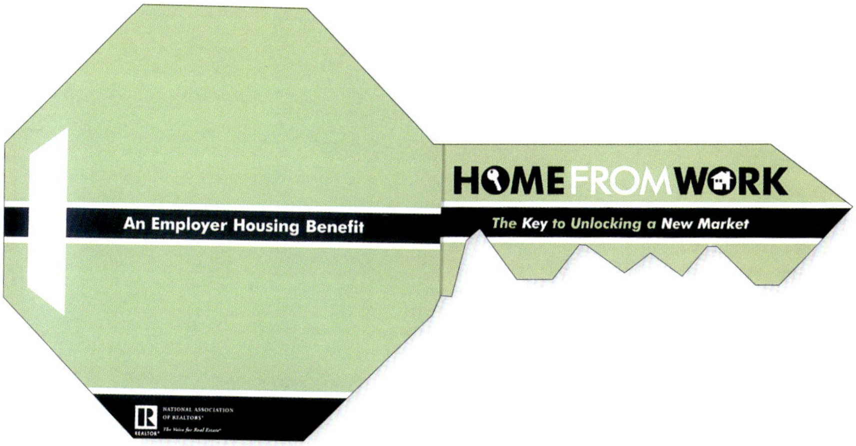

client
National Association of Realtors®
design firm
Crabtree + Company
designers
Susan Angrisani, Rod Vera

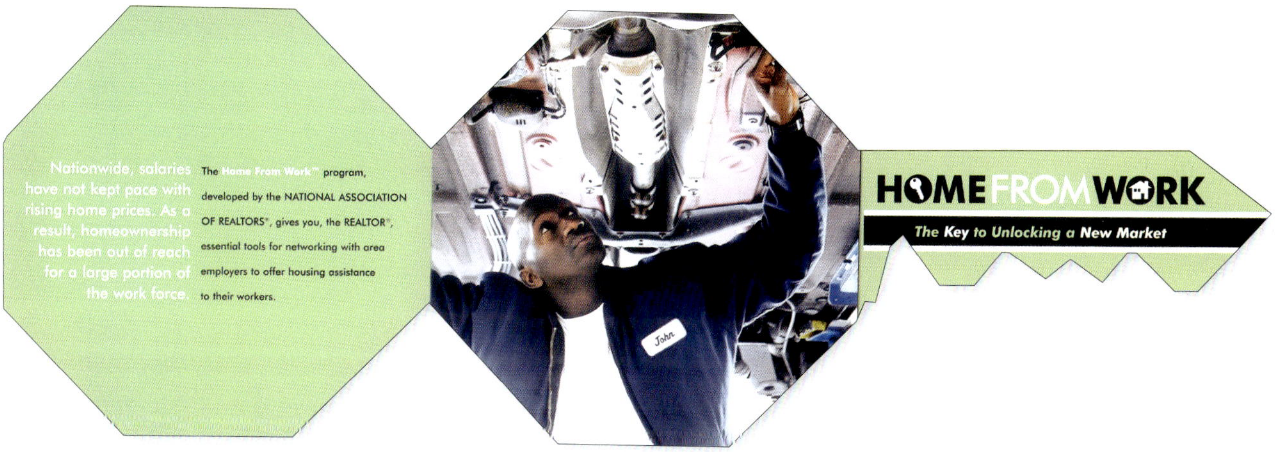

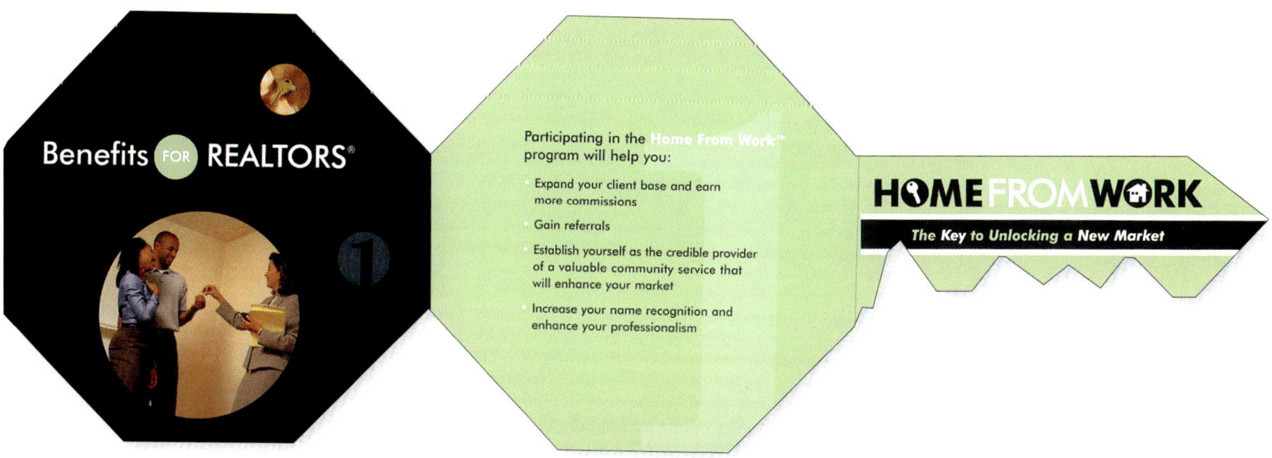

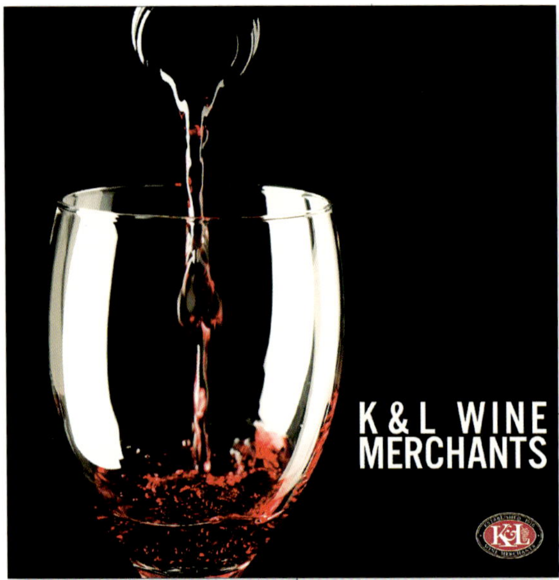

client
K & L Wine Merchants
design firm
IE Design + Communications
www.iedesign.net
creative director
Marcie Carson
designer
Christine Kenney

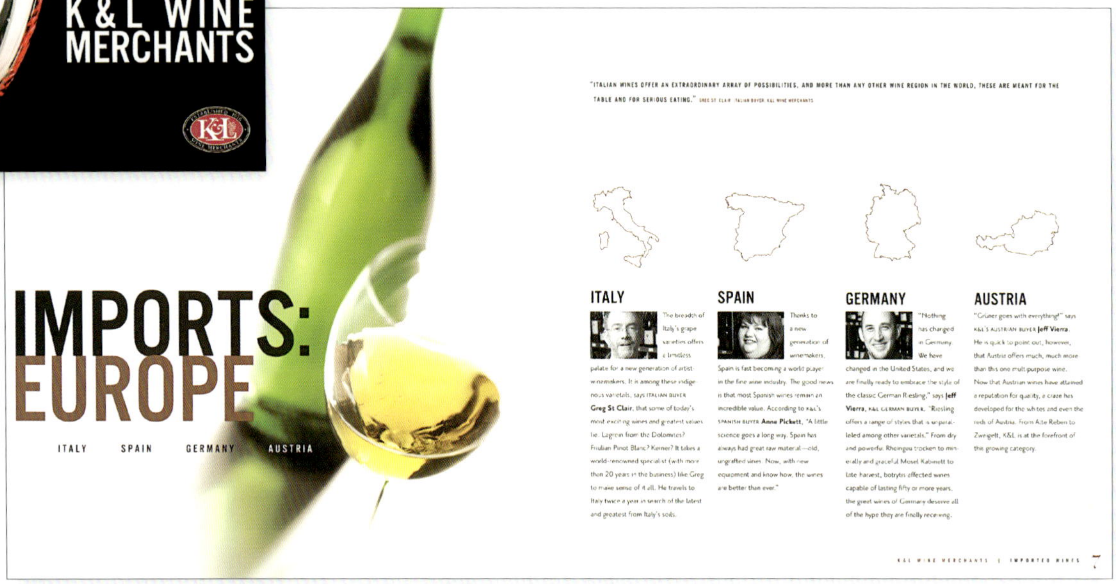

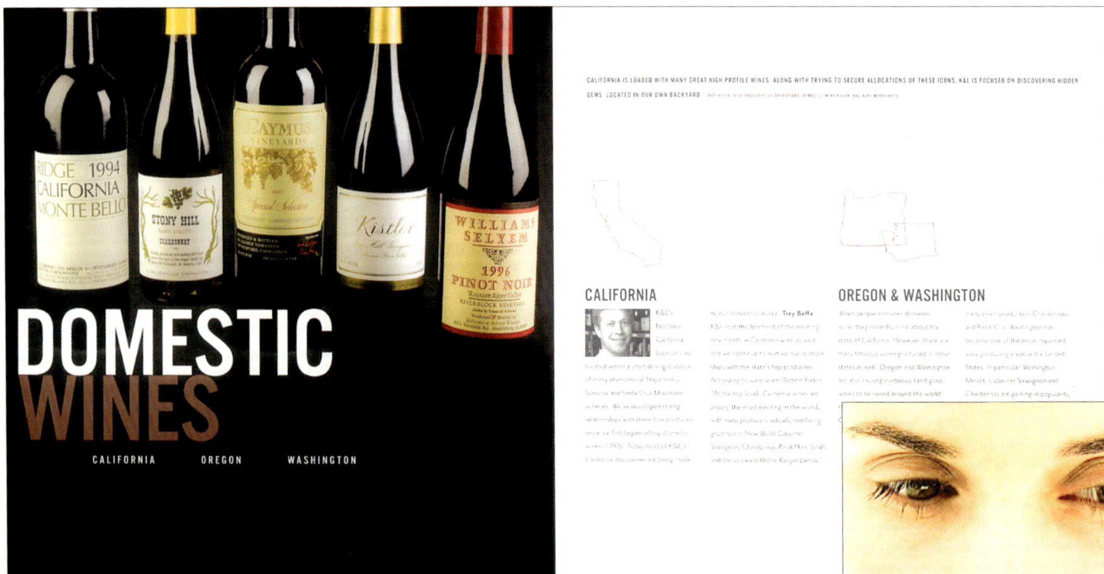

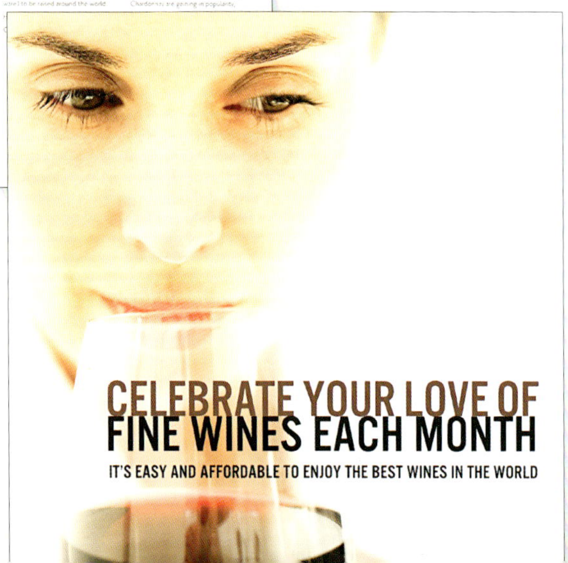

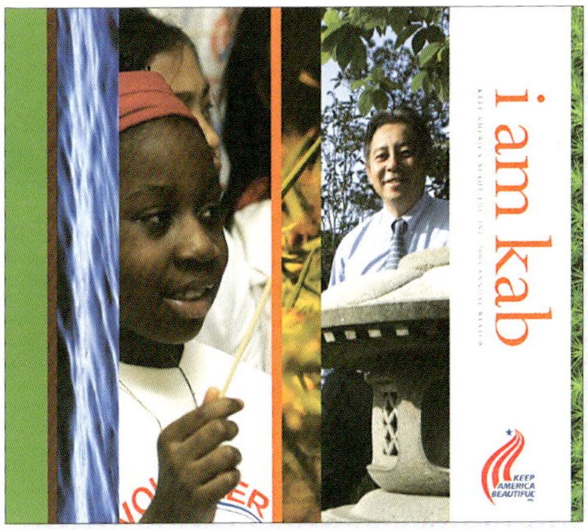

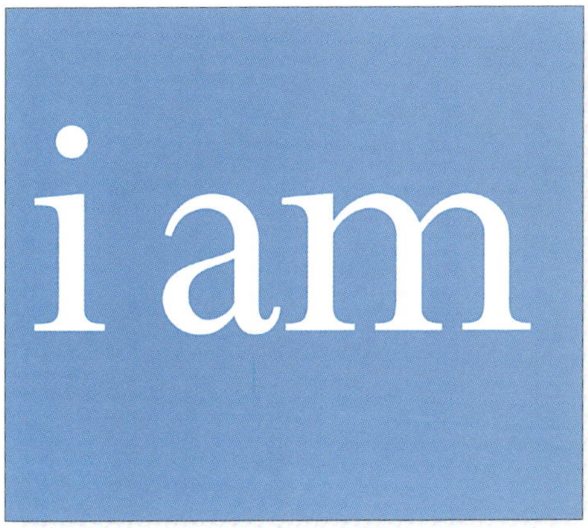

client
Keep America Beautiful
design firm
Taylor Design
www.taylordesign.com
designer
Mark Barrett

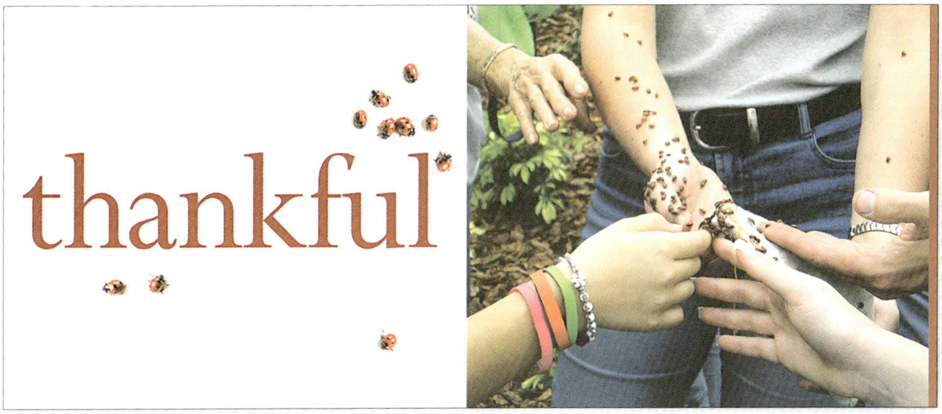

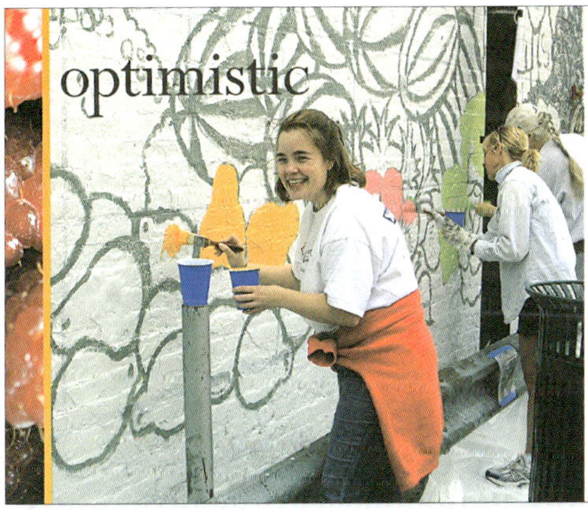

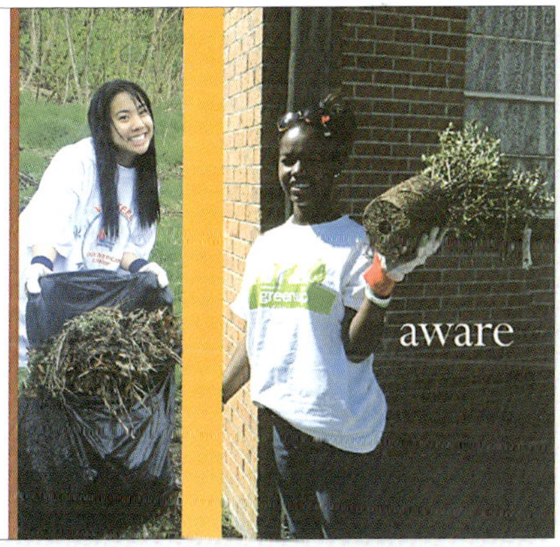

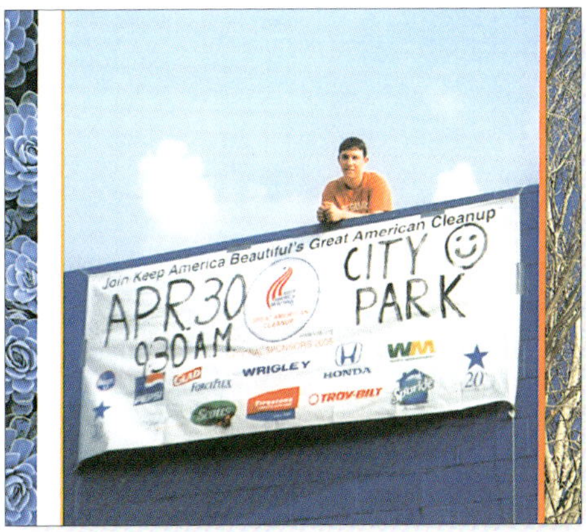

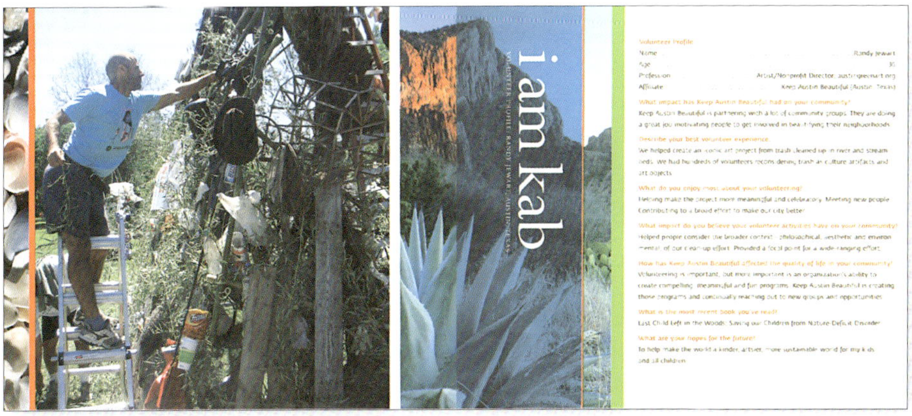

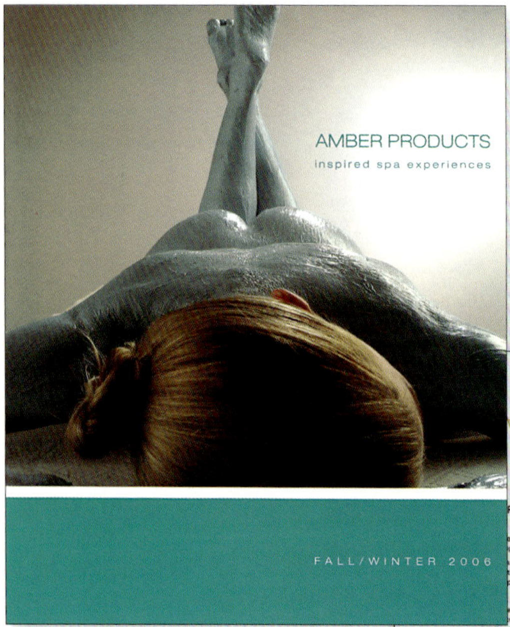

client
Amber Products Company
design firm
Reinnov8 Design Group
www.reinnov8.com
designer
Richard A. Hooper

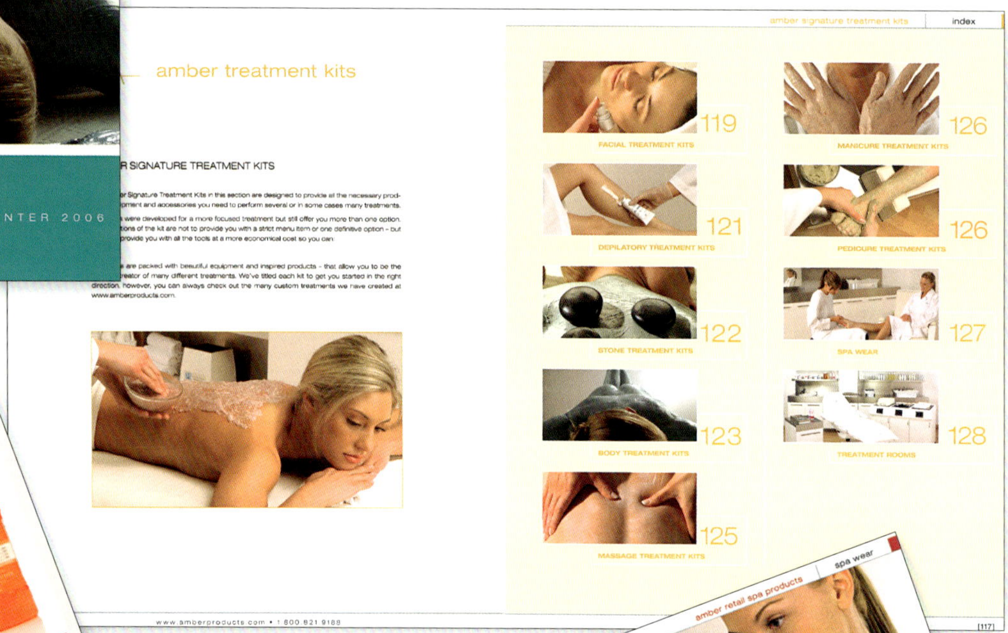

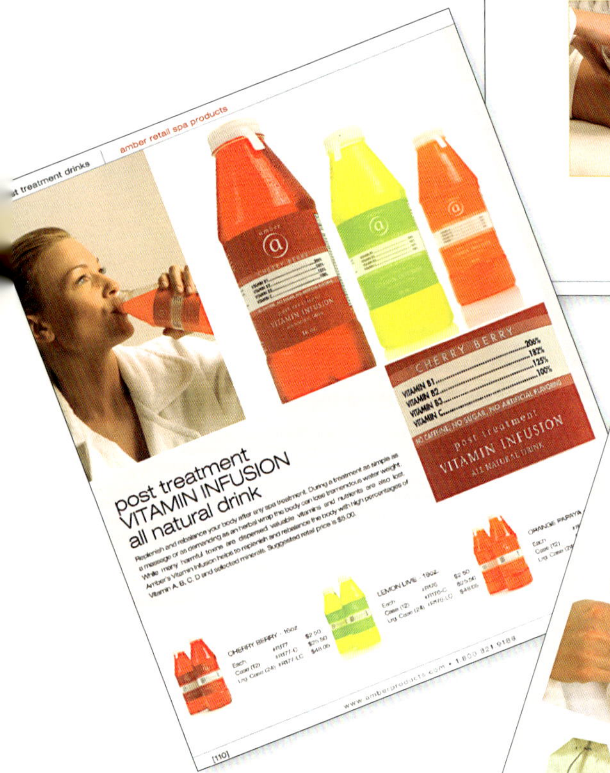

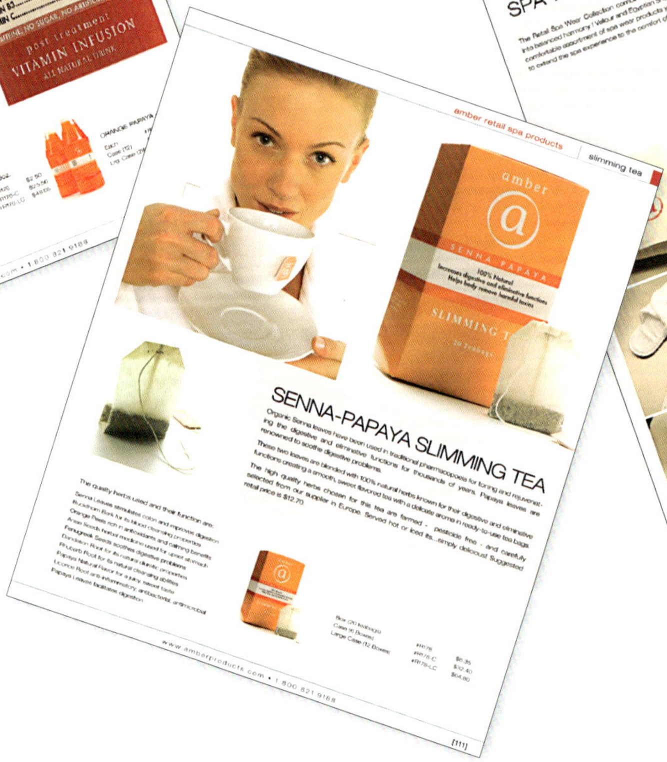

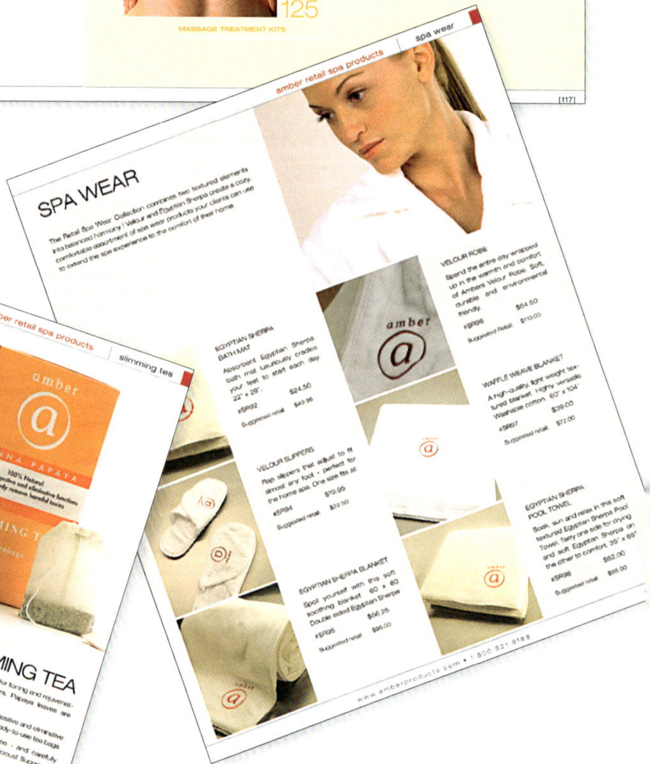

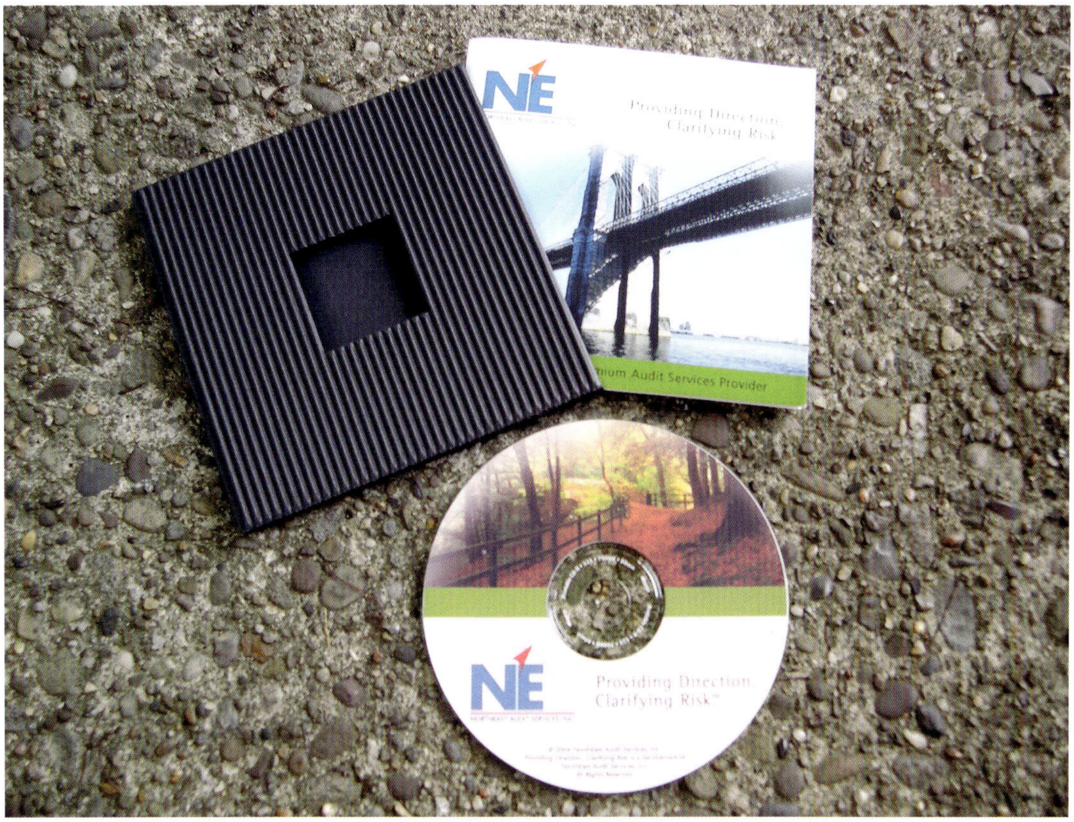

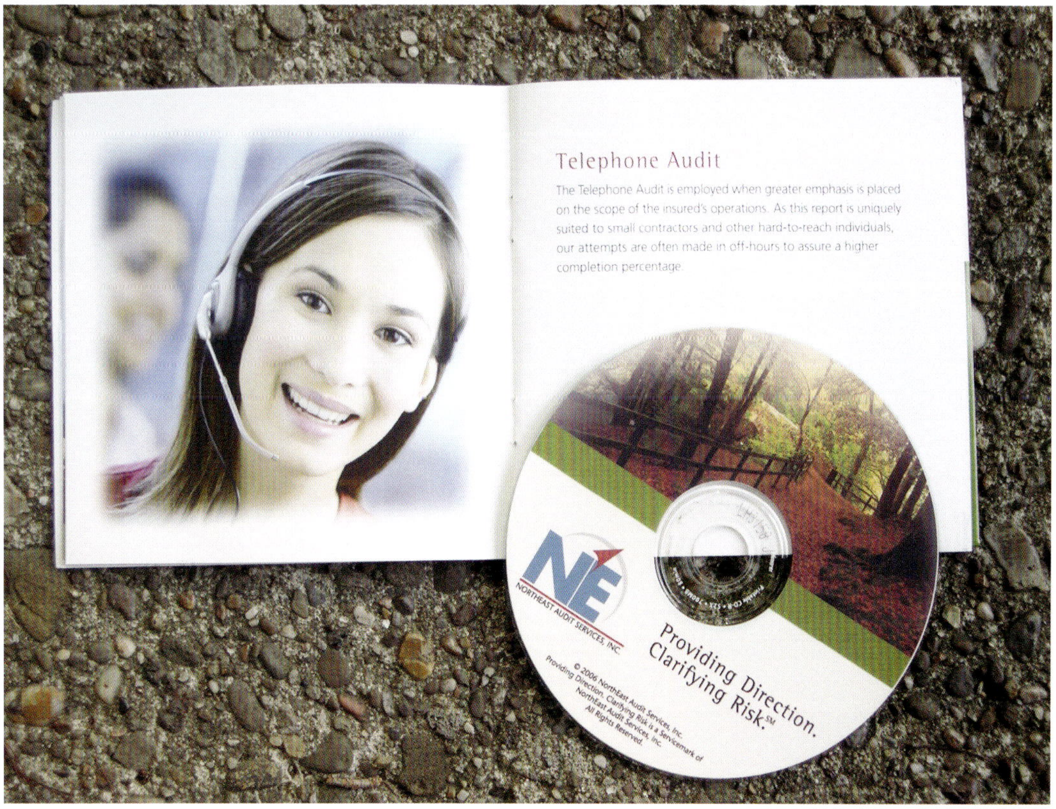

client
NorthEast Audit Services
design firm
Icon Graphics Inc.
thinkfeelchoose.com
designers
Icon Graphics Inc.

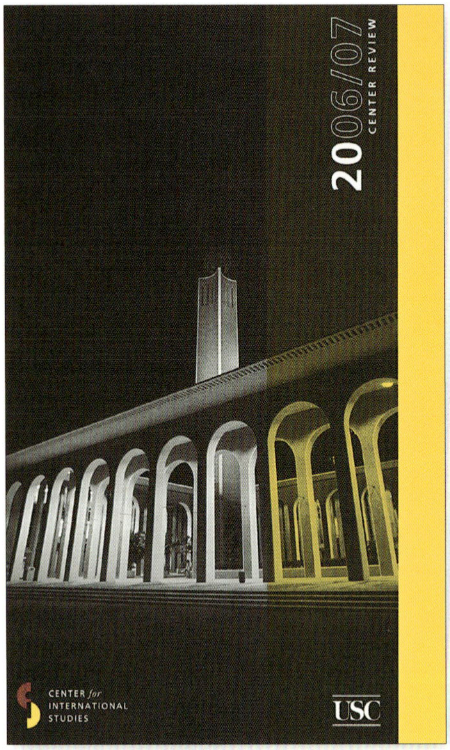

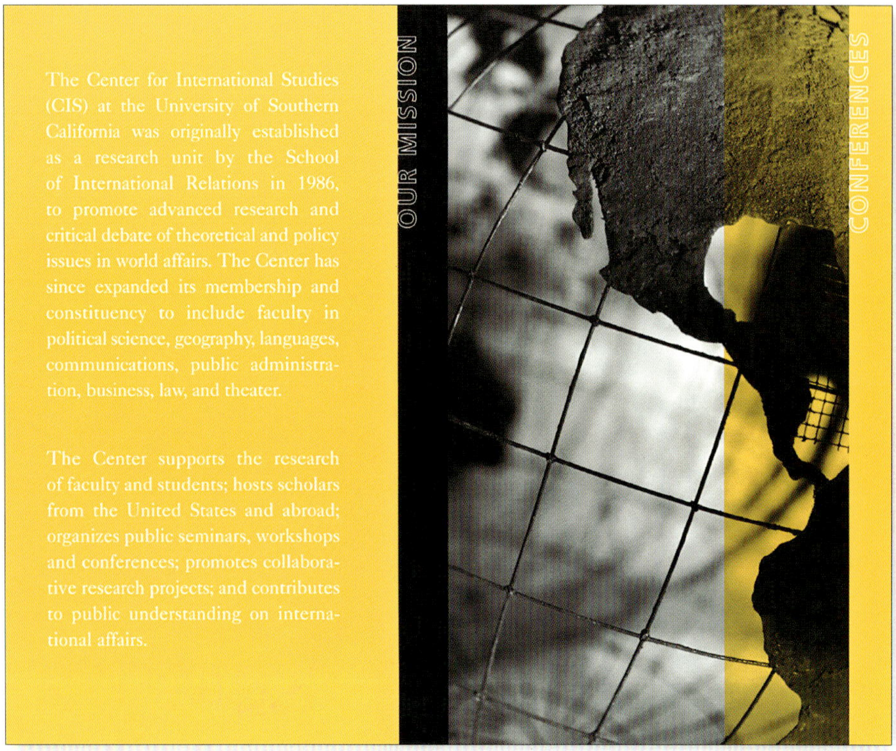

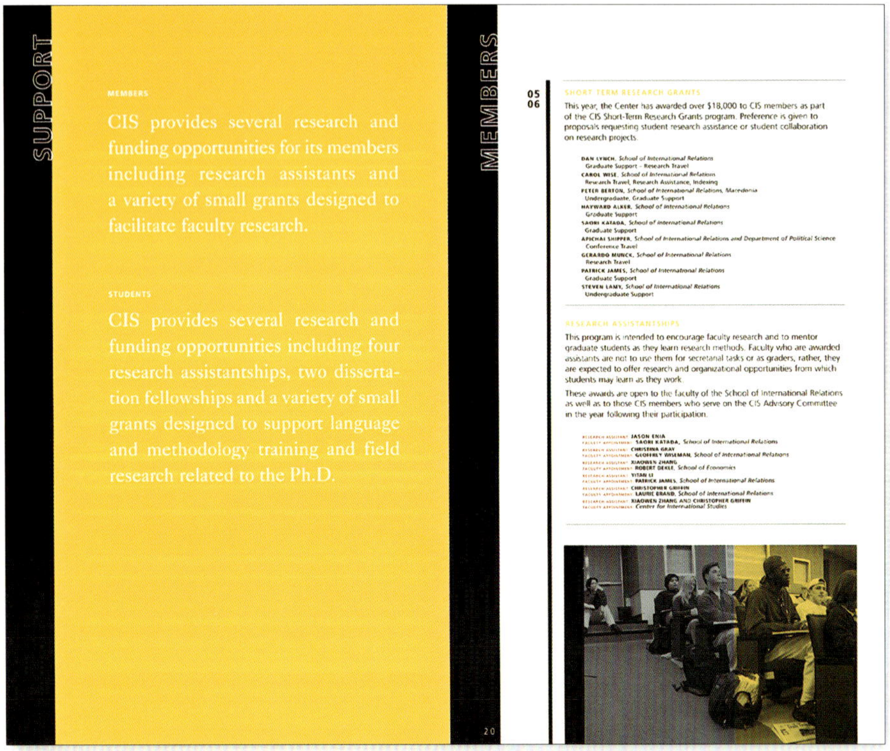

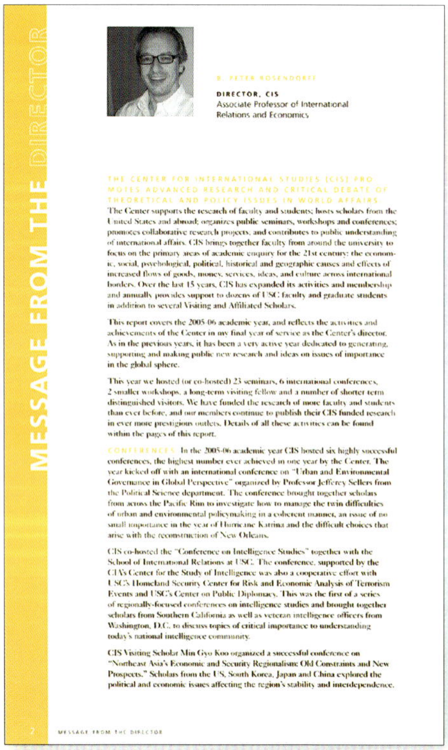

client
USC Center for International Studies
design firm
IE Design + Communications
www.iedesign.com
creative director
Marcie Carson
designers
Nicole Lehmann, Jane Lee

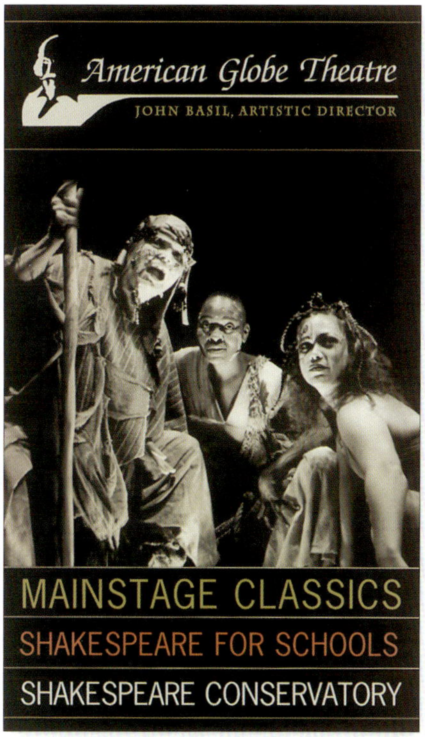

client
American Globe Theater
design firm
WestGroup Creative
www.westgp.com
designer
Chip Tolaney

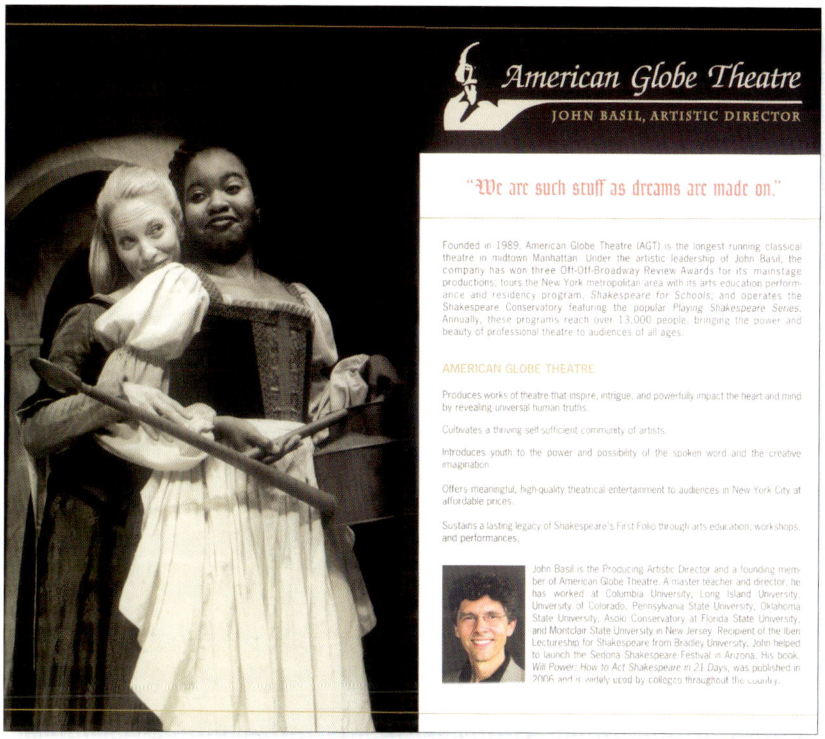

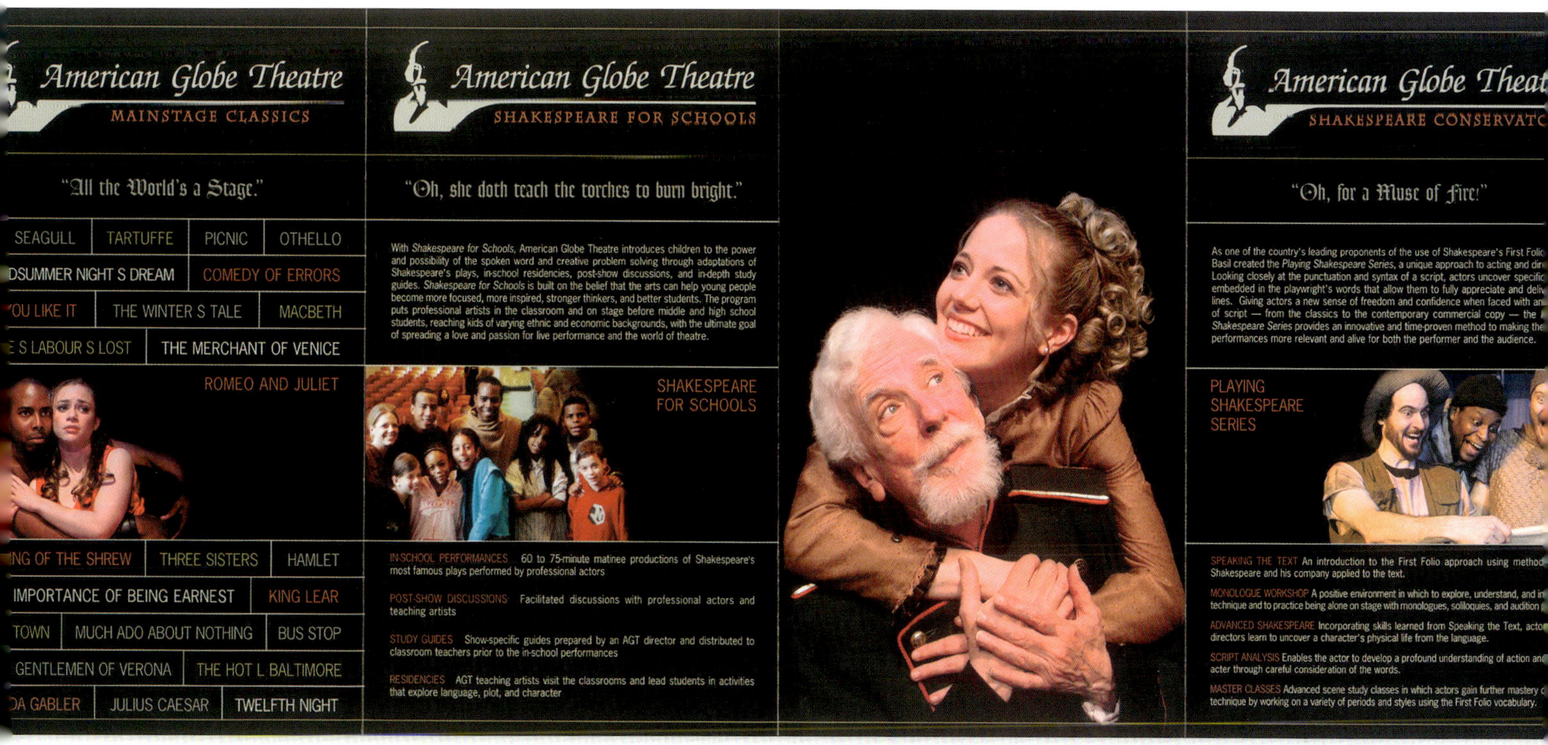

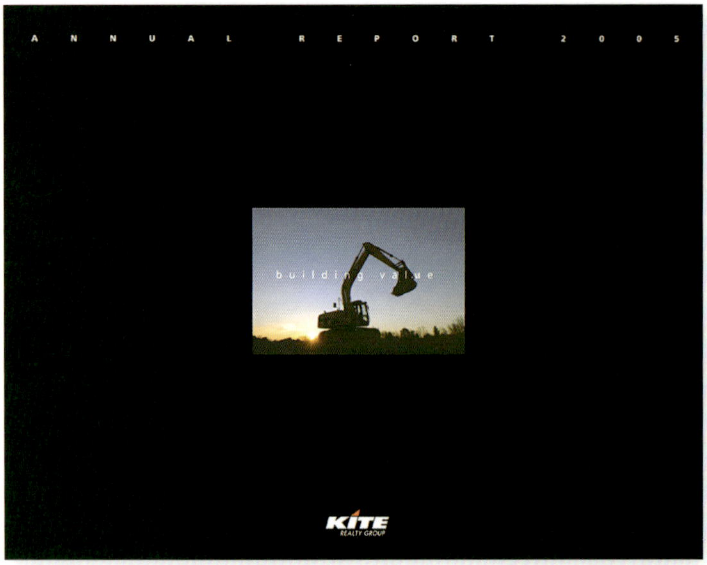

client
Kite Realty
design firm
Gibson Group
www.gibsongrp.com
designer
Diane McGuire

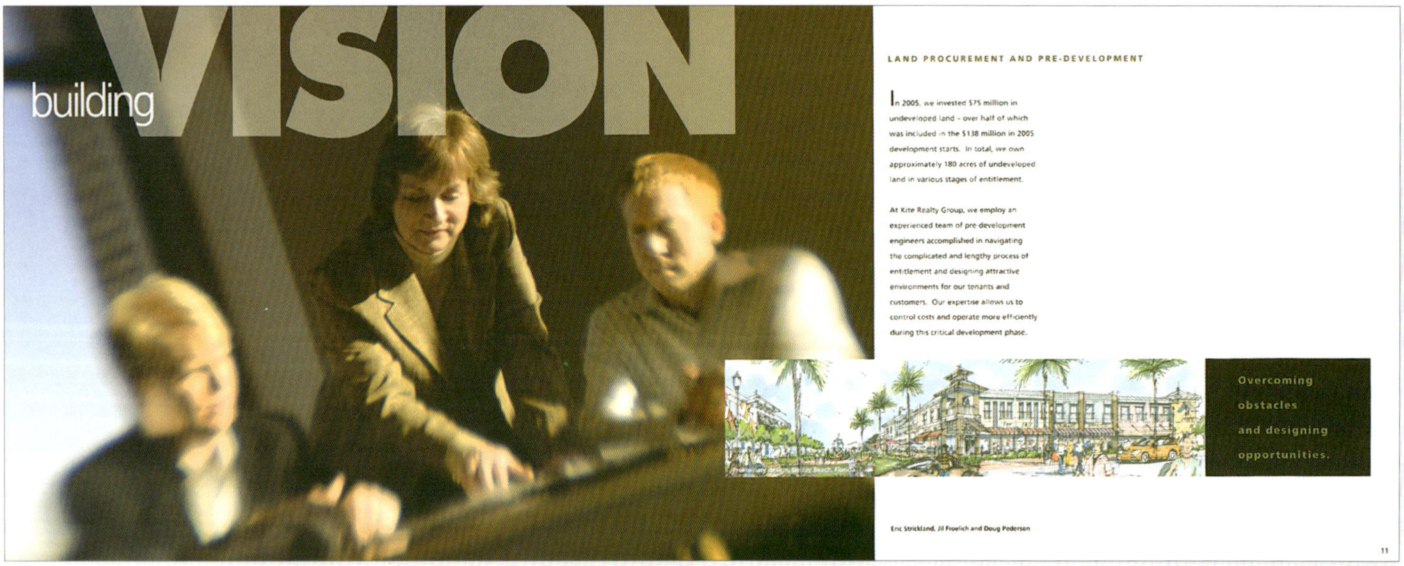

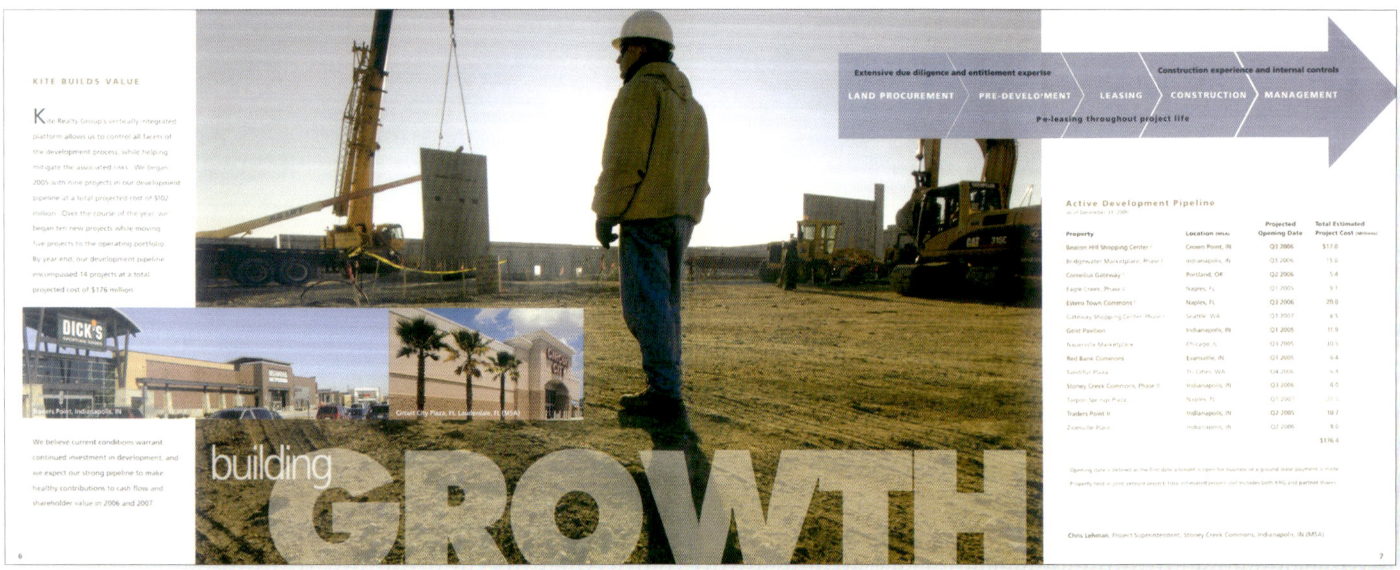

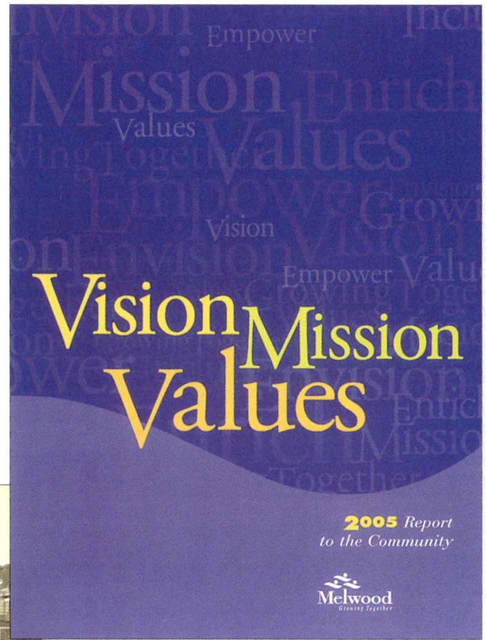

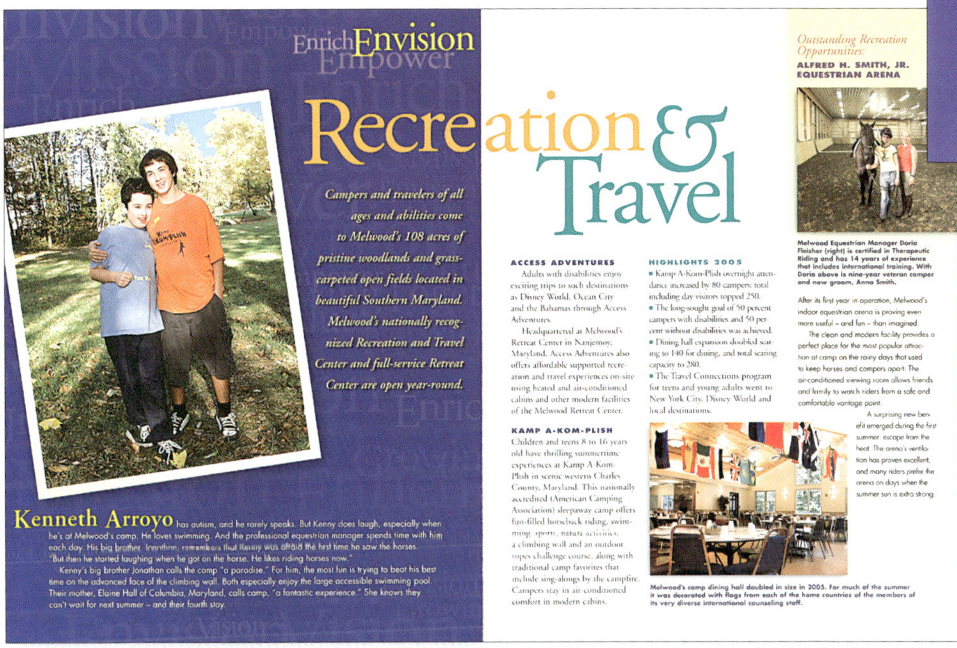

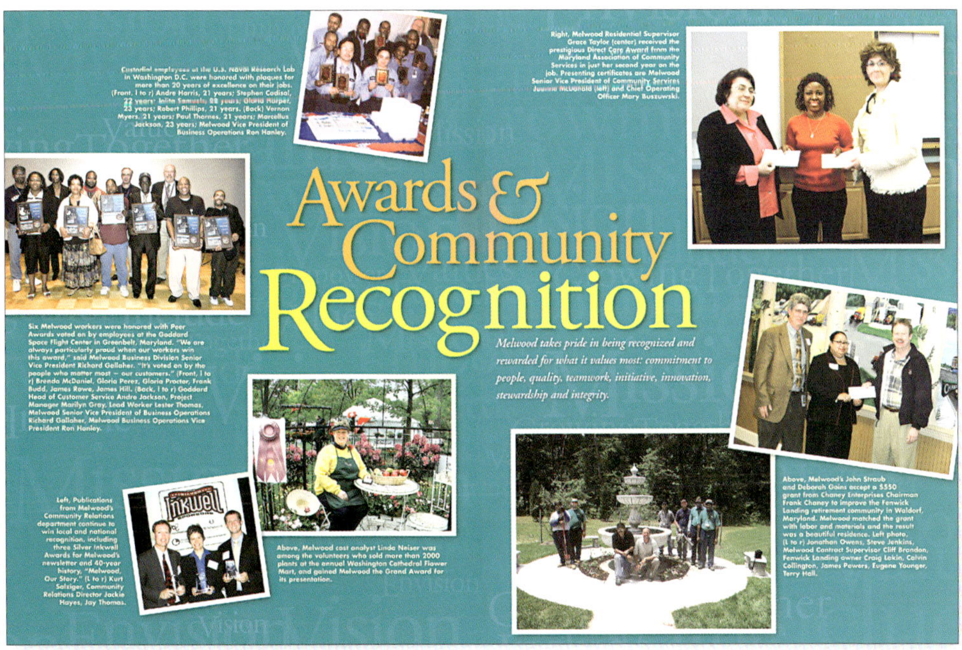

client
Melwood
design firm
Dever Designs
www.deverdesigns.com
art director
Jeffrey L. Dever
designer
Fatima Ameen

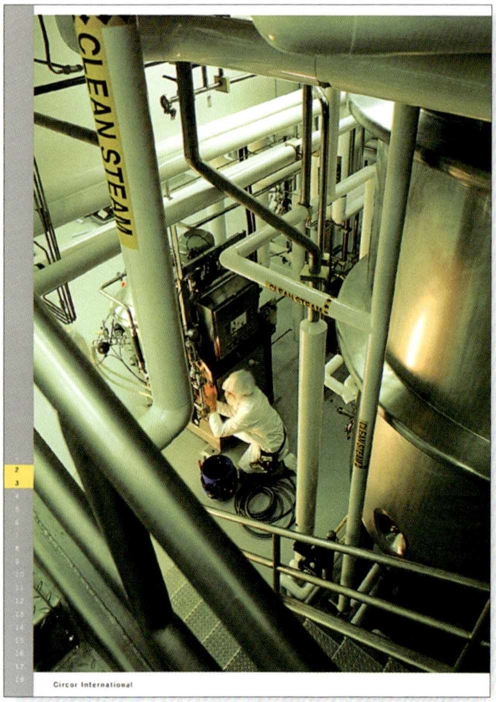

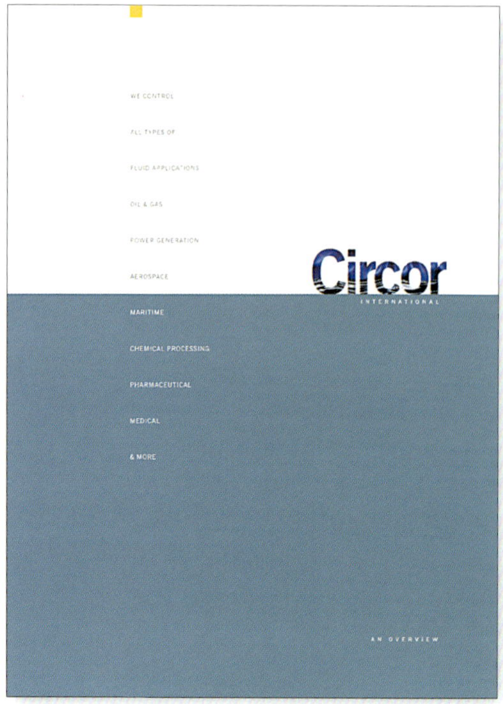

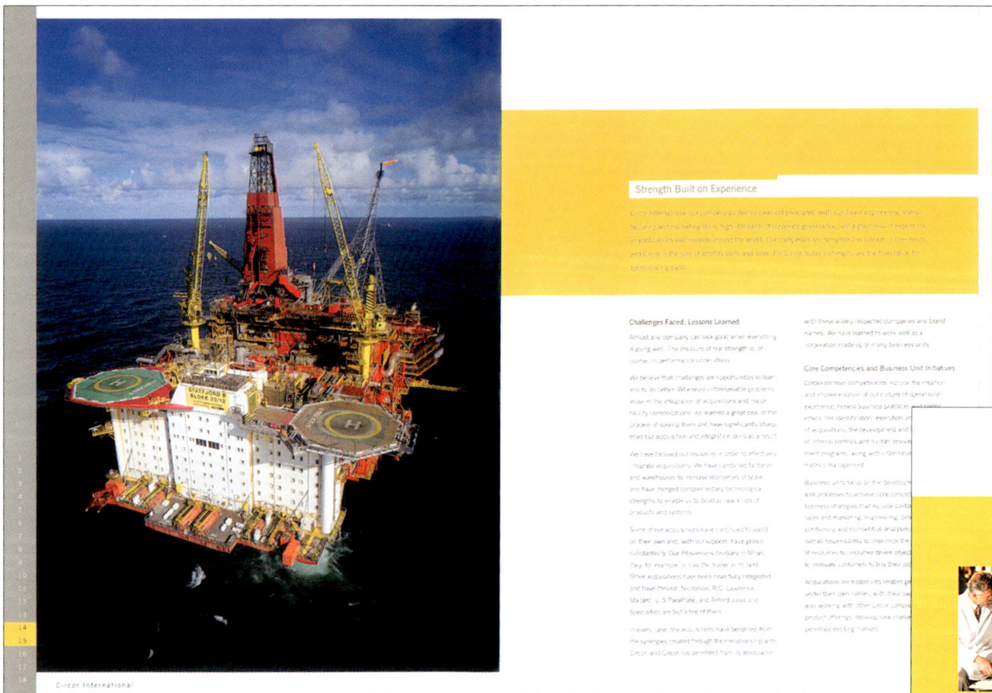

client
Circor, Inc.
design firm
Gill Fishman Associates
www.gillfishmandesign.com
designer
Tammy Torrey

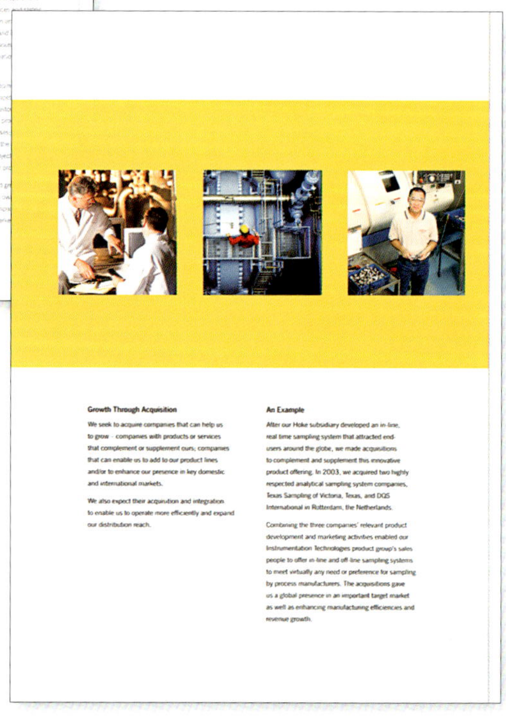

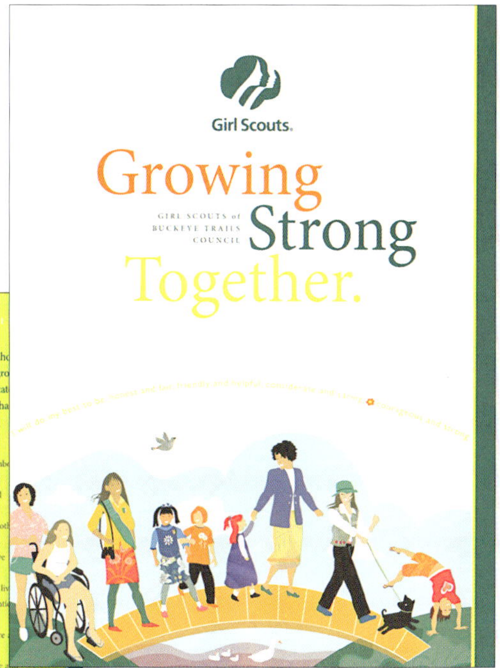

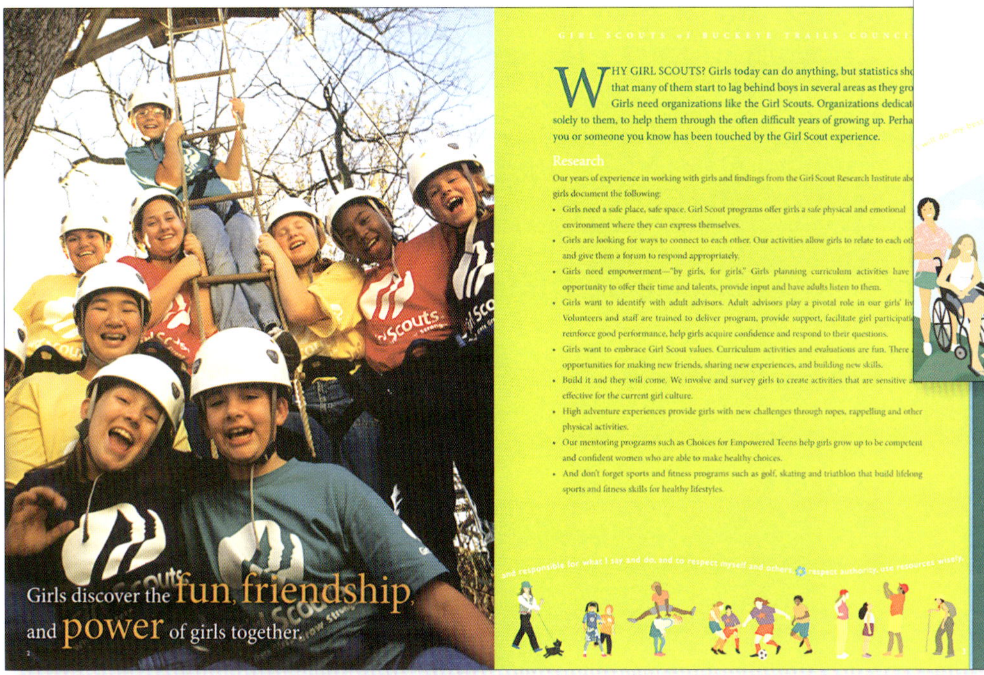

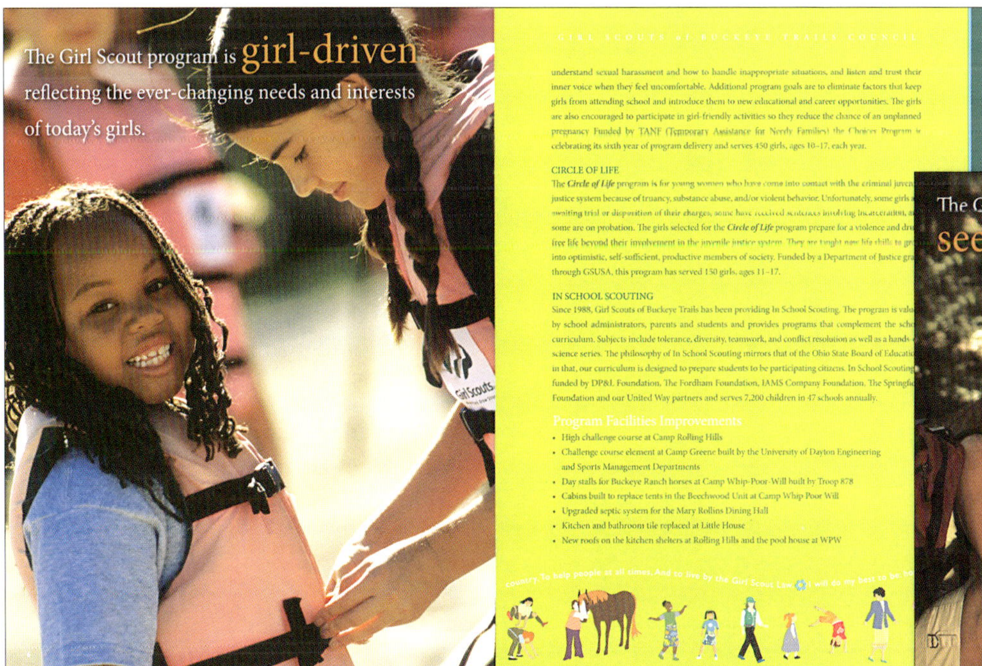

client
Girl Scouts of Buckeye Trails Council
design firm
V.M.A., Inc.
vmai.com
designers
Doug Knopp, Amritha Ward

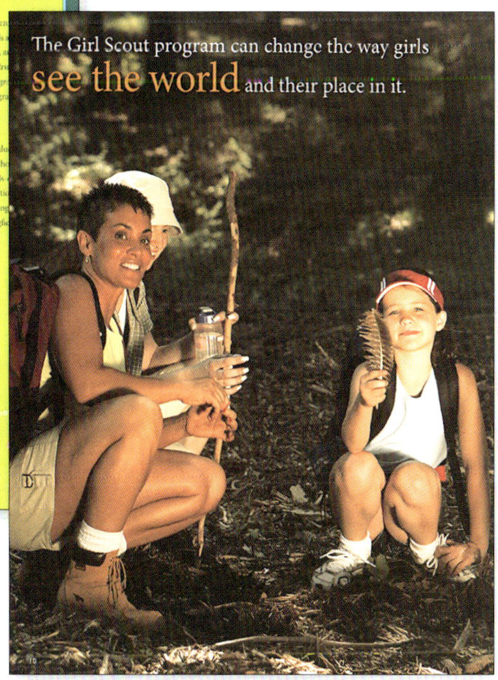

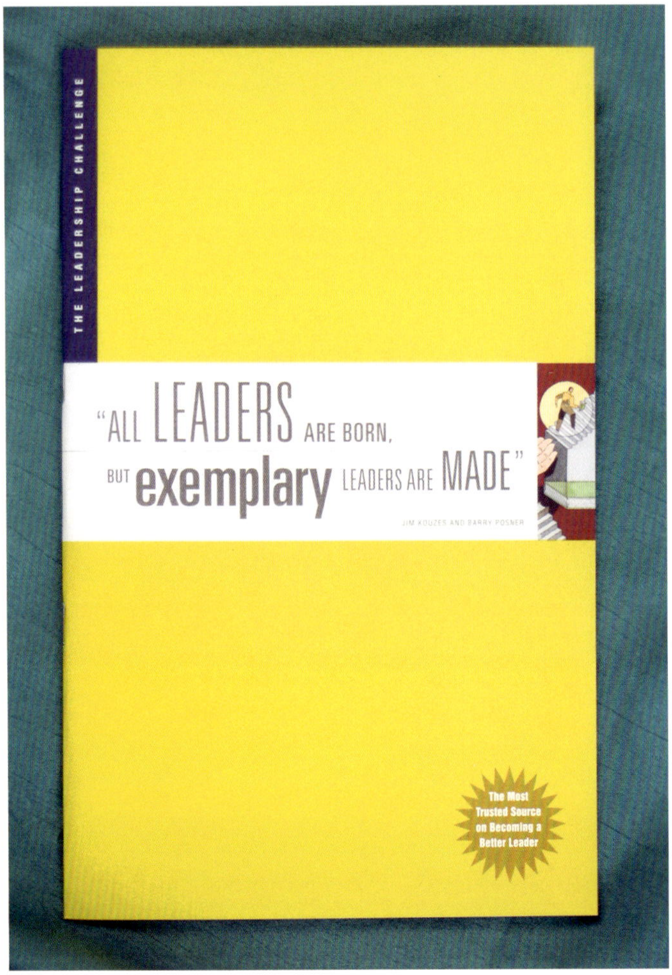

client
John Wiley & Sons, Inc.
design firm
Mortensen Design, Inc.
www.mortensendesign.com
art director
Gordon Mortensen
designer
Patricia Margaret

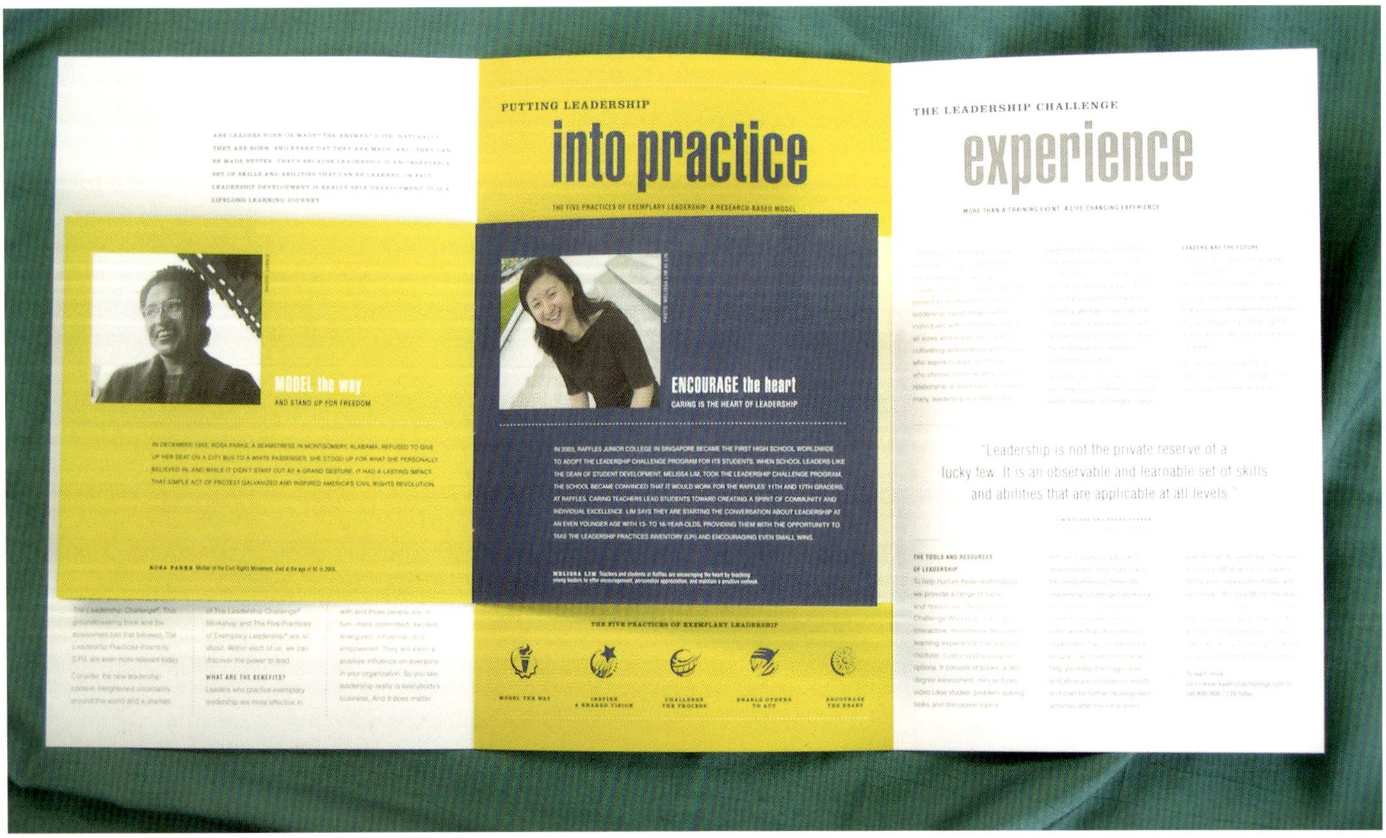

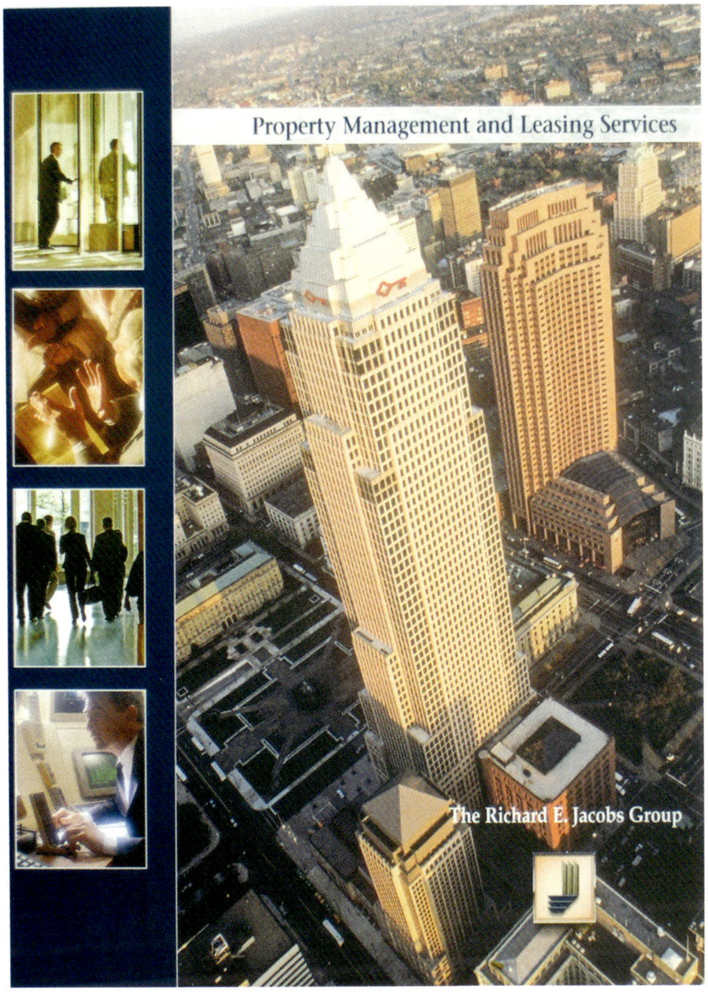

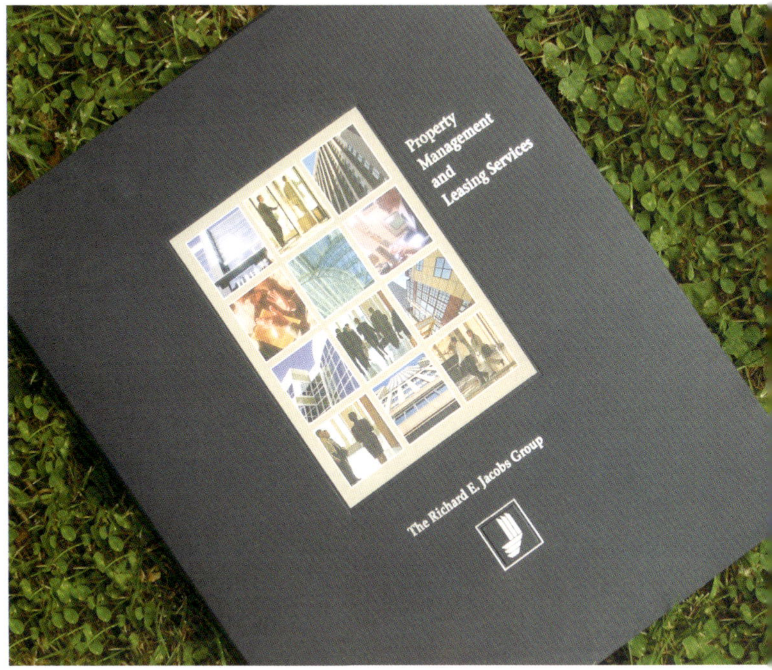

client
The Richard E. Jacobs Group
design firm
Herip Design Associates, Inc.
www.heripassociates.com
designers
Walter M. Herip, John R. Menter

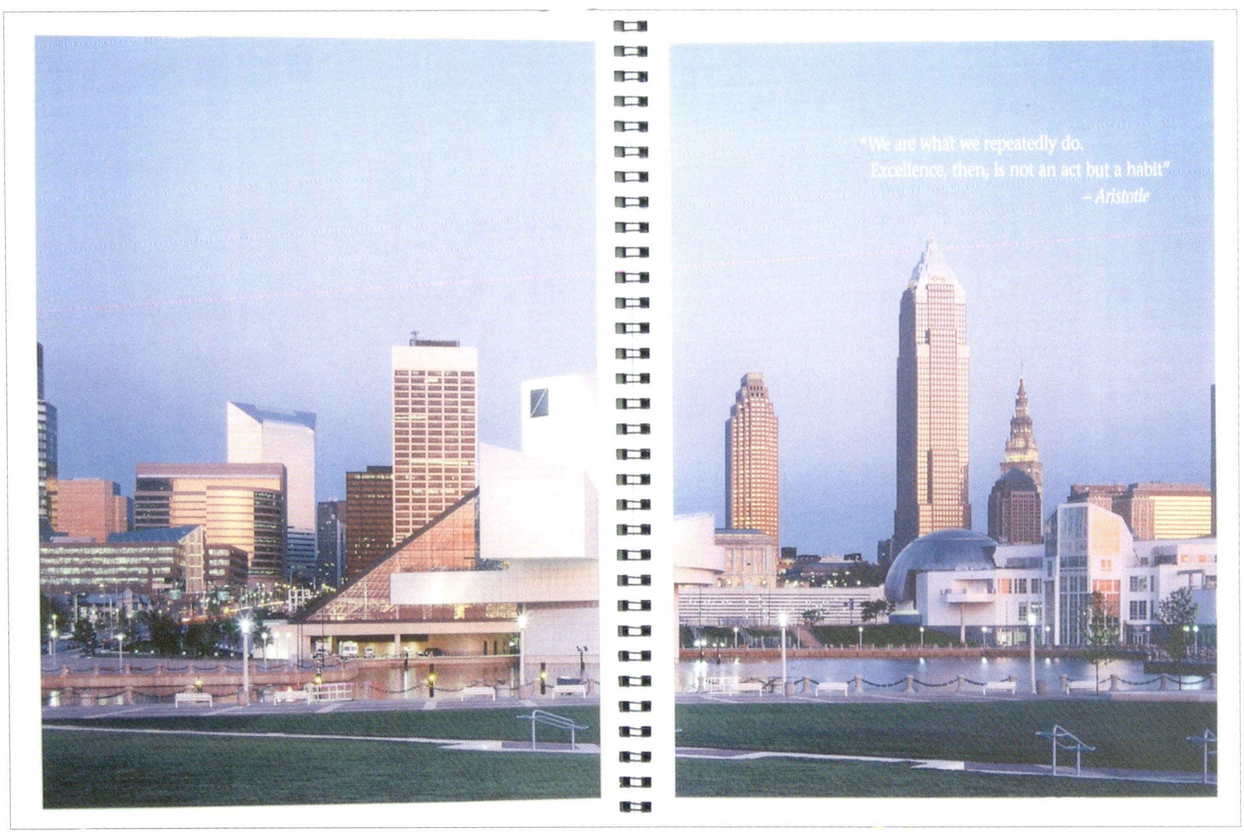

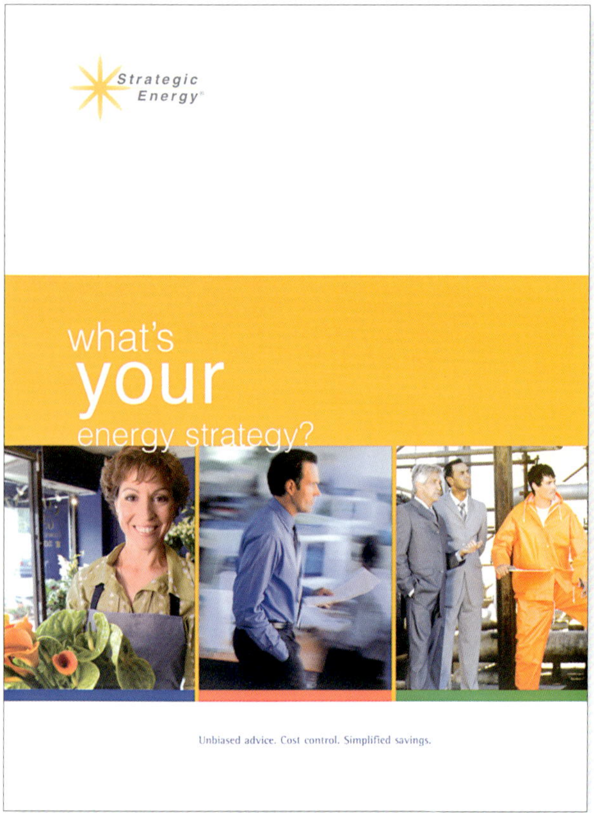

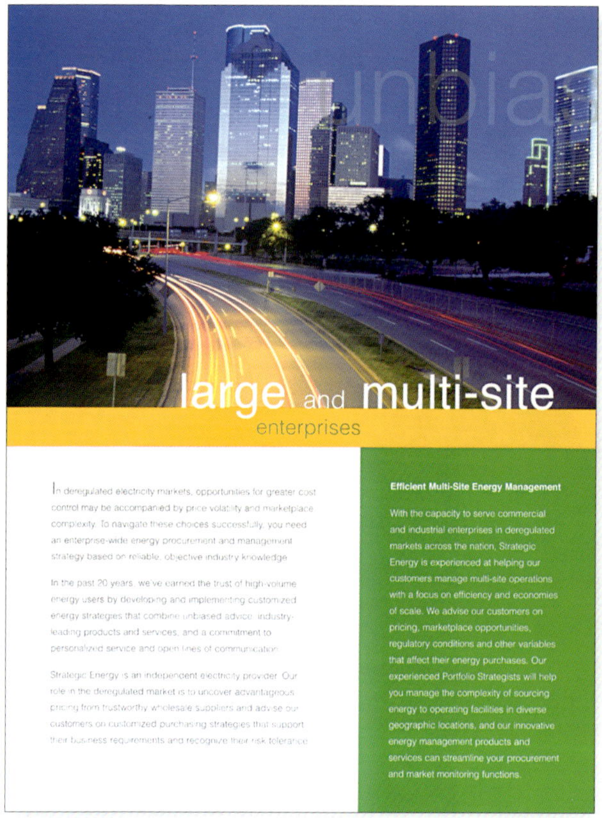

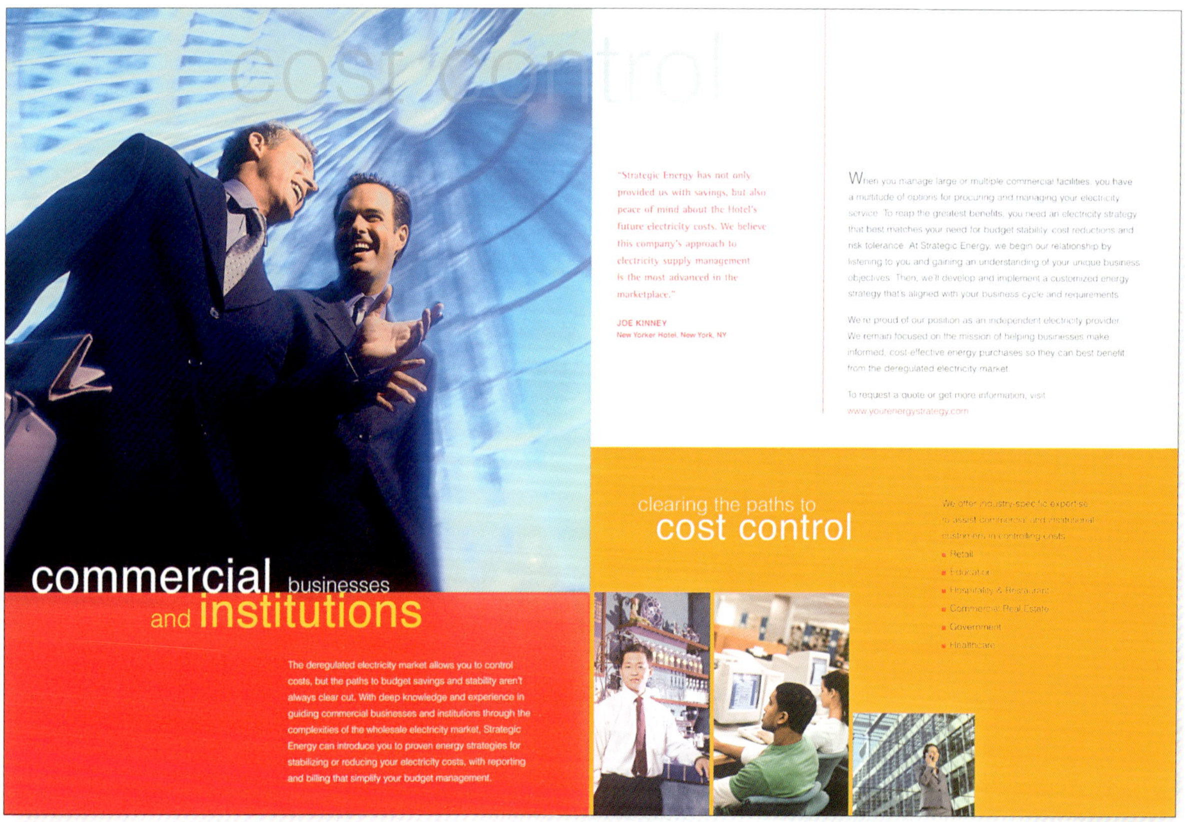

client
Strategic Energy
design firm
Desbrow
desbrow.com
designers
Kimberly S. Miller, Brian Lee Campbell

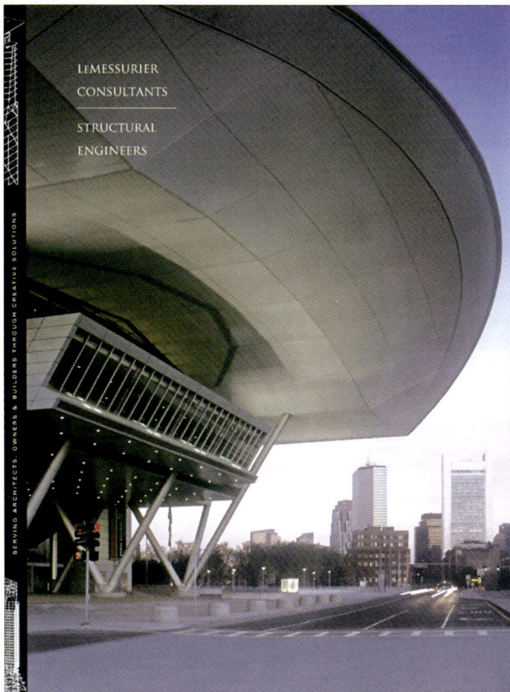

client
LeMessurier Consultants
design firm
Gill Fishman Associates
www.gillfishmandesign.com
designer
Tammy Torrey

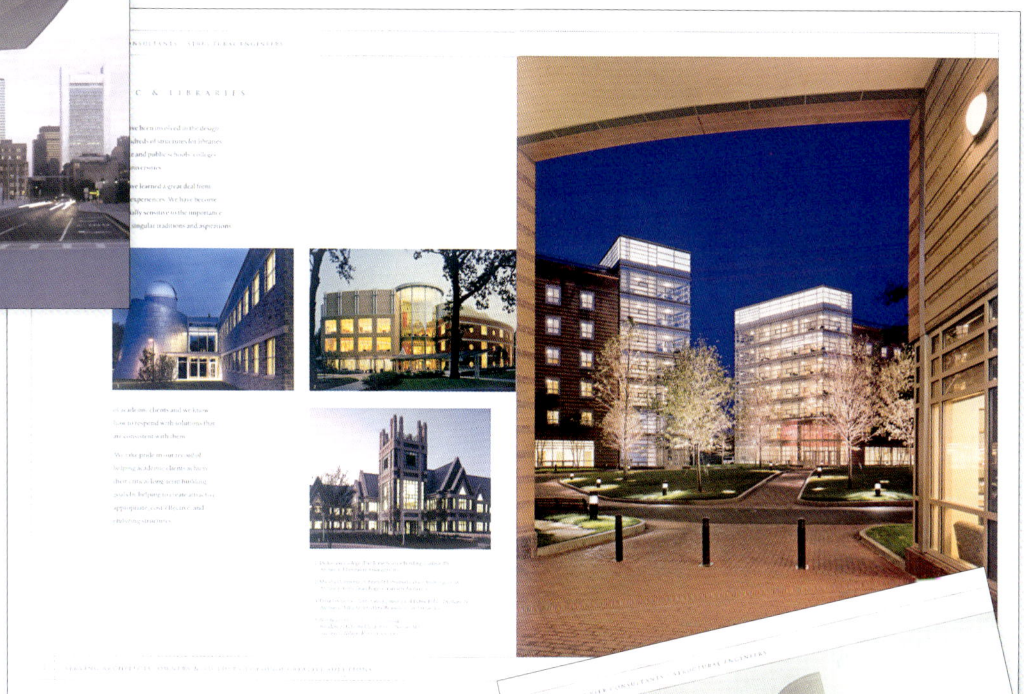

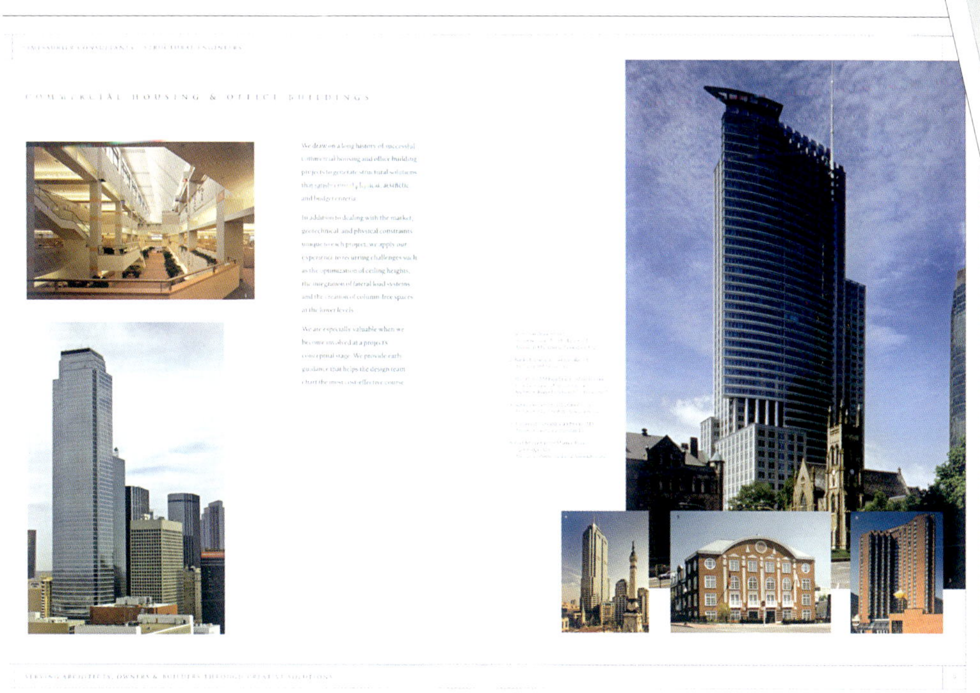

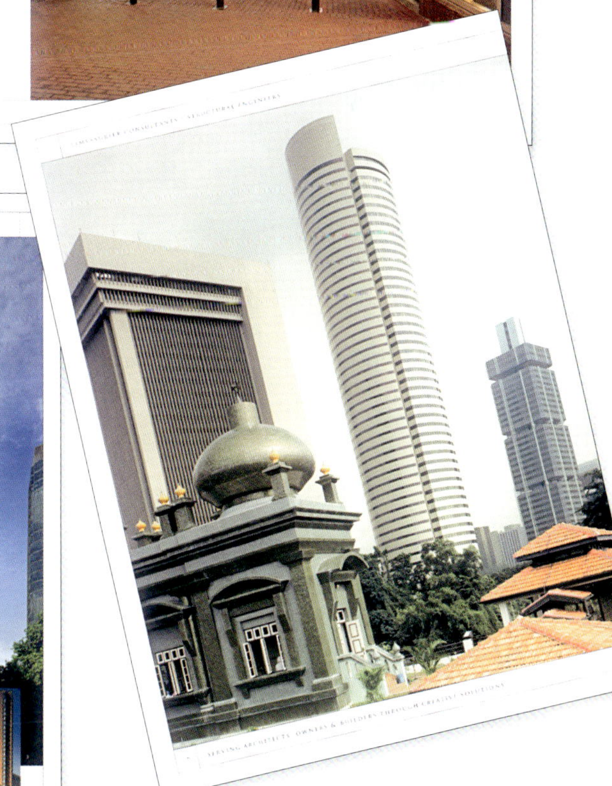

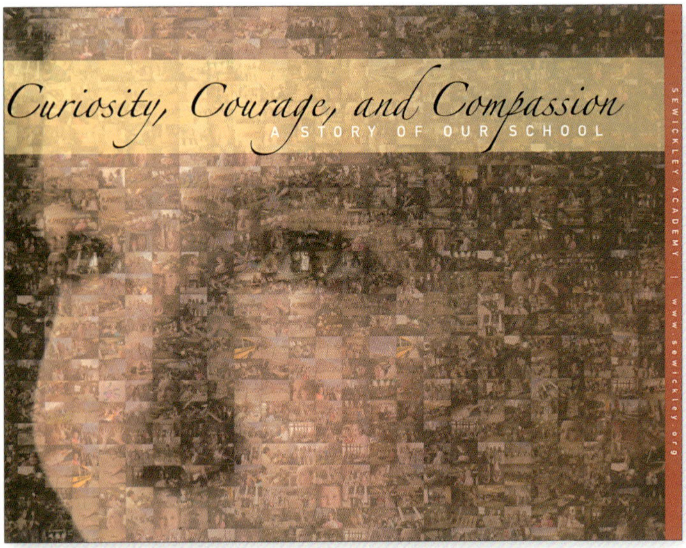

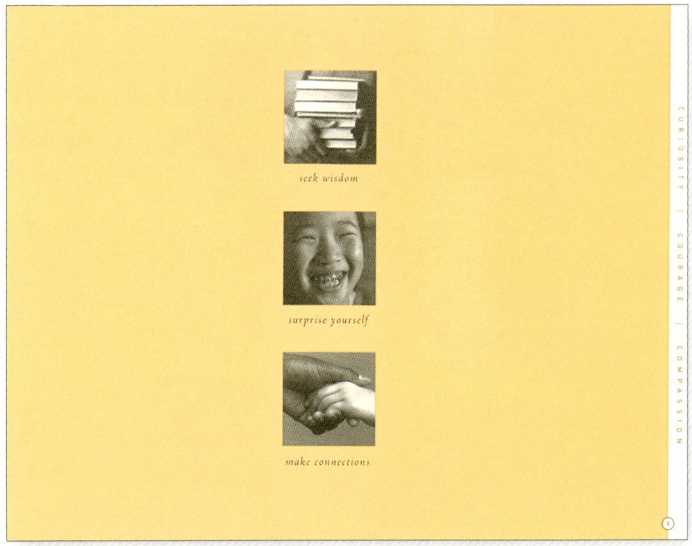

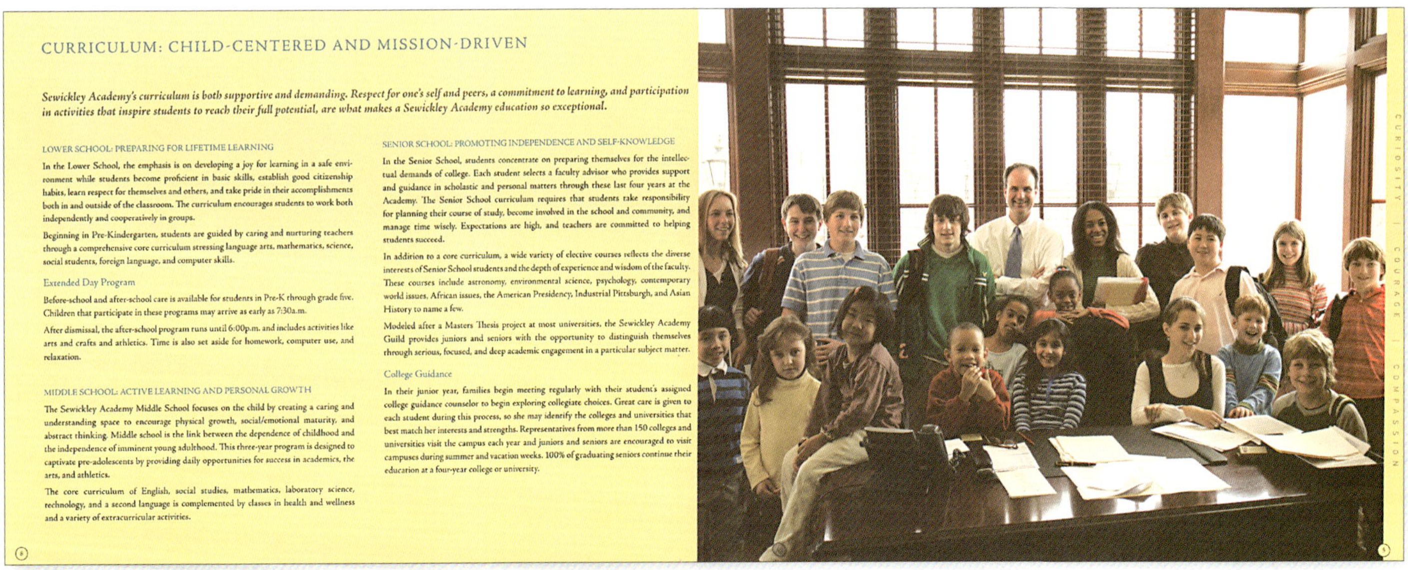

CURRICULUM: CHILD-CENTERED AND MISSION-DRIVEN

Sewickley Academy's curriculum is both supportive and demanding. Respect for one's self and peers, a commitment to learning, and participation in activities that inspire students to reach their full potential, are what makes a Sewickley Academy education so exceptional.

LOWER SCHOOL: PREPARING FOR LIFETIME LEARNING

In the Lower School, the emphasis is on developing a joy for learning in a safe environment while students become proficient in basic skills, establish good citizenship habits, learn respect for themselves and others, and take pride in their accomplishments both in and outside of the classroom. The curriculum encourages students to work both independently and cooperatively in groups.

Beginning in Pre-Kindergarten, students are guided by caring and nurturing teachers through a comprehensive core curriculum stressing language arts, mathematics, science, social students, foreign language, and computer skills.

Extended Day Program

Before-school and after-school care is available for students in Pre-K through grade five. Children that participate in these programs may arrive as early as 7:30a.m.

After dismissal, the after-school program runs until 6:00p.m. and includes activities like arts and crafts and athletics. Time is also set aside for homework, computer use, and relaxation.

MIDDLE SCHOOL: ACTIVE LEARNING AND PERSONAL GROWTH

The Sewickley Academy Middle School focuses on the child by creating a caring and understanding space to encourage physical growth, social/emotional maturity, and abstract thinking. Middle school is the link between the dependence of childhood and the independence of imminent young adulthood. This three-year program is designed to captivate pre-adolescents by providing daily opportunities for success in academics, the arts, and athletics.

The core curriculum of English, social studies, mathematics, laboratory science, technology, and a second language is complemented by classes in health and wellness and a variety of extracurricular activities.

SENIOR SCHOOL: PROMOTING INDEPENDENCE AND SELF-KNOWLEDGE

In the Senior School, students concentrate on preparing themselves for the intellectual demands of college. Each student selects a faculty advisor who provides support and guidance in scholastic and personal matters through these last four years at the Academy. The Senior School curriculum requires that students take responsibility for planning their course of study, become involved in the school and community, and manage time wisely. Expectations are high, and teachers are committed to helping students succeed.

In addition to a core curriculum, a wide variety of elective courses reflects the diverse interests of Senior School students and the depth of experience and wisdom of the faculty. These courses include astronomy, environmental science, psychology, contemporary world issues, African issues, the American Presidency, Industrial Pittsburgh, and Asian History to name a few.

Modeled after a Masters Thesis project at most universities, the Sewickley Academy Guild provides juniors and seniors with the opportunity to distinguish themselves through serious, focused, and deep academic engagement in a particular subject matter.

College Guidance

In their junior year, families begin meeting regularly with their student's assigned college guidance counselor to begin exploring collegiate choices. Great care is given to each student during this process, so she may identify the colleges and universities that best match her interests and strengths. Representatives from more than 150 colleges and universities visit the campus each year and juniors and seniors are encouraged to visit campuses during summer and vacation weeks. 100% of graduating seniors continue their education at a four-year college or university.

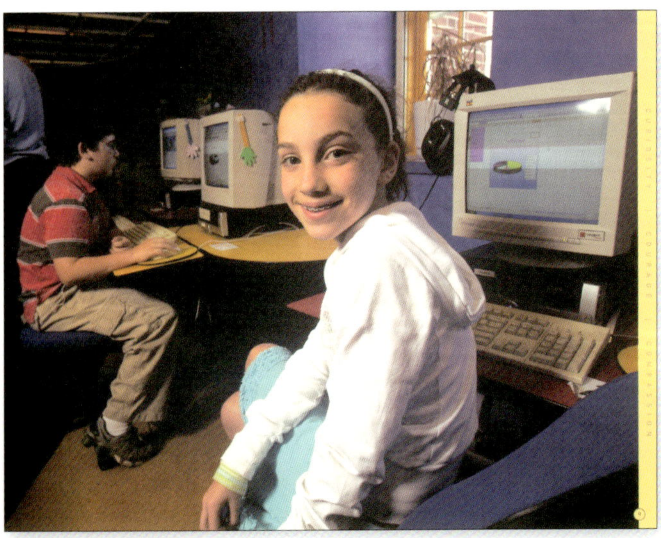

client
Sewickley Academy
design firm
Reinnov8 Design Group
www.reinnov8.com
designer
Richard A. Hooper

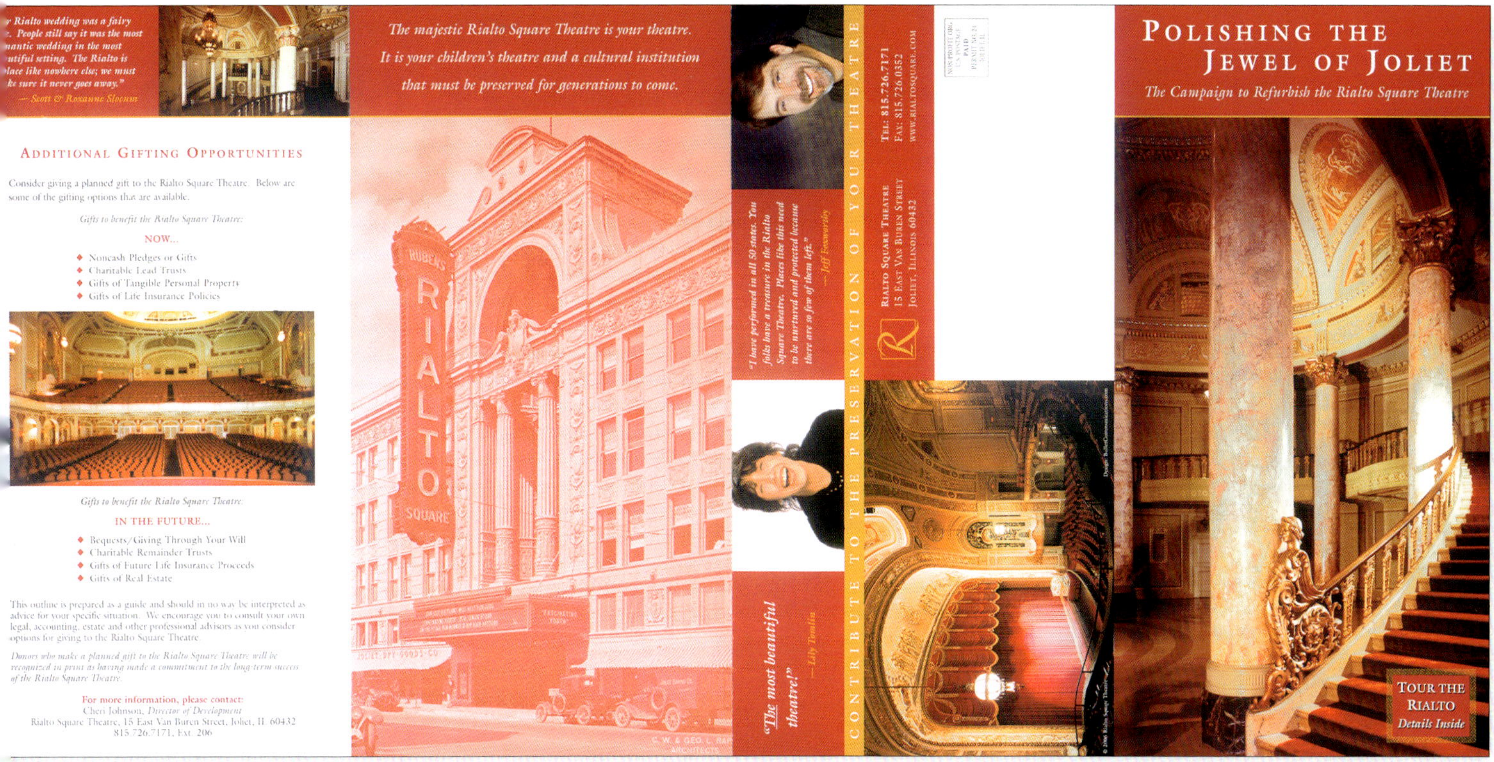

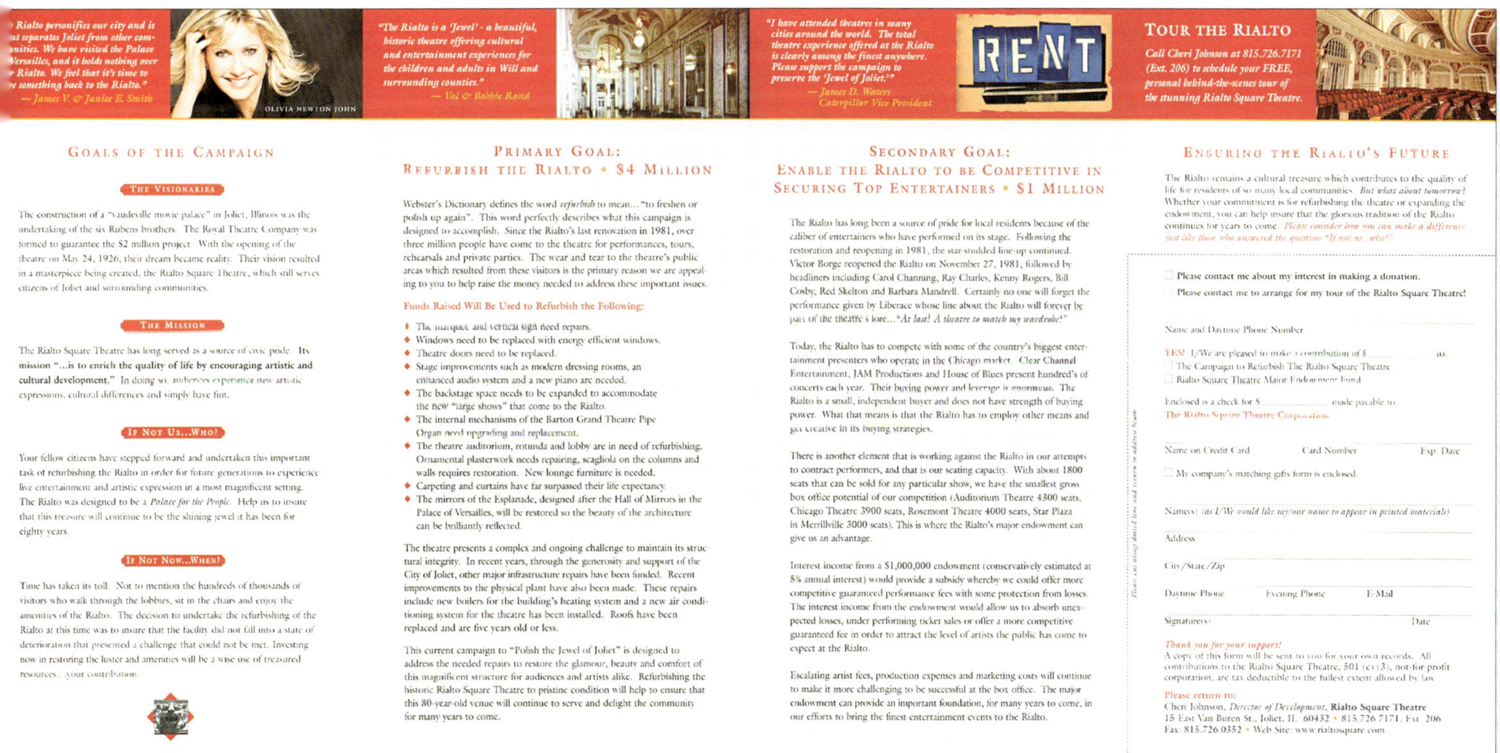

client
Rialto Square Theatre
design firm
Bullet Communications, Inc.
www.BulletCommunications.com
designer
Tim Scott Kump

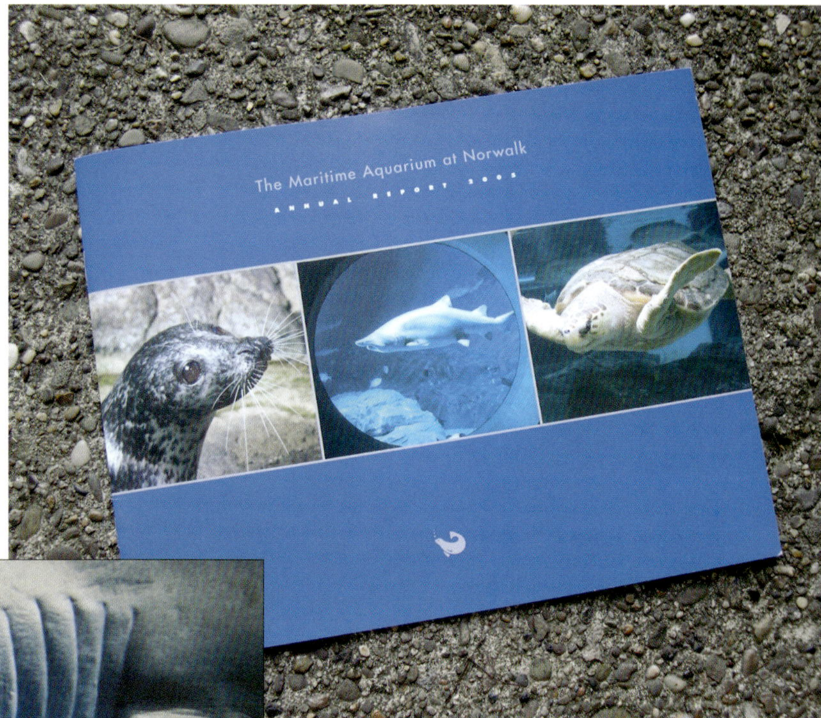

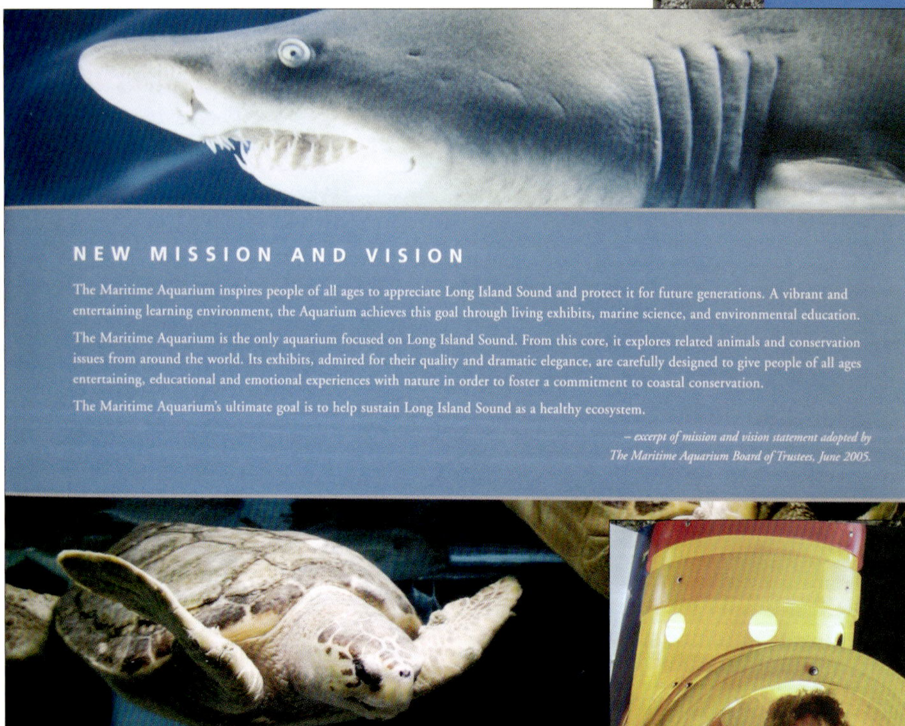

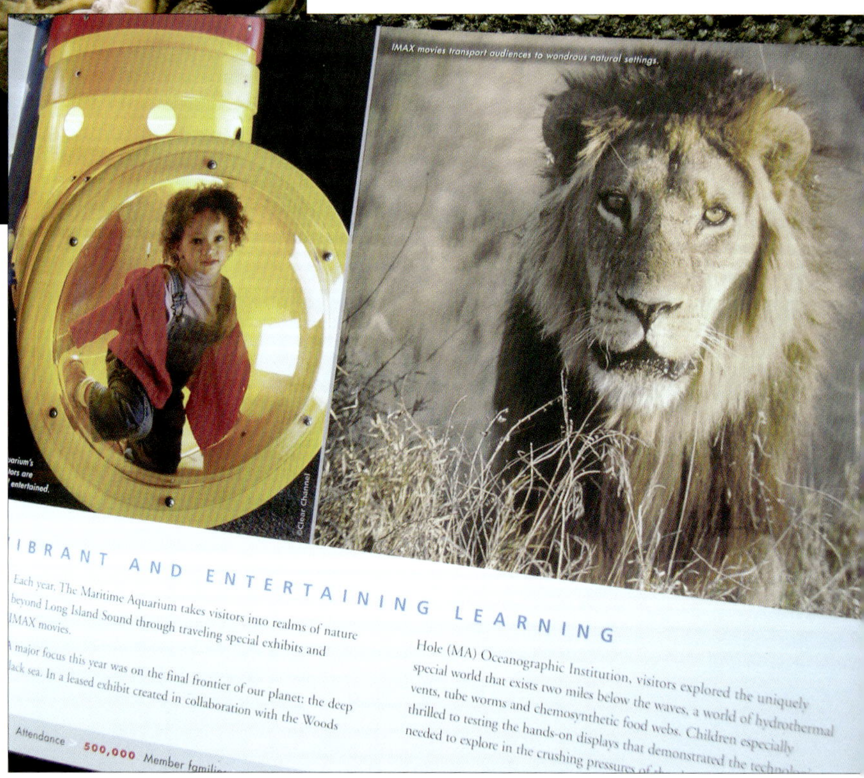

client
The Maritime Aquarium at Norwalk
design firm
Tom Fowler, Inc.
www.tomfowlerinc.com
art directors
Elizabeth P. Ball,
Brien O'Reilly

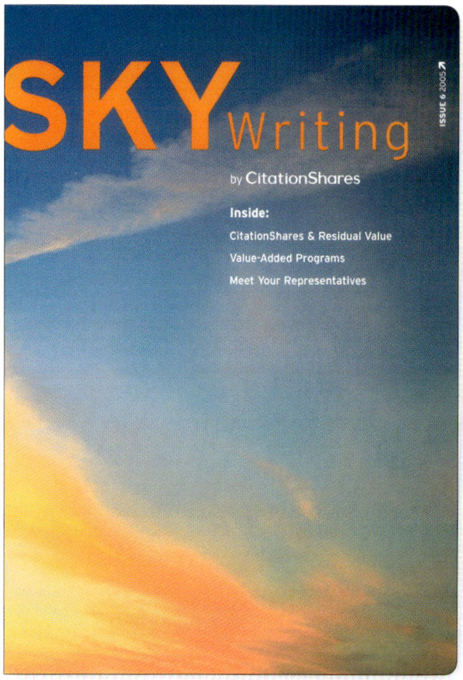

client
CitationShares
design firm
Hornall Anderson Design Works
www.hadw.com
designers
Jack Anderson, Kathy Saito,
Peter Anderson, Ed Lee, Chris Freed

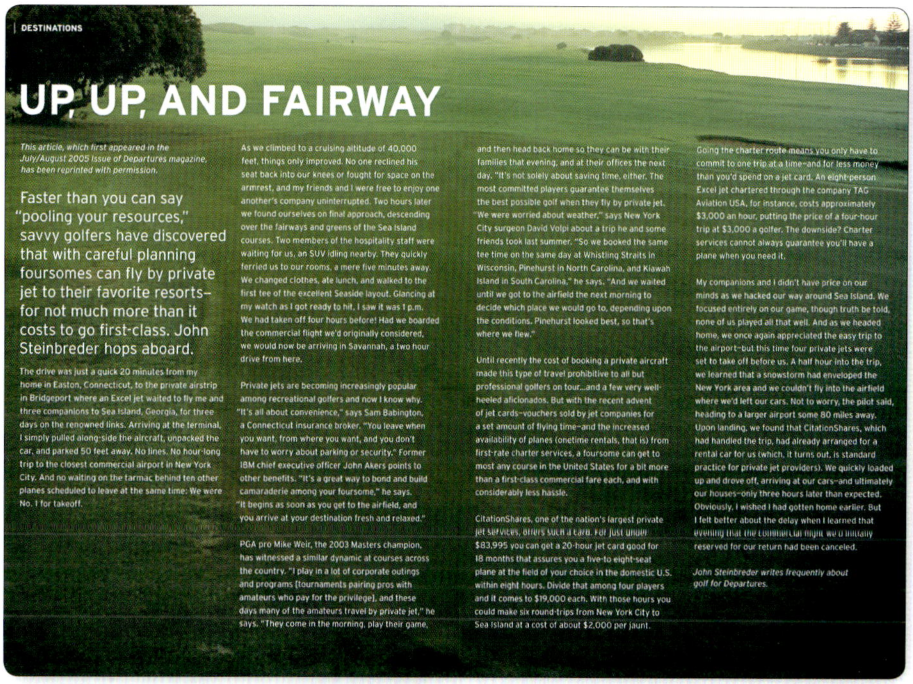

DESTINATIONS

UP, UP, AND FAIRWAY

This article, which first appeared in the July/August 2005 issue of Departures magazine, has been reprinted with permission.

Faster than you can say "pooling your resources," savvy golfers have discovered that with careful planning foursomes can fly by private jet to their favorite resorts–for not much more than it costs to go first-class. John Steinbreder hops aboard.

The drive was just a quick 20 minutes from my home in Easton, Connecticut, to the private airstrip in Bridgeport where an Excel jet waited to fly me and three companions to Sea Island, Georgia, for three days on the renowned links. Arriving at the terminal, I simply pulled along-side the aircraft, unpacked the car, and parked 50 feet away. No lines. No hour-long trip to the closest commercial airport in New York City. And no waiting on the tarmac behind ten other planes scheduled to leave at the same time: We were No. 1 for takeoff.

As we climbed to a cruising altitude of 40,000 feet, things only improved. No one reclined his seat back into our knees or fought for space on the armrest, and my friends and I were free to enjoy one another's company uninterrupted. Two hours later we found ourselves on final approach, descending over the fairways and greens of the Sea Island courses. Two members of the hospitality staff were waiting for us, an SUV idling nearby. They quickly ferried us to our rooms, a mere five minutes away. We changed clothes, ate lunch, and walked to the first tee of the excellent Seaside layout. Glancing at my watch as I got ready to hit, I saw it was 1 p.m. We had taken off four hours before! Had we boarded the commercial flight we'd originally considered, we would now be arriving in Savannah, a two hour drive from here.

Private jets are becoming increasingly popular among recreational golfers and now I know why. "It's all about convenience," says Sam Babington, a Connecticut insurance broker. "You leave when you want, from where you want, and you don't have to worry about parking or security." Former IBM chief executive officer John Akers points to other benefits. "It's a great way to bond and build camaraderie among your foursome," he says. "It begins as soon as you get to the airfield, and you arrive at your destination fresh and relaxed."

PGA pro Mike Weir, the 2003 Masters champion, has witnessed a similar dynamic at courses across the country. "I play in a lot of corporate outings and programs [tournaments pairing pros with amateurs who pay for the privilege], and these days many of the amateurs travel by private jet," he says. "They come in the morning, play their game, and then head back home so they can be with their families that evening, and at their offices the next day. "It's not solely about saving time, either. The most committed players guarantee themselves the best possible golf when they fly by private jet. "We were worried about weather," says New York City surgeon David Volpi about a trip he and some friends took last summer. "So we booked the same tee time on the same day at Whistling Straits in Wisconsin, Pinehurst in North Carolina, and Kiawah Island in South Carolina," he says. "And we waited until we got to the airfield the next morning to decide which place we would go to, depending upon the conditions. Pinehurst looked best, so that's where we flew."

Until recently the cost of booking a private aircraft made this type of travel prohibitive to all but professional golfers on tour...and a few very well-heeled aficionados. But with the recent advent of jet cards–vouchers sold by jet companies for a set amount of flying time–and the increased availability of planes (onetime rentals, that is) from first-rate charter services, a foursome can get to most any course in the United States for a bit more than a first-class commercial fare each, and with considerably less hassle.

CitationShares, one of the nation's largest private jet services, offers such a card. For just under $83,995 you can get a 20-hour jet card good for 18 months that assures you a five-to eight-seat plane at the field of your choice in the domestic U.S. within eight hours. Divide that among four players and it comes to $19,000 each. With those hours you could make six round-trips from New York City to Sea Island at a cost of about $2,000 per jaunt.

Going the charter route means you only have to commit to one trip at a time–and for less money than you'd spend on a jet card. An eight-person Excel jet chartered through the company TAG Aviation USA, for instance, costs approximately $3,000 an hour, putting the price of a four-hour trip at $3,000 a golfer. The downside? Charter services cannot always guarantee you'll have a plane when you need it.

My companions and I didn't have price on our minds as we hacked our way around Sea Island. We focused entirely on our game, though truth be told, none of us played all that well. And as we headed home, we once again appreciated the easy trip to the airport–but this time four private jets were set to take off before us. A half hour into the trip, we learned that a snowstorm had enveloped the New York area and we couldn't fly into the airfield where we'd left our cars. Not to worry, the pilot said, heading to a larger airport some 80 miles away. Upon landing, we found that CitationShares, which had handled the trip, had already arranged for a rental car for us (which, it turns out, is standard practice for private jet providers). We quickly loaded up and drove off, arriving at our cars–and ultimately our houses–only three hours later than expected. Obviously, I wished I had gotten home earlier. But I felt better about the delay when I learned that evening that the commercial flight we'd initially reserved for our return had been canceled.

John Steinbreder writes frequently about golf for Departures.

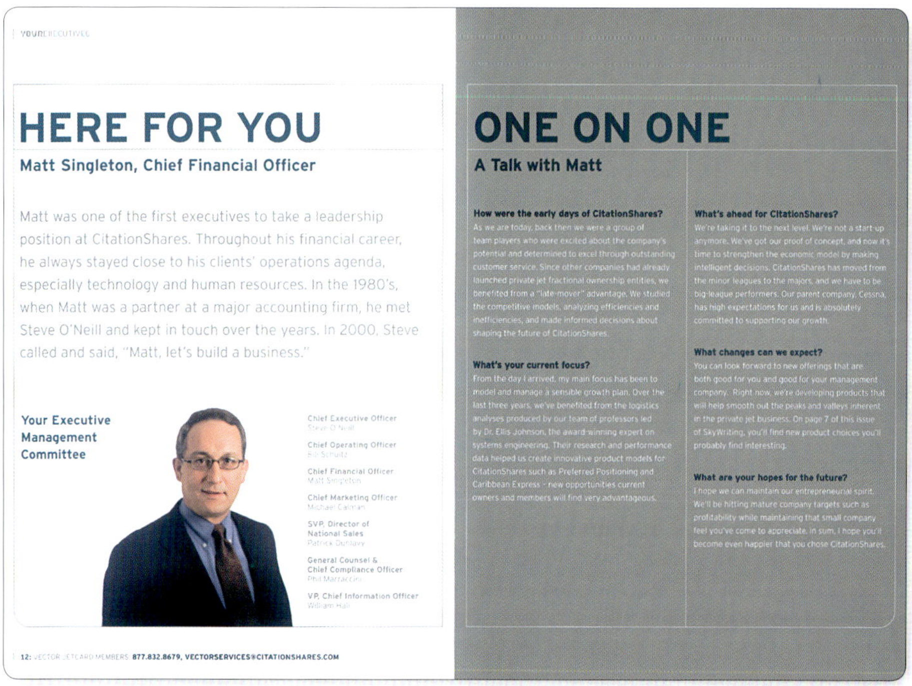

YOUR EXECUTIVES

HERE FOR YOU

Matt Singleton, Chief Financial Officer

Matt was one of the first executives to take a leadership position at CitationShares. Throughout his financial career, he always stayed close to his clients' operations agenda, especially technology and human resources. In the 1980's, when Matt was a partner at a major accounting firm, he met Steve O'Neill and kept in touch over the years. In 2000, Steve called and said, "Matt, let's build a business."

Your Executive Management Committee

Chief Executive Officer
Chief Operating Officer
Chief Financial Officer
Chief Marketing Officer
SVP, Director of National Sales
General Counsel & Chief Compliance Officer
VP, Chief Information Officer

12 | 877.832.8679, VECTORSERVICES@CITATIONSHARES.COM

ONE ON ONE

A Talk with Matt

How were the early days of CitationShares?
As we are today, back then we were a group of team players who were excited about the company's potential and determined to excel through outstanding customer service. Since other companies had already launched private jet fractional ownership entities, we benefited from a "late-mover" advantage. We studied the competitive models, analyzing efficiencies and inefficiencies, and made informed decisions about shaping the future of CitationShares.

What's your current focus?
From the day I arrived, my main focus has been to model and manage a sensible growth plan. Over the last three years, we've benefited from the logistics analyses produced by our team of professors led by Dr. Ellis Johnson, the award-winning expert on systems engineering. Their research and performance data helped us create innovative product models for CitationShares such as Preferred Positioning and Caribbean Express - new opportunities current owners and members will find very advantageous.

What's ahead for CitationShares?
We're taking it to the next level. We're not a start-up anymore. We've got our proof of concept, and now it's time to strengthen the economic model by making intelligent decisions. CitationShares has moved from the minor leagues to the majors, and we have to be big-league performers. Our parent company, Cessna, has high expectations for us and is absolutely committed to supporting our growth.

What changes can we expect?
You can look forward to new offerings that are both good for you and good for your management company. Right now, we're developing products that will help smooth out the peaks and valleys inherent in the private jet business. On page 7 of this issue of SkyWriting, you'll find new product choices you'll probably find interesting.

What are your hopes for the future?
I hope we can maintain our entrepreneurial spirit. We'll be hitting mature company targets such as profitability while maintaining that small company feel you've come to appreciate. In sum, I hope you'll become even happier that you chose CitationShares.

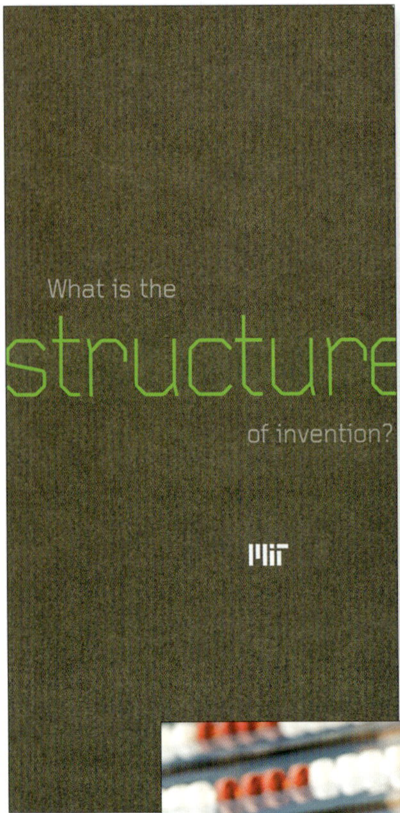

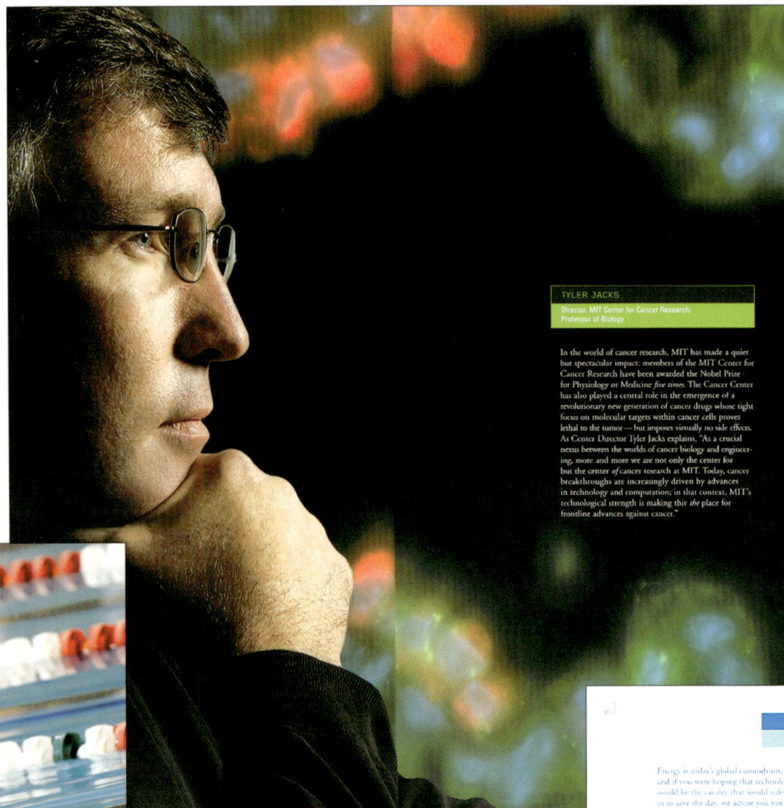

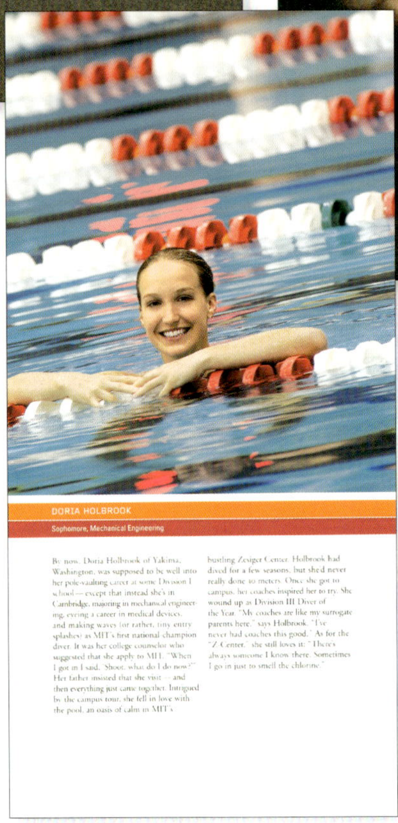

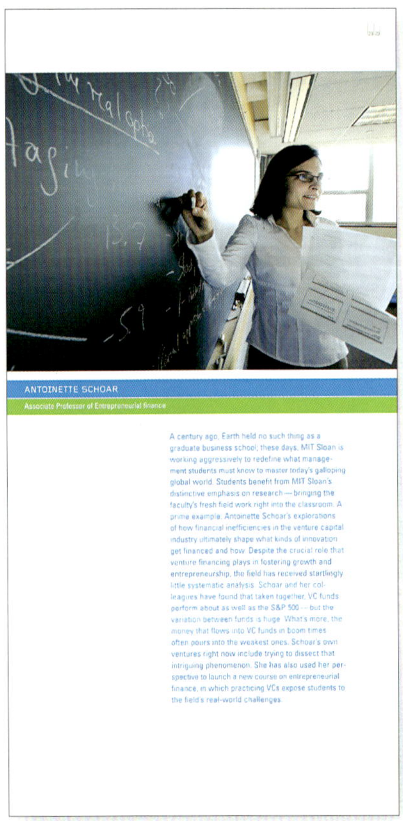

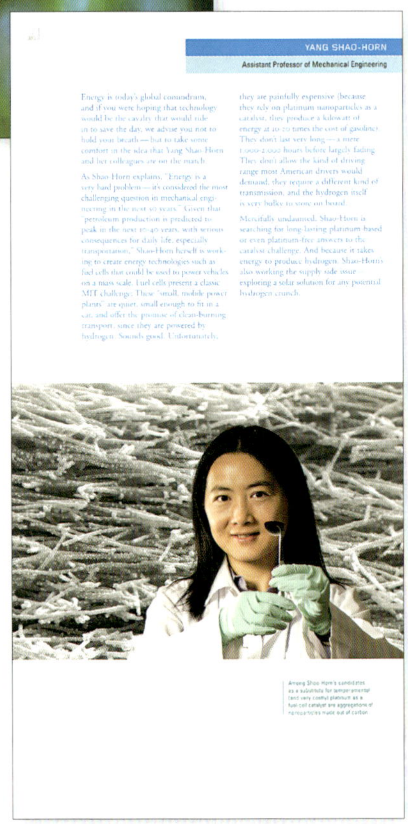

client
Massachusetts Institute of Technology
design firm
kor group
www.kor.com
designers
Jim Gibson, James Grady, Karen Dendy Smith

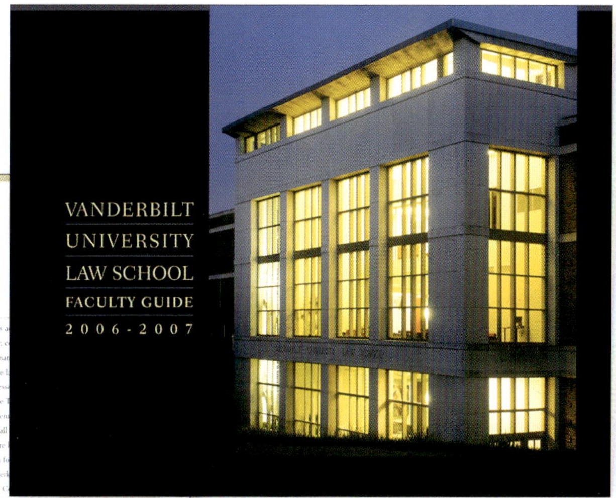

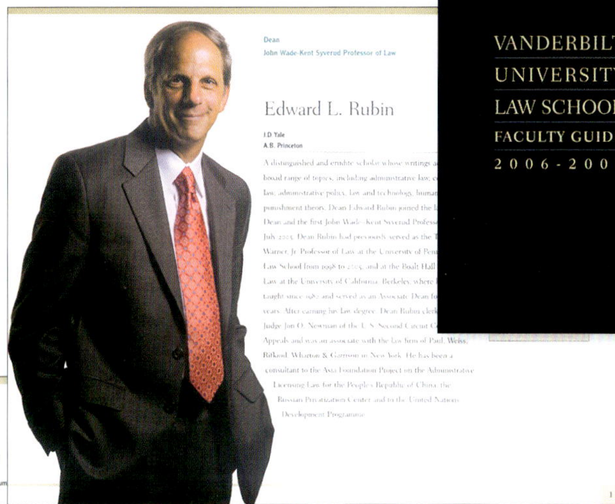

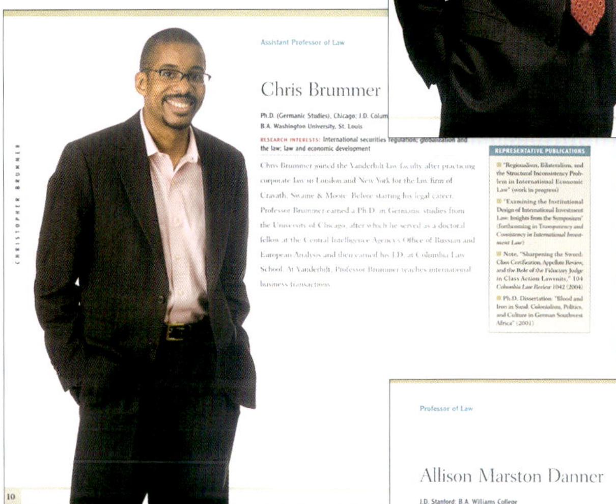

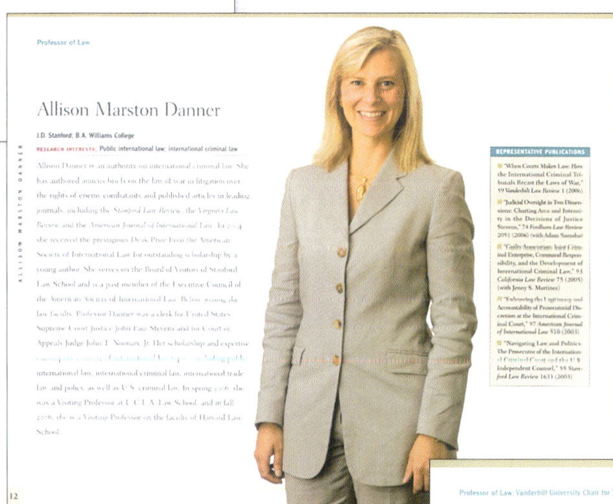

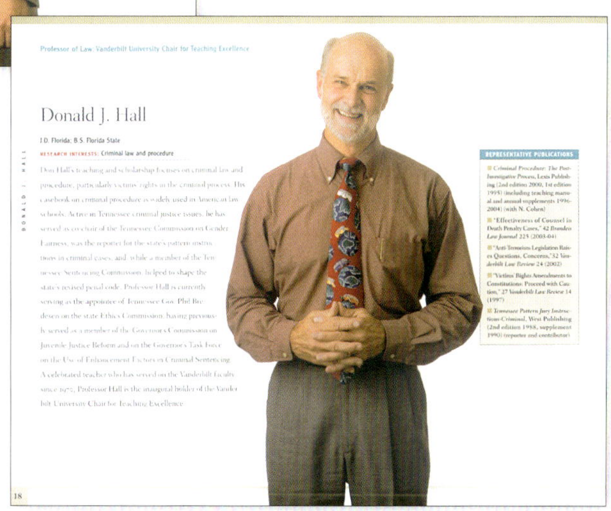

client
Vanderbilt University Law School
design firm
Ventress Design Group
www.ventress.com
designer
Tom Ventress

client
Ramapo College
design firm
kor group
www.kor.com
designers
Jim Gibson, Anne Callahan

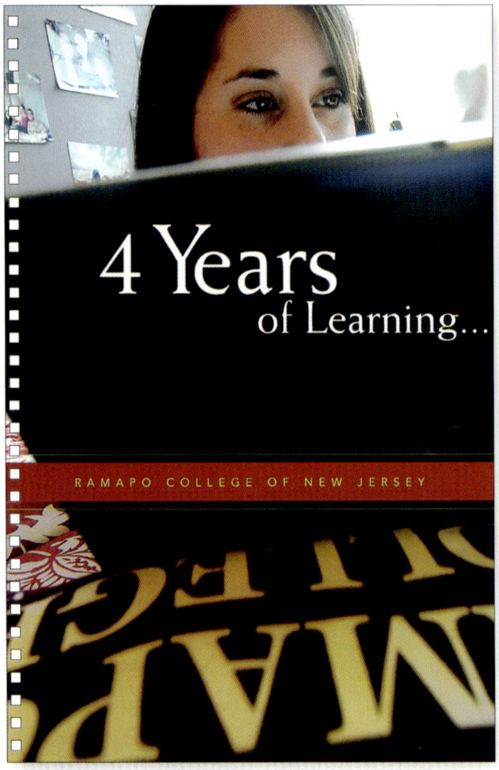

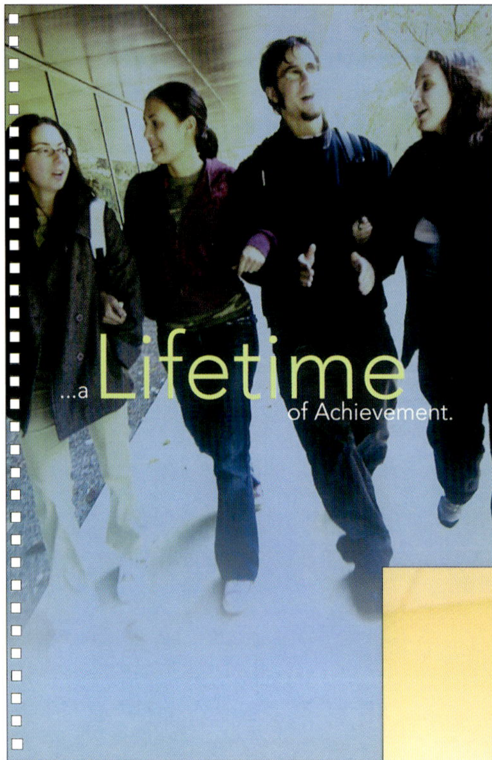

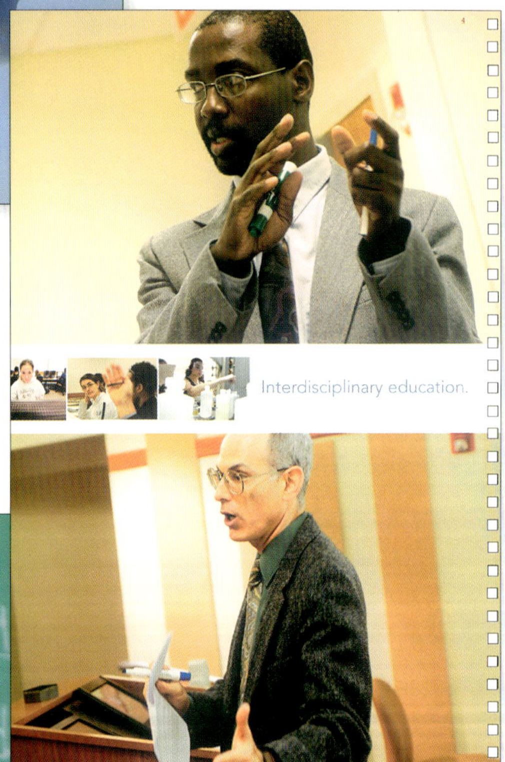

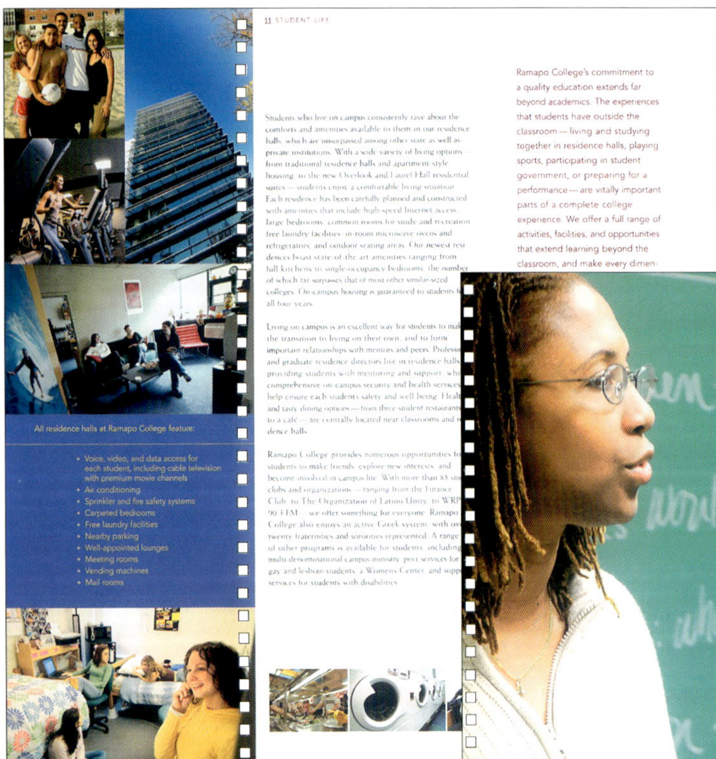

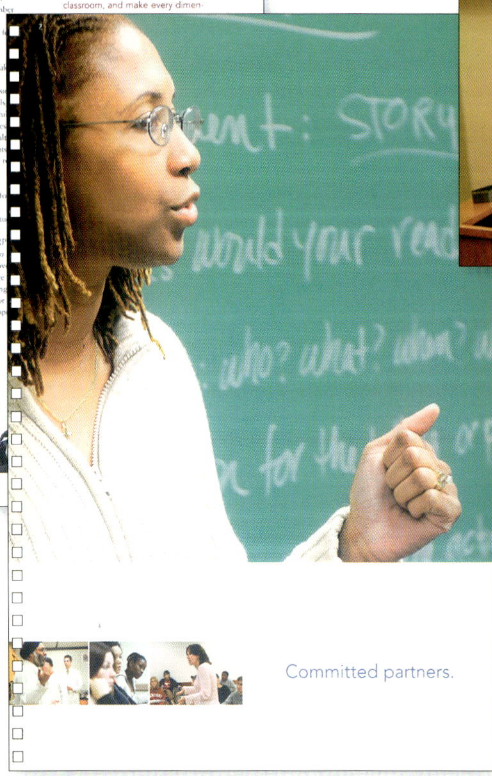

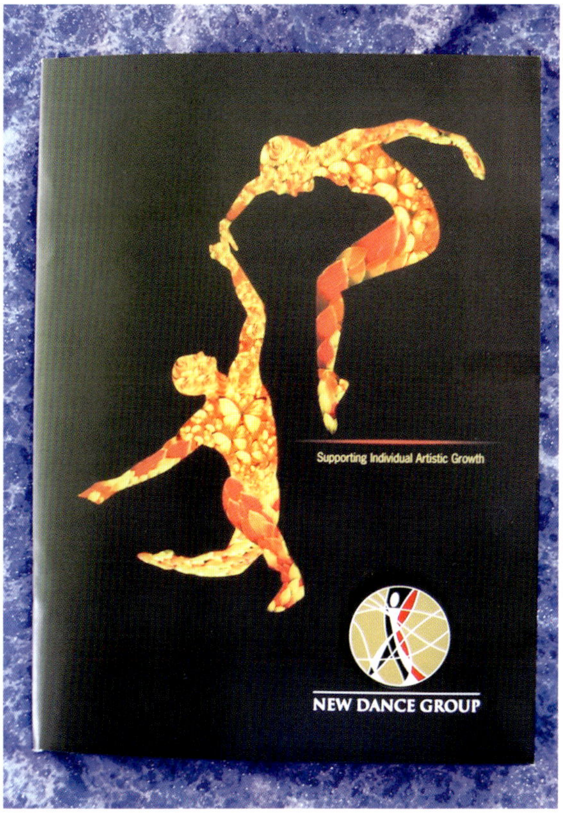

client
New Dance Group
design firm
WestGroup Creative
www.westgp.com
designer
Chip Tolaney

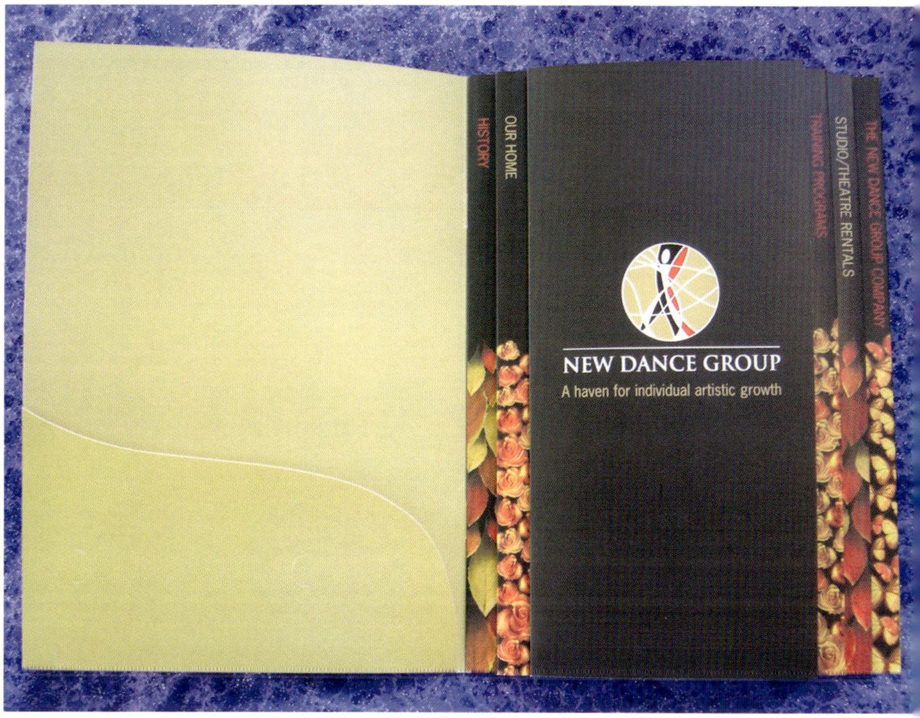

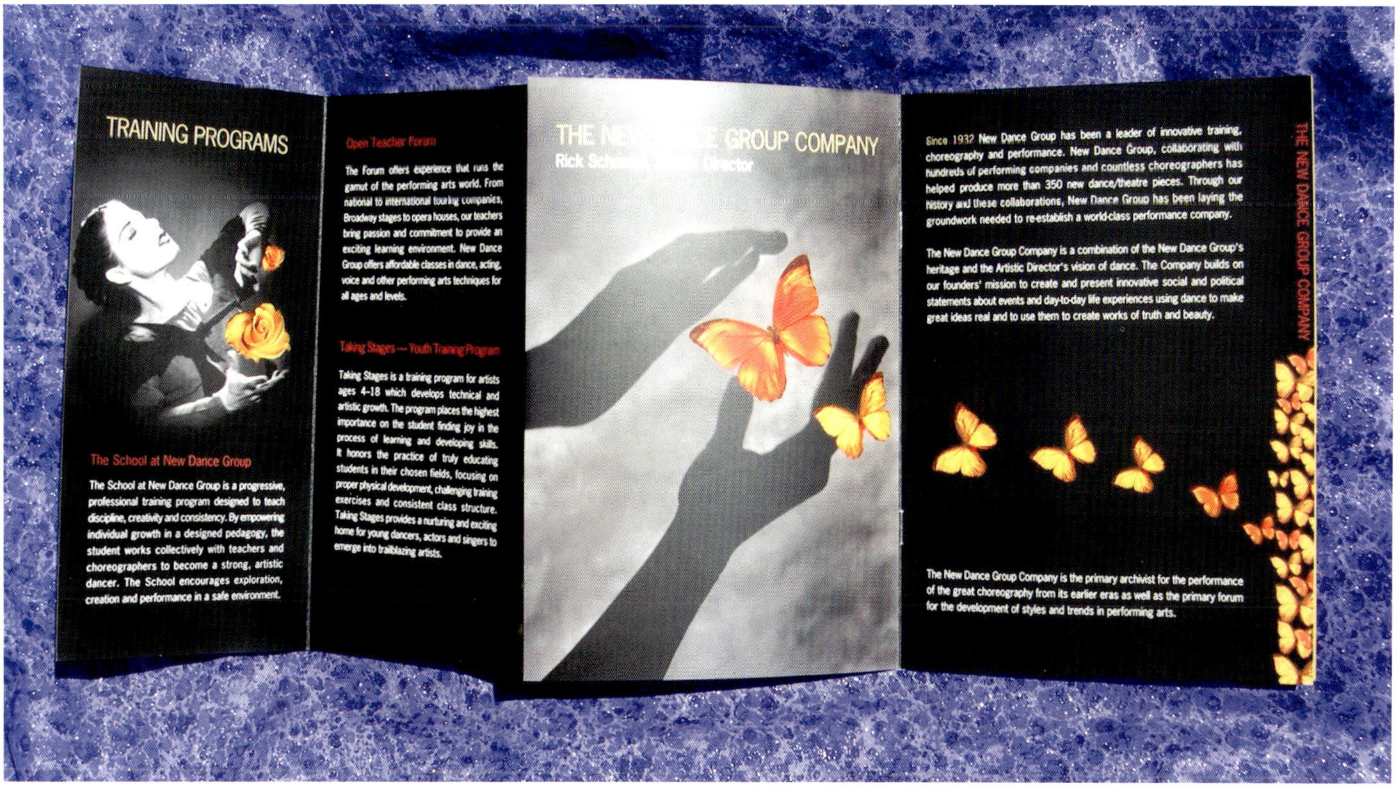

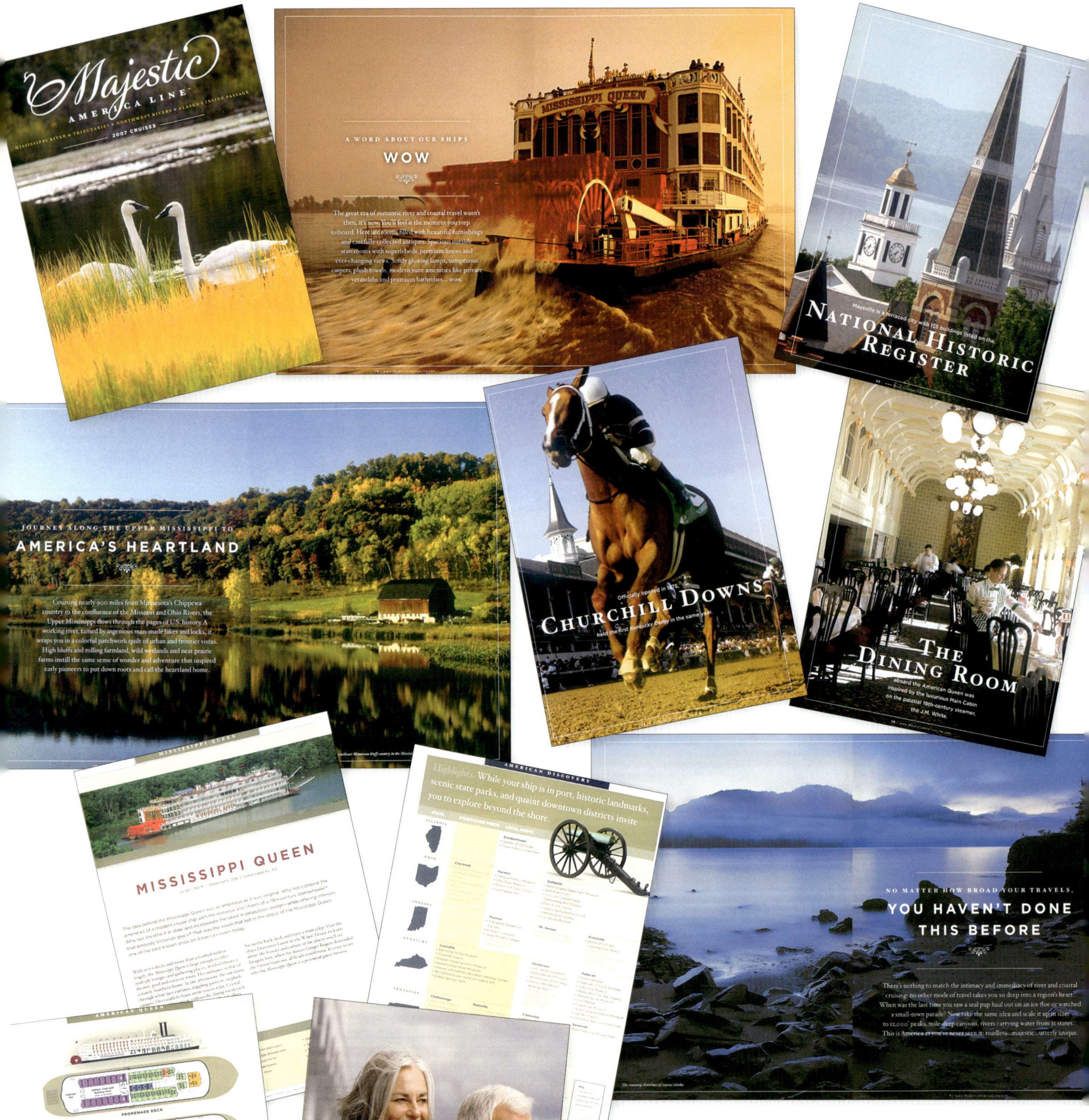

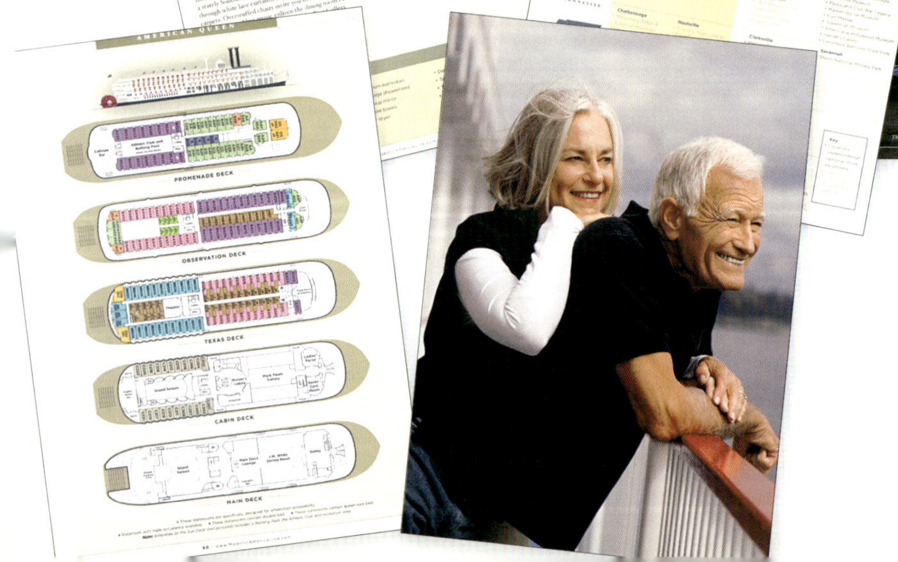

client
Majestic America Line
design firm
Hornall Anderson Design Works
www.hadw.com
designers
Jack Anderson, Andrew Wicklund, Peter Anderson, Belinda Bowling, Kathleen Gibson, Ensi Mofasser

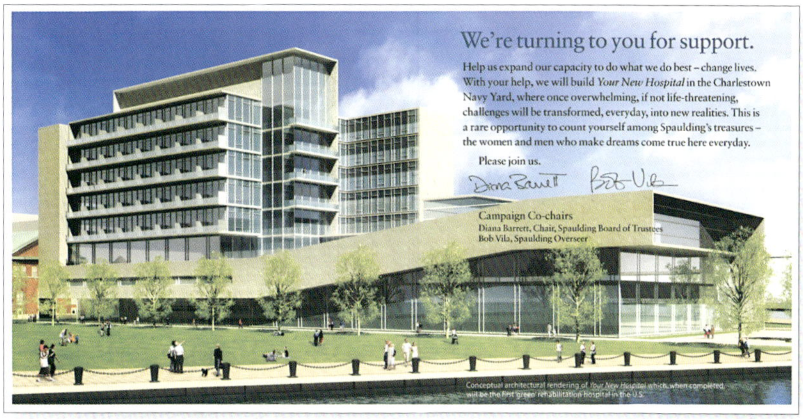

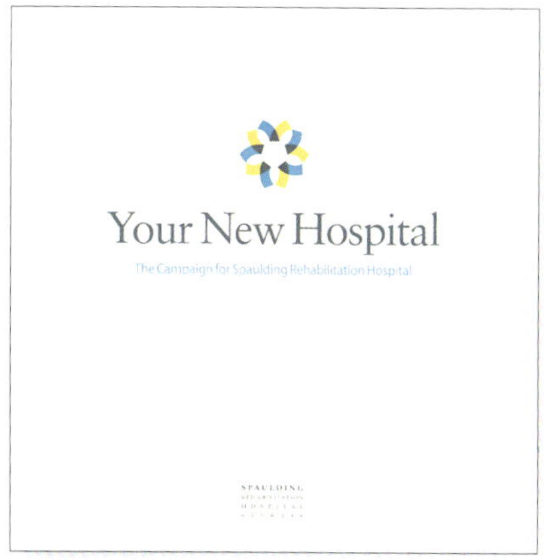

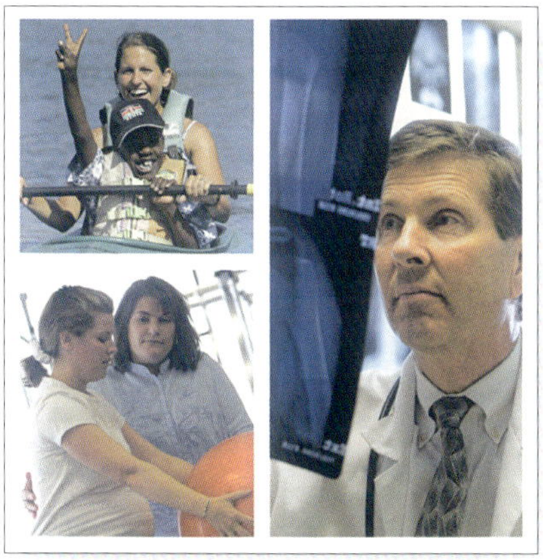

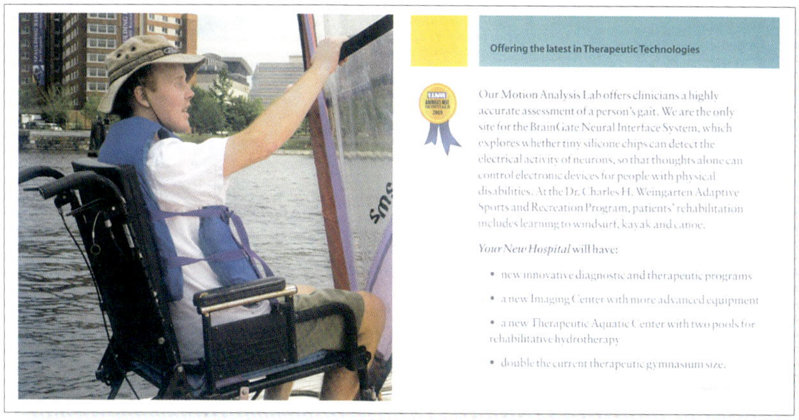

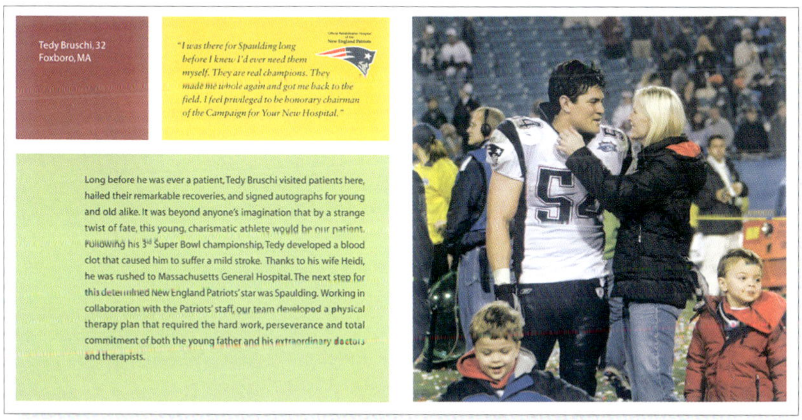

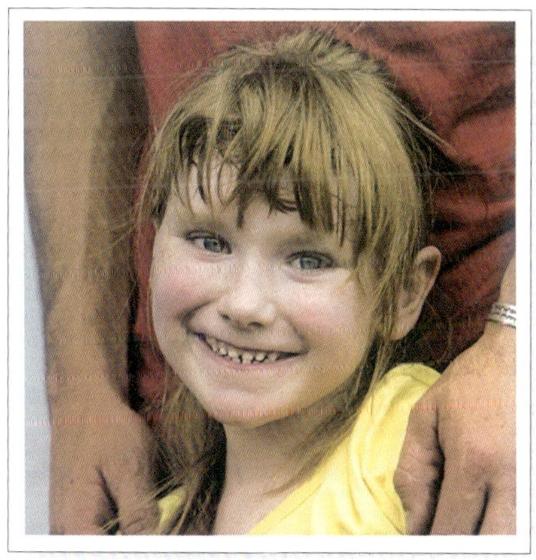

client
Spaulding Rehabilitation Hospital
design firm
Gill Fishman Associates
www.gillfishmandesign.com
designer
Michael Persons

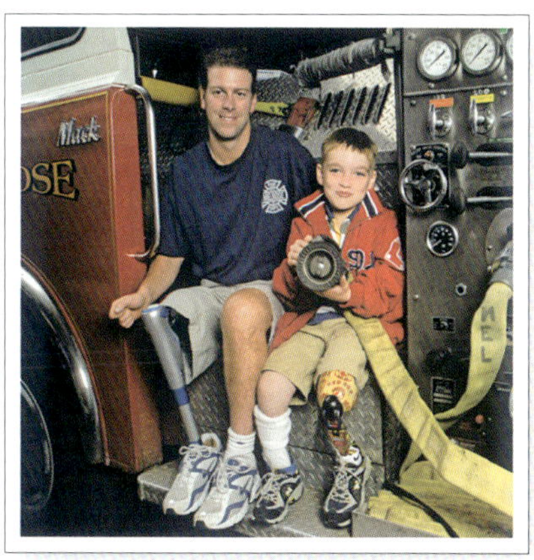

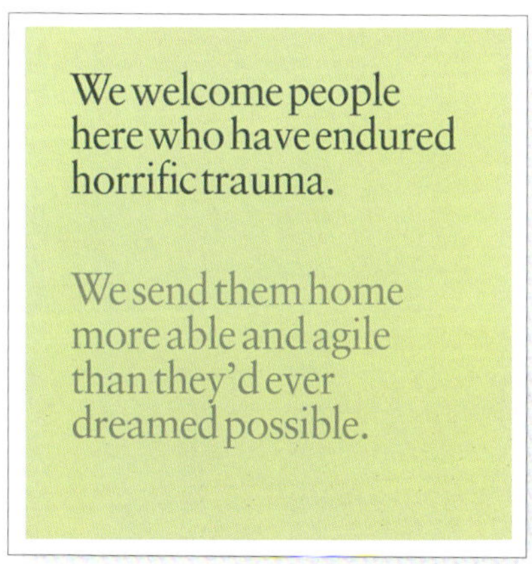

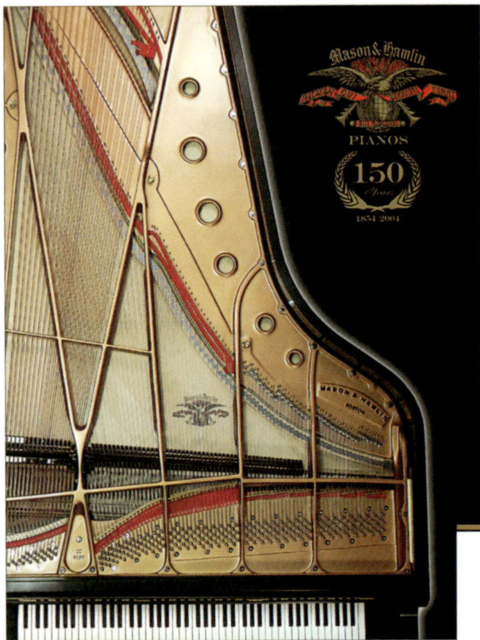

client
Mason & Hamlin
design firm
JC-Evans, Inc.
www.jc-evans.com
designer
Jeff Evans

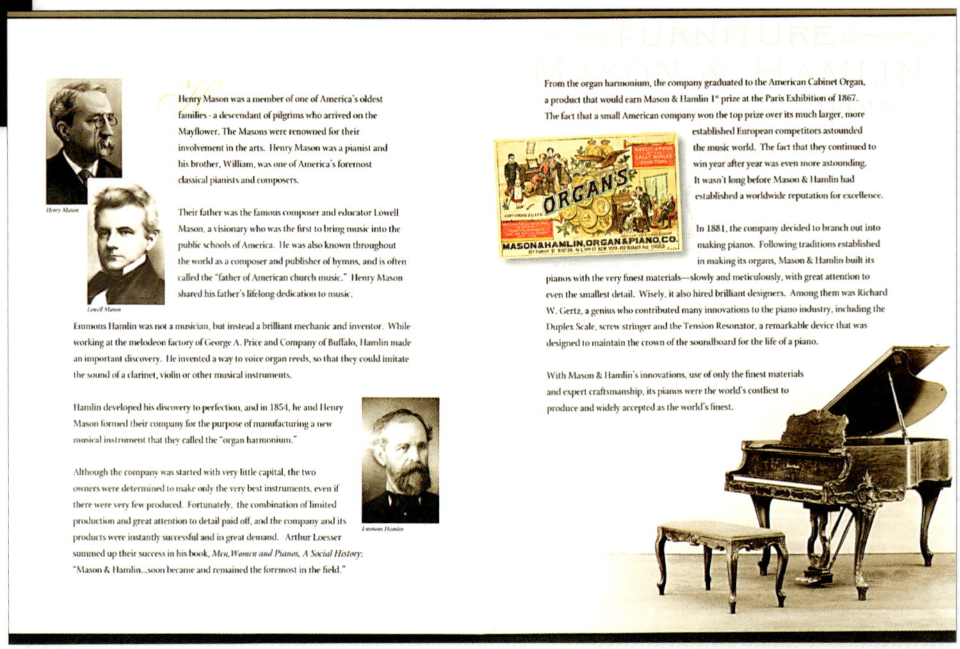

Henry Mason was a member of one of America's oldest families - a descendant of pilgrims who arrived on the Mayflower. The Masons were renowned for their involvement in the arts. Henry Mason was a pianist and his brother, William, was one of America's foremost classical pianists and composers.

Henry Mason

Their father was the famous composer and educator Lowell Mason, a visionary who was the first to bring music into the public schools of America. He was also known throughout the world as a composer and publisher of hymns, and is often called the "father of American church music." Henry Mason shared his father's lifelong dedication to music.

Lowell Mason

Emmons Hamlin was not a musician, but instead a brilliant mechanic and inventor. While working at the melodeon factory of George A. Price and Company of Buffalo, Hamlin made an important discovery. He invented a way to voice organ reeds, so that they could imitate the sound of a clarinet, violin or other musical instruments.

Hamlin developed his discovery to perfection, and in 1854, he and Henry Mason formed their company for the purpose of manufacturing a new musical instrument that they called the "organ harmonium."

Although the company was started with very little capital, the two owners were determined to make only the very best instruments, even if there were very few produced. Fortunately, the combination of limited production and great attention to detail paid off, and the company and its products were instantly successful and in great demand. Arthur Loesser summed up their success in his book, *Men, Women and Pianos, A Social History*: "Mason & Hamlin...soon became and remained the foremost in the field."

Emmons Hamlin

FURNITURE
MASON & HAMLIN

From the organ harmonium, the company graduated to the American Cabinet Organ, a product that would earn Mason & Hamlin 1st prize at the Paris Exhibition of 1867. The fact that a small American company won the top prize over its much larger, more established European competitors astounded the music world. The fact that they continued to win year after year was even more astounding. It wasn't long before Mason & Hamlin had established a worldwide reputation for excellence.

In 1881, the company decided to branch out into making pianos. Following traditions established in making its organs, Mason & Hamlin built its pianos with the very finest materials—slowly and meticulously, with great attention to even the smallest detail. Wisely, it also hired brilliant designers. Among them was Richard W. Gertz, a genius who contributed many innovations to the piano industry, including the Duplex Scale, screw stringer and the Tension Resonator, a remarkable device that was designed to maintain the crown of the soundboard for the life of a piano.

With Mason & Hamlin's innovations, use of only the finest materials and expert craftsmanship, its pianos were the world's costliest to produce and widely accepted as the world's finest.

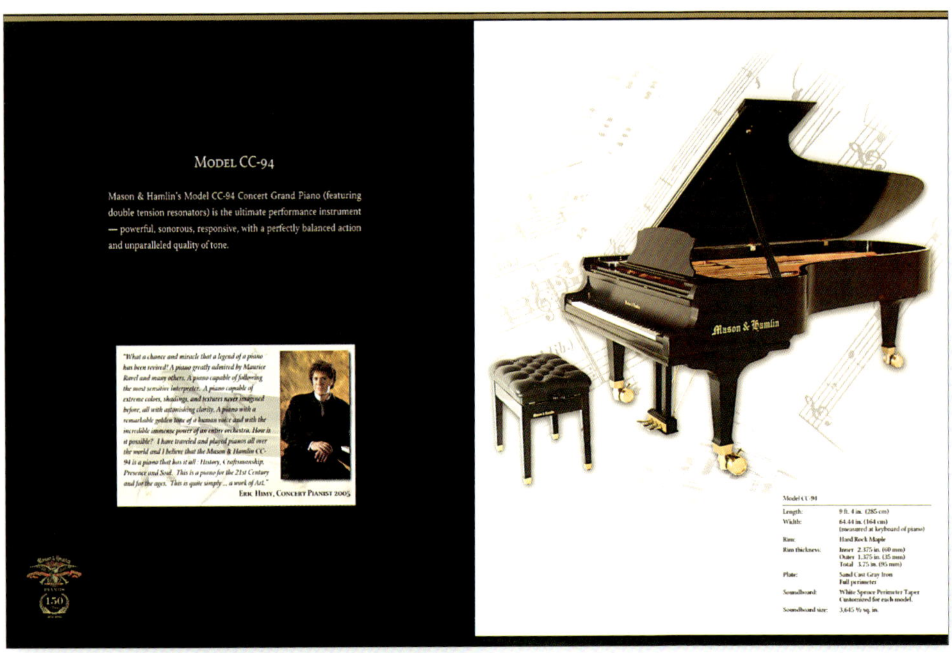

MODEL CC-94

Mason & Hamlin's Model CC-94 Concert Grand Piano (featuring double tension resonators) is the ultimate performance instrument — powerful, sonorous, responsive, with a perfectly balanced action and unparalleled quality of tone.

"What a chance and miracle that a legend of a piano has been revived! A piano greatly admired by Maurice Ravel and many others. A piano capable of following the most sensitive interpreter. A piano capable of extreme colors, shadings, and textures never imagined before, all with astonishing clarity. A piano with a remarkable golden tone of a human voice and with the incredible immense power of an entire orchestra. How is it possible? I have traveled and played pianos all over the world and I believe that the Mason & Hamlin CC-94 is a piano that has it all: History, Craftsmanship, Presence and Soul. This is a piano for the 21st Century and for the ages. This is quite simply ... a work of Art."
ERIC HIMY, CONCERT PIANIST 2005

Model CC-94

Length:	9 ft. 4 in. (285 cm)
Width:	64.44 in. (164 cm) (measured at keyboard of piano)
Rim:	Hard Rock Maple
Rim thickness:	Inner 2.375 in. (60 mm) Outer 1.375 in. (35 mm) Total 3.75 in. (95 mm)
Plate:	Sand Cast Gray Iron Full perimeter
Soundboard:	White Spruce Perimeter Taper Customized for each model.
Soundboard size:	3,645 ½ sq. in.

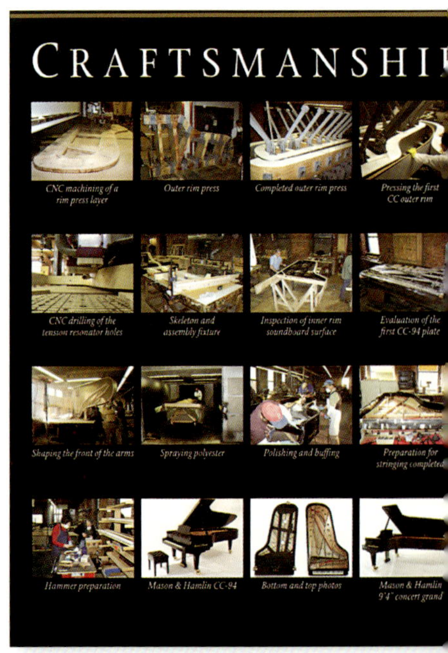

CRAFTSMANSHIP

CNC machining of a rim press layer · *Outer rim press* · *Completed outer rim press* · *Pressing the first CC outer rim*

CNC drilling of the tension resonator holes · *Skeleton and assembly fixture* · *Inspection of inner rim soundboard surface* · *Evaluation of the first CC-94 plate*

Shaping the front of the arms · *Spraying polyester* · *Polishing and buffing* · *Preparation for stringing completed*

Hammer preparation · *Mason & Hamlin CC-94* · *Bottom and top photos* · *Mason & Hamlin 9'4" concert grand*

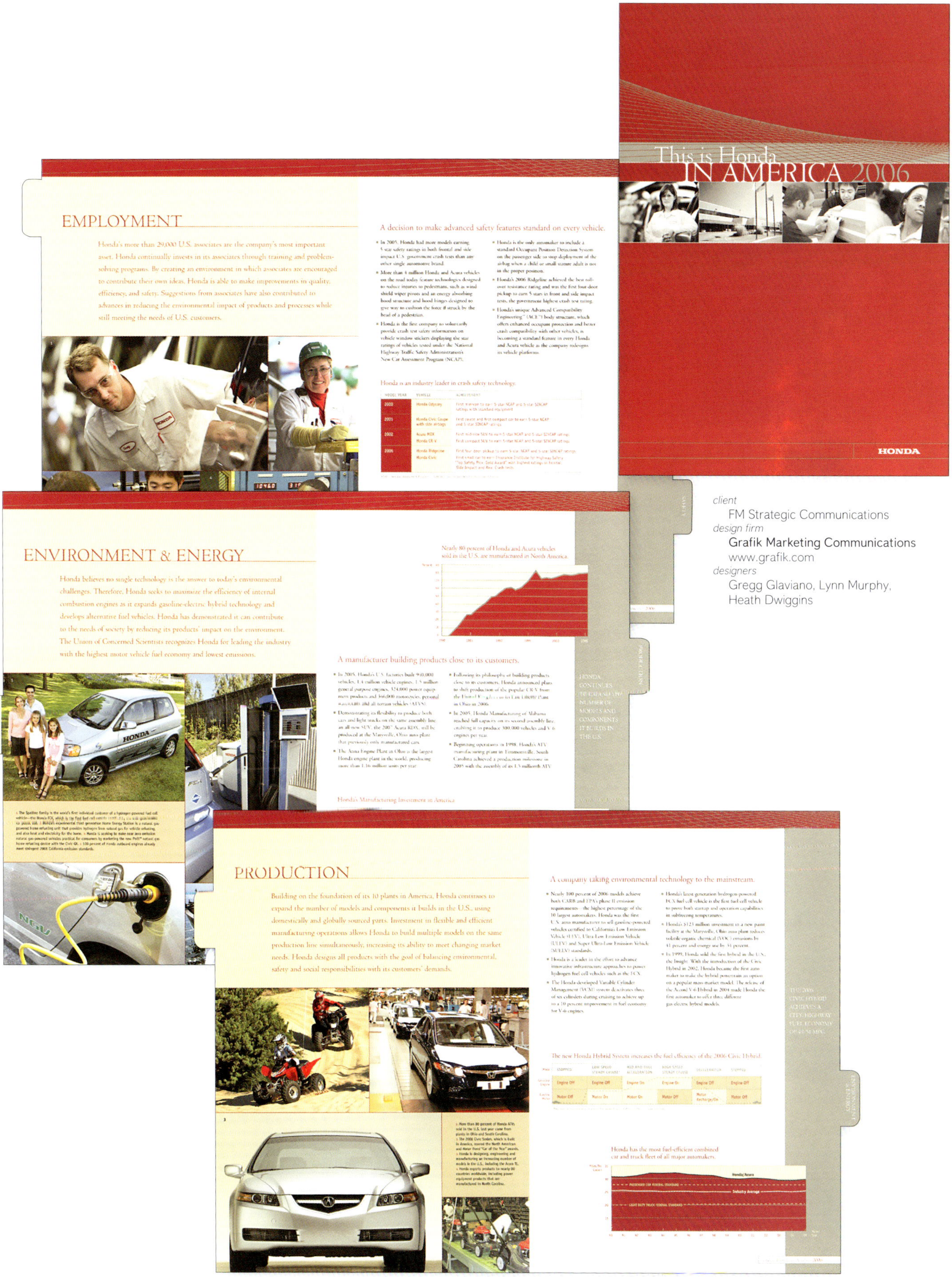

client
FM Strategic Communications
design firm
Grafik Marketing Communications
www.grafik.com
designers
Gregg Glaviano, Lynn Murphy, Heath Dwiggins

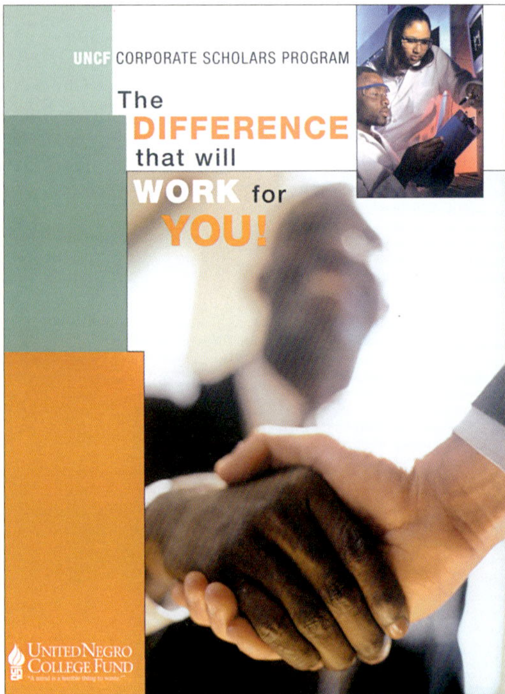

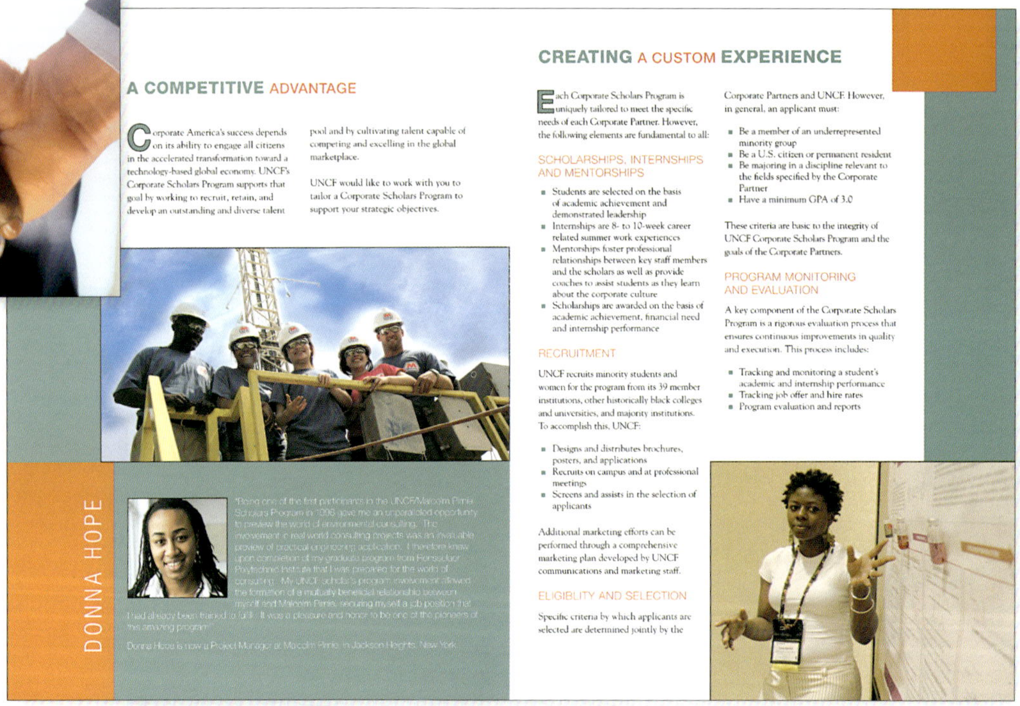

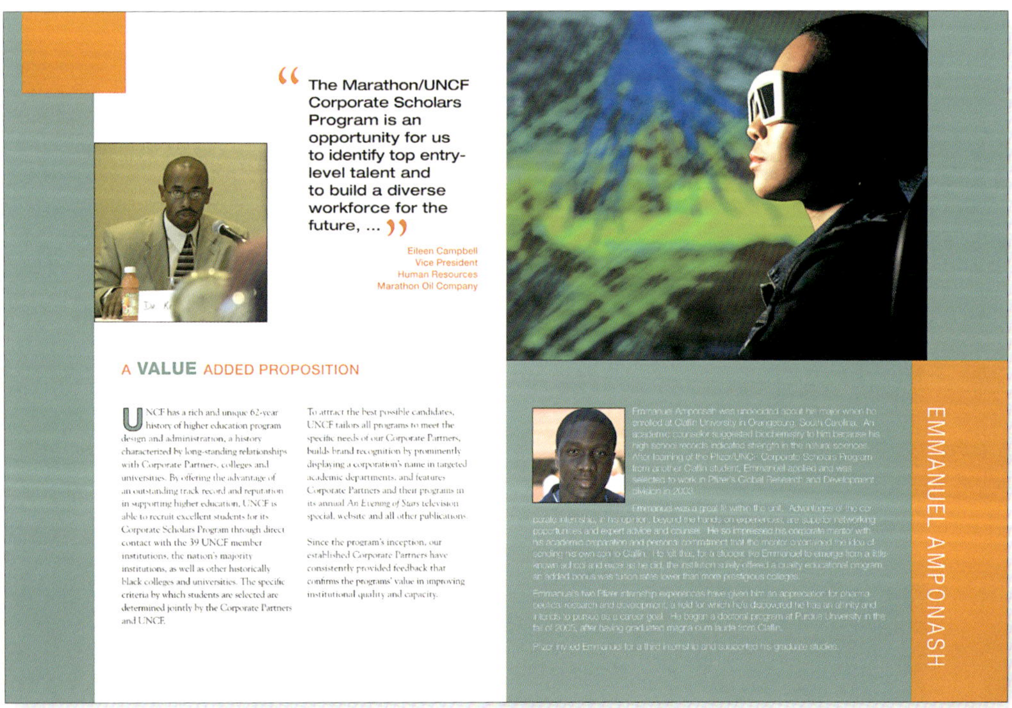

client
United Negro College Fund
design firm
RCW Communication Design, Inc.
www.rcwinc.com
designers
Rodney C. Williams, Michele Thomas, Anna Blazejcyk

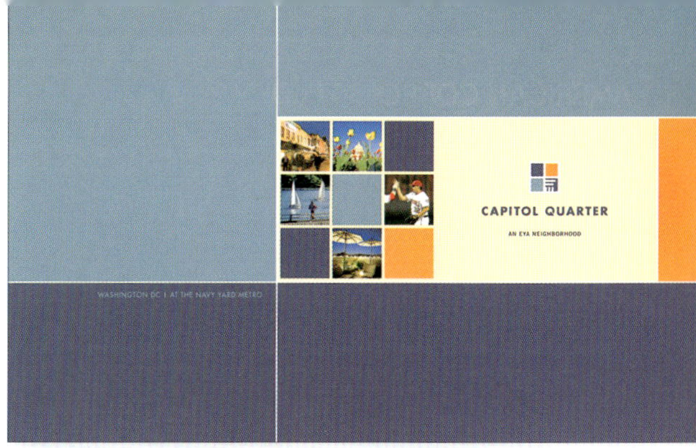

client
EYA
design firm
Grafik Marketing Communications
www.grafik.com
designers
Michelle Mar Collins, Johnny Vitorovich, Lynn Murphy, Regina Esposito

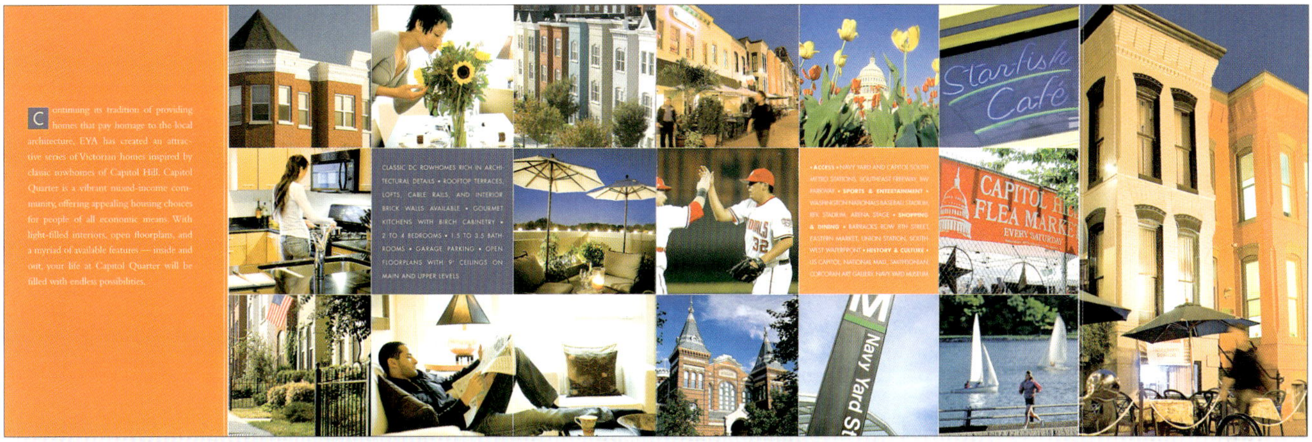

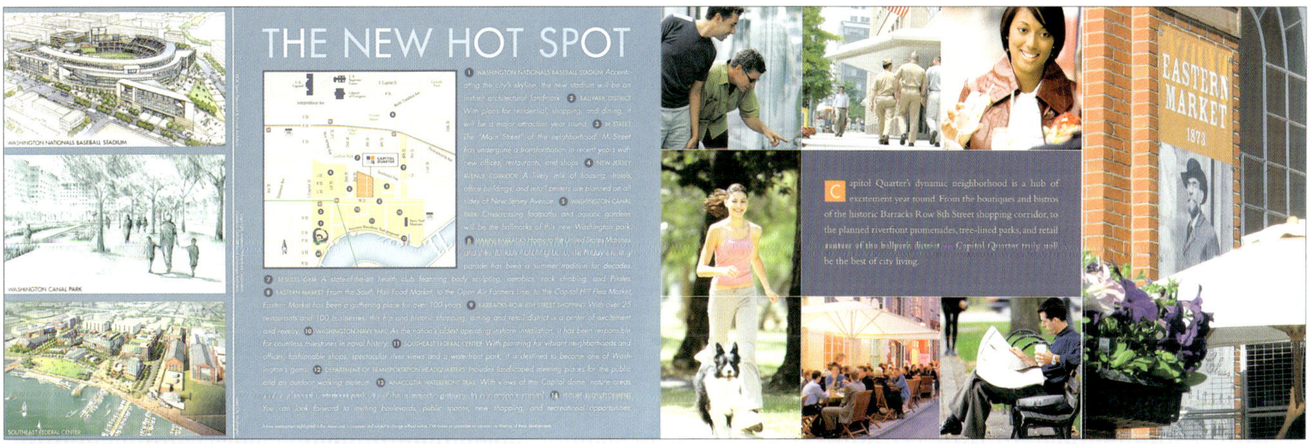

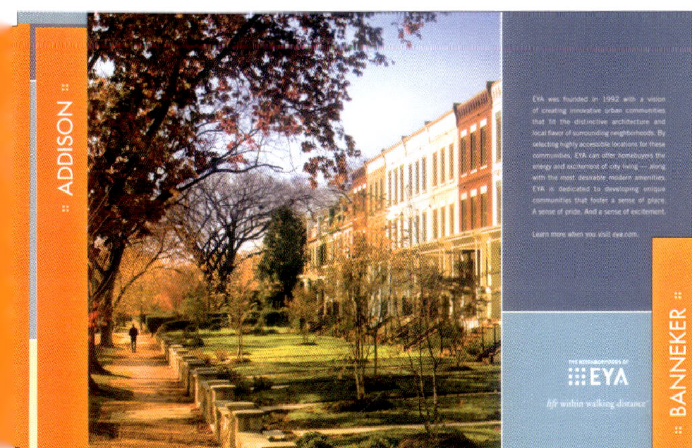

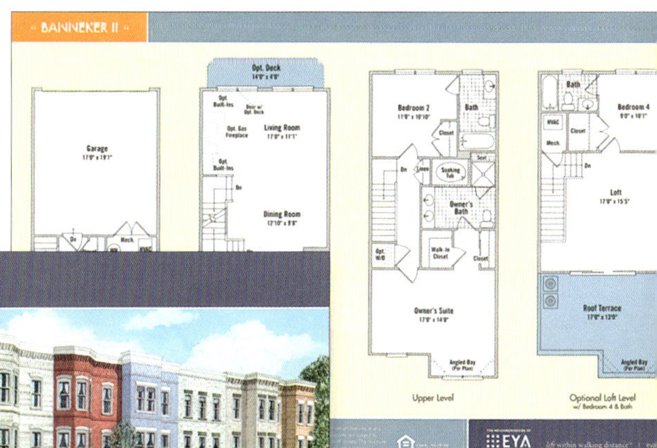

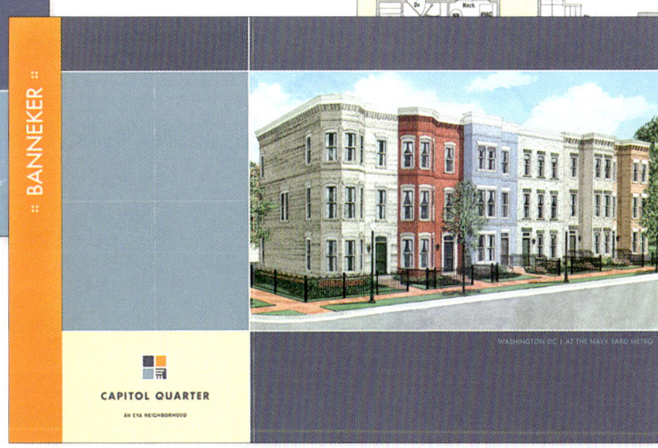

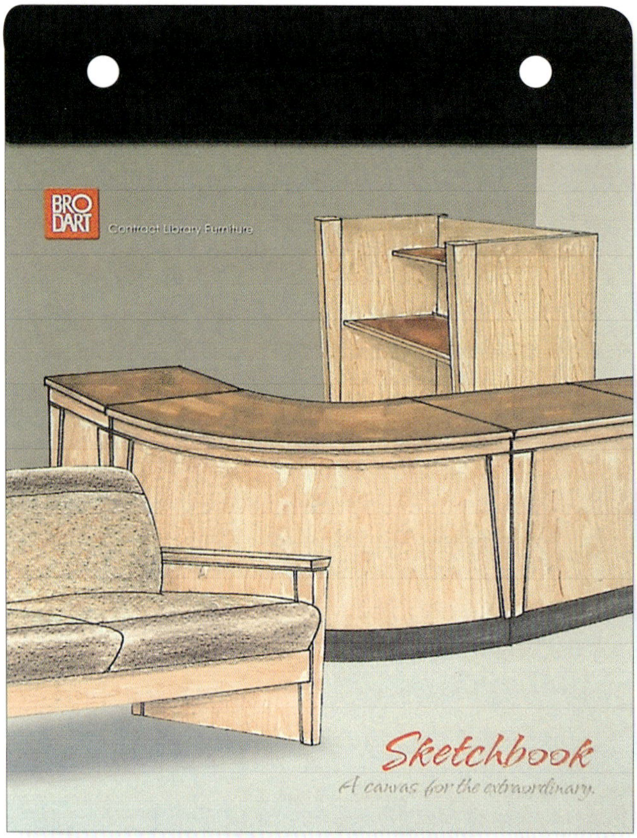

client
Brodart Furniture Company
design firm
Sire Advertising
www.sireadvertising.com
creative director
Shawn Felty
designer
Jordan Chappell

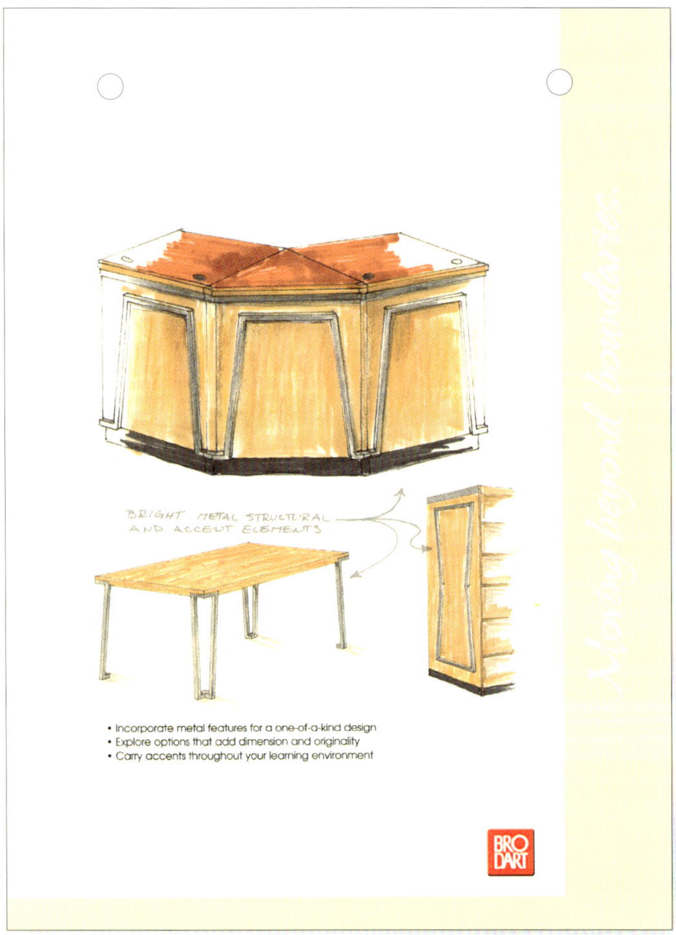

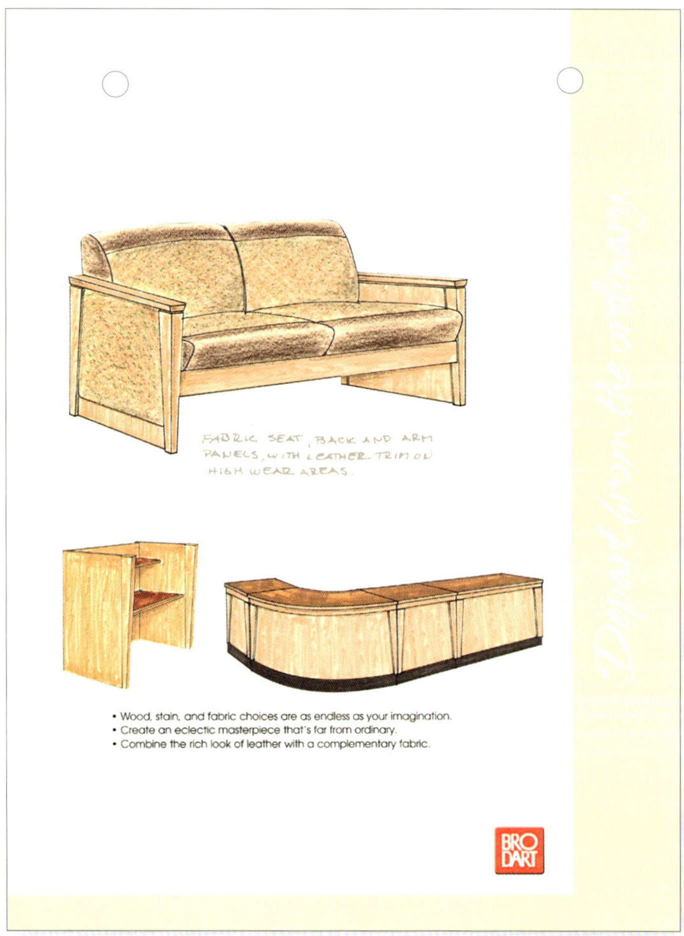

client

Co-exprise Technology

design firm

Desbrow

desbrow.com

designers

Kimberly S. Miller,
Brian Lee Campbell

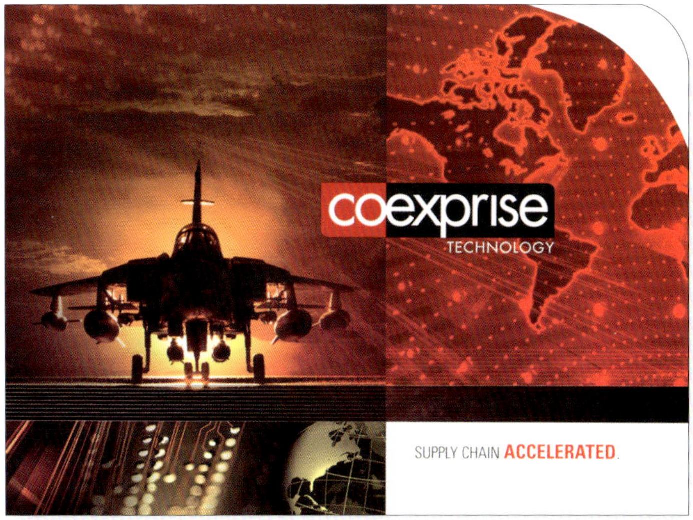

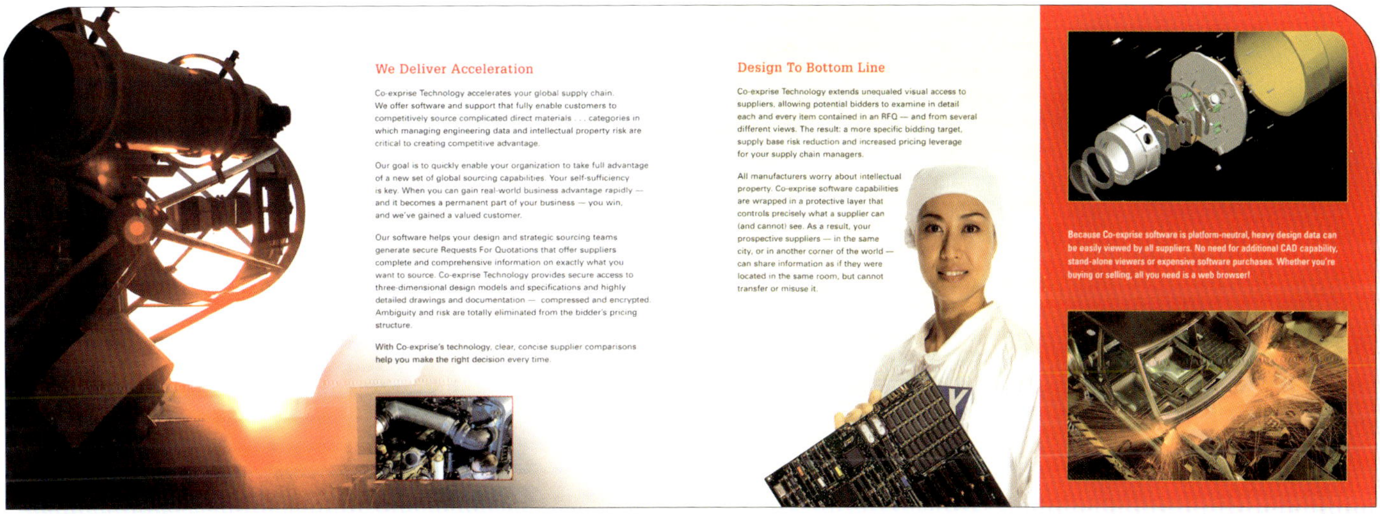

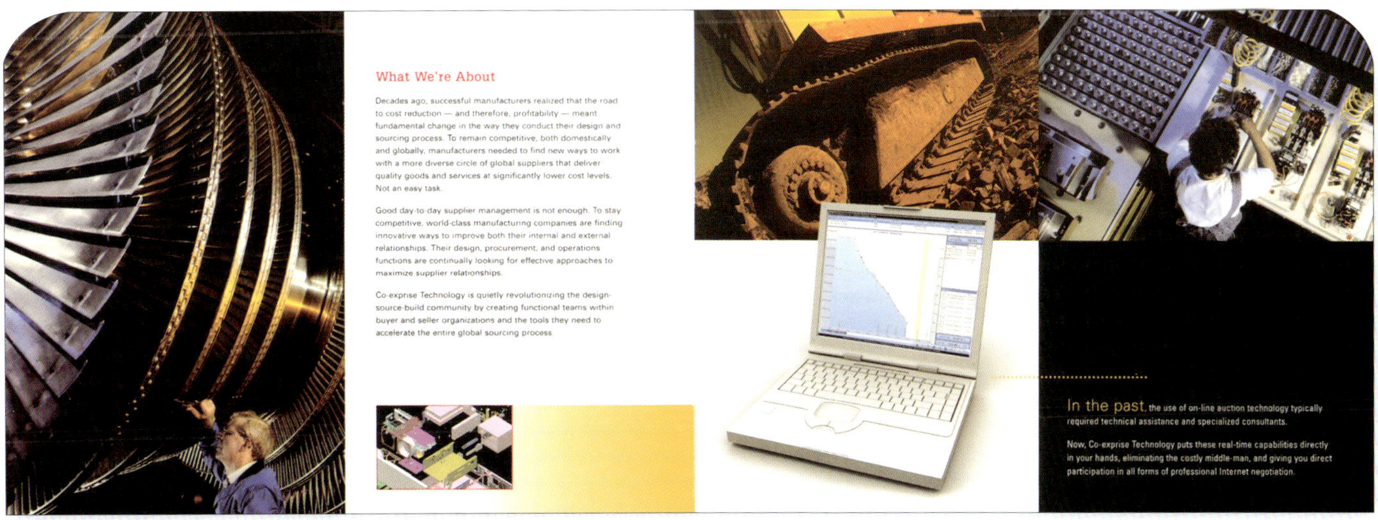

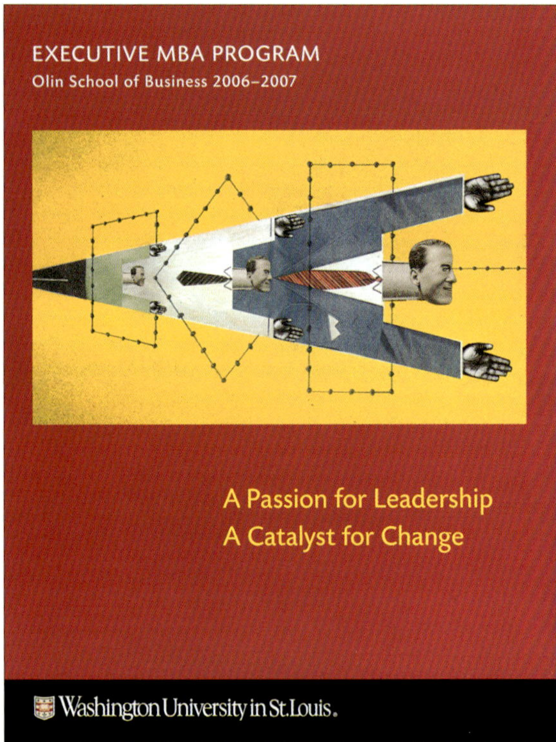
EXECUTIVE MBA PROGRAM
Olin School of Business 2006–2007

A Passion for Leadership
A Catalyst for Change

Washington University in St. Louis

client
Olin School of Business
design firm
Kiku Obata + Company
designers
Amy Knopf, Carole Jerome

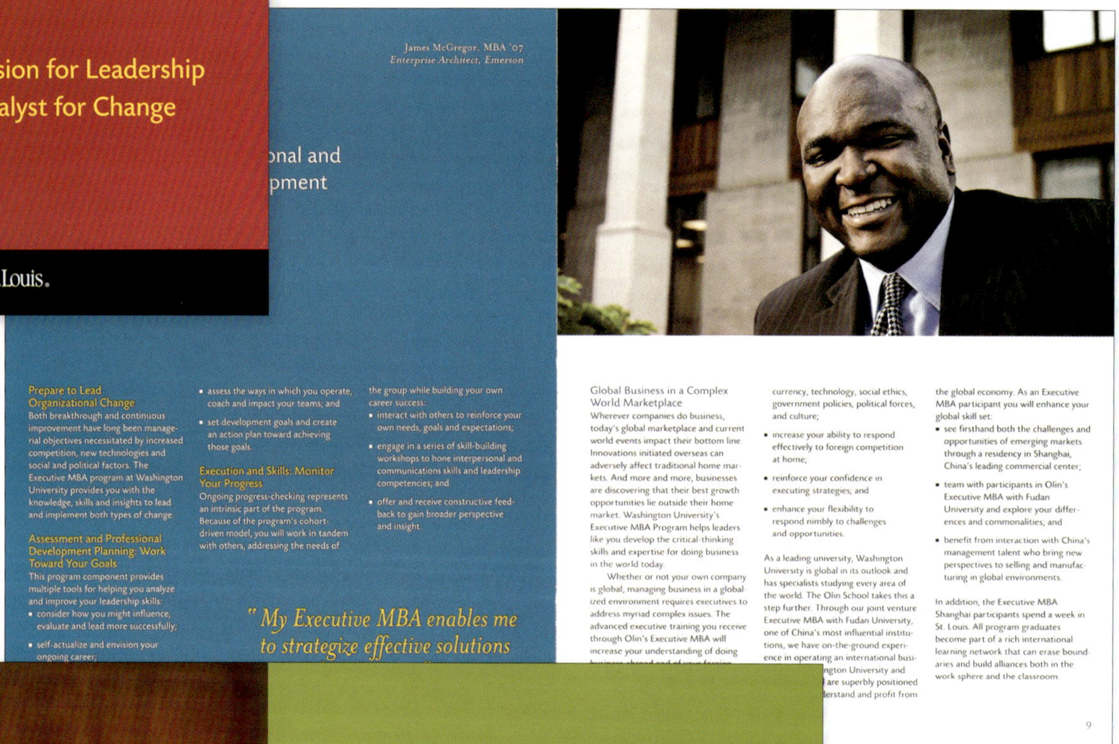
James McGregor, MBA '07
Enterprise Architect, Emerson

…onal and
…pment

Prepare to Lead Organizational Change
Both breakthrough and continuous improvement have long been managerial objectives necessitated by increased competition, new technologies and social and political factors. The Executive MBA program at Washington University provides you with the knowledge, skills and insights to lead and implement both types of change.

Assessment and Professional Development Planning: Work Toward Your Goals
This program component provides multiple tools for helping you analyze and improve your leadership skills:
- consider how you might influence, evaluate and lead more successfully;
- self-actualize and envision your ongoing career;
- assess the ways in which you operate, coach and impact your teams; and
- set development goals and create an action plan toward achieving those goals.

Execution and Skills: Monitor Your Progress
Ongoing progress-checking represents an intrinsic part of the program. Because of the program's cohort-driven model, you will work in tandem with others, addressing the needs of the group while building your own career success:
- interact with others to reinforce your own needs, goals and expectations;
- engage in a series of skill-building workshops to hone interpersonal and communications skills and leadership competencies; and
- offer and receive constructive feedback to gain broader perspective and insight.

"My Executive MBA enables me to strategize effective solutions

Global Business in a Complex World Marketplace
Wherever companies do business, today's global marketplace and current world events impact their bottom line. Innovations initiated overseas can adversely affect traditional home markets. And more and more, businesses are discovering that their best growth opportunities lie outside their home market. Washington University's Executive MBA Program helps leaders like you develop the critical-thinking skills and expertise for doing business in the world today.

Whether or not your own company is global, managing business in a globalized environment requires executives to address myriad complex issues. The advanced executive training you receive through Olin's Executive MBA will increase your understanding of doing … currency, technology, social ethics, government policies, political forces, and culture;
- increase your ability to respond effectively to foreign competition at home;
- reinforce your confidence in executing strategies; and
- enhance your flexibility to respond nimbly to challenges and opportunities.

As a leading university, Washington University is global in its outlook and has specialists studying every area of the world. The Olin School takes this a step further. Through our joint venture Executive MBA with Fudan University, one of China's most influential institutions, we have on-the-ground experience in operating an international busi… …ngton University and … are superbly positioned … …erstand and profit from the global economy. As an Executive MBA participant you will enhance your global skill set:
- see firsthand both the challenges and opportunities of emerging markets through a residency in Shanghai, China's leading commercial center;
- team with participants in Olin's Executive MBA with Fudan University and explore your differences and commonalities; and
- benefit from interaction with China's management talent who bring new perspectives to selling and manufacturing in global environments.

In addition, the Executive MBA Shanghai participants spend a week in St. Louis. All program graduates become part of a rich international learning network that can erase boundaries and build alliances both in the work sphere and the classroom.

9

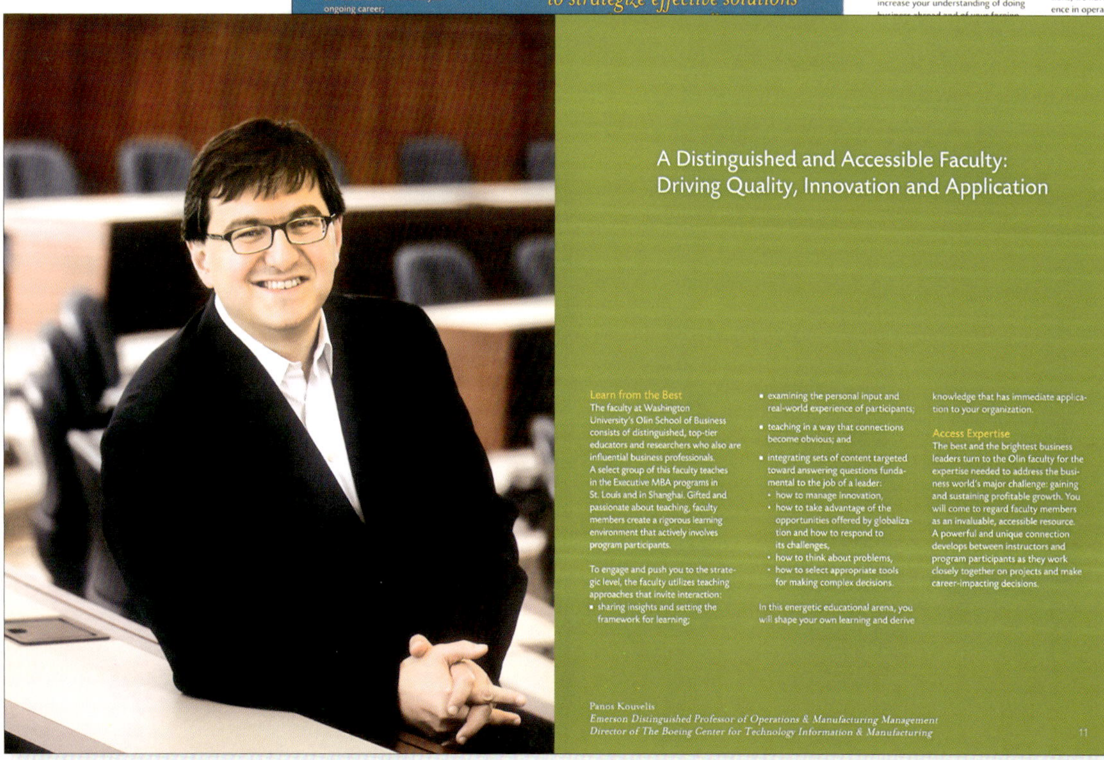
A Distinguished and Accessible Faculty:
Driving Quality, Innovation and Application

Learn from the Best
The faculty at Washington University's Olin School of Business consists of distinguished, top-tier educators and researchers who also are influential business professionals. A select group of this faculty teaches in the Executive MBA programs in St. Louis and in Shanghai. Gifted and passionate about teaching, faculty members create a rigorous learning environment that actively involves program participants.

To engage and push you to the strategic level, the faculty utilizes teaching approaches that invite interaction:
- sharing insights and setting the framework for learning;
- examining the personal input and real-world experience of participants;
- teaching in a way that connections become obvious; and
- integrating sets of content targeted toward answering questions fundamental to the job of a leader:
  - how to manage innovation,
  - how to take advantage of the opportunities offered by globalization and how to respond to its challenges,
  - how to think about problems,
  - how to select appropriate tools for making complex decisions.

In this energetic educational arena, you will shape your own learning and derive knowledge that has immediate application to your organization.

Access Expertise
The best and the brightest business leaders turn to the Olin faculty for the expertise needed to address the business world's major challenge: gaining and sustaining profitable growth. You will come to regard faculty members as an invaluable, accessible resource. A powerful and unique connection develops between instructors and program participants as they work closely together on projects and make career-impacting decisions.

Panos Kouvelis
Emerson Distinguished Professor of Operations & Manufacturing Management
Director of The Boeing Center for Technology Information & Manufacturing

11

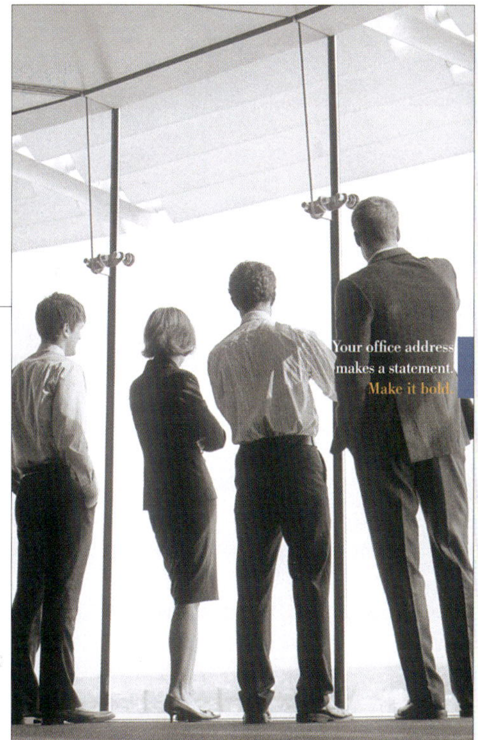

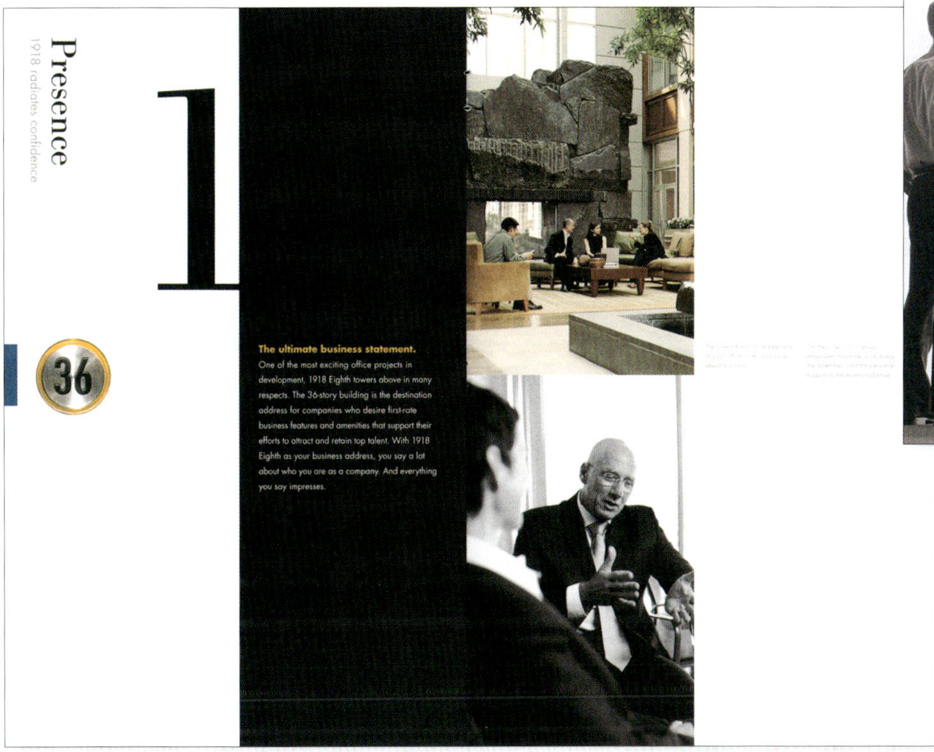

client
Schnitzer Northwest
design firm
Hornall Anderson Design Works
www.hadw.com
designers
John Anicker, Andrew Wicklund, Vu Nguyen, Leo Raymundo

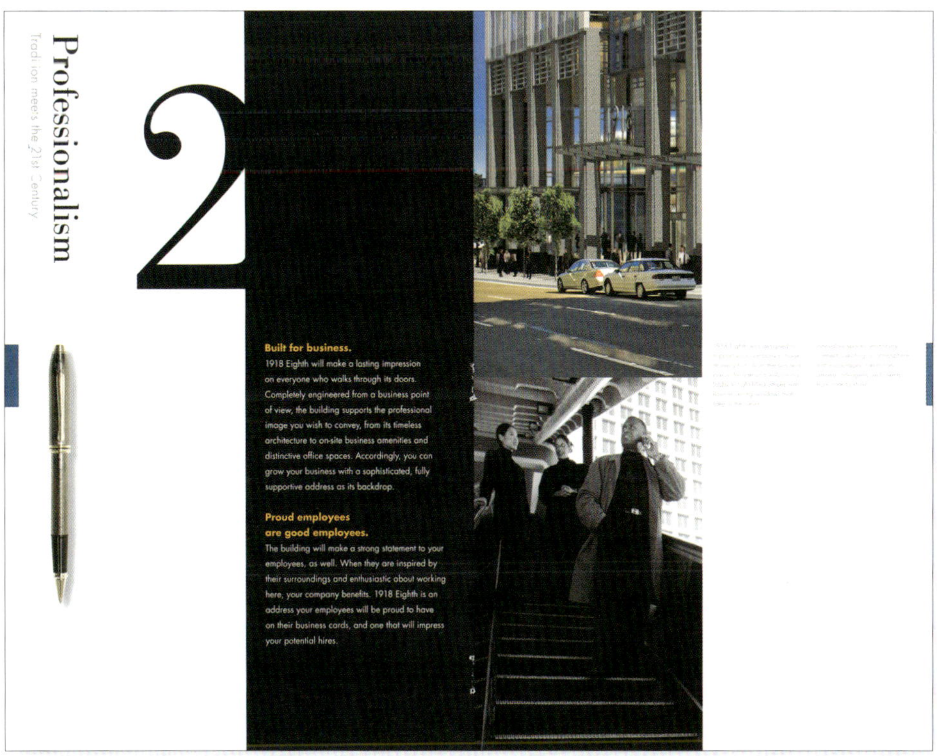

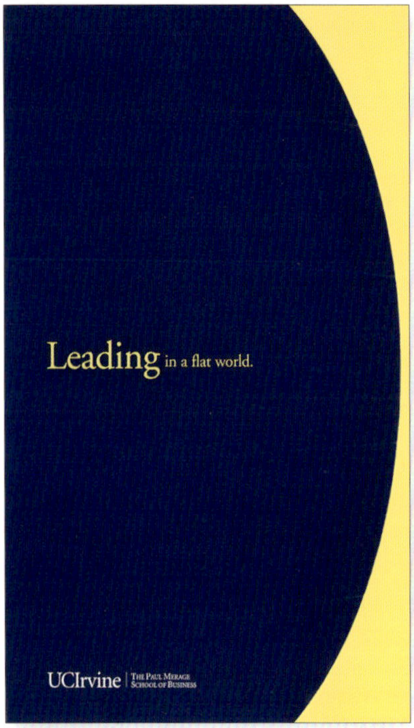

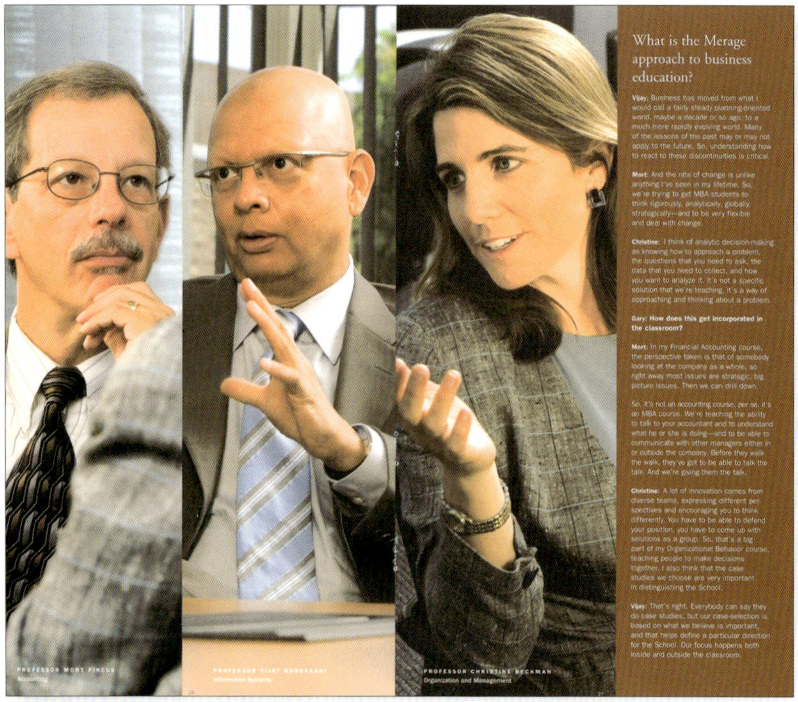

client
UC Irvine, Paul Merage School of Business
design firm
IE Design + Communications
www.iedesign.net
creative director
Marcie Carson
designer
Jane Lee

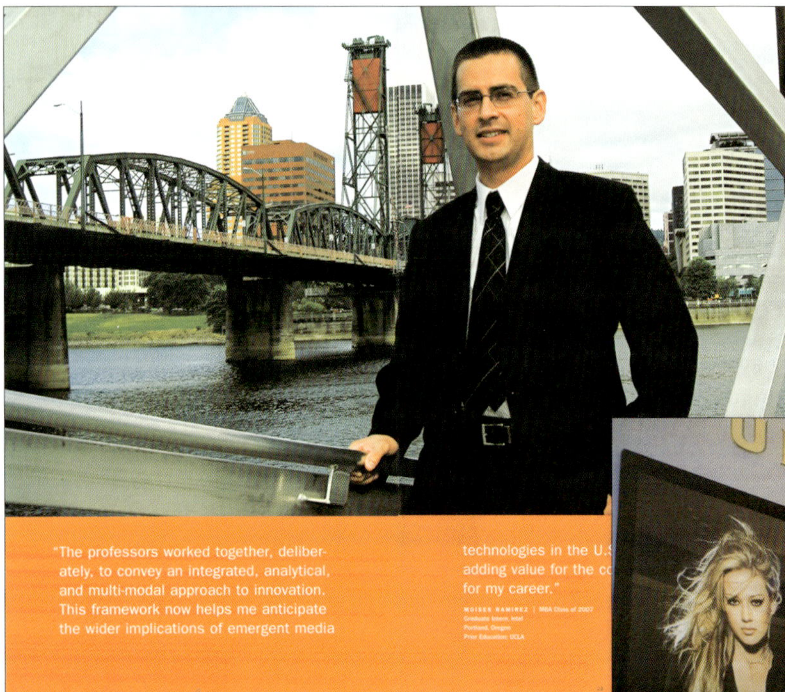

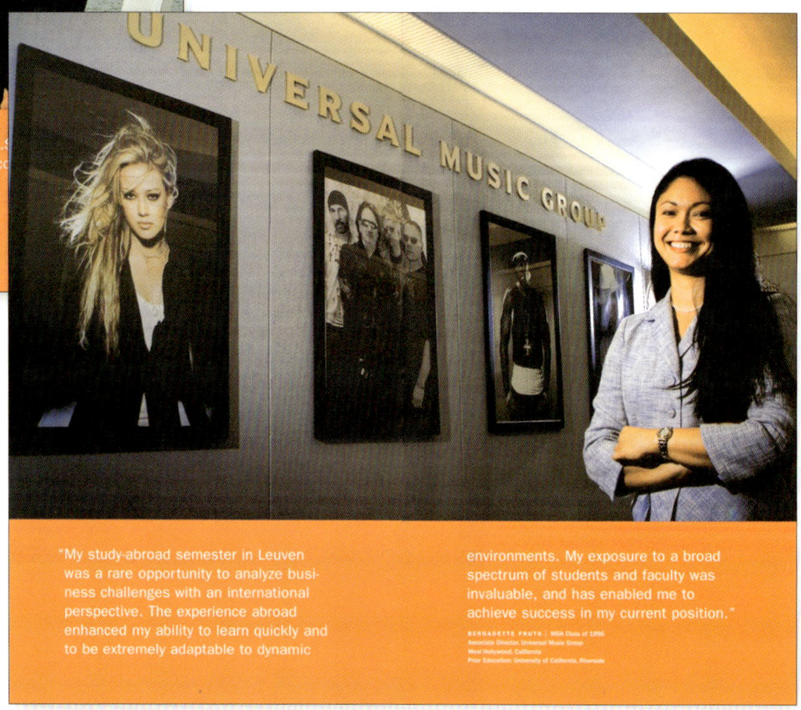

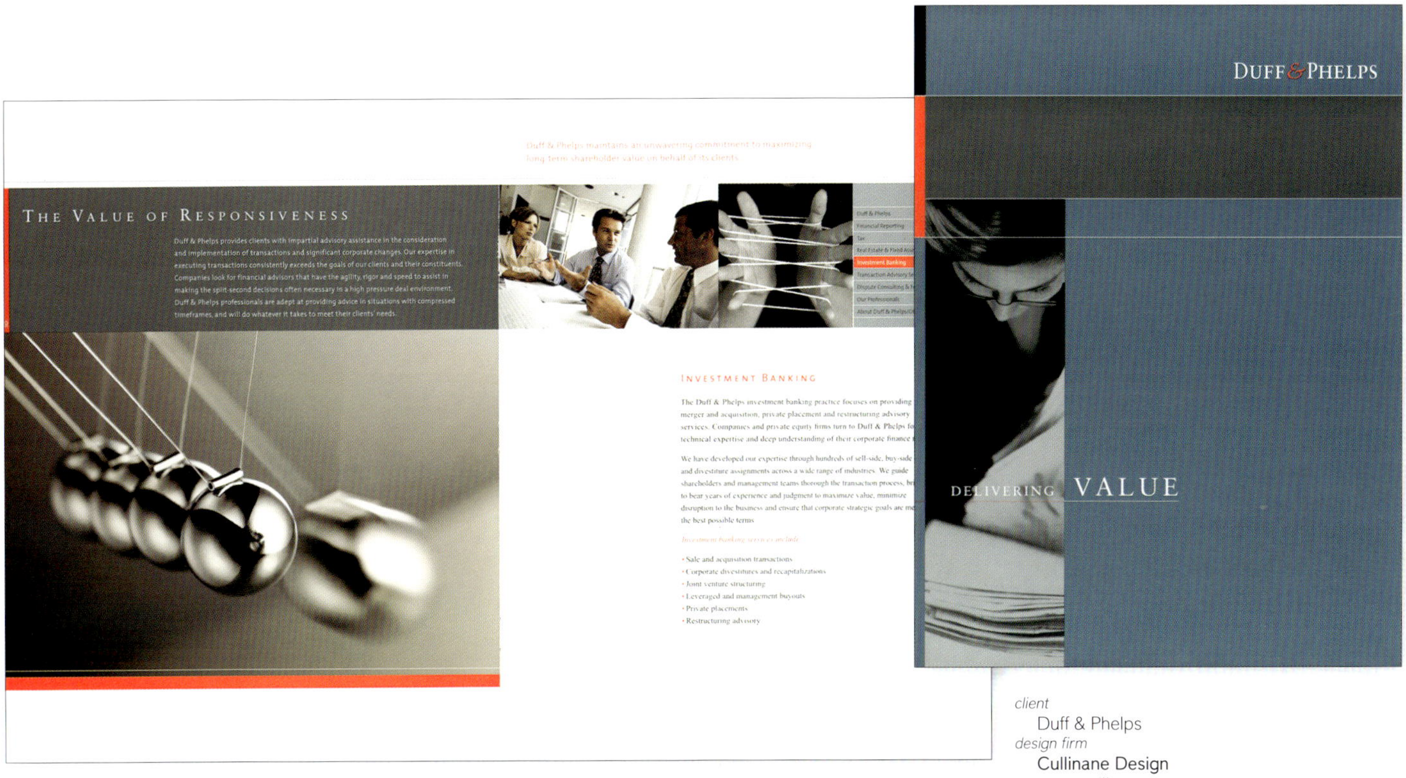

client
Duff & Phelps
design firm
Cullinane Design
www.cullinane.com
designers
Jia Kang Sung, Bob Cullinane

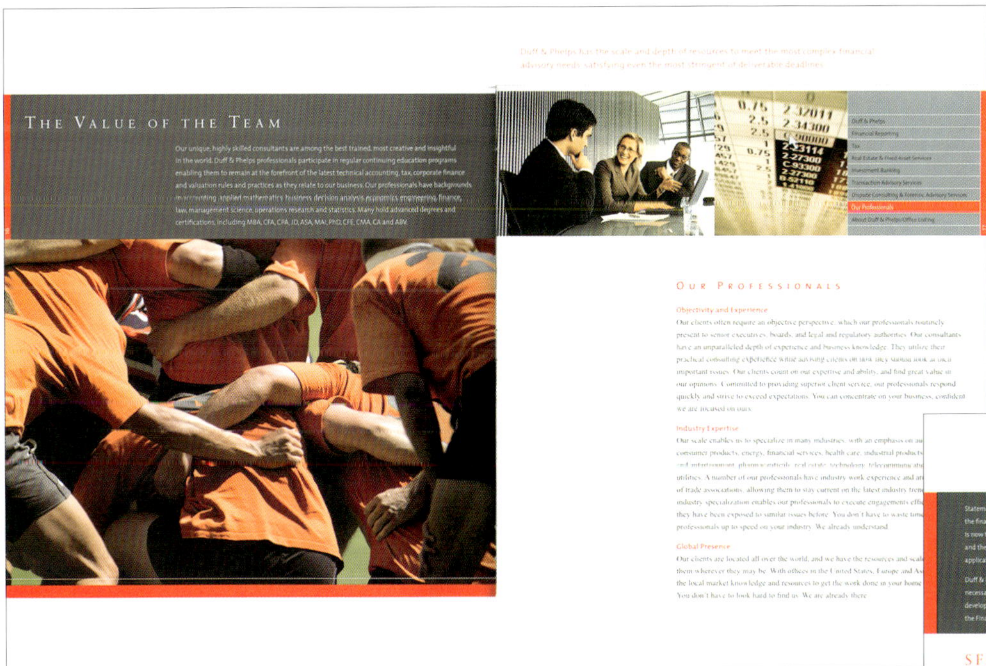

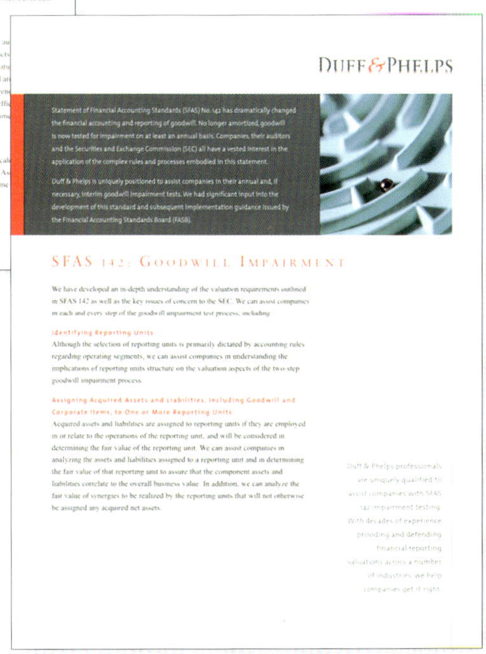

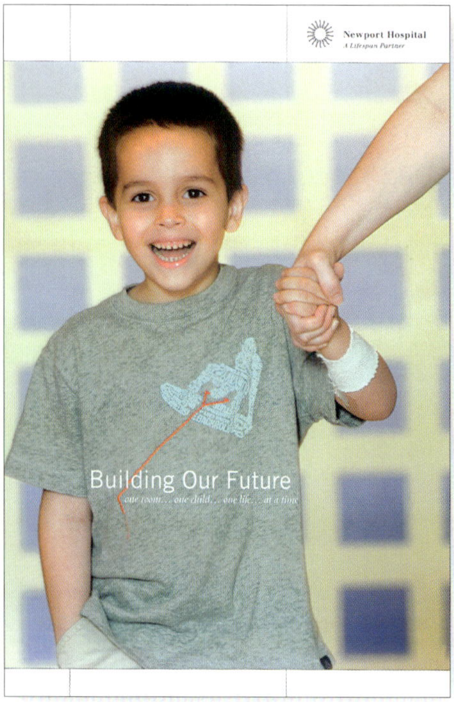

client
Newport Hospital
design firm
Gill Fishman Associates
www.gillfishmandesign.com
designer
Meredith Maluchnik

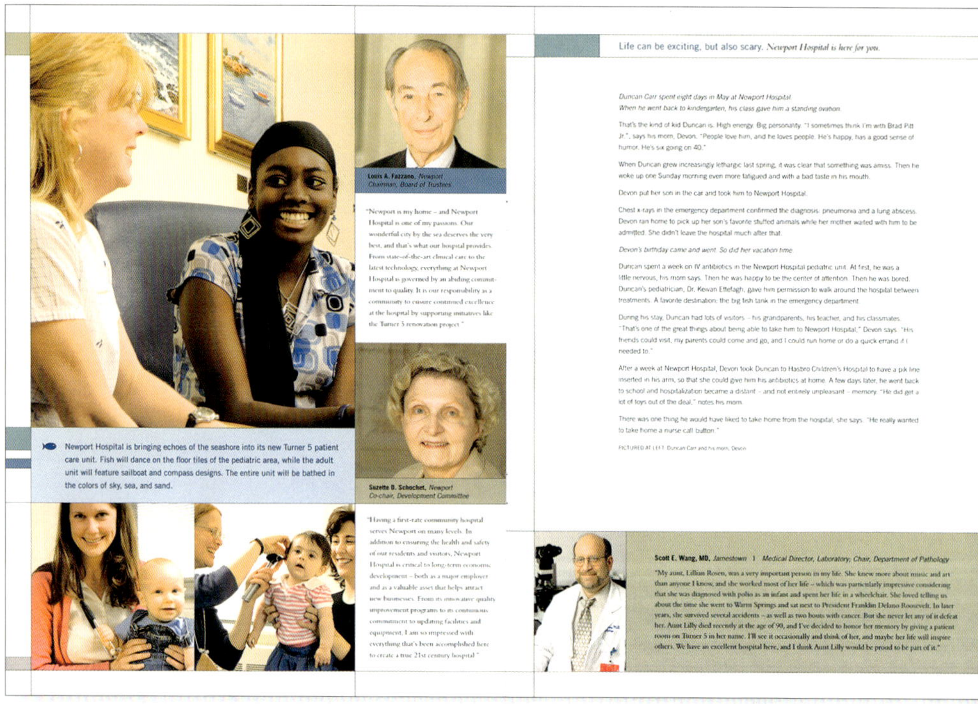

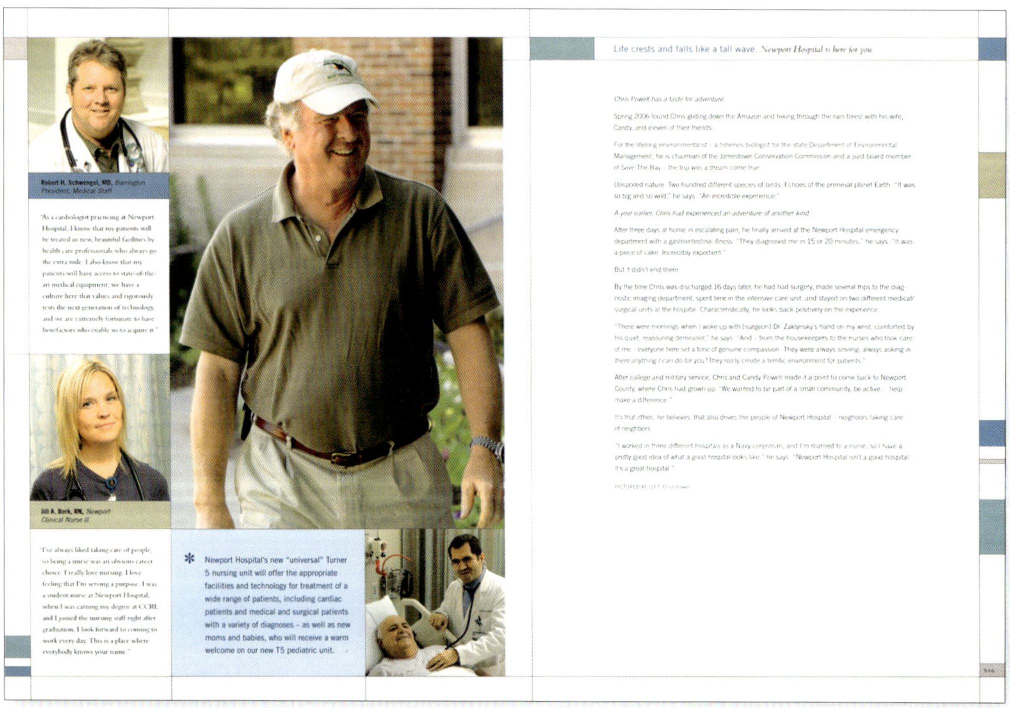

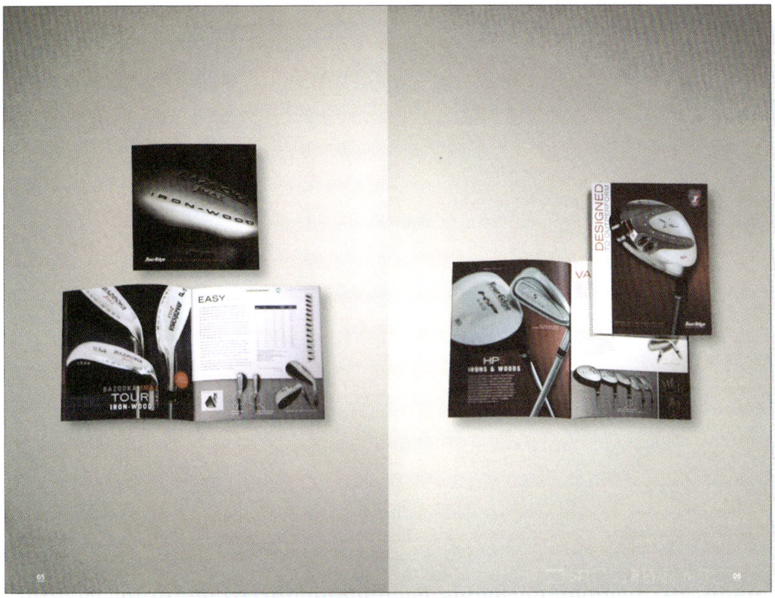

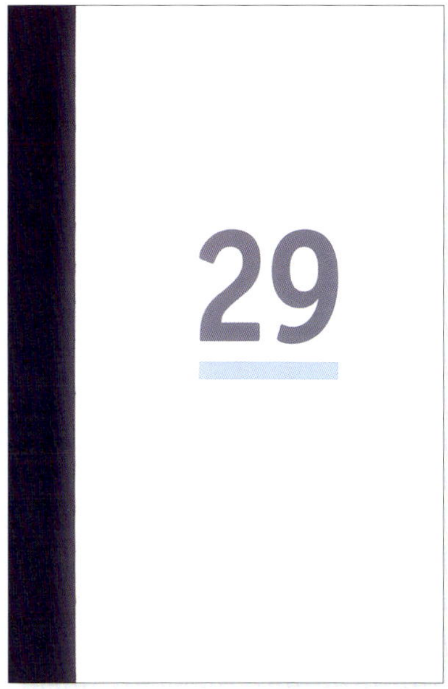

client
Rule29 Creative
design firm
Rule29 Creative
www.rule29.com
designers
Justin Ahrens,
Josh Jensen,
Billy Carlson

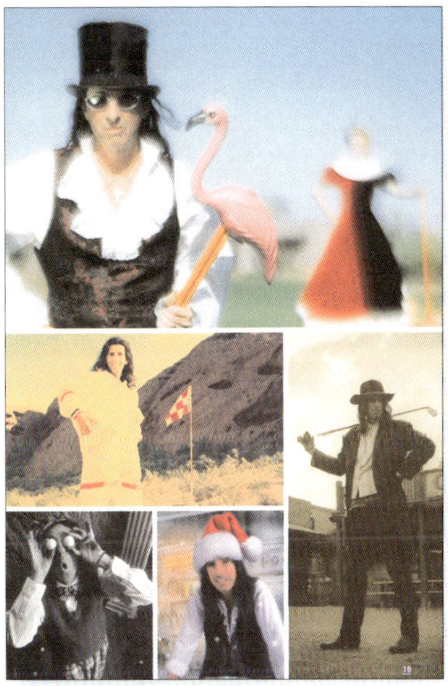

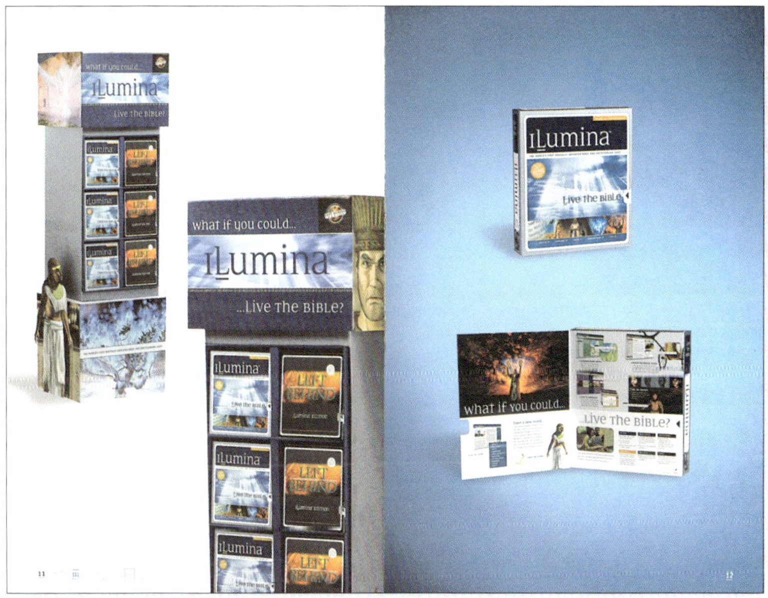

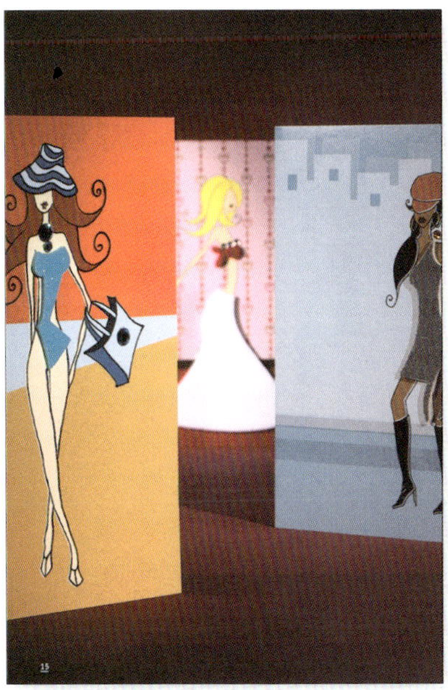

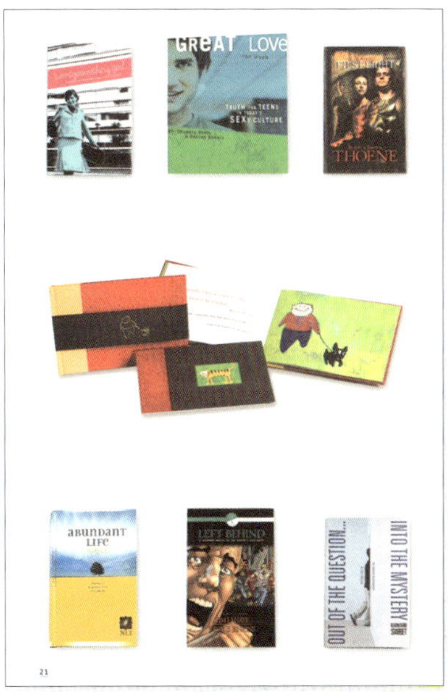

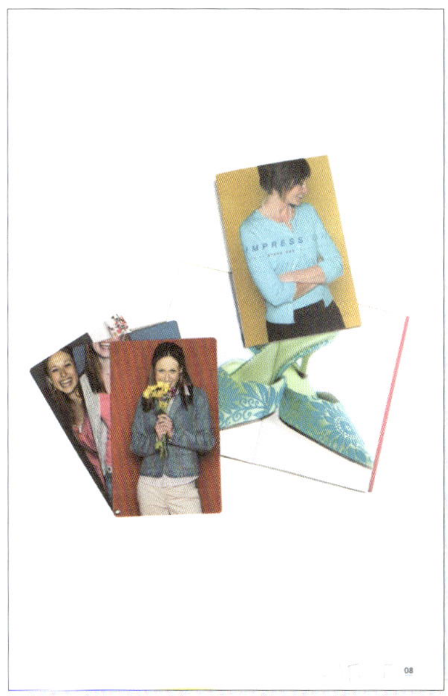

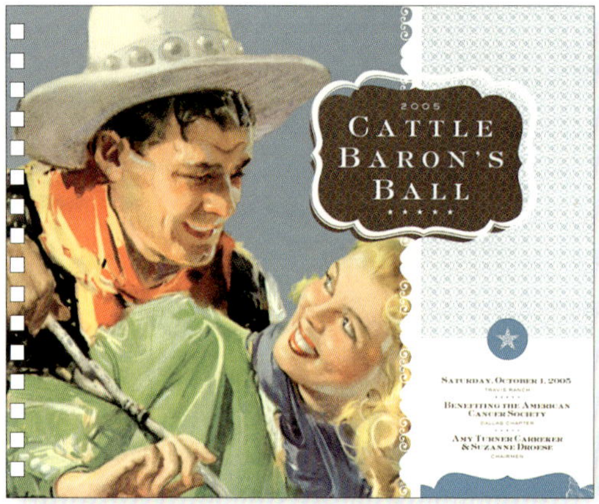

client
Cattle Baron's Ball '05
design firm
Kendall Creative Shop, Inc.
kendallcreative.com
designers
Tim Childress, Mark Platt

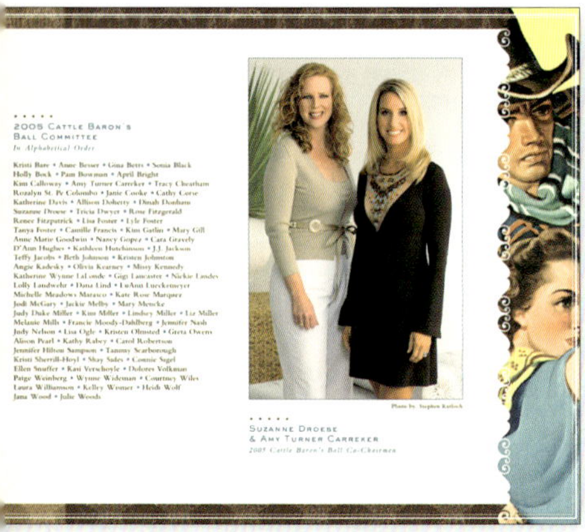

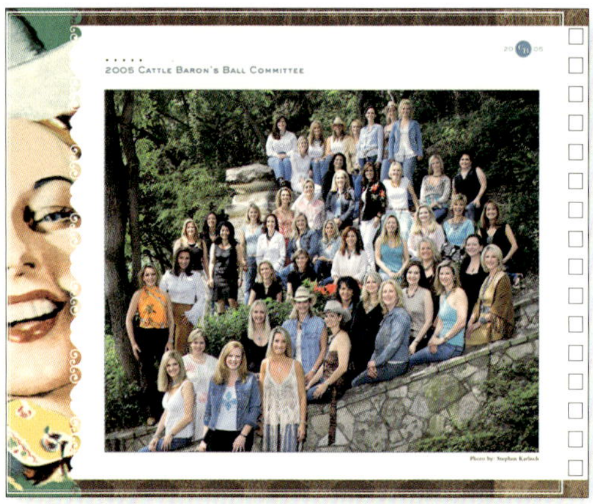

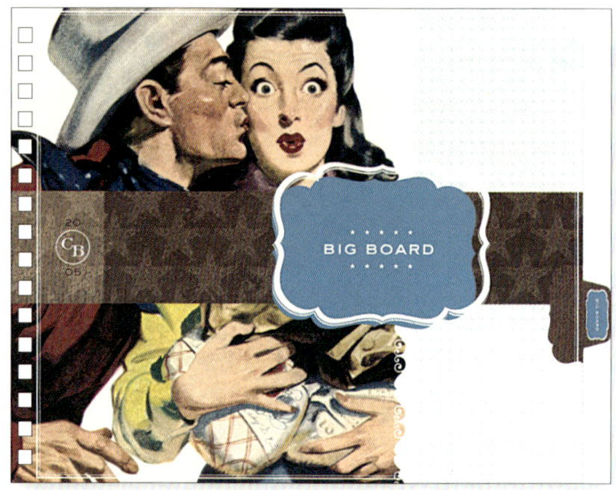

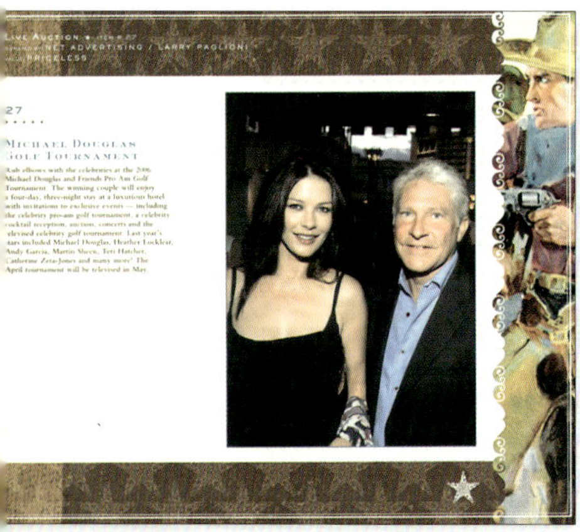

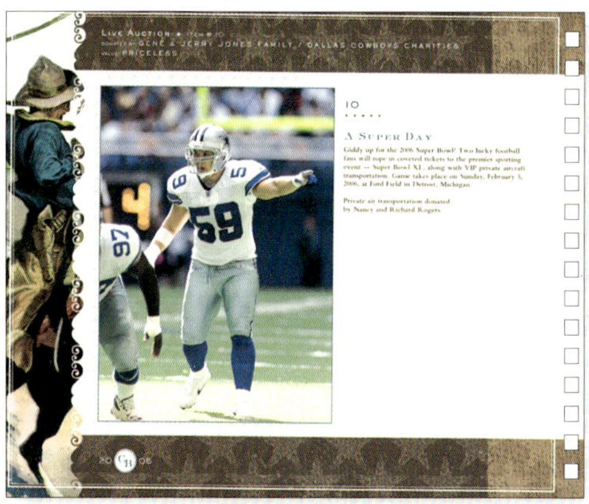

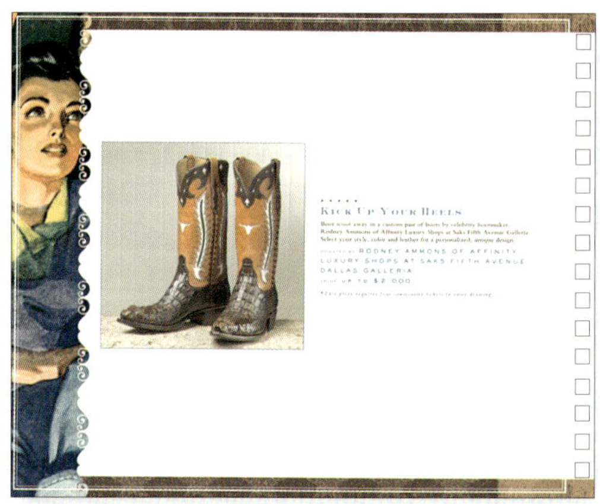

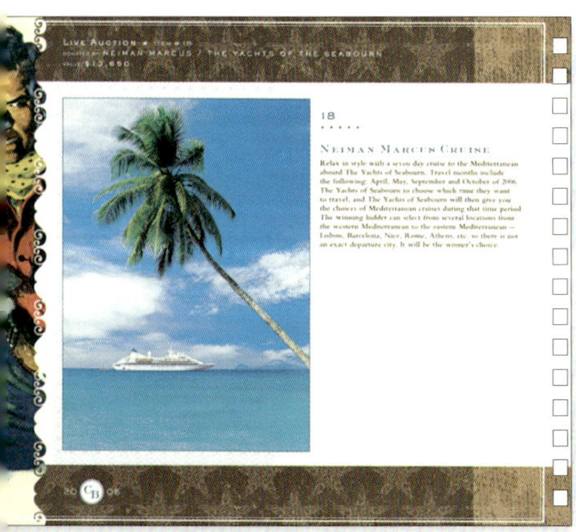

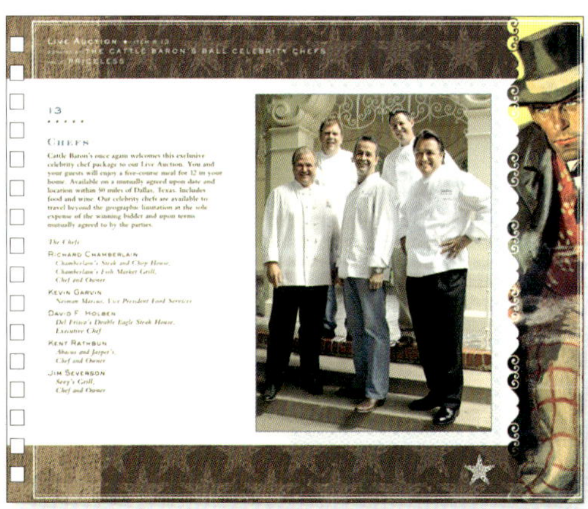

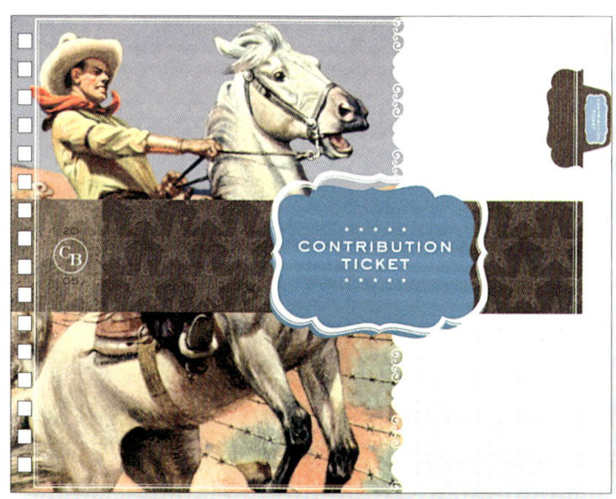

client
Society for Neuroscience
design firm
Dever Designs
www.deverdesigns.com
art director
Jeffrey L. Dever
designer
Kim Pollock

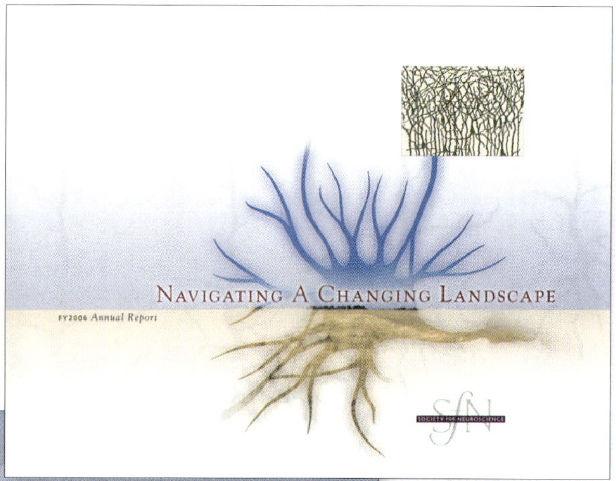

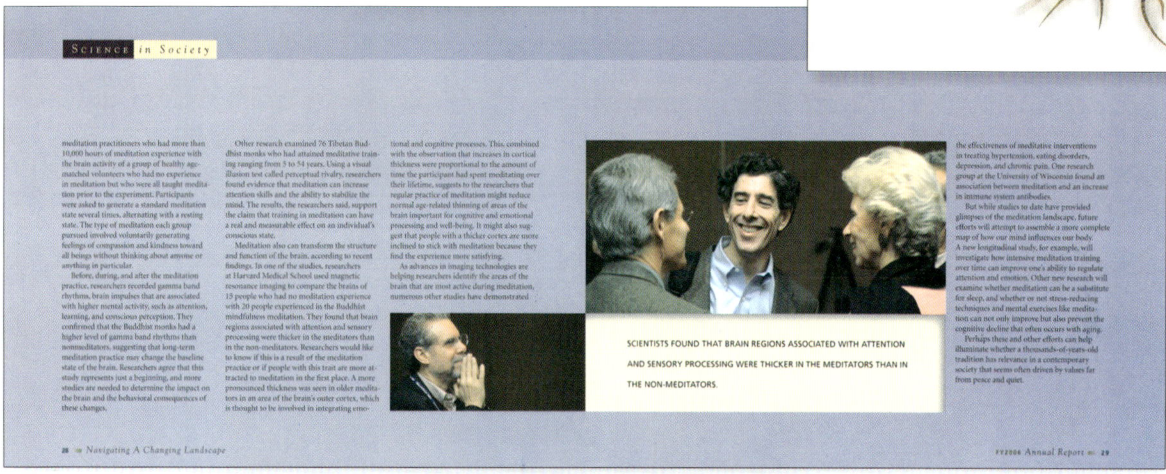

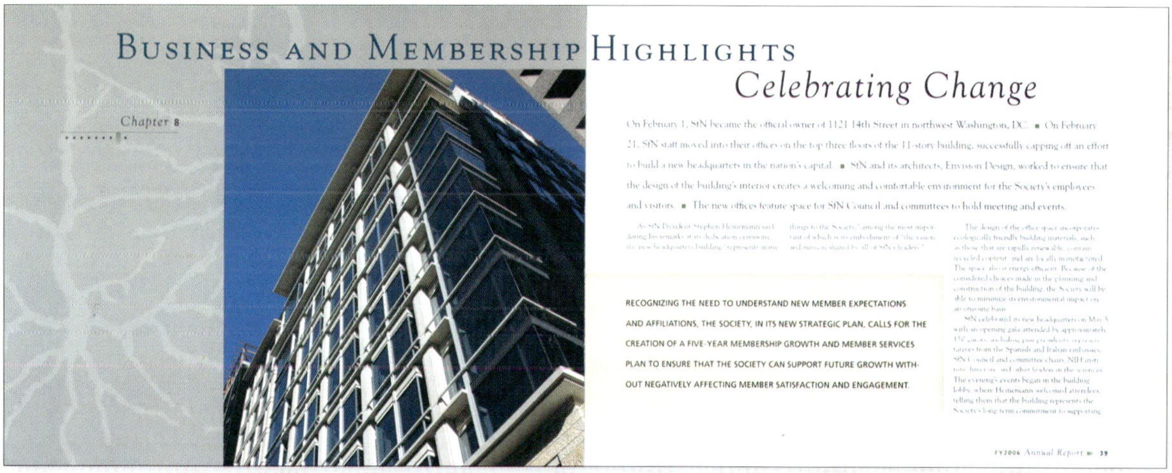

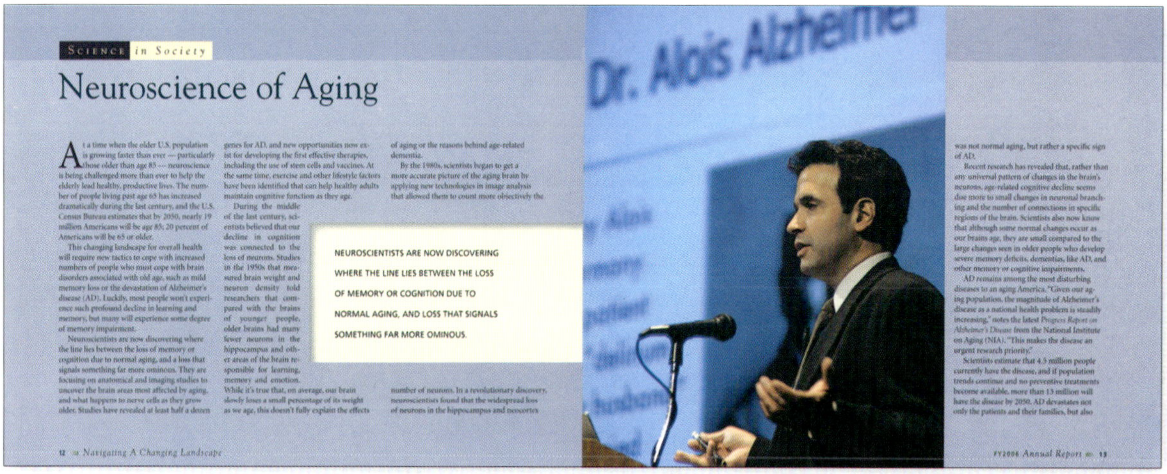

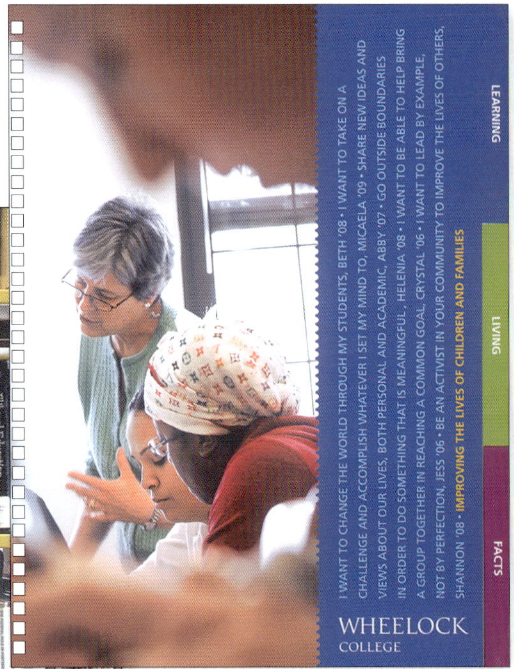

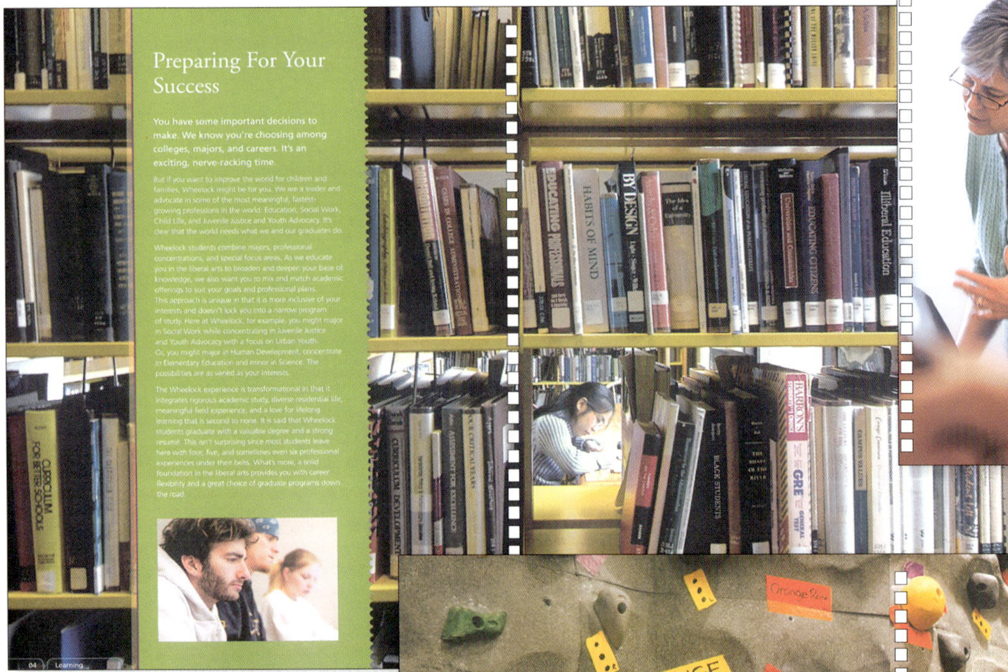

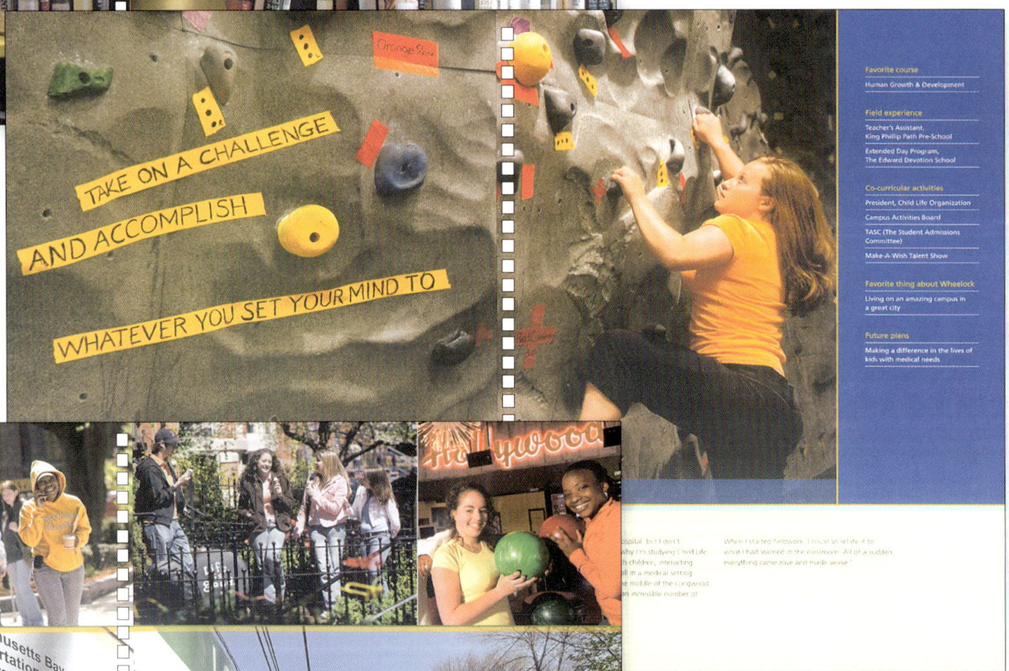

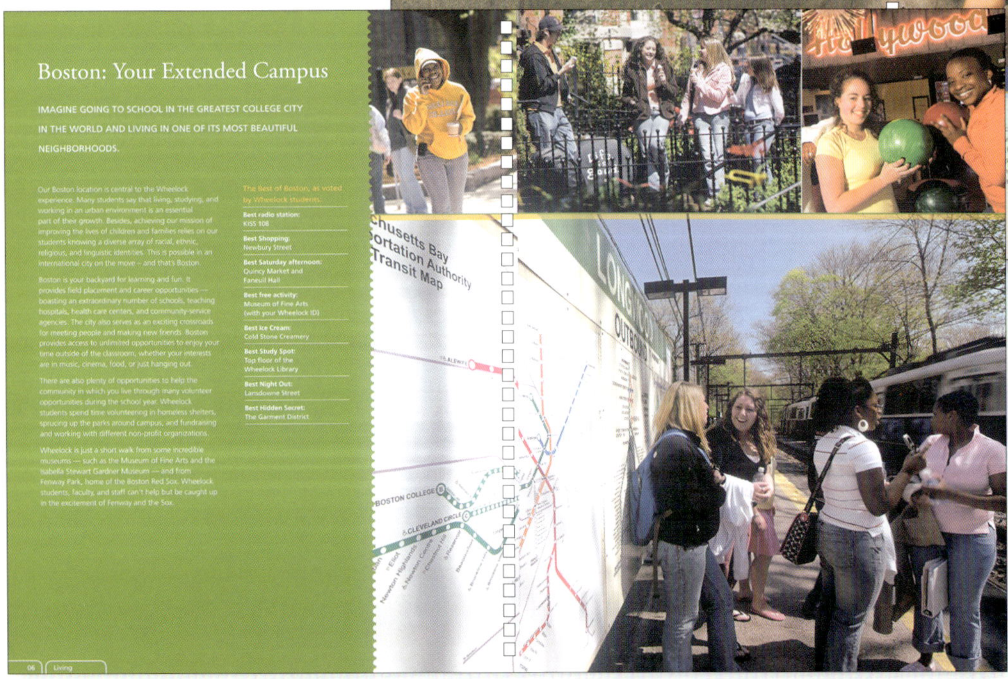

client
Wheelock College
design firm
kor group
www.kor.com
designers
Kjerstin Westgaard Oh, Brigitte Ting, Karen Dendy Smith

client
Co-exprise MarketPlace
design firm
Desbrow
desbrow.com
designers
Kimberly S. Miller,
Brian Lee Campbell

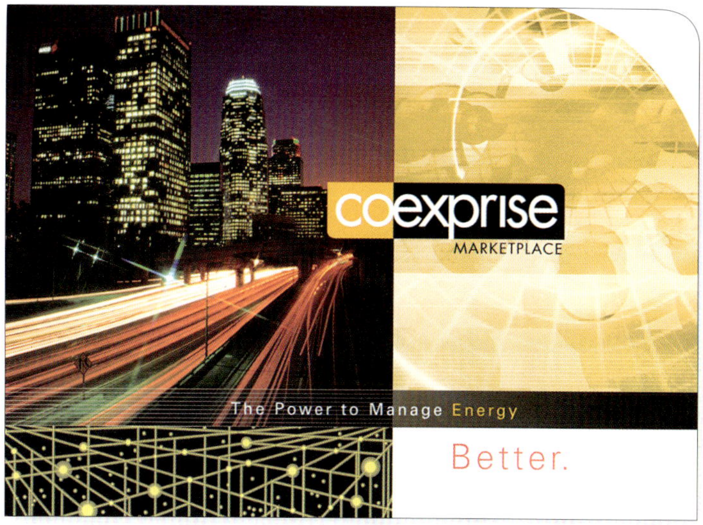

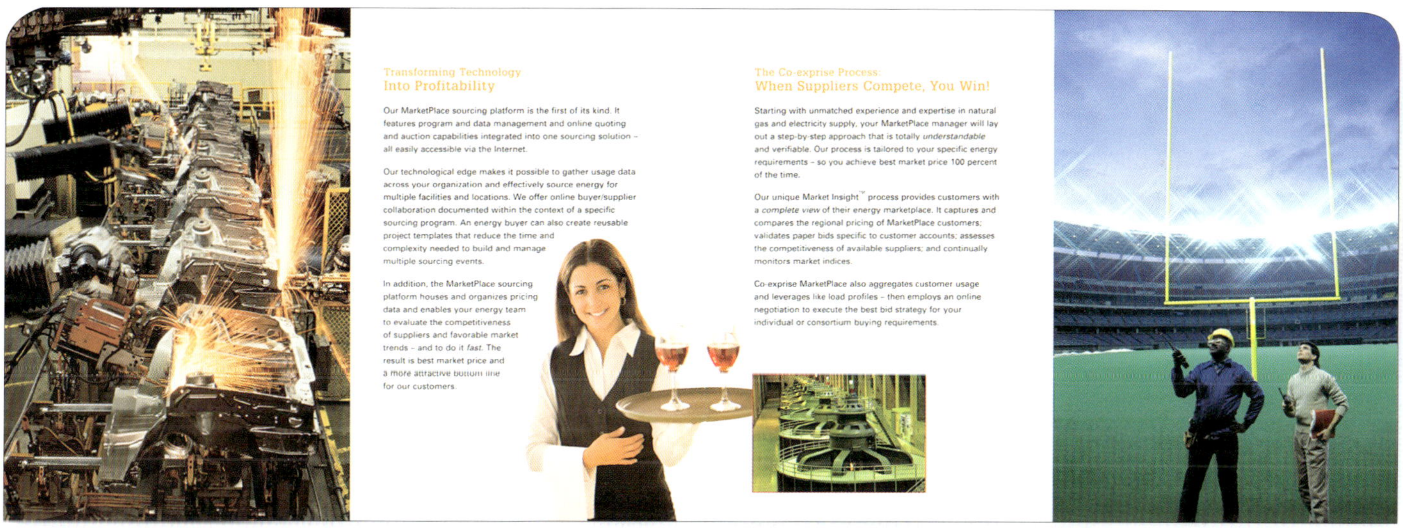

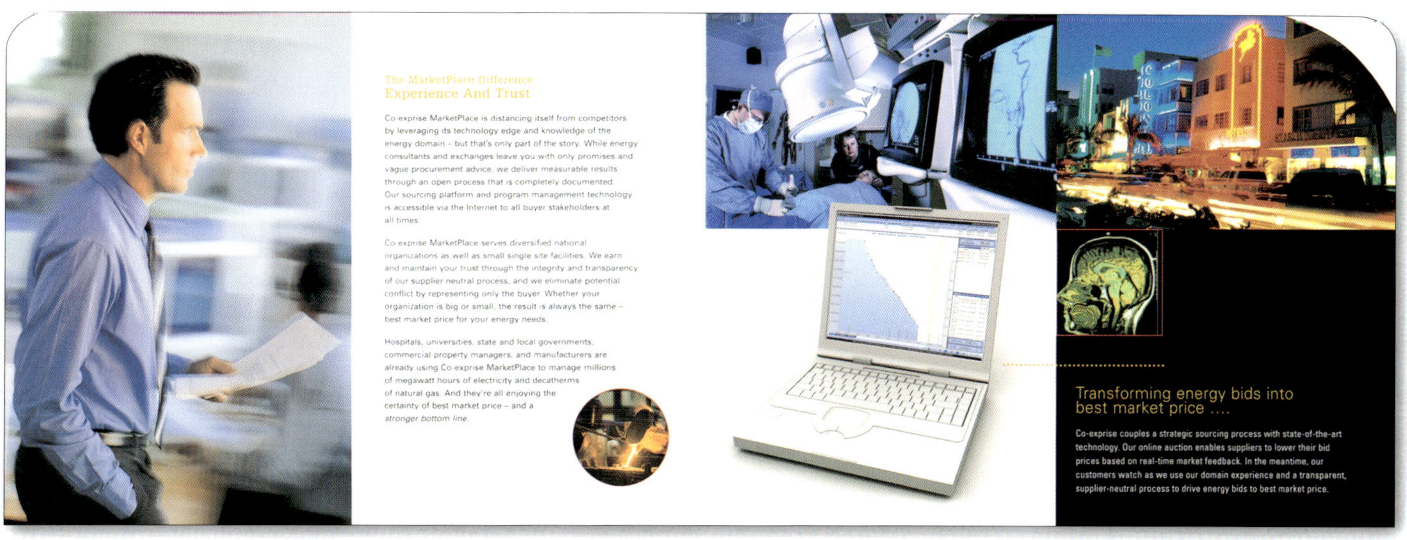

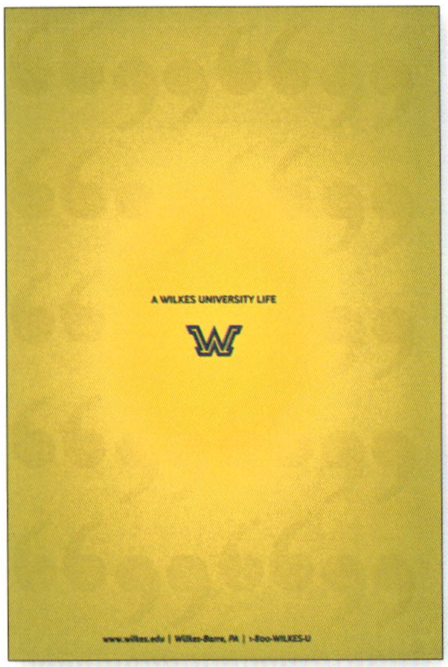

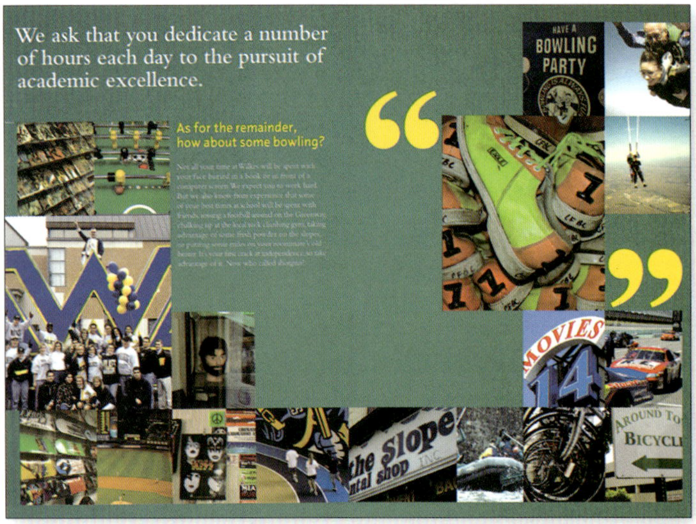

client
Wilkes University
design firm
160over90
designers
Giac Ciminello, Adam Flanagan, Jim Walls, Darryl Cilli

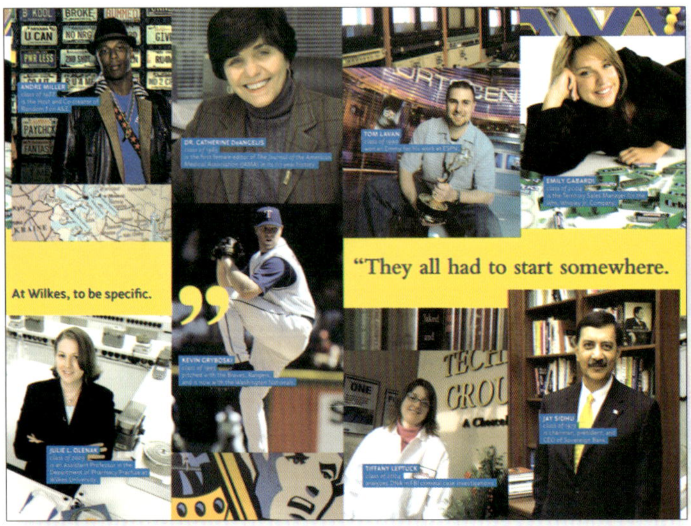

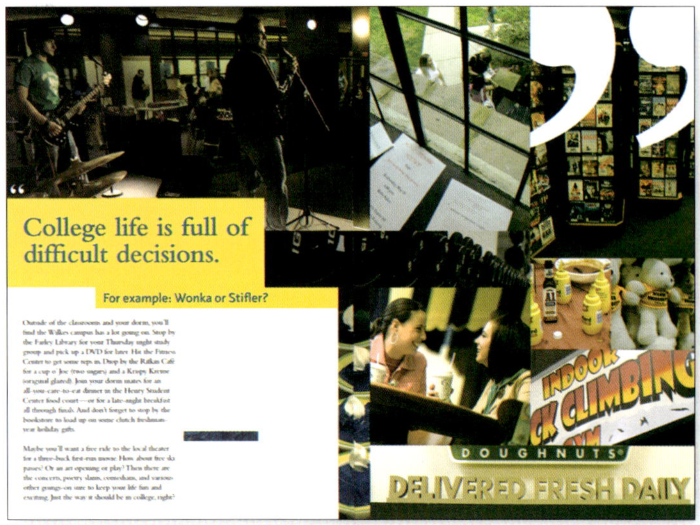

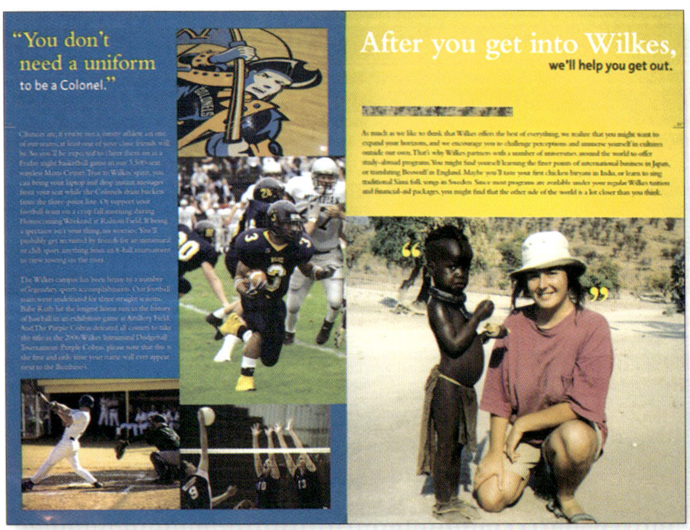

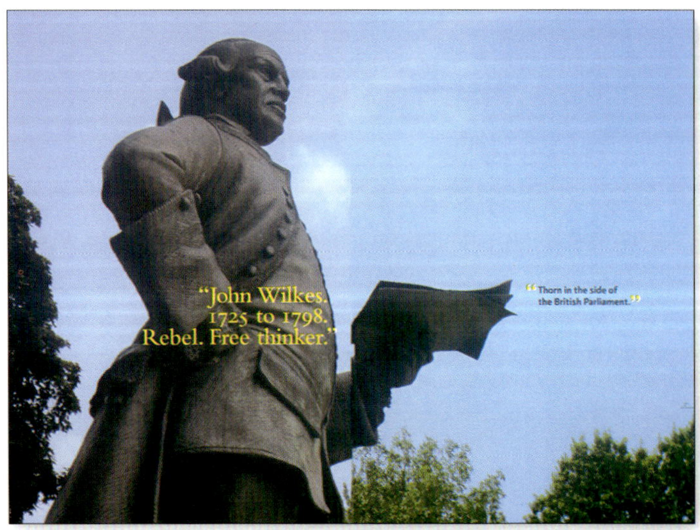

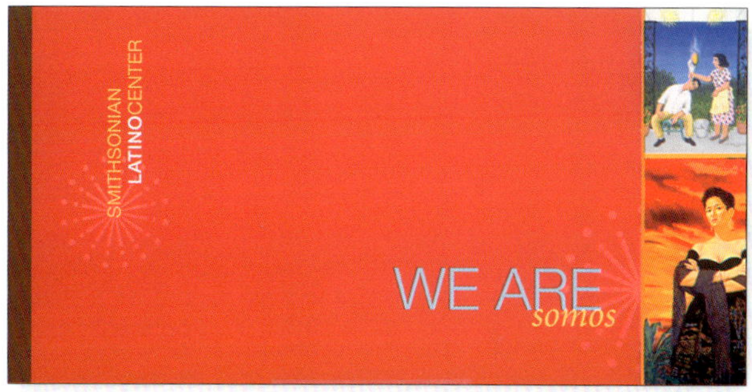

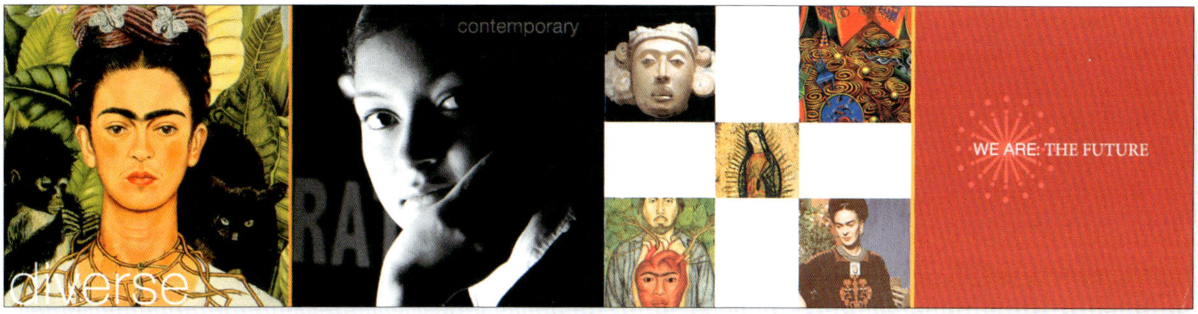

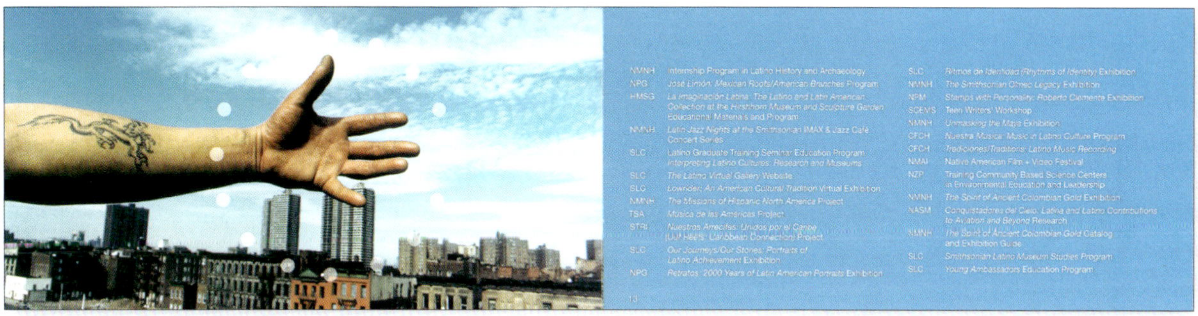

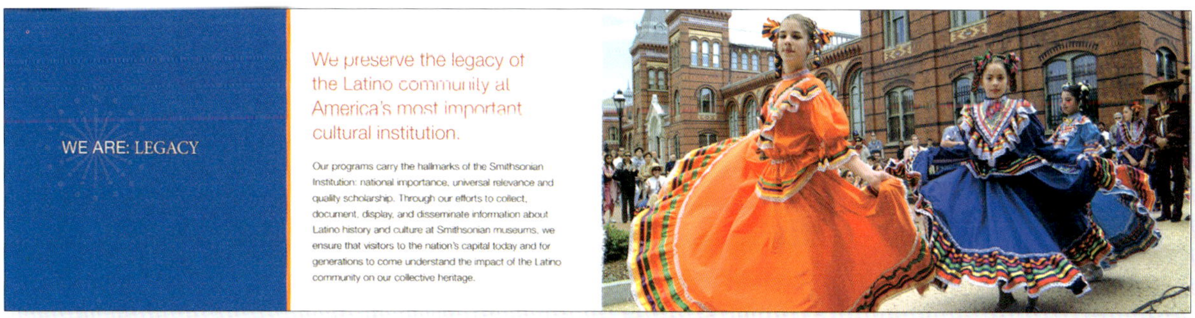

client
Smithsonian Latino Center
design firm
Grafik Marketing Communications
www.grafik.com
designers
Gregg Glaviano, Lynn Murphy, Heath Dwiggins

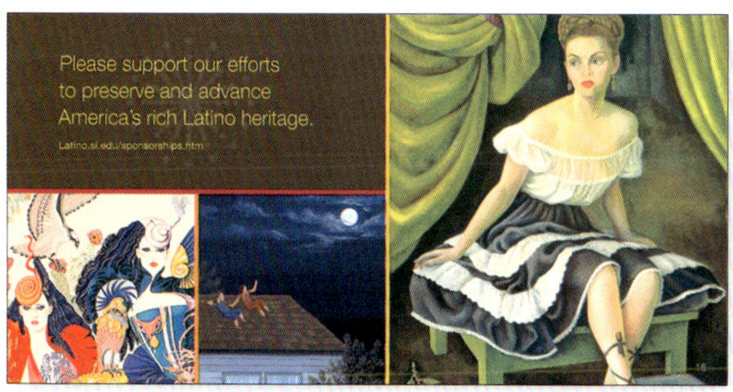

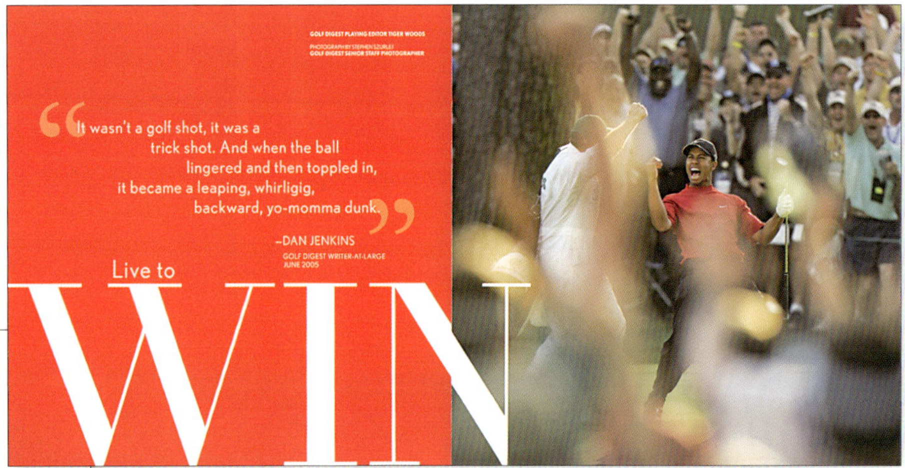

Golf Digest
Live to Play

client
Golf Digest
design firm
Golf Digest Marketing Promotion
golfdigest.com
designers
Lance Hertzbach, Deb Chute

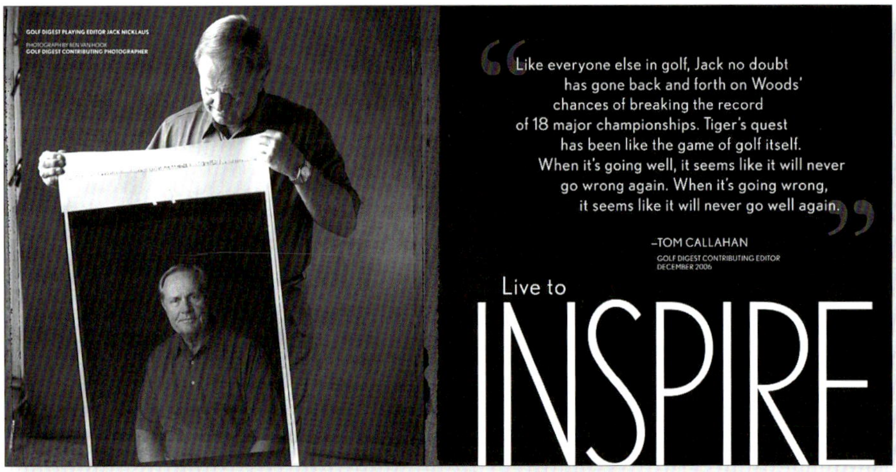

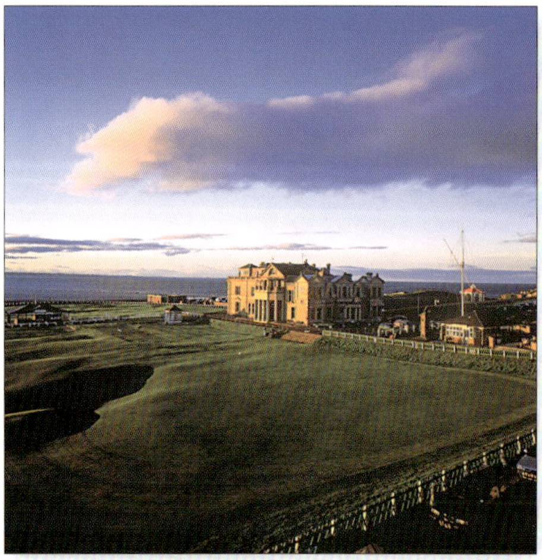

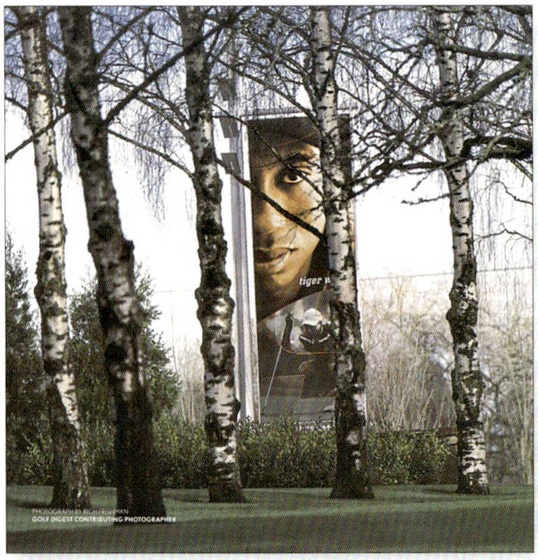

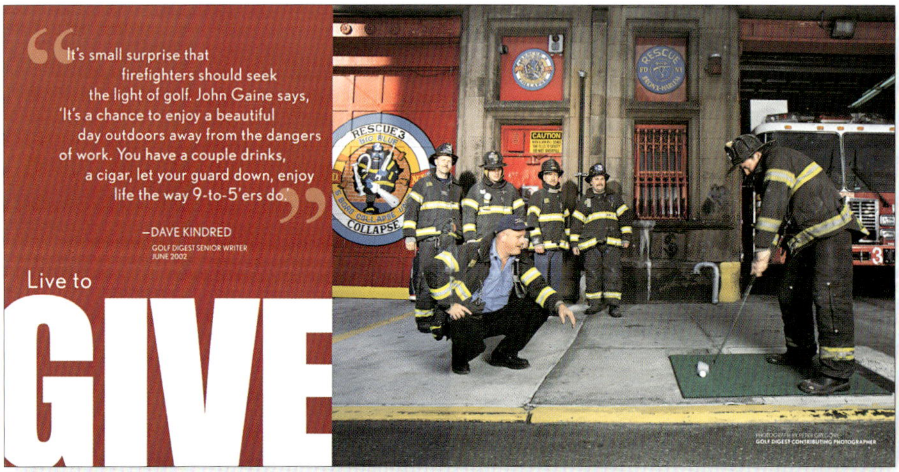

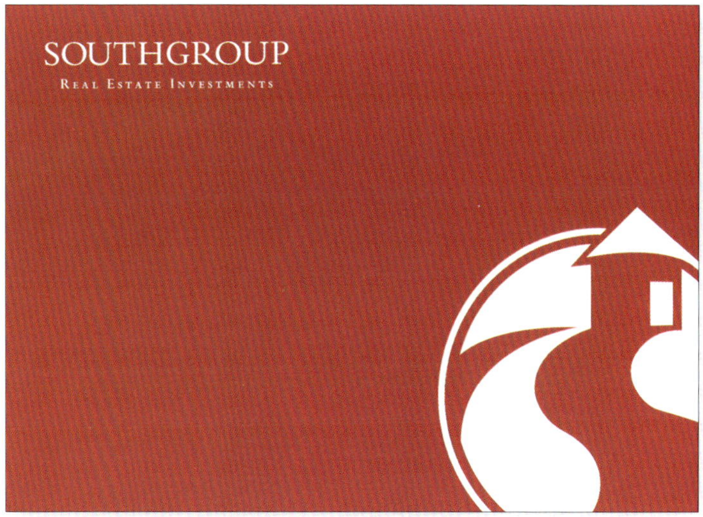

client
South Group Investments
design firm
A3 Design
www.athreedesign.com
designer
Amanda Altman

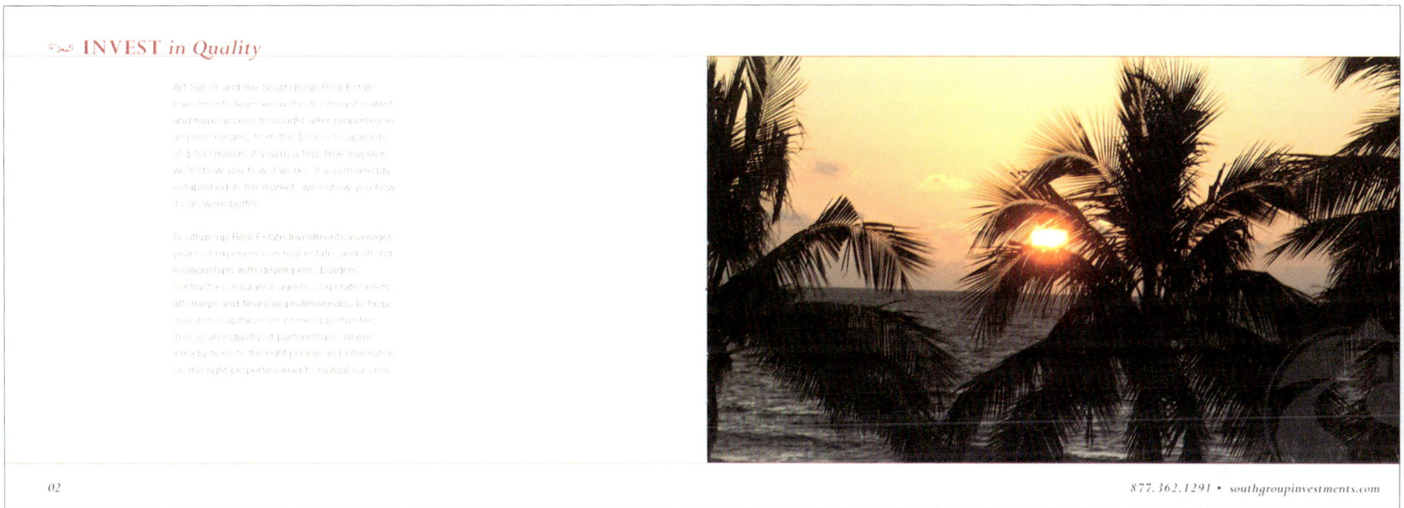

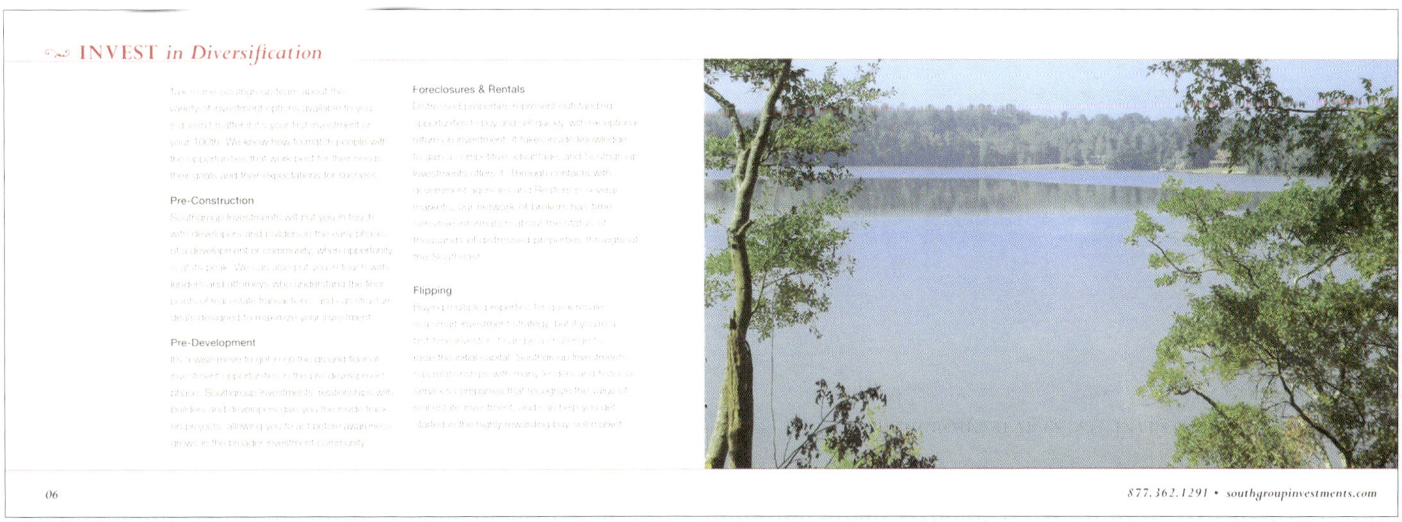

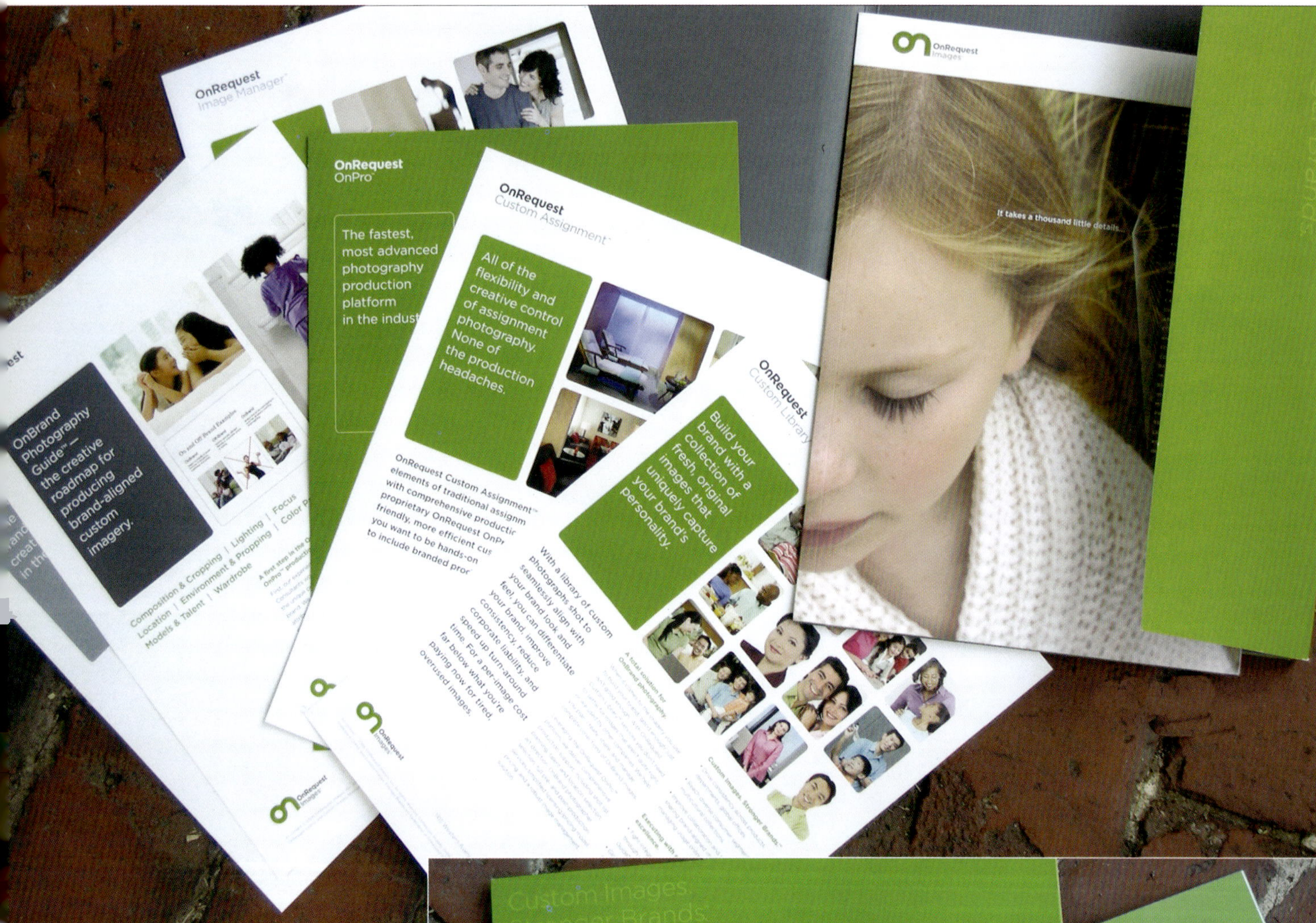

client
OnRequest Images
design firm
Hornall Anderson Design Works
www.hadw.com
designers
Jack Anderson, Mark Popich,
Peter Anderson, Yuri Shvets,
Michael Brugman, Mignonne Lysiak

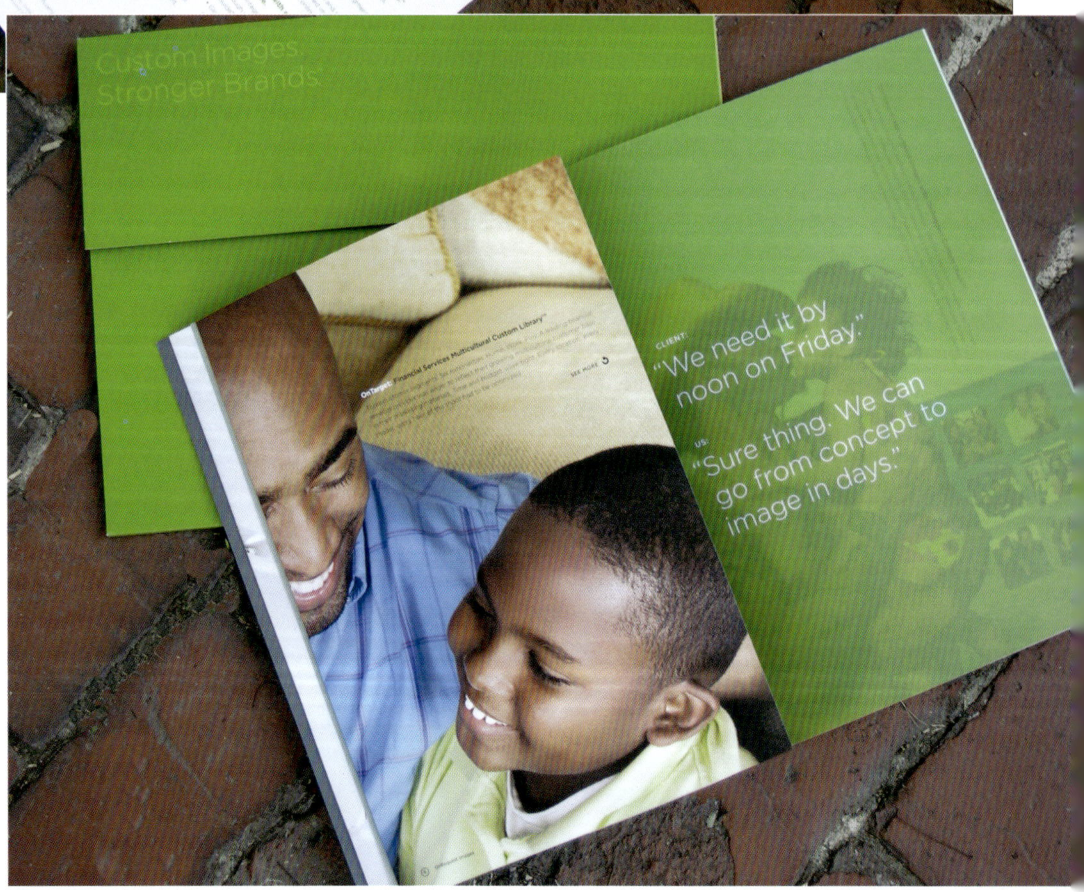

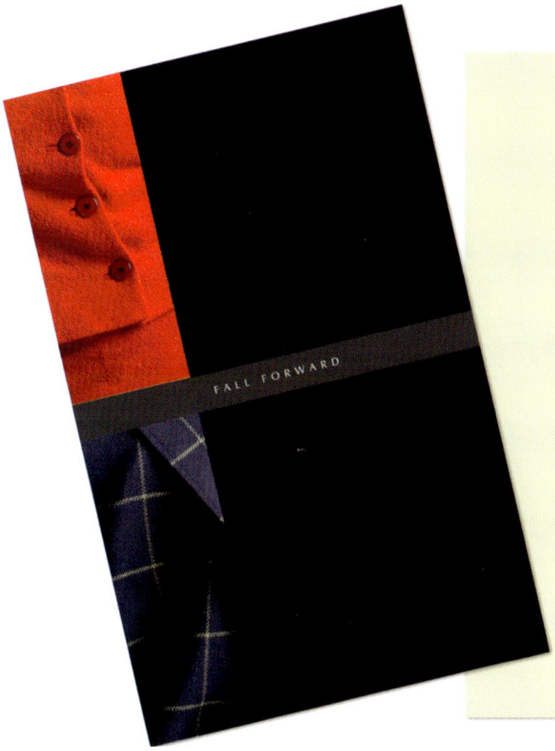

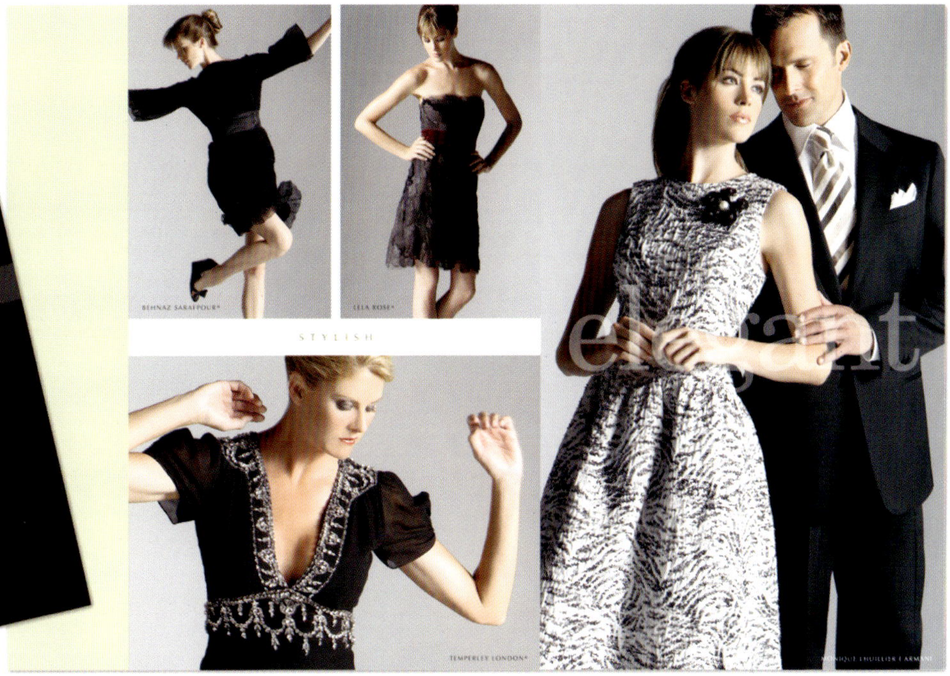

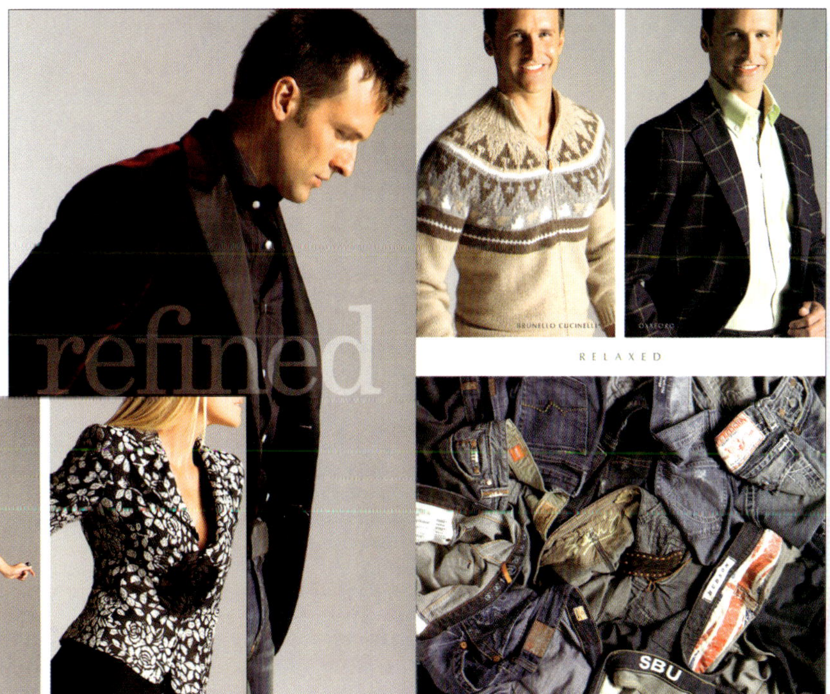

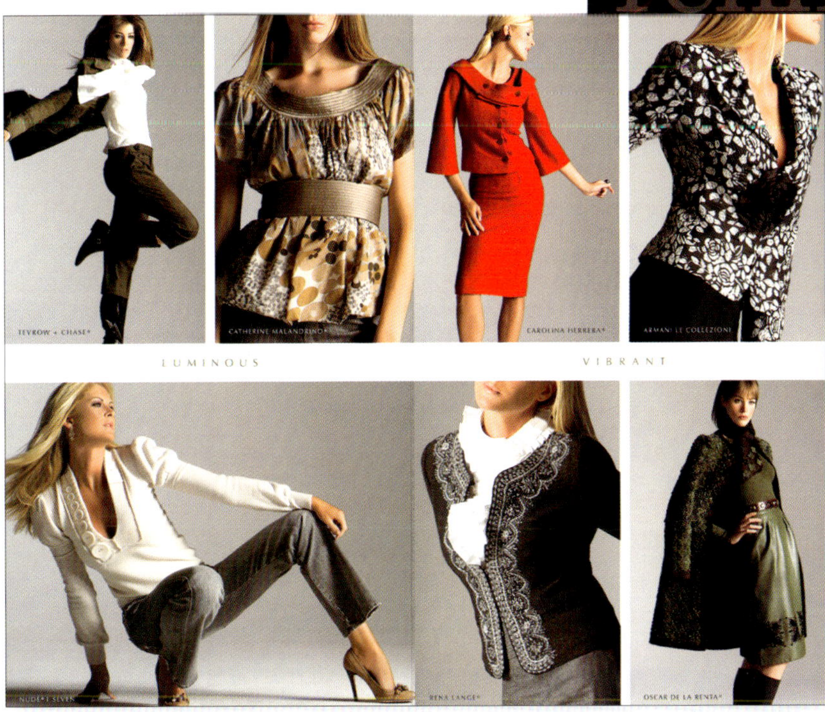

client
Andrisen Morton
design firm
Rassman Design
www.rassmandesign.com
designer
Lyn D'Amato

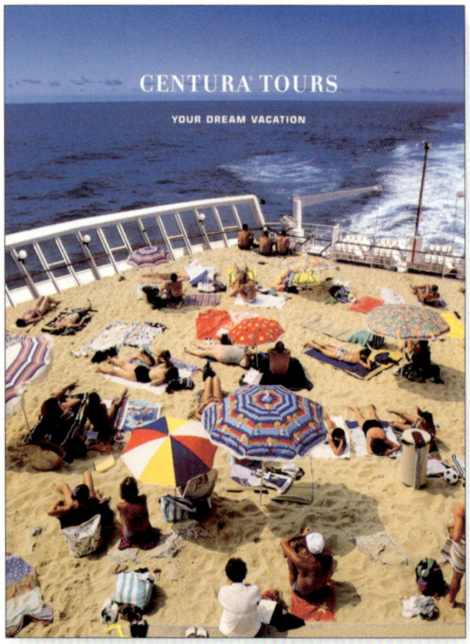

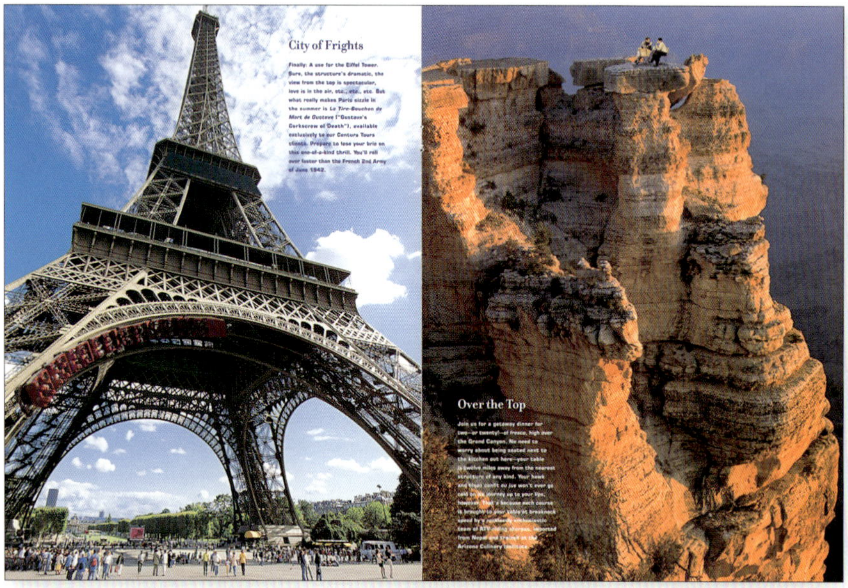

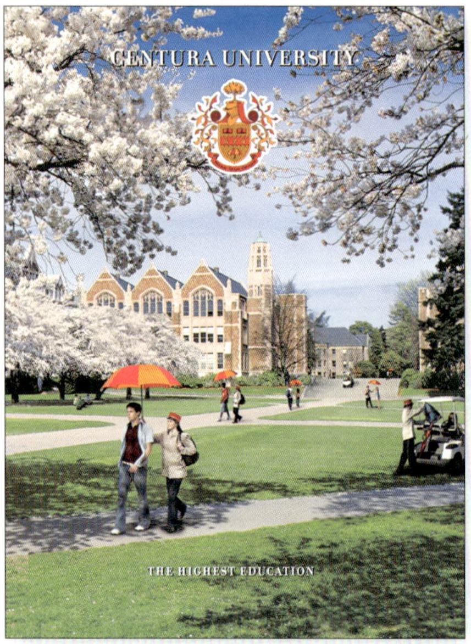

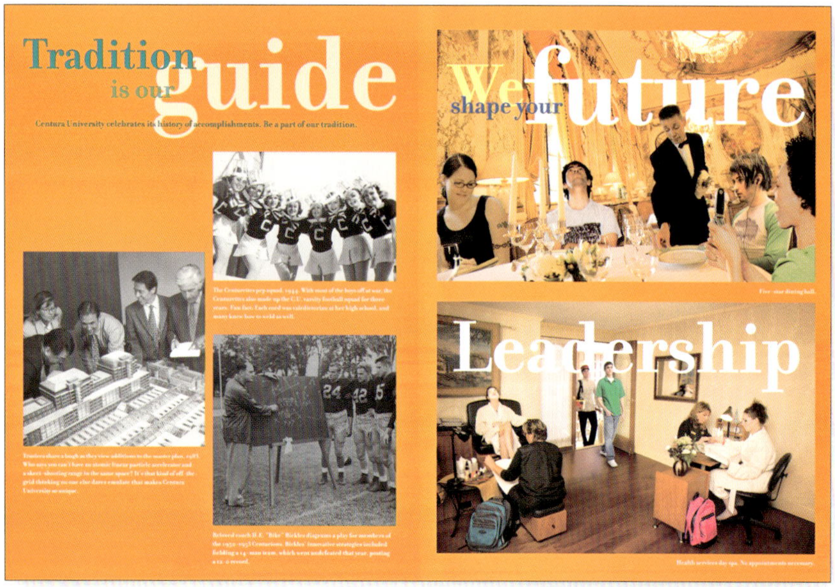

client
Stora Enso
design firm
Alexander Isley inc.
www.AlexanderIsley.com
designers
Alexander Isley,
George Kokkinidis,
Cherith Victorino

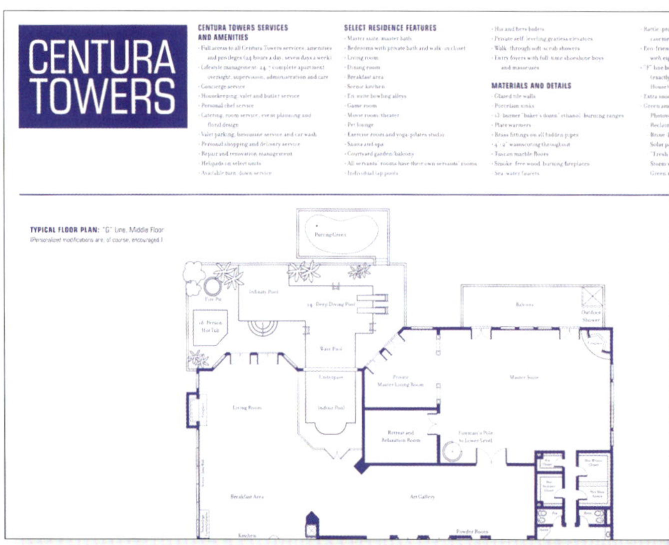

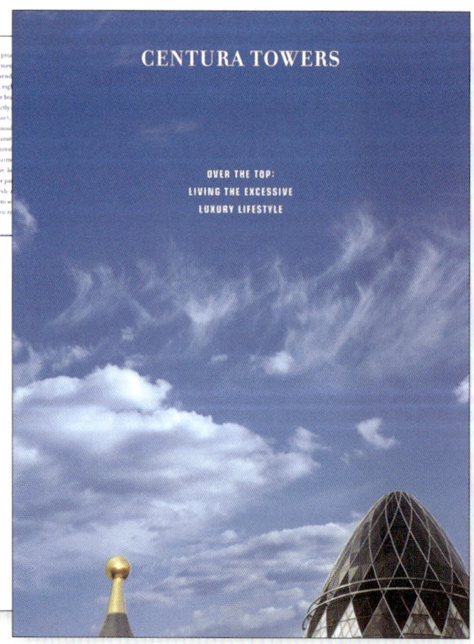

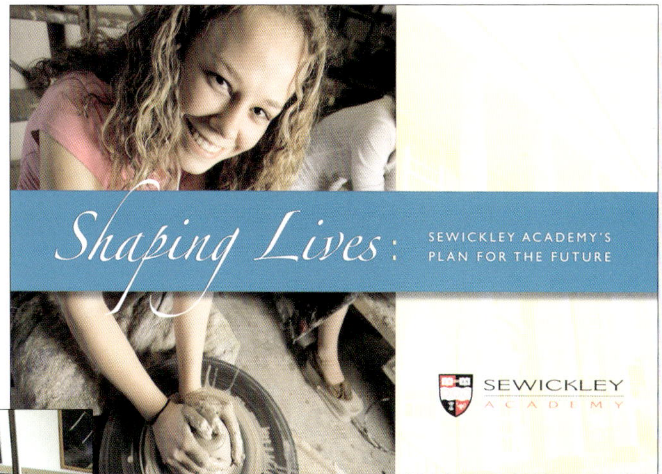

client
Sewickley Academy
design firm
Reinnov8 Design Group
www.reinnov8.com
designer
Richard A. Hooper

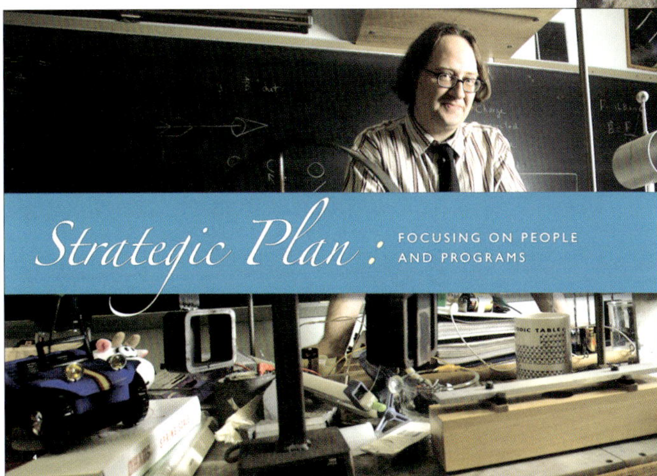

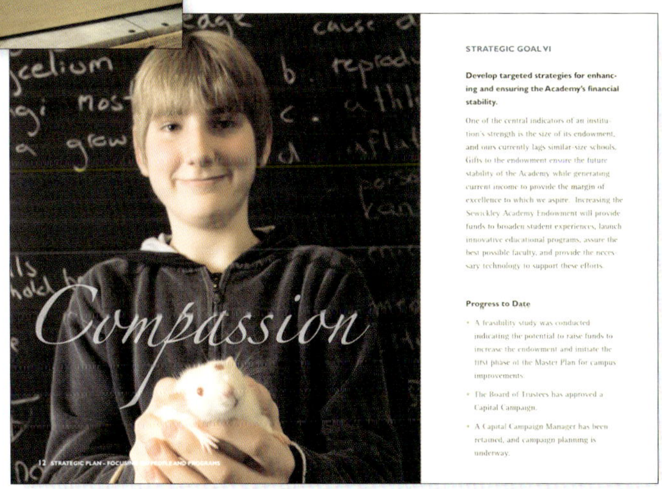

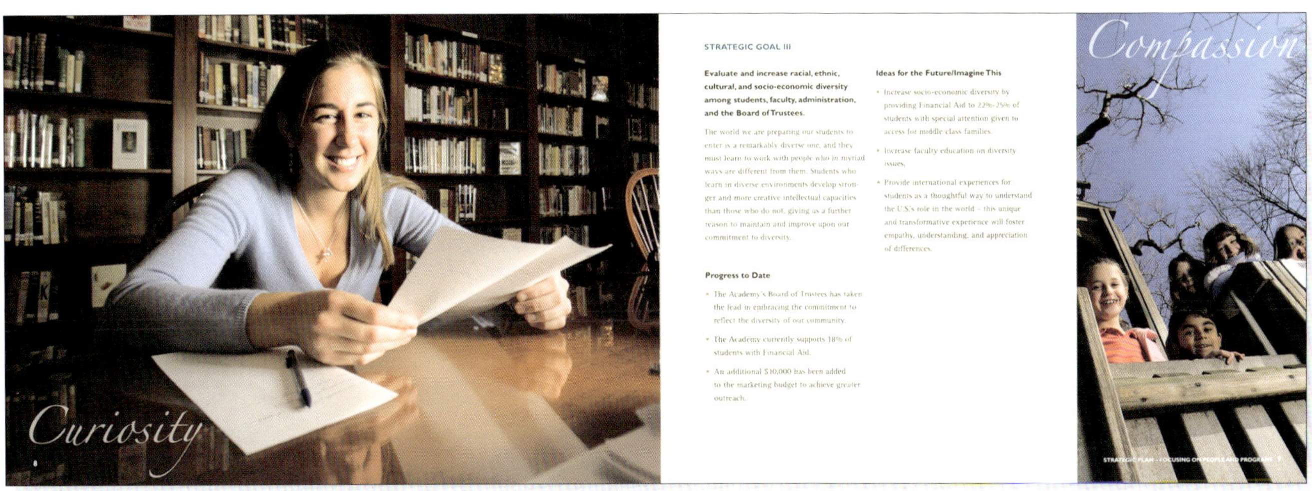

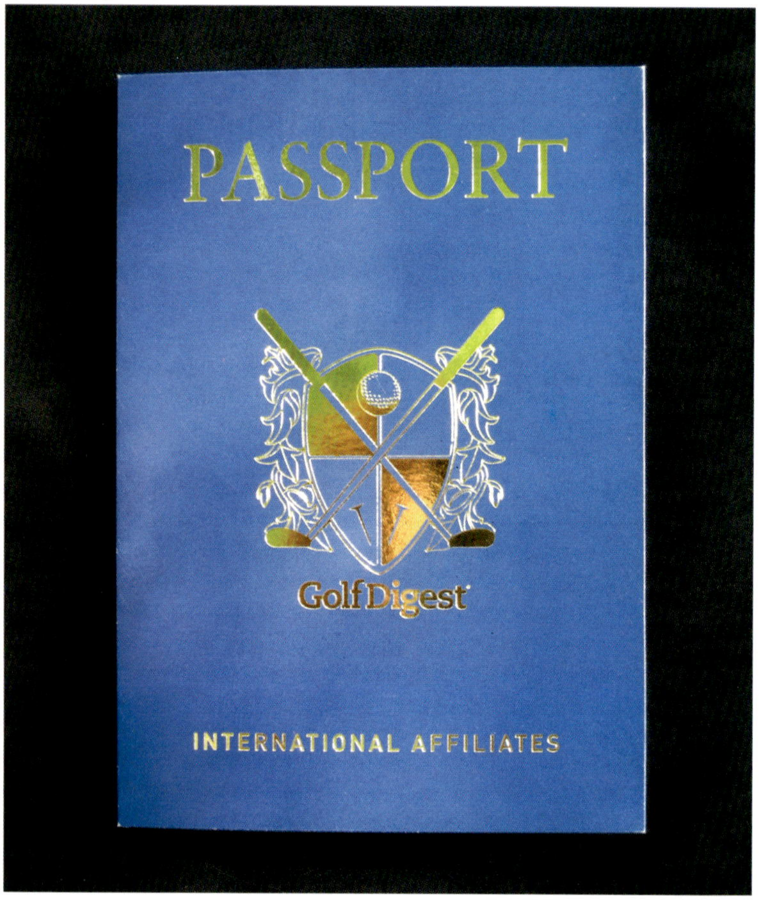

client
Golf Digest
design firm
Golf Digest Marketing Promotion
golfdigest.com
designers
Lance Hertzbach, Deb Chute

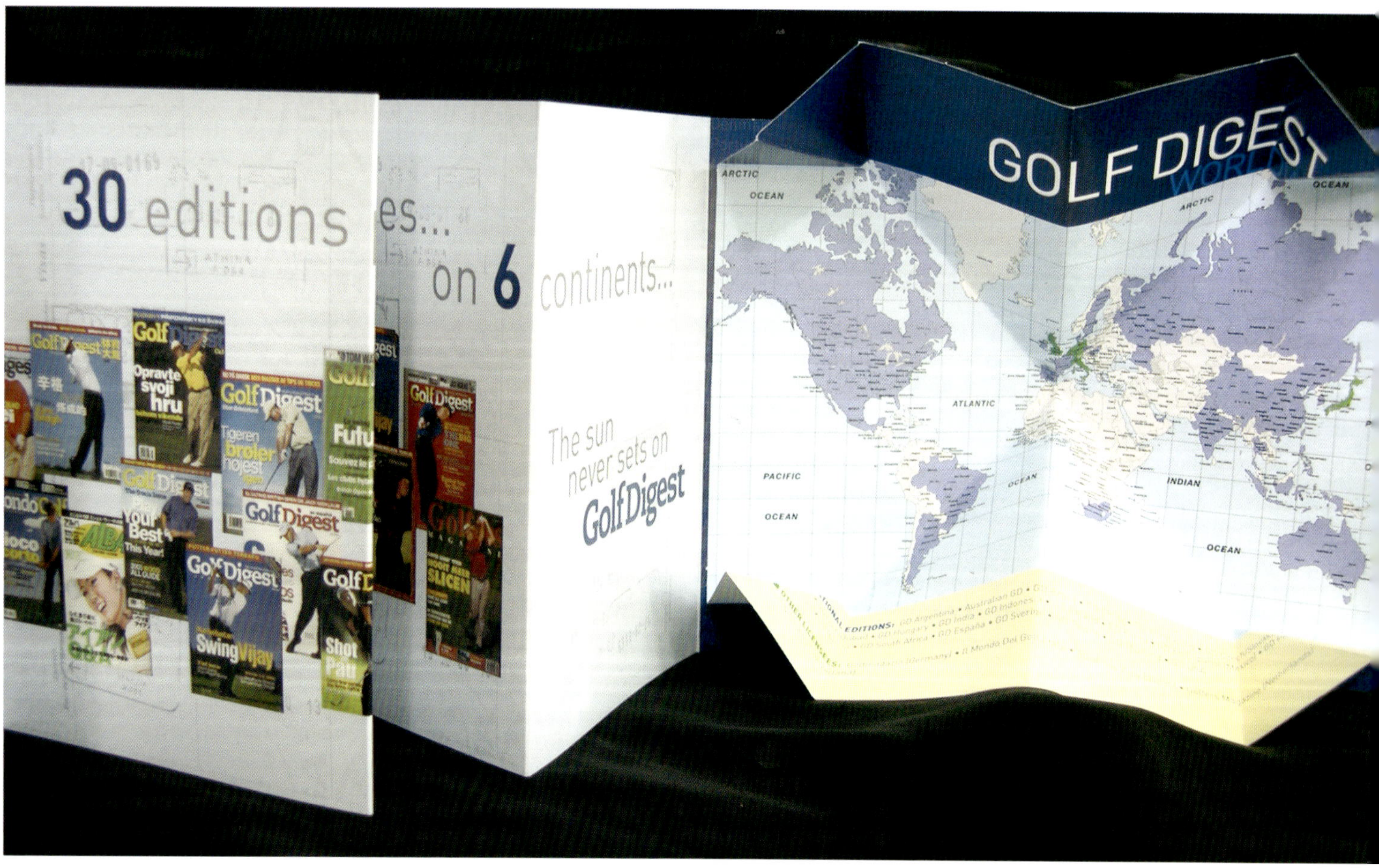

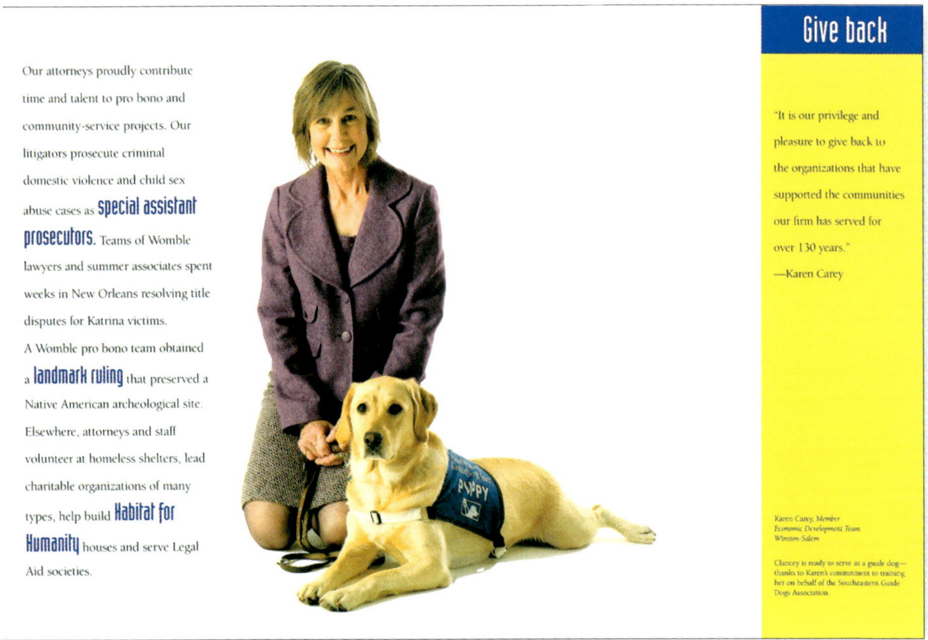

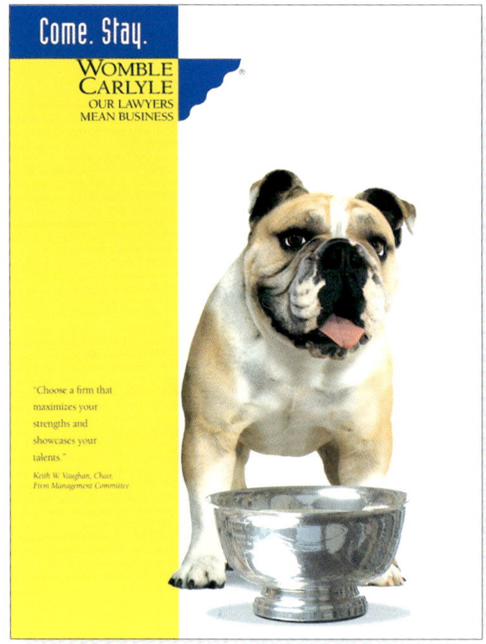

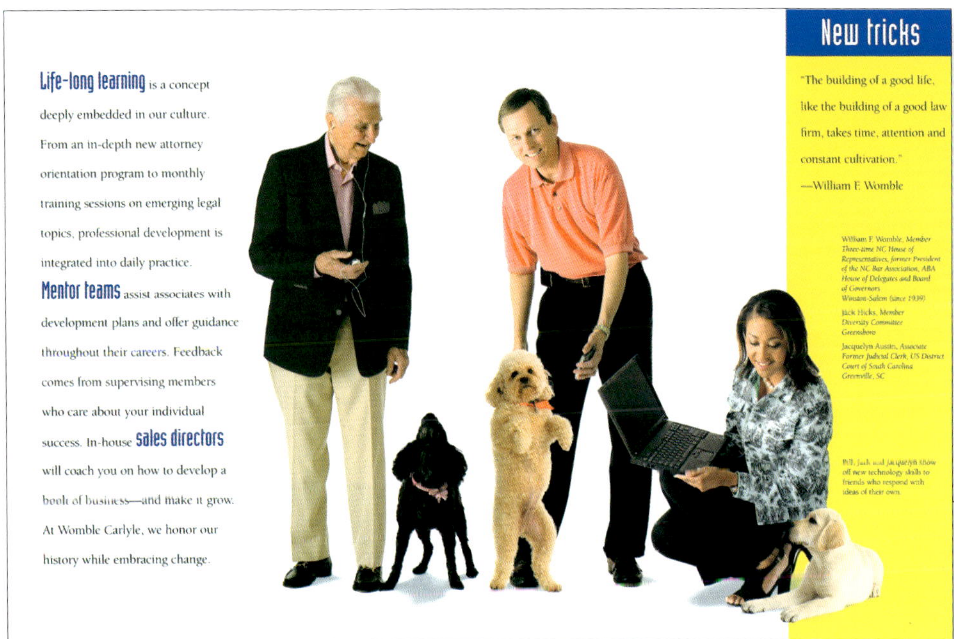

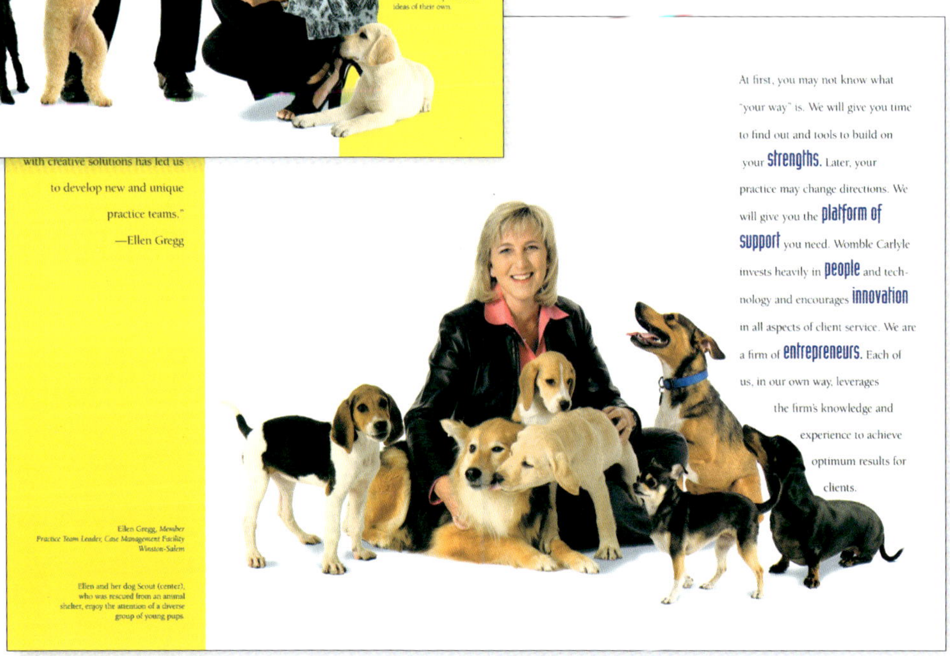

client
Womble Carlyle Sandridge & Rice
design firm
Greenfield/Belser Ltd.
www.gbltd.com
designers
Aaron Thornburgh, Burkey Belser

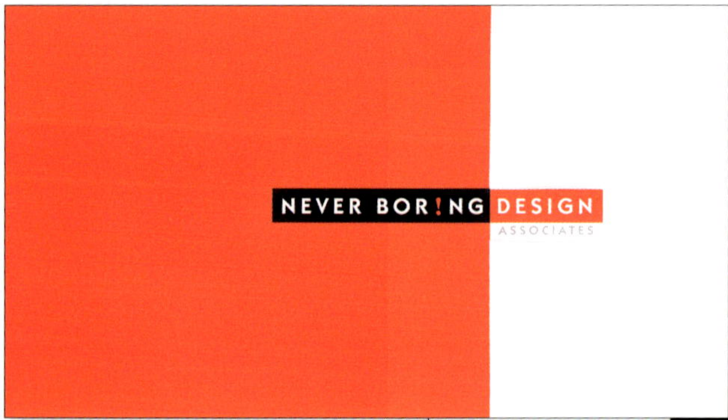

client
Never Boring Design Assoc.
design firm
Never Boring Design Assoc.
www.neverboring.com
designers
Julie Orona, Katrina Furton,
Shawna Bayers, David Boring

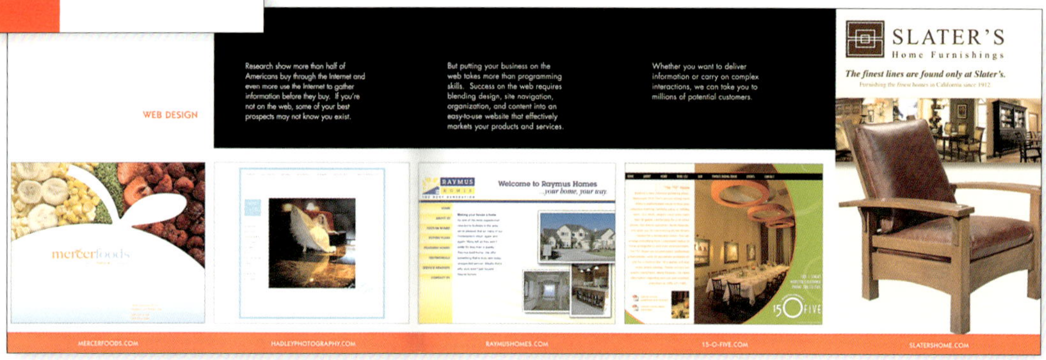

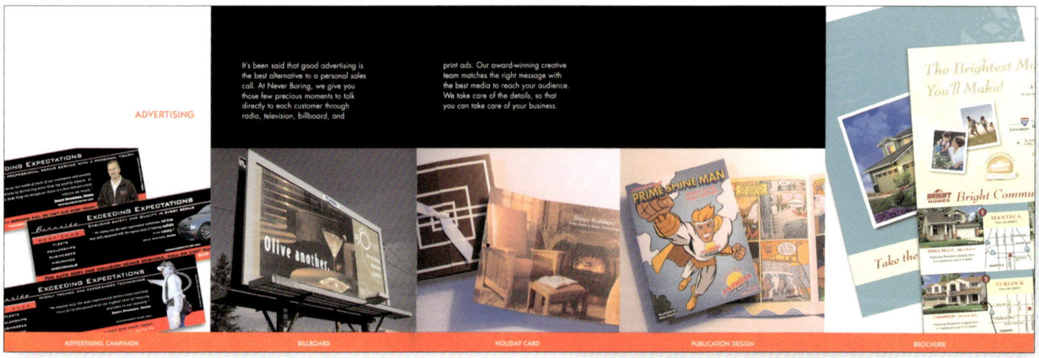

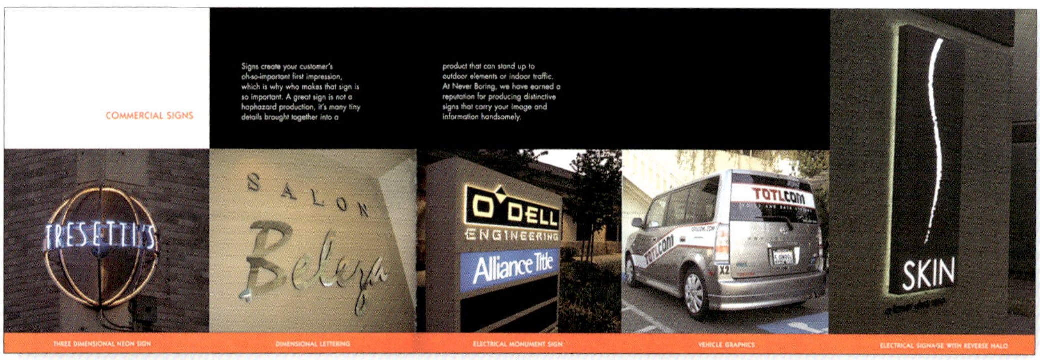

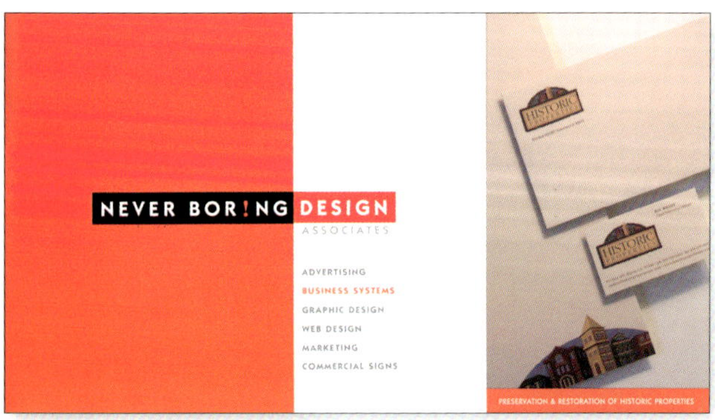

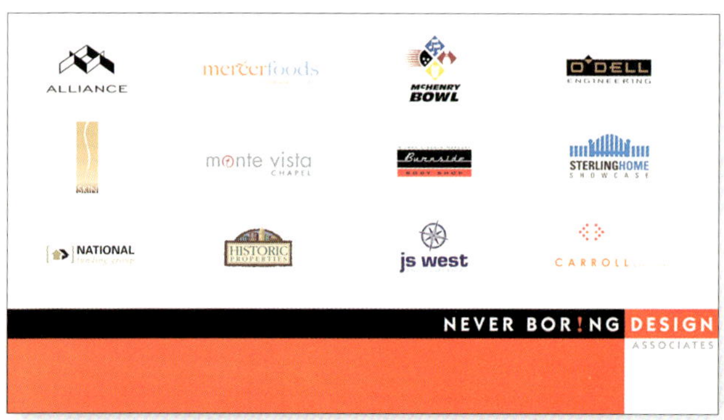

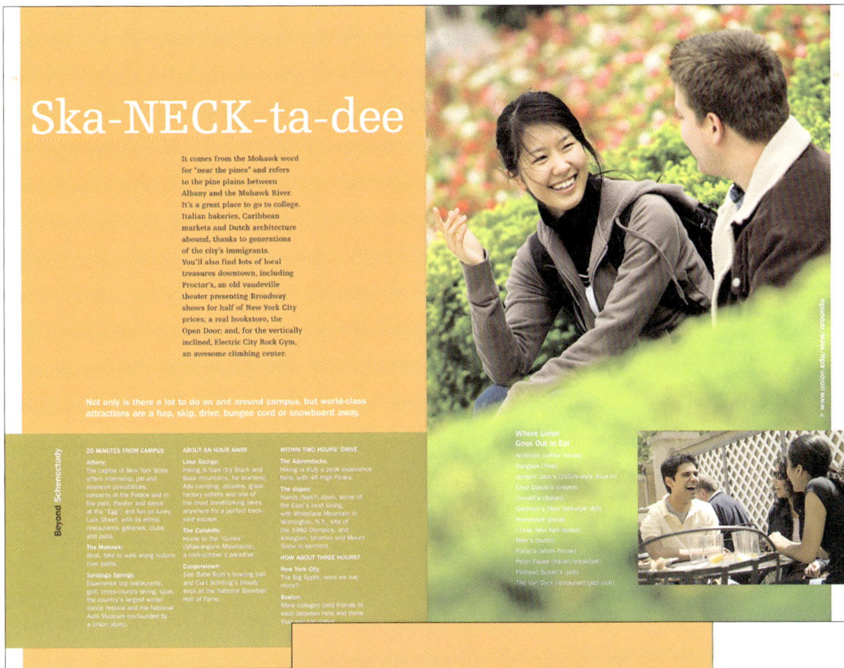

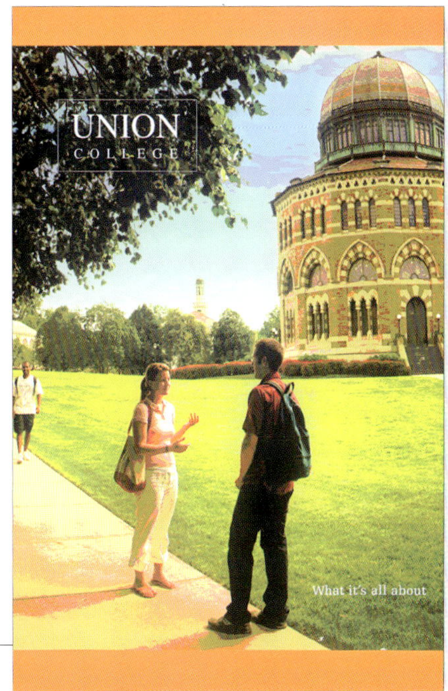

client
Union College
design firm
kor group
www.kor.com
designers
Jim Gibson, MB Jarosik

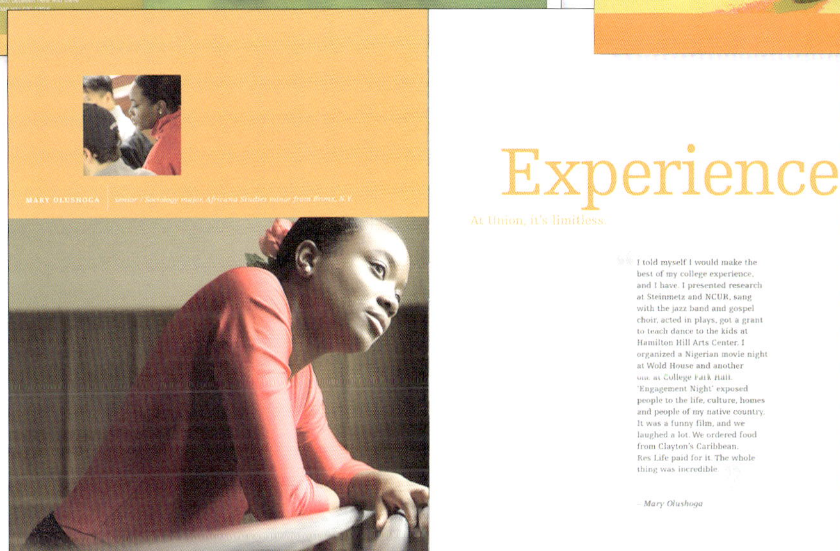

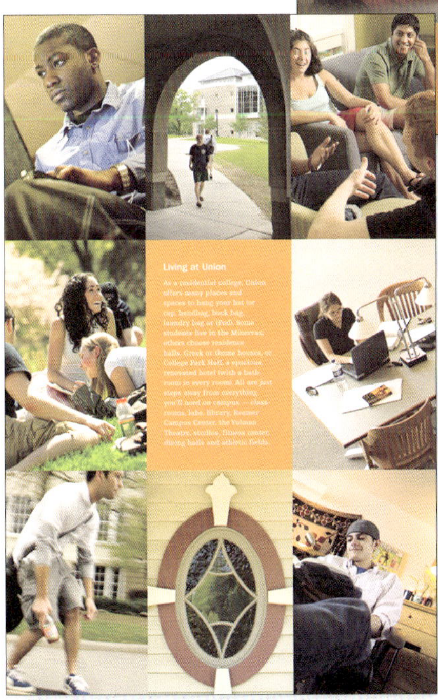

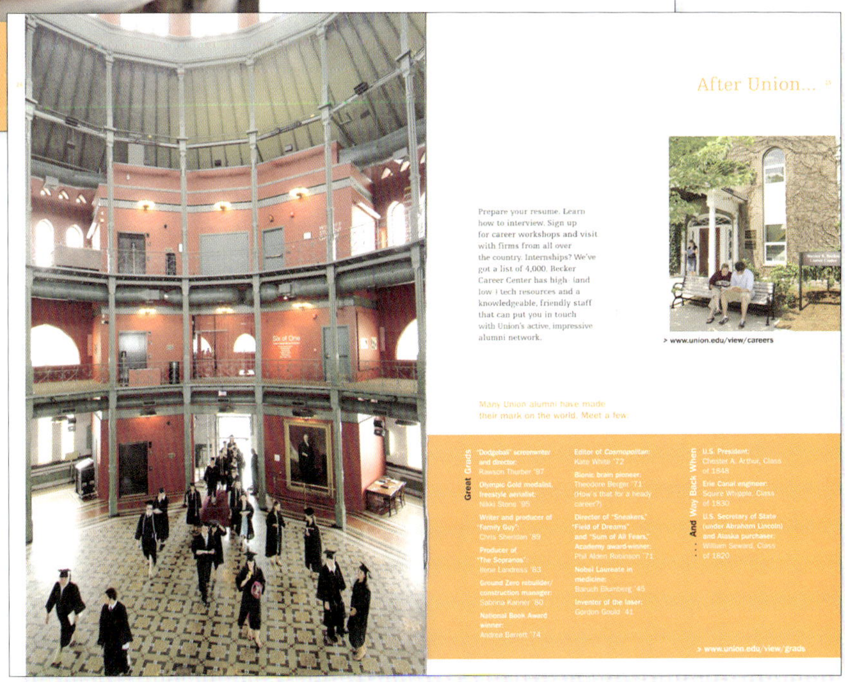

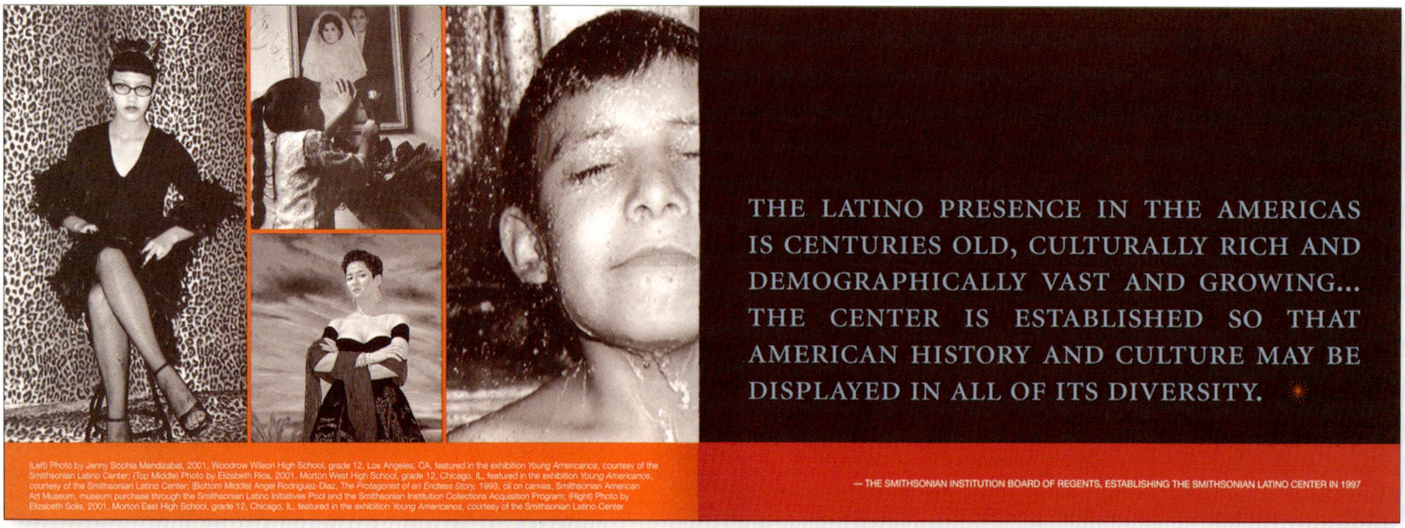

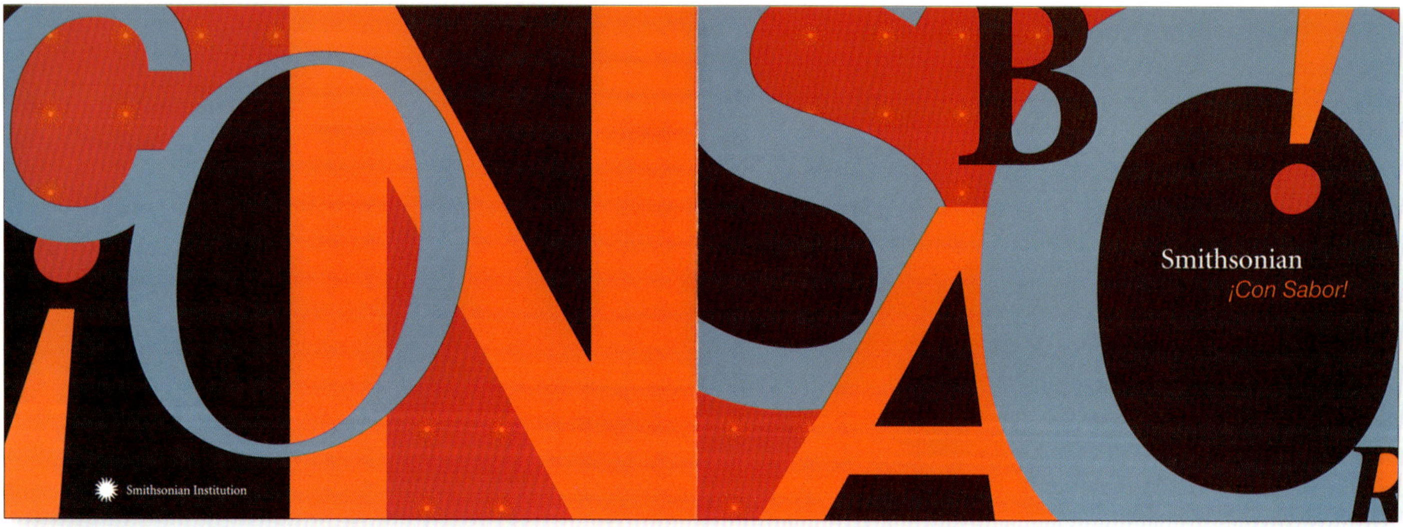

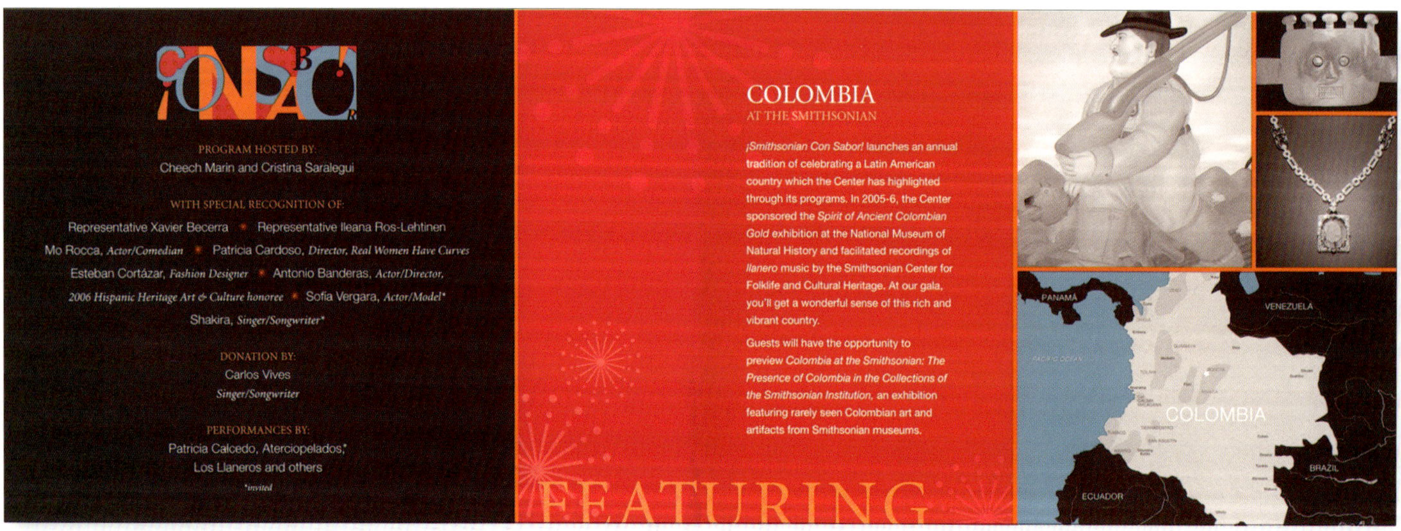

client
Smithsonian Latino Center

design firm
Grafik Marketing Communications
www.grafik.com

designers
Gregg Glaviano, Mila Arrisueno, Lynn Murphy, Regina Esposito

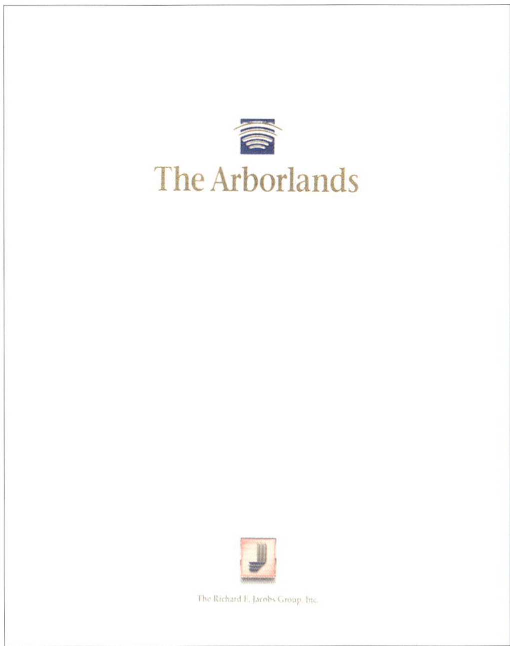

client
The Richard E. Jacobs Group
design firm
Herip Design Associates, Inc.
www.heripassociates.com
designers
Walter M. Herip, Jen Hollo Crabtree,
John R. Menter

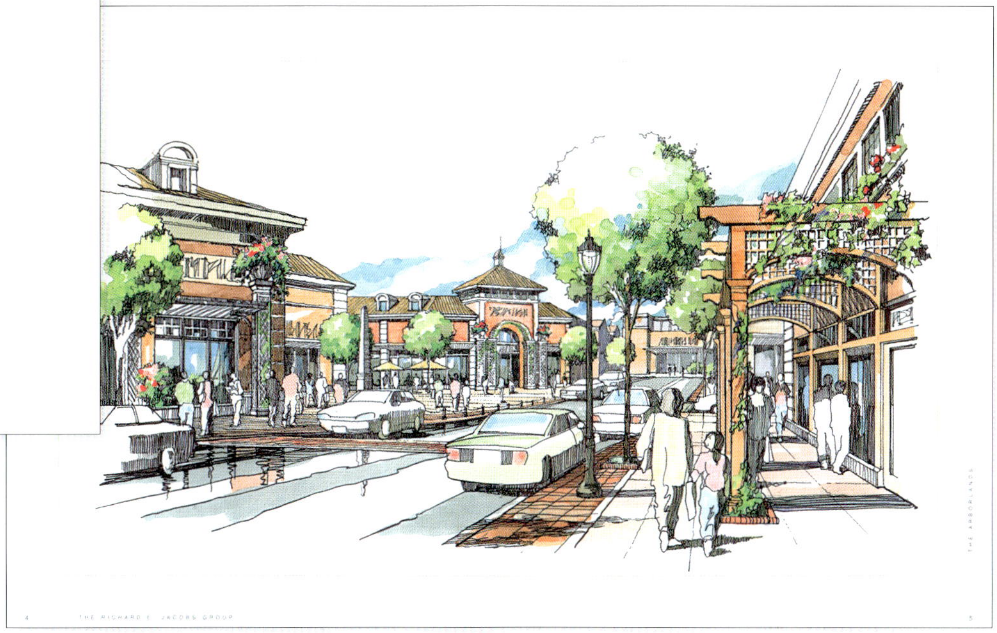

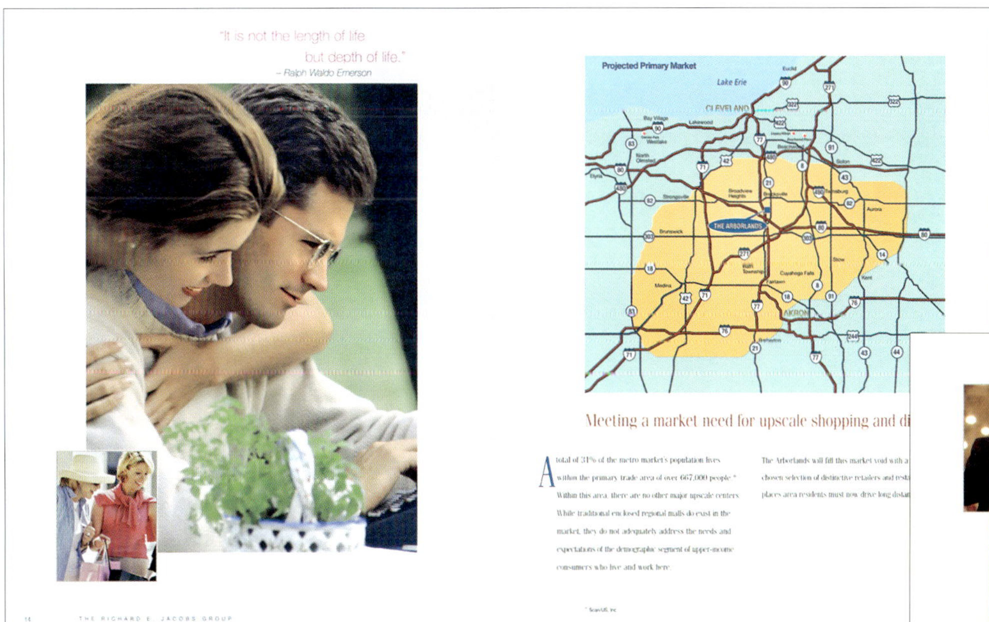

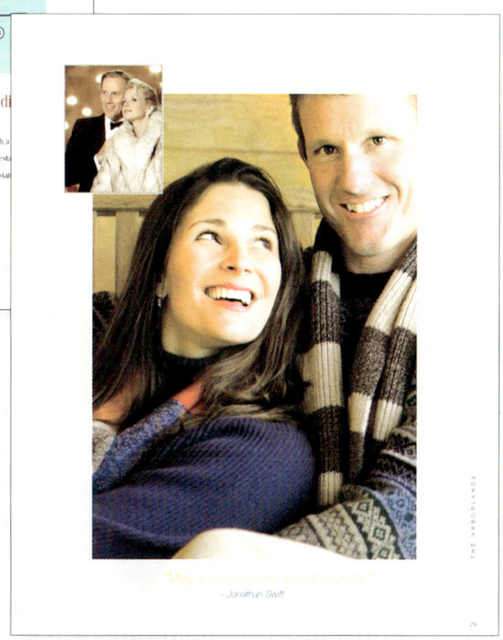

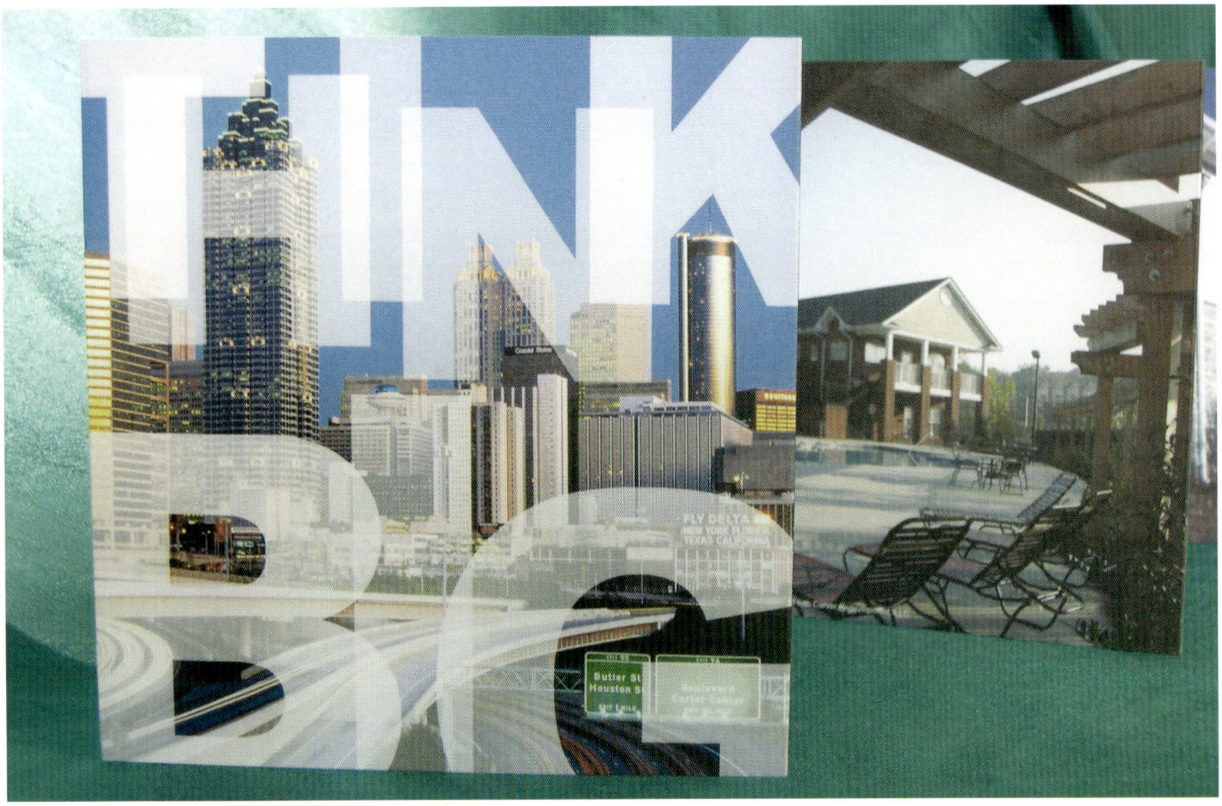

client
Atlanta Housing Authority
design firm
Chris Cottos
www.chriscottos.com
designer
Chris Cottos

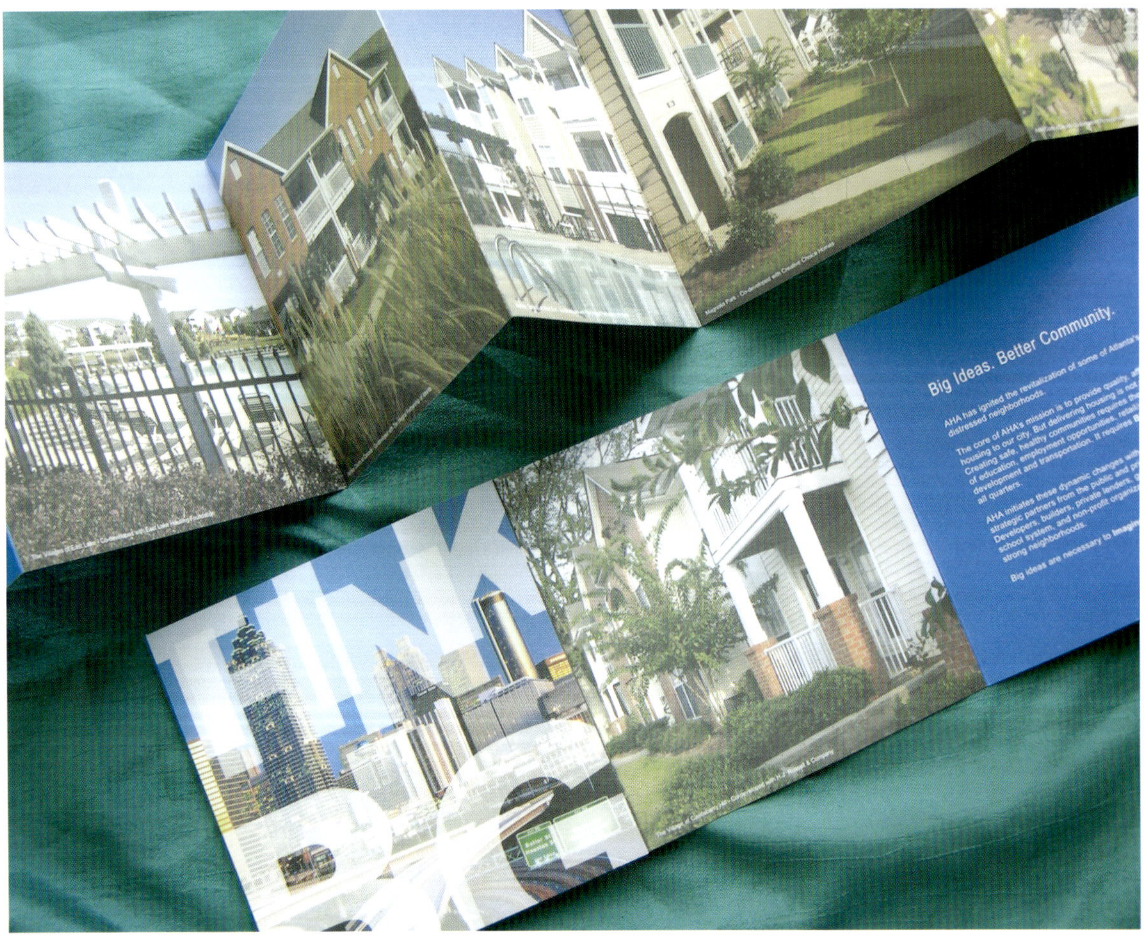

client
Schnitzer Northwest
design firm
Hornall Anderson Design Works
www.hadw.com
designers
John Anicker, Andrew Wicklund, Leo Raymundo, Kathleen Gibson, Holly Craven

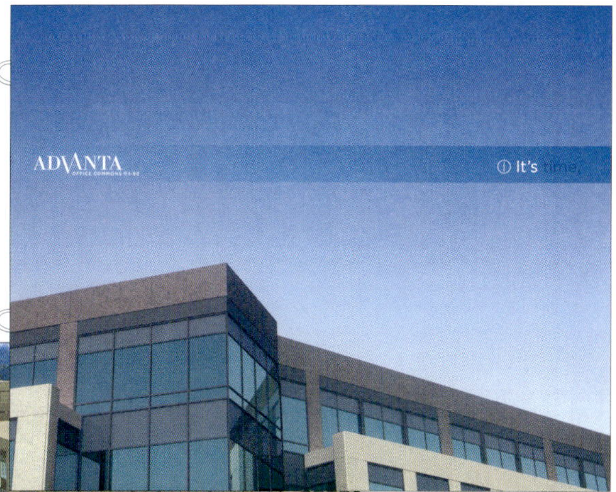

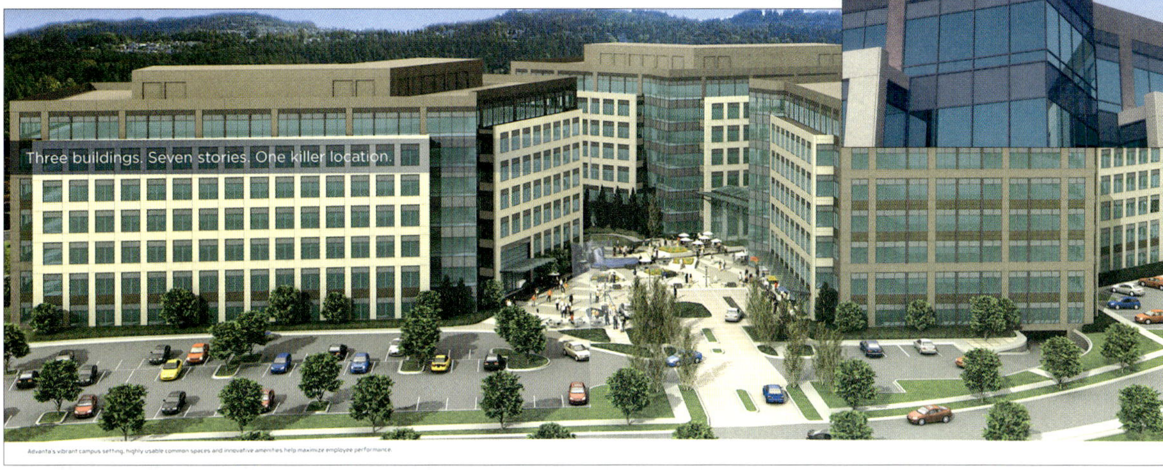

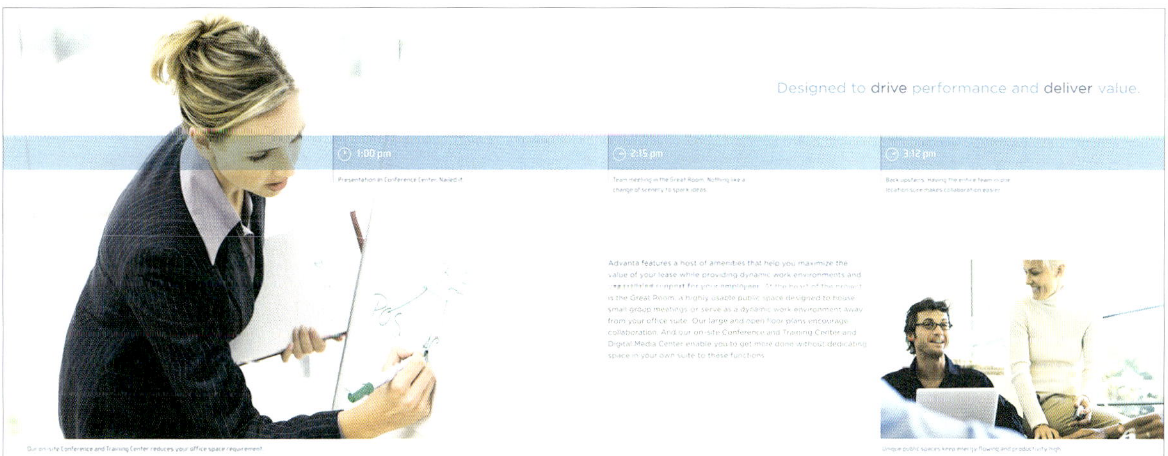

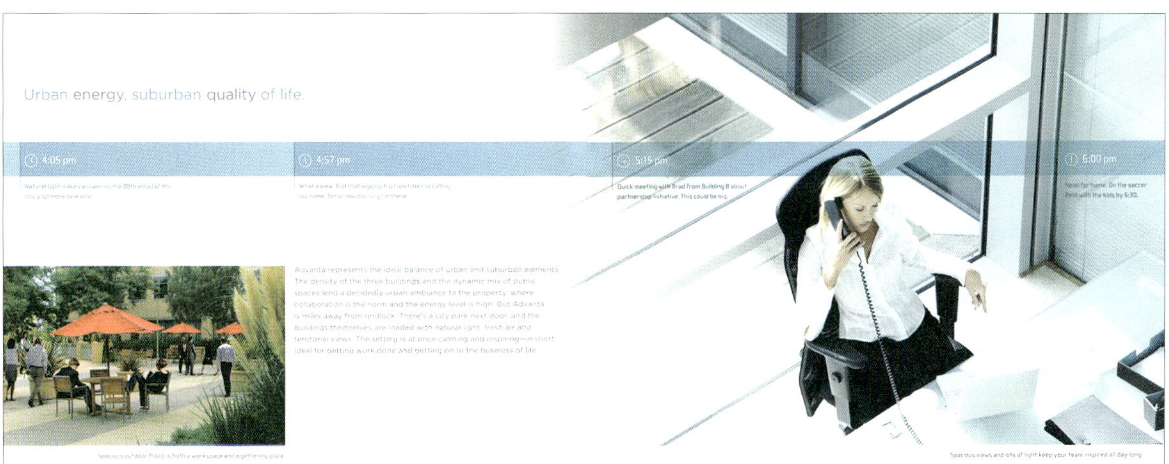

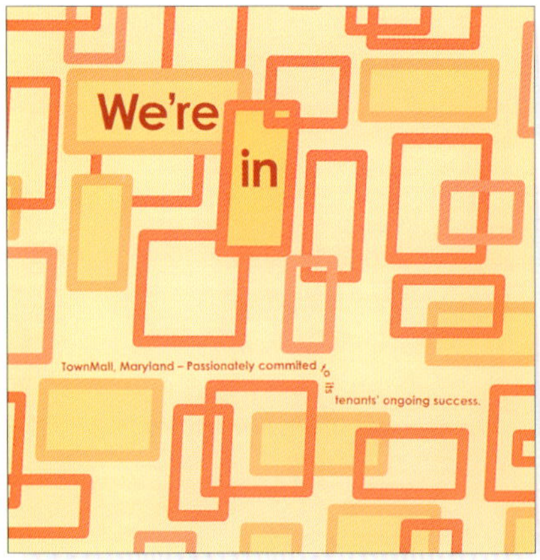

client
TownMall of Westminster
design firm
Gibson Group
www.gibsongrp.com
designer
Andrew Lautner

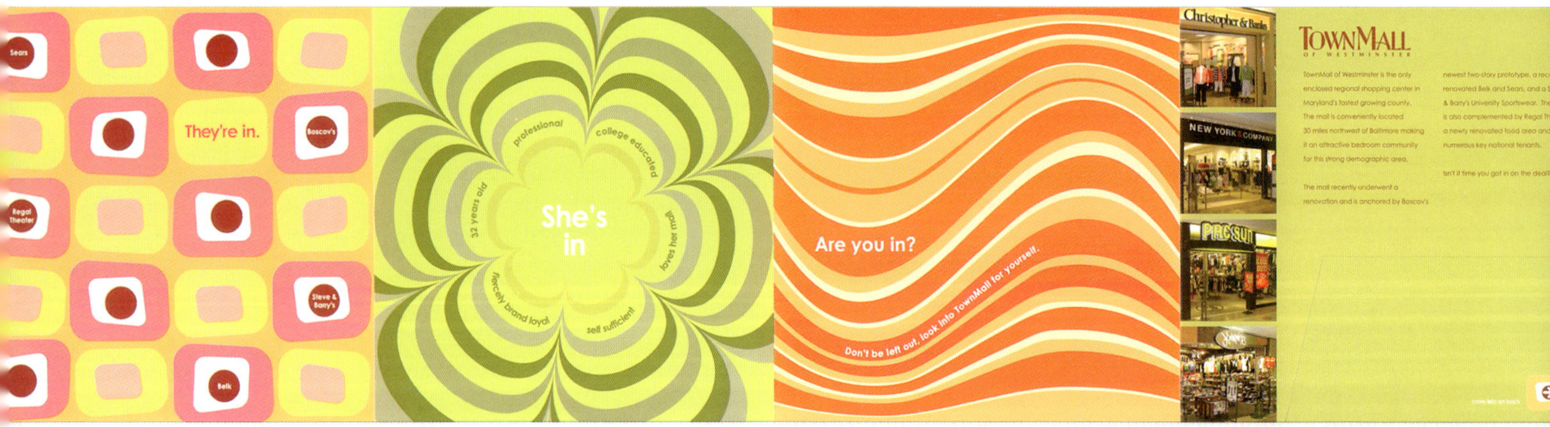

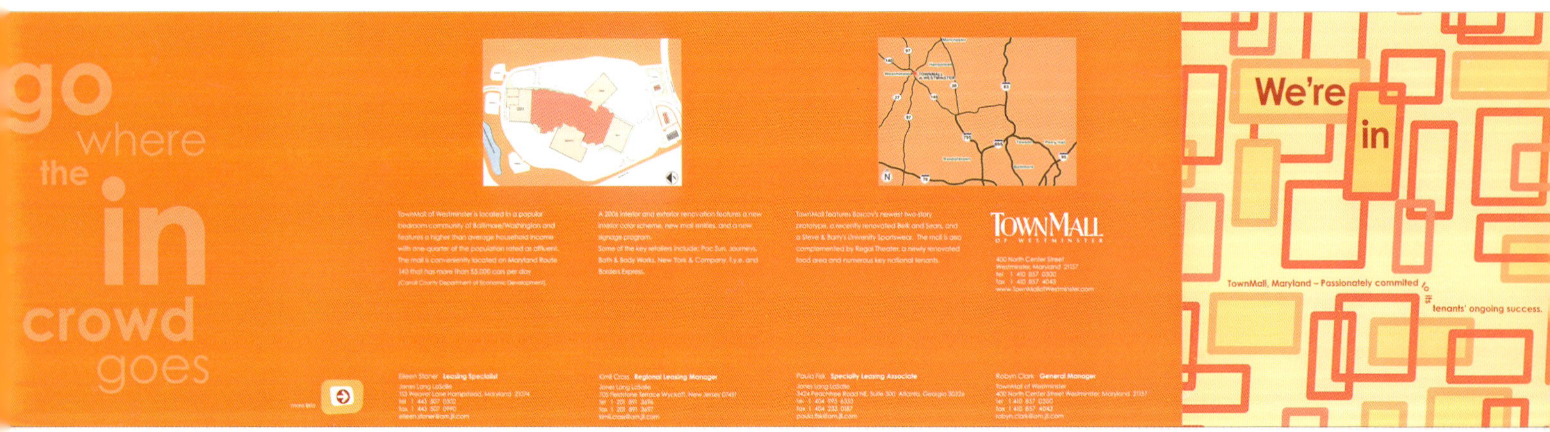

client
Vectrix
design firm
The Bailey Group
www.baileygp.com
designers
Gary LaCroix, Eric Yeager

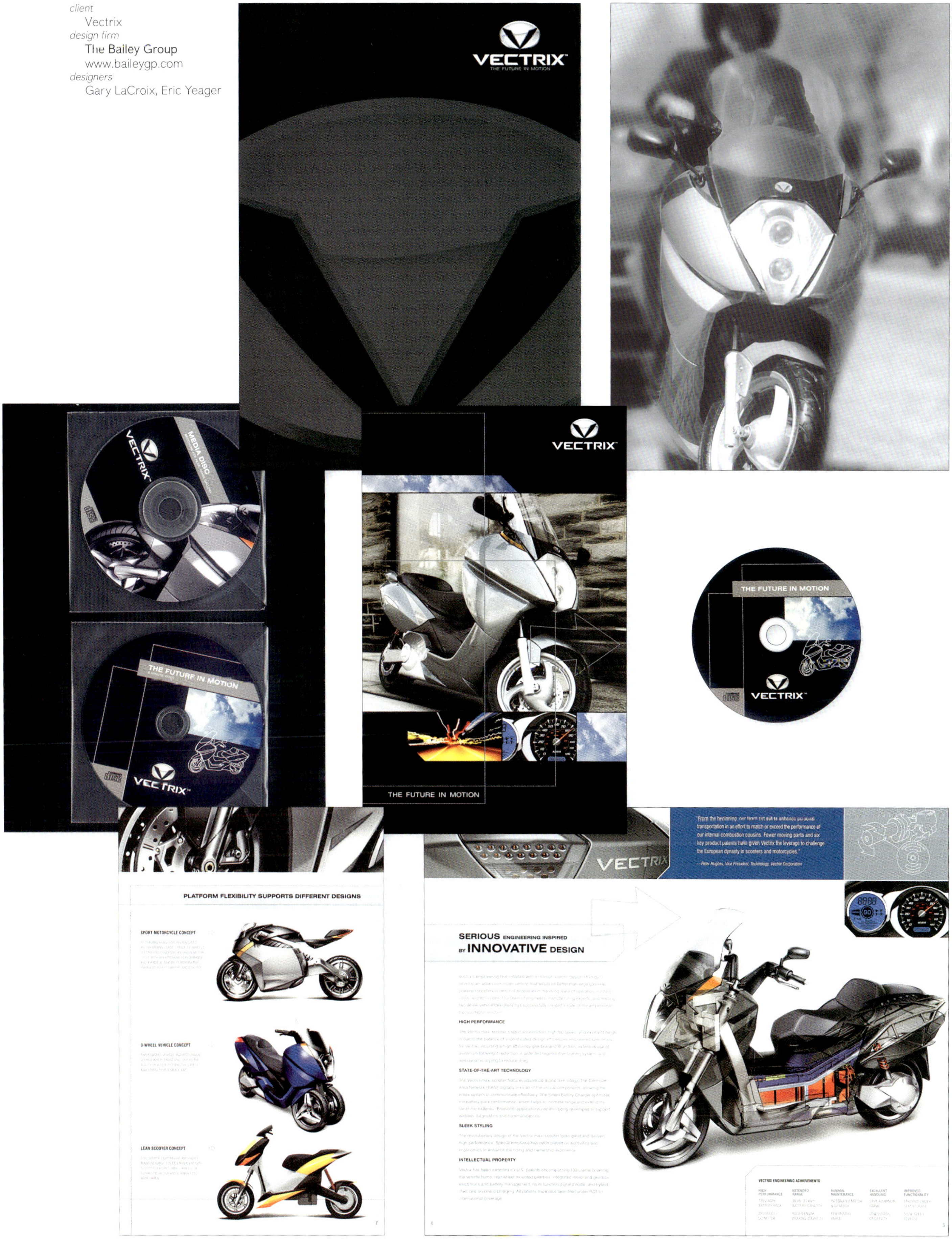

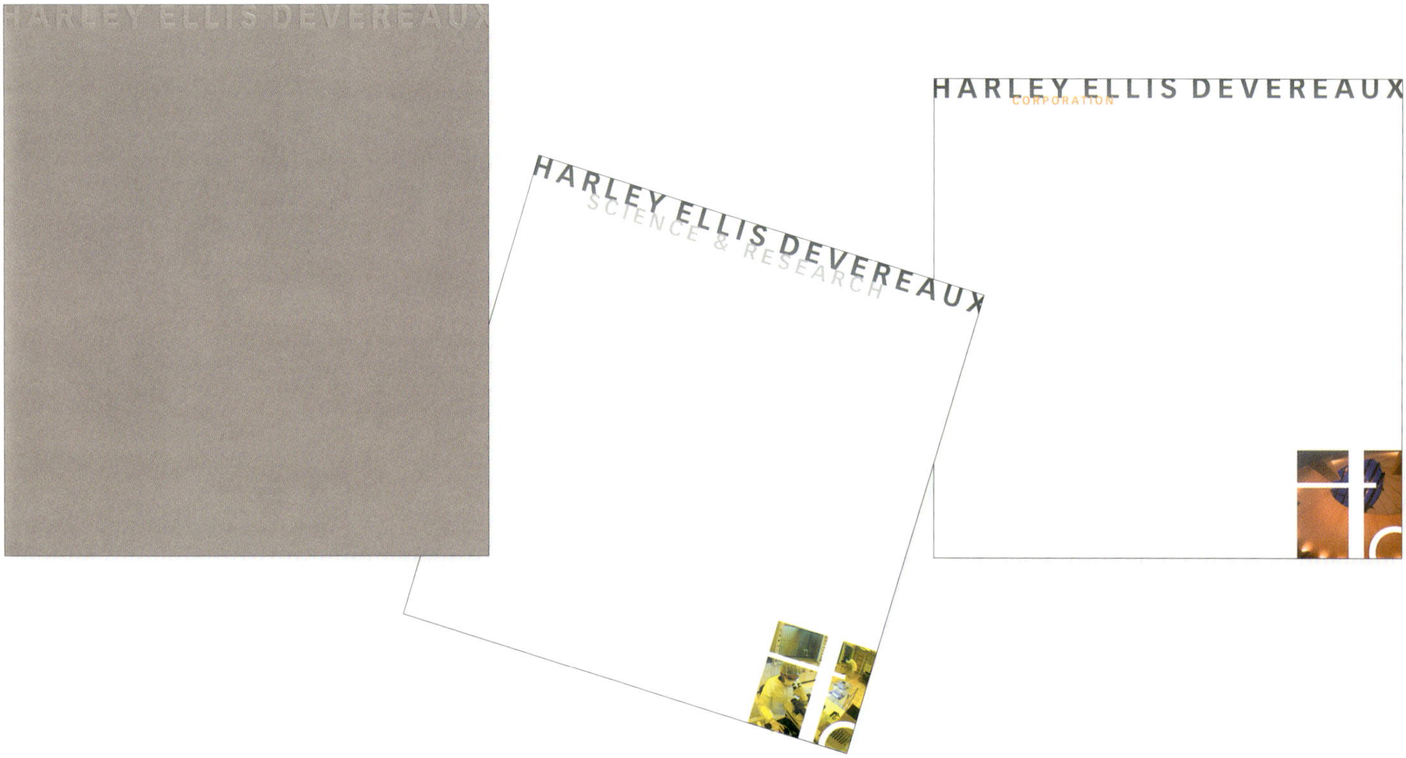

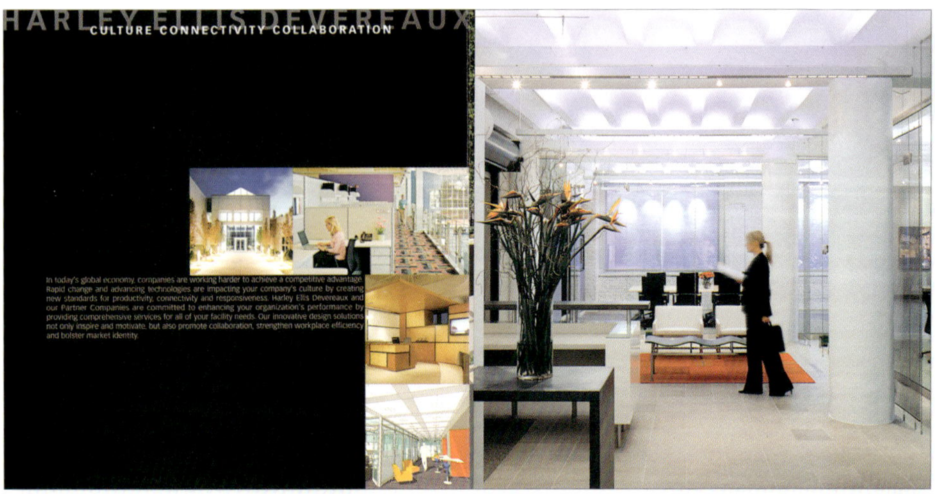

client
Harley Ellis Devereaux
design firm
Skidmore, Inc.
www.skidmorestudio.com
designer
Pete Nothstein

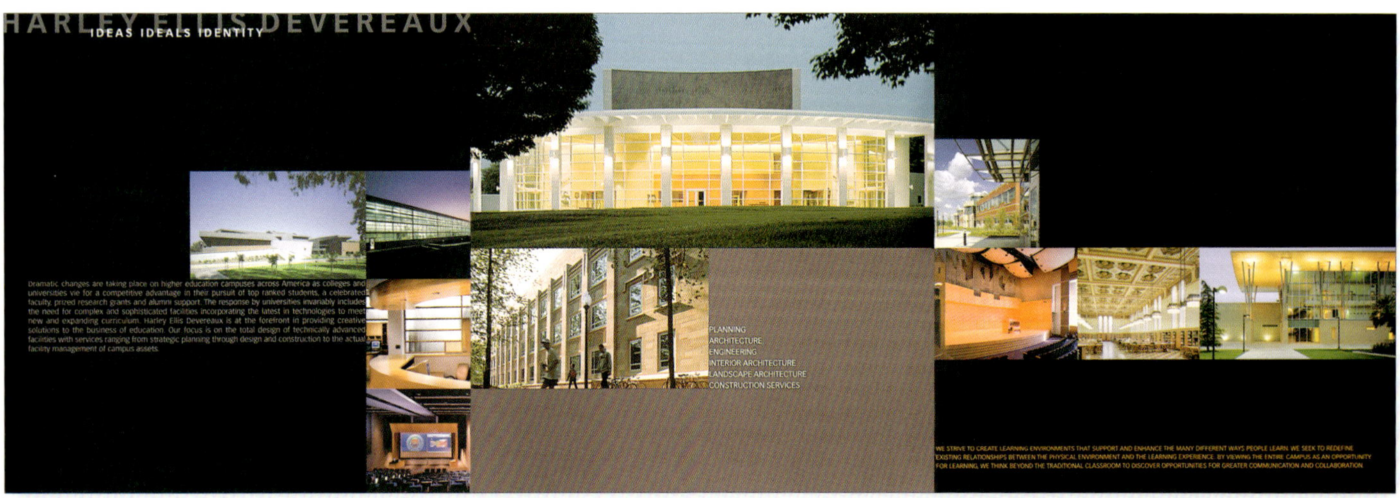

client
Heister House Millworks
design firm
Sire Advertising
www.sireadvertising.com
creative director
Shawn Felty
designers
Bob Henninger,
Jordan Chappell
photographer
The Wild Studio

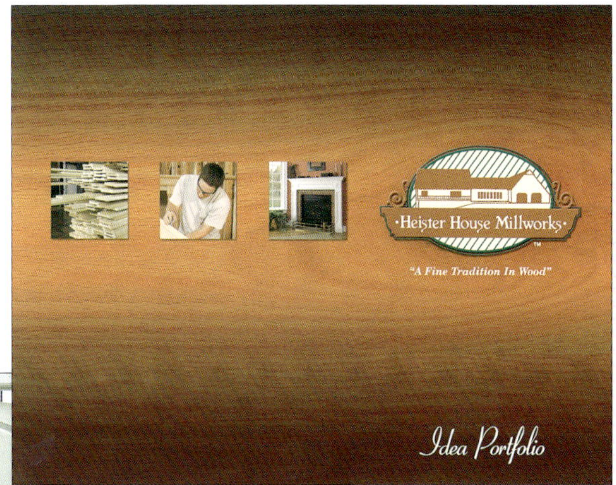

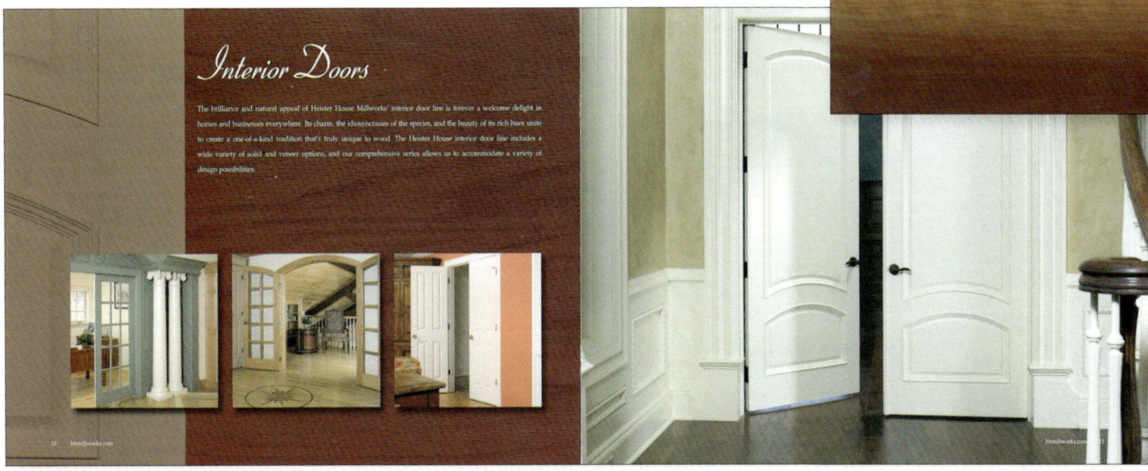

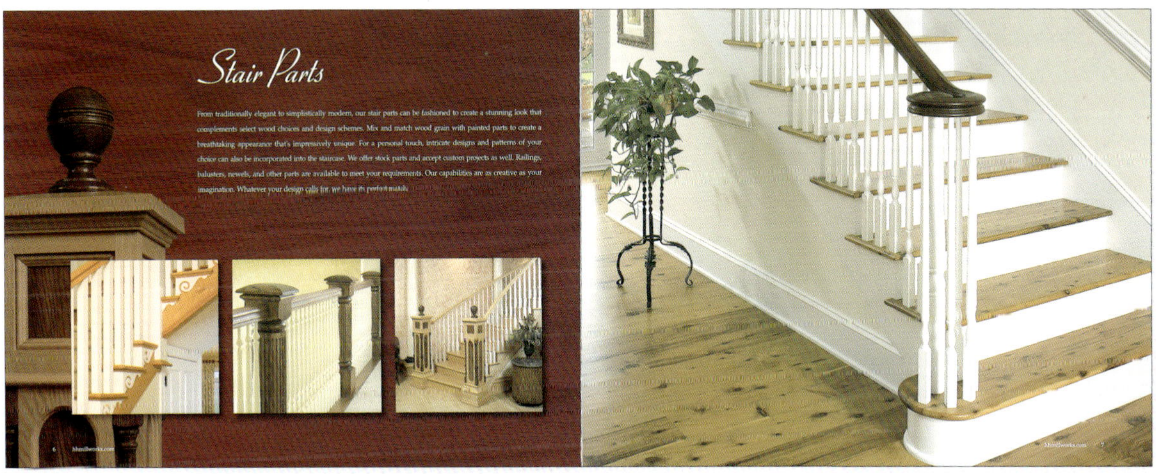

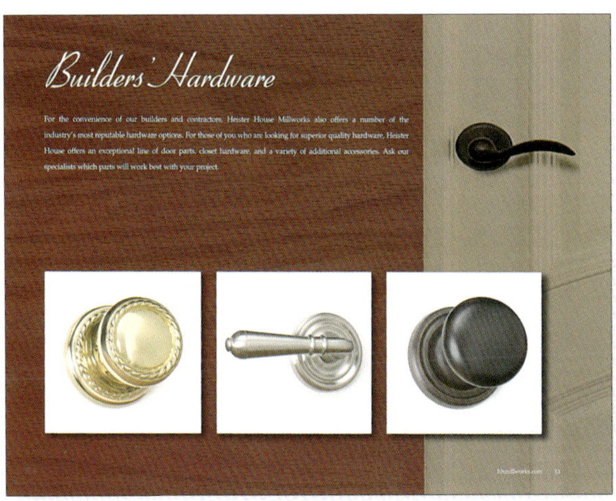

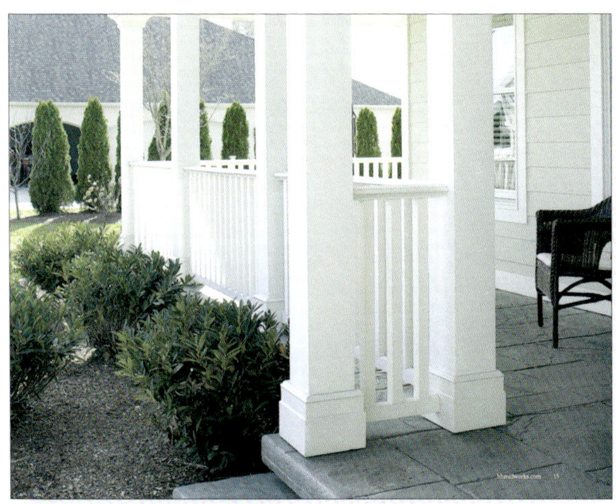

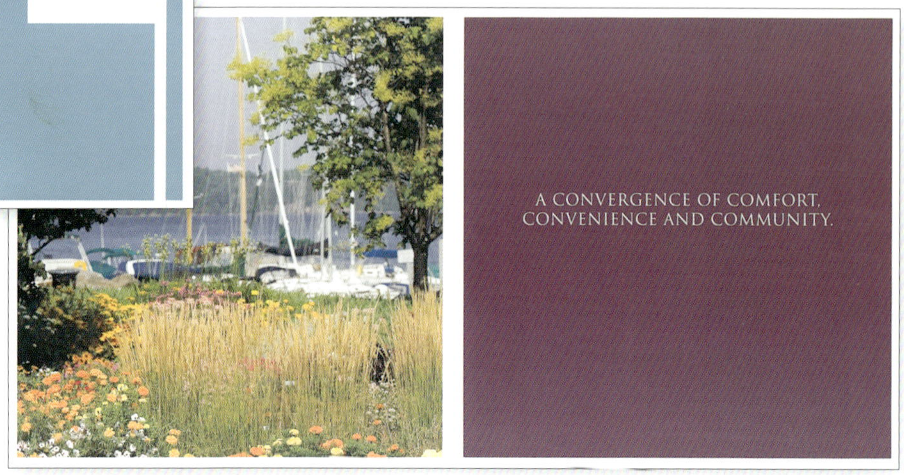

client
Keen's Crossing
design firm
Paul Kaza Associates
www.paulkaza.com
designer
Carissa Butler

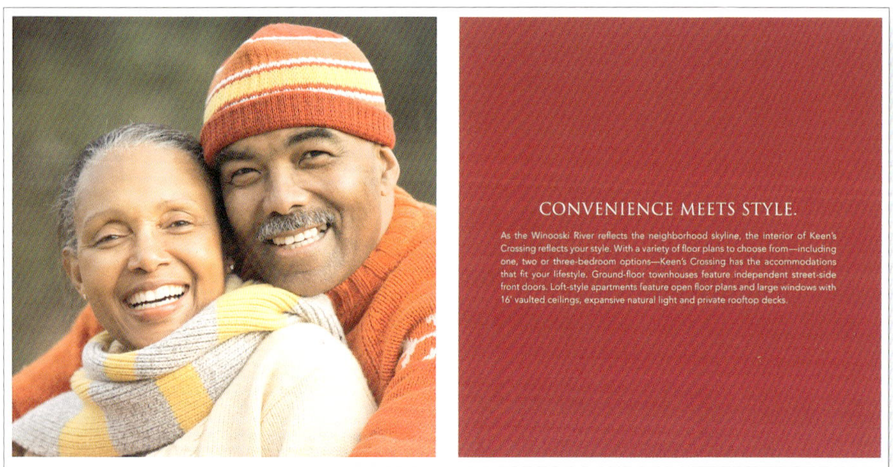

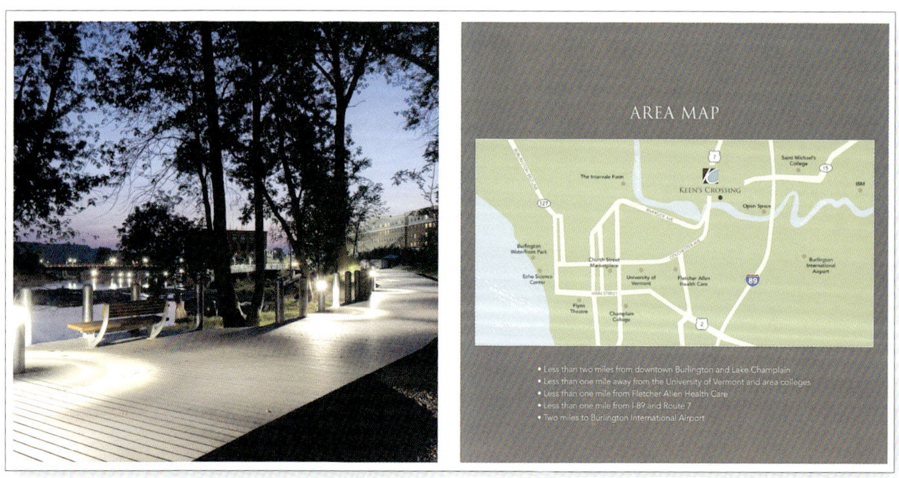

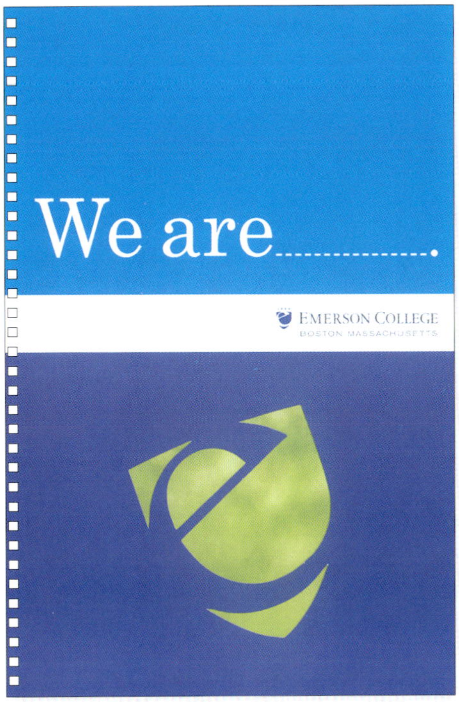

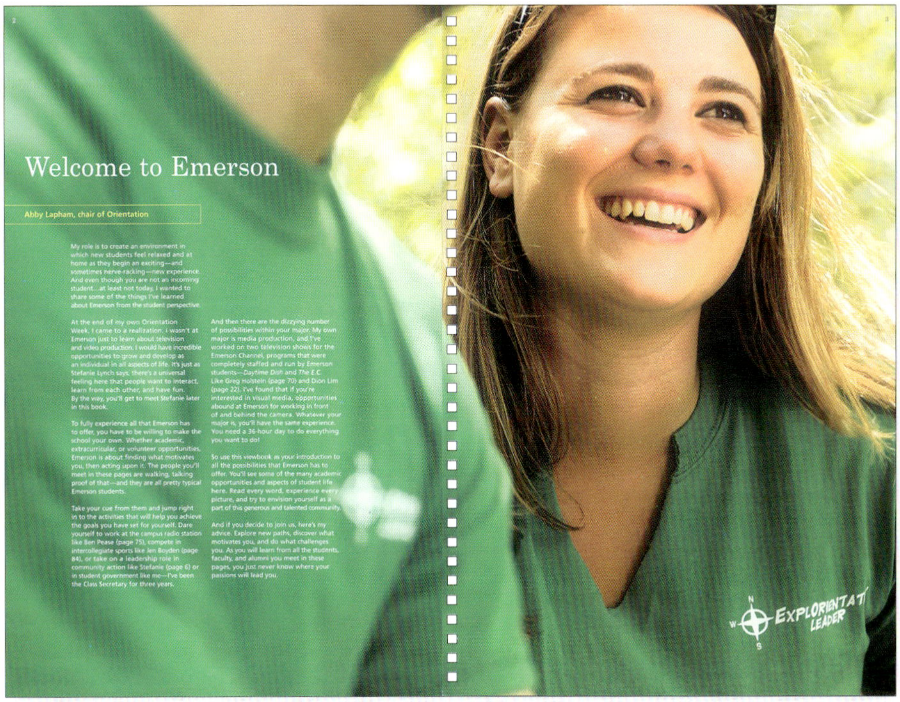

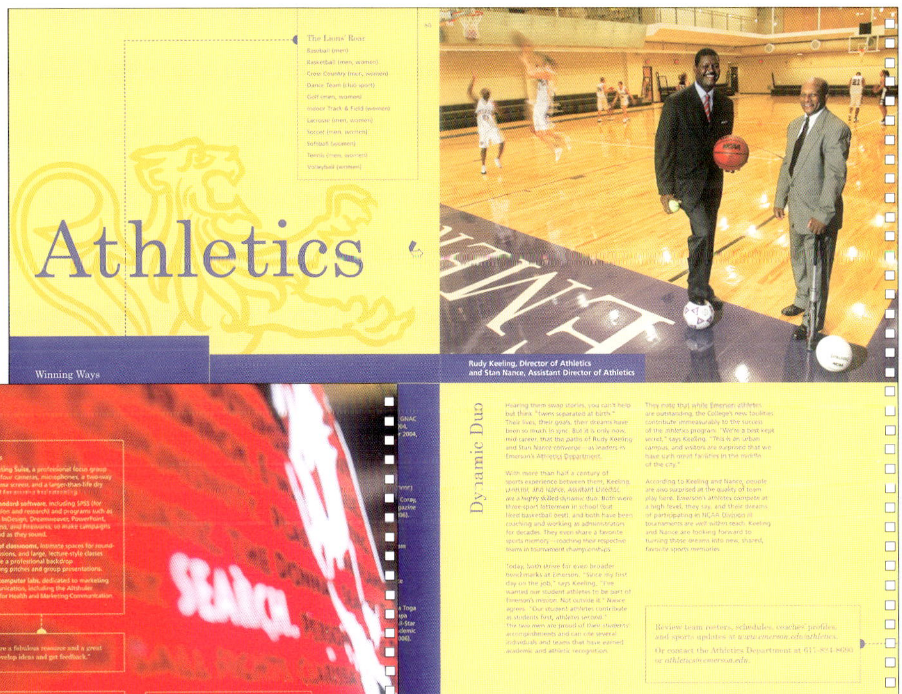

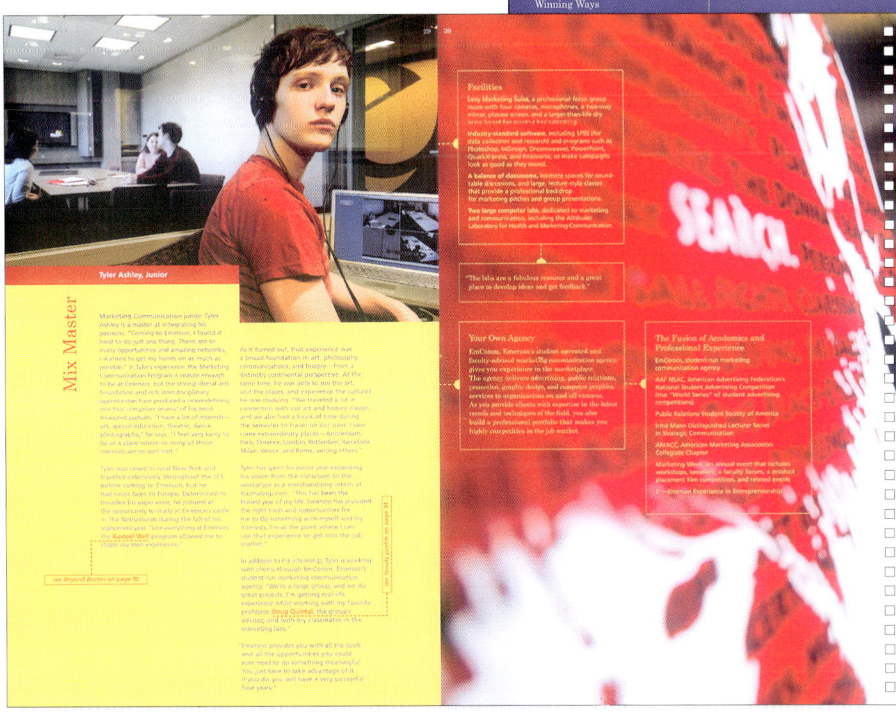

client
Emerson College
design firm
kor group
www.kor.com
designers
James Grady, MB Jarosik

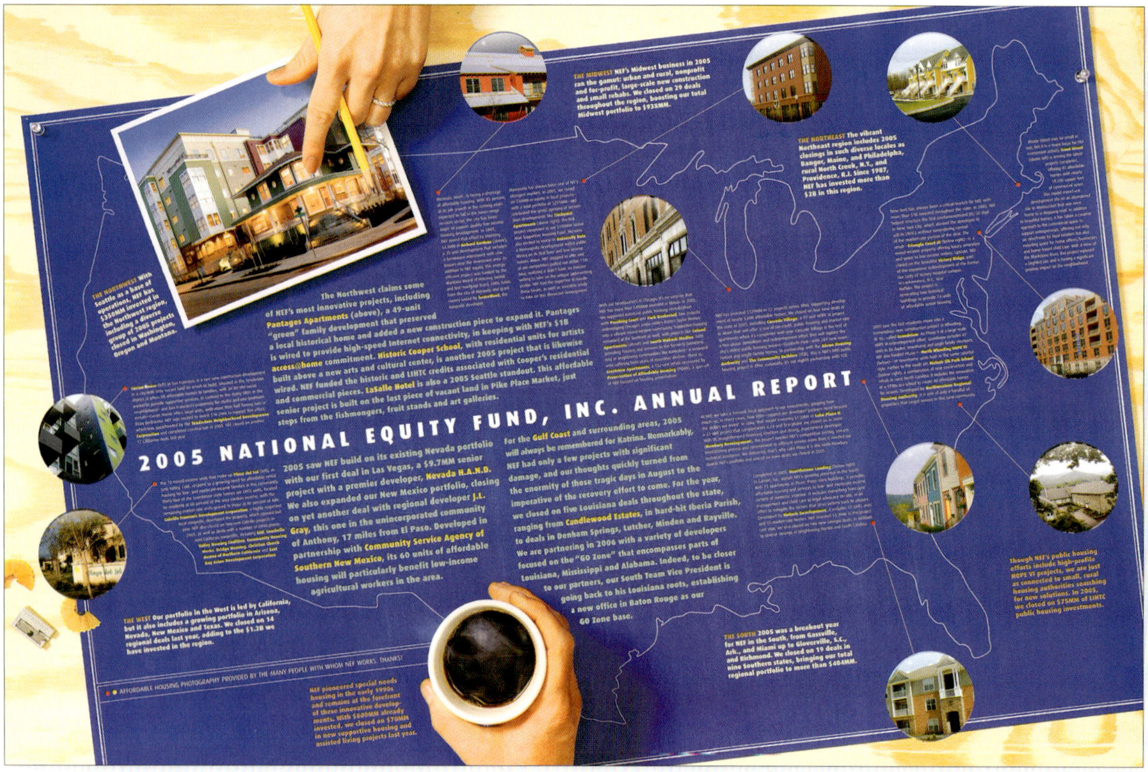

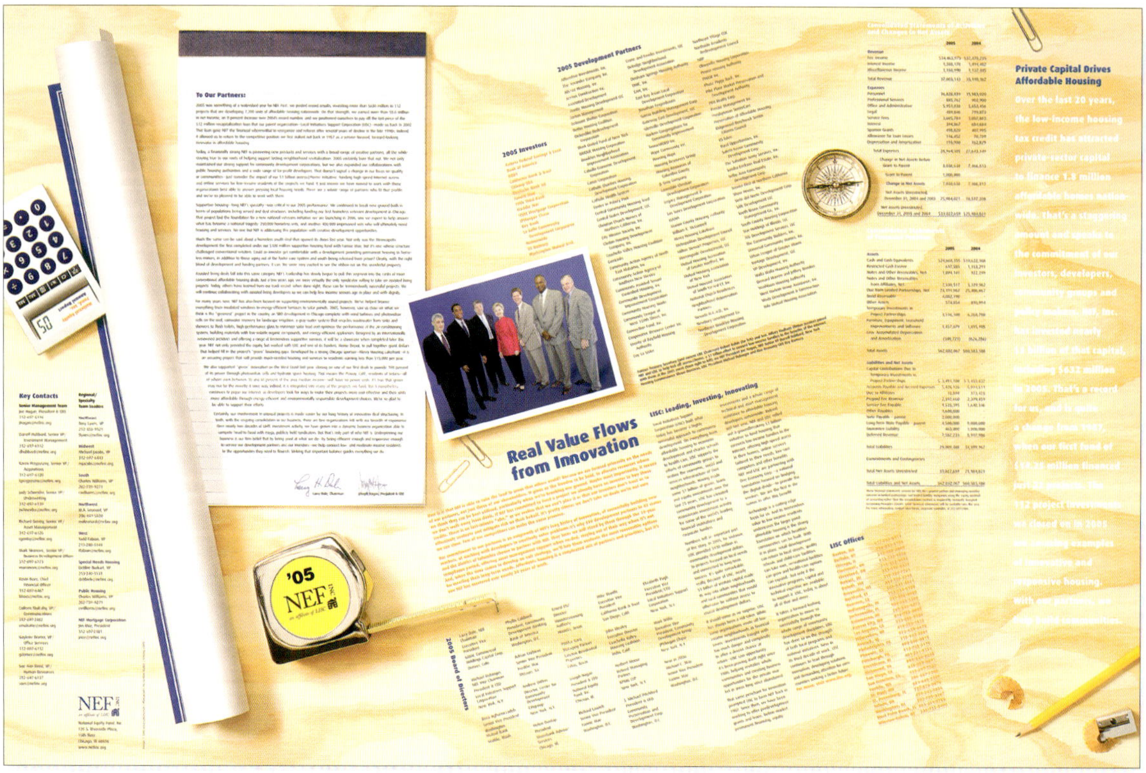

client

National Equity Fund, Inc.

design firm

Namaro Graphic Designs, Inc.

namaro.com

designers

Nadine Robbins,

Wendy Macomber

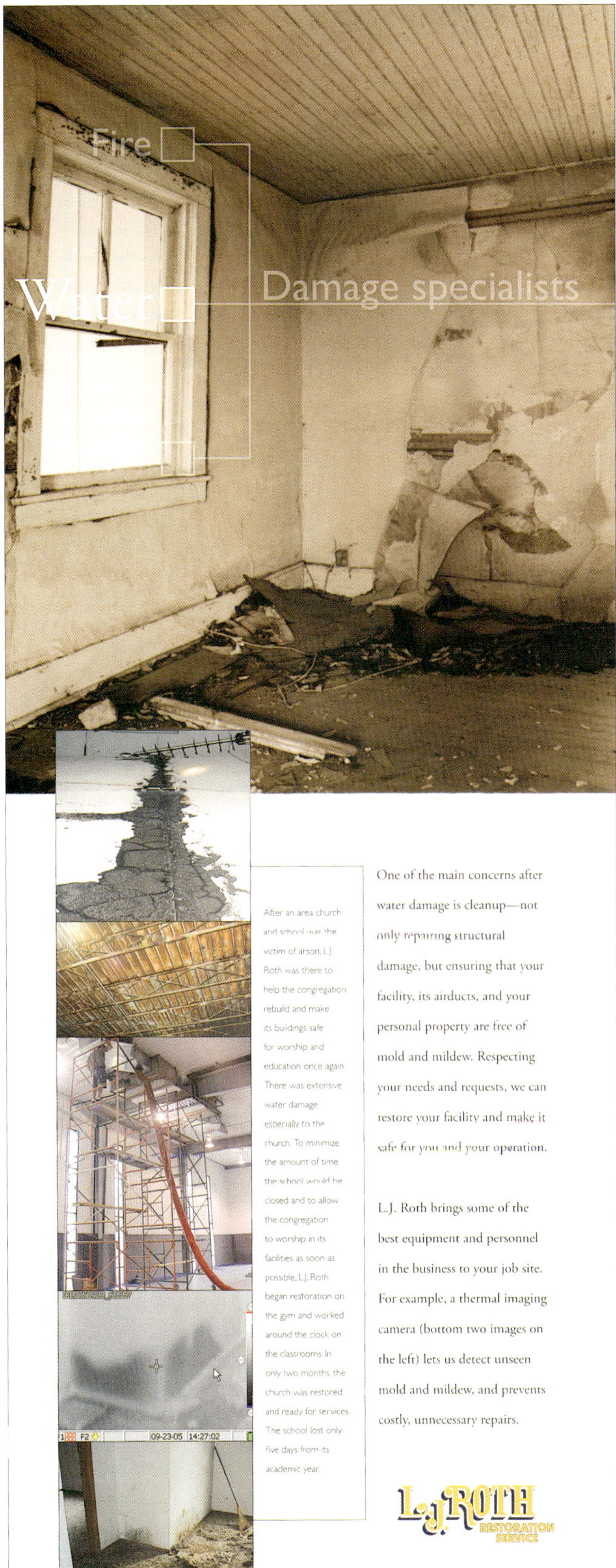

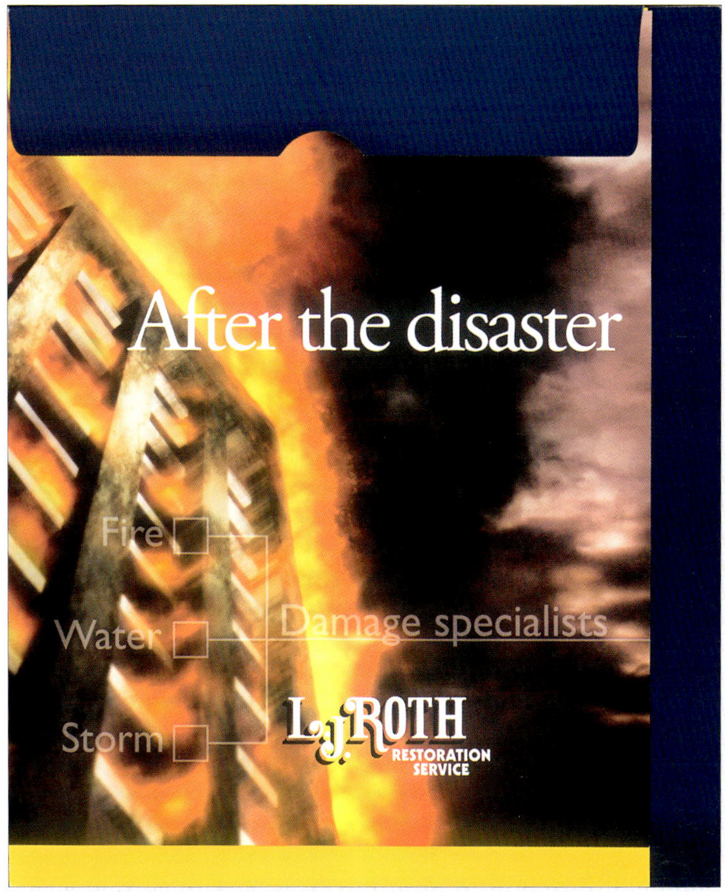

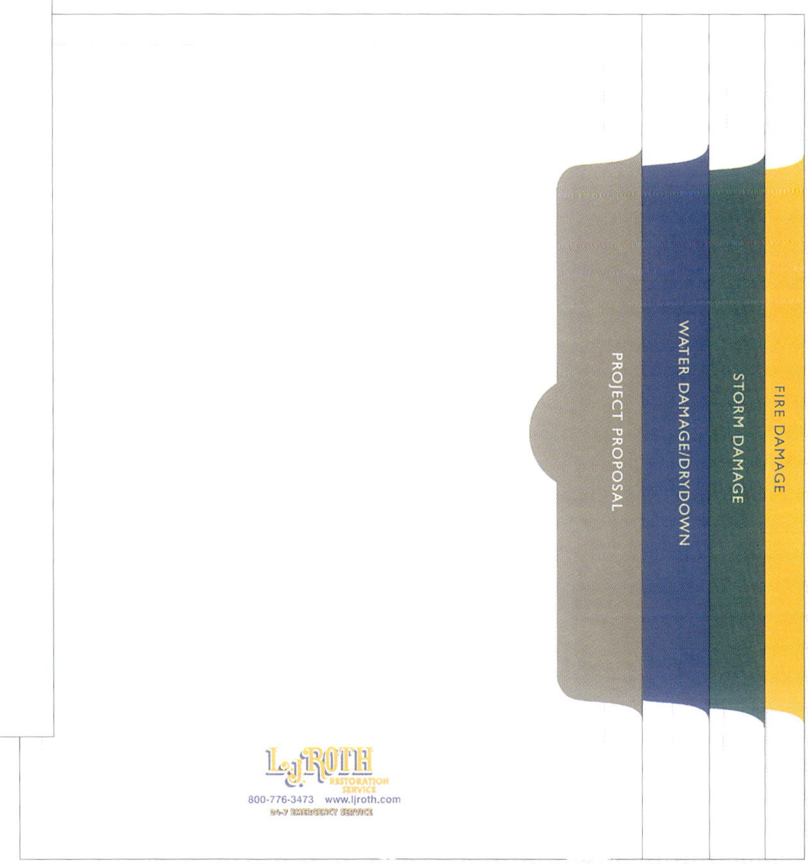

client
L.J. Roth
design firm
Benson & Hepker Design
www.bhdesign.com

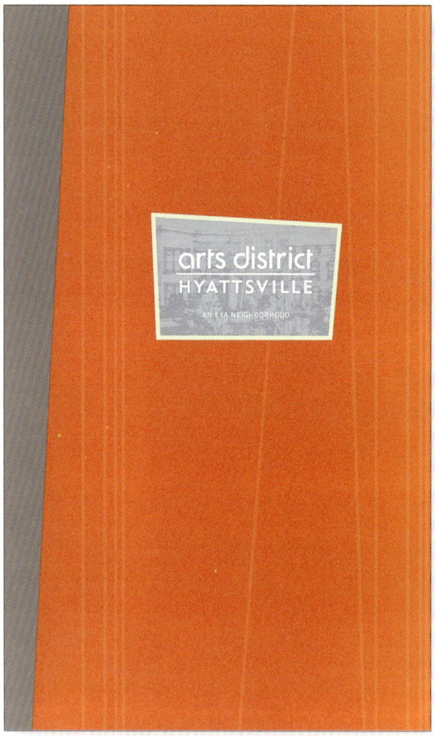

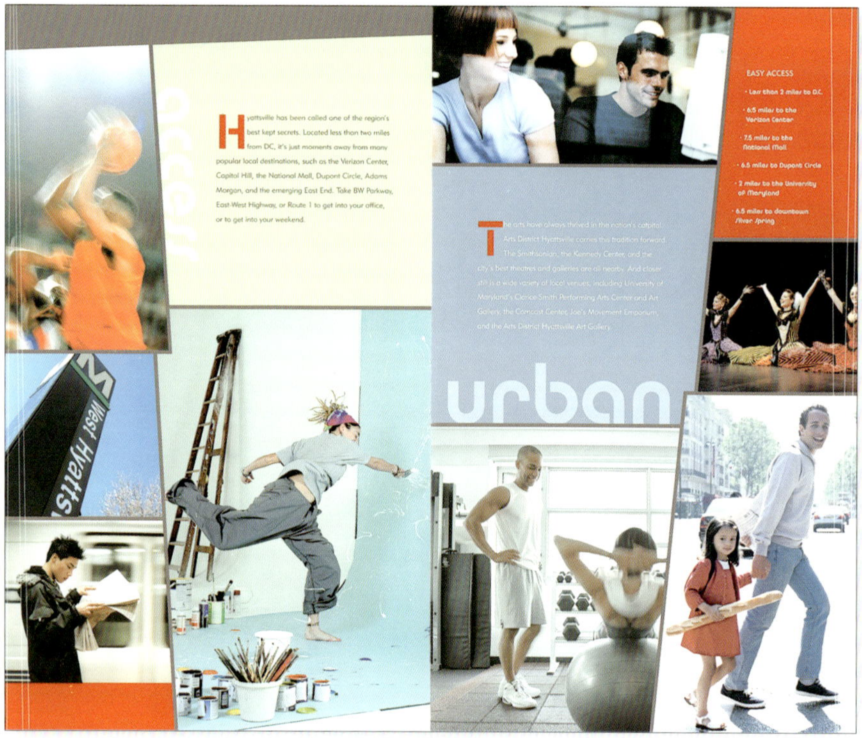

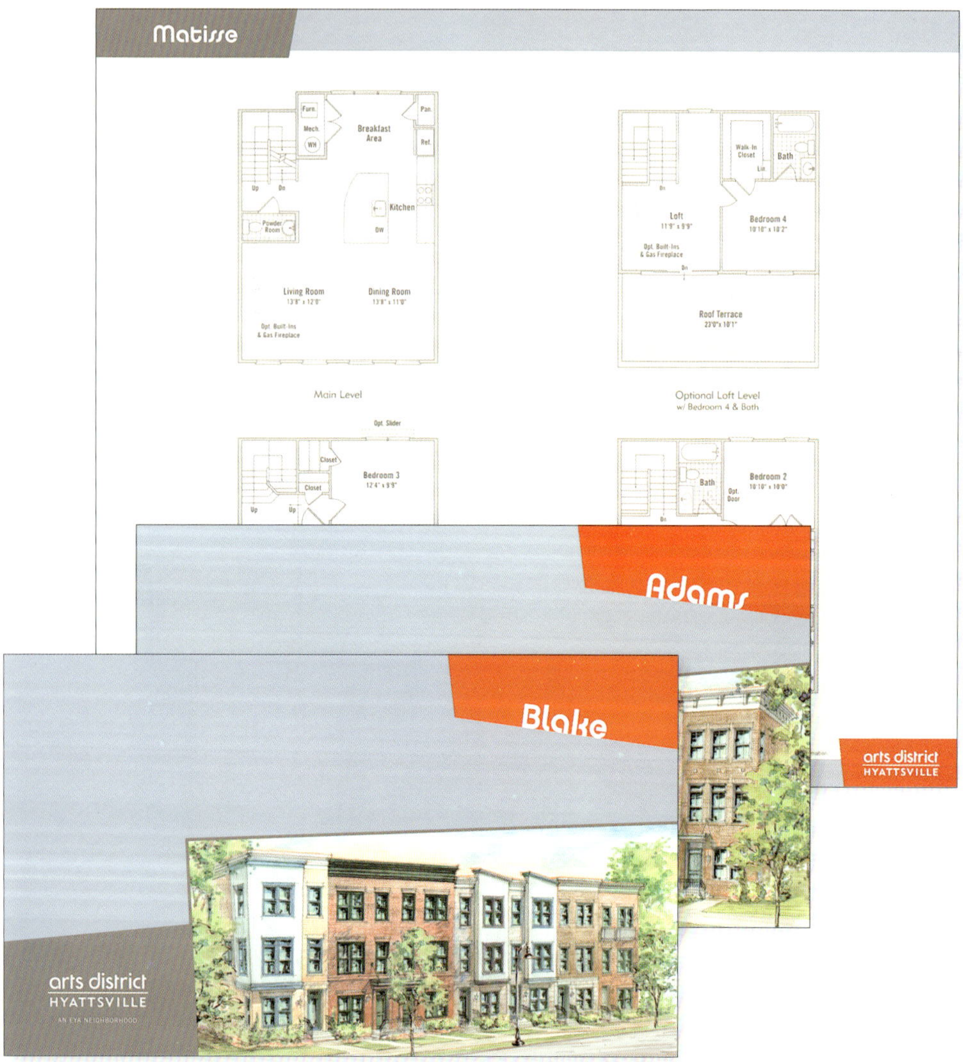

client
EYA
design firm
Grafik Marketing Communications
www.grafik.com
designers
Michelle Mar Collins, Lynn Murphy, Johnny Vitovovich, Hal Swetnam, Regina Esposito, Ivan Hooker

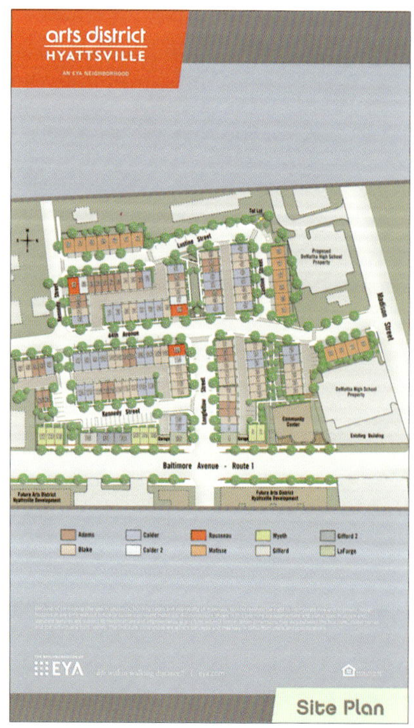

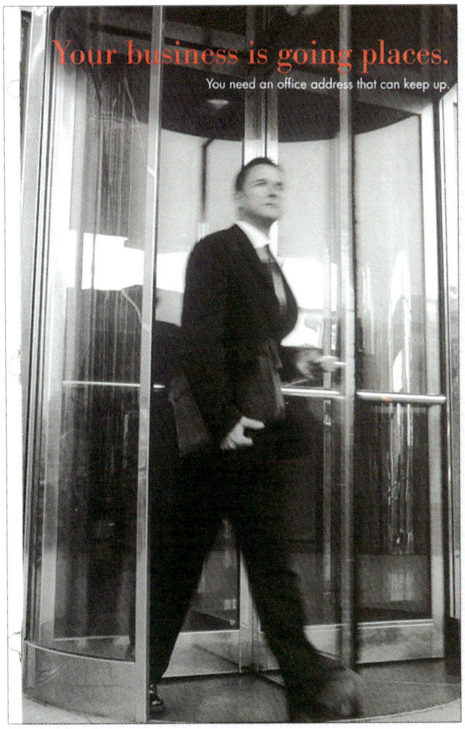

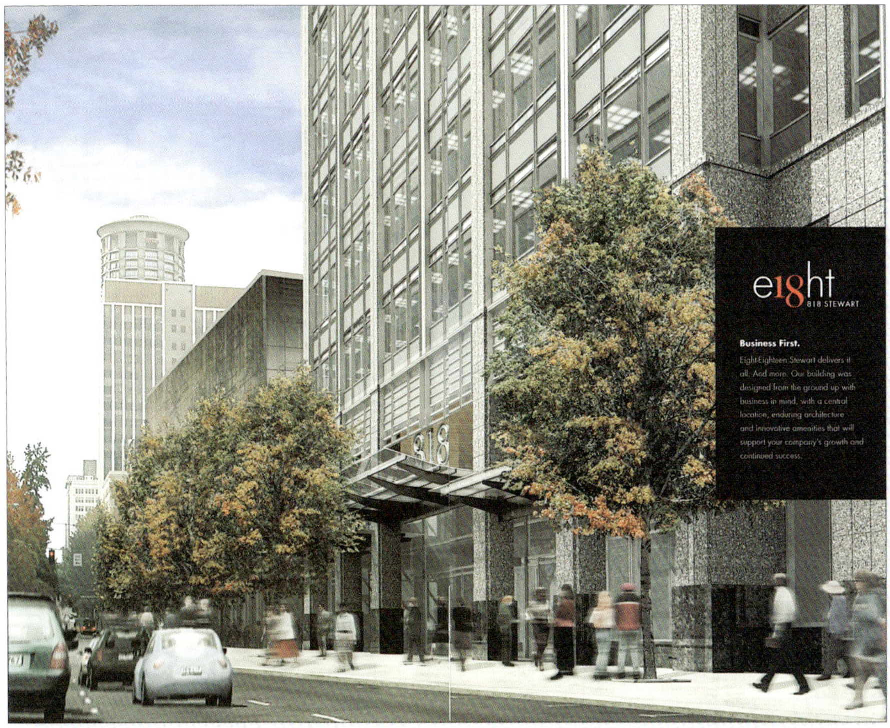

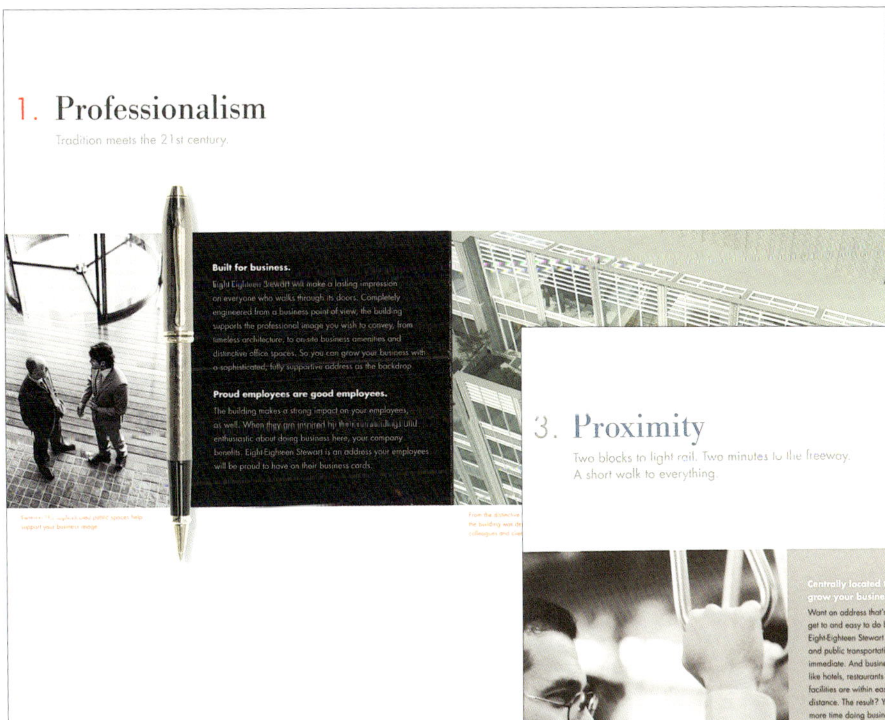

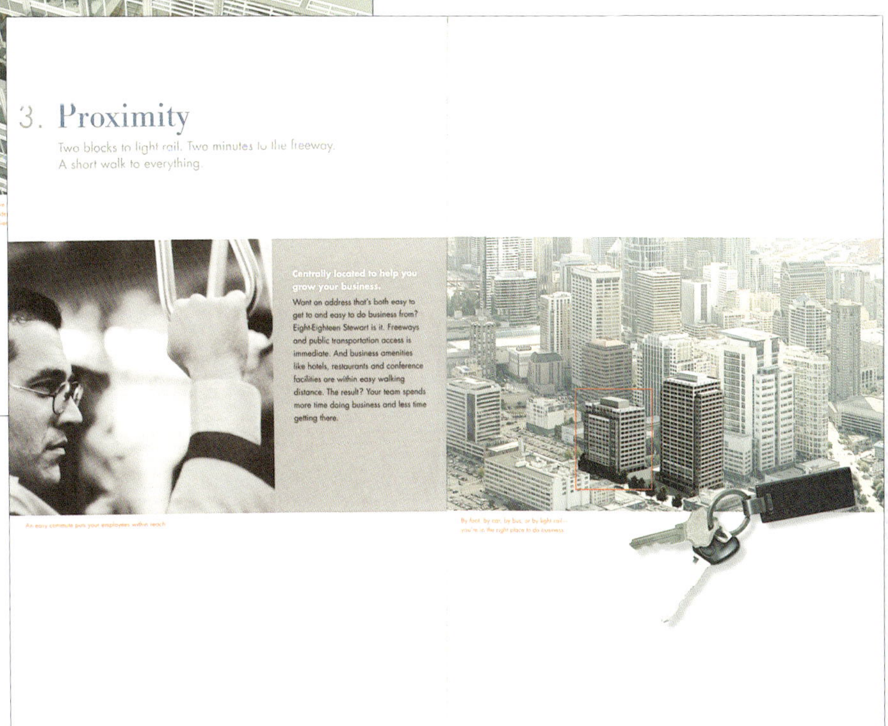

client
Schnitzer Northwest
design firm
Hornall Anderson Design Works
www.hadw.com
designers
John Anicker, Andrew Wicklund, Leo Raymundo, Chris Freed, Kathleen Gibson

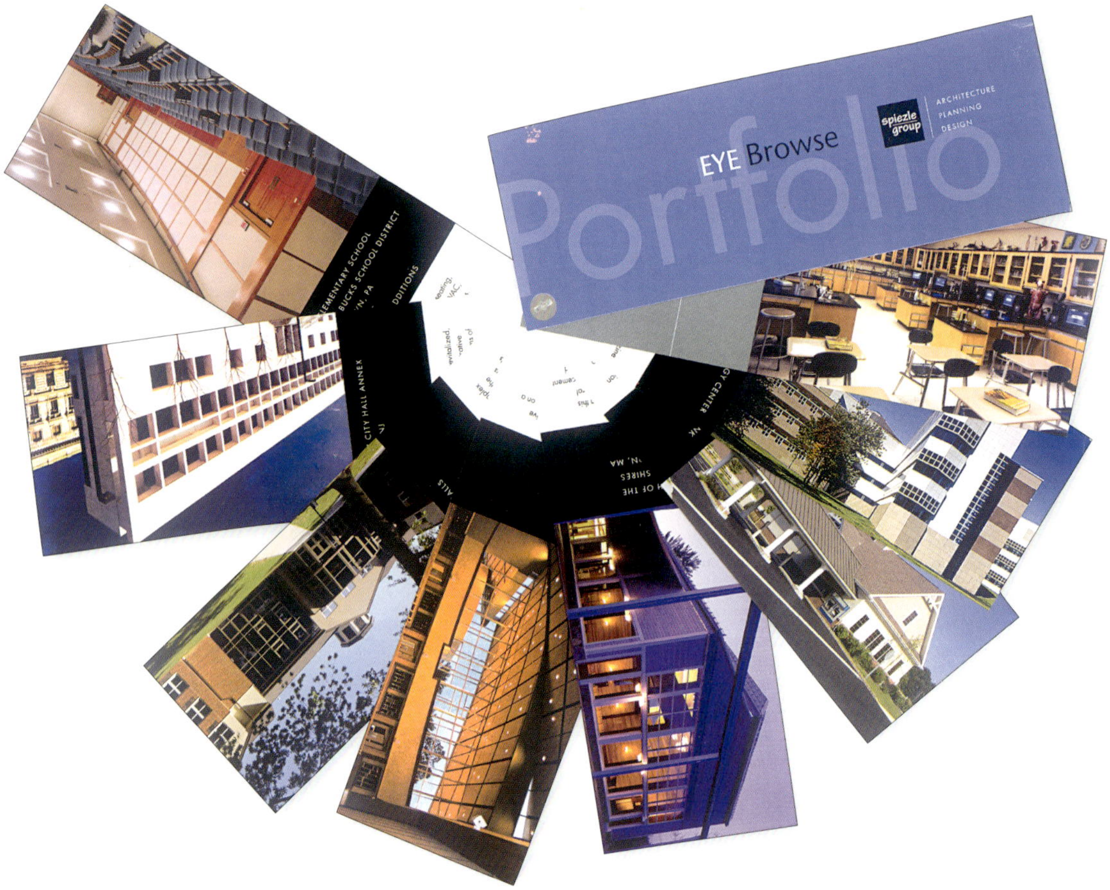

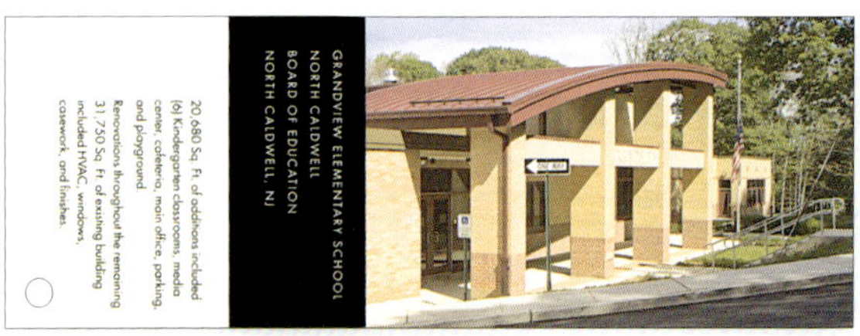

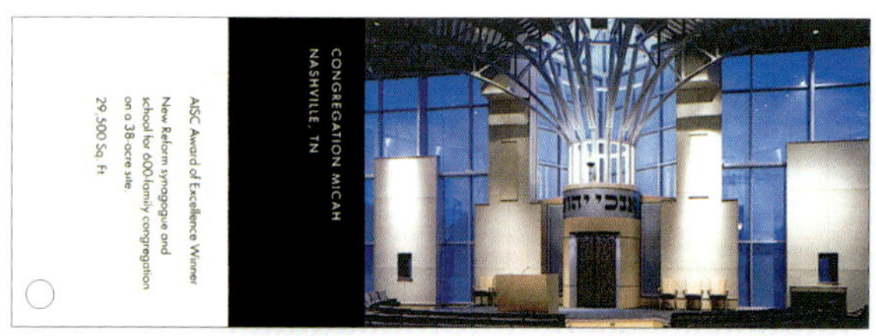

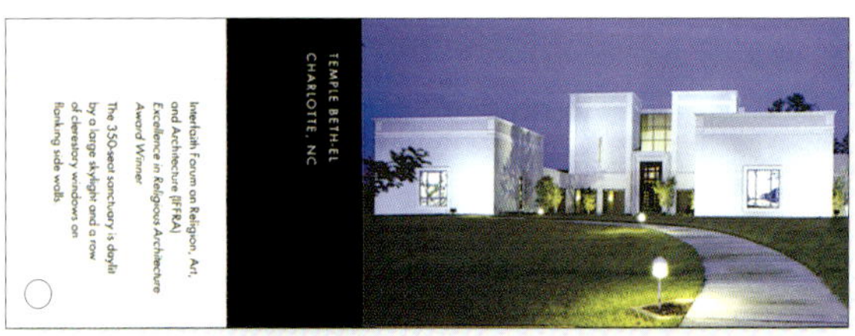

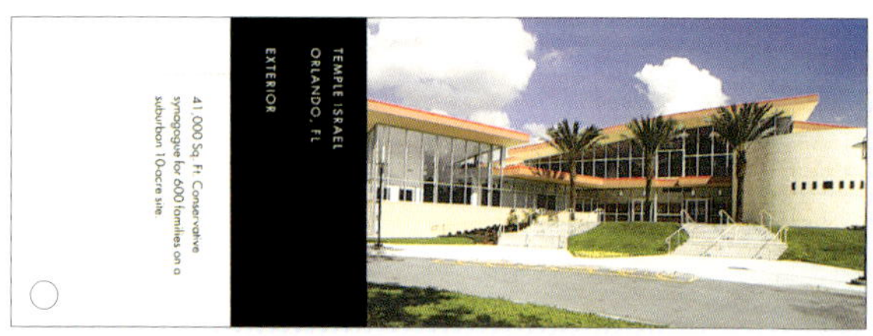

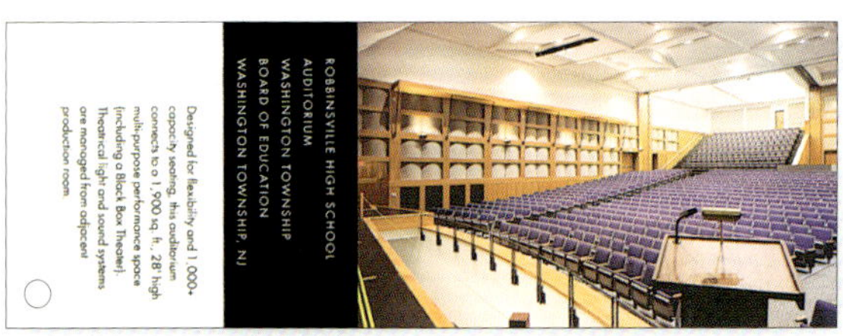

client
Spiezle Group
design firm
Gill Fishman Associates
www.gillfishmandesign.com
designer
Alicia Ozyjowski

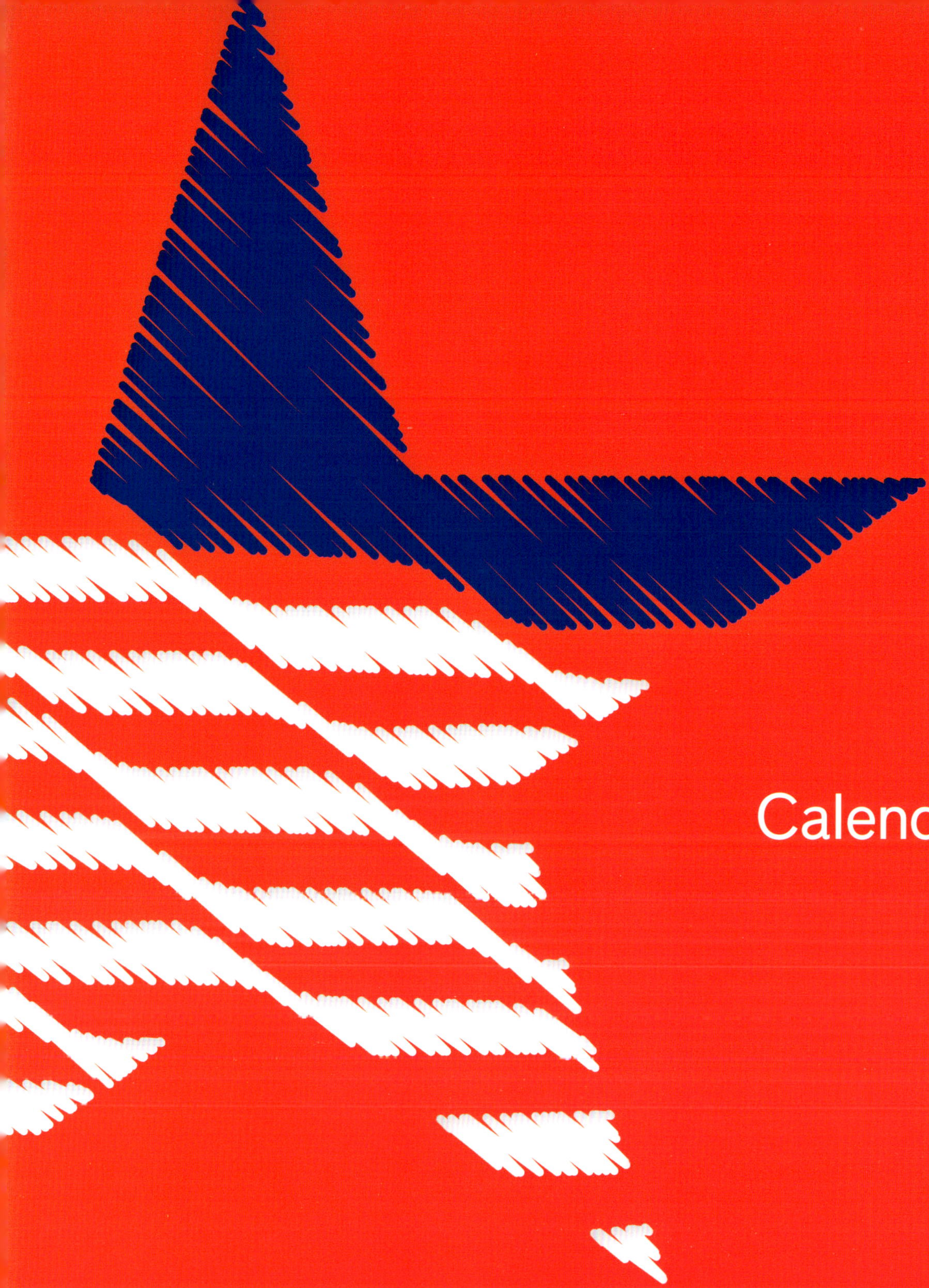

Calendars

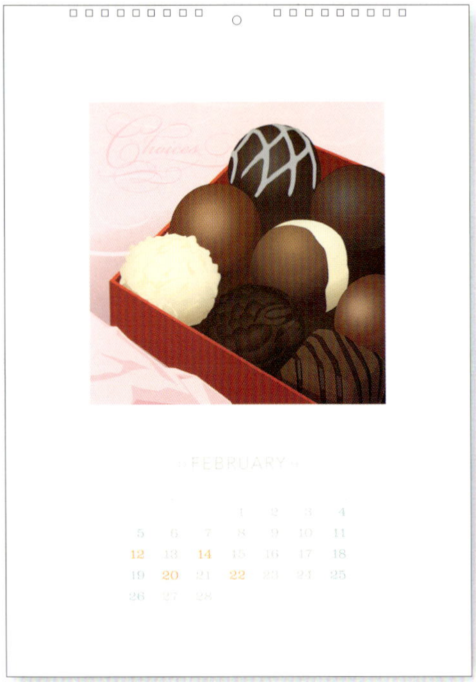

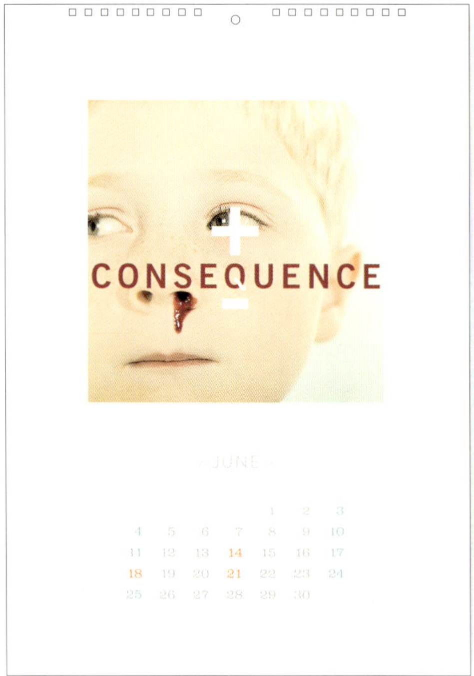

client
ARC Paper
design firm
eurie creative
designers
Victor Rodriguez, Debra Heiser

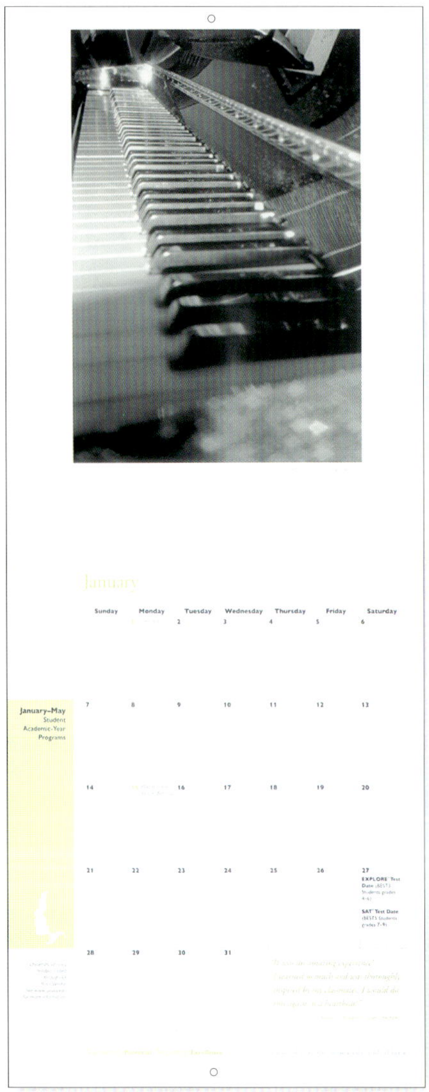

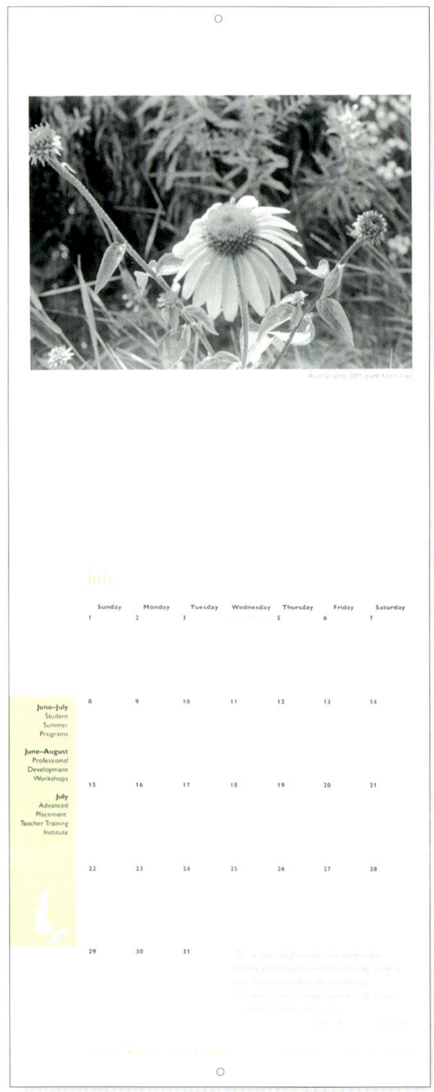

client
Belin-Blank Center
design firm
Benson & Hepker Design
www.bhdesign.com

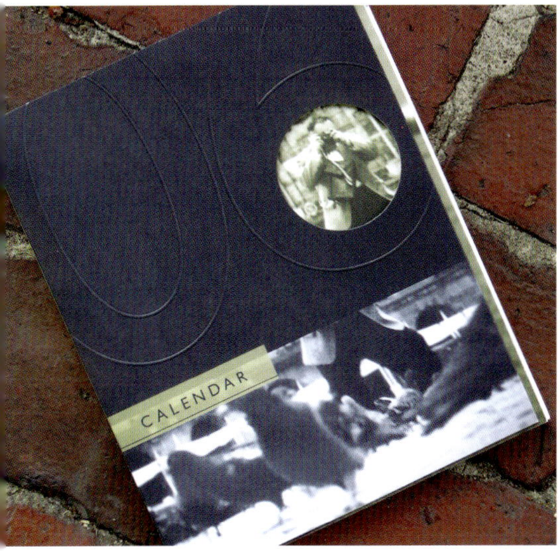

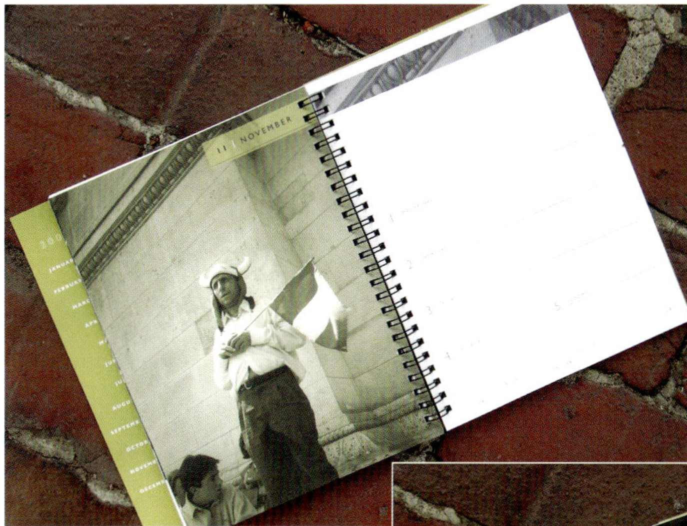

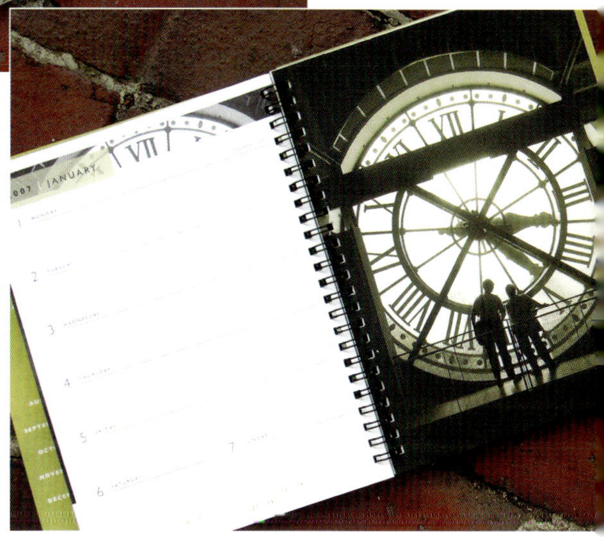

project

collaborative holiday client gift calendar to promote photographer, designer, printer, paper company, and marketing company

design firm

Defteling Design

www.defteling.com

designer

Alex Wijnen

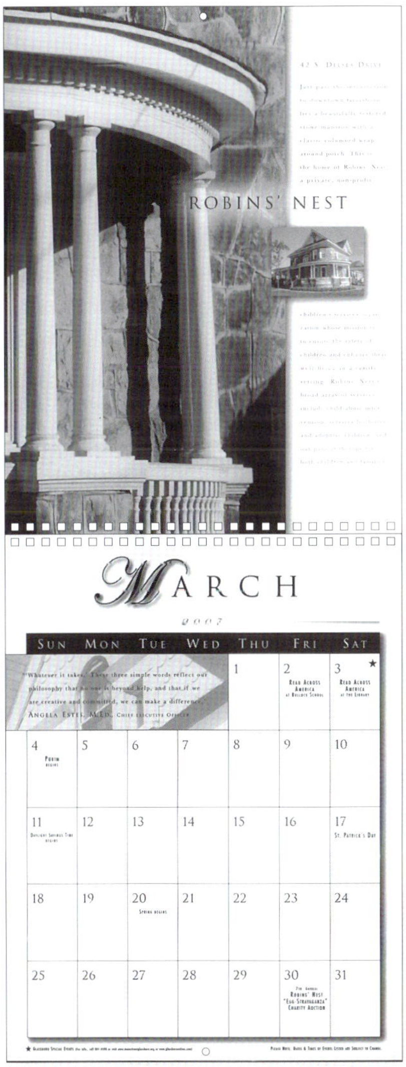

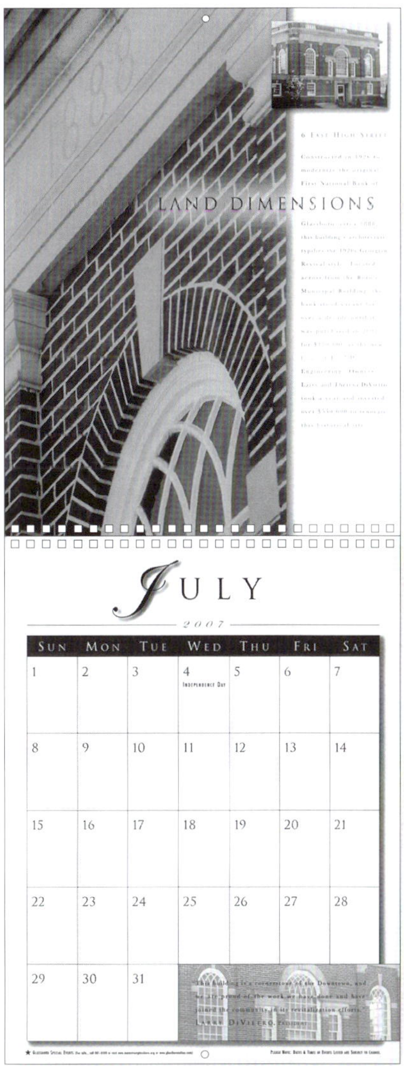

client

Main Street Glassboro

design firm

Randi Wolf Design

www.randiwolfdesign.com

designer

Randi Wolf

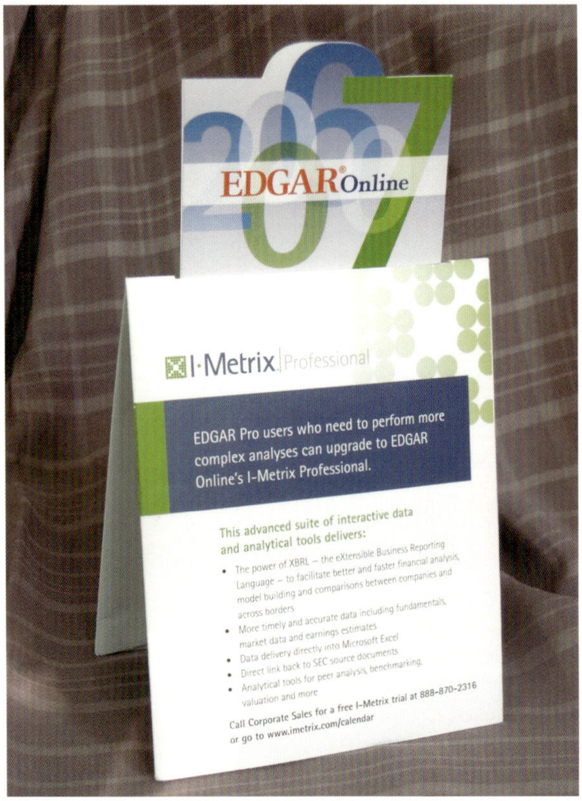

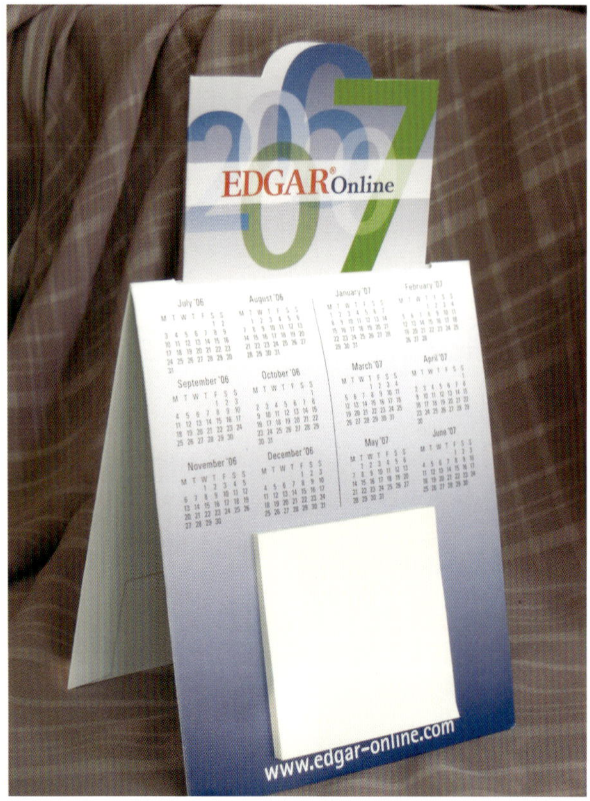

client
Edgar Online
design firm
Cullinane
www.cullinane.com
designers
Jia Kang Sung, Paul Patrick

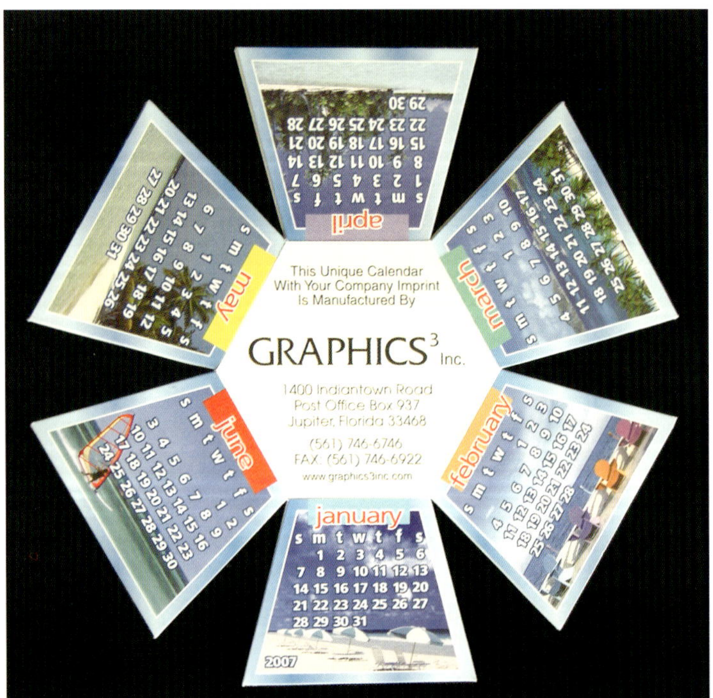

client
Graphics Three, Inc.
design firm
Tom Fowler, Inc.
www.tomfowlerinc.com
designer
Elizabeth P. Ball

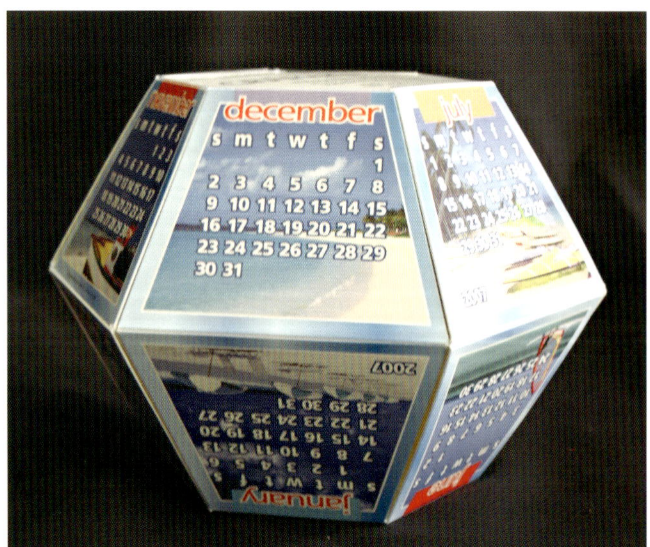

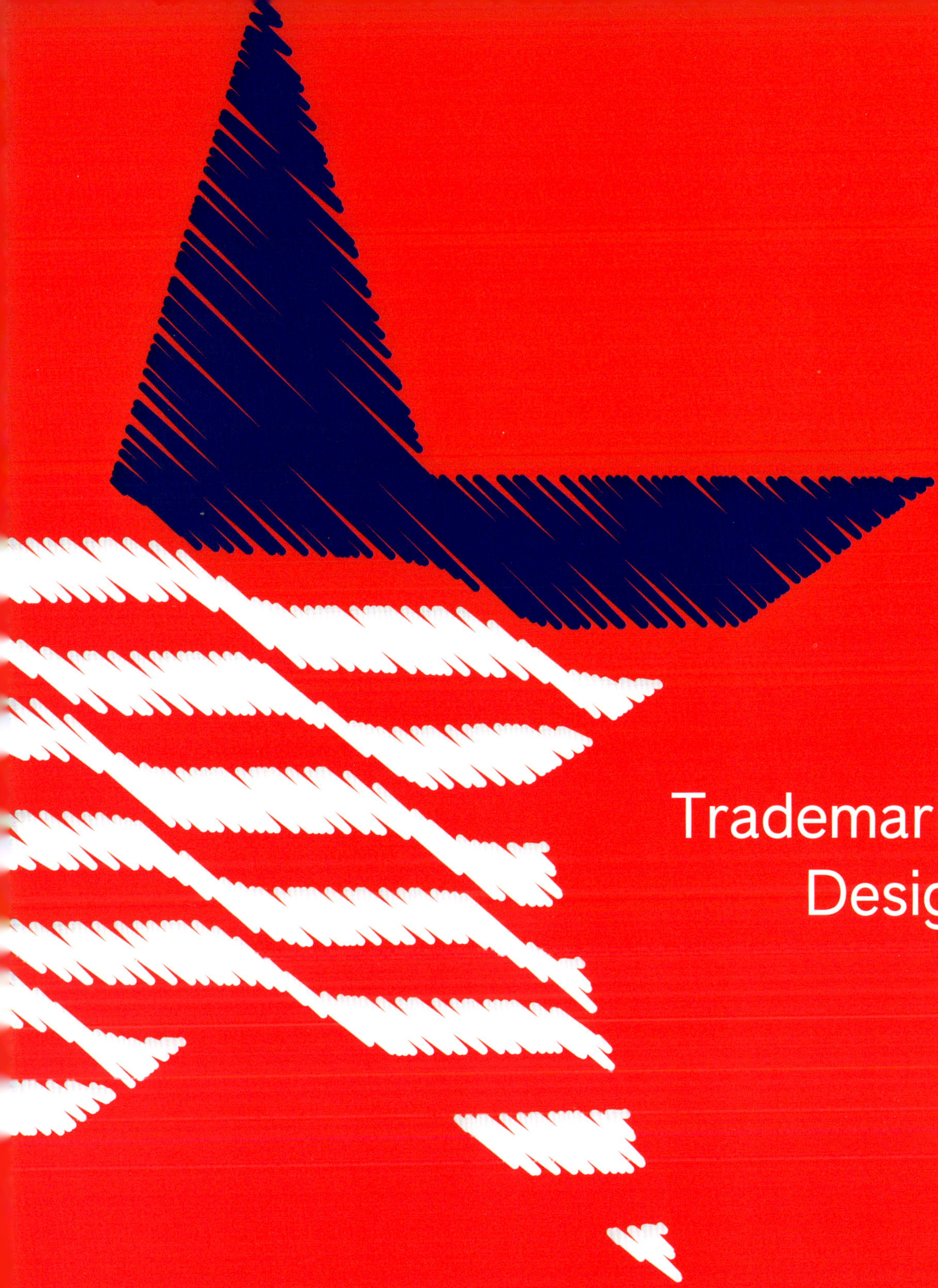

Trademark/Logo Design

client
Keith Mill
design firm
art270, Inc.
www.art270.com
designers
Carl Mill, John Opet

FIVE IN SIX
THE GREAT LAKES TOUR

client
Jobster
design firm
Hornall Anderson Design Works
www.hadw.com
designers
Jack Anderson, Michael Connors,
Leo Raymundo, Ensi Mofasser

jobster

client
Bean Creative
design firm
Bremmer & Goris
www.goris.com
designers
Li-Chow, Miki Lo

extension
more mind reach

client
Cowley College
design firm
Insight Design Communications
Insightdesign.com
designers
Tracy Holdeman,
Steve Cranford

COWLEY
COLLEGE

client
Cognisage
design firm
Keng's Designs
www.kengsdesigns.com
designer
Robert Keng

COGNISAGE
REDEFINING TECHNICAL INGENUITY

client
Velocity Broadcasting
design firm
Elias/Savion Advertising
elias-savion.com
designer
Ronnie Savion

VELOCITY
BOX
OFFICE

client
EXCELL Cement Technologies
design firm
Desbrow
desbrow.com
designers
Brian Lee Campbell,
Kimberly S. Miller

client
Vivendi Development
design firm
Helena Seo Design
www.helenaseo.com
designer
Helena Seo

client
Renaissance Theatre Company
design firm
Fifth Letter
www.fifth-letter.com
designer
Elliot Strunk

client
Abel/Noser
design firm
Cullinane
www.cullinane.com
designer
Kristin Romano

client
Dillion Property Pros
design firm
MillerWhite, LLC
www.millerwhite.com
designer
Lori Lucas

client
Campbell's Nutrition
design firm
Sayles Graphic Design
www.saylesdesign.com
designer
John Sayles

client
Nature Corps
design firm
Pierre Rademaker Design
www.rademakerdesign.com
designers
Pierre Rademaker,
Debbie Shibata

client
San Diego Museum of Man
design firm
Design Group West
www.dgwest.com
designer
Jim Naegeli

client
Tribeca Kitchen, LLC
design firm
Brand Engine
designers
Andrew Otto, Meghan Zodrow, Konrad Tse

client
The Rumley
design firm
Insight Design Communications
Insightdesign.com
designer
Tracy Holdeman

client
World Import Gallery
design firm
Insight Design Communications
Insightdesign.com
designer
Tracy Holdeman

client
Everyone Counts
design firm
Design Group West
www.dgwest.com
designer
Jim Naegeli

client
Alman Group, LLC
design firm
Options By Design
www.optionsbydesign.com
designers
Jeff Wright, James Benes,
Kathryn Schlesinger

client
Teens for Safe Cosmetics
design firm
Axion Design
axiondesign.com

client
Council on Library and Information Resources
design firm
Bremmer & Goris
www.goris.com
designers
Li Chow, Miki Lo

client
Clean Choice Professional Services
design firm
Octavo Designs
designers
Sue Hough, Mark Burrier

client
The Richard E. Jacobs Group
design firm
Herip Design Associates, Inc.
www.heripassociates.com
designers
Walter M. Herip,
Jen Hollo Crabtree

client
William Dunn
design firm
William Dunn Design
designer
William Dunn

client
Rhino Products
design firm
Ted DeCagna Graphic Design
www.tdgraphicdesign.net
designer
Ted DeCagna

client
The Launch Crew
design firm
Rubin Cordaro Design
www.rubincordaro.com
designer
Jim Cordaro

client
Will Call Express
design firm
Lorenc+Yoo Design
designers
Jan Lorenc, Jisun An, David Park

client
Denver Public Schools Foundation
design firm
Rassman Design
www.rassmandesign.com
designers
John Rassman, Glen Hobbs

client
Green Bay East High Soccer Booster Club
design firm
Daniel Green Eye-D Design
designer
Daniel Green

client
The Overfors Group
design firm
Rubin Cordaro Design
www.rubincordaro.com
designer
Jim Cordaro

client
Hillside Children's Center
design firm
A3 Design
www.athreedesign.com
designers
Alan Altman,
Amanda Altman

client
Hearth, Patio & Barbecue Association
design firm
Fixation Marketing
www.fixation.com
designers
Bruce E. Morgan, Randy Guseman

client
Polar Delight Group
design firm
Radi Design, Inc.
www.radidesign.com
designers
Art Baez, Robert Radi

client
Wirz & Associates
design firm
Kevin Hall Design
designer
Kevin Hall

client
Queen City Capital
design firm
A3 Design
www.athreedesign.com
designers
Alan Altman, Amanda Altman, Lauren Gualdoni

client
Green Bay East High Soccer Booster Club
design firm
Daniel Green Eye-D Design
designer
Daniel Green

client
Opera Colorado
design firm
Rassman Design
www.rassmandesign.com
designer
John Rassman

client
Yogali-fun yoga for kids
design firm
Niza Hanany Design
designer
Niza Hanany

client
PMO Wildwood
design firm
Brand Engine
designers
Coralie Russo, Robert Burns,
Meghan Zodrow, Andrew Otto

client
Fieldman Rolapp & Associates
design firm
Design Group West
www.dgwest.com
designer
Jim Naegeli

client
Brand Engine
design firm
Brand Engine
designer
Eric Read

client
WetPaint
design firm
Hornall Anderson Design Works
www.hadw.com
designers
David Bates, Yuri Shvets, Jacob Carter

client
RealtyProf, Inc.
design firm
Keng's Designs
www.kengsdesigns.com
designer
Robert Keng

client
Olmsted Parks Conservancy
design firm
Crowley Webb and Assoc.
crowley-webb.com
designer
Kelly Gambino

client
John Michael Kohler Arts Center
design firm
Liska + Associates
www.liska.com
designer
Steve Liska

JOHN MICHAEL KOHLER ARTS CENTER
expect the unexpected

client
Peck Shaffer & Williams LLP
design firm
Greenfield/Belser Ltd.
www.gbltd.com
designers
Burkey Belser, Shikha Savdas

PECK SHAFFER

client
Schiff Farms
design firm
Dean Design Marketing Group, Inc.
www.deandesign.com
designer
Jeff Phillips

Schiff Farms
Since 1945

client
Geyer Pathology Solutions
design firm
Elias/Savion Advertising
elias-savion.com
designer
Ronnie Savion

GEYER PATHOLOGY SOLUTIONS

client
Cable in the Classroom
design firm
Beth Singer Design, LLC
www.bethsingerdesign.com
art director
Beth Singer
designers
Chris Hoch,
Sucha Snidvongs

client
TransLore
design firm
Insight Design Communications
Insightdesign.com
designer
Tracy Holdeman

TRANSLORE
TRANSMIT. TRANSACT. TRANSFORM.

client
Charmalot Elegant Collectables
design firm
Ted DeCagna Graphic Design
www.tdgraphicdesign.net
designer
Ted DeCagna

client
Harlem Symphony Orchestra
design firm
Hopscotch Studio
designer
Dawn Hachenski

client
Forest City Washington
design firm
Herip Design Associates, Inc.
www.heripassociates.com
designers
Walter M. Herip, Jen Hollo Crabtree, John R. Menter

client
Printed Culture
design firm
ZGraphics, Ltd.
www.zgraphics.com
designers
Andy Matznick,
Joe Zeller

client
JBE Tile & Stone
design firm
Options By Design
www.optionsbydesign.com
designers
Jeff Wright, James Benes, Kathryn Schlesinger

client
Hidden Farms
design firm
Gill Fishman Associates
www.gillfishmandesign.com
designer
Alicia Ozyjowski

client
Red Lantern Restaurant
design firm
Keng's Designs
www.kengsdesigns.com
designer
Robert Keng

client
Conservatory of Music
design firm
MillerWhite, LLC
www.millerwhite.com
designer
Noah Ostby

client
Majestic America Line
design firm
Hornall Anderson Design Works
www.hadw.com
designers
Jack Anderson, Andrew Wicklund, Peter Anderson, Ensi Mofasser, Belinda Bowling, Kathleen Gibson

client
The Glad Products Company
design firm
Clorox Creative Services
designer, illustrator
Tim Ferdun

client
Child Health Association
design firm
Reinnov8 Design Group
www.reinnov8.com
designer
Richard A. Hooper

client
Home Connecticut
design firm
Fathom Applied Strategy
designer
Michelle Guilmette

client
Versant
design firm
Vince Rini Design
vincerinidesign.com
designer
Vince Rini

client
Fat Duck Inn
design firm
Perlman Company
designer
Robert Perlman

client
Verse Group
design firm
Verse Group
www.versegroup.com
designer
Michael Thibodeau

verse
the narrative branding company®

client
Alzheimer's Drug Discovery Foundation
design firm
Graphic Expression, Inc.
www.TGENYC.com
designer
Kurt Finkbeiner

Alzheimer's Drug Discovery Foundation

client
Market Tools
design firm
Michael Patrick Partners
www.michaelpatrickpartners.com
designer
Eko Tjoek

MarketTools™

client
Zippo Manufacturing Co.
design firm
Icon Graphics Inc.
thinkfeelchoose.com
designers
Icon Graphics Inc.

Zippo®
Unmatched.
1932-2007

client
Goosey Press
design firm
Defteling Design
www.defteling.com
designer
Alex Wijnen

Goosey Press

client
Nuvoiz
design firm
Michael Patrick Partners
www.michaelpatrickpartners.com
designer
Sabrina Li

nuvoiz

client
Associated Physicians and Surgeons Clinic
design firm
MillerWhite, LLC
www.millerwhite.com
designer
Jenny Hoffeditz

AP&S CLINIC

PERSONAL. COMPREHENSIVE. INNOVATIVE.

client
Alliance for Regional Stewardship
design firm
art270, Inc.
www.art270.com
designers
Carl Mill, John Opet

ALLIANCE FOR REGIONAL STEWARDSHIP

client
Silicon Image
design firm
Addison Whitney
www.addisonwhitney.com
designers
Kimberlee Davis, Trey Walsh, Kristin Hager

SimplayHD™

client
28 Saint Thomas
design firm
Liska + Associates
www.liska.com
designer
Steve Liska

28SAINTTHOMAS

client
First Community Foundation of Pennsylvania
design firm
Sire Advertising
www.sireadvertising.com
designers
Shawn Felty, Jessica Varner

FIRST COMMUNITY FOUNDATION OF PENNSYLVANIA

client
The Killjoys
design firm
Sayles Graphic Design
www.saylesdesign.com
designers
John Sayles,
Aaron Petersen

The Killjoys

client
Sabingrafik, Inc.
design firm
Sabingrafik, Inc.
tracy.sabin.com
designer
Tracy Sabin

client
Chez Thuy Restaurant
design firm
Lightspeed Commercial Arts
www.lightspeedca.net
designer
Michael J. Hamers

client
Glabeebers—SarahBear
design firm
Lorenz Advertising
lorenzadvertising.com
designer
Arne Ratermanis

client
Common Threads Farm
design firm
Migrant
designer
Kent Smith

client
Carl Mill
design firm
art270, Inc.
www.art270.com
designer
John Opet

client
San Luis Obispo Sesquicentennial
design firm
Pierre Rademaker Design
www.rademakerdesign.com
designers
Pierre Rademaker,
Debbie Shibata

client
Raimondo Construction
design firm
Desbrow
desbrow.com
designers
Brian Lee Campbell,
Gabrielle Holleran

client
CORE Building Company
design firm
Hummingbird Creative Group
www.hummingbird-creative.com
designer
Juli LaDuc

client
Coldwell Banker Previews International
design firm
Verse Group
www.versegroup.com
designers
Michael Thibodeau,
Mark Landry,
Marina Binns

client
Swift & Company
design firm
Insight Design Communications
Insightdesign.com
designer
Tracy Holdeman

EST. 1855 BRAND CERTIFIED

client
Attwood Equestrian Surfaces
design firm
Zero Gravity Design Group
www.zerogny.com
designers
Zero Gravity Design Group

EQUESTRIAN SURFACES

client
Partners Bank of California
design firm
Design Group West
www.dgwest.com
designer
Jim Naegeli

PARTNERS BANK OF CALIFORNIA

client
Hubbard Business Interiors
design firm
Rule29 Creative
www.rule29.com
designers
Justin Ahrens, Josh Jensen

HUBBARD™ BUSINESS INTERIORS

client
RMC, Inc.
design firm
SiMPLE DESIGN
simpledesigninc.com
designer
Robert Mitchell

CoyoteCreek STEAKHOUSE & SALOON

client
Crimson Capital LLC
design firm
Smith Design
smithdesign.com
designer
Laura Markley

WHITECAP PARTNERS

client
The Cascades
design firm
Paul Kaza Associates
www.paulkaza.com
designer
Donda Thibault

the Cascades at Winooski Falls

client
Aurum Wealth Management
design firm
Innis Maggiore
www.innismaggiore.com
designer
Jeff Monter

AURUM WEALTH MANAGEMENT GROUP

client
Shore to Shore
design firm
VMA, Inc.
vmai.com
designers
Doug Knopp, Amritha Ward

SHORE TO SHORE
BRAND PACKAGING SOLUTIONS

client
Stash Pirates
design firm
Rassman Design
www.rassmandesign.com
designers
John Rassman,
Jonathan Wheeler,
Andy Schneider

PLUNDERING THE HIDDEN POWDER
Stash Pirates
PILLAGING THE SECRET STASHES

client
Savidge Housing Group
design firm
Sire Advertising
www.sireadvertising.com
creative director, designer
Shawn Felty
illustrator
Bob Henninger

PHEASANT
RIDGE
A Savidge Development

client
Lipsitz Green Scime Cambria LLP
design firm
Crowley Webb and Assoc.
crowley-webb.com
designer
Kelly Gambino

Lipsitz Green Scime Cambria LLP

client
Skincare Revolution, LLC
design firm
Jensen Design Assoc. Inc.
designers
Alyssa Igawa, Dave Jensen

nuLase™
LASER ENHANCED SKIN CARE

client
Genesee Valley Plein Air Painters
design firm
Icon Graphics Inc.
thinkfeelchoose.com
designers
Icon Graphics Inc.

GENESEE VALLEY
PLEIN AIR PAINTERS

client
East Bay Homes For You
design firm
Keng's Designs
www.kengsdesigns.com
designer
Robert Keng

East Bay Homes For You
We Make It Happen

client
Endologix Powerlink
design firm
Lorenz Advertising
lorenzadvertising.com
designer
Brian Lorenz

Powerlink®

client
Carbon House
design firm
A3 Design
www.athreedesign.com
designers
Alan Altman, Lauren Gualdoni

client
Visit Charlotte
design firm
A3 Design
www.athreedesign.com
designers
Alan Altman, Amanda Altman, Lauren Gualdoni

client
Idaho Terrace Tenants Association
design firm
Pat Taylor
designer
Pat Taylor

client
Eric Fisher Academy
design firm
Insight Design Communications
Insightdesign.com
designer
Tracy Holdeman

client
Griffith Choppers
design firm
A3 Design
www.athreedesign.com
designers
Alan Altman,
Amanda Altman

client
The Dial Corp.
design firm
Wallace Church, Inc.
www.wallacechurch.com
creative director
Stan Church
designer
John Bruno

client
J. Spargo & Associates, Inc.
design firm
Fixation Marketing
www.fixation.com
designers
Bruce E. Morgan, Randy Guseman

client
Stay
design firm
Liska + Associates
www.liska.com
designers
Kim Fry,
Stephanie Meier

client
Enertech
design firm
Hornall Anderson Design Works
www.hadw.com
designers
Jack Anderson, James Tee, Beth Grimm,
Elmer dela Cruz, Sonja Max, Lauren DiRusso

client
Pennsylvania Ballet
design firm
art270, Inc.
www.art270.com
designers
Alexis Van Saun,
Carl Mill, Sue Strohm

client
CBS SportsLine.com
design firm
Elias/Savion Advertising
elias-savion.com
designer
Ronnie Savion

client
Vision Financial
design firm
Cullinane
www.cullinane.com
designers
Bob Cullinane, Jon Lyness

client
Southern Virginia Recreation Facilities Authority
design firm
Kendall Creative Shop, Inc.
kendallcreative.com
designers
Ben Dolezal, Mark Platt

client
Victor 8
design firm
Ghengis Design
ghengisdesign.com
designer
Dale Monahan

client
Splash, Ltd.
design firm
Kevin Hall Design
designer
Kevin Hall

client
Spaulding Rehabilitation Hospital
design firm
Gill Fishman Associates
www.gillfishmandesign.com
designer
Michael Persons

client
Downtown Middle School
design firm
Fifth Letter
www.fifth-letter.com
designer
Elliot Strunk

client
Saint Thomas Aquinas
design firm
Kendall Creative Shop, Inc.
kendallcreative.com
designers
Ryan Briggs,
Mark Platt

client
Media Consultants
design firm
Stephen Longo Design Associates
designer
Stephen Longo

client
Crescent Beach Productions
design firm
Zero Gravity Design Group
www.zerogny.com
designers
Zero Gravity Design Group

client
Data Comm Electronics, Inc.
design firm
Design Resource Center
www.drcchicago.com
designers
John Norman, Melanie Gibb

client
Flaming Fresco Mexican Cuisine
design firm
Keng's Designs
www.kengsdesigns.com
designer
Robert Keng

client
Beaverdale Books
design firm
Sayles Graphic Design
www.saylesdesign.com
designers
John Sayles,
Jessi O'Brien

client
Our Story
design firm
Michael Patrick Partners
www.michaelpatrickpartners.com
designer
Eko Tjoek

client
Okun Holdings
design firm
Gibson Group
www.gibsongrp.com
designer
Diane McGuire

client
Juvenile Diabetes Research Foundation
design firm
eurie creative
designer
Victor Rodriguez

client
Widmer Brothers Brewery
design firm
Hornall Anderson Design Works
www.hadw.com
designers
Jack Anderson,
Larry Anderson,
Jay Hilburn,
Bruce Stigler,
Elmer dela Cruz,
Hayden Schoen,
Daymon Bruck

client
Mophie
design firm
reduced fat
www.reduced-fat.com
designer
John Bolster

client
Anvil Knitwear, Inc.
design firm
Creasia LLC
creasiadesign.com
designer
Carmen Li

client
Carmel Clay Parks and Recreation
design firm
MillerWhite, LLC
www.millerwhite.com
designers
Lori Lucas, Atsu Kpotufe

client
McBride Development
design firm
Migrant
designer
Kent Smith

client
Junior Diabetes Research Foundation
design firm
Kendall Creative Shop, Inc.
kendallcreative.com
designer
Tim Childress

client
Brightwater Fly Angler
design firm
William Homan Design
williamhomandesign.com
designer
William Homan

client
Olivia's Gift
design firm
Square One Design
designers
Anna Huddleston, John Totten, Lin Ver Meulen

client
Lorelei Enterpises and Events, Inc.
design firm
Whet Design, Inc.
www.whetdesign.com
designer
Cheryl Oppenheim

client
City of Redwood City, California
design firm
Keng's Designs
www.kengsdesigns.com
designer
Robert Keng

client
Colorado Ice Football
design firm
Genghis Design
www.genghisdesign.com
designer
Dale Monahan

COLORADO ICE

client
Zia Music Production
design firm
Ventress Design Group
www.ventress.com
designer
Tom Ventress

ZiA

client
Crossroads Coffeehouse & Music Co.
design firm
Peterson Ray & Company
www.peterson.com
designer
Scott Ray

client
Dermatologic Laser Institute
design firm
Mayhem Studios
www.mayhemstudios.com
designer
Calvin Lee

DLI
dermatologic Laser institute

client
Strada
design firm
Defteling Design
www.defteling.com
designer
Alex Wijnen

STRADA
Training | Adventure | Discovery

client
American Board of Certification of Teacher Excellence
design firm
Fixation Marketing
www.fixation.com
designers
Bruce E. Morgan, Randy Guseman

MASTER TEACHER

client
Motorola
design firm
Liska + Associates
www.liska.com
designer
Sabine Krauss

client
Microgravity Enterprises
design firm
Lightspeed Commercial Arts
www.lightspeedca.net
designer
Michael J. Hamers

client
Douglas Elliman
design firm
Liska + Associates
www.liska.com
designer
Scott Devondorf

client
National Datacast
design firm
Grafik Marketing Communications
www.grafik.com
designer
Arthur Hsu

client
Old Market Sourdough
design firm
Pierre Rademaker Design
www.rademakerdesign.com
designers
Pierre Rademaker, Debbie Shibata

client
NNAP (Natural Native American Products)
design firm
Laurel Black Design, Inc.
designer
Laurel Black

client
Cosmetic Cafe
design firm
Insight Design Communications
Insightdesign.com
designer
Tracy Holdeman

client
Emerge Medical Spa at Bridgeport
design firm
Jeff Fisher LogoMotives
www.jfisherlogomotives.com
designer
Jeff Fisher

client
Besso's
design firm
Levine & Associates
www.levinedc.com
designer
Monica Snellings

client
Mayberry Moonshine
design firm
A3 Design
www.athreedesign.com
designers
Alan Altman, Amanda Altman, Lauren Gualdoni

client
Orthopedic Surgery Center of Orange County
design firm
Vince Rini Design
vincerinidesign.com
designer
Vince Rini

client
Apple Growth Companies
design firm
Innis Maggiore
www.innismaggiore.com
designer
Jeff Monter

client
DNH Homes, LLC
design firm
Designing Words
www.designing-words.com
designer
Julianne Nardone

DNH HOMES
CUSTOM BUILDERS

client
East Bluff Health Group
design firm
MFDI
designer
Mark Fertig

East Bluff Health Group
MENTORING PROGRAM

client
The Mission Inn Hotel
design firm
Winter Ad Agency
www.winteradagency.com
designer
Mary Winter

Bella Trattoria
ITALIAN BISTRO

client
Cardinal Gas
design firm
Kendall Creative Shop, Inc.
kendallcreative.com
designer
Jennifer Brehm

CARDINAL
gas solutions

client
University Orthopaedic Group
design firm
art270, Inc.
www.art270.com
designers
Nicole Ganz, Carl Mill, Reid Smith

University
Orthopaedic Group

client
Actual Size
design firm
Migrant
designer
Kent Smith

actualsize

client
Vivendi Games
design firm
Vivendi Games
designer
Nathan Gruppman

MEDIA
PRODUCTIONS
@ VIVENDI GAMES

client
Baird Brothers
design firm
Innis Maggiore
www.innismaggiore.com
designer
Brian
Bradway

BAIRD
BROTHERS
FINE HARDWOODS

client
Package Design Magazine Makeover Challenge 2005
design firm
Brand Engine
designers
Meghan Zodrow,
Aileen Kendle-Smith,
Robert Burns

client
University of San Diego
design firm
Design Group West
www.dgwest.com
designer
Jim Naegeli

client
Inspire Properties
design firm
Kendall Creative Shop, Inc.
kendallcreative.com
designer
Ryan Briggs

client
Global 20/20
design firm
Icon Graphics Inc.
thinkfeelchoose.com
designers
Icon Graphics Inc.

client
SmartCare
design firm
Kiku Obata & Company
designer
Eleanor Safe

client
Soundtanker
design firm
silver creative group
silvercreativegroup.com
designer
Bonnie Harriman

client
HDiQ
design firm
Kendall Creative Shop, Inc.
kendallcreative.com
designer
Mark Platt

client
Wolff Properties
design firm
Kiku Obata & Company
designer
Jim Redington

client
Saccuzzo Coffee
design firm
Fathom Applied Strategy
designer
Joe Philippon

client
Benchmark, Inc.
design firm
Gill Fishman Associates
www.gillfishmandesign.com
designer
Michael Persons

client
Shaser
design firm
Gill Fishman Associates
www.gillfishmandesign.com
designer
Michael Persons

client
The Pittsburgh Glass Center
design firm
Desbrow
desbrow.com
designers
Kimberly S. Miller,
Brian Lee Campbell

client
University Park United Methodist Church
design firm
Jeff Fisher LogoMotives
www.jfisherlogomotives.com
designer
Jeff Fisher

client
TCI
design firm
Beth Singer Design, LLC
www.bethsingerdesign.com
art director
Beth Singer
designer
Sucha Snidvongs

client
Marilyn Mantor, CPA
design firm
Laurel Black Design, Inc.
designer
Laurel Black

client
Sunbury Broadcast Corporation
design firm
MFDI
designer
Mark Fertig

client
Zelco
design firm
silver creative group
silvercreativegroup.com
designer
Tracy Waxenberg

client
Sugar Bowl Bakery
design firm
Brand Engine
designers
Robert Burns,
Aileen Kendle-Smith,
Coralie Russo

client
OpVista
design firm
Michael Patrick Partners
www.michaelpatrickpartners.com
designer
Eko Tjoek

OPVISTA™

client
John L. Fox Construction
design firm
William Dunn Design
designer
William Dunn

John L. Fox Construction
GENERAL & ELECTRICAL CONTRACTOR

client
Paul Zanecchia, Esq.
design firm
Mastrogiannis Design, Inc.
designer
Peter Mastrogiannis

client
National Nursing Centers Consortium
design firm
Murphy Design
www.murphydesign.net
designer
Rosemary Murphy

STUDENTS RUN
PHILLY STYLE
GO FARTHER!

client
Hopscotch Studio
design firm
Hopscotch Studio
designers
Dawn Hachenski, Ronn Daniel

HOPSCOTCH
HOPSCOTCH*STUDIO*

client
Trombetta's Farm
design firm
Compago Creative
www.compagocreative.com
designer
Sandra Pirie-St. Amour

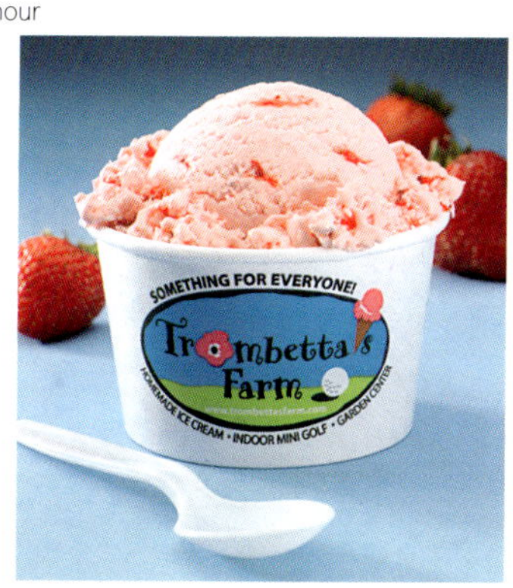

client
Microgravity Enterprises
design firm
Lightspeed Commercial Arts
www.lightspeedca.net
designer
Michael J. Hamers

Microgravity™
ENTERPRISES, INC.

client
Dermatologic Laser Institute
design firm
Mayhem Studios
www.mayhemstudios.com
designer
Calvin Lee

DERMATOLOGIC
LASER INSTITUTE

client
Hafner
design firm
Options By Design
www.optionsbydesign.com
designers
Jeff Wright,
Kathy Smyth

Hybrid
by Hafner

client
Hafner
design firm
Options By Design
www.optionsbydesign.com
designers
James Benes, Kathryn Schlesinger

THINSkin
by Hafner

client
University Church of Christ
design firm
Jonathan Wheeler/Freelance
designer
Jonathan Wheeler

WINTER PEAK

client
Ox Restaurant
design firm
Creasia LLC
creasiadesign.com
designer
Carmen Li

ox
RESTAURANT : JERSEY CITY

client
Schnitzer Northwest
design firm
Hornall Anderson Design Works
www.hadw.com
designers
John Anicker,
Andrew
Wicklund,
Chris Freed,
Leo Raymundo,
Kathleen
Gibson

e18ht

client
Susan Jane
design firm
Kollar Design Associates, Inc.
www.kollardesign.com
designers
Candice Kollar,Paul Nojima

SusanJane™

client
Michael Hauser
design firm
Patrick Redmond Design
www.PatrickRedmondDesign.com
designer
Patrick Redmond

client
Weckerle Cosmetics
design firm
Graphic Advance
www.graphicadvance.com
designer
Aviad Stark

client
Velocity Broadcasting
design firm
Elias/Savion Advertising
elias-savion.com
designer
Ronnie Savion

client
Blake, Cassels & Graydon LLP
design firm
Greenfield/Belser Ltd.
www.gbltd.com
designers
Tae Jeong, Mark Ledgerwood
calligrapher
Tim Girvin

client
Lutéce
design firm
Octavo Designs
designer
Sue Hough

client
Direct Access Partners
design firm
Zero Gravity Design Group
www.zerogny.com
designers
Zero Gravity Design Group

client
The Pittsburgh Ballet
design firm
Elias/Savion Advertising
elias-savion.com
designer
Ronnie Savion

client
Connecticut Grand Opera & Orchestra
design firm
Tom Fowler, Inc.
www.tomfowlerinc.com
designer
Elizabeth P. Ball

client
Solusoft
design firm
ID Group
idgrouppr.com
designers
Mayra Maldonado,
Abner Gutiérrez

client
Ditech Networks
design firm
Michael Patrick Partners
www.michaelpatrickpartners.com
designer
Eko Tjoek

client
Global Presenter
design firm
Design Group West
www.dgwest.com
designer
Megan Boyer

client
Ocean Atlantic
design firm
Sightline Marketing
www.sightlinemarketing.com
designer
Emily Wilson

client
Biotechnology Industry Organization
design firm
Fixation Marketing
www.fixation.com
designer
Bruce E. Morgan

client
Rivertown Business Builders
design firm
Alien Identity
www.alienidentity.com
designer
Dennis Derammelaere

client
N-Gas
design firm
Kendall Creative Shop, Inc.
kendallcreative.com
designers
Ben Dolezal, Mark Platt

client
Hip To Bamboo, LLC
design firm
Jing Zhou Studio
designer
Jing Zhou

client
Tronic's Microsystems
design firm
Loomis Group
www.loomisgroup.com
designer
Petra Andersson

client
Strategic Partnerships International
design firm
Octavo Designs
designers
Mark Burrier, Sue Hough

client
Clickshift
design firm
Michael Patrick Partners
www.michaelpatrickpartners.com
designer
Eko Tjoek

client
Fox Resources, LLC
design firm
Ted DeCagna Graphic Design
www.tdgraphicdesign.net
designer
Ted DeCagna

client
Forest City Military Communities
design firm
Herip Design Associates, Inc.
www.heripassociates.com
designers
Walter M. Herip,
John R. Menter,
Jen Hollo Crabtree

client
Stock Artists Alliance
design firm
Liska + Associates
www.liska.com
designers
Tory Knappenberger, Steve Liska

client
LMAP
design firm
Axion Design
axiondesign.com

client
Mega Brands
design firm
Smith Design
smithdesign.com
designers
Glenn Hagen, Carol Konkowski

client
American Israel Public Affairs Committee
design firm
Beth Singer Design, LLC
www.bethsingerdesign.com
art director
Beth Singer
designer
Sun Yu

client
Windham Mountain
design firm
Smith & Jones
www.smithandjones.com
designers
John Missale,
Sara Tack

client
Shawn Lynch
design firm
Fifth Letter
www.fifth-letter.com
designer
Elliot Strunk

client
Military Mothers
design firm
Kendall Creative Shop, Inc.
kendallcreative.com
designers
Ben Dolezal, Mark Platt

client
Lake Local Schools
design firm
Innis Maggiore
www.innismaggiore.com
designer
Jeff Monter

client
Pietragallo, Bosik & Gordon LLP
design firm
AF&A Brandtelligence
Brandtelligence.com
designers
Robert Adam, Ralph James Russini,
Blair Good, Charles Heza

client
Dallas Dental
design firm
MFDI
designer
Mark Fertig

client
The Advisor Group
design firm
Desbrow
desbrow.com
designers
Kimberly S. Miller,
Brian Lee Campbell

client
The BrickYard
design firm
The Prime Time Agency LLC
designer
John Seymour

client
Meathead Movers
design firm
Pierre Rademaker Design
www.rademakerdesign.com
designers
Pierre Rademaker, Debbie Shibata

client
LaGrange County Community Foundation
design firm
MillerWhite, LLC
www.millerwhite.com
designer
Lori Lucas

client
Bucks County Historical Society
design firm
art270, Inc.
www.art270.com
designers
John Opet,
Carl Mill,
Dianne Mill

client
Akron Art Museum
design firm
Nesnadny + Schwartz
www.nsideas.com
designers
Mark Schwartz, Greg Oznowich,
Nick Watts, Shawn Beatty

client
Keen's Crossing
design firm
Paul Kaza Associates
www.paulkaza.com
designer
Carissa Butler

KEEN'S CROSSING
at Winooski Falls

client
Allegiance Development
design firm
Kendall Creative Shop, Inc.
kendallcreative.com
designers
Mark Platt, Tim Childress

client
Ambrilia Biopharma
design firm
Addison Whitney
www.addisonwhitney.com
designers
Trey Walsh, Kristin Hager, Kimberlee Davis

ambrilia
BIOPHARMA

client
American Film Network
design firm
VMA, Inc.
vmai.com
designer
Doug Knopp

AFN
American Film Network

MPFA
Motion Picture Fund of America

IMPG
Independent Motion Picture Group

client
Acme United Corporation
design firm
Tom Fowler, Inc.
www.tomfowlerinc.com
designer
Mary Ellen Butkus

client
Opera Colorado
design firm
Rassman Design
www.rassmandesign.com
designer
John Rassman

client
New Haven County Cutters
design firm
Kevin Hall Design
designer
Kevin Hall

client
Goody's Paint
design firm
A3 Design
www.athreedesign.com
designer
Alan Altman

client
Colorado Colfax Marathon
design firm
Rassman Design
www.rassmandesign.com
designer
John Rassman

client
Speedy Motorcycle Studio
design firm
Speedy Motorcycle Studio
www.speedymotorcycle.com
designer
E. June Roberts-Lunn

client
Pittsburgh Glass Center
design firm
Robert Meyers Design
www.robertmeyersdesign.com
designer
Robert Meyers

client
American Institute of Architects Minnesota
design firm
Rubin Cordaro Design
www.rubincordaro.com
designer
Jim Cordaro

client
iConclude, Inc.
design firm
Connie Hwang Design
www.conniehwangdesign.com
designer
Connie Hwang

client
Harris Day Architecture
design firm
Innis Maggiore
www.innismaggiore.com
designer
Lee-Ann Demeo

client
Cattle Baron's Ball '06
design firm
Kendall Creative Shop, Inc.
kendallcreative.com
designer
Jennifer Brehm

client
Flying Penguin Pictures
design firm
Stephen Longo Design Associates
designer
Stephen Longo

client
Schnitzer Northwest
design firm
Hornall Anderson Design Works
www.hadw.com
designers
John Anicker, Andrew Wicklund, Leo Raymundo, Holly Craven, Kathleen Gibson

client
The Armor All Products Company
design firm
Clorox Creative Services
art director
Chris Twilling
designers
Tim Ferdun, Anthony Luk, Jose Rodriguez

client
Community Initiative
design firm
Ventress Design Group
www.ventress.com
designer
Tom Ventress

COMMUNITY INITIATIVE

client
Aspen Dental
design firm
Crowley Webb and Assoc.
crowley-webb.com
designer
Katie Hazel

AspenDental®
More reasons to smile.

client
Harriette's Song
design firm
Rule29 Creative
www.rule29.com
designer
Justin Ahrens,
Josh Jensen,
Kerri Liu

HARRIETTE'S
SONG

client
Westchester Sports and Wellness
design firm
Tom Fowler, Inc.
www.tomfowlerinc.com
creative director
Thomas G. Fowler
designer
Brien O'Reilly

WESTCHESTER
SPORTS & WELLNESS

client
Orthopaedic Associates of Southern Delaware
design firm
Dean Design/Marketing Group, Inc.
www.deandesign.com
designers
Jeff Beck, Cantrell Lau

ORTHOPAEDIC
ASSOCIATES
of Southern Delaware, P.A.

client
Boston Properties
design firm
kor group
www.kor.com
designers
Kjerstin Westgaard Oh, Karen Dendy Smith

PRUDENTIAL CENTER

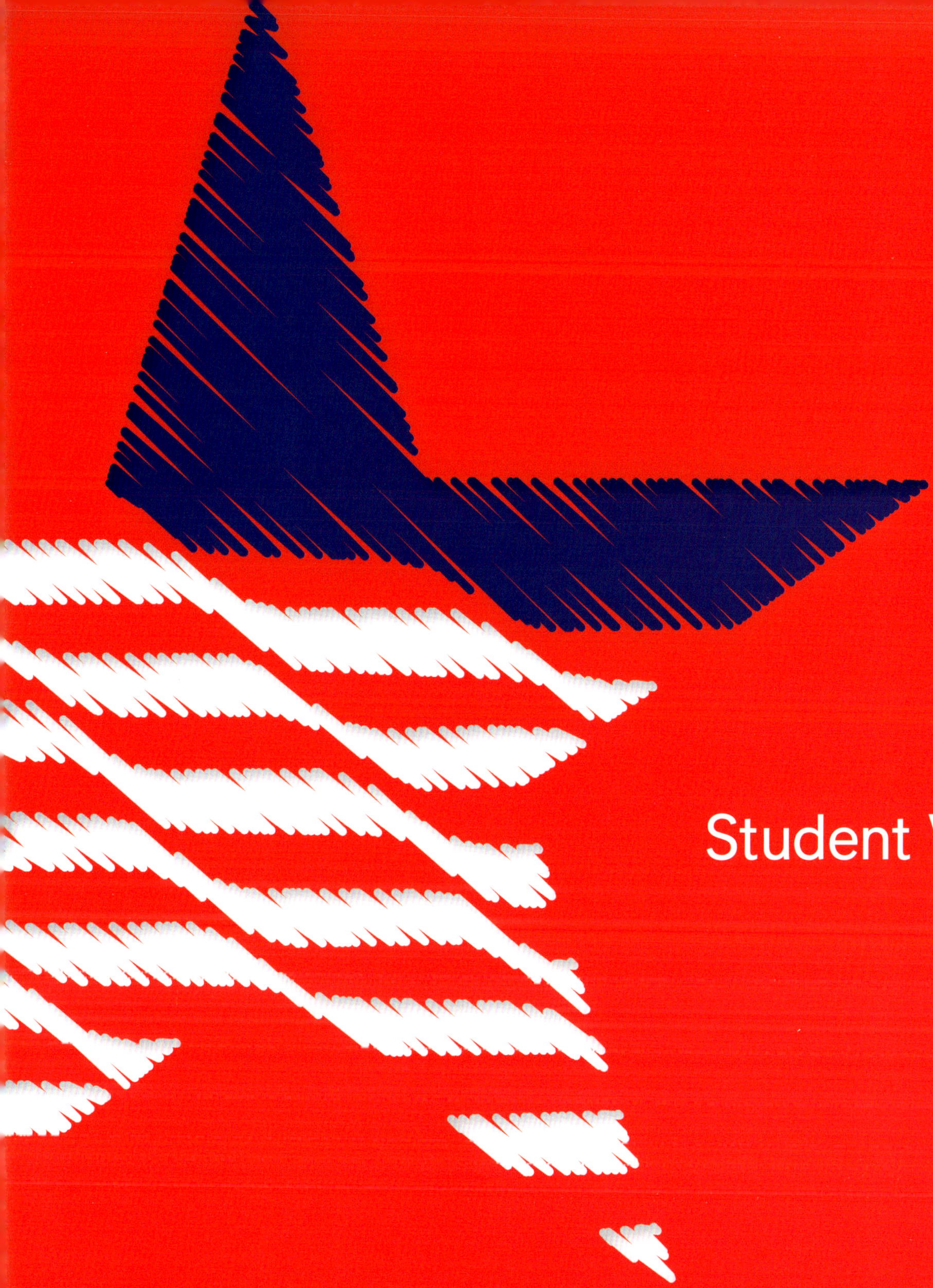

Student Work

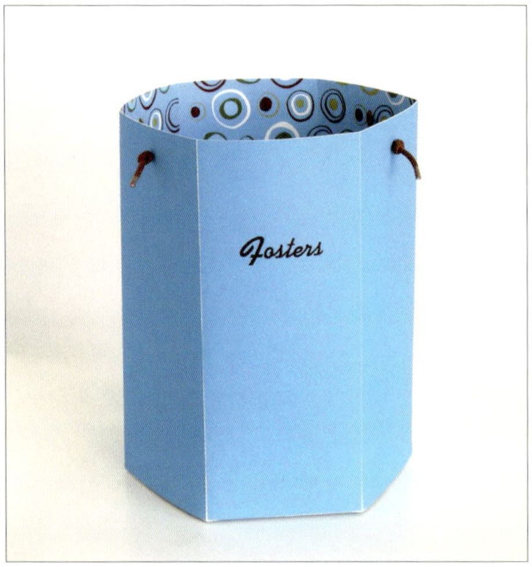

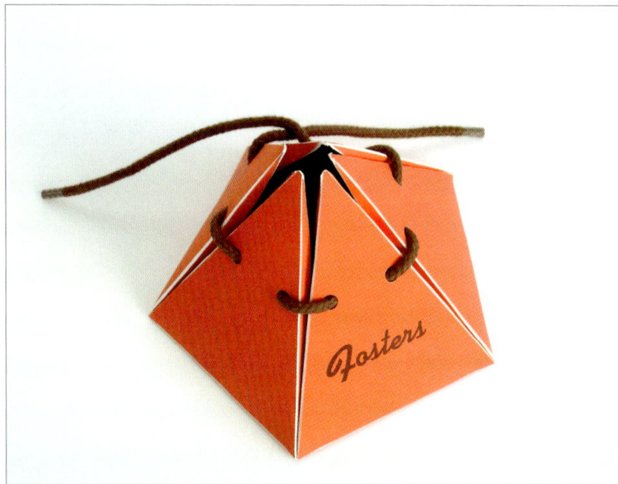

project
Fosters Urban Hardware for Kids
(Bags, Tags, Labels, & Boxes)
school
Drexel University
Antoinette Westphal College
of Media Arts & Design
instructor
Sandy Stewart
designer
Georgette Klotz

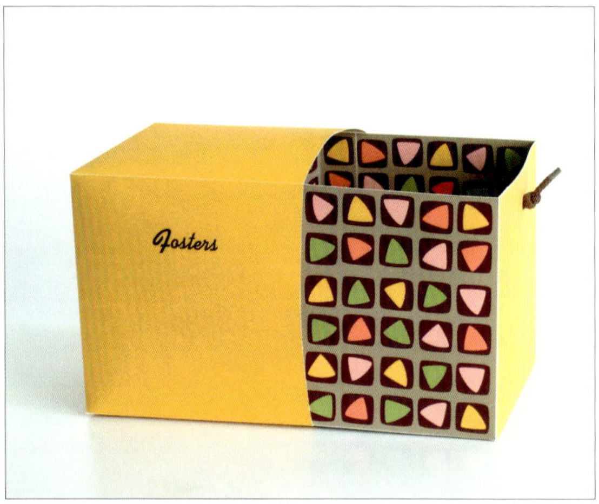

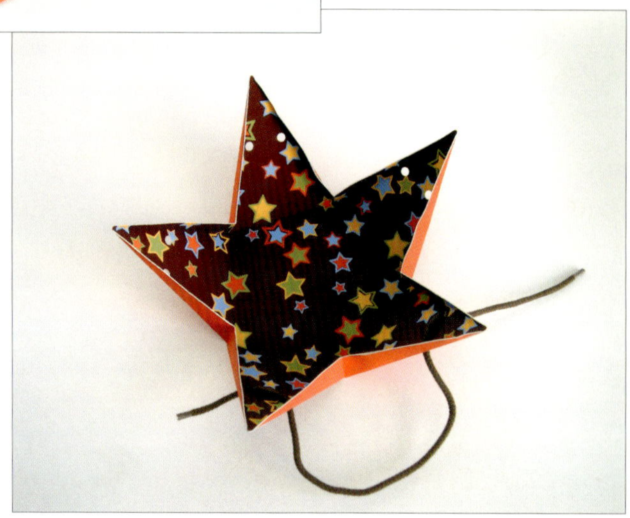

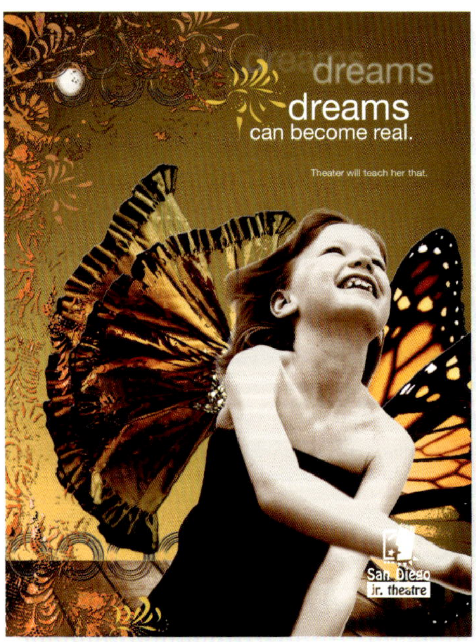

project
San Diego Junior Theater Ad Series
(Promotional Design)
school
Marshall University
instructor
Jenette Williams
designer
Jessica Cox

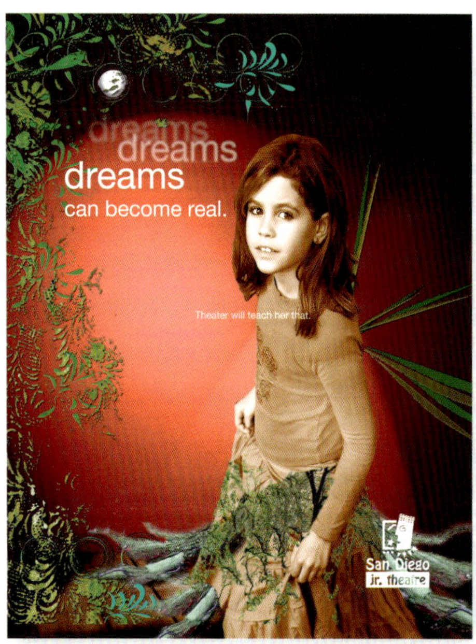

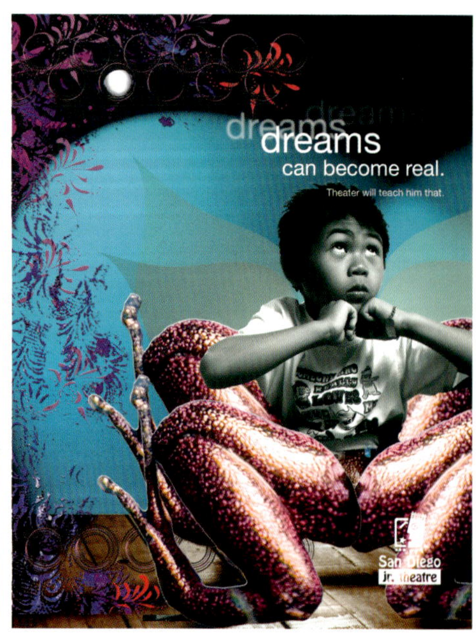

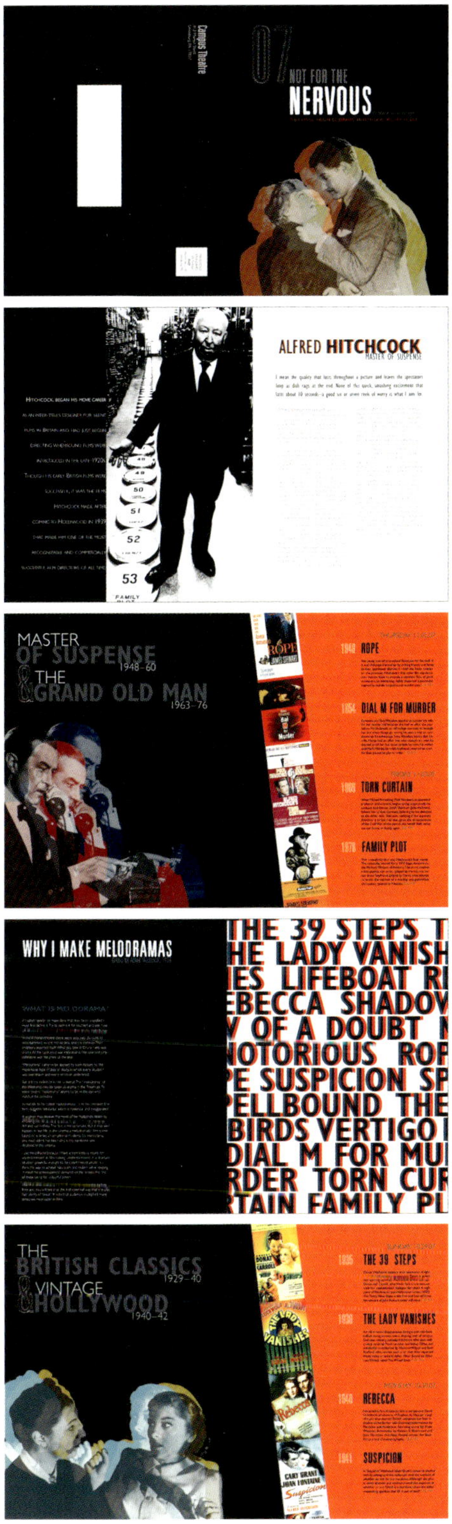

project
Not for the Nervous Brochure
(Promotional Design)
school
Susquehanna University
instructor
Mark Fertig
designer
Katie Lesser

project
Christian Children's Fund
(Stationery Design)
school
Texas State University—
San Marcos
instructor
Michelle Hays
designer
Whitney Leigh Wiedner

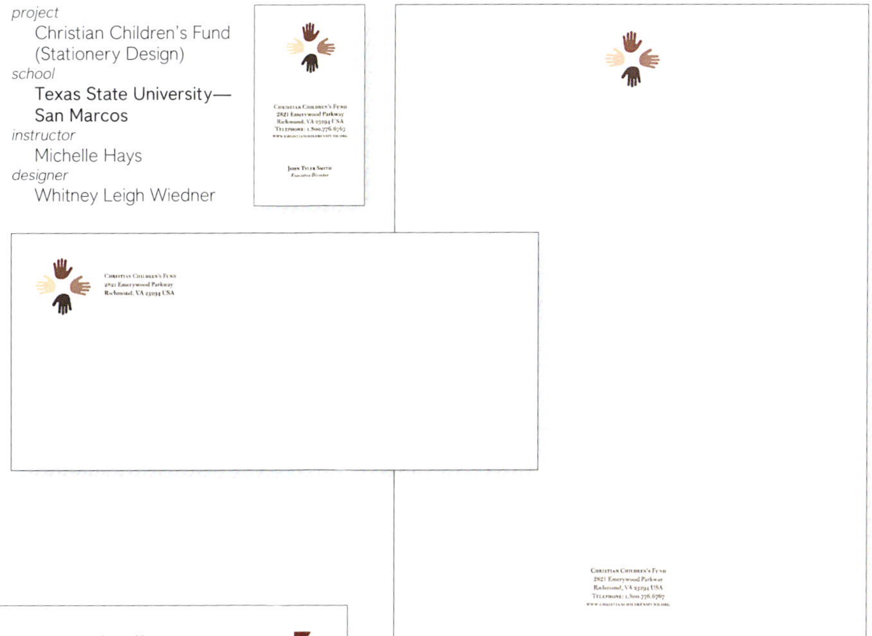

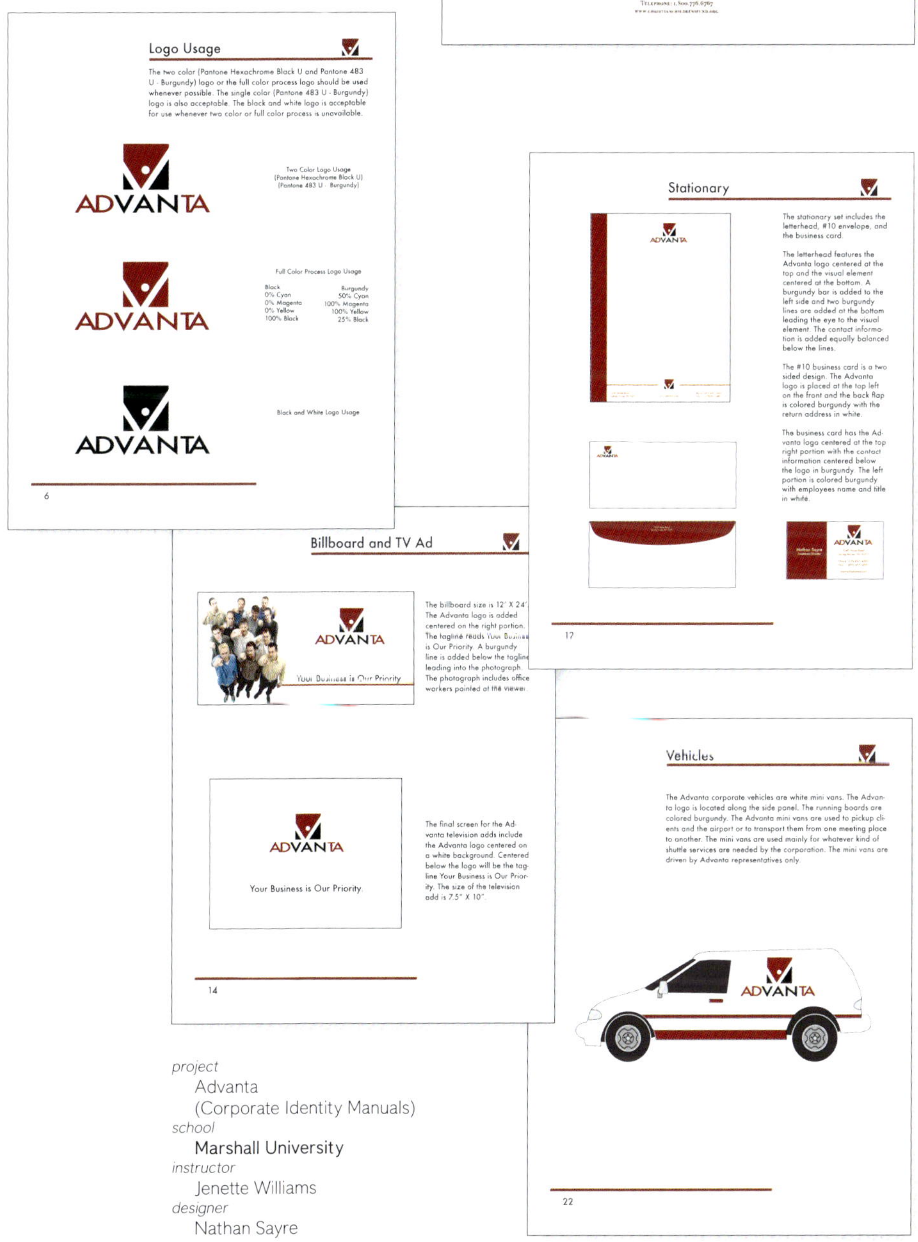

project
Advanta
(Corporate Identity Manuals)
school
Marshall University
instructor
Jenette Williams
designer
Nathan Sayre

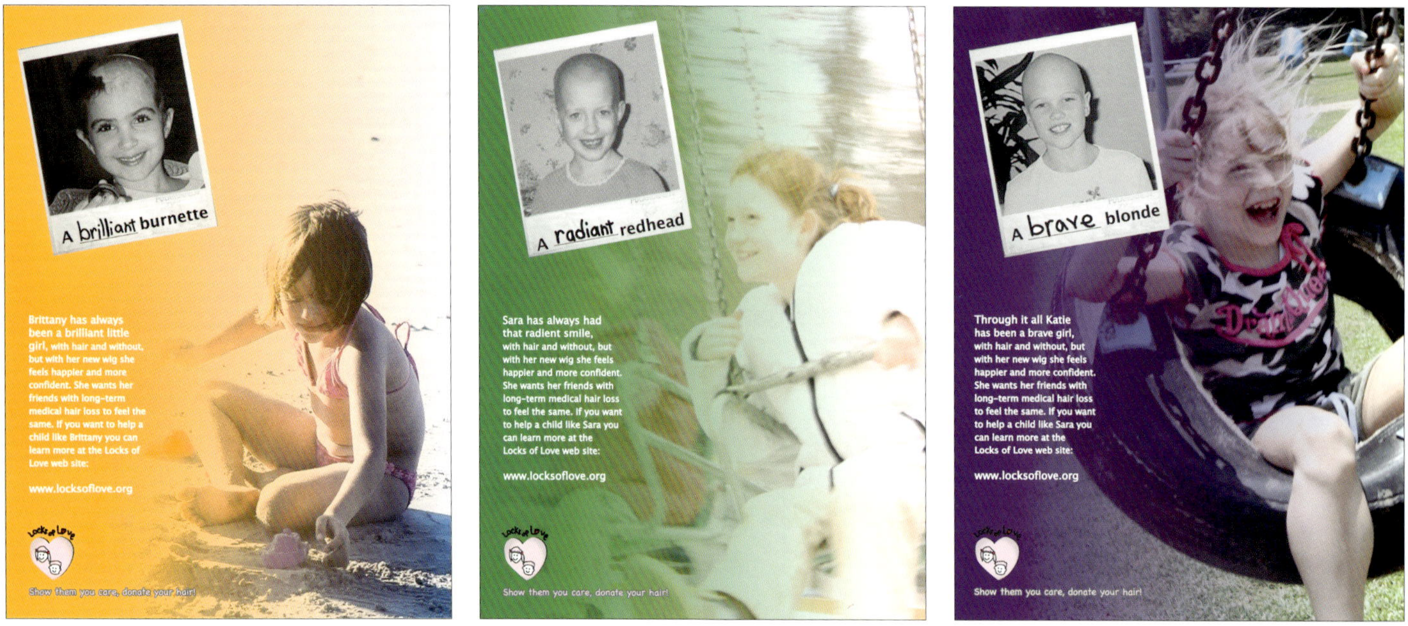

project
Locks of Love Ad Series
(Promotional Design)
school
Marshall University
instructor
Jenette Williams
designer
Lisa Affolter

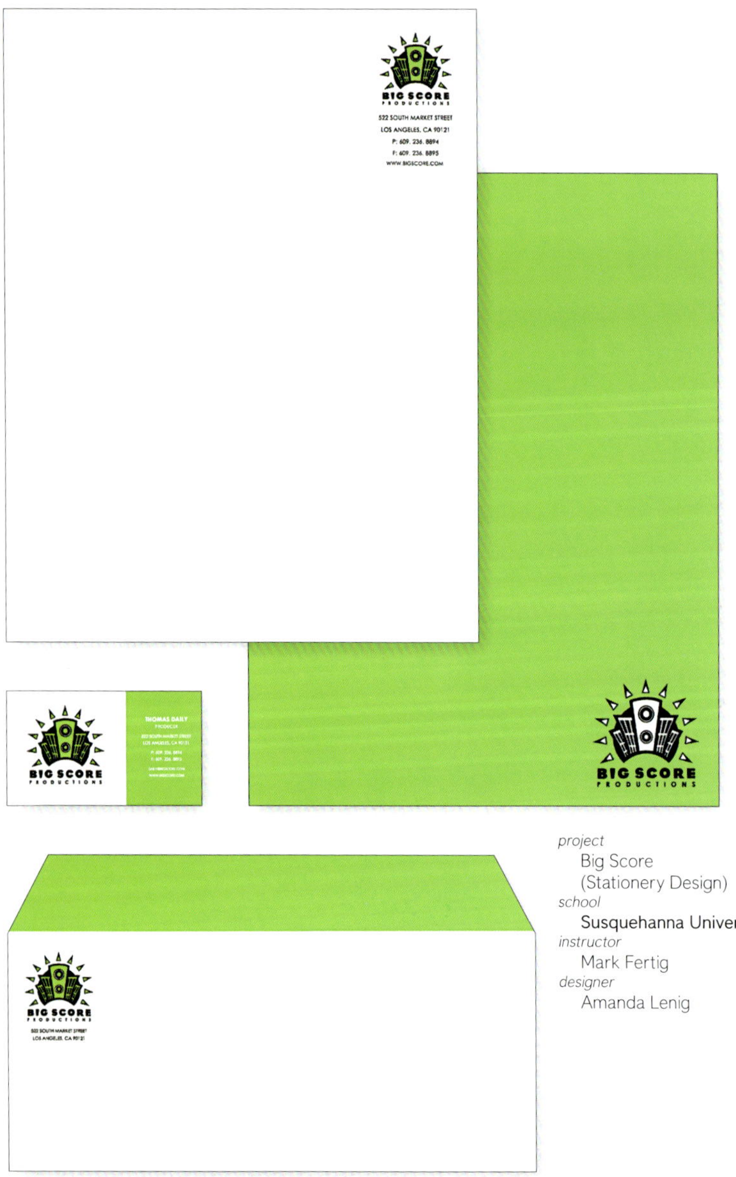

project
Big Score
(Stationery Design)
school
Susquehanna University
instructor
Mark Fertig
designer
Amanda Lenig

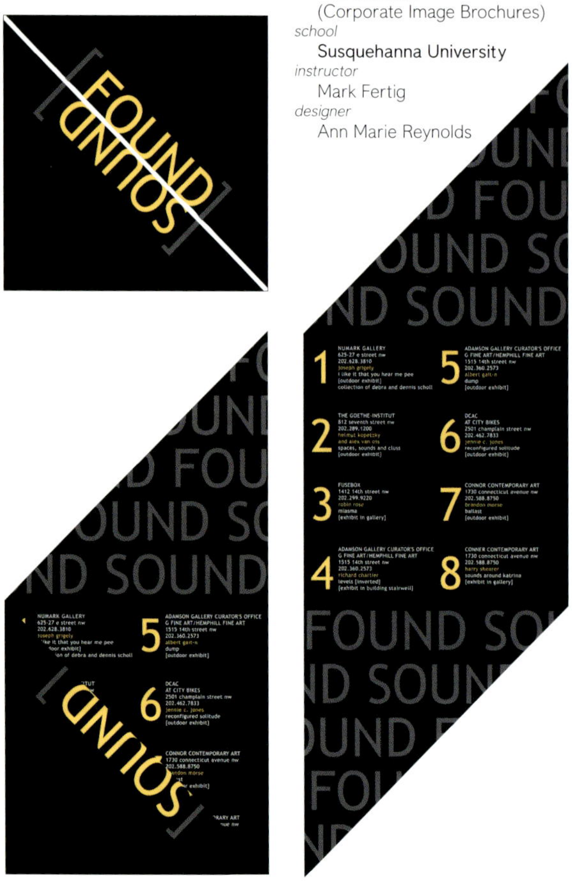

project
Found Sound
(Corporate Image Brochures)
school
Susquehanna University
instructor
Mark Fertig
designer
Ann Marie Reynolds

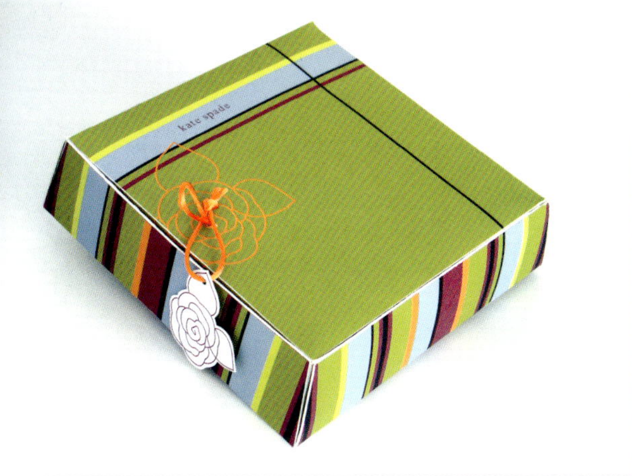

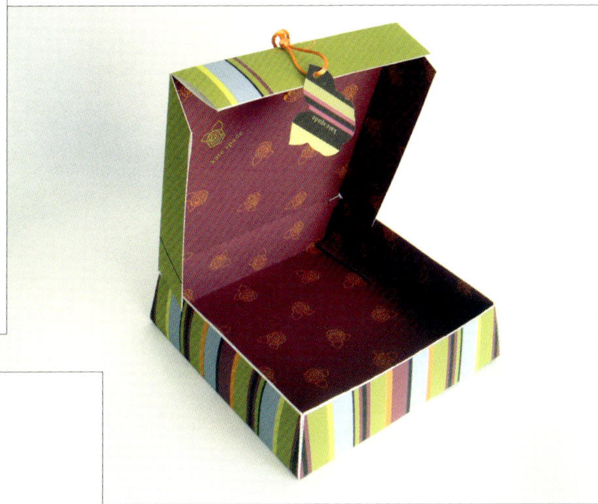

project
Kate Spade
(Bags, Tags, Labels, & Boxes)
school
Drexel University
Antoinette Westphal College
of Media Arts & Design
instructor
Sandy Stewart
designer
Marcella Zuczek

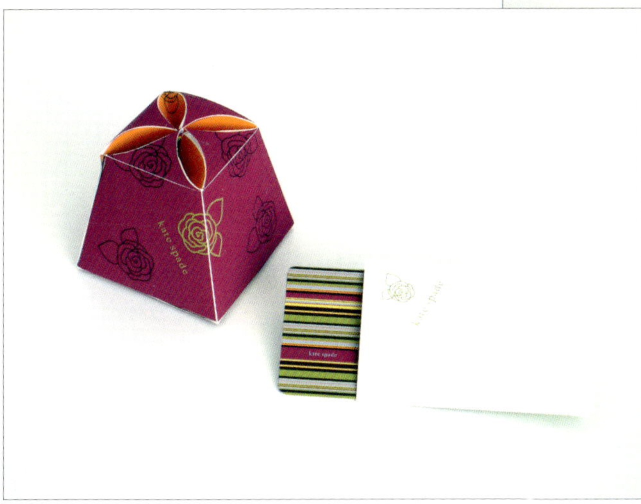

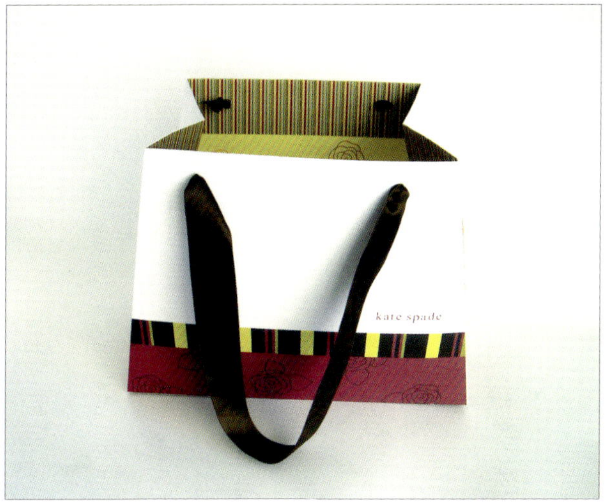

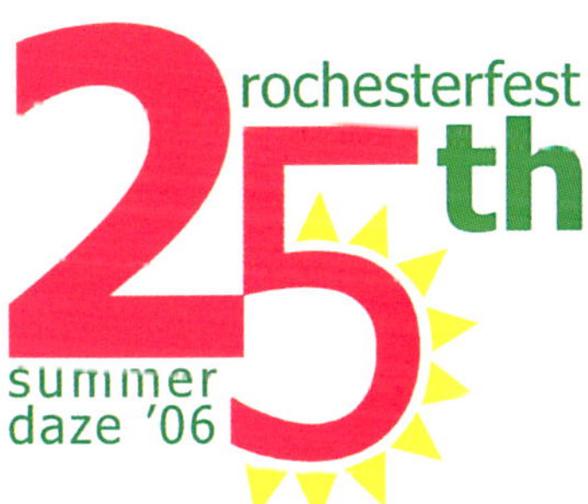

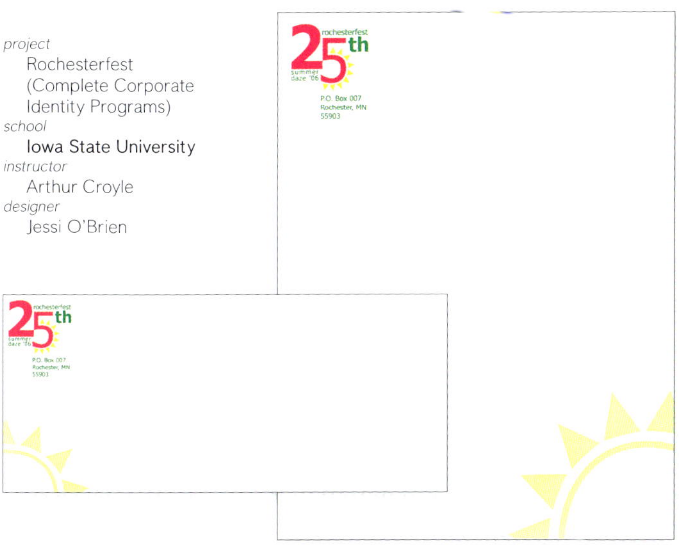

project
Rochesterfest
(Complete Corporate
Identity Programs)
school
Iowa State University
instructor
Arthur Croyle
designer
Jessi O'Brien

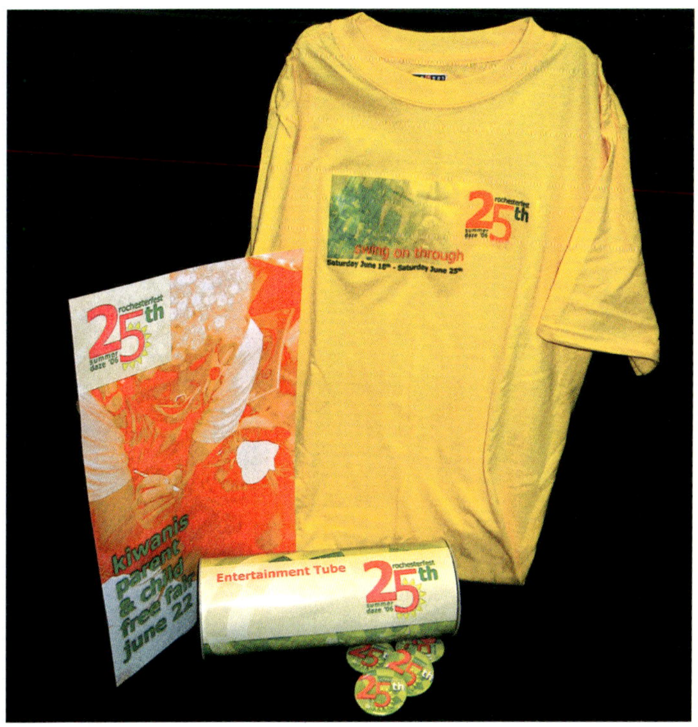

project
Rubio's Grill
(Trademark/Logo Design)
school
Susquehanna University
instructor
Mark Fertig
designer
Joe Pilcavage

project
Good Dog
(Trademark/Logo Design)
school
Drexel University
Antoinette Westphal College
of Media Arts & Design
instructor
E. June Roberts-Lunn
designer
Caitlin Anderson

project
Disney Grad Nite
(Trademark/Logo Design)
school
Texas State University
instructor
James Howe
designer
Aline Forastieri

project
Authentic West
(Trademark/Logo Design)
school
Susquehanna University
instructor
Mark Fertig
designer
Jordan Mollot

project
Mother Earth Foods
(Trademark/Logo Design)
school
Susquehanna University
instructor
Mark Fertig
designer
Lauren Fasnacht

project
Love Joy's Tea Room
(Trademark/Logo Design)
school
Texas State University—San Marcos
instructor
Jeff Davis
designer
Whitney Leigh
Wiedner

project
Wildman Productions
(Trademark/Logo Design)
school
Susquehanna University
instructor
Mark Fertig
designer
Steve Semanchik

project
Heartland Pasta
(Trademark/Logo Design)
school
Susquehanna University
instructor
Mark Fertig
designer
Christine Ottley

project
National Airlines of South Africa
(Trademark/Logo Design)
school
University of Hartford
instructor
John Nordyke
designer
Stephanie Trainor

project
National Airlines of Zimbabwe
(Trademark/Logo Design)
school
University of Hartford
instructor
John Nordyke
designer
Tim Bayon

project
Breathe Spa
(Trademark/Logo Design)
school
Susquehanna University
instructor
Mark Fertig
designer
Kyle Nalls

project
Windy City Bistro
(Trademark/Logo Design)
school
Susquehanna University
instructor
Mark Fertig
designer
Tracy Brauner

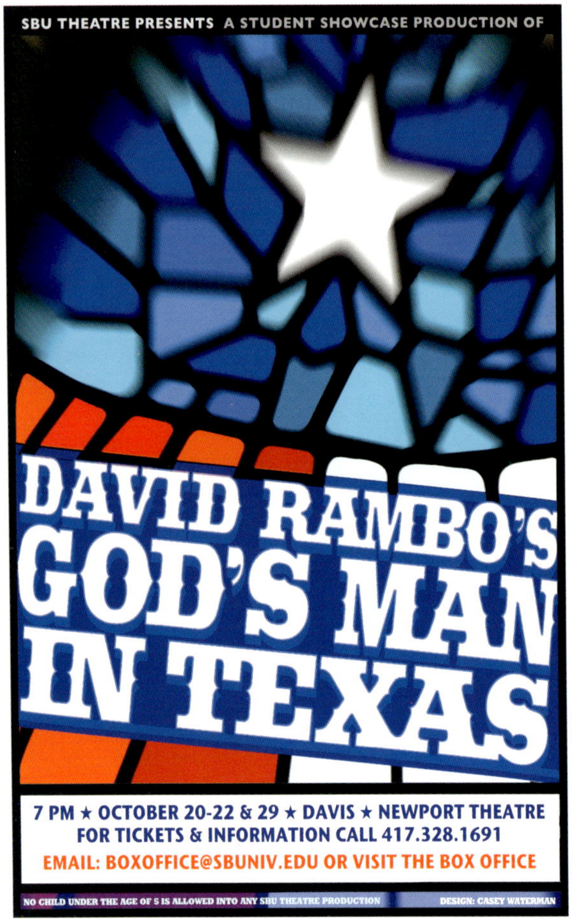

project
God's Man in Texas (Promotional Design)
school
Southwest Baptist University
instructor
J. Gruber
designer
Casey Waterman

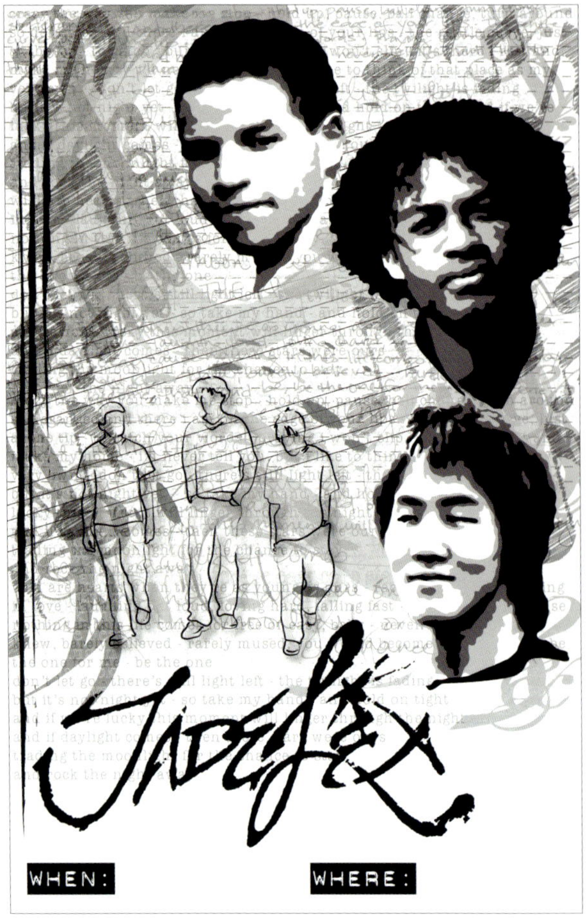

project
Jade Lea Poster (Promotional Design)
school
Iowa State University
designer
Kelly Leaman

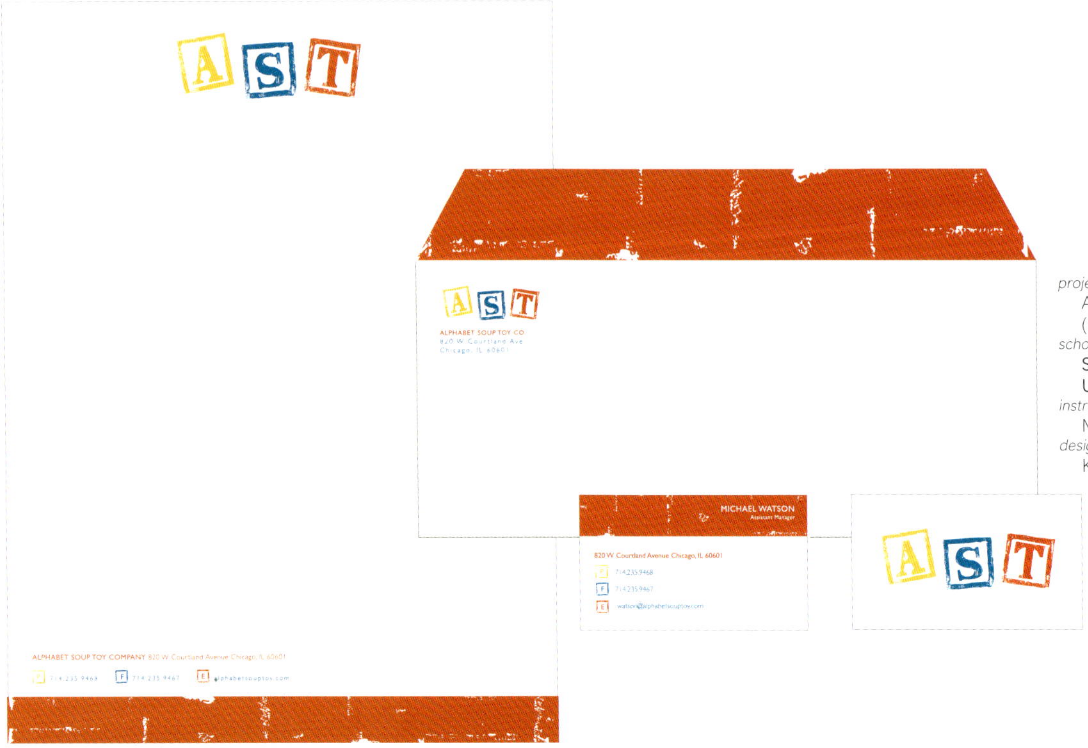

project
Alphabet Soup (Stationery Design)
school
Susquehanna University
instructor
Mark Fertig
designer
Katie Lesser

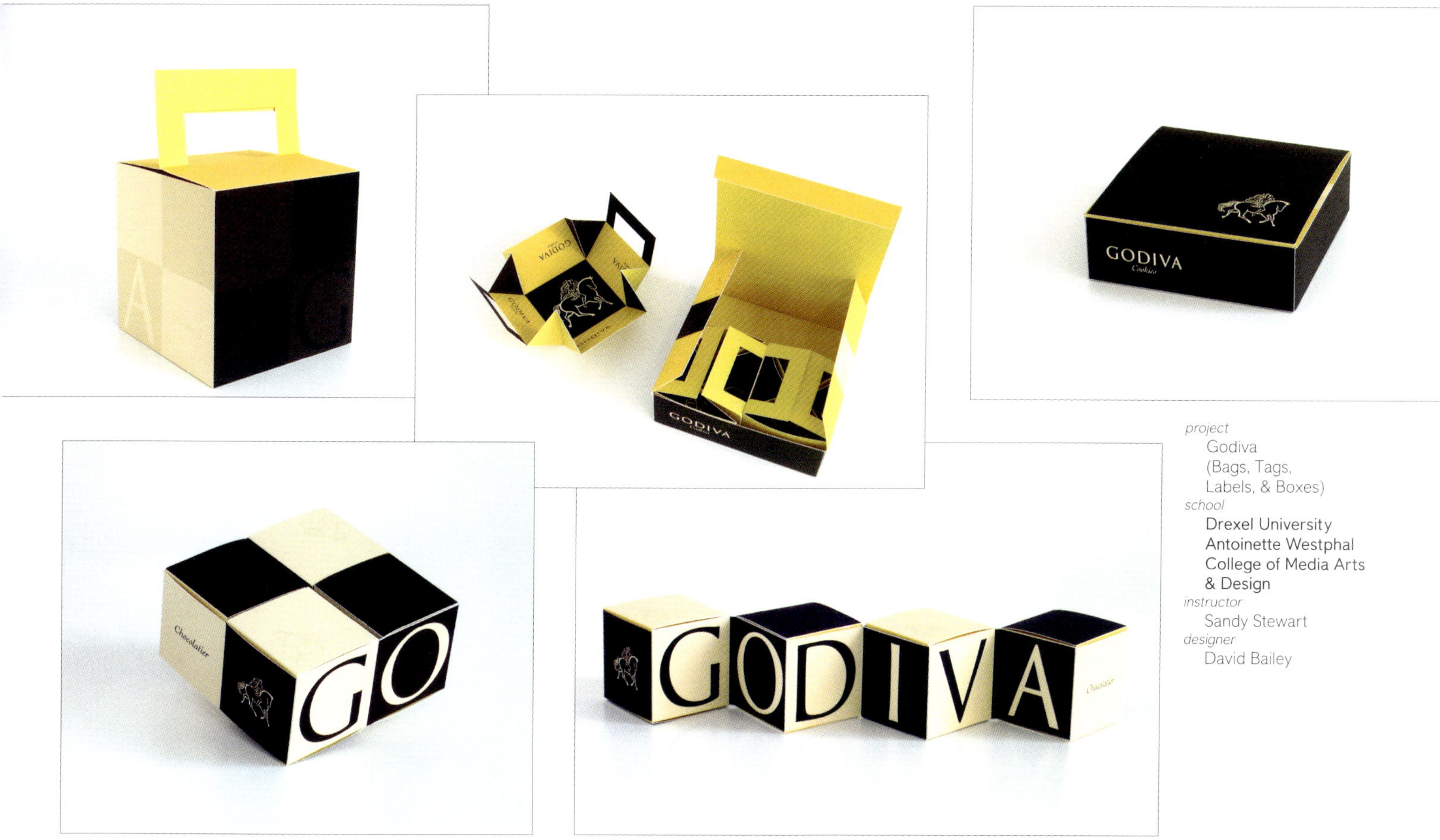

project
Godiva
(Bags, Tags,
Labels, & Boxes)
school
Drexel University
Antoinette Westphal
College of Media Arts
& Design
instructor
Sandy Stewart
designer
David Bailey

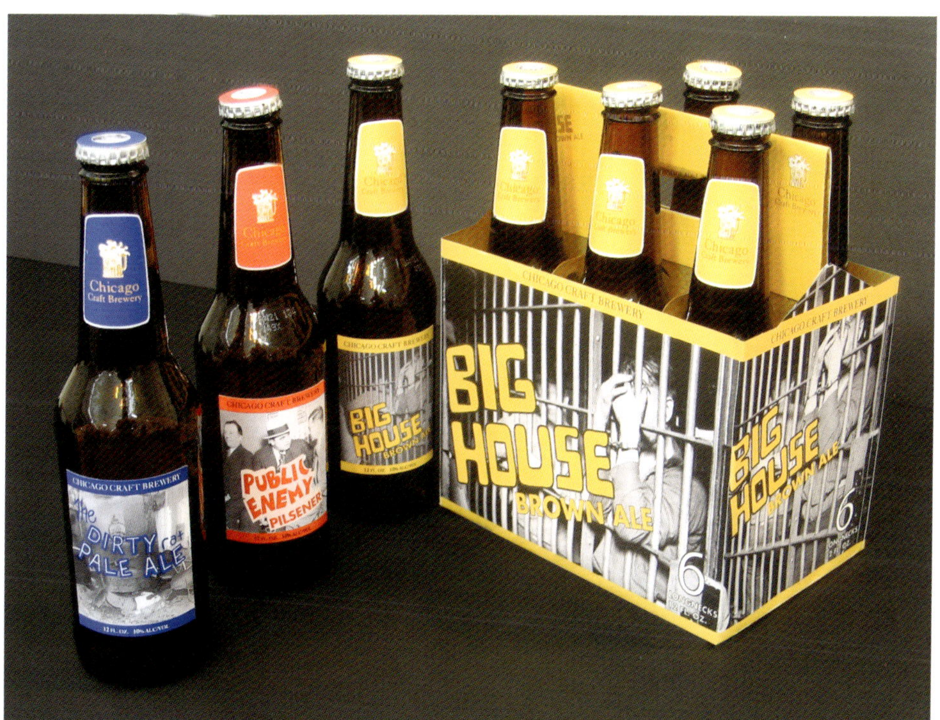

project
Big House Beer
(Package Design)
school
Susquehanna University
instructor
Mark Fertig
designer
Angelique Markowski

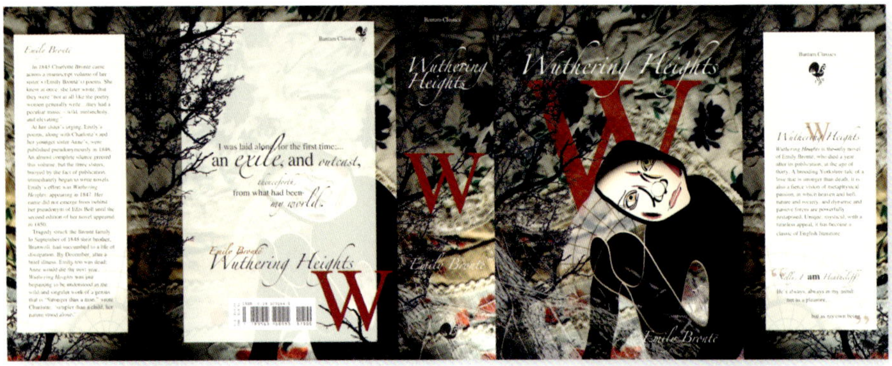

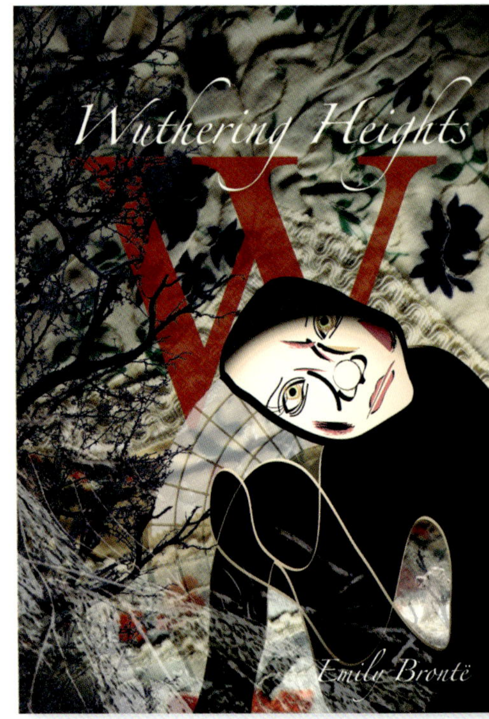

project
Wuthering Heights Book Jacket (CDs, DVDs, & Books)
school
Marshall University
instructor
Jenette Williams
designer
Jessica Cox

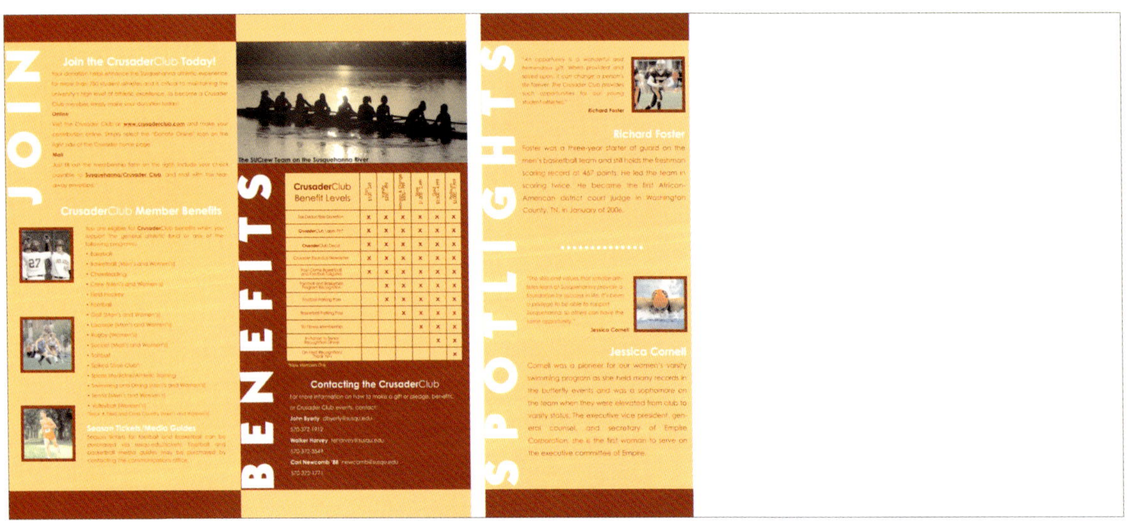

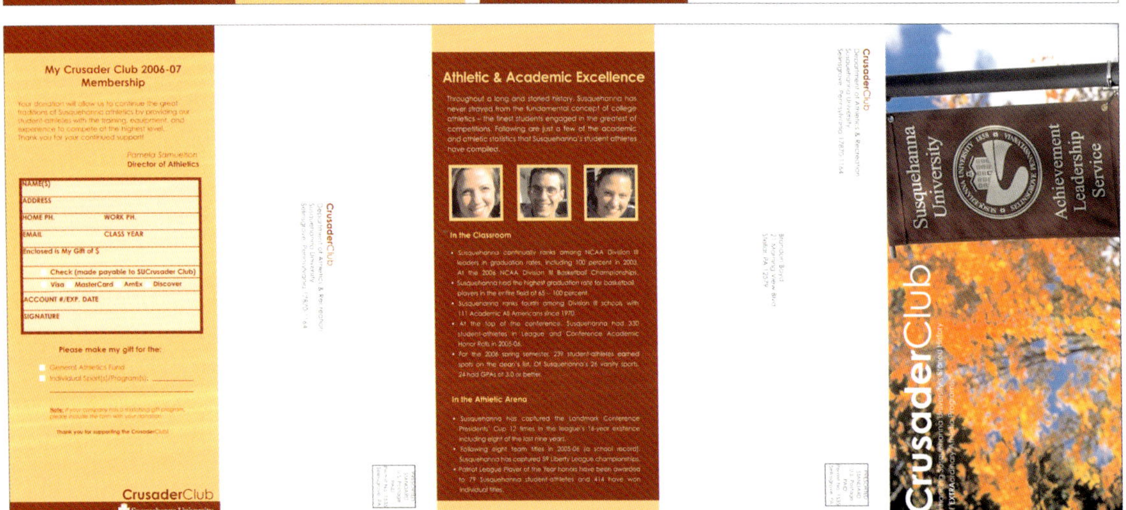

project
Crusaders Club (Corporate Image Brochures)
school
Susquehanna University
instructor
Mark Fertig
designer
Ann Marie Reynolds

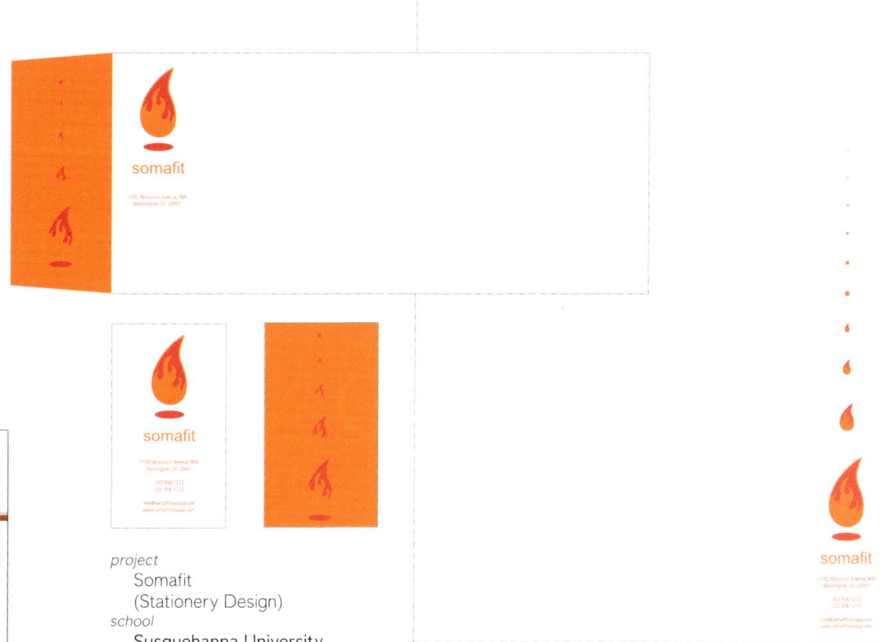

project
Somafit
(Stationery Design)
school
Susquehanna University
instructor
Mark Fertig
designer
Angelique Markowski

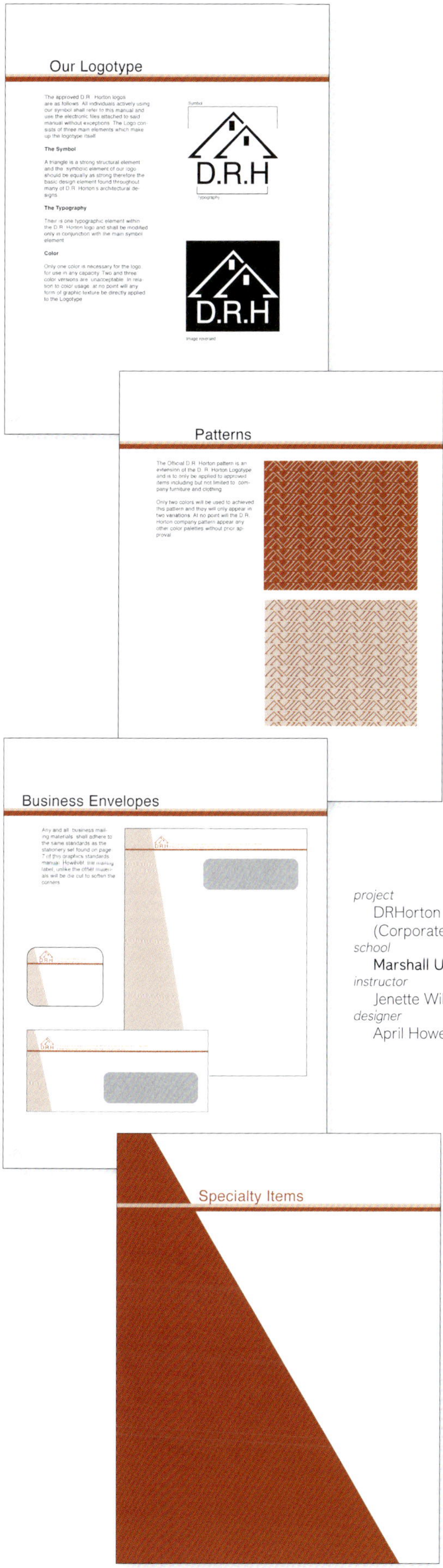

project
DRHorton
(Corporate Identity Manuals)
school
Marshall University
instructor
Jenette Williams
designer
April Howe

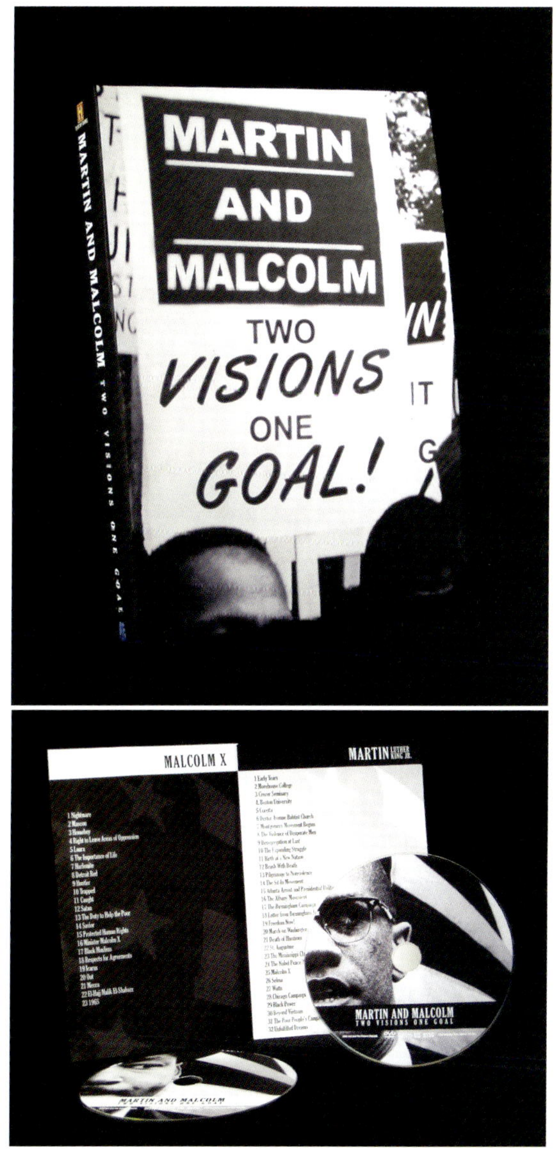

project
History Channel
(CDs, DVDs, & Books)
school
Susquehanna University
instructor
Mark Fetig
designer
Katie Lesser

project
National Airlines of Italy
(Trademark/Logo Design)
school
University of Hartford
instructor
John Nordyke
designer
Julie Coleman

project
Airgas
(Trademark/Logo Design)
school
Marshall University
instructor
Jenette Williams
designer
Tonya Rayburn

project
Women's Bowling Association
(Trademark/Logo Design)
school
Texas State University
instructor
Bill Meek
designer
Aline
Forastieri

project
Water's Edge Camp
(Trademark/Logo Design)
school
Susquehanna University
instructor
Mark Fertig
designer
Andrew Goodsell

project
Night Owl Recording
(Trademark/Logo Design)
school
Texas State University—San Marcos
instructor
Michelle
Hays
designer
Whitney
Leigh
Wiedner

project
Black Box
(Trademark/Logo Design)
school
Marshall University
instructor
Jenette Williams
designer
Alan Fairchild

project
AutoLiv
(Trademark/Logo Design)
school
Marshall University
instructor
Jenette Williams
designer
Casey Pauly

project
Wildman Productions
(Trademark/Logo Design)
school
Susquehanna University
instructor
Mark Fertig
designer
Lauren Fasnacht

project
Mother Earth Foods
(Trademark/Logo Design)
school
Susquehanna University
instructor
Mark Fertig
designer
Angelique Markowski

project
National Airlines of Greenland
(Trademark/Logo Design)
school
University of Hartford
instructor
John Nordyke
designer
Kyle Green

project
Out of Focus Entertainment
(Trademark/Logo Design)
school
Iowa State University
instructor
Alan Mickelson
designers
Jessica Hamilton, Gretchen Anderson, Lucia Keller, Matthew Starks

project
Culture Shock
(Trademark/Logo Design)
school
Drexel University Antoinette Westphal College of Media Arts & Design
instructor
E. June Roberts-Lunn
designer
Kyle Cook

project
Prima Energy
(Trademark/Logo Design)
school
Marshall University
instructor
Jenette Williams
designer
David Kendall

project
Beer Icon Series
(Trademark/Logo Design)
school
Susquehanna University
instructor
Mark Fertig
designer
Jessie Stoltzfus

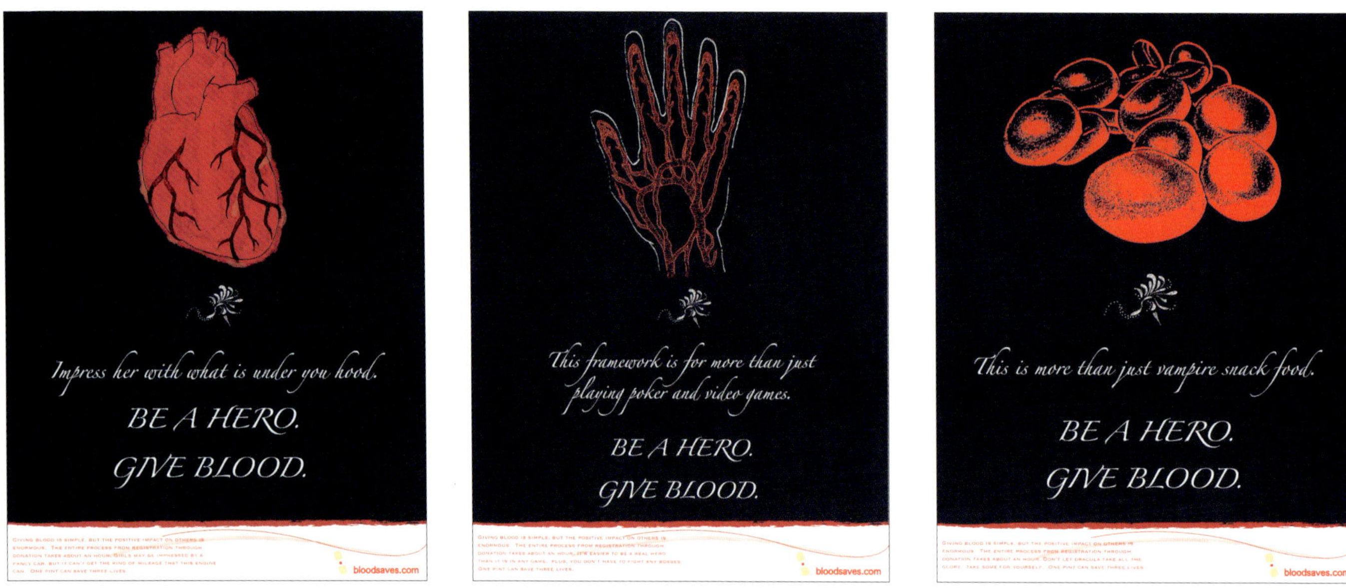

project
Give Blood Ad Series
(Promotional Design)
school
Marshall University
instructor
Jenette Williams
designer
April Trimboli

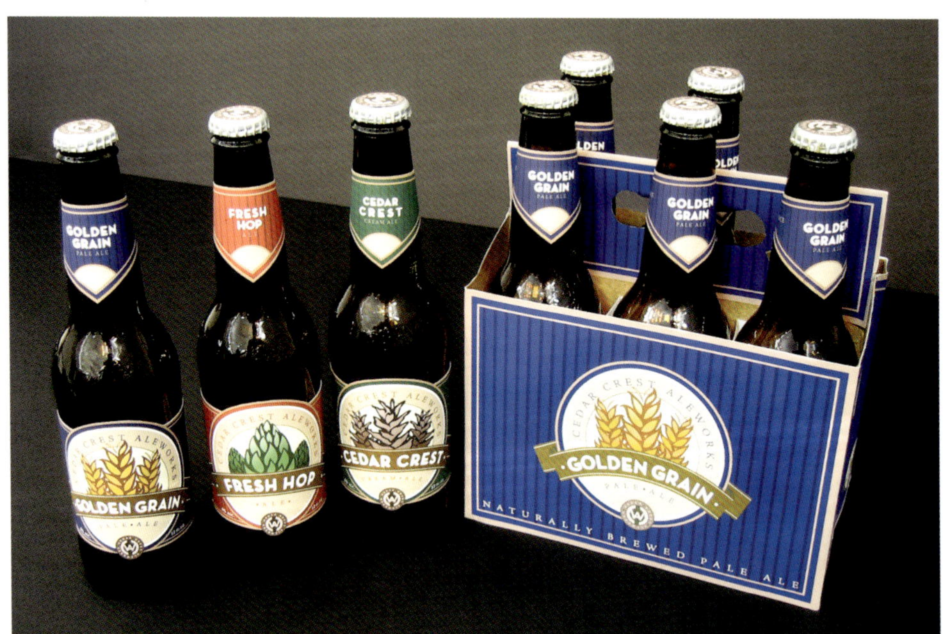

project
Cedar Crest Beer
(Package Design)
school
Susquehanna University
instructor
Mark Fertig
designer
Amanda Lenig

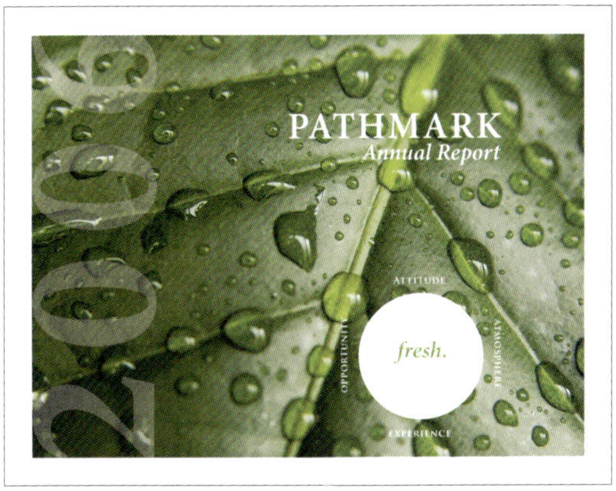

project
Pathmark Annual Report
(Corporate Image Brochures)
school
Marshall University
instructor
Jenette Williams
designer
Bethany Sharp

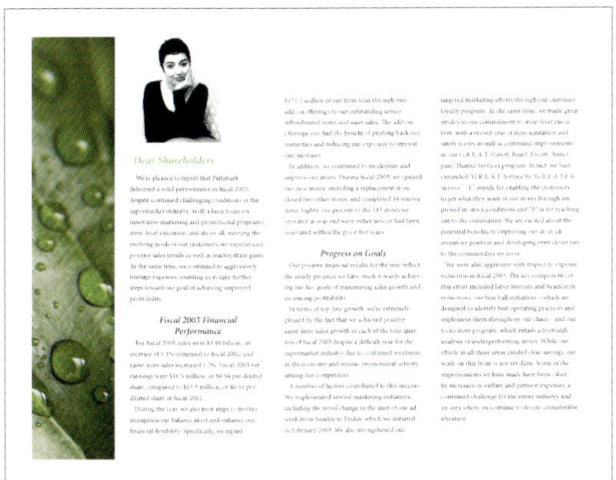

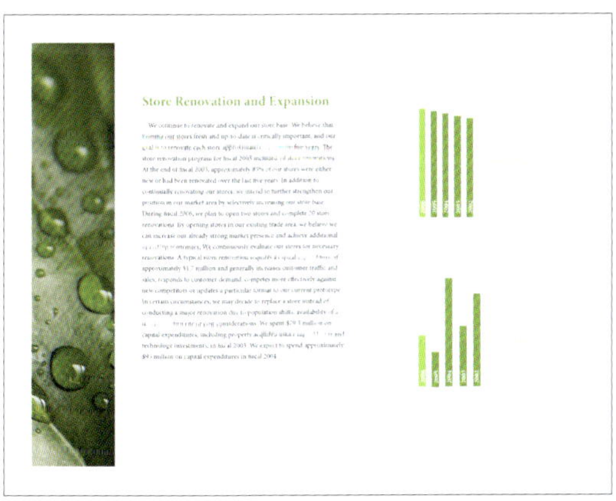

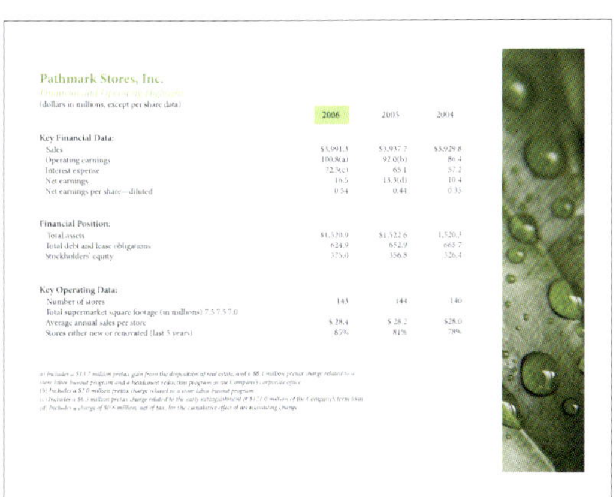

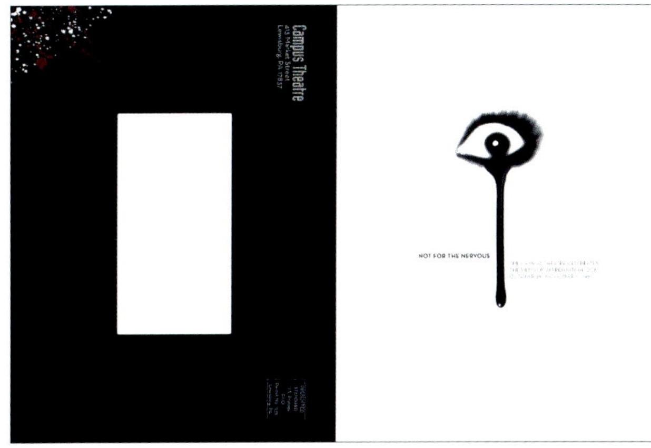

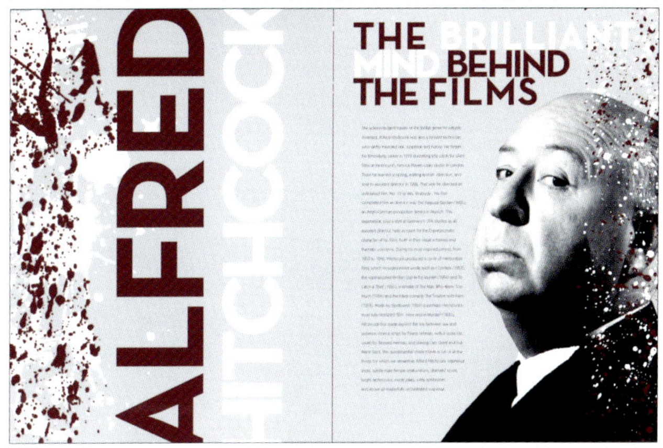

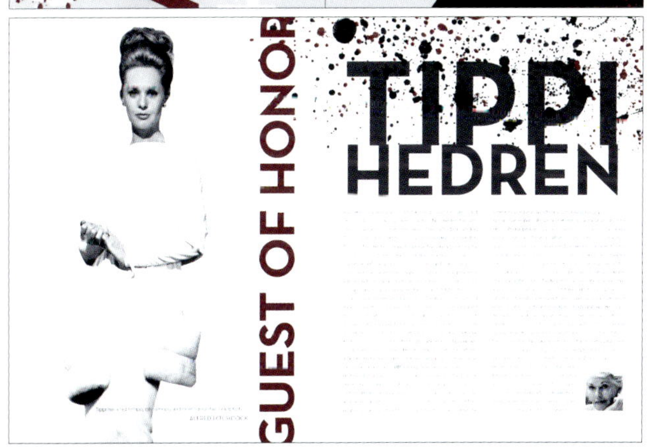

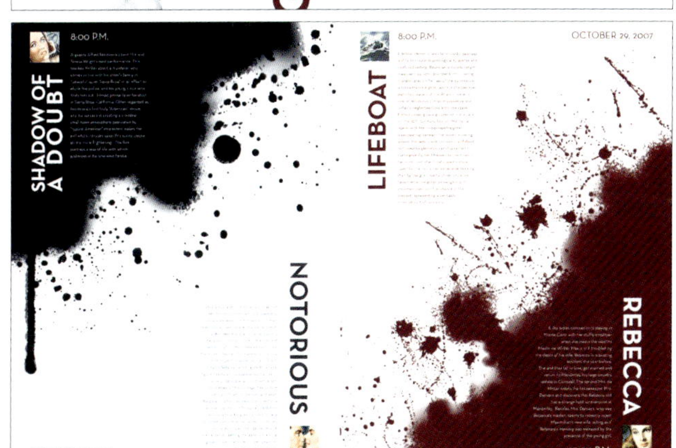

project
Film Festival Brochure
(Promotional Design)
school
Susquehanna
University
instructor
Mark Fertig
designer
Ann Marie Reynolds

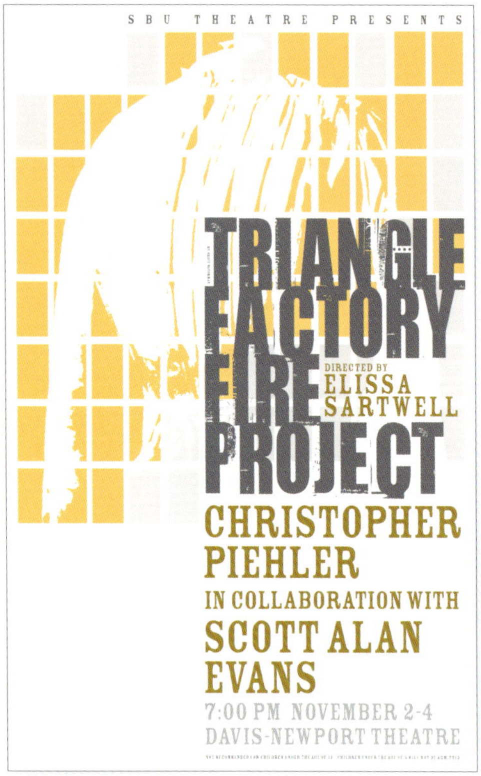

project
Triangle Factory Fire Project (Promotional Design)
school
Southwest Baptist University
instructor
J. Gruber
designer
Casey Waterman

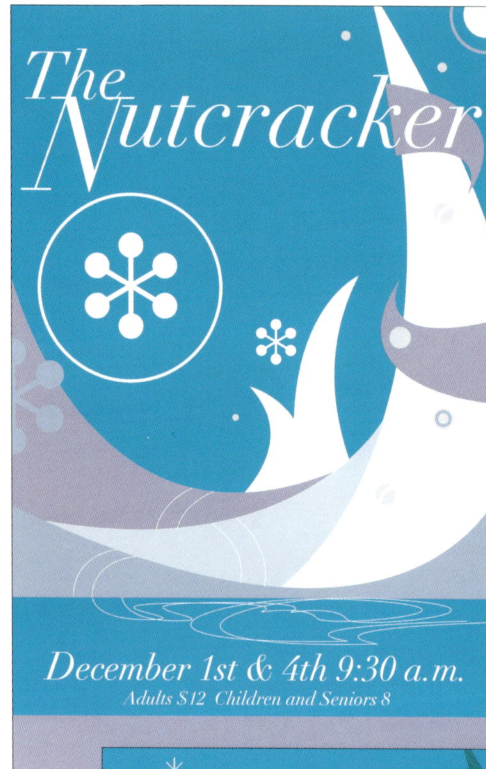

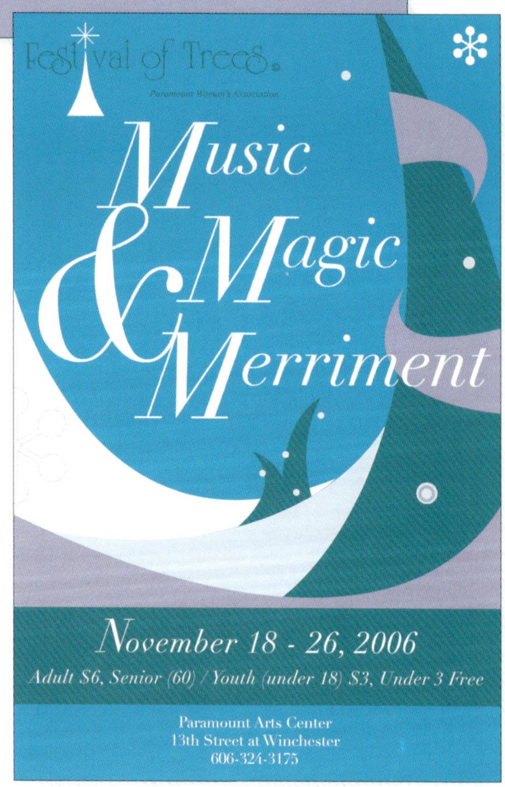

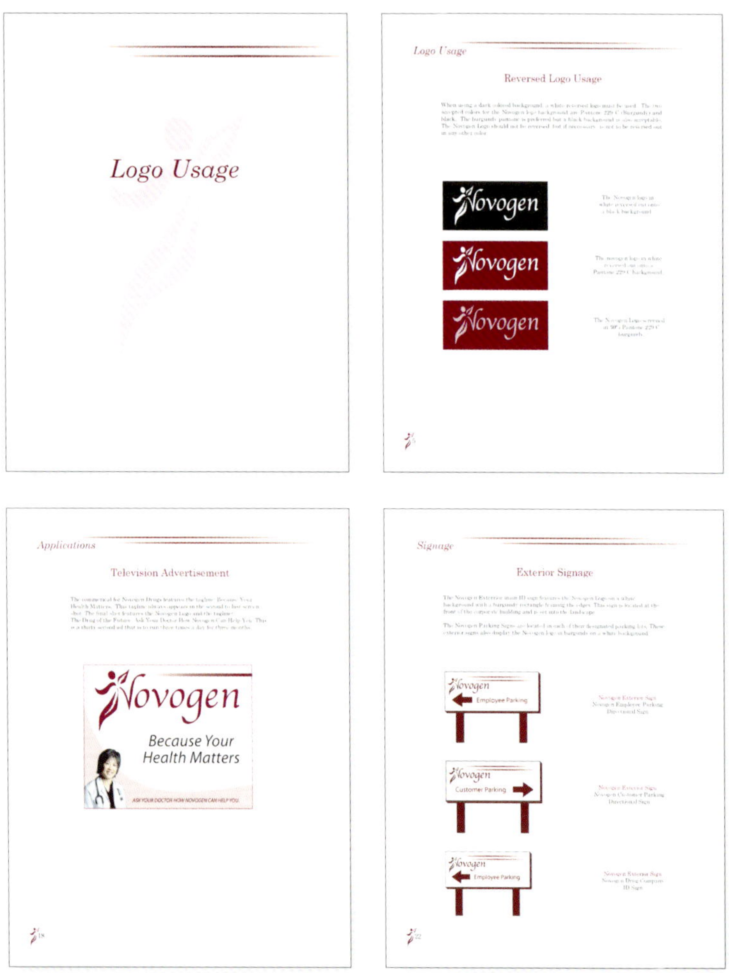

project
Festival of Trees (Promotional Design)
school
Marshall University
instructor
Jenette Williams
designer
Casey Pauly

project
Novogen (Corporate Identity Manuals)
school
Marshall University
instructor
Jenette Williams
designer
Kelli Marakovits

Index